ISBN 978-0-260-15560-3
PIBN 10931271

THE

Knickerbocker,

OR

NEW-YORK MONTHLY MAGAZINE.

VOLUME XXVIII.

NEW-YORK:
JOHN ALLEN, PUBLISHER,
No. 139 Nassau-street.

1846.

THE KNICKERBOCKER.

VOL. XXVIII.   JULY, 1846.   No. 1.

AMERICAN SCHOLARSHIP.

BY J. F. JACKSON.

IT must be admitted that many of the most successful and distinguished men have been self-made. Wealth, rank in society and powerful friends, which in some cases apparently open a royal road to distinction, have never enticed them into exertion, nor refreshed them during their toil. They have rather been thrust forward by an indomitable will, along a steep and slippery path, crossed with torrents, overhung with rocks, and clouded by storms. As it has been with individuals, so it may be with nations. A young people may start into life, possessing in itself all the elements of physical and moral greatness. To be sure, time alone can bring unity and steadfastness of purpose, the full development of its resources, and the perfection of concentrated powers. All other wants, however, its native richness will supply; all other obstacles the wild sweep of its energies will lay prostrate. As an example of this truth, America stands before the eyes of the world.

It is however our present intention to speak of but one of the forms in which our nation has developed its self-making energies. We mean SCHOLARSHIP; an object of national ambition upon which the peculiar disadvantages of youth have more influence than upon any other.

There are those who are ever ready to decry our claims to scholarship, while others are not wanting to cry them up extravagantly. These extremes are of course undesirable. A rational and careful estimate of the attainments of the United States in scholarship has, so far as we know, never been attempted.

It has been truly said that ' our country is indeed a giant, leaping forth in his strength.' Only a little more than two centuries have elapsed since the wild woods of America resounded for the first time with the footsteps of the white man; since the forests disappeared from the places where now have risen with a kind of majesty

ORIGINAL PAPERS.

no eminent divines, has been expressed. But the absurdity of this assertion will be manifest if we take a brief survey of facts.

Among those belonging to our first and second ages, we would mention Cotton, the Mathers and Thompson, as men of fervent piety, sound in thought, acute in reasoning, and powerful in argument. After these came President Stiles, a profound scholar, equally distinguished for his attainments in both sacred and profane learning; Dr. Samuel Johnson, the father of the American Episcopal Church; Hopkins, who contributed much to theological science during the last century; Jonathan Edwards, the acutest analyst that the world has known since the days of Plato. Robert Hall considers him 'the greatest of the sons of men.' 'His power of subtle argument,' says Sir James Mackintosh, 'was perhaps unmatched, certainly was unsurpassed among men;' and it was joined, as in some of the ancient mystics, with a character which raised his piety to fervor. Among the followers of Edwards we would refer to Dr. Dwight, a thorough scholar, a fervent and profound thinker, an advocate of the highest principles of religion and philosophy, in whose character was combined the rarest and noblest of human virtues.

Not to extend our catalogue, we dare assert that the nation does not exist which can furnish a list of divines more distinguished for thorough scholarship, originality of mind, force of expression and superior talents and acquirements, than that which includes the names of Emmons, Fisk, Channing, Stuart, Robinson, and others whose names are closely identified with the New-England theology of the last and present century.

Among those who have contributed to and enlarged the boundaries of metaphysics, James Marsh, formerly of Hampden and Sidney College, deserves mention. Most of his writings are devoted to those pure and spiritual principles of philosophy of which Kant was the most distinguished European supporter. Before the works of Kant were known in this country, Marsh had formed theories similar to his, and taught them to his classes.

Among our contemporary philosophical writers, Ralph Waldo Emerson is perhaps the most distinguished. He is an original and independent thinker. He carries you through no long process of dim reasoning, upon certain premises, but jumps at once to his conclusions. He perceives the evils in society, but does not attempt to make any reformation; he is content to be an observer and a prophet. We pretend not to discuss his ethereal subtilties.* Whether we believe or disbelieve in his semi-pantheism is nothing to the point. We merely mention him as an American scholar of distinction. Some would doubtless reckon Orestes A. Brownson in this category. We would hold him up before the eyes of foreign nations only as we would send Tom Thumb to France. His philosophy seems to consist in keeping his mind in as unsettled a state as possible, while hurling the most absolute dicta from every resting-

* 'This word is often written *subtleties*, but less correctly.' — Webster.

place which he finds in the erratic march of opinion. In early life a rank infidel, he has passed through different phases of conviction until he has reached the most bigoted of all religious creeds.

Let us now glance at the state of legal science in our country. The fact that different codes exist in the different states operates as a strong barrier against the scientific culture of the law, as a national study. Beside, the profession of law among us necessarily exhausts itself almost entirely in legal practice. We make no extensive claim to the historic law-learning of the old world. Yet in all that relates to the science of English law, the works of our writers would well bear a comparison in learning and authority with those of any nation. We hesitate not to say, that for legal acumen and skill, for luminous method, for profound research, for purity of diction, for comprehensive brevity, for pregnancy of matter, for classical embellishments, for apt illustration, for clear and manly style, and for extent and variety of knowledge of jurisprudence, American judges and lawyers stand second to none in the world. The opinions of some of our authors are as highly appreciated, and considered as good authority in the courts of England as in those of the United States.

Who is the author of the treatise on international law which serves as a manual for European diplomatists ? An American, who represents his country at the most learned court in Europe. We can boast of lawyers who would sustain with honor to their country and credit to themselves, the weight and dignity of Westminster Hall. Our reports contain decisions which for sound learning, for force and logic, for skill and practical knowledge, have not been excelled, even in the proudest days of the law. The reports of Massachusetts, Connecticut and New-York are most respectable as authorities all over the Union, and are treated with much respect abroad. Until within the last quarter of a century, we had done but little more than adapt a few English law works to suit the condition of our country ; but during the last twenty-five years we have vied with the old world in the number and in the value of treatises on legal subjects. As evidence of this fact, of the legal treatises, digests and reports, the very list of which would frighten an ex-chancellor, we need only mention the works of PHILLIPS on Insurance and on Patents ; SWIFT's Digest ; WHEATON on International Law ; DANE on American Law ; HOFFMAN, whose book ' contains by far the most perfect system for the study of the law which has ever been offered to the public ;'* and above all, the Commentaries of Chancellor KENT, the American Blackstone, and the works of Judge STORY on Bailments, Constitutional Law, the Conflict of Laws and Equity Jurisprudence, all of which have won for their authors a reputation which is not confined to one hemisphere. The Commentary of Judge STORY on National and Commercial Law is one of the first text-books put into the hands of the young barrister of the Temple ; and his opinions are quoted as good authority, both

---

* Judge STORY.

our houses, our cities, our seminaries of learning, and the temples of the living God. For more than a century and a half the colonies were dependent on the mother country. With our national freedom commenced our peculiar national development, which has advanced with a rapidity that has no parallel in the history of the world. Instead of thirteen feeble colonies, we now number twenty-seven states, together with immense tracts of territory, and Texas; instead of a population of three and a half millions of souls, we now number seventeen millions; no portion of our vast territory, from the Atlantic to the Pacific, remains unexplored, and the sails of our commerce whiten every sea.

Situated as we have been, it could not be reasonably expected that the cultivation of the national mind would keep pace with these wonderful physical developments, or that we should be inspired with enthusiasm for the more quiet pursuits of literature and science. Such a state of things would have been an anomaly among nations. We have made more progress in letters within the last half century, than during the whole period of our previous existence. The colonists were more engaged in levelling the forests and securing an external prosperity, than in searching for native dryads and nymphs in their primitive shades. There were, it is true, among the pilgrims a WINTHROP, a BRADFORD and a HUTCHINSON to commemorate their deeds; a ROGER WILLIAMS and a COTTON to 'beat the drum ecclesiastic;' a WOLCOTT and a TRUMBULL to 'give to airy nothing a local habitation and a name;' but the productions of these men are now placed in our libraries as mere curiosities, and are seldom referred to. In fact, with the exception of the writings of ADAMS, JEFFERSON, HAMILTON and JAY, the works of FRANKLIN and the State Papers of WASHINGTON, all that we have accomplished in literature and science has been done within the last thirty years. It can scarcely be said that we have a class of men devoted exclusively to letters and the sciences; or at most, we had better speak very modestly on this topic. The very circumstances of our condition and character tend to prevent the formation of a literary class.

One of these circumstances is the vast extent of our territory in comparison with the amount of our population. The demand is for laborers in the *practical* departments of society. Such being the case, could it be expected that a large number would be found who love science and pursue it for its own sake, and depend upon it for bread? The relative number of those who obtain even a liberal education is very small, and they pursue their elementary course, not for the sake of cultivating letters, or enlarging the boundaries of science, but because it is necessary to obtain for them wealth, influence, and eminence in a profession.

Another feature in our condition which operates against the formation of a literary and scientific class, is the form of our government. It is, both in theory and in practice, in the hands of the people; and therefore the sentiment of the whole community is the regulator of all public measures, and this sentiment encourages the culture of literature and science only so far as they subserve more practical ends. In short, the cultivation of literature and science, except so far as they have a practical bearing, is left to the operation of the voluntary principle. The very nature of our institutions prevents the government from calling forth and patronising a literary class. Their tendency is to diffuse a practical education throughout the whole mass of the people; and the voluntary principle, for want of opportunity and means, has not as yet been called into exercise to any considerable extent.

Some may think that we have spoken thus far in terms too derogatory to ourselves; but it must be remembered that we have spoken only of the means and facilities of learning among us. If however we take a brief survey of the actual attainments of the United States in scholarship, notwithstanding there have been and still are, from the very nature of our condition and character, many powerful causes operating against us, we shall not fail to perceive, if we mistake not, that we are, in many respects at least, on an equality with the countries of the old world.

We grant that in those branches of learning in which success depends on long training and access to libraries, the scholars of the old world occupy the front rank; but we do maintain that in those departments which are connected with practical duties, or which depend on personal effort and observation, and in the application of the various sciences to the arts and the uses of practical life, the United States need not shrink from any comparison. A brief review of facts will show how far this assertion is borne out.

Let us consider for a moment the condition of the learned professions in the United States and in Europe.

Look first at Theology: indeed it is asserted by one whose long experience, profound learning, and close observation have well qualified him to judge correctly, that the clergy of the United States, as a body, hold a higher rank, both in the science and in the practice of their profession, than do those of any country of the old world, with the single exception perhaps of Germany. In that country there are men who devote their whole lives to the science of theology, but they do not usually preach. From this fact we derive the conclusion by *à priori* reasoning that the American clergy really merit a higher rank than even those of Germany. The American student takes but one path when seeking for theological truth; the German student, guided by an unsteady and flickering light through the hazy regions of metaphysics, finds her now on the surface, now in the clouds, and now — where the fable places her — 'in the bottom of a well.'

The causes of the emigration of our forefathers were religious, and their literature was of a religious cast. They were free, independent thinkers, unshackled by foreign authorities, acknowledging no head but the Supreme Being, no guides to the duties of religion except the holy prophets and apostles, together with CHRIST, the perfect exemplar of a spotless life.

We are aware that the opinion that our country has produced

no eminent divines, has been expressed.   But the absurdity of this assertion will be manifest if we take a brief survey of facts.

Among those belonging to our first and second ages, we would mention COTTON, the MATHERS and THOMPSON, as men of fervent piety, sound in thought, acute in reasoning, and powerful in argument.   After these came President STILES, a profound scholar, equally distinguished for his attainments in both sacred and profane learning; Dr. SAMUEL JOHNSON, the father of the American Episcopal Church; HOPKINS, who contributed much to theological science during the last century; JONATHAN EDWARDS, the acutest analyst that the world has known since the days of Plato.   Robert Hall considers him ' the greatest of the sons of men.'   ' His power of subtle argument,' says Sir JAMES MACKINTOSH, ' was perhaps unmatched, certainly was unsurpassed among men;' and it was joined, as in some of the ancient mystics, with a character which raised his piety to fervor.   Among the followers of EDWARDS we would refer to Dr. DWIGHT, a thorough scholar, a fervent and profound thinker, an advocate of the highest principles of religion and philosophy, in whose character was combined the rarest and noblest of human virtues.

Not to extend our catalogue, we dare assert that the nation does not exist which can furnish a list of divines more distinguished for thorough scholarship, originality of mind, force of expression and superior talents and acquirements, than that which includes the names of EMMONS, FISK, CHANNING, STUART, ROBINSON, and others whose names are closely identified with the New-England theology of the last and present century.

Among those who have contributed to and enlarged the boundaries of metaphysics, JAMES MARSH, formerly of Hampden and Sidney College, deserves mention.   Most of his writings are devoted to those pure and spiritual principles of philosophy of which Kant was the most distinguished European supporter.   Before the works of Kant were known in this country, MARSH had formed theories similar to his, and taught them to his classes.

Among our contemporary philosophical writers, RALPH WALDO EMERSON is perhaps the most distinguished.   He is an original and independent thinker.   He carries you through no long process of dim reasoning, upon certain premises, but jumps at once to his conclusions.   He perceives the evils in society, but does not attempt to make any reformation; he is content to be an observer and a prophet.   We pretend not to discuss his ethereal subtilties.*   Whether we believe or disbelieve in his semi-pantheism is nothing to the point.   We merely mention him as an American scholar of distinction.   Some would doubtless reckon ORESTES A. BROWNSON in this category.   We would hold him up before the eyes of foreign nations only as we would send Tom Thumb to France.   His philosophy seems to consist in keeping his mind in as unsettled a state as possible, while hurling the most absolute dicta from every resting-

* ' THIS word is often written *subtleties,* but less correctly.' — WEBSTER.

place which he finds in the erratic march of opinion. In early life a rank infidel, he has passed through different phases of conviction until he has reached the most bigoted of all religious creeds.

Let us now glance at the state of legal science in our country. The fact that different codes exist in the different states operates as a strong barrier against the scientific culture of the law, as a national study. Beside, the profession of law among us necessarily exhausts itself almost entirely in legal practice. We make no extensive claim to the historic law-learning of the old world. Yet in all that relates to the science of English law, the works of our writers would well bear a comparison in learning and authority with those of any nation. We hesitate not to say, that for legal acumen and skill, for luminous method, for profound research, for purity of diction, for comprehensive brevity, for pregnancy of matter, for classical embellishments, for apt illustration, for clear and manly style, and for extent and variety of knowledge of jurisprudence, American judges and lawyers stand second to none in the world. The opinions of some of our authors are as highly appreciated, and considered as good authority in the courts of England as in those of the United States.

Who is the author of the treatise on international law which serves as a manual for European diplomatists? An American, who represents his country at the most learned court in Europe. We can boast of lawyers who would sustain with honor to their country and credit to themselves, the weight and dignity of Westminster Hall. Our reports contain decisions which for sound learning, for force and logic, for skill and practical knowledge, have not been excelled, even in the proudest days of the law. The reports of Massachusetts, Connecticut and New-York are most respectable as authorities all over the Union, and are treated with much respect abroad. Until within the last quarter of a century, we had done but little more than adapt a few English law works to suit the condition of our country; but during the last twenty-five years we have vied with the old world in the number and in the value of treatises on legal subjects. As evidence of this fact, of the legal treatises, digests and reports, the very list of which would frighten an ex-chancellor, we need only mention the works of PHILLIPS on Insurance and on Patents; SWIFT's Digest; WHEATON on International Law; DANE on American Law; HOFFMAN, whose book 'contains by far the most perfect system for the study of the law which has ever been offered to the public;'* and above all, the Commentaries of Chancellor KENT, the American Blackstone, and the works of Judge STORY on Bailments, Constitutional Law, the Conflict of Laws and Equity Jurisprudence, all of which have won for their authors a reputation which is not confined to one hemisphere. The Commentary of Judge STORY on National and Commercial Law is one of the first text-books put into the hands of the young barrister of the Temple; and his opinions are quoted as good authority, both

* Judge STORY.

in the courts of the mother country and in those of the United
States at the same moment.   While we write, it is in contemplation
to erect in Lincoln's Inn a monument to this great American law-
yer, who has recently passed away from the scenes of earthly bick-
erings and strifes to contemplate Eternal Justice, before the most
august of all tribunals.

We might continue, and notice at length those who in their res-
pective departments have enlarged the boundaries of science, and
contributed much toward building up the Republic of Letters in
the western world; but our limits do not permit, nor does our plan
require it.   A brief reference to a few of the votaries of science
and literature among us must suffice.

And first we mention Noah Webster, whose great American
Dictionary of the English language, 'the product of thirty years
labor,' has been reprinted in Europe, and pronounced by competent
judges to be the most comprehensive and useful one extant.   In
the learned languages, Prof. Anthon, of Columbia College, stands
preëminent.   Nearly a dozen of his elaborate works are text-books
in the universities of Great Britain.   In pure mathematics our au-
thors have rarely made themselves known beyond the text-books
used in our seminaries of learning.   Yet to show that this depart-
ment is not wholly neglected, we would mention that Nathaniel
Bowditch, the self-taught cabin-boy, afterward a navigator, trans-
lated and published at his own expense, in four large quartos, La
Placé's Mècanique Cèleste, and added a valuable commentary of
abstruse calculations and problems, equal in amount of matter to
the original text.   Bowditch's Practical Navigator is of inestimable
value to the mariner, and is now found on every sea.

The most magnificent and accurate work that has yet appeared
on Ornithology was written by John James Audubon, a native of
South Carolina.   Our chemists and geologists have won for them-
selves an European reputation.   They are known and highly res-
pected abroad as well as at home.   Our meteorologists hold a con-
spicuous place among the lords of storms.

Dr. Lieber, of South Carolina College, editor of the 'Encyclopæ-
dia Americana,' has written a profound work on political ethics, and
also a valuable treatise on hermaneutics.   As a historian, Prescott
stands unrivalled among contemporary writers.   Careful and in-
telligent in research, master of composition as an art, profound and
yet graceful, he has succeeded in imparting to history all the noblest
qualities of romance, without trenching one inch upon fidelity and
precision.   Titian's colorings cannot be warmer, or Reynolds' out-
lines more exact.   Bancroft, with some faults, is not without much
merit as a historian.   His accurate and philosophical history of
the United States has won for him a just meed of applause, and se-
cured for him the reputation of being an excellent historical writer.
Enough has been said to show that the writers of our country are
not deficient in any of the essential qualities which should charac-
terize historians.   We would not neglect to mention here the name
of Washington Irving, who, it is not too great praise to say, is the

best living writer of English prose. His style possesses all the characteristic beauties of ADDISON'S, its ease, grace, simplicity and elegance. While he has great accuracy, point, spirit and dignity, the mere ornaments of a good style, he exhibits in an eminent degree the sense, or as Shakspeare calls it, the *soul*.

Nor is America without her great men in the department of eloquence. To say nothing of her OTISES, her HENRYS, her RUTLEDGES, and her AMESES, whose eloquence was 'as a flame of fire,' we mention only the greater orators of the present age — WEBSTER, CLAY and CALHOUN,

'UPON whose lips the mystic bee hath dropped the honey of persuasion.'

When their speeches, breathing as they do the liberal spirit of our free institutions, shall have been hallowed by time, they will form one of the proudest monuments of our nation's literature. For elegance and purity of diction, chasteness of style, cogency of argument, force of expression; for splendid rhetoric and for solidity, strength and power of reasoning, WEBSTER stands without a rival. He 'wields the club of Hercules entwined with flowers.' CLAY's chief excellence consists in his *practicalness*. His great power is passion, the basis of which is a strong common-sense conviction of what he utters. His productions, exhibiting as they do broad and liberal views of policy, an earnestness of conviction, and a heartiness of purpose, entitle him to his high reputation. For sententious and close reasoning, for power of analysis, simplicity and dignity, CALHOUN has no superior.

It is one of the sentences of the popular cant, that America has given birth to no poets. But have we not a BRYANT, whose poetry delights the inhabitants of Scotland as well as the wanderer on the romantic borders of the Rhine? Have we not a DANA, who gives us 'thoughts that breathe and words that burn?' Have we not a PERCIVAL, a devoted scholar, who 'writes with fluency all the modern languages of Europe;' who makes reports to the state legislature on geology, and yet finds time to court the Muses, and tell us that

'THE world is full of poetry ; the air
Is living with its spirit ; and the waves
Dance to the music of its melodies,
And sparkle in its brightness?'

We have, too, a HALLECK, who, amid a thousand duties, finds occasional leisure to throw off lyrics so thrilling that they find their way to every heart. We might speak of LONGFELLOW, WILLIS, BRAINARD, WILLIS GAYLORD CLARK, and others of merit in this department, did our limits permit.

As for novelists, we mention only the names of COOPER and CHARLES BROCKDEN BROWN, whose writings have been translated into French, German and Italian, and are very popular on the continent. Their productions are fit to be ranked among the best works of their kind written in the most highly cultivated nations of modern times. They will 'live as long as the sea-surges sound, and the heart of the old woods is silent.'

The attainments of America in *classical* scholarship, Oriental research, and the philology of modern languages, together with the departments of natural philosophy and criticism, we omit for want of time; but we cannot forbear mentioning incidentally, that it is in mechanical invention, and the strong grasp on fundamental principles, and their felicitous application to the public interests, that America has borne her richest fruits; fruits richer than the similar products of any other soil. The invention of the cotton-gin has had a powerful influence for good on the prosperity of our Southern states, and has greatly improved the condition of—we had almost said *created*—the middle class in Great Britain. To say nothing of the wonderful inventions of FRANKLIN and FULTON, our locomotives traverse the plains of Germany and Russia, and architects from the old world visit our shores to study the models of our ships and the construction of our rail-roads. The Magnetic Telegraph, the wonder of the age and pride of our nation, has been put in successful operation in the countries of the old world by Americans.

Enough has been said to show that much has been done toward building up a Republic of Letters in America. In fact, the Anglo-Saxon race in the United States have done as much in the domains of thought in the present century as any twelve millions of people in the world. But while we congratulate ourselves on having made such progress, we would not forget that much remains yet to be done. Our country is young; our scholarship in its comparative infancy; nor can we expect of youth the strength of manhood. All that we have accomplished has been done while laboring under many disadvantages, and as we think some defects in our system of education.

One great obstacle which tends to impede the successful cultivation of literature and science in our country, is the absence of an International Copy-right Law, which shall recognise and protect literary property. This subject is too well understood to require examination here. We want too more genuine and lofty national feeling, more intelligent and earnest effort to foster the good we have, and acquire the good we need. The standard of scholarship among us should be raised to a higher point, and this important duty devolves upon our seminaries of learning. This naturally leads us to inquire, what is the influence which American colleges are exerting on American scholarship? To answer this question correctly, it will be necessary to consider the system of college education pursued in the United States. We have spoken of this system as being defective. And defects certainly there are; for a *perfect* system would satisfy the demands of the public; and the frequent changes that have been made in the present system, added to the fact that in order to support our colleges it is necessary to give away a large portion of our education, are sufficient proof that it does not meet the wants of the people. We would here guard against all novelty: we do not purpose to suggest any new theory of education, nor to recommend any wild Utopian scheme of instruction. It shall be our endeavor to consider dispassionately some of the principal features in the present system of college education in the United States ; and if on examination we find it really defaced by blemishes, to attribute the errors and defects to those to whom they are due, and then, so far as we have ability, to suggest improvements, or point out proper remedies.

The appointment and the power of the board called trustees, directors or the corporation of the college, claims our attention first. The general direction of the affairs of the institution is intrusted to this corporation. It is their duty to attend to the pecuniary interests of the college, appoint and remove officers, confer degrees, and in *some* of the New-England colleges, together with those in the south and west, it is made a part of the duty of the corporation to mark out the course of instruction to be pursued.

This body in most cases (time-honored Yale is a bright exception) is composed of men who have had no experience in teaching ; who are more distinguished for their wealth or high standing in society than for literary and scientific attainments ; men who are not competent to judge of the qualifications of the instructors they appoint, or their success in teaching after they have been appointed ; who never made the science of education a special study ; who are not particularly interested in science and letters ; who devote but very little time to the discharge of their duty ; who are chosen not unfrequently for their sectarian principles ; who in most cases meet only once a year ; who are not obliged to consult the Faculty of the college in regard to proposed changes ; who accept the office perhaps only to gratify the friends of the institution they represent ; who have very limited opportunities of becoming familiar with the management of the business committed to their hands ; men who do not feel that they are in any measure responsible for the failure or the success of the institution ; who do not exercise the power vested in them, and whose attention is absorbed in interests other than those of education. Is then, we ask, such a body of men, forming as they do the most powerful but least efficient part of the government of a college, fit to have the entire control of the discipline, the choice of text-books, and the general plan of instruction in a college ? If this body is of an innovating spirit, and exercises the power which it alone has a right to use, then changes are introduced, experiments are tried, instructors are made dependent upon them, and if they resist the proposed changes they are removed, and others of a more pliant disposition, but less competent to teach, are sought to fill their places. If, on the contrary, the board of Trustees is inactive and negligent, and the reputation of the institution is not established and sustained, then the instructors free themselves from all censure or blame, by saying that they had not the power to act, and that the want of success is owing to the bad management of the corporation.

This is true in its full extent in regard to certain portions of our country where this system prevails.

We are aware that in a very small number of our colleges the business of the corporation is faithfully attended to by a committee, consisting of three of their number. This is well. And we are told that in point of *fact* the members of the corporation listen to the advice of the Faculty of the college, and that they are guided in all their proceedings by the suggestions of the Faculty, granted. The corporation *nominally* possess the power. In *reality*, the Faculty of the college possess it. Now is it not reasonable and just that the responsibility should rest upon those who exercise the power ? We speak not of the members of the corporation; it is of the system that we complain. That the whole plan of education should be under the control of such a board of Trustees, is a defect in the constitution of American colleges. And would it not be an improvement if the members of this board, instead of being chosen for life as they now are, should be chosen for a term of years ? The - reasons for such a change will be manifest, if we consider how natural it is for office-holders, when the office is a permanent one, and requires but little of their time, to become dilatory in the discharge of their duty. We would have the period of office sufficiently long to show the effect of new measures and incumbents proving themselves worthy, should be reëligible.

Again : would it not be a still greater improvement if the members of the corporation were few in number ? Every one knows how difficult it is to make a large number of men feel the weight of responsibility. Let the responsibility which now rests upon the twenty members of a corporation fall upon five competent and judicious men, and we venture to affirm that the duties of that body would be more perfectly discharged than they are at present. In short, we think that the power which the corporation possess, but which they do not exercise, should be vested in the instructors of the college. They are the men, actuated by high motives and aiming at noble ends, who care most for their own reputation and that of the college ; who have had years of experience in teaching ; men who are most competent, in the very respects in which the corporation are most deficient, to control the college; who are zealous for the advancement of letters, and who are best qualified to arrange the general scheme and minutiæ of the work to be done in a literary and scientific institution.

Another serious defect in the constitution of American colleges is the unequal qualifications of instructors in equally important branches of education. We grant that the professorships in our colleges are in the main filled by men who are in every respect competent to discharge the duties of their office. · But there are exceptions. It cannot be denied but that there are instructors in some of the American colleges who are wholly unfit, for want of natural ability, learning or industry, to discharge the duties of their office in a proper manner; who are in fact destitute of some of the most important qualifications of instructors; who keep down the departments of which they have charge under the pressure of their own inability or stupidity; who consult their own convenience and ease rather than the good of their pupils, and who waste the time and ruin the intellectual habits of all who are so unfortunate as to come under their instruction.

The intellectual character of the student is necessarily shaped to a great extent by that of his instructor; and it is obvious that the evil of which we speak — the unequal qualifications of instructors in equally important branches of education — must have a baneful influence upon him. The student imbibes wisdom from the instructor who conveys his knowledge gracefully and intelligibly, whether the science taught be worth his eager attention or not. But he shrinks with impatience from coarse language, obscure expressions, want of enthusiasm and palpable mediocrity of talent, although these forbidding means are applied to convey the most delectable and useful knowledge. Who would thrust his hand into a hive of living bees though he might extract thereby the very honey of Hymettus?

This inequality of instructors is no more than might be reasonably expected under the present plan of appointment. Are they chosen hastily? Are any measures taken to ascertain who is the most competent person who would accept the office? Is the electoral body influenced by parties? — for there are parties in the literary and scientific as well as the political world. Are they removed from their office when found incompetent to fill it? Do any of them owe their appointment to some accident or caprice? Do the appointments always give satisfaction? Are they made in such a manner as to add dignity to the office, and render it an object of virtuous ambition? Is the field of selection a very limited one? The answer to these grave questions it is unnecessary that we should suggest. We think a change might be made in the mode of appointing professors which would greatly improve the present system of college education. When a vacancy occurs let a public announcement of the fact be made. Let the office be open to free and honorable competition. Let the appointment depend upon the result of a strict and searching examination, conducted without partiality, by men competent to act as judges in the case; and let the tenure of the office depend on industry and success in teaching. . This is the method pursued in Germany and other European countries, and centuries of experience testify to its superior excellence. Is it not worthy of trial in the United States? If adopted it would enhance the dignity and increase the respectability of the situation. It would secure the public against imposition. It would induce the candidates for the vacant chair to study and fit themselves to act in that department. It would secure the greatest amount of talent and learning. It would add a stimulus to the cultivation of literature and science. It would place professors under the same obligations to labor as any other class of men; and knowing that the tenure of their office depended on their personal efforts and success in teaching, and that the cause of letters would be advanced, and their own reputation increased in proportion to their exertions, they would devote themselves zealously to their high calling, and students would delight to derive lessons of wisdom from such enthusiastic and pleasing instructors. This is not mere idle speculation. These results might reasonably be expected from such a change.

We come now to speak of an evil far-reaching in its effects, and perhaps the most difficult of all to be remedied. We mean the great number of our colleges. The last number of the American Almanac gives the names of one hundred and seventy-three colleges in the United States, containing sixteen thousand two hundred and thirty-three students. According to a table published recently in a German journal, there are but one hundred and seventeen universities in all Europe, and they contain ninety-four thousand six-hundred students. The single state of New-York, with a population of two millions and-a-half, has twelve colleges and one thousand two hundred and eighty-five students. Prussia, (her universities are among the best in the world,) with a population of fourteen millions, has seven universities and five thousand two hundred and twenty students. France, with a population of thirty-five millions, has fourteen colleges and twelve thousand one hundred and eighty students. Pennsylvania, with a population of less than two millions, has twenty colleges and two thousand and thirty-four students. Great Britain has nine universities and seventeen thousand seven hundred and fifty students, for a population of twenty-seven millions. The New-England states have nineteen colleges and two thousand eight hundred and fifty-seven students for a population of about two millions and a quarter.

From these statistics, which are not without their connection with our subject, it appears that if the number of our institutions was reduced to only twenty, we should still have a greater number in proportion to our population than any country in the old world. And it is not too much to say, that if the money which has been given by legislative grants and private donations to nearly two hundred colleges, had been distributed among only twenty of these institutions, we should now possess universities as wealthy and as well provided with all the facilities and *essential* means of instruction as even Oxford or Cambridge. The number of our colleges is constantly increasing. It is now in contemplation to establish one in Oregon, even before Great Britian has released her claim to that territory. And how can this rage for multiplying colleges be checked? We answer, let those institutions which already possess the confidence of the public, raise the standard of scholarship. Let the standard for admission be higher than at present. Let a comprehensive course of study be adopted, and let instruction be thorough. Then the petty electioneering institutions, bearing the name but destitute of the essential characteristics of a college, which now infest our country, will go down. They will not be able to enter into competition with the older colleges; while their narrow and popular course of study will secure for them their proper position; namely, that of high schools.

Another defect in our system of college education is the absence of established scholarship, similar to those that exist in Oxford and Cambridge. The course of study, in our best institutions at least, is comprehensive enough, but would it not be an improvement if the time for studying before receiving a degree was prolonged? The object of a college institution is to direct and discipline the mind, develope its faculties, and fit the student 'for all the offices, both public and private, of peace and war.' It is to teach him how to study and draw from the depths of his own mind. Certainly the cultivation of the mental faculties requires as much time as the art of a mechanic or a silversmith. Those who are destined for one of the mechanical trades are required to serve an apprenticeship of seven years, and should not the student give the same time to the Muses before receiving a diploma? Let the time spent within college walls be extended. Let the requirements for a degree be higher than at present, and let its reception depend on the actual amount of knowledge which the candidate on examination is found to possess. Then the diploma will be proof, of no dubious character, that the individual whose name it bears has not 'gone through college in vain,' but that he has been a faithful and punctual student, and received all the instruction he could obtain from his Alma Mater. Such a change would require no additional studies or instructors.

Thus we have endeavored to advance a few practical thoughts on our system of college education, as it is and as it ought to be; and should the changes which we have ventured to suggest ever be made, we hesitate not to predict that a new era will dawn upon American colleges, and a brilliant chapter be commenced in their history. Most of the defects which injure the American system of collegiate education can, we imagine, be traced to the want of a proper standard of scholarship. The qualities which ought to characterize such a standard, are to be found only in a NATIONAL UNIVERSITY. The condition of our country demands the establishment of such an institution. Let the nation make provision for a literary class who may devote their whole lives to science and letters; ·let their wants be supplied; let them have a place to which they may retire from the busy throng; let them receive encouragement and sympathy from a generous people; and then we shall have an institution which will command the respect of the world, and be a standard by which to try others in our own country. Within its walls will be found the genius of the nation, the most gifted men of the land. And by their mutual efforts they will beget a thirst for knowledge and stengthen each other. This fountain of wisdom will give an impulse to the energy, and vitality to the intellect of the nation. The store-house of nature will be opened, the treasury of knowledge unsealed, and important truths discovered; the boundaries of science and letters will be extended, and a higher and more healthful tone will be given to THE SCHOLARSHIP OF AMERICA.

New-Haven, Conn.

AN ANGEL ON EARTH.

Die when you will, you need not wear
At Heaven's court a form more fair
   Than Beauty at your birth has given;
Keep but the lips, the eyes we see,
The voice we hear, and you will be
   An angel ready-made for Heaven.

THE TEACHING OF NATURE.

WHY dost thou o'er thy sorrows mourn,
  As if to mourn were all thy duty?
Why think'st thou only on the thorn,
  And not upon the rose's beauty?

Is not the GOD of Heaven and Earth
  Creator of the sparkling river;
Of Nature? — and of Nature's mirth —
  The truest thanks to GOD the Giver?

Is GOD a GOD of sighs and tears?
  His ocean moved by storms forever?
And answers to the sailor's cheers
  The laughter of the billows never!

Oh, yes! there's joy for all that GOD
  The breath of life on earth has given;
There's not a rock, there's not a clod,
  That seeth not the *light* of heaven!

That seeth not, and thanketh not
  Of beauty and of joy the MAKER;
There's not on earth so lone a spot,
  That is not of that joy partaker.

Then why should man do nought but mourn,
  And never copy Nature's smiling?
As if the world were given to turn
  Our better soul with false beguiling?

And is not flesh the heir of joy,
  A joy transcending every sorrow?
Where outward wo cannot destroy
  The bliss that from our faith we borrow?

Yes! GOD has given us lessons there,
  And stars to guide our steps to Heaven;
Midst all that's bright and all that's fair,
  There's not one false allurement given.

The streams, the flowers are monitors,
  But monitors of blithsome bearing;
All breathing things one feeling stirs —
  Is not that feeling worth the sharing?

How could we of the GIVER know,
  Untokened in all Nature's brightness!
How could we to HIS goodness bow,
  Who ne'er had given our hearts a lightness!

How could we pray? how could we praise?
  How could we dream of Heaven hereafter?
When all lays else were joyous lays,
  And only man's forbidden laughter?

                                      W. M.

LIGHTS AND SHADOWS OF FASHIONABLE LIFE.

BY PETER SCHLEMIHL.

'ICH habe gesehen, was (Ich weiss das) ich nicht würde geglaubt haben auf ihre Erzählung.'
TREVIRANUS, TO COLERIDGE.

'I have seen what I am certain I would not have believed on your telling.'

MRS. SMITH hid her face in her hands, until she had regained her self-possession; when, looking up, she requested the Gentleman in Black to tell her more about his system of labor; and asked:

' What is the prevailing religion among your slaves ?   I presume they are, as all slaves are said to be, very religious ?'

' The religion of my slaves is various indeed,' replied the Gentleman in Black, with great vivacity, and an air of the utmost frankness. ' They are at liberty to worship as many gods as they please, for I pride myself in being tolerant.   Some of them are rather lax, but most of them are very devout, and delight in macerations, stripes, pilgrimages; some again are exceedingly dogmatical, and ready to fight for abstractions which no human sagacity can make palpable even to themselves.   It do n't matter much to me what they worship.   The idols of the imagination are just as real as the idols of gold and silver, and those who deem themselves too wise to worship the creations of Art, are those most devoted to the creations of Fancy.'

' You just now spoke of the efforts of the *Abolitionists* among your slaves.   And do you allow them to come upon your plantations ?'

' I can 't help it, Madam; they will come, in spite of all I can do; and so I do the best I can to weaken their influence, by showing my slaves the folly of giving up the known for the unknown, the seen for the unseen; and I am rarely unsuccessful, I assure you.   I must, however, confess to you, with much mortification on my part, that at the outset of their irruption into my territory, I allowed my agents to apply LYNCH LAW to them pretty actively and extensively; but I found that so far from securing my object, it made my slaves believe that that which was told them by stealth, and at the risk of life and limb, must be something specially desirable; and in consequence of this mania, lost my slaves in great numbers.   Finding out my mistake, I changed my policy: though on some of my plantations my agents still adhere to this plan, believing it to be best to compel submission; but I assure you, my dear Madam, it is against my enlightened judgment in such cases, and which I every where disclaim and deny as any part of my code of government.   But

what can I do? I can't be every where at once, and my agents
will act as they please when I'm away.'

'That's true,' said Mrs. Smith; 'your plan is certainly the best,
and I do wish our southern planters would adopt it; we should not
then have this hateful slave question with all its enormities, alien-
ating one section of the country from the other.'

'I am satisfied it is not only wisest, safest and best for the slaves,
but for the masters, who have the curse of slavery resting upon
them.'

'And do *you* speak of slavery as a curse resting upon the masters?'

'Yes, Madam, I do. The fetter and the chain which binds the
ankle of the slave is fastened to a galling collar encircling the neck
of the master;* and the only method I have found successful in
relieving myself from inquietude was to adapt my service to an ex-
act accordance with the tastes and temperaments of my bondsmen.'

'I am sure you are amply repaid for any losses you may have
sustained, by the delightful consciousness that they feel your ser-
vice to be one of choice and not of compulsion.'

The Gentleman in Black bowed, with an air of extreme modesty,
of one who blushed at the hearing his own praise so sweetly spoken,
and replied:

'It would not become me to speak in commendation of my own
lenity, but it is not uncommon for those who have left my service
to return; and I assure you, in no instance have I, or my agents,
ever punished their delinquencies, but rather received them as re-
turning prodigals; and of such I can truly say, that their zeal in
my service is greatly increased by such a course of treatment.'

'Indeed, Sir, for one, I do not doubt it; and only wish our South-
ern gentlemen would take you for a pattern, in the management of
their poor slaves, who if they are recovered or return, from a fond
desire of their old homes and associates, are too often sold into
some distant state, so that 'their last state is worse than their first.'

My dear Madam, that's just what the Abolitionists tell my bonds-
men, but they themselves never complain of their reception and
subseqent treatment, so that all these representations of a condition
they never realize to be true, have only the effect to rivet their at-
tachment to my service the stronger.'

'And are all your slaves productive workers? This is contem-
plated, I believe, in all the *Phalansteries* of Unitative Associationists.'

'Oh no, Madam, this making every man and woman a mere
working machine, is no part of my plan, and would be, as I believe
it ever will be, impracticable. But all my slaves doing just what
they please, please me in doing what they do.'

'And yet you must have some very idle and worthless creatures
among them, and such as you must find it hard to turn to any good
account. Is it not so?'

'It is indeed so; and sometimes I'm puzzled to find out the way
of making some of my young girls of any sort of use whatever.

---

* St. Pierre.

Their whole souls are devoted to the gratification of their vanity, their love of admiration, dressing and undressing of themselves; and such is the wretched effect of pursuits so trivial and contemptible, that their souls have no expansion, and their hearts become incapable of any generous emotions. The sacrifice of a single opportunity to exhibit their prettinesses causes a tempest of passion hardly to be conceived of.

' I fear you are too severe upon the poor creatures. They have but few objects to interest them, and naturally seek to attain that grace and beauty which is the secret of their strength and influence.'

' But it is not, if they knew it; they would be irresistible could they but know that the attractions they covet are shallow and worthless, and the beauty they so sedulously seek to heighten, is only permanently influential when they possess those graces of the mind and affections, and that gentleness and loveliness of demeanor which they know is the highest attraction; but of which they rarely seek more than the shadow. One of their greatest favorites, and whose poems they place under their pillows, and on their centretables, has said of them: ' Women were ever fated to be my bane. Like Napoleon, I have always had a great contempt for women; and formed this opinion of them not hastily, but from my own fatal experience. My writings, indeed, tend to exalt the sex, and my imagination has always delighted in giving them a *beau ideal* likeness, but I only drew them as a painter or a sculptor would do — as they should be. The Turks and Eastern people manage these matters better than we do: they lock them up, and they are much happier. Give a woman a looking-glass and a few sugar-plums and she will be satisfied.'* This picture is drawn by one who has seen society in its highest forms, and may be considered a capable judge. ' Tis true, there are a few who are susceptible of a strong passion, which takes them out of themselves, and whatever direction this takes, it is a sure indication of a superior nature. Now, as I have said, they get sometimes weary of the worthlessness of their pursuits, and an abolitionist will sometimes inspire them with a strong desire for the homes and skies of their forefathers, by picturing the beauty and happiness they may attain by leaving my service; and they give me some trouble to reclaim them, though I am made to feel that they are hardly worth the cost of the gew-gaws by which they are won, and the exercise of the little arts by which they are to be retained.

' But why keep them in your service? Why not let them run, if they are desirous of going?'

' Ah, Madam, whatever may be my real estimate of their characters, they are after all essential and necessary to me.'

' For what purpose, if they are so worthless in themselves?'

' I must have them for wives and mothers. They are useful to

---

* Lord Byron's Conversations with Lieutenant Medwin.

me in this way, that they keep up my stock of slaves, who take their characters from their mothers; and you can readily see that I cannot afford to lose them. Now there is nothing I so much dread as the influence of an intellectual female; one whose soul is the seat of all pure and generous emotions; whose highest happiness is found in the discharge of the domestic duties of life; whose sympathies are alive to all that is beautiful and true, and whose mind is actively occupied in the attainment of all that knowledge and literature which gives grace and charm to her conversation, and makes her the companion and counsellor of her husband and his friends; who enriches every topic by the beauty of her imagination, and inspires in others the love of all that gentleness, purity and peace which hallows and glows in her own soul; such a female mind is the most attractive and most noble of all the creations of DEITY; but they are not the sort of daughters, wives and mothers that suit me, for they give me more trouble than a thousand of such as I have described. Their children seem formed for a higher condition than that to which they are born, and are full of aspirations, which 't is hard for me to repress or subvert; so you can readily see, that it would be greatly to my injury to propagate a class of minds which I am compelled to reverence and admire. Fortunately for me, most of my women are 'pleased with a rattle and tickled by a straw.'

'I fear, Sir,' said Mrs. Smith, 'you are a woman-hater. Were you ever married?'

The Gentleman in Black changed color, and for an instant his eye fell on the carpet; and, in a tone so low as to be almost inaudible, he replied: 'I am no woman-hater. I had hoped the sentiments I have just expressed would have satisfied you that there are women whose virtues I appreciate, and whose worth I acknowledge.' And musing for a moment, he continued—'I believe that if Christianity should be compelled to flee from the mansions of the great, the Academies of the philosophers, or the throng of busy men, we should find her last and *purest* retreat with WOMAN at the fireside; her last altar would be the *female* breast; her last audience, the children gathered around the knees of a *mother;* her last sacrifice, the secret prayer, escaping in silence from her lips, and heard only at the throne of GOD.'

The Gentleman in Black remained silent, as if absorbed by recollections which were full of tender and sad remembrances of the past; and Mrs. Smith felt she had unconsciously pained her visitor by questions which were too sacred to be prosecuted further; and to change the subject, inquired:

'In what forms do the religious tendencies of our nature exhibit themselves among your slaves?'

'They are so various, Madam, that it were a hard task to tell you,' replied the Gentleman in Black, with somewhat of his former cheerfulness of manner.

'Will you not be pleased to tell me of some of them?'

'They are, Madam, characterized by penances of various sorts, and especially as practised by those whom they style 'Tapas;' whose prayers are earnestly solicited by those around them, who minister to their wants and passions in every way possible. The more painful and difficult these penances are, the more they are revered. And these consist of standing on one foot and holding the other at the same time, with their eyes fixed on the sun. This is quite a distinguished penance. Others stand on the top of their toes for a length of time, which Fanny Ellsler has never attempted; others are buried in the earth, with a pipe which supplies them with air and food; some stand on their heads, others hang by the hands on a tree, or hang from the tree with their heads downward; all these penances are prescribed in their books, which they style the *Puranas.* Some go about with their heads turned upward to the heavens, and others with their arms crossed on their breasts, in a thoughtful posture, and with downcast looks, as if in profound meditation; others, with their arms stretched out horizontally, and some who are called *Muni's,* are doomed to perpetual silence.

'But while some of my slaves·are doomed to a state of painful immobility, others, called the *Choura-asin* are in constant activity, going through eighty-four sitting postures or changes, remarkable for their difficulty; but the most singular of all their penances, which they call the *Kassali,* and which is exquisitely painful, consists in their standing with their bare feet upon the *areka,* or betel-nut.'

'Can't these be boiled soft ?' inquired Mrs. Smith. 'Would it not be a kindness to translate for them Peter Pindar's Pilgrim and the Peas ?'

'It would doubtless be a kindness,' replied the Gentleman in Black, smiling; 'but these creatures are excessively attached to these extreme tortures; the least and most common of which is, the elevation of the hands above the head, which is persevered in till they become immoveable, the finger-nails perforating the palms. The *Batsiri* sit, never lying nor rising. Others hold their breath for an incredible length of time, and others again sit surrounded with four fires, at the cardinal points, intense as they can be borne. Such are the favorite austerities of my Eastern serfs; and though they are of no value to me as producers, yet they keep the rest of my slaves in due subjection to my overseers by their frightful pictures of the future destinies of such as are refractory, and which it is their province to avert, and for which they are well paid : and as most of these penances are necessarily of short duration, the devotees gain by them a full scope for the indulgence of their passions, without losing any of the respect of their devotees. On other plantations, the exhibition of the·religious sentiment differs, and the most sensible of them all, is the form adopted and practised by the rudest of my bondsmen.* Their GOD is an ugly image, before which their priests set a huge wheel on which they nail the prayers for the day, which the priests turn round with the utmost indifference, leaving it to the option of the image to take notice of them or not, as it chooses.'

---

* THE Calmuc Tartars.

' Your people are most miserably debased truly, and I wonder you can consent to the continuance of such practices, which would be deemed a disgrace in any age or country under the influence of the Christian religion,' said Mrs. Smith, with some asperity of manner.

' Not so unlike those practised by the christian church as you may suppose,' replied the Gentleman in Black, tartly.

'Indeed! In what dark age and country have ever such enormities been practised ? No, Sir, you must pardon me; I can't believe you.'

' You may believe me or not as you please, but as you think so highly of 'the pure and pristine ages of the Church,' I will, if you please, enlighten you on this subject. I have the materials at hand,* said the Gentleman in Black, looking toward the fathers of the church.

Mrs. Smith shook her head incredulously.

' I shall not undertake to show you the same disgusting exhibitions of self-inflicted tortures, imposed under the idea of propitiating heathen idols, but *penances* as utterly at war with the spirit of Christianity, practised and praised by the saints in those early ages of the Church, which some persons are so pleased to regard as the purest and the best. A system of self-immolation not unlike what I have described to you as existing among my own slaves, originated with Paul the Egyptian, who in the seventh persecution retired to a private cave, and lived unseen, till St. Anthony discovered him just before his death and buried him, and took possession of his cave. The notion that the soul is clogged by the body, and its virtues impeded by its connection with it, operating on the indolent and melancholy turn of many persons in the southern climate of Asia, especially of Egypt, led them to affect an austere and solitary life, as destitute as possible of every thing that might pamper the body, or gratify those appetites and passions which were supposed to have their seat in the flesh. Hence arose the notion of the greater purity and excellence of celibacy, of which I have spoken. It is the same principle which has made Essenes among the Jews, Monks among the Christians, Dervises among the Mahommedans, and Fakirs among the Hindoos.* Finding so many followers, St. Anthony drew up his famous RULES and ORDERS, of which Erasmus speaks of in his colloquies, and which are but transcripts of those institutes which Pythagoras imposed on his collegiates in order to their monastic life, and which he brought out of Egypt when he forbade matrimony to those of his sect, and constituted a cloister of nuns, over which he placed his daughter.†

' And so utterly corrupt had the state of the church and the christian world become, that a distinguished writer speaking of this subject, says : ' Within two hundred years from the death of Chrysostom, Mahomet broke upon the world, and the tempest of heresy which he raised *came as a blast of health upon the nations*. What Mahomet and his Caliphs found in all directions, whither their cimetars cut a path for them, was a superstition so abject, an idolatry

---

* CORRUPTIONS of Christianity, Vol. II., p. 386.—See MOSHEIM, Vol. I. p. 307.
† GALE's Court of the Gentiles, Vol. II., p. 212.

so gross and shameless, church doctrines so arrogant, church prac-
tices so dissolute and puerile, that the strong-minded Arabians felt
themselves inspired anew, as God's messengers, to reprove the errors
of the world, and authorized as God's avengers to punish apostate
christendom.'*

'All this is very startling,' said Mrs. Smith; 'but how are such
rhetorical assertions sustained? Give me, if you please, a bill of
particulars.'

'That is easily done;' and rising from his seat, the Gentleman in
Black went to the cases and selected several of those old *patristic*
folios, and laying them on the table, continued the conversation, by
saying:

'In order to show you how nearly the self-sacrificing devotions of
my slaves resemble the practices of the early ages of the Church,
permit me to state to you the prevailing customs as they are here
stated,' laying his hands on the volumes before him. 'According to
their faith and zeal, these Recluses employed their days, which were
passed in their cells, either in vocal or mental prayer: those asso-
ciated in monasteries assembled in the evening, and they were
awakened in the morning, for the public worship of the fraternity.
Even sleep, the last refuge of the unhappy, was rigorously measured:
the vacant hours of the monk rolled along without business or plea-
sure; and before the close of each day he had repeatedly accused
the tedious progress of the sun. In this comfortless state Supersti-
tion still pursued and tormented her wretched votaries. The repose
they sought was disturbed by a tardy repentance, profane doubts and
guilty desires; and while they considered each natural impulse as
an unpardonable sin, they perpetually trembled on the edge of a
flaming and bottomless abyss. From the painful struggles of disease
and despair, these unhappy victims were relieved by madness or
death. Their visions, before they attained this extreme and acknow-
ledged term of frenzy, have afforded ample materials of supernatu-
ral history. It was their firm persuasion that the air they breathed
was peopled with invisible enemies; with innumerable demons, who
watched every occasion and assumed every form, to terrify, and above
all to tempt their unguarded virtue.†

'In the performance of the penances they practised, stimulated by
applause and emulation, they sunk under the painful weight of crosses
and chains; and their emaciated limbs were confined by collars,
bracelets, gauntlets and greaves, of massy and rigid iron. All
superfluous incumbrance of dress they contemptuously cast away;
and some savage saints of *both sexes* have been admired, whose
naked bodies were only covered by their long hair; they allowed
their beards and nails to grow, and sometimes became so hirsute, as
to be actually mistaken for hyænas and bears.‡ Thus they aspired
to reduce themselves to the rude and miserable state in which the

---

* Taylor.
† The Devils were most formidable in a female shape. — Roswerde.
‡ Taylor, p. 427, quoting Palladius.

human brute is scarcely distinguished above his kindred animals: and a numerous sect of anachorets derived their name from their humble practice of grazing in the fields of Mesopotamia with the common herd.* And so late as the tenth, eleventh and twelfth centuries, the forests of France and Germany were haunted by naked anachorets, who round the year, roamed about, refusing even the comforts of a cavern, and were wont to repose on the fresh-fallen snow.†

'It is said of some of the Abbots of Egypt, that they had five, seven, and even ten thousand monks under their direction; and the Thebais, as well as certain spots in Arabia, are reported as literally crowded with solitaries. Seventy thousand, at the end of the fourth century, of all classes, were at one time to be found in Egypt alone,‡ so small a country as you well know this to be; and the writings of these fathers leave no doubt as to the prevalence of the ascetic system throughout all the countries to which they belonged; namely: Syria, Egypt, Arabia, Asia Minor, Thrace, Italy, Gaul, Spain and North Africa. They recount with fervid eloquence their utter neglect of the body. In certain instances, the leathern girdle was found, after death, to have lodged itself in the integuments of the loins, so as in ordinary cases to have occasioned intense sufferings; yet never had they betrayed the secret to any one by any indications of uneasiness. And instances still more extreme and far too revolting to describe, abound in these records of Monachism.'§

'What could have induced this horrid state of things?' inquired Mrs. Smith.

'It arose, Madam, from the idea of *expiation* by these self-inflicted torments.

'The doctrine of expiation, by penance in this life, of the pains otherwise to be endured in purgatory, had taken fast hold of the religious mind; and in their pictures of purgatorial pains, the fathers drew largely upon that special knowledge of the infernal regions which the privileged commerce of the ascetics with devils had so well supplied them; and some idea, Madam, of their extent and character may be attained by reading the ' *Lives of the Saints,*' by Rev. ALVAN BUTLER, (a comparatively *recent work,*) who says, ' a soul, *for one venial sin,* shall suffer more than all the pains of distempers, the most violent cholic, gout and stone, joined in complication; more than all the most cruel torments undergone by malefactors, or invented by the most barbarous tyrants; *more than all the tortures of the martyrs summed up together.* This is the idea,' he says,‖ ' which the Fathers give us of purgatory; and how long many souls have to suffer there, we know not.' Now, if a small part of all this was believed, and it was doubtless received in all its

---

* GIBBON, chap. 37.— THEODORET has in a large volume the lives of these *grazing* monks.

† FANATICISM, p. 75.

‡ FLEURY Hist. Eccl., quoted in ' Corruptions of Christianity,' Vol. II., p. 391.

§ FANATICISM, p. 74.

‖ LIVES: for November 2. This work is now being reprinted in this country.

fulness by these poor naked and half-starved hermits, who regarded their bodies as their chiefest of enemies, why should they not sacrifice their bodies here, so as to save their souls from such inconceivable wretchedness hereafter ?'

'And were all these multitudes of recluses subjected to like destitution ?'

'Certainly not, as I will show you;' so saying, he opened SAINT CHRYSOSTOM.* 'It seems that the customs of the third century, against which CYPRIAN inveighed, had not improved in the days of CHRYSOSTOM. Not only did the *aged* monks avail themselves of the offices and society of young women in their cells, but *young* monks also did the same; while, on the other hand, the young nuns entertained a cortége of 'philosophic' paramours, under various pretexts, which are described on page 310, and the pages following, of this the first volume of *Chrysostom's works.* It may amuse you to know something of the customs of these 'pure and pristine days of *the* church;' permit me to read you a passage or two from pages of this volume.

' 'The pious Father exclaims : 'What a sight it is, to enter the cell of a SOLITARY monk, and to see the apartment hung round about with female gear, shoes, girdles, reticules, caps, bonnets, combs and the like, too various to mention; but what a jest it is to visit the abode of a rich monk, and to look about you : for you find the *solitary* surrounded with a bevy of lasses, one might say, just like the leader of a company of singing and dancing girls. What can be more disgraceful ? — and, in fact, the monk is all day long vexed and busied with the petty affairs proper to a woman · · · · not merely is he occupied with *worldly* matters, contrary to the apostolic precept, but with even *feminine* cares; these ladies being very luxurious in their habits, as well as imperious in their tempers.' He goes on to give the particulars : 'The good man is liable to be sent on fifty errands; 'to the silversmith, to inquire if my lady's mirror is finished; if her vase is ready; if her silver cruet had been returned; and from the silversmith's to the perfumer's, and thence to the linen-drapers, and thence to the upholsterer's; and at each place he has twenty particulars to remember.' Then the father goes on to describe in addition to all these cares, 'the jars and scoldings that are apt to resound in a house full of pampered women;' and urges them, 'as the warriors of the church, to be clad with spiritual armor, and not take on themselves the office of waiting like menials upon worthless girls, or to busy themselves with their spinnings and sewings, and spend the livelong day by their side, while at work, imbuing their minds with effeminate trifles.''

'Truly, this is a strange picture !' exclaimed Mrs. Smith, with real astonishment and unaffected surprise, 'of *The Lights and Shadows of Fashionable Life,*' as it existed fourteen hundred years ago.'

'Yes, indeed; and CHRYSOSTOM makes an acknowledgment not

---

* CHRYSOSTOM, tom. I., p. 279.

so complimentary as I could wish it, as to the authors of all this licentiousness,' said the Gentleman in Black.

'Is it in that volume ?' Mrs. Smith inquired, with some hesitation.

'Yes, it is here,' turning to page 304. 'Shall I read it ?'

'I am rather doubtful as to hearing any more of these *morceaux.* And yet, if you think it readable, you may go on. I shall in this instance trust to your discretion.'

'It is a very eloquent and powerful passage, in the Father's best style, and I am sure there is nothing in it which can pain you save the melancholy confession it makes of the authors of this reign of riot and misrule in the church.' So saying, the Gentleman in Black read as follows :

'Alas, my soul! well may I so exclaim, and repeat the lamentable cry with the prophet! Alas, my soul! Our virginity has fallen into contempt; the veil is rent with impudent hands, that parted it off from matrimony; the holy of holies is trodden under foot, and its grave and tremendous sanctities have become profane, and thrown open to all; and all that which was once held in reverence, as far more excellent than matrimony, is now sunk so low, as that one should rather call the married blessed, than those who profess it. *Nor is it an enemy that has effected all this ; but the* VIRGINS *themselves !'* '

'Poor dear girls ! how truly they were to be pitied !' said Mrs. Smith. '*After all,* this state of hopeless seclusion of gentle and loving girls in the days of infancy and childhood, and which is still practised, seems to me, now that I think of it, as more to be detested than any of the austerities practised among your slaves. I think I must confess, the superstitions engrafted upon Christianity are the most dreadful of all others.'

'I beg you to believe I have not exhausted the subject.'[*]

'Pardon me ; though you may not have exhausted the subject,' said Mrs. Smith, very kindly, and smiling, 'you have my capacity to hear any more on a topic so full of horrors. I had much rather you should speak to me of yourself than of others.'

Mrs. Smith could not have been conscious of the very gentle tones in which these words were expressed, though they were winged with flames, if the flush which glowed on the face of the Gentleman in Black spoke truly.

---

[*] THE manners of the days of CHRYSOSTOM seem to have come down with the monastic institutions to later days; old FULLER, in his ' History of the Church,' Book VI., p. 315, says, amours were very general among the English nuns, and he speaks of very extensive powers of absolution for certain vices : writing of love-letters, interviews at grated windows, employing smiths to remove bars, as well as '*holy contemplations* in the church at night between two lovers ;' and that even the confessor of the nuns, usually and seemingly a very austere and devout monk, whose office, he quaintly remarks, ' was that of a midwife, whose duty it was to eradicate sin from the heart, that it might afterward bring forth *the new man ;* but these confessors,' he adds, 'often attended only to the latter part of the injunction in a corporeal sense,' FOSBROOKE, in his History of British Monachism, (quarto, London, 1817,) has given a full view of the rise and progress, manners and customs of Monachism as it was, and still exists in Great Britain.

L I N E S

SUGGESTED BY A PICTURE OF JEPTHA'S DAUGHTER, IN A GALLERY OF PAINTINGS.

BY MRS. S. L. SCHERMERHORN.

DAUGHTER OF JEPHTHA ! with thy fair head bowed,
As droops the flower, when from the burdened cloud
In fierce assault has burst the stormy shower ;
Why hangs this gloom upon thy life's young hour ?
Bent is thy brow ; beneath the drooping lid,
Like jewels shrined, thy sparkling eyes are hid ;
Clasped are thy fairy fingers, half in prayer,
Half in the anguish of thy soul's despair :
Oh ! not more sad the lovely Peri sate,
Who sought admittance at bright Eden's gate,
Yet doubted if her offered gifts could win
From watching Angels leave to enter in.
And yet thou wear'st no drooping mourner's guise,
Veiled is thy form in robe of glowing dyes ;
Amidst the braided richness of thy hair
Bright pearls are beaming, and the jewelled star
Gleams on thy shoulder ; as when stars arise,
Ere evening's blush has faded from the skies ;
A branch unblighted on thine arm is thrown,
But where's the thrilling of thy song's proud tone ?
When forth thou led'st the fair and virgin choir,
To hail with song and dance thy conquering sire ?

Rash JEPHTHA ! what an awful vow was thine,
To pour in sacrifice upon the shrine
The blood of whomsoe'er thou first might'st meet !
And lo ! a virgin bright, with bounding feet,
Springs forth to meet thee, with her fond caress ;
Why turn away ? hath she no power to bless ?
Is there a father, who can coldly spurn
A daughter's kiss, that welcomes his return ?
Swift through his soul this thought of horror flies,
JEPHTHA is saved, but JEPHTHA's daughter dies !

Oh ! dark Idolatry ! whose fearful rite
In human blood hath ever found delight ;
JEPHTHA ! from idol altars thou hadst turned,
But not of ISRAEL's GOD the worship learned ;
Past is thy bloody vow, with guilt defiled —
The first to meet thy coming is thy child !
'T is but a picture that I see, and yet
Illusion, distance, time — all I forget ;
I wait to see her trembling tear-drops start,
And hear the pulses of her throbbing heart ;
Spreads o'er her head a sky of sunny hue,
Soft from the valley swell the mountains blue ;
I cannot think the knife's descending blow
Shall stain with blood her bosom's spotless snow :

Oh ! gracious Heaven, avert the fearful hour !
Drench not in blood this fair, unfolding flower.
What was her prayer ? ' Oh ! Sire, since GOD has heard
Thy vow, and passed thy lips the fatal word
That dooms thy daughter, to my fate I bow,
And JEPHTHA's child shall meet her father's vow.
I ask but this : while two bright moons shall rise
And fade with waning crescent from the skies,
Far from my childhood's happy scenes away,
On the lone hills, with weeping eyes, to stray
And wail with mournful lyre, and plaintive song,
The fate that tears me from the virgin throng.'

Daughter of JEPHTHA ! comfort would it be
To hearts that through all time shall bleed for thee,
If on the lonely mountains thou hadst died,
With weeping virgins kneeling by thy side ;
Thy heart's last sigh, thy lyre's last dying tone,
In mingled breathings on the wild winds thrown ;
A faded flower, yet lovely to the last,
Thy parting spirit on thy MAKER cast ;
The earth thy couch, thy last look on the skies,
When from the hills the parting daylight dies :
Night's falling dews their crystal tears to weep,
And stars of light their silent watch to keep.

SKETCHES AT CONSTANTINOPLE.

BY JOHN P. BROWN, ESQ.

SOME time ago I took Doctor S —— to Abdul Hak Effendi, the *Hakim Bashi,* or chief physician of the Sultan, to obtain from him a permit for the former to practice medicine in Constantinople and its environs.   I informed the Effendi, who is an old fat man, fond of a joke, that Doctor S ——, being an Armenian by birth, wished to practice only among his own people, and would not *molest* the Turks.

'Oh ! I understand !' exclaimed the Effendi, laughing; 'he will *spare* us !'

I remarked in the course of conversation that an American vessel had arrived Smyrna from Boston in twenty-nine days; this one of the foreign professors present confirming, ' Mashallah !' exclaimed the old man ; ' perhaps the world is folding up, and thus lessening in extent;' then after making some observations about space, he added : ' It is remarkable that places which during our childhood seemed to us so extensive and ample, in after years, or in older age, appear diminished in size.   For instance,' continued he, ' I was born and spent my childhood near the quarter of Eyoub, on the harbor. Behind my father's house was a garden, in which, when a boy, I was fond of racing a Mytylene pony I owned, the gift of an uncle.   The garden was large and spacious, and I could run the pony in it to my heart's content. It was my world, and I knew not of, nor wished for, an ampler field for amusement. Some months ago, being near the quarter of Eyoub, the idea came into my head to visit the scene of my youthful achievements. How changed! My father's old house was a mass of crumbling fragments; and pained with its dreary and desolate appearance, I hastily passed by it and entered the vast and ample garden. This seemed so small that I even doubted its identity, and wondered how I ever could have raced a pony in it. I felt shocked with the change, which of course had taken place only in myself and my own mind. As we acquire knowledge, we need space, and what in our youth was sufficient for the scope of our ambition and necessities, in after years becomes too small for us.'

It struck me that the Effendi's remarks were applicable to nations as well as to individuals.

Doctor S —— took his diploma from a tin case in which he preserved it, and handed it to the Effendi, who, not being acquainted with Latin, referred it to the foreign professors near him. They in turn passed it in examination, and one of them on reading it aloud reached the word *Albanaie.* 'Albania!' suddenly exclaimed the old man, who had been listening; ' what have the American doctors to do with our province of Albania?' The diploma was given in the city of New-York, and the professors, as well as Doctor S ——, could offer no explanation of the reason why *Albania* was mentioned in it; neither could I offer any; and in the midst of the embarrassment Doctor S —— luckily recollected that Albany was the seat of government of the state of New-York, which being interpreted to the Effendi, relieved him very effectually, and improved the Doctor's prospect of receiving a permit considerably. While the Effendi's secretary was making out the permit, I took my leave of the Effendi and left the Medical College. An hour or two later I met an *employée* of the college proceeding in great haste to Dr. S —— 's dwelling, to inquire whether or no he possessed any curious objects from the New World, which would serve to amuse the Effendi, who intended passing the night at the college.

You have doubtless heard of the great benefits this country has received from its present sanitary system. It was established with great difficulty, and against the opposition of the more bigotted of the Mussulman community. The head of the Board of Health was an elderly Turk, certainly not chosen with any reference to his liberal principles; the members were the first dragomans of each of the foreign legations, and a number of physicians. When the subject of quarantine was broached, the old President was greatly shocked by a suggestion that ' *all* persons arriving from places suspected of contagious disease should be required to perform quarantine.'

' Suppose,' said he, 'the Capudan Pacha, or any of the higher officers of the government, were to arrive here from Syria or Egypt; you would certainly not expect him to remain away from his harem, or other home-comforts, for fifteen or twenty days in the lazzaret?'

The members of the Board of course explained to him the necessity of an indiscriminate quarantine; but the old man would not

listen to them; and in defiance of their united protests, drew up and
sent to the Porte a warm recommendation that the chief dignitaries
of the empire should be distinguished from the common herd of tra-
vellers, and be allowed to perform their quarantine by proxy. The
Porte, fortunately for humanity, took a different view of the subject.

Among Oriental governments it has always been customary to
supply the embassies which are sent to them with a residence, and a
bountiful ration of provisions; sometimes even a sum of money is
daily sent for the expenses not included in the preceding items.
The last embassy sent to the Porte by the Shah of Persia was dis-
missed in a manner quite unique. It had, according to the prece-
ding custom, been in the daily receipt of a supply of provisions; but
as the coolness between the Sultan and the Shah increased, the sup-
ply in the same ratio diminished; until one morning, in place of the
customary quantum of sheep, loaves of bread, vegetables, etc., the
Porte sent to the Shah's representative a bag of onions. The hint
was too *strong* not to be taken; so, packing up his baggage, he left
the 'Gate of Felicity,' as the Turks call their capital, in wounded
dignity.

Some years ago there was an envoy sent from Mongrelia on the
Caspian Sea to the Porte, for the purpose of negotiating a treaty
of amity. The envoy was a prince, who under the feudal system of
his government had the entire selection of the *personnel* of his em-
bassy, and consequently each member of it were his own slaves.
The secretary of legation it is supposed was a slave better educated
than the others, and able to serve his master as scribe, in case of
need. This may well have been the case, as at present the white
slaves in Constantinople are elevated with their master's children,
and receive the same education as they; and two of the present
Sultan's brothers-in-law were the slaves of his father or officers.
Their *kismet*, or fate, has however been very different from that of
the poor secretary in question. The negotiation having been pro-
longed later than the envoy anticipated, and his government failing
to make him remittances, or what is more probable, (the Asiatic
sovereigns seldom allowing their ambassadors any other compensa-
tion than a *Bakshish* or present at parting with another, if they return
with success,) his own resources failing, he was compelled to have
recourse to the sale of the said *personnel* of his embassy for a sub-
sistence. In the course of a few months he had sent to the slave-
market all his *attachés*, under-secretaries, etc.; and the first Secre-
tary of Legation was at length destined to follow the same fate. A
Russian ambassador, having visited the prince for the purpose of
communicating a document from his government, and finding his
colleague from Mongrelia about to copy it himself, suggested the
propriety of calling in the secretary.

'Alas!' remarked the Prince, 'poor fellow! I have had to *eat*
him also.'

'Eat him!' exclaimed the astonished Russian, who could think of
no greater dainty than a tallow candle, 'what do you mean?'

'I kept him until the last,' replied the Prince, 'hoping daily to receive relief from my government, or to terminate my mission ; but last week I had to sell him, and have already consumed the proceeds.'

You are aware, I presume, of the Eastern tradition, that the world is supported on the back of certain animals; for instance, a great turtle, bull, etc., and of the dilemma in which philosophers yet are, to learn what they find a foot-hold on.   Some days ago, dining at the table of an illustrious foreign representative, at which were present several Englishmen, the conversation chanced to turn on this subject; and some one happening to remark that the people of Turkey generally believe that the world rests on a bull's horns, the host replied that it was very likely that they do believe it *now*, and that the horns were those of one JOHN BULL !

A LOVER'S ORISONS.

AVE MARY ! I am bending,
　　With true devotion fraught ;
On my heart's blest rosary, counting
　　One by one, the beads of thought.
Telling o'er my heart's blest rosary,
　　Radiant MARY ! all divine !
Every thought an aspiration
　　From my spirit breathed to thine.
Ave MARY !—Ave MARY !
　　My spirit prays to thee ;
Oh, Sister of the Angels !
　　Look tenderly on me.

Look tenderly upon me,
　　Oh ! pure and gentle eyes !
Orbs passionate and holy,
　　Where I have made my skies !
Blue skies ! bend down in brightness !
　　Let thy fair and beauteous face
Beam on my soul's dark fountain,
　　Radiant MARY ! full of grace !
Ave MARY !—Ave MARY !
　　My spirit prays to thee ;
Oh ! Sister of the Angels !
　　Look tenderly on me !

I would kneel for intercession
　　To the saints above me now ;
But o'er all my memory's calendar
　　I find no saint but thou !
Thou to whom in secret worship
　　I the strain thus fondly pour
From th' heart whose true chords are the lute
　　That shall praise thee evermore.
Ave MARY !—Ave MARY !
　　My spirit prays to thee ;
Oh ! Sister of the Angels !
　　Look tenderly on me !

IONE.

THE THUNDER-BOLT.

A BALLAD.

THERE is an artless tradition among the Indians, related by IRVING, of an Indian warrior who saw the thunder lying upon the ground, with a beautifully-wrought moccasin on each side of it. Thinking he had found a prize, he put on the moccasins, but they led him away to the Land of Spirits, from whence he never returned.

LOUD pealed the thunder
  From arsenal high;
Bright flashed the lightning
  Athwart the broad sky.

Fast o'er the prairie,
  Through torrent and shade,
Sought the red hunter
  His hut in the glade.

Fierce swept the wild-horse
  O'er mountain and plain;
On rolled the tempest,
  And fast fell the rain:

Breaking and changing,
  The clouds gathered o'er,
Like surges that beat
  On a rock-bound shore.

Deep roared the cannon
  Whose forge is the sun:
Blood-red was the chain
  The thunder-bolt spun.

O'er the thick wild-wood
  There quivered a line;
Low mid the green leaves
  Lay hunter and pine.

Clear streamed the sunshine,
  The hurricane past,
And fair flowers smiled on
  The path of the blast.

Still in the forest
  Lay rent the huge tree,
Up rose the red man,
  Still unharmed and free.

Bright glittered each leaf
  With sun-shine and spray,
And close at his feet
  The thunder-bolt lay:

With moccasins wrought
  With the beads that shine,
Where the rainbow gleams
  With a smile divine.

Wondered the hunter
  What spirit was there,
Then donn'd the strange gift
  With a shout and prayer:

Quickly the wild wood
  Reëchoed the strain;
Heard it the red man
  Oh! never again!

Up o'er the mountain
  As torrents roll down,
Marched he o'er dark oak
  And pine's soaring crown:

Far in the bright west
  The sunset grew clear;
Crimson and golden
  The hunting-grounds near.

Light trod the chieftain
  The tapestried plain;
There stood his good horse
  He'd left with the slain:

Gone were the sandals
  And broken the spell;
A drop of clear dew
  From either foot fell.

Long the dark maiden
  Sought tearful and wide;
Never the red man
  Came back for his bride!

With the fork'd lightning
  Now hunts he the deer;
Where the GREAT SPIRIT
  Smiles ever and near.

Shelter-Island.

MARY GARDINER.

ADVENTURES OF A YANKEE-DOODLE.

NUMBER FOUR.

'KAPTING, is that a mounting?'

'Certingly!'

Mr. Stubbs was on his way home from school. The person who asked the question, which he accompanied with a knowing leer at a prodigious peak of the mountain, meant to pass after this fashion a commentary upon the grandeur of the scene. How different are the styles of eloquence, and what is called 'the power of description!' I suppose a novelist would thus convey the scene which was spread at that evening hour before the eyes of Stubbs: 'And now the glorious sun, sinking behind the far stretching line of mountains, rested for a moment on the summit of their grandeur, and crowned it with a diadem of fire;' and so on to the end of a chapter, implanted like a garden of rhetoric with all the graces of composition. But mark how five words, and one of these a single letter, shall put all this figuring to the blush, and fetch out to your mind's eye the gigantic picture of the mountain in bold relief.

'Kapting, is that a mounting?'

'Certingly!'

The person who made this inquiry was named Dobbs, an itinerant lecturer on Animal Magnetism, who was going on that night to convince the skeptics of Jig-Town; with which view he had already got his bills printed, and was taking a pleasant walk to the place in question. He was in outward figure not unlike O'Callaghan in the play of 'His Last Legs;' otherwise his nationality was clear, as he wiped his brow with a 'Star-spangled Banner-of-America' pocket-handkerchief. His cheek was protuberant with that which is expressed by the neuter gender of the interrogative pronoun, *quis;* and it was wonderful how he hit the heads of the simple flowers which grew by the wayside, defiling their fair cheeks with spittle, and thrashing them down in his path like a north-east storm.

'Schoolmaster?' said he, inquisitively, eyeing Stubbs, who carried a dictionary under his left arm.

'Ain't northen else.'

'Young man, I 'm pleased to hear you say so. Eddication! that 's the crëowning glory of the United'n States'n. Ain't your name Cobias?'

'Try again.'

'Wal, I did n't know but what it was. I guess it 's somethin' like it, any how. You 've got the Cobias nose, and gooms too. Maybe your name ain't Spalding, then?'

'Jist about as much like it as a kettle is like a shaving.'

'Yeö pshaw! Let 's look at that dictionary. Oh! ah! Holy Bible, eh?

'HOLY Bible, book divine,
Precious treasure, thou art mine!'

You need n't look at me so like Thomas à Kempis, Esquire. I ain't agoing to hook it. Twenty-five from forty-five, twenty remains. You 're twenty years of age; your name 's Thomas Stubbs, eh? 'Thomas Stubbs, His Book. Do n't steal this book, my Christian friend; for if you do, the gallows will be your end.' Ho! ho! ho! — he! he! he! To be sure! to be sure!'

'Look-a-here,' said Stubbs; 'just let me ask you one question, will you?'

'Certingly; five hundred, my feller citizen.'

'Wal, where would you be if you was where you was a year ago?'

'In the middle of an attack of typhus fever, pretty nigh death's door, I tell yer!'

'Wal, and what other door beside death's door?'

'My tender Sir, I was gi'n up: the barber was sent for.'

'That 's comin' to the p'int. You was gi'n up by the authorities of Tuscaloosy, Alabammy, and the barber was sent for to shave your creöwn. I 've seen a daguerreotype of your picter!'

'You 're a Hottentot!'

'You 're another! Say the indefinite article *a*, and I 'll spile your parsin' forever!'

'Come, come! draw it mild. You do n't want for mother wit. What 'll you ax to train up a little boy of mine, (Philetus William,) about three year old, and a leetle older, and about as tall as a shingle?'

'How 's that?'

'There 's such an infant now living in North Car'lina.'

'I wan' know?'

'It 's the truth: I ai'nt tellin' you nothin' else. I 'm goin' to fetch him North put' soon.'

'What series of spellin'-books has he been 'customed to?'

'Cobb's fust; arterward he took to Noser Webster's.'

'That 's just what we use in our district.'

'Do you attend to their morals?'

'Fust-rate!'

'Very good. I 'll talk to you about him after the lectur'.'

'What you goin' to lectur' about?'

'Wal, I guess Magnetism.'

'I 've heerd somethin' about that. I believe it as much as I believe that 'ere hoss is a dollar-bill.'

'The human mind is so constituted that the grandest truths make their way slowly through the mists of prejudice. Religion and science, geography and the use of the globes, together with the application of art, bears witness to the fact, and shallow ignorance is loud in her opposition, in proportion as that ignorance is deep and abiding.'

' That 's *wrote !*'

' Thanks to the spirit of the age, a better day is approaching.   A republican country will burst the shackles of creeds, and the heredi- tary dogmas of ages.   The grasp of mind is onward.   The flight of knowledge is not to be poisoned by the streams of religious error and the narrow-minded bigotry which stops the enginery of the age.   ' GOAHEAD !' as the great German, Teufelsdröck, well expressed it, is written in the frontals of science; 'GOAHEAD !' is the plain cry of lisping infants as well as of inveterate old age; 'Go- AHEAD !' is heard from early in the morning until the Gulf of Mexico !'

' Ha ! ha ! ha !—he ! he ! he !   Lectur' ! lectur' !'

' What will be the sum total of the results of Magnetism ?   I predict that fifty years will not elapse before the diagnoses of medi- cine will be decided by that art.   Treasures shall be drawn up from the vasty deep, and it shall be told to a man in Cincinnati that his son that instant has broken his leg in Canton.   The augurs pre- dicted by the flight of birds and the entrails of animalcula; *we* hold converse with the spirit of a man, and establish an identity by a manipulation as certain and infallible as the law of nations. Borne up by the wing of a cognate spirit, a man shall travel to the planet Mars, and behold the waterfalls of that region.   Divested of flesh, and yet tolerably corpulent, your alderman shall flit like a butterfly among the stars ; behold teeth drawed without a struggle ; the cries of infants hushed, and age made to die easily.   Bandage the eyes with cotton-battens, and he will read the finest print of Brattleboro', in Vermont.   Now he shall go to the eyrie of the eagle, or swoop into the cultivation of the valley.   Plough-shares shall be contrived in a trice, and patents invented of a different fashion.'

' I swan to man !' exclaimed Stubbs, in amazement.

Doctor Dobbs, for such was the cognomen of the lecturer, halted in the middle of the highway, thrust his two thumbs into the eylet- holes of the schoolmaster's coat, and having first bent down his head, opened his jaws like a steel-trap, and let fall therefrom a great quid of tobacco, fastened his two eyes upon the orbs of Stubbs' eyes, and held them fixed with a glance of fascination.

' Hallo!' exclaimed Stubbs, almost squealing out with a night- mare-effort; ' you want to stop my blood from running ?'

' Young man !' said the conjuror, mitigating his stare, yet speak- ing earnestly, ' I reckon you 're above the spirit of the age.   We could make our fortunes together.'

Stubbs' eyes glistened with the brilliancy of a judicious man's when a bottle of the choicest wine is in the process of uncorking. His motions assumed a sudden quickness ; he treated his nose to a cruel tweak, snapped his fingers in the elastic air, rubbed the cotton cover of his Bible, leaped the fence, seized a casual stray urchin who was depredating in a small way, turned him over the knee, chastised him with the palm of his hand, overleaped the fence again, approached the lecturer, spat, slapped him upon the shoulder;

'May-be,' says he, 'we do n't know nothin' abŏout the geography of the United'n States'n !'

Doctor Dobbs smiled.

'Howsoever,' proceeded the other, coming back to a cooler state of mind, 'I 'd like to see a little of that 'ere sort of thing before I believe it, jist like Calvinism.'

'You shall,' said the Doctor.

'Not on me !' exclaimed Stubbs.

A small jackass was browsing in the adjoining field. He was in high spirits, with a belly full of oats, and had refused to stir a step in harness for two weeks. He was impregnable to whip-lashes, and tolerated with exemplary indifference the battering of a stout club. His forte was to stand stock-still and twitch his ear. Pull him, and his feet were riveted to the round earth as if the attraction of gravity held him fast. He looked as grave as the chief-judge of the county. Doctor Dobbs approached the ass, and poked his fingers in his ribs, when he immediately crumpled, twitched and corrugated the skin of his back, as much as to say, 'Hands off, and let me alone, will you ?'

'Pray,' said the Doctor ——

The ass brayed with a brassy gloriousness of flourish, which shook off the blossoms of the orchard. It was like a hard asthma, carried on by powerful machinery. Mr. Stubbs looked surprised.

'Nay,' exclaimed the magnetizer ——

The animal modulated his notes into a neigh not quite so musical as that of the ancient ass we read of in story, who browsing in a retired lane breathed over a flute which had been lost 'by accident.' An account of this may be found in the 'Life of Pickenbrunner.'

Stubbs' eyes swelled out of his head with superstitious amazement. 'Beelzebub,' said he, 'has crossed over the Connecticut River ! A dollar would n't tempt me to look him in the face — not as money now is.'

'I will make the passes,' said Doctor Dobbs, ' from his ears downward, shaking off the magnetism at every pass. So ho ! my little cheärmer ! So ! so ! so ! Let us see if we can git up a little extronary sympathy. May-be we ain't both afeered of ——'

'A halter,' exclaimed Professor Stubbs.

So it would appear. The jackass got into a positive state of electricity. He brayed (if the figure is not inapplicable) with an effulgent clearness, displayed a lurking humor of expression, and cut an eccentric fandango for an ass. Turning his hind-quarters impolitely, he managed to stand for a second of time upon his front legs, while he jerked out his other hoofs with an elastic unanimity of aim which swept off the Doctor's hat, leaving him a bare-headed philosopher in the open air.

'Look-a-there,' said the Doctor, spitting at a small bush ; 'I 'd like to get that hat kind o' fixed up like, before evening, if there 's a hatter would do it any way reasonable.'

'He 'll cheärge yer abeŏut two-and-six-pence,' said Stubbs, ' and that ain't as much as trepannin' would could come to.'

A clarion voice came out of the ass's throat, like that italicized *'flourish of trumpets'* in the stage directions of plays, or *'alarum'* in the battle-scenes of Richard. The magnetized ass stood bewitched under an apple-tree. He jumped up like an electrical shilling in a tumbler. His eyes glanced wildly at the apple-blossoms, and he danced with an exhilarating motion which had in it something of a spiritual grace. Not Ellsler, when she waved her arms in the be-witching Cracovienne, and caused to twinkle her steel-clad feet, and smiled with gay allurement, could have more agitated the be-whiskered and cane-sucking heads, than would our present actor upon his grassy stage, could he have been surrounded with a com-pany of asses. It looked as if some sort of a communication were established with the Doctor, and that the flighty ideas of Yankee ingenuity were somehow conveyed to the cranium of the beast. He who formerly stood mum as a cow in green pastures, frolicked about as if in a play-ground of elves, or rendered nervous by the appreciation of a harvest of dollars. Doctor Dobbs again ap-proached, but this time somewhat carefully, and began to make the magnetic passes. Two negroes, who were overseeing the whole matter from a hay-loft, and were so amazed that nothing but the whites of their eyes remained, went and told their master that a horse-thief was in the act of stealing the ass, Rosinante. Before he could take measures accordingly, a new-comer, who had been standing about ten paces off, rushed up suddenly to Doctor Dobbs, seized him by the collar, which he crumpled roughly. The latter turned red in the face, and looked around, with surprise and guilt depicted in his countenance.

' You need n't be afeered,' said the stranger, ' I ain't a-going to *charge* you any thing!' So saying, he began to chafe and rub the collar of his coat, where he had detected a grease-spot afar off, as a hawk sees a small fish from the clouds. He was a seller of a patent ' Vestamental Soap ;' for such was the elegant name given to a substance which was advertised to remove grease-spots at a mo-ment's warning, and restore the pristine splendor of colors. He rubbed away with perfect success, and then desired to sell Doctor Dobbs a cake for a shilling. He refused, but liked the looks of the patentee, and encouraged him to be present that evening at the lec-ture on Magnetism, to be delivered at the Assembly-room at Jig-Town, previous to his departure, when he should develope some remarkable phenomena of that science.

Mr. Stubbs and the magnetizer now proceeded on their walk, when the latter more than hinted that some kind of a partnership between the two might be rendered profitable to both. He told him all his successes and adventures at the South; among others, the singular one of THE GYANOUSA.

' I want you should go with me,' said Dobbs, kindly ; ' I think I could soon show you a *lusus naturæ.'*

' A what !' screamed Stubbs, erecting each ear into a pinnacle of observation.

' A LUSUS NATURÆ !'

CHAPTER SIX

The Gyanousa.

If taken out of the Doctor's mouth, and related in plain language, the story of *The Gyanousa* is simply this. Not long ago, some Yankees who had been exercising their various gifts and ingenuities through the state of Georgia, met in one of the larger towns, to which they had come to attend the fall races, where they put their heads together and formed as remarkable a coalition of rascality as ever collected without the walls of the college at Sing-Sing. Some of them had been driving at one trade, some at another; but what they had all been doing for some time past, was nothing. They had come to town to relax their intellects, to combine their capitals, or to see how diamond could cut diamond. They put up at the greatest hotel of the place, where they cursed and swore, drank and frolicked, and for ten days filled the place with uproar. Sometimes they vapored about the streets, and stared the pretty girls out of countenance; at others, they smoked in the sitting-room of the hotel, which was fronting the main street, where they placed their heels upon the window-sills, at a considerable elevation above their heads, presenting a worthy object of observation to the passers-by. Here they were calling perpetually for 'juleps,' which they imbibed out of a long straw, or even stronger waters; and by their continual appearance of carousing, greatly scandalized an advocate of the temperance cause who had put up at the same house. They would be bawling out at all hours, ' What 'll you take?' ' I 'll take a julep.' ' I 'll take a cobler.' ' Waita'! waita'! Brandy and water, julep and sherry-cobler.'

The landlord indeed admired their facility of spending, and thought there would be a fine bill to foot-up. It was nothing to him. If the gentlemen chose to be liberal in their expenditures, he was bound to give them what they asked. In this manner things proceeded with the club, and every individual member lived for the present moment, not reflecting that the time might come when they must resort to a friend to ' lend them five shillings.' The hour of distress must indeed soon come to the extravagant, a state of Beau Brummell neediness and extremity, when washerwomen stand trembling over the well-whitened linen and a thousand petty accounts lift up their hands in despair. The evil day may be beckoned off, and the ancient *cloak** of extravagance remain as with the beau; when that is gone, hurrah for the rags!

This jolly club, six in number, all went out to the races on the last day, in a barouche. There were fifty dollars remaining among them. They had a glorious time, amused themselves with faro and thimble-rigging, and on returning at night begged the toll-keeper to lend them the amount of the toll. The next day they were in

---

* See Brummel's ' Life.'

great spirits; convened a council of war, called for their bill : 'Two hundred and fifty dollars.' 'Very good; all right. Was n't the landlord doing himself injustice? Only three dollars a bottle for his wines! Too moderate — would n't have grumbled at twice that sum. It was n't right to be cheating himself; however, that was his own look-out.'

The President of the club put the bill in his pocket-book. The next day it was published in the place that a monstrous curiosity had been brought into town over night; 'THE GYANOUSA, from the disputed territory of Penobscot; a monster of gigantic proportions. He vegetates on the tops of trees, and gets his living on the tallest branches of the poplar.' All this accompanied by a vast demonstration of a picture, a wood-cut, or rather a would-be cut, which one of the club carved out with his pen-knife from a block of wood, while the printer set up the types of the advertisement. Tusks, horns and humps of a singular model were represented, such as belong to no recognized class in Liberia, the Southern continent, or the 'United'n States'n.' This creature would be exhibited in the theatre, accompanied by a band of music and several curiosities, the whole presenting an entertainment of which the most fastidious need not be afraid. 'Clergy and Professors of Natural History respectfully invited to attend, gratis.'

The whole announcement created a buzz of excitement as great as that produced among the population down South ' without visible means' when it was announced by large placards in the streets : 'To arms! to arms! General Taylor is surrounded by the Mexicans, and no man can leave his camp without running the gauntlet. Come up to the stars and stripes, and enrol your names!' The fair population were on the *qui vive*. The editors came, with their reporters. The scientific man of the place was prepared to take notes for Silliman's Journal. The theatre was crowded; and when the foot-lights were raised, an audience really brilliant for beauty and gems and jewels, was presented, and an excited flutter of fans began.

'Who had heard of this animal? Was he well secured in his cage? What would be the consequence if by any means he should break loose? Charles, do n't leave me a minute! Dear me! I am so nervous! What was that!'

The musicians crawled into their places, and began the discordant twanging of their instruments. They played an overture very familiar to theatre-goers. Then came a long pause, broken by cat-calls and an impatient stamping of feet. Another overture, tolerated with extreme unwillingness. When that was finished, a dead pause succeeded. Not a word was spoken. Not a fan moved, not a ribband fluttered in the breeze. The curtain was about to rise. The monster was at hand. A rumbling like distant thunder was heard, and at the same time faint shrieks in various parts of the theatre. Suddenly a tumultuous bellowing, like ten bulls, filled the whole house with alarm, and in the midst of fainting and consternation the curtain rose. The stage presented nothing but the tattered scenery of a house and balcony like that under which the Seguin's used to sing when the opera required a serenade. Expectation was at a painful pitch; nor was it long left unsatisfied. An alarm resounded from without, and a man rushed upon the stage from the left wing, his eyes blood-shot, his hair dishevelled and standing on end, horror depicted in all his features. He made violent gesticulations, and clasped his hands above his head in agony. 'Ladies and gentlemen! leave the house immediately! Save yourselves! THE GYANOUSA AM LOOSE!'

CHAPTER SEVEN.

STUBBS left the Doctor to pursue his walk, while he himself entered the enclosures of a rich and pretty widow. She possessed a farm of many acres, and all things presented an aspect of neatness, thrift and consummate tact. The crops looked as if they had all been washed by that miraculous shower

'Which JULIA to EMMA conveyed.'

The grass was green and luxuriant as an English sward. Sweetly the flowers grew around the neat mansion, all trained and cultivated by the widow's hand. Perhaps the Kentucky rose is not excelled by any plant in America for the plenitude of its blossoms. It is by itself small and sweetly modest, but cluster gushes above cluster in such gorgeous profusion, that the place where it grows becomes a paradise on earth. It is a great climber, and I have seen it rising with its crown of flowers above the majestic head of the oak, twined with its classic leaves, a combination more graceful than the poplar and the vine. There was a plant before the widow's door deliciously interwoven with the branches of a young willow, drooping into a clear stream which mirrored it on the same face with the tints of heaven, cluster for cluster and rose for rose.

Mistress Wadman sat before her porch in the light of maturer widowhood. All around her, as I have said, bore witness to her management and skill, for her husband had been fifteen years deceased — *poor man!* His righteousness and fair dealing had insured him during his life-time the respect of all men. He was the friend of the fatherless, and broke his heart over the afflictions of the needy. He loved the whole world, but more than all the world he loved his wife and child — *poor man!* Perhaps he was too fond a husband. Perhaps he was too loving a father. For people did but smile at his affection when he showed it forth in all his tender conduct, and spoke continually of his dear wife and child — *poor man!* The little boy perished in his eleventh summer, when he could just reach upon tiptoe the blushing fruits of the garden. The sound of his little feet no longer told of his approach upon the creaking stairs. He left his mother utterly disconsolate, and his father too — *poor man!*

When this link of attachment was broken between the parents, and Time by taking the case into his own hand made it no longer needful that they should resort to each other for consolation, the superior temper of the wife blazed forth with vigor, to the discomfiture of the husband's peace —*poor man!* It is dreadful where the acid so prevails as to destroy the fruit which were otherwise sweet and welcome. It is dreadful to see a man as meek as Moses bound in the same yoke with a domineering woman, and the bone of contention continually to be picked. Now this was the case of the person at present alluded to. For passing through the vale of misery, he could not call it a well, and so he died —*poor man!*

Could it be possible that the thoughts of matrimony suggested themselves to Stubbs with this fascinating, tempting, yet dangerous widow? It was even so. He took one look over the fields, blew his nose without his pocket-handkerchief, and resolved to pop the question. Two difficulties presented. To mention the first; a very unpleasant animosity existed between himself and the widow's dog. This animal saw him coming through the gate and growled accordingly. He was as large as a Newfoundland, and fixed himself in a cockpit attitude, his head down, the broad, white band of hairs around his handsome throat standing out like a collar full of nails. Mr. Stubbs' little black eyes darted from side to side very quickly, watching the moment when he should spring, when he intended to receive him upon the left arm and plant a forcible blow in the pit of the stomach with his right, which he fancied would operate like lead; but seeing reason to change his tactics, he depressed the column of his ribs suddenly, rammed his whole arm into the dog's throat, and grasping the roots of his tongue, held him with a perfect mastery. At comparative ease, he now waited patiently for help, and thought over in what phrase he might salute the widow. Could he find words to express his ideas? Could he represent his prospects? But he was so bashful before women! Here was the second difficulty. He could make a bargain with a dozen men at once, cheat eleven of them, and get the better of the twelfth, but one woman was enough to confuse him prodigiously.

'There comes the class-leader. Brother Kikle! Brother Kikle! jist give us your help a minute. Boos and me's got into a leetle quarl. I got no time to be feeling the pulse of the roots of his tongue here. Sha'nt you call for help? No, I 'm 'blige to yer. If you 'll jist prize open his meöuth while I take out my hand. Feel in my side-pocket, Brother Kikle, and you 'll find somethin' to prize open his meöuth with. No, no. That ar'nt it. That 's a Bobble. In the other pocket, there 's a small patent gate. That 's it, brother Kikle. Neöw, jist screw that into his jeäws. How 's the backsliders? Is the widow Wadman to hum?'

Mr. Stubbs was liberated, but the dog choked to death. The widow knew nothing of it when he went in to pop the question of marriage. She was playing on a harpsichord and accompanying the same with her voice. She smiled on Stubbs, and then sang brilliantly:

'OH tis love, tis love, tis love,
Which makes the world go round;
And oh tis love, tis love, tis love,
Which makes the world go round.'

Stubbs listened for some moments with admiration, and then that singular eccentricity of his physical nature which I have already mentioned began to show itself. ' Oh!' said he, ramming his fingers down his throat, and turning a little pale, ' that 's too good. I 'm sick, by jingo.'

The widow desisted, and Stubbs recovered himself and sat by her side. A pause of many minutes intervened, during which he pinched his trowsers, and could not find words even to hint at his desire to be a suitor. ' Widow,' at last, said he, ' I – I – I – I – I.' The perspiration rolled from his features. ' You what,' quoth she, with emphatic sharpness. Stubbs' head went right down between his shoulders, like a big sinker. His sharp knees cracked against his sharp chin; ' I – I – I – I – I – I.'

' Well,' said she, good-humoredly, ' I think I may venture to hint at what you mean to say.'

' Hold on !' roared Stubbs, as quick as lightning, recovering courage, and fearful of being taken too quick. Perhaps more lucrative schemes might yet suggest themselves to his mind. Could I venture to insinuate the possibility that the fair neck and glossy curls of Alice Wynn came back like a vision of loveliness among the calculations of his sordid mind? ' Widow,' said he, his eyes brightening with an idea which held fast the hopes of the present, kept in store the future, and relieved him from his dilemma; 'will you — will you — will you —— *gin me the refusal of you for six months ?*'

CHAPTER EIGHTH.

THE inhabitants of Jig-Town are a lively race, and fond of money-making. They turn out fifty thousand wooden bowls per annum; a great total of figures to be put down in the statistics of the United States. But then the wood is soft and the tools sharp. They have no complaint but the inflammatory rheumatism, and that sometimes ends with a disease of the heart. While they do live they are as active as circus-riders. The air is so sharp and the sun is so bright that it is almost impossible to speak two consecutive words without sneezing.

Doctor Dobbs arrived before night, and was very glad to see his placards headed ' MAGNETISM' posted up on all the willow trees. He acted with much promptness; put on a white neck-cloth, and walked right into the house of the Presbyterian minister as an AD-VOCATE OF SCIENCE. He said that piety was a jewel, and the cause of religion dear to him as a ' 'fessor of 'ligion.' He hoped the minister had giv' out that notice in his church. Magnetism was now taking its place on an adequate platform. It was good for the youth of a village to have their minds divested who were wrapped up in dissipation and nine-pins. How was the cause of temperance advancing? He had lately received the interesting intelligence that fifteen young ladies under the age of ten had signed the pledge against ' King Alchy,' in that one cod'ngregation. It would do his heart good to see those fifteen young ladies march in a procession

with white spencers, with a motto on their little bosoms, and with
a flag with ' No Dram-drinking or no Husbands.' The next step
would be that they would jine the church. Let individooals put
their shoulder to the wheel, or lisping infancy would cry shame to
the furrowed locks of age.' Doctor Dobbs opened the palm of his
hand, and then opening his mouth, let fall therein a beautifully round
quid of tobacco, and flung it with an electric jerk through a heart
which attracted his notice in a delicately scissored grate apron.
We *do* think a smile of triumph *might* have passed over his face :
it was almost cruel to regard his own dexterity so coldly. Nothing
of the kind; with such a moral certainty was the act accomplished.
The clergyman's family were sitting down at the table to feast on
some radishes and bread-and-butter. His daughters were all in a
titter at the outlandish appearance of the Doctor. The lady of the
house was kind and hospitable : ' Would n't he draw up and take
a cup of tea ?'

' No, I 'm 'blige' to yer; but I 'll take a bed with you this even-
ing, if one of the girls,' said he, ' will get me some shavin' tacklin'.
I 'll look on and *see you eat*, and polish off my statooary.'

The shaving tackle was brought. ' Would n't he have a looking-
glass ?'

' Oh no, he thanked them. He could guess put' nigh where the
beard oughter be, unless he had made some bad bargain, which he
guessed he had n't. He was not the individooal to be imposed
upon by ' Vestamental Soap,' or any composition or compoûund
mixtur' of that natur'. He would advise them to be on the look-
out ; such a personage would be along presently.'

He jerked his handkerchief about his throat. In an instant his
face was covered with soap-suds, and nothing stuck out but his ca-
daverous nose, like a macaroon in a whip-syllabub. He dragged
the razor six times over his throat and chin, and the work was done.

' He would find water in the kitchen area.'

' He did n't want any such thing.'

He tore off his handkerchief, which was tucked under his chin,
rubbed it over his visage, and put the ' shavin' tacklin' upon the
tea-table.

' If this evening's lectur' succeeds,' said Doctor Dobbs, ' I 'll bring
my clairvoyant, and *put-up with you*, and deliver a full course of
lectur's, in the *church*.'

' Oh ! ah ! but would the church be a suitable place —— '

' Do n't make no 'pologies. Good *enough*. Too good, for that
matter. Don't keer about the cushions. Large, *large* — that 's what
I look at. Hold a good many. I should reckon that buildin' would
hold fifty dollars, and not take nothin' for the parson, the sexton, and
the rulin' elders. We calculate to put *them* on the free list. Any
how, that 's the plan all over the United'n States'n. Look-a-here,'
said the Doctor, ' I don't care if I *doo* take a dish of tea.' He
bolted from his chair like a hart panting for a water-brook, seized a
radish, dipped it in the salt-cellar, and sticking it into his throat, the
green head of it fell upon his plate, bit off with a sharp precision.

'Would he have milk in his tea ?'

'He would n't have nothing else. He could drink up the milky way.'

The cup was given him. He took it, and with a mighty suction imbibed the whole at a single gulp.

''Pears to me,' said he, ' you did n't put no sugar in to 't.'

'I ask your pardon. I understood you to say milk and nothing else.'

'Jus' so. I 'll thank you for some sugar this time. When I was a boy I eat up seven links of a sugar cable. I 'm death on sugar.'

He swallowed the tea again in an instant, drained the saucer, dug out the dregs with the spoon, and passed it back with a matter-of-course-air to the lady of the house. ' Fine little girl, that. Fessor of 'ligion ?'

'Oh, yes.'

'That 's good. Sing in the quire ?'

'Yes.'

'Wal. Come-a-here, my little dear ; what red cheeks you've got ! ' Little bloomer ! give all to the LORD !' When I was young I went into the catechism. What is the chief end of man ? What is the work of effect*oo*al callin' ? How many commandments are there, and all that ? Yaas ; I was taught early, for which I owe a debt of gratitude-ah, to pious parents-ah !'

The Doctor drank seven cups of tea in succession, until the young ladies were all in a titter. Then he placed his feet at a convenient angle, threw back his head, shut his eyes, and apparently went to prayer. Such was his first letter of introduction at the village of Jig-Town.

H E   I S   C O M I N G   H O M E.

BY MRS. M. E. HEWITT.

I.

A SHIP is on the Indian main —
  Be kind ye gales that o'er her sweep!
For never Spanish galleon bore
  A richer freight across the deep.

II.

She looseth from the Orient Isles,
  And like a dove comes o'er the sea;
And oh ! among her noble hearts,
  Is one that beats for me — for me!

III.

I know his cheek is bronzed and changed
  With burning clime and many a care ;
And he hath dwelt beneath the palm
  Till silver threads are in his hair.

IV.

Yet ever to my memory
  He comes as when in childhood's hours
With ringing laugh and bounding feet
  We chased the bee among the flowers.

V.

But I shall know him 'mid the band
  That leap with eager feet on shore;
For can my heart e'er fail to trace
  The lineaments his boyhood wore ?

VI.

Oh ! like the faithful dove of old,
  To meet her ark upon the sea,
My soul is springing toward the bark
  That bears the loved one home to me !

'MATCHES ARE MADE IN HEAVEN.'

MARY, how beautiful the faith, which holds
Matches are made above!— that human souls
Are formed in pairs, and start from heaven together
To 'seek their fortune ;' but earth's stormy weather
Drives them asunder, and through life they stray,
Sad from their loss, tired of the lonesome way,
Until perchance kind Providence provides
Another meeting. All the world beside
Is then forgotten! How the sweet surprise
Wakes up their hearts to rapture! arms their eyes
With harmless lightnings! fills the world around
With melody and beauty! Each has found
What the heart yearned for. Hand in hand, they go
Through life's short journey ; share each joy and wo ;
Together sink into the silent tomb ;
And, borne on angel's wings, together find their home!

MARY, when I, on that sweet summer day,
First chanced to see your image in my way,
First sunned me in the glory of your eyes,
First heard that voice, and drank its melodies,
Thrilled with delight, my spirit said to me :
' This is no stranger, but a friend to thee !'
And *had* I seen that lovely face before ?
Or was it in a dream, and nothing more ?
O no, dear girl ! it was not in a dream
I heard that dove-like voice, and saw the gleam
Of that bright eye. It was long, long ago,
When we left heaven for this world below.

O ! do you not remember how we sailed,
And with a gentle motion neared the earth ?
And with what joy our future home we hailed,
Not dreaming we should part ? But at our birth
We missed each other. The years dragged on,
Even life was dull, for lonely was the road ;
Pleasure was heartless — labor was a curse.

But on that summer day, when first I found
My long-lost treasure ; when I heard the sound
Of that loved voice, and saw that radiant eye
Flash forth the splendors of our native sky,
Joy seized my soul ; Hope gave me back my wings ;
Pain fled away, and from the trembling strings
Of my heart's harp did gentle music creep,
Courting each fear unto a wakeless sleep.

Matches *are* made in heaven ! There ours was made !
I claim thee, dearest ! as my heavenly bride.
Together our young spirits first surveyed
The starry route to earth, and side by side
Shall we not now remain, and part no more !
Together we will smile — together weep ;
One life will live ; one GOD we will adore ;
And when grim Death shall close our eyes in sleep,
Like forked flame, our souls shall pierce
The heavens' blue deep.   F. W. F

CAUSES OF EARLY CONSUMPTION.

BY PROF. JAMES J. MAPES.

THE question is often asked, why it is that those who live at or near the level of the sea are more subject to that scourge of mankind, *Consumption,* than the hardy mountaineer? And it is as often answered, ' that it is due to the difference in their food and exercise.' To this, as well as to many other trite sayings, the adage that ' Public Report is a public Liar' may be justly applied.

The true cause of narrow chests and small and feeble lungs is easily defined by the naturalist. BUFFON tells us that all animals inhabiting high altitudes have larger lungs and more copious chests than those residing in valleys. AUDUBON and WILSON both agree in stating that such birds as are accustomed to the highest flights have the largest air-receptacles for respiratory purposes. The same class of animals which inhabits the mountains, if brought into the valley, although exercised in the same manner, will often become pulmonic; while an animal removed from the valley to the mountain, without any change in diet or exercise, expands its chest, and obtains a corresponding increased action of the lungs. Nature has so adapted the physiological configuration, that it may undergo these changes as occasion may require; and if it were *not* so, every mountaineer on visiting the valley would lose his life by a collapse of his lungs; and every inhabitant of the lowlands would die of suffocation for want of sufficient oxygen, while breathing the lighter dilated atmosphere of the mountain.

All this is easily accounted for, and the *rationale* is within the comprehension of the meanest intellect.

From the height of the atmosphere it is well known that at the level of the sea its superincumbent weight is fifteen pounds to every square inch of surface exposed to its action; and that consequently, as air is very elastic, that which we breathe in low regions is in a very compressed state. One of the great objects of respiration is to enable the blood to rob from the air received within the lungs the oxygen contained in it; and the blood will not be content, nor continue to perform its proper offices, with any less than its necessary quantity of this important element.

Now suppose a cubic foot of air to be enclosed in a tight and fragile vessel, and then to be carried to the top of a mountain, or other high elevation. It will be found to expand as it loses its superincumbent weight by being elevated, and at no impracticable height to double its bulk and to burst its prison-wall. If then a cubic foot of air of the valley contains two proportionals of oxygen, that of the mountain, from being expanded, will contain but one; and therefore the resident of these high altitudes is compelled to breathe double the bulk of air to supply the blood with the same weight of oxygen. Nature enables the configuration of man, as well as of all other animals, to meet this change. And the chest and the lungs, from natural causes alone, enlarge themselves for their new office.

The city of Mexico is nine thousand feet above the level of the sea; and in this locality narrow chests and diseased lungs are unknown; while from the extreme dilation of the atmosphere, animal substances never become putrid; notwithstanding its proximity to the equator, and consequent high temperature.

It must not be supposed, from this extreme case, that slight elevations are not serviceable. The difference of elevation between the basement and garret stories of a high house may be taken advantage of for the use of the early consumptive; and the heights at Weehawken, and the Kaätskill and other mountains, are fully sufficient for the restoration of the *incipient* pulmonic.

Those invalids who visit the West Indies and remain in Matanzas, Havana and other *low* localities, die; while those who reside on the Highlands of Cuba, St. Croix and elsewhere, recover, without reference to any other fact than mere elevation and moderate temperature.

There are other advantages which will arise to invalids from high elevations. The exhalations from the surface of their bodies should be got rid of with the greatest possible degree of rapidity. If they are surrounded by an atmosphere of nearly the same weight as that of the gasses given off from the surface of the body, these gasses will mix with and be carried away by the atmosphere but slowly; whereas when surrounded by the light atmospheres of high elevations the heavy exhaled gasses fall off with greater rapidity, for the same reason that a cannon-ball will fall more rapidly through water than through melted lead; the upper atmosphere being lighter and thinner than the lower.

These facts will be more clearly understood, when we reflect that if the body be enclosed in a varnished silken bag, such as balloons are made of, and tied around the neck, so as to prevent the escape of gasses given off from the surface of the body, notwithstanding the mouth is free to breathe the outside atmosphere, the person so encased will die in a short time.

The missionaries who report the state of health of the poor inhabiting the basements and cellars of our city, inform us that life is shortened by such residences and dormitories more than one half. The reports of Dr. Edwin Chadwick, of London, and Doctors Griscom and Stevens, of New-York, corroborate these facts; they all attribute it however to want of sufficient ventilation; but as most of these sufferers die of pulmonary diseases, it is equally fair to suppose that it is from want of sufficient elevation.

Take a farther and more familiar illustration of these principles: those who descend in diving-bells to the depth of thirty feet under water, the bell being supplied with air by the operation of force-pumps and flexible tubes, are under a pressure, first, of fifteen pounds to the inch from the atmosphere; second, to a still farther pressure of fifteen pounds to the inch from the compression exerted by the height of the column of water surrounding and above the bell; and the lungs are then breathing against an accumulated pressure of thirty pounds to the inch, instead of fifteen, as when at the surface of the water. Although the time necessary for this descent is but a few minutes, still in this short space of time the lungs so configure themselves that they lessen the size of their cavity, and no inconvenience is felt in breathing. But if, when in this state, the bell is suffered to rise too suddenly to the surface, not giving time to the lungs to adopt their former configuration, they will not only be injured, but from the sudden relief of pressure and consequent sudden internal expansions, the blood will rush from the nose, mouth and ears, and in many instances cause death.

INVOCATION.

BY M. A. MERRITT.

DESTINY!
Hast thou darker paths for me?
Hast thou deeper gloom to shed
O'er thy child's devoted head?
I can tread thy paths though lone,
  I can meet thy skies though dark,
So no tempest yet unknown
  Greet the loved one's wandering bark.

II.

Thou hast frowned
On each tie in love that bound;
Thou hast rent each link apart,
Binding mine to kindred heart;
But I bow without a tear
  To the ills thou hast in store,
For my heart disdains to fear
  Griefs the loved have known before.

III.

Be but kind
To the lingerers behind —
Sad survivors of the lost,
Treading paths by shadows crossed;
Come in Sorrow's hues arrayed,
  I can bow to thy behest,
So thy gloom forbear to shade
  Paths by kindred footsteps pressed.

THE WAY THEY DO THINGS IN NEW-YORK.

IN A LETTER FROM A RUSSIAN TO A FRIEND AT HOME.

FEW things are more ridiculous than the attempt to force the manners of a foreign country upon another, when they are totally inapplicable to the habits and general character. The light, gay manners of France can never be engrafted or thrive on the character of the plodding Americans; the dress is not appropriate to the climate, neither is the mode of cooking adapted to their naturally plain taste. A people may be improved by receiving a tincture, who would be spoiled by taking the crude substance; a total change deranges the system, beside producing unsteadiness in the temper. In this city these abortive attempts are most discernible in the winter-evening reünions; in the article of dress; in affectation of foreign manners; in a display of foreign terms when the party speaking has an imperfect knowledge of the language and misapplies words; in imitation of the fashionable hours of meeting, as is observed by the rich and idle among the beau-monde abroad, totally hostile to the regular routine of a sober-minded people.

We will suppose a sedate man—one who carefully counts his clothes when they are to be washed, who rakes up his own fire at night, and goes to bed at ten—in short, an 'exemplary character,' who requires a given number of hours of quiet sleep, that he may be at his customary labors early the next day; how can he bear to be deranged by transforming himself into a man of fashion, perhaps a leader of the 'haut ton,' by retiring at two in the morning, after the excitement of a 'soirée dansante?' I say nothing of the conversation held at these places, for this must conform to the tastes of the various persons who there assemble. It generally turns upon foreign travel; little dandies with big moustaches and little ladies with pretty lips descant on the pleasure of Parisian society; the grandeur of the Alps; the soft beauties of Como, or the picturesque charms of Terni; yet when they are closely questioned, it may be discovered that their profound knowledge of Parisian society came to them through a formal dinner at their banker's, or by being two or three times at the ambassador's regular soirées; the grandeur of the Alps flashed before their senses as they passed over them in all haste in a vetturina; and the guide-books found at Milan or Rome are the true sources whence are derived their admiration of the classical associations of Como or Terni. Sentimentality may be had at the book-seller's, fitted to all temperaments, while Eustace and Byron furnish elements of classical knowledge, to the great relief of wearied limbs, beside saving in tavern-bills and coach-hire. These are sufficient for your dainty little travellers to say, with apparent feeling, 'When I crossed the Alps,' 'When I was in Italy,' etc.; although they may have crossed without seeing intellectually these monuments of nature, while they saw Italy, *not* the Italians.

It must be admitted that a portion of the time passed at an American soirée has the full stamp of reality, where the natural character expands. This is the hour of supper. Here all are equal; the travelled gentleman and the home-keeping youth are on a level. Sentimental conversation ceases; the beauties of the mind are suffered to lie dormant; young and old seek relaxation from mental labor by playful dalliance with ice-creams or jellies, or dwell with satisfaction on the more solid charms of tongue and stewed oysters. Neither Como nor Terni, with all their delights, are to be compared to Prince's Bay; Byron and Eustace fade from the mind when in presence of a dish of Downing's best Chingaroras. Here every thing is matter-of-fact; and if any thing can make one see the character of the people in its unsophisticated state, it is when they exercise their gastronomic privileges at a supper-table loaded with the indigenous productions of their own favored land.

Another way they have of aping the customs of Europeans is by putting their servants into livery and painting armorial bearings on their carriages. Before the revolution which separated this country from the parent state, these trappings were common, because the people were English, with English feelings; but when the two countries became distinct, a desire manifested itself among the Americans to eradicate these early impressions, and to sweep away all that remained of the customs of their immediate progenitors. They affected primitive manners; they passed laws to encourage simplicity and to repress luxury, or even any old leaning to former opinions. The state and the church were new-modelled, and even old things were called by new names, that no remembrance should be held of the aristocratic notions they had inherited and once cherished with so much satisfaction. But pride ever lurks in the human heart, although forms may be changed and names be altered. At first the attempts were feeble, so as to avoid display. The coachman had an outside coat of a peculiar cut, with colored trimmings; as yet, the footman was not. When this last was ventured upon, he was made to appear in the same costume. After this came a bordering to the hat; then a cockade; afterward, all the garments were livery, more or less ornamented, according to the taste or ostentation of the modern prodigals. The same slow approaches were made in the arms. At first a modest crest, then the field with the escutcheons, were painted on the panels of the coach. At last, when the public mind was accustomed to the view of these objects, the full emblazonment of heraldry was seen in silver or gold on the hammer-cloth. Thus far these patterns of simple republican manners have advanced; but it is not to be presumed they will long stop at this point. Chasseurs and out-riders are yet to come, and one footman will not be found sufficient to display the wealth or maintain the dignity of the rising nobility.

There is one thing wherein the Americans show great modesty, and I speak it to their praise : they make no effort to hunt up pedigrees.   They have a maiden coyness in looking into the past ; they speak of their ancestors with respect, but are silent as to the castles they stormed, the captives they delivered, what conqueror they came over with, or the battles wherein they acquired renown, with the right to have their arms quartered.   There are not wanting however malicious persons who assert that this shyness is more the result of prudence than of modesty ; that the unwillingness to refer to the deeds of their ancestors arises, from a difficulty in discovering the renown that attaches to mechanical labors, some of them of the lowest cast.   Be this as it may, this modesty, if it do exist, is a great bar in the way of selecting suitable coats of arms as fit symbols of ancestral distinction or of actual merit.   No herald's-office is yet established in the country ; and as for Garter-King of Arms, he is not known in his heraldic capacity.   In a plebeian sense, he is familiar to chamber-maid as well as mistress ; but his daily presence, though very necessary to individual convenience, so far from being thought an ennobling appendage, is concealed with great care.   Young aspirants for honors are so much at a loss to find distinguishing marks by which their families may be known, that out of pure regard, and to show a little gratitude for many acts of friendship performed in my favor, I now offer a few emblems, which I respectfully think very applicable to the condition of the present ambitious generation :

For a lordly-minded Dame, with amplitude of person, I would propose, *Argent,* three peacocks in their pride *proper.*

For one whose ancestor was a Tailor : *Gules,* a cabbage in its compliment *Or,* supporters ; on the dexter-side a pair of shears *rampant,* on the sinister-side a goose *gorged Or.*

For a Shoe-maker : *Azure,* on a *Fess diamond* between three shoes *proper,* an awl erect *Gules.*

For an Oil-man : *Argent,* three whales'-heads erect, surmounted by an oil-flask in *bend-sinister.*

For a Druggist or Apothecary : *Argent,* a gallipot *proper,* two syringes in *Fess Or.*

For a perfect Gentleman, whose fortune consists of lands gently sloping from the Rocky mountains toward the Pacific : *argent,* three empty purses in their *detriment sable.*

For another Gentleman of easy manners, with large mustaches and no particular occupation : *or,* a jack-ass's head *erased sable.*

For one whose ancestor was elevated to a post far above his expectation : *sable,* a hangéd-man with his arms and legs extended *proper.*

I have little doubt these arms will be acceptable to many who are now seeking to be illustrated ; and I am sure I derive much satisfaction in being thus able to administer to a laudable pride.   Gentlemen and ladies may now see the origin and foundation of the dignities by which they are raised above the rest of mankind ; and by means of these emblems are at once able to embody many historical facts which without them would be lost to the world.

It is at dinner festivals, where their wealth may best be displayed, that the Americans depart farthest from the simplicity of their ancestors, and where is most conspicuous the predilection for foreign customs. In the dishes wherewith the table is loaded, you see the products of all climes arranged by the hand of foreign cooks into new forms that disguise the substance, called by foreign names which none but gourmands understand, and which give a very imperfect idea of the substance itself. It is amusing to see the wry faces made by one of the uninitiated when a dish with an unintelligible name is presented to him. A simple-hearted man, who has grown gray under the solid material of beef and mutton, looks at the dish with distrust; yet to avoid being ignorant or rude, asks quietly of his neighbor what it is that he is called upon to eat; his neighbor is probably quite as ignorant as himself; he then casts an anxious look round the table, in the hope that his accustomed food may form part of the feast. He looks in vain; still not without hope, he asks for a slice of the surloin, with a piece of the fat. The Major Domo regards him with pity, and hands an ' *Entre côte à la sauce piquante ;*' the novice in French names and French dishes rejects this as incomprehensible, and asks for a wing and a piece of the breast of the chicken. The poor man is as wide of the mark as ever, for there comes before him a ' *Suprême de Volaille.*' His patience is put to a severe trial, yet he must eat something; accordingly he makes a third attempt to get a dinner, and demands in a voice a little sharp, the thigh of a partridge with the back-bone and a little of the dressing. Here he is as badly off as he was before; thigh-bones and back-bones are vulgar and out of fashion; so he finds himself helped to a kind of porridge called ' *Purée de Perdreaux.*' The good man is almost in despair; his good nature grows weaker while his appetite grows stronger; and in a tone as angry as the place will admit, he begs the waiter for Heaven's sake to give him something he can eat. No sooner said than done; and '*Côtelettes de Veau en Papillotes*' are placed before him, the gravy well preserved. The hungry man's knowledge of French is not at all increased by hearing all these foreign names while undergoing his trials, and this new dish is not better understood than the others; yet what can he do? Time presses, and ' the inward parts give signs of wo :' if hunger can, as they say it will, break through stone walls, surely paper can offer no resistance; so he swallows greedily the côtelettes, papillotes and all, in order to appease a craving that long abstinence, added to great mental anxiety, has now rendered insupportable.

' How shall the young preserve their ways,' and how shall the old satisfy their hunger, by modern cookery? The temptations offered to youth are numerous and not easy to resist; but alas! the trials of the old in these modern times of improvement are past endurance! The Americans are not a refined people; their march of mind is wonderful; yet why need they march into the stomach so unmercifully as they do, especially when the land abounds in luxuries? Bear's ham is excellent eating, and bears' claws *bien traitées* are equal to '*Pieds de cochon farcis ;*' beaver's-tail is far superior to the English ox-tail, and no tongues in the world can be compared to those of the buffalo, not forgetting moose's lip, which is far more delicate than '*Dinde aux Truffles.*'

If the ignorant could by any means be enlightened by a slight fore-knowledge of the kind of fare to be set before them, they might by previous preparation fortify the inward man in a way to enable him either to eat or fast, as the lights or shadows of gastronomic life might fall upon him.   I have bethought me of a method, which I submit to the consideration of those who take the lead in fashionable din-ner-giving, with a hope that they will have pity on the benighted per-sons whose education has been neglected, but who are yet thought worthy of being received into the circles of refined society.

I would suggest to the exclusives, when they intend to produce an effect, to make known to the invited guests, by means of billets of a particular color, the fare they may expect to find.   For example, when an ordinary family dinner is meant, plain white paper may be used, and if the person invited be a country cousin, or an old friend from the Prairies, a wafer is sufficient ; sky-blue paper should be chosen for a distinguished stranger to meet a select party of friends ; but for a display of the perfection of gastronomic art, with all its appliances, pink paper, with a ' *Poulet saute*' as a vignette, should be considered as an indication that a refined repast is to be offered. In this way no person would be unprepared, 'and he might safely trust himself to one who kindly provides him a feast or carefully guards him against a famine.

If I were an American, I should lament that so little is done to shake off dependence on Europe for customs, fashion in dress and modes of thinking.   Very few things are purely national ; almost all are borrowed ; and climate, education and domestic relations are made to swerve from their place to conform to novelties brought from abroad.   Literature and works of art are but slightly valued till they have passed through the ordeal of foreign criticism, and come back stamped with the judgment of writers and artists who are apt to measure such works by the standard they themselves have raised for the meridian of their own country.   This dependence on others in matters of taste indisposes the Americans to invention in the higher branches of art ; creates a deficiency of stability in their opinions, and so far a distrust of their own judgment as to produce an unfavorable effect upon their character.   Every country of Eu-rope has its modes and customs ; even in districts and villages may be seen usages that give a distinctive character to the inhabitants ; but in America, vast as it is, with a numerous people scattered over an immensely extensive surface, all are alike in appearance and general habits — and these are English.

It is not to be supposed that this sameness is never to end ; yet as no attempt is made to produce a change, years must elapse before America will contain a population as dense as that of Europe, and have it in her power to show to others a model of manners and na-tional taste.   Till that period arrive, she will quietly remain subser-vient to the English for manners and literature, and to the French for cooks and milliners.

L I N E S

ON SEEING THE PICTURE OF 'NAPOLEON MUSING AT SAINT HELENA'

BY A NEW CONTRIBUTOR.

I.

BID your guard begone and leave me! free me from their loathed sight,
Nor their hated presence longer o'er me cast its with'ring blight:
Is the wo of fallen greatness subject meet for menial stare?
Must the espial's eye pursue it with its cold and heartless glare?
Have I the eagle's pinion or the falcon's arrowy spring,
To sweep yon broad blue ocean with the curlew's tireless wing,
That ye fear alone to leave me, girt with rock and rolling wave,
Prison direr far than tyrant ever doomed rebellious slave?

II.

Hirelings, back! this hour Remembrance claims from Fate as all her own,
Bought with loss of life-won glory at the cost of crown and throne:
Then away with orders given! tell me not of stern decree —
This is all of life that's left me, and this day I will be free:
All the shadowy past recalling, now the visioned hopes review,
Crushed before thy iron tempest, sad and fearful Waterloo!
GOD! how showed my bearded veterans, ranked upon that fatal plain,
Like the reapers at the harvest ere they cut the bending grain!

III.

How I scanned the grim battalions, all alike inured to war,
And above their measured tramping hearkened to the wild 'Hurrah!'
Long my ardent gaze dwelt on them, joyed to see the squadrons ride
Gleaming in the battle harness, hero-pomp and warrior pride:
Noted on the banners blazoned each renowned and noble name,
Jena's fight, Marengo's story and dread Lodi's bridge of flame:
Blent with these, Arcola deathless, Austerlitz's radiant sun,
Red Eylau and Hohenlinden, and old Wagram's thunder-gun!

IV.

How they trod, those iron legions! who by far Aboukir's wave,
In the pyramid's deep shadow heaped the Mameluke's bloody grave!
Saw the domes of distant Moscow reel amid her ocean fire,
And the mighty Kremlin piling high to heaven a Nation's pyre:
Braved the shock of Borodino, Beresina's madd'ning swell,
When the howl of desperation echoed back the Cossack yell,
And the broken battered columns whelmed beneath the torrents roar,
Rolled in blood and headlong carnage on that hope-abandoned shore!

V.

Now with rage and indignation kindled on each bronzéd face,
Met arrayed the gathered Allies of the scornful Bourbon race:
And among the hostile ensigns waving 'neath the clouded sky,
Saw the English leopard standard, chiefest of their foemen, fly;
Stormy wrath and rankling hatred, shouts for vengeance pealing wide,
Burst as from the rent volcano springs the lava's flashing tide;
All before me rolls the battle; from the heights of Houguemont,
Like the broad and strong tornado, JEROME pours upon their front!

VI.

Forward now, my noble brother! strike for crown and kingly name,
'T is a sceptre beckons onward, guides the path through blood and flame;
Think of all the deep contumely, think of all the bitter scorn
Heaped on Elba's throneless exile, world-abandoned and forlorn;
And let levelled lance and sabre, rattling shot and blazing gun,
Tell the foes of France and Frenchmen, 'Once again her 'chosen' come!'
Think of Acre's reeking slaughter, Badajos, Sebastian's cry —
To the brim the cup is filling, red revenge is foaming high!

VII.

Hark! the cannon's jarring thunder! — rank and square together reel,
D'ERLON, charge with all thy riders! give the horse the rein and heel!
Yonder, where the smoke is lifting, bid the bugles sound afar:
Oh for him! my peerless swordsman, for one hour of wronged MURAT;
But again to see his white plume tossing 'mid the colored smoke,
While around like darting lightning, flashed and fell his sabre stroke:
Crashing rolls another volley! onward now in full career,
On, as speeds the wingéd whirlwind, wild dragoon and cuirassier!

VIII.

Marshal all the bristling columns! wake the trumpet's deepest tone!
Bid the drum beat, strike the onset, 'up and at them,' brave CAMBRONNE!
Let them hear 'THE GUARD are coming?' let them see *thee*, gallant NEY!
Warrior-guide in blood and combat, beacon-star in stormy fray!
On they rush, and loud above them rings the eagle's vengeful strain,
Like the song of Denmark's ravens, grim rejoicers o'er the slain:
Overweening, haughty England, who shall now thy doom arrest,
Who shall bar the red bolt dashing low to earth thy lofty crest!

IX.

Vainly for the laggard Prussian listen 'mid the battle hail,
At the last the Gaul hath grasped thee — thou art clutched in hand of mail!
Not the hour that saw the Roman and imperial Austrian kneel
Matches this, that shrouds thee, Britain, in yon hurricane of steel:
Vengeance quaffs the brimming banquet; hark that cry of wild despair,
Mingling with the shock of cannon bellowing through the darkened air;
Those are surely GROUCHY's squadron's! No? Oh GOD! I see them now,
These are Prussia's swarming thousands — that is BLUCHER's sullen brow!

X.

Oh! for eyes to view the battle! would the curtained smoke were torn!
Do my gallant columns falter, by these numbers overborne?
Ah! the front is broke and rending! — havoc stern and deep dismay
Scatter wide the flying remnants, and the wreck of their array:
All forsake the hopeless combat, in confusion quit the field,
All but those, the brave, heroic, who could die but could not yield!
Loss of empire, loss of glory, all I met with firm regard,
But these drops of bitter anguish fall for ye, my noble Guard!

XI.

Passed the dream and visioned contest; gone the tumult of the fight,
Like the sleeper's air-drawn phantoms with the wasting of the night:
Still the Era hastens onward, prophet-like I see the day
When the veil shall rend asunder and the sceptre pass away:
When like ocean's dashing billows, thrones and kingdoms shall be tost,
'T il amid the wreck of empires slave and tyrant shall be lost:
Then shall Europe's cowering millions bend alone to Freedom's nod,
And fair France shall hail her hero as the noblest 'Sword of GOD!'

THE SAINT LEGER PAPERS.

NUMBER TWELVE.

THE next morning found me up betimes; nor was Hubert behind me. He had planned an excursion with Christie, in which I was to be a party if I chose; but my services were not insisted upon. As I was desirous to make one more visit to the 'Glen,' have one more interview with my strange kinsman, and take one more last look (was it to be the *last?*) at the enchanting Leila, I excused myself from joining my cousin. I could scarcely wait for a seasonable hour in which to present myself at the stone grotto. When I did arrive there, I found Leila *alone* in the apartment before described. She received me almost cordially; and to my inquiries about her father, she replied that he had passed a very restless night, and was far from well; at the same time she stepped into the adjoining room, and after a few moments returned, saying that if I would have patience for a short time, her father would see me. She turned again to leave the apartment. As the present was the only opportunity I might have for a private interview, I determined to make a desperate effort to realize it. 'Patience,' said I, 'is a virtue I have not of late particularly indulged in, and it is especially difficult to exercise it alone. Pray, my fair cousin, (excuse my calling you so for the first, the last, the *only* time — here too away behind the world,) pray, my fair cousin, have you any very serious objections to gratifying my curiosity upon a subject nearly concerning yourself?'

'What would you know?' said Leila, quietly, yet as I thought not indifferently; at the same time taking her seat. 'At a last interview much certainly may be allowed.'

'Lovers at least say so,' I replied; 'but I have a claim a thousand times stronger than that. A lover may be in despair; but I am bewildered! My brain is turned; I am crazed, positively crazed! I came to St. Kilda through love for adventure merely, but I have been so completely baffled, perplexed, confounded during my very short sojourn, that on the first fair wind I shall 'up sail' and away.'

'I certainly regret any incipient symptoms of insanity,' interrupted Leila, rather tartly, 'at least on your own account, and would recommend an immediate return to some place which can boast of civilization and a lunatic asylum. Still, I do not call some three or four weeks a very short sojourn at St. Kilda.'

'Three or four weeks!' exclaimed I, in amazement; 'three or four weeks! I have scarcely been in St. Kilda as many days!'

'Nor in its vicinity?' asked Leila, quickly.

'Certainly not,' I replied. 'I have not made a single landing at any of the contiguous islands.'

'Then you did not come——' Leila suddenly checked herself, and left the sentence unfinished.

'No, I did not,' replied I, coolly.

'Nay,' said Leila, 'but you know not what I was about to ask. It was really of no importance, and did not at all concern me.'

'You were about to ask,' continued I, speaking very slowly, 'if I did not come with one Vautrey, and I reply, *No! I did not!*'

'Hush! hush! Not so loud!' exclaimed the maiden, in a low but excited tone; 'breathe not *that* name here! Yĕt tell me; did you not really come in his company? Do you not know him? Are you not his friend?'

'Leila,' said I, 'I will answer your question seriously. I *do* know Count Vautrey, but I came not hither *with* Count Vautrey; I have no fellowship nor communion with him, for I believe him a deep, designing, selfish, cold-hearted villain; a fiend in human shape! I in *his* company! Nay, I had rather go to the bottomless pit in company with the foul fiend. And now let me be questioner once again: why do you avoid me, as if I were some repulsive object, to loathe and to shrink from? What have you to do with this Vautrey? Why do you start and become agitatĕd at the mention of his name, and bid me '*hush!*' as if it were guilt to mention it? Nay, nay; interrupt me not, but tell me—may I not ask this?—tell me why you are here, in this strange spot?—when do you leave it, and where do you go? There is some strange mystery connected with all this. Will you not explain it?'

'When I better understand your right to demand such explanation,' said Leila, haughtily. 'The private history of every one has its peculiarities, yet that is no warrant to the curious to pry into them.'

'None whatever,' returned I, in the same tone; 'and I am not at all surprised at being refused that confidence as a kinsman which you would doubtless have granted to me as a friend of Count Vautrey!'

'What mean you?' said Leila.

'And,' continued I, without noticing the interruption, 'I beg to state explicitly that I claim no right to ask you a single question, nor to allude to a single event of your life. Surely I can have nothing to do with the affairs of yourself and Count Vautrey. Excuse the presumptuous boldness of detaining you for a moment.'

As I concluded, Leila turned upon me a look so desolate, so full of sadness, that my conscience smote me for what I had uttered.

'*And you* HATE *this Vautrey!*' said Leila, slowly.

'If ever man can honestly hate his fellow-man, I do!' was my reply.

'*Then I love you!*' exclaimed the girl, passionately, starting up and advancing near me. 'And, oh!' continued she, bursting into a flood of tears, 'oh! if you knew me, knew my history—all that I have suffered and endured, what my fate has been and what my destiny surely, oh! surely *will be!*—but why do I speak thus to a stranger? Yet you are my kinsman. Alas! my kinsmen have ever proved my worst enemies! When shall I have peace? whither, whither shall I fly? Even in this remote spot I am persecuted by the importunities of that wretch. Oh, St. Leger! not one friend have I in the wide world! Tell me, what *shall* I do? In this moment of agony, when a sense of *utter* desolation overshadows my soul—alone! alone!—'t is fearful to live *always* alone—even at this moment, I come to you, to you whom I have beheld but once before—to you whose heart is young, and not like mine, burnt up within my bosom—to you I come; I *must*, I WILL have one friend; and may Heaven help me, if this last hope shall fail!'

The young girl abandoned herself so completely to her grief that it was impossible either to soothe or arrest it. Tears rolled down her face; her dark hair, breaking loose from its fastening, fell dishevelled upon her shoulders; her hands were clasped together, and her arms, partly upraised, were extended toward me. Never have I beheld so beautiful and so affecting a spectacle. My astonishment and the novelty of my situation for a while kept me speechless; my cold English temper could not immediately sympathise with the passionate exhibitions of a nature warmed and fostered under the influence of a more genial clime, and to which circumstances had unundoubtedly given additional cause for such violent emotions. But I soon found myself yielding wholly to the influence of so exciting a scene. A sympathising chord in my own heart was struck, and it responded. For all that, my manner was cold; I felt that it was cold; and it seemed almost unfriendly when contrasted with the ardent temper of Leila. I took advantage of the first pause in her pathetic appeal to reässure her. 'Leila,' said I, 'judge me not from this cold habit that I wear about me; it belongs to my race; but judge me by the heart that beats under it. And by its strong pulsations, by my faith, and by my hopes, I swear to you that I will be your friend henceforth. For your own sake compose yourself. Nay, you must be calm and tell me how my friendship can best serve you. Surely you forgot your father when you declared yourself quite friendless.'

'My father!' said Leila, mournfully, resuming her seat as she spoke, and burying her face in her hands: 'Alas! I am doubly wretched, doubly sinful, in having a parent whom I cannot love, and who loves not me!'

I shrunk with horror at such an avowal from one so young and so beautiful. The words of Scripture, 'without natural affection,' rose to my lips, but I repressed them. Leila perceived that I was shocked, and said:

'Do not in your mind accuse me unjustly. When I speak thus of my father, I am unburthening the load that weighs heaviest at my heart. To him I owe every thing that can minister to my personal comfort. I know not what it is to have a want ungratified. To him honor and obedience are due; but if you knew my history, and you shall know it ere long, you would not judge me harshly for not adding love.'

'I will not judge at all, till I do know,' said I; 'but your mother — is she not living?'

'May Heaven forgive you for mentioning the name!' exclaimed Leila, relapsing into her former emotion; 'mother! mother! Oh! I know not if I had a mother. Strange surmises crowd upon me; dreadful illusions pass before me; horrible suspicions force themselves upon me, at that word — *mother!* Never have I beheld a mother's face, never experienced a mother's love; and now I would barter for a mother's smile all that I hold dear in life, even though the lips that smiled upon me were guilty and polluted!' I saw that I had innocently touched upon a most delicate topic, and fearing the effects of farther excitement, I attempted to calm her spirit by my assurances of sympathy and friendship. Expecting an interruption every moment from the father, I asked Leila when we should meet again. 'I fear we shall not again meet alone here,' said she; 'my father is strange, very strange; and it is owing solely to his indisposition that he has left us so long together. No, not here; not here. Yet remember, *we shall meet again.* I too leave this gloomy island ere the moon wanes. Then you shall hear from me, and only let me feel that there is one solitary being in the wide world who will sympathise with me and I am grateful. I ask no more.' An old female at this moment made her appearance at a side-door which I had not before noticed, and beckoned hurriedly to Leila. The latter quickly obeyed the summons without bidding me adieu, and the door closed upon both. At the same instant, another door opened from the adjoining room and the Wœdallah entered the apartment.

So completely was his aspect changed that I scarcely recognised him. His countenance bore marks of extreme physical suffering and mental anguish. He looked ten years older than on the preceding day. Advancing slowly toward me, he took my hand, and in a kind but saddened tone asked me how I was. I was touched by his manner, and in return inquired as to his indisposition. 'It was nothing,' he replied, 'nothing but the effect of heavy heart-pains which occasionally afflicted him, and which were past cure.' As he said this, he sighed deeply, and asked me if I would not take a turn with him into the fresh air. He put his arm within mine, and we left the dwelling.

Passing out, we walked some distance along the coast, until it began to rise to a precipitous height. Here my kinsman paused. The swell from the sea under the influence of a strong west wind was tremendous. The waves mounting on high dashed furiously against the cliffs, and then retreating as if to renew their strength, returned again and were again thrown back into their ocean bed. We stood for some moments contemplating the grandeur of the scene in silence. At length my companion spoke:

'My son,' exclaimed he; 'my son, look around you and behold this isolated spot. Who would have thought that busy man should have come hither to make it his own? Yet here Virtue may dwell secure and uncontaminated, for there is no place for the pomp and circumstance of this world to stand upon. But look away yonder, far, far away; nay, you see it not, save with the *mind's* eye; behold crowded together the habitations of the children of men. See the buildings close-cemented as if all were under a single roof. Must not peace and þrotherly love and happiness dwell there ? Surely there can be no discords, no dissensions, no unhappy conflicting interests. Is it possible that those firm and strong walls between each dwelling separate the bitterest enemies, divide the good man from the assassin, the innocent from the vile, the honest from the knave ? Men herd together for mutual *concealment*, not for any good, assuredly. Those cities of the plain, mark me, should be destroyed, and fire from the LORD out of heaven should fall upon them, even as it fell upon Sodom and Gomorrah ! But let us turn from the contemplation of so revolting a picture. Let me speak something of myself and you. Know you the relation we bear to each other ?'

I replied that I did not; that I had learned but little of our family history, although I was eager to learn more of it.

' Then know,' continued my kinsman, 'that I am the son of Wilfred St. Leger. Ay, of Wilfred the rash, Wilfred the unfortunate; a younger brother, as you doubtless know, of old Hugh St. Leger, the Lion-hearted, your father's father. William Henry, I am calm now,' continued he, for the first time calling me by name. ' I fear the unhappy effect of our last interview upon your mind, and I would do what I may to counteract it. As I said before, I have dreadful heart-pains which quite unman me. For what I say when suffering under this terrible affliction I am not, I cannot be, accountable. You carry truth within your bosom; your sentiments I honor; I bow to them; I would that I could make them mine. But 't is too late. Do not speak to me farther on this head. I WILL NOT hear you !'

' But will you not,' said I, deeply interested, 'tell me why you are here, and explain to me the strange selection which you have made for a home ?'

' Home !' said the other; ' *home !* My home is *there !*' pointing down into the deep abyss of waters which foamed beneath us; ' for no mortal shall hereafter tread upon my grave, nor shall any monument stand up to say, ' This man once lived upon the earth !' But you shall be satisfied. Sit we down upon these rough stones ; turn your face away from mine, and most briefly will I sketch my life.'

I did as directed ; and my kinsman began :

' You doubtless have heard,' said he, ' how Wilfred St. Leger, my father, in company with Julian Moncrieff of Glencoe, made their way to Paris with the fair Isabella Seward, a rich heiress, and a ward of the Earl of Venachoir; how Wilfred St. Leger wedded the young girl, and how they lived happily together; how in some three years the lovely lady grew pale, saddened and *died*, leaving one child, a boy—myself. I have no recollection of my mother; sometimes I fancy I can bring to mind her sweet pale face, as she pressed me closely to her bosom, and weeping commended her infant to GOD. It was a sin to leave a guardian's roof and elope as she did; but how sorely was she punished, and how surely ! *Thank God, she died !* Ay, died, instead of carrying the crushing weight of a broken heart and an agonized spirit through a long life-time. My father was always a slave to the gayeties of Paris. From my boyhood, on the contrary, I detested them. I longed to get upon English ground. I determined never to adopt any other country for my own. At the age of ten, my father, more to avoid the restraint which a young boy's observation would naturally bring upon a parent desirous of casting it off, sent me to England to his brother, Hugh St. Leger, your grandfather, having previously got the consent of my uncle that he would take charge of me. I spent in England the only happy days of my life. Your noble father was about my own age, and we rode, we hunted, we read and we studied together. How I loved him then! and if my heart was not stone, how I should love him now! For seven long, (to children years are long,) happy, happy years was England my home. Of that time, three years were spent at Eton, and one year at Oxford. Previously to that we were attended by private masters at Bertold Castle. Through the whole time your father was my constant playmate and companion; and never was there any serious difference between us. I now considered myself permanently located in England. From my father I heard three or four times a year; his letters generally contained some half-dozen lines expressing his approbation of the course I was pursuing under my uncle's direction, with some common-place remark about 'duty,' and the like. Nevertheless, his remittances were always punctually made, and I soon came to regard one epistle as the *fac simile* of the other, the date being altered.

'I had been at Oxford a year. I was ambitious as a student, without being a book-worm, and I began to feel that I had that about me which would lead to an honorable distinction among my fellows. My habits were good, and much did I owe to your father's influence that they were so. Still, there was that about me of which . I trembled thoughtfully to consider. There was a latent desire to know and to experience the pleasures of life, and to taste its follies. The *Untried* was constantly before me with its temptations, but I resisted them all; yet I felt how necessary it was for me to keep as far as possible beyond their reach. Just then—mark me, for the Devil's hand was in it!—just then, I received a letter from my father, written in great haste, commanding me to come immediately to Paris. I cannot describe my feelings at this unexpected announce- . ment. For a time I was completely beside myself. I raved and swore, and cursed my destiny; nay, I fear I cursed my parent! At length I became calm. I sat down and wrote him a long letter, stating my situation, what I had accomplished, what I hoped to accomplish; and concluded by begging him to allow me to remain where I was. I received in return a short, decisive note, stating that none but the most urgent reasons had influenced his decision; that it was unalterable, and that he was already suffering through my delay. I left Oxford at once for Bertold Castle, and asked my uncle's advice. His view of the relation of parent and child was severe. He said that he regretted my father's decision, but advised me to bow to it; and that it might be in my power speedily to re-turn. Much more he said, which I need not repeat; but the con-clusion was, that I was persuaded.

'The next day I left for Paris. Arrived there, I drove to my father's hotel in *Rue Montmartre*, and found it *closed*. A sick-ening apprehension came over me as I leaned against the ponder-ous gate which commanded the entrance to the court-yard. Not even the *portier*, who almost always remains a fixture on the pre-mises, was in his accustomed place to answer questions, and the door to the *conciergerie* was shut and fastened. I knew not what to do in such a dilemma. My mind was sorely perplexed; and as I looked up at the high walls of the gloomy building, rendered ten-fold more gloomy by being tenantless, I felt that I was indeed 'a stranger in a strange land.'

'I had nothing to do but to drive to some proper place for lodg-ings, and find my father as I best might. As I was about giving the necessary directions, an old fellow with a patch on his eye hobbled up to me as if to ask charity, and prayed me for the love of GOD to read a dirty paper which he thrust in spite of me into my hands. I opened it and read as follows :

' ' *This evening, at eight o'clock, Rue Copeau, No.* 4, *unaccompanied.*
                                                        W. ST. L.'

' ' There is a franc for you, my poor fellow,' said I, handing back the paper; and without waiting to hear a reply, I drove to Rue Vivienne to find lodgings. Surmises being useless, I waited pa-tiently until after seven, when I set out on foot, to elude observa-tion, for Rue Copeau. This was a short street far away on the other side of the Seine, leading into the Garden of Plants. I passed slowly into Rue St. Honoré, and followed it through its whole extent into Rue St. Denis; down that to the Seine, thence along the Quai till I reached the Isle St. Louis, where I crossed; thence along the Quai again to Rue de Seine, and up that to Rue Copeau. Do you wonder at the minuteness of this detail? I tell you that every step of that walk is as fresh to me now as on the day it was taken. I remember the faces of thousands who passed me; I see them now—now before me. There was a little old man with a long cue extending half-way down his back, whom I thoughtlessly jostled as I passed, and who at once turned and beg-ged my pardon. There were pretty grisettes, who stared at me with naïve wonder as I pushed unheedingly on; there were old women on the Quai; there were soldiers about the gardens; there, there are they all!—and hark! just as I reached the ap-pointed number in the appointed street, the chimes from the nun-nery of the 'Sisters of Universal Concord,' situated just in the rear, pealed merrily forth the hour of eight.'

Here my relative paused for some minutes. I turned partly round, alarmed at his silence. Large drops of sweat were standing on his forehead, and his whole appearance was that of one in mor-tal agony. Shortly, however, he resumed.

LAYS OF A PEDESTRIAN.

BY LUCIUS E. SMITH.

My path winds up the steep hill-side,
    Fanned by the morning breeze,
That dimples with smiles the leafy pride
    Of the huge o'er-shadowing trees :
All fringed with light, the fleecy clouds
    Brood o'er the mountain's brow,
And the softened hum of busy crowds
    Comes up from the vale below ;
Where a village rests in the warm embrace
    Of hills that gird it round,
Rejoicing in Nature's loveliness,
    And with Nature's riches crowned !

Hark ! 't is the steam-pipe's whistle shrill !
    It sounds through yonder glen,
And the startled echoes from the hill
    Repeat the sound again ;
And now through the tunnel's darkened gorge
    The rattling car has fled,
With a sullen roar, as of VULCAN's forge
    Under Ætna's heaving bed !
Swift ! for the iron horse is strong,
    And proud of his strength is he ;
But the shaded walk and the robin's song
    By the violet-bank for me !

True, 't is exulting thus to be
    Sped like an arrow forth,
To ' take the wings of the morn' and flee
    To the uttermost parts of earth !
Is it in fear the high hills quake
    As the fiery train sweeps by ?
Methinks the mountains wildly shake
    Their tresses in the sky !
The firmament seems to writhe in dread
    Above the iron way,
And the brave old trees from the burning steed
    In terror flee away !

'T is gone ! — the smoky trail alone
    Creeps through the spreading trees ;
Again I hear the soothing drone
    Of insects on the breeze ;
There 's not a voice but seems to bless
    And cheer me as I go,
My thoughts are full of pleasantness,
    Calm as deep rivers' flow.
And thus with Nature's joy around,
    Led by the rising sun,
With Hope's exulting banner crowned,
    My journey 's well begun.

NED BUNTLINE'S LIFE-YARN.

'BEAUTIFUL! how beautiful!' was half-involuntarily murmured by
every body on the next morning, as each eager eye glanced through
the misty veil of early dawn, upon the lofty bluffs which arose on
either side of the harbor's mouth.   Like the bold outline of an un-
finished picture, sketched by a master hand, the ridged land lay in
wild relief against the blue sky beyond ; and down under its shadow
lay little islands, scattered here and there, their palmy foliage
waving in the morning breeze, looking like signals of welcome to
the toil-worn and ocean-tossed.   A sailor can but faintly conceive
how sweetly looked that land to the sea-weary ones on board the
schooner.   To a seaman even, there is at times music in the cheery
cry of ' Land ho !' and to him the land sometimes seems like a rest-
ing-place ; yet so accustomed does he become to his billowy home,
that ever with a sad sigh he leaves, with a glad smile he returns to,
its restless bosom.

With an old navigator there was no need for the services of a
pilot in entering the harbor of Rio, so bold are its shores and so
deep its channels ; therefore, as soon as daylight opened every thing
to view, all sail was made on the schooner, and with the star-span-
gled robe of liberty floating from the peak, she glided in toward the
town, before a light zephyr-breath from sea-ward.   Soon the heavy
sea-swell gave place to the smoother surface of the harbor, and the
Mary C —— bore on more swiftly than before, passing close under
the shade of the tall 'Sugar-Loaf,' between it and the island-fort,
gliding smoothly past the frowning batteries of Santa-Cruz ; on, until
the whole of that beautiful bay, its islands, cones and inlets opened
like a fairy scene before her.   Magnificent indeed is the view which
the eye embraces on a first entrance into Rio Janeiro.   In the far
back-ground, like the rising clouds of a distant storm, appear lofty,
irregular mountains ; then nearer, all that gentler variety of hill and
dale, cot and village, which a lover of rural scenery could wish for ;
and here and there, imbedded in green and lofty foliage, were beau-
tiful country-seats ; some resting close upon the margin of the bay,
others back upon the wooded knolls.   Oblong in its shape, very ex-
tensive, dotted plentifully with islands, covered with rich and flowery
vegetation, and fringed with well-cultivated gardens, the harbor of
Rio exhibits every charm which may link land and sea together.

As soon as the schooner passed the castle Santa-Cruz, a large
barge rowed toward her, having a yellow flag flying over her stern-
sheets.   As the boat came near, the Mary C —— was hove to, and
in a moment more the port-physician was pacing her deck with all the
pomposity of medicinal authority, with the dreadful power of qua-

rantine confinement in his possession. But fortunately she had left
Philadelphia with a ' clean bill of health,' and we were excused from
the lazaretto and its many disagreeabilities; and the health-officer
with his sickly-looking crew of bargemen left her to proceed up to
the anchorage. As we rounded-to before the city, lowered away
and brailed up our sails ready for furling and dropped our anchor,
the custom-house boat boarded us, while a perfect fleet of little boats,
which dare not come alongside until the revenue search had been
made, lingered around in every direction. Our papers having been
examined, and two revenue guards left to prevent any contraband
mischief, the passengers' passports were countersigned and all inter-
diction between us and shore-going was removed. Then came the
crowd of shore-boats with their motley gangs : merchants, clerks,
hotel-keepers, fruit-venders, provision men, Jews and washer-wo-
men, all in a huddle, each speaking of his or her particular business
in some half-dozen different keys and tongues, giving us an infantine
idea of Babel before the strange tongue-machinery had got fairly
under head-way. ·

The consignees having come on board with our permit, we hauled
in to the shore to discharge cargo and to give our passengers a
chance to get on shore conveniently; an opportunity at once taken
advantage of by Mr., Mrs. and the little Marleys, who hated our craft
worse than his Satanic Majesty dislikes the portals of Paradise. In
fact, Mr. Marley had smiled but twice since we had sailed ; once
when he had a prospect of getting a good dinner of fresh meats,
from a boat when we were off the coast of Brava ; the second time
when his blue eyes had made out the land ahead on that morning.
He and his family left without much ceremony, unregretting and
unregretted. 'But as the ' stranger' came up from the cabin, pre-
paratory to leaving, a stir was seen among the crew, each striving
to have the honor of carrying his luggage on shore ; for his kindness
to poor Bill Hanson when sick had brought up the true sailor's
gratitude from their heart-lockers. Bill, still pale and wan, stood
by the companion-way, twisting his tarpaulin about in his left hand,
and pulling his recollection-curl with the other, trying to express
himself as he felt :

' We all wish your honor was a-goin' back with us, Sir,' said Bill ;
'for we do n't like to leave a real true-grit American, who has come
to be like a ship-mate in this 'ere short v'yage with us, in this out-
landish country, among a lot of cowardly Diegos that would stick a
knife into a white man for a doubloon, and kill a half-a-dozen nig-
gers in the bargain. If your honor will only make up your mind to
go back with us, we 'll be right joyous, and it sha'n't cost your
honor a red cent !'

Here Bill paused in his speech, and looked around among his
messmates to see if he had spoken rightly, and their looks earnestly
asked the stranger not to leave them, but to seek again the land of
his nativity.

' No, my good lads, it cannot be ; I thank you for your kind and
honest offer, but I have left the land of my birth forever !'

He did not wait to hear their renewed solicitations, but with a painful effort turned away and passed on. He was soon followed by Mr. Amadinna and his daughter. Mr. Amadinna hoped and expected to finish his business in time to go home in the schooner on her return trip.

When night came its shadow brought joy to the heart of NED, for with it came that cessation from the labor of discharging cargo which would enable him to glance over the city. He rigged himself in his 'shore-going togs' after supper, and under the convoy of the captain, started on a land cruise. First, they made their way to the Plaza del Populo, in front of the palace, where Ned was quite enchanted with the music of the military band and the flashing black eyes which glanced out from the shadow of the silken mantillas, like stars through little peep-holes in a thunder-cloud. Throngs of gay cavaliers, fair maidens, old men and little children, were enjoying the cool night air, the soft, clear moonlight, the dashing, sparkling fountains and sweet music on their favorite Paséo. But Ned decidedly objected to the walking dress of the ladies, a sort of sack that muffled up all the fair proportions of their figures, leaving nothing visible save *one* eye, and their pretty tiny feet. But 't is said that Imagination is a better painter than Reality; on this principle therefore we may picture (as tourists generally do) the Brazillian ladies beautiful as the thrice angelic Houris of a Mussulman's paradise.

In that equatorial clime* evening is a great luxury. It is only then that one can walk with pleasure; it is only then that the better and fairer half of creation make the air musical with their merry laugh and dulcet tones. It is only then that from the dull castle-like houses and narrow streets life seems to issue; and as you pass along, the strum of the sweet guitar, the clang of the lively castanet and the voice of song, all speak of peace, joy, love and happiness. Late in the evening, Ned and the captain returned on board, after a lengthened tramp among the squares and fountains, and retired to their welcome berths.

For the first three or four days, all hands were busy in discharging the cargo; so that Ned had but little chance to look around him, save in the short but delightful evenings. He had made no new acquaintances here, nor had he, as is the sailor's privilege, fallen in love.with any new beauty. A fair poet of our own clime sings:

> 'THEY say it is a sailor's boast
> That, fickle as a child,
> He lights Love's torch on every coast
> Along the waters wild ::
> With hopes and fears he maketh sport,
> Of vows an idle jest;
> He hath a sweetheart in each port,
> North, South and East and West.'

But we think the lady rather too severe and a little unjust in this general charge; although it is but natural that he who in his life of toil and peril is deprived of her society nearly all of his time, should

---

* ALTHOUGH Rio is but a little farther from the equator than the southern portion of Florida, the warmth of the climate is much greater in the former place.

be more attentive to, and the better appreciate, dear WOMAN than the tame landsman, who being ever near her, gazes upon her as a common sight, and cares for her not as a seldom-to-be-seen blessing, but as an earthly convenience, made to assist the 'lords of creation' in the laborious vocations of their daily life. Fickle as they are said to be, show me any men in the world who place a higher estimate upon 'GOD's last best gift' than sailors do; show me one isolated case, one instance, where a true thorough-bred seaman has abused the trust of the weaker sex, and I shall see a sight never as yet to me unveiled.

Pardon me, reader, if in defence of my slandered brethren I 'yaw from the course' of my yarn. I'll return to it.

Each day the 'Stranger' came down to look at the schooner, and every time, as he gazed upward at the 'meteor-flag' that waved from her mast-head, his eye looked brighter, even as with the moisture of the dew of death; and his cheek more pale, his step less firm, spoke of that within which was like to the worm nested in a frail flower's centre, eating its life away. He seemed to love to see his countrymen, yet avoided much converse with them. Once or twice had the captain and Ned in their evening walks met him with Jane Amadinna and her father, enjoying the promenade of the Plaza, but each time a change in his appearance was apparent. Mr. Marley too they had met, with his weightier half and group of duplicates; but now that his foot was once more on terra-firma, he did not condescend to notice the 'Yankees,' which neglect was borne by them with singular fortitude and composure.

At last the cargo was out, and then one day's 'liberty' was allowed to all hands. Each according to his disposition availed himself of this chance for 'a spree;' some, making a straight wake for a livery-stable, were soon mounted on horse-back, steering toward the country, stopping at every *Fonda* which they came in sight of, to lay in a fresh supply of '*ballast*,' of which before night many of them had an overplus, if we may judge from the fact that they very often tumbled overboard from their strange crafts, and complained of great difficulty in steering their 'lubber-rigged' conveyances. The black cook had fully realized the force of the poet's idea of being 'Darkie' 'beautifully blue,' and many others of the crew, if not as dark as he, were quite as blue.

Ned and the captain had the pleasure of a volanté trip, in company with the Amadinnas and the 'Stranger,' to a mountain in the vicinity called the 'Parrot's Head;' so named probably because it looked less like the head of that bird than any thing else in creation. From this elevated spot they had a beautiful view of the city, the surrounding villas, and the rich plantations; the broad and glassy bay covered with ships at anchor, and little white sails skimming here and there, looking like young swans sporting in a lake of liquid silver; and in the dim north-eastern distance, the peak of the 'Organ' range arose like hoary monuments of the world's birthday against the sky. Down below, along the sunny hill-sides and beside rushing streams in the valleys, the peasantry were at their

labors among the fruits and flowers. Oh! in such a scene, could any
one live and not be happy? Ask the pale laborer there; ask the
gaunt, attenuate slave if he is happy? Where is the bright, free
eye; the clear, joyous carol; the firm, steady step, and the upright
form that speaks the freeman? Oh! it is not here!

The scene below and around them was indeed glorious. Had
man done but half his duty there; had he done but half as much
for himself as GOD has done for that glorious country, there would
be no spot on earth which could vie with it. The 'Stranger's' wan
face brightened with the sun of enthusiasm as he gazed forth, and
turning to the lady, said:

'This land is much fairer than that which we have left.'

'Yes, Sir, it is fairer, yet here we cannot feel as we have felt at
home. Our land hath winter snows, chilling storms and barren
spots, but LIBERTY is there; we there are *free.* Here, bright though
nature be, fairy as are all the scenes, the cloud of cold tyranny
blasts all happiness, darkens and destroys all soulful enjoyment,
leaving nothing to sate the weary life-wanderer save a few fleeting
sensual pleasures. No man here dare say that he is free! No one
can go to his rest at night with a calm security that before morning
flashing steel, lurid flames and hireling soldiery will not awaken
him. Give me a desert if liberty is there, rather than a paradise
where tyranny reigns! Let me hear the sound of the bleak winds
of winter in my own land, rather than the Æolian breathings of
these flower-scented zephyrs, which bring the clank of chains and
the groans of the oppressed to my ear!'

'And yet to such a land, lady, have I come to *die!*' said the
Stranger.

'Oh, no! you must not stay here to die! Here, where you have
no friends; where they will not let your Protestant corse lie in the
burial-place of christians.* You must return; and *if* you die, die
where friends may soften your pathway to the tomb by acts of kind-
ness and love; die where religion may breathe hope to your de-
parting soul; die where your remains may be sepulchred with
respect. It were far better to die out upon the stormy ocean than
here in this land, where the sun shineth yet warmeth not the hearts
of men; where houses are erected to worship GOD in, and yet
where those who believe in a blessed SAVIOUR cannot have christian
burial, because they differ in sectarian points from those who pro-
fess the same holy JESUS.'

'You see, Sir, it's no use to try to stay here,' said the captain
playfully to the 'Stranger;' 'you have your *orders* to return with
us, and it would be very ungallant in you to disobey orders from a
source so fair and good.'

'It would give me pleasure to obey those orders, captain; but I

* REFERENCE is here made to the custom in Catholic countries of not permitting Protestants to be
buried in consecrated ground. Of this the poet YOUNG complains in his ' Narcissa,' alluding to his
daughter, whom he buried secretly at night in a garden:

'WHILE Nature melted, Superstition raved;
That mourned the dead, and *this* denied a grave!'

fear my sailing-orders for man's last port are too nearly made out for me ever to hope to look again upon my native land ; and yet I shall be very lonely here after your vessel sails. I shall then feel that my *friends* are gone, and the last link that chains me to earth will be broken.'

' Oh ! nonsense, my young friend ! never give up to the blues ! Your 're worth a dozen dead men yet. A sweet calm always comes after a storm, and the sun shines a great deal brighter after it has had its face washed by a cloud.'

Night was coming on with rapid shade, and they descended to the town.

———

CHAPTER TENTH.

NEARLY three weeks had elapsed after the arrival of the Mary C —— before her ' clearance' was made out from the Rio custom-house. But the day came ; her last bag of coffee had been stowed in the hold, her provisions and water re-supplied, and the fruit-net-ting over the stern amply filled with the products of that luscious land.

It was a brilliant Sabbath* morning when the seamen ran aloft to loose the schooner's sails, and on the quarter-deck stood Jane Am-adinna and her father ; but the ' Stranger' was not there. Our captain, with trumpet in hand, had just given the order to ' Let fall ! sheet home ! hoist away ! stand by to clear away the shore-fasts !' when his quick eye glanced up the ' Calle del Rey,' a street leading up from the water, and he shouted :

' Hold on a bit, my boys ! avast sheeting home ! By old Nep. ! there comes our friend, yet ! I 'm devilish glad he 's made up his mind to go back ; I do believe he *would* have died in this outlandish hole.'

In fact, the ' Stranger' was hastily approaching the vessel, with his luggage following him. Stepping on board, he bowed to Jane and her father, and faintly smiling, said :

' You see, even at the eleventh hour, I have taken your advice, fair lady. I could not bear to be alone among so many people, and I *felt* alone when you and your good father left me ; and—I am here !'

' Now our party is complete,' said she, joyfully, ' and I can leave this land without one regretful sigh, without one sad thought.'

If looks could speak, both captain and crew were delighted that he had returned ; and now, all being ready, sail was made, the lines let go, and out shot the beautiful craft, moving along the silvery bay like a single snowy cloud athwart a summer sky. Again her keen prow threw up foam-flakes beneath the shade of the frowning ' Sugar-Loaf ;' soon once more she rose and fell upon the heaving waves of old ocean, softly, gently as an infant upon its mother's heaving bosom.

———

* SAILORS have not many superstitions, yet they always regard starting on a Sunday as a propi-tious time, and sailing on a Friday as an unlucky day.

Seamen and landsmen were glad, for were they not homeward-bound? *Homeward-bound!* Oh! how the heart leaps at that sound!—the heart that for weary years has been absent from those it hath loved and still loves! The pictures that are painted, the joys that are anticipated; the hopes that arise to brighten, the fears that come to darken, the future—all, all these can be felt, but they cannot be expressed!

STANZAS TO MY SISTER.

God bless thee, dearest! on thy brow
  Earth has no shadow cast;
The future is all bright to thee,
  No cloud rests o'er the past.
Light is thy step and bright thine eye,
  Where mirth and gladness beam;
Thy every look is joyousness,
  Where peace and radiance gleam.

Oft do I tremble as I gaze,
  For fear thou 'lt pass away,
Like all the bright and fairy things
  Of earth that cross my way;
For fear thou art some vision fair,
  A spirit from the land,
The '*better* land,' of Hope and Love,
  Strayed on Time's barren sand.

To light this dark and chilling world
  For but a fleeting day,
And then as wane the stars at morn
  Fade from my sight away;
As the sweet bird is to the wood
  Where oft the wild winds moan,
Art thou unto my spirit here,
  My bright, my joyous one!

Thou knowest nought of earthly care,
  Of sorrow's bitter tears;
How burning love and freezing hate
  And fervent hope and trembling fears
Are mingled in the cup of life
  With many a bitter wo:
How often preys the secret grief
  The world will never know.

Oh! I would kneel and ask my God
  That I might always bear
Whatever in thy lot shall be
  Of grief or pain or care;
That as some glad and placid stream
  Sweeps to its parent sea,
So may thy peaceful days e'er flow
  On to eternity!

Shelter Island.

The soul is like the viewless harp
  Where the winds love to play,
That vibrates to the softest breath
  That passes on its way;
Beneath the dark and threat'ning storm
  The spirit's chords are bent,
And the frail and wildly-thrilling strings
  Are by the tempest rent.

I would not have thee live to bow
  Beneath earth's stormy clime;
I would not have thy spirit touched
  By the dark hues of time.
The forest-bird forsakes its wood
  When first the winter lowers,
And seeks a fairer, brighter home
  In the sweet southern bowers.

So like that bird, if e'er thy sky
  Presage a wint'ry night,
I 'd have thee flee from earth away
  To realms of fadeless light;
I 'd have thee pass as fade the stars
  Before the dawning day,
Or as the snow beneath the sun
  Unsullied melts away.

But oh! it is my fervent prayer
  That no dark cloud arise
To throw a shadow on thy brow,
  Or dim thy youthful skies:
That when my soul is called away
  From earth, thou wilt be nigh,
To bless me with thy joyous smile,
  And close my dying eye.

God bless thee, dearest! He who led,
  Amid the desert land,
His wand'ring sons by cloud and fire
  Through Egypt's burning sand;
Oh! He will guide and guard thee here
  From every sin and care;
Then call thy spirit up to Him,
  Eternal love to share.
                    MARY GARDINER.

THE PEOPLE. By M. MICHELET. Translated by G. H. SMITH, F. G. S. In one volume. New-York: D. APPLETON AND COMPANY.

WE sincerely wish that one of our publishers would have the good taste, to say nothing of honor and honesty, when a book is republished, to give some hint in the title-page of the source whence it was derived. If our, republishers of other people's books have no sense of justice due to the owners whose property they appropriate, they should at least have a sense of what is due to their own customers. We do not make this remark with any particular reference to the republication before us, for the custom of reprinting English works without any allusion to their origin we know to be universal among our book-sellers; but we never open an English work published in this country without feeling a sense of national degradation at the utter disregard of human rights manifested by our people in refusing to allow to foreigners the privilege of controlling their own property on our soil. It is true that a majority of the traders in books are beginning to perceive that honesty is the best policy in their business as well as in all others, but this was not always the case; and had it not been for the opposition of a few book-sellers, we believe that congress would long ago have passed a bill for the protection of foreign authors. As the matter now stands there is no law on the subject; and we believe that if proper steps were taken a legal stop might be put to the Algerine practices of our book-printers. The least that could be done would be to acknowledge, on the part of our publishers, the original source of their borrowed goods, by stating on the title-pages of the books that they were re-published from such and such editions.

M. MICHELET in this volume has chosen a theme worthy of a philosopher; but we find, on a closer examination of his pages, that he has treated it like a Frenchman. Although his work contains a good deal of truth, expressed in his peculiar manner, it also contains a vast amount of error, and is consequently the reverse of a philosophical treatise. But perhaps he aimed at nothing more than to give an exposition of the 'people' of France. If so, he has doubtless performed his task well; but he appears to have aimed at something higher than this, and if so he has failed. The most interesting portion of the book is the dedication to EDGAR QUINET, wherein M. MICHELET gives a touching history of his own life, which compels us to love him and reverence him for the hardships which he endured in his youth, and the purity of his soul, which enabled him to keep himself above the evils that surrounded him. The liveliness of his imagination, the rapid elegance of his style and his high moral feelings, joined to extensive erudition, render him the most readable of the brilliant historical writers by whom France is distinguished at this time. But withal, he is thoroughly French, and has that shocking, unmanly, unchristianlike and unphilosophical admiration for bloody finery and gew-gaws which characterizes his nation, and which we grieve to acknowledge is fearfully rife among our own countrymen at this time. He believes that swords and bayonets do as much good as sermons and books, and has great admiration for men-killers. 'Sacred bayonets of France!' exclaims M. MICHELET, 'that light which hovers over you, which no eye can sustain, watch that nothing dims its brightness!' These sacred bayonets happen to be engaged just now in letting out the entrails of Arabs, a people on whom the 'people' of M. MICHELET have made war for mere pastime, and to prevent the men who have been trained to blood-shed from making war on each other. 'Sacred bayonets of France!' What have the colporteurs of our Foreign Evangelical Society been about, that they have not sent M. MICHELET a copy of the Bible? We hope that Doctor BAIRD or Doctor CHEEVER will see that this popular author is kept no longer in ignorance that there was once a greater Teacher in this world, whose lessons yet remain among us, called JESUS CHRIST.

LIFE IN PRAIRIE-LAND. By ELIZA W. FARNHAM. In one volume, 12mo. pp. 408. New-York: HARPER AND BROTHERS.

THE author of this volume is well known to a large circle of friends, many of them among the ablest of our public men, as a lady of strong mind, and one who ranks among the best writers of her sex in this country. Her anonymous contributions to the press on prison discipline and kindred subjects, and her labors in the post she now occupies, would, if known to the public as they have been to these friends, give her a high reputation. Mrs. FARNHAM received a thorough education in one of our highest female seminaries, since which she has resided several years at the West. She has not in her work drawn much from her imagination, but has chosen rather to present graphic sketches of real scenes and actual incidents. She says in her preface: 'The writing of these sketches has been to me a labor of love. While engaged upon them, I have lived again in the land of my heart. I have seen the grasses wave, and felt the winds, and listened to the birds, and watched the springing flowers, and exulted in something of the old sense of freedom which these conferred upon me. Visions prophetic of the glory and greatness which are to be developed here have dwelt in my mind and exalted it above the narrow personal cares of life. It is the enjoyment afforded by this kind of emancipation which so endears the Western country to those who have resided in it. It steals upon the heart like what it is, the very witchery of nature; so that those who are susceptible to it feel the charm but not the inconvenience through which it is invoked. Such persons delight in the perfection and beauty of the natural, and these suffice them.' As a book of humor, the volume will amuse; as one of true information, it will instruct; possessing a distinct order of literary merit, it will interest; and in all respects it will well repay perusal. Mrs. MARY CLAVERS' delightful works depicting the multiform scenes and events of forest-life in occidental regions have created quite a demand for sketches in a kindred vein; and we are well pleased to find that Mrs. FARNHAM is so much at home in so fresh and fruitful a field. It is one which can scarcely be over-cultivated by competent laborers.

ADDRESSES AND MISCELLANEOUS WRITINGS: BY CHARLES B. HADDOCK, D. D., Professor of Intellectual Philosophy and Political Economy in Dartmouth College. In one volume. pp. 574. Cambridge: METCALF AND COMPANY.

THIS volume, we are informed by the author in his preface, is published at the request of a large number of his pupils, to whom we may add the work is dedicated. It professes to be 'nothing more than a memorial of an early guide and companion in study, who has ventured now and then beyond the scene of academic life to contribute his mite in stimulating enterprise or improving education in the community around him. 'It is now,' continues our author, 'five-and-twenty years since I adopted the resolution never to refuse to attempt any thing consistent with my professional duties in the cause of learning and religion, which I might be invited to do. This resolution I have not at any time regretted, and perhaps I may say I have not essentially violated it. However this may be, I have never suffered for want of something to do; and the work now offered to you is mainly a selection from the numerous addresses which I have had occasion to deliver on a considerable variety of subjects, but remotely connected with my principal studies. If it answer the purpose of reviving pleasant memories of college days and college friendships in my pupils, already constituting more than a third part of the whole number who have gone out from the bosom of our Alma-Mater, I shall be quite satisfied without any other mark of favor for a volume which seeks no higher or more public regard.'

We cordially welcome the volume of Professor HADDOCK; and notwithstanding the small pretensions it makes to the notice of the world, we shall be much mistaken if it does not command wide and general attention. We believe a great error prevails as to the duties and responsibilities of clergyman, scientific men and men of letters. By almost general opinion the former are strictly confined to the cure of souls within the limits of their respective parishes, and the latter employed in schooling young men and in writing books, treatises and essays, or in superintending their publication for what is called 'the reading community.' No one thinks that these same clergymen, scientific men, literary men, have any interest in, or care a groat about the *pratique* of this vain world. What to them are internal improvements, national rights, or for that matter, private rights? What have they to *do* with the duties of a good citizen? What have they to do with the Gog and Magog of this world? And if at some unlucky moment one of their number, who cannot exactly understand why he should be disfranchised and every right of manhood virtually taken from him, should venture to meddle with sublunary affairs, or make any suggestion as to their administration, the cry is raised of 'priestcraft,' 'all theory, no practice,' 'visionary men,' 'moon-struck,' and so on. Now we must confess that we cannot understand what should prevent a clergyman from being a good citizen and a patriot beside; and withal, from expressing his views with freedom on subjects touching the common weal. Again, we are rash enough to suggest that scientific and literary men, if only allowed an opportunity, can exert a very great and a very good influence in the world. For all practice being referable to theory, it certainly ought to follow that they who thoroughly understand the latter may become best versed in the former. It is because they are not allowed this privilege that they do not make good our assertion.

As we have before remarked, Professor HADDOCK's book contains a great variety of subjects, which are treated after the manner of one who thoroughly understands his work. In one place we find the Professor giving an instructive lesson upon the proper standard of education for the pulpit ; in another, showing before a large convention of his own and a neighboring state the great utility of a proposed line of railway. Here he descants most eloquently upon the duties of the patriot citizen ; next we find an address full of practical truth, delivered before the Vermont Medical Society. Every page in the volume shows that the writer has lived a thoughtful life, and that one great object of it has been how his thoughts might most benefit mankind. We think he has in himself happily illustrated the true connection between the theoretical and the practical ; showing them to be as inseparable as are the soul and body in this life. We subjoin as many extracts from the volume as our limits will permit. Professor HADDOCK's style is remarkable for great beauty and correctness. His sentences are all finished sentences ; not a verbal criticism can attach to one ; not a mistake of any kind ; not a grammatical error. As a model for study and improvement, we commend his writings to the student of polite literature. In some few places, and few we acknowledge them to be, we think that this perfection of style (so to call it) has been obtained at the expense of force of expression ; and that an occasional adjective or expletive, while it makes a perfect balance in the sentence, somewhat weakens its tone. Speaking of the connection between the several branches of knowledge, a subject by the way too generally overlooked, he remarks :

'THE object of all science is one ; the improvement and elevation of human nature. And thought, directed to this common end, receives a unity of character from its unity of purpose.

'It is therefore natural and necessary that the sciences which *one and the same mind* creates, concerning *one and the same world*, for *one and the same end*, should be bound together by intimate and visible relations and dependencies. In many instances, the connection is too palpable to escape the most careless observation ; in all, it is real, and has engaged the notice of wise men of every age.

'Thus affiliation of the numerous branches of knowledge is far from being mere matter of curiosity. It is an instance of that beneficent general provision by which we so often realize a double reward of our labors !'

From the ' Patriot Citizen' we take the following passage. Its truth is as undeniable as its style is felicitous :

' HE who so lately discovered that it is just as far round the bail of a kettle when it stands up as when it lies down, and applied the principle to our turnpike roads, is entitled to the thanks of men and beast. The kind citizen who says an encouraging word to fainting industry, or hesitating ambition, or tempted integrity, is a benefactor of his country. To introduce a new fruit or a new grain, a new instrument or a new mode of culture, does the state some service. The example of a neator husbandry, of more durable architecture, of more tasteful ornaments, of improved education, of rational enterprise, is not lost on the community. It is a public benefit to plant a tree by the roadside or on one's own grounds. The hand is not busy to no purpose which rears a flower or trains a vine. It is a narrow spirit that calculates the probabilities of living to sit under ' our own vine and fig-tree.' What matter is it if we do not ? others will enjoy what we leave behind us. The children for whom our life is so much spent will think of us with kindness when they succeed to the places we improve and beautify. The tree will cast a cooler shadow for being planted by a father's hand. The rose will be sweeter which a mother reared. We may die, and children may not come into our places ; not a drop of our blood may run in any man's veins. But still our country will remain ; our liberties, our schools, our arts, our fields, our houses will survive us, and will bear the impress of our taste and our charities down to posterity.'

In the discourse on rural ornament, we find the following exquisite description :

' A TREE is in itself eminently beautiful. There is something wonderful in its history. Beginning in a little germ, under the surface of the earth, it pushes up a delicate shoot, expands a fresh, green leaf to the vital air, and year after year follows the seasons round, casting down its honors to battle with the winter winds, and renewing them again to engage in the rivalry of beauty through the glorious summer.

' The tree has an organization like that of an animal ; vessels conveying to its remotest extremities the fluids from which its nutriment is elaborated, by a process similar to that which draws the food of animals from the blood. It has an evident irritability, amounting almost to the sensibility of the lower order of animals ; turns to the light, sleeps and breathes ; and exhales from its flowers and leaves and thousand pores the varied odors of the vegetable year. In its branches multitudes of innocent creatures gayly spend their little day of sunny bliss ; under its shadow the ox and the lamb ruminate and rest. Fifty generations of men come and look upon it, and go away. Still it stands, towering upward, and stretching far and wide its sinewy arms, the oldest living thing upon the earth. I do not wonder that the Druid venerated the tree, or that the Turk still cherishes it upon the shores and islands of his beautiful seas.'

We close our extracts with the following extract from one of Prof. HADDOCK's speeches in the New-Hampshire House of Representatives, on the bill providing for the appointment of commissioners for public schools :

'WE talk of the sin of idleness ; and undoubtedly it is neither rare nor venial. But, Mr. Speaker, there is a sin of labor as well as of sloth. Does any man imagine that a human creature was made for no higher destiny than to work ? Can delving in the dirt be the end of any class of men ? Why, Sir, labor, though necessary and honorable in all, connected in our present state with health and happiness ; labor in its lowest form, as in its highest, is but a means, a means of nobler, better ends. Unremitted, unrelieved toil is by Providence the necessary lot of no man. A portion only of our waking hours is needed for the purposes of our animal life ; intelligent industry soon provides for ordinary living ; a man should labor to live, not live to labor. It must be that something more is intended for us, even here, than to be hewers of wood and drawers of water, though it be all for ourselves. The mind that shoots forth here and there, from all ranks and conditions of life, is but a sign of what from unpropitious causes lies unawakened every where. Untold treasures of reason and moral power are yet to be opened in the great soul of humanity. And if our age may be said, in the French phrase, to have ' a million' assigned to it, is it not plainly this, to bring out the character and disclose the capacities of the common mind ? Education, education in its broadest sense, the education of the many, is, next to the spiritual salvation of the race, and ultimately even as a means of this salvation itself, the work, the appropriate, the primal work of our day.

'Our part of this delightful and truly glorious work is here, among the hills, along the rivers of our native state. I covet no better place; I know no better. I ask for no fitter material; for no other, and no more.'

We should not omit to add that Prof. HADDOCK's volume is characterized by an external purity and neatness quite in character with its contents. It is admirably printed upon fine white paper, and is rendered farther attractive by a finely-engraved portrait of the author.

NAPOLEON AND HIS MARSHALS. By J. T. HEADLEY. Two volumes. pp. 647. New-York : BAKER AND SCRIBNER.

WE find ' third edition' upon the title-page of this work, and can very easily account for the flattering fact which these two words herald. First, the spirit of the time, owing to the remarkable contest with which our own country is occupied on the confines of a neighboring nation, is favorable to the wide circulation of the volumes ; and secondly, the very graphic and spirited manner in which Mr. HEADLEY describes all military movements, and the evident goût with which he engages in the most terific battles of NAPOLEON and his marshals, will arrest and secure the attention of our countrymen. Mr. HEADLEY has aimed in the work before us to correct as far as possible the erroneous impressions which prevail respecting NAPOLEON and the wars he carried on ; to clear his character from the aspersions of English historians and the slanders of his enemies ; and to group together some of the most striking events of that dramatic period when he was marching his victorious armies over Europe. Having himself visited in person many of the battle-fields he has described, Mr. HEADLEY has been enabled the more vividly to recall the scenes enacted upon them. In reference to the distinguished men whom BONAPARTE gathered around him, and with whom he obtained and held the vast power he wielded, our author well observes: ' The mighty genius of NAPOLEON has so overshadowed all those beneath him, that they have not received their due praise nor their proper place in history. Their merits have been considered mere reflections of his : and to one intellect and one arm is attributed the vast results they accomplished. But with weak men NAPOLEON never could have unsettled Europe and founded and maintained his empire. The marshals who led his armies and governed his conquered provinces were men of native strength and genius ; and as they stand grouped around their mighty chief, they form a circle of military leaders, the like of whom the world has never at one time beheld. To show what these men were ; unfold their true characters and illustrate their great qualities, it was necessary to describe the battles in which they were engaged. A man is illustrated by his works; if an author, by his books; if a politician, by his civil acts and speeches; if a ruler, by his administration of public affairs, and if a military man, by his campaigns and battles. To mention merely the actions in which a military man has been engaged, and the victories he won, without describing the manner in which they were conducted and the genius which gained them, is like illustrating an author by giving a list of his works, or a ruler by naming over the measures he suggested or carried out.'

THE NEW ILLUMINATED PICTORIAL BIBLE. From the press of Messrs. HARPER AND BROTHERS, Number Eighty-two, Cliff-street, New-York.

WE were about to sit down to convey to our readers our high estimate of this most admirably printed and illustrated book, when the following notice from the competent pen of the editor of the 'Courier and Enquirer' arrested our attention. We endorse its commendations with no 'mental or other reservations' whatsoever: 'We regard it as not simply the most magnificent edition of the Word of GOD which has ever been offered to the American public, but as one of the most sumptuous productions of the typographic art, and as a most noteworthy monument of the high degree of perfection which the skill of artists and the enterprise of publishers have reached in this country. It forms a very large and very thick quarto volume, printed in the very highest style of the art, upon the very best of fine white linen paper. The engravings are exceedingly numerous, embracing an immense number of large illustrations of noteworthy scenes in the Sacred History, a still larger number of small pictures scattered throughout the pages, and an initial letter, executed always elegantly and sometimes very elaborately, for every chapter throughout the work. These engravings, numbering nearly *two thousand*, are all upon wood; and they illustrate in a more striking manner than any other work we have seen, the rapid advances which the art of wood engraving has recently made toward perfection. It is but a few years since engravings upon wood were universally and justly regarded as caricatures of art rather than its genuine productions. Now however they are among the finest in the world. Except the very finest and most costly steel engravings, those upon wood, when executed as are those in this Bible, by artists of merit, have a softness and a finish combining the best features of mezzotint and steel, and decidedly superior to either. Many of the illustrations of this work have been repeatedly mistaken by persons of the most accurate taste for the most highly-finished steel engravings; and their superiority to copper-plate is universally acknowledged. The illuminated title-pages, registers for marriages, births and deaths, and other parts of the work, are also admirably done; and the whole typographical appearance of the book gives it rank as by all odds the most magnificent production of the publishing art in the United States. The binding has been adapted in all respects to the character of the letter-press; it is at once strong, durable and elegant, to a degree unequalled in any other work within our knowledge. The Bible is a book which should be a *family possession*, and every family throughout the Union should possess itself of a copy, not to be worn-out or laid aside, but handed down from generation to generation as an enduring family memorial. Of course the excellence of the edition becomes in this case a matter not of minor, but of prominent and preëminent importance.'

THE MONUMENT TO GEORGE FREDERICK COOKE. — Our KNICKERBOCKER metropolis dare not aspire to the renown of a 'monumental city.' We have no Bunker-Hill column, like that of Boston; no WASHINGTON monument, like that of Baltimore. Neither our feelings nor 'the fashion' seem at present to tend that way: honorable reputation, whether achieved amidst the contentions of political distinction, on the broad arena of patriotism, or by effective labors in science and the arts, has scarcely any other memorial to perpetuate its glory than the canvass of the painter or the humble stone of the church-yard. True it is, the worthy fathers of our municipal government are not indifferent to the fame of their meritorious associates; the spacious apartments of our City-Hall, filled with the effigies of a long line of governors and mayors, afford sufficient proof that talents in one sphere of action, and among one order of men, are to be duly honored; are to make 'that first appeal which is to the eye' in after times. We object not to this proceeding on the part of our enlightened corporation: the town-hall in due season may be filled to overflowing with these mementoes of the defunct magistrates of our empire state and commercial metropolis; yet we have sometimes pensively reflected, that a city of the Union which has given birth to so many of the illustrious men who have adorned our national annals, should yet be so deficient in suitable works of art recording the great deeds of their noble lives in enduring marble, as a lasting legacy to their countrymen. Two or three exceptions to this total neglect of conspicuous merit may indeed be found; but singularly enough, and quite unfortunately for our patriotism, nearly all that has been done has been confined to illustrious individuals who were strangers from abroad, and who by their indomitable perseverance and attainments secured glory to themselves and proved benefactors to their adopted land. The monument of MONTGOMERY in the edifice of St. Paul's, and the column to EMMET in the fore-ground of that church, are worthy of the hero of Quebec, and of the great civilian of the New-York bar. An appropriate tablet in memory of the author of our military tactics during the revolutionary contest, Baron STEUBEN, a native of Prussia, once occupied a prominent place in a venerable though humble church in Nassau-street; but we believe it would be a perplexing question for a majority of our inhabitants to answer where lie the remains of that ingenuous benefactor of both worlds, ROBERT FULTON; where the appropriate spot designated as the sepulchre of that distinguished citizen, ROBERT R. LIVINGSTON; where the mural tablet or column commemorative of the services of PHILIP FRENEAU, another of our city-born worthies, the patriotic poet of our revolutionary struggle, whose writings Lord JEFFREY thought would at some future day command a commentator such as HUDIBRAS had in GREY ; where is a memorial to be found of LINDLEY MURRAY, the grammarian, who was also a native of New-York ? Perhaps the period may not be far distant when the capacious and beautiful grounds of the Greenwood Cemetery may be deemed a fitting resting-place for some at least of the future dignitaries of our Anglo-Saxon race. The removal of all that was mortal of our illustrious CLINTON to this delectable place of final repose is auspicious of a consummation so devoutly to be wished.

It is partly on account of this paucity of demonstration of regard for the memory of exalted characters once conspicuous among us, who have honored us in their high career, and partly because we have been greatly gratified by services lately done in behalf of professional excellence in a peculiar line of art, that these desultory thoughts are thrown together. Hereditary talents associated with those substantial qualities which evince that the heart of the possessor has riches of its own, induce us to pay a passing tribute to the chaste marble monument situated in the centre of St. Paul's church-yard in this city, to the memory of the great dramatic hero, GEORGE FREDERICK COOKE, and which has lately been renovated and beautified. The late WILLIAM DUNLAP, shortly after the death of Mr COOKE, wrote a memoir of his erratic yet instructive life ; and in his ' American Theatre' he increased our obligations to him by a record of subsequent events in the history of COOKE. It is well known that the late EDMUND KEAN entertained an exalted opinion of the intellectual and histrionic powers of COOKE ; that he formed the determination, toward the close of his first dramatic visit to this country, to ascertain the whereabout of his mortal remains, and to cause a monument, in a suitable place, to be erected to his memory. A surviving personal friend of COOKE, and one of his medical attendants, who had often administered to the relief of his physical sufferings, and watched over the last flickerings of his departing life, Dr. JOHN W. FRANCIS,* was enabled from personal knowledge of all the circumstances connected with the death and interment of the great tragedian, to furnish Mr. KEAN with every particular necessary to carry out his praiseworthy design. COOKE died at the Park-Place House ; and his body, accompanied to the grave by several members of the three liberal professions, a number of gentlemen of high reputation in the army and navy, and a numerous train of distinguished citizens, was deposited in the ' Stranger's Vault' of St. Paul's Church-yard, in September, 1812. Nearly nine years after, in May, 1821, Mr. KEAN expressed to his friend and physician, Dr. FRANCIS, his desire to leave some token of his regard for his illustrious predecessor, the great actor, before he departed for Europe ; and he at once concluded that a marble monument in a conspicuous place would best correspond with his wishes. Mr. KEAN, accompanied by Dr. FRANCIS, waited upon the late eminent prelate, Bishop HOBART, in order to lay before him his intended plan, and to obtain his assent thereto. Bishop HOBART received the representative of SHAKSPEARE with the greatest suavity, and readily acceded to his views, upon learning that the contemplated memorial to COOKE was not a mural tablet *within* the church, but a sepulchral work *without*, in the venerable burial-ground. KEAN, alive to the propriety of his solicitation, intimated that our country ' had as yet no Westminster Abbey in which the actor's deserts might be confirmed by posthumous fame ; he would that Mr. COOKE, though dead, might still bear the palm of superiority which by acclamation was accorded him when he ' majestic trod the stage.' The good bishop

* DRS. HOSACK, MCLEAN and FRANCIS were the medical advisers of Mr. COOKE.

rejoined, that Mr. COOKE, of whom he had *heard* much, could hardly, he thought, in his most serious moments, ever have expected to find his memory pepetuated within the walls of an Episcopal Church ; but nevertheless, he added, he himself was ever ready to favor the erection of becoming memorials of departed greatness; and he freely consented to a location of the proposed monument in any portion of the extensive burial-ground which might be selected. KEAN assured the bishop that he would not profane the site chosen by an ordinary specimen of sculpture ; and thereupon took his leave, with much courtesy. As he walked off, he turned to the Doctor, and in emphatic accents observed : ' I am somewhat familiar with the ' right reverend fathers of the church,' but what a vast difference, FRANCIS, between your unvarnished Yankee bishop and my old pedantic Grecian friend, SAM. PARR, with his enormous wig ! Does this holy man whom you have introduced me to exhibit the same earnestness in his pulpit-labors that he has just shown in our business transactions ?' No man ever contemplated with greater satisfaction than did Mr. KEAN a work raised for a like purpose. On the third of June, 1821, Mr. KEAN superintended in person the removal of the remains of COOKE by Dr. FRANCIS. We borrow the language of Mr. DUNLAP descriptive of this event :

' IN June, 1821, the body of Mr. COOKE was removed from the 'Stranger's Vault' in ST. PAUL's church-yard to a most eligible spot in the centre of that extensive burial-ground. Mr. COOKE died in September, 1812, and the monument over his remains was erected on the fourth of June, 1821. It is a well-executed work in marble, by the FRAZEES, consisting of a square pedestal, on two steps, surrounded by an urn, from the top of which a flame issues toward the Park Theatre, the scene of Mr. COOKE's greatest efforts in this country. The inscription on the tomb, which was furnished by Dr. FRANCIS, who had superintended the removal of his remains, is as follows:

· ERECTED to the memory of GEORGE FREDERICK COOKE, by EDMUND KEAN, of the Theatre-Royal, Drury-Lane, 1821.'

' THREE kingdoms claim his birth,
Both hemispheres pronounce his worth.'

'Several engraved representations of this monument have been published, in which the figures of Mr. KEAN and Dr. FRANCIS, and a medallion with a portrait of Mr. COOKE, are introduced. As a specimen of this species of work, the monument is as worthy of the subject as it is illustrative of the liberality of Mr. KEAN. If what old FULLER says be correct, that ' the shortest, plainest and truest epitaphs are the best,' no fault can be found with the inscription on COOKE's tomb. The place of his nativity is yet disputed ; each portion of the United Kingdom claims him as its own, although there is no doubt that he was born in Westminster, as he told us, and we have recorded. He long enjoyed an unrivalled reputation, both in the old and in the new world ; and although it may hereafter be found that his surgeon possesses his skull, and his successor, KEAN, the bones of the fore-finger of his right hand — that dictatorial finger ! — still the monument covers the *remains* of GEORGE FREDERICK COOKE.'

After this explicit narrative of facts, we pause not to animadvert upon the ridiculous details which CROLY has published on the same subject in his work denominated ' The Life of EDMUND KEAN.' The dramatic world, and the admirers of genius every where, will thank the present descendant, now among us, of that graphic expositor of the passions, and the acknowledged possessor of many of his finest and rarest qualities, CHARLES KEAN, for the liberality and kind feelings which he has recently displayed in repairing this beautiful monument to the honor of COOKE. The younger KEAN has by this disinterested act enhanced the claims so justly due him, while treading with acknowledged ability in the footsteps of his honored father ; and every lover of SHAKSPEARE will rejoice that the circle of his renown is widening ; that the substantial rewards of talent, whether innate or acquired, await with certainty the professional exercise of his lofty powers. It abates little from the manliness of Mr. KEAN, that the short period he remained in New-York previously to his reëmbarkation for his native land should have been spent in contemplating his cherished monument, beneath which were entombed the ashes of his great forerunner. Neither the bustle of day nor the stillness of night weaned him long from his reflections. The chimes of old Trinity called up the memory of by-gone days, when the plaudits of BYRON followed his utterance; when from the lips of MOORE he first learned to sing the ' Evening Bells ;' and with an occasional monologue on the fickleness of popular favor, and his felicitous solo execution of that beautiful melody, he loitered in St. Paul's grounds till the last moment had arrived of the time for his departure, after his first sojourn among us. The then recent disasters at Boston, which he had encountered and ineffectually resisted, doubtless had their share in creating this state of remarkable pensiveness. The proclamation had been issued which declared his once powerful kingdom divided. The press groaned under the issues of abuse and ribaldry. A sudden darkness had overwhelmed the dazzling brightness of his professional renown; he sought alleviation in abstraction; he felt that New-York and the excellent Mr. SIMPSON had appreciated at their sterling value his histrionic efforts; that his health had been assiduously watched over by his skilful and accomplished physician; and he was willing to extricate himself from all farther American associations.

The monument of which we have been speaking is but one of the many generous acts of the late EDMUND KEAN, for the humanities of his nature ceased but with the last pulsations of his bosom. The affections were inherent in his very blood; and so cordial were his sympathies, that it might seem extravagant to say how many wretched and unfortunate beings he rendered happy, at least for a season. Let us hope that the younger KEAN will neither forget the excellencies of his father's heart nor how much his father loved him; how transported were his father's feelings upon receiving the first Latin epistle of that son, then a student, addressed to him across the wide waters, in America. Let him also remember his inimitable study, his perfect keeping, his harmony, his consummate performance of every part he assumed; the distinctiveness, the integrity of character, of every dramatic personation he undertook; how entirely he was transformed into the very being, and none other, he would represent. True art! faithful nature! When reflecting on the responsibilities of the actor's part, let him dwell at times upon his father's method of procedure, the better to obtain a mastery in the delineation of that embodiment of qualities of the more refined order, King LEAR. St. Luke's hospital for a period of nearly three years was the collegium he visited; in that place he clinically observed the physical changes of disordered intellect. Here he investigated with philosophical scrutiny, idiocy; then the displays of insanity, in all its Protean forms, from brooding melancholy to ' laughter holding both his sides.' The scholar he knew would read BURTON for his erudition, and the painter would visit Rome in order to improve his art by the study of RAFFAELLE; for *his* especial purpose, a just conception of the secrets of his science, and the development of its manifestations in unsound minds, the Hospital of St. Luke was his studio, his Vatican, his Sistine Chapel. Thus graduated, he ventured a public demonstration of the distracted monarch; with what success need not now be mentioned.

We are reluctant to think how long a period may elapse before we shall again witness the counterpart of this extraordinary genius; and we shall console ourselves with the reflection that the pure light by which he illuminated the dramatic art, although perhaps at times less intense, is still imparted to us by his accomplished son. Mr. CHARLES KEAN, however, needs no expression of assurance of the high estimation in which his private worth and professional excellence are held: fortunately he is independent of it. Like all who have by their efforts secured the object of their ambition, he is aware that the toils of application must precede the rewards of success. No alchemy has hitherto transmuted lead into mercury ; and the purest metals demand the refiner's art. Eclecticism is no less inadmissible in the drama than in architecture. His father's once sumptuous intellectual board furnished sustenance sufficient for a thousand jejune intellects ; the want of original stamina in most of these recipients has ended in depraved assimilation and fatal dyspepsia. Mr. KEAN will most wisely draw from the resources within himself ; the material is abundant for every purpose, and of the best quality: yet with a full knowledge of his constitutional powers, should the exigency ever occur, he might safely exercise the prerogatives of an hereditary claimant. Mr. KEAN's calling is to educate, refine and exalt the mind. He is destined to secure an abundant recompense, in the full fruition of his highest aspirations. If the chronicles correctly tell us, his career through the United States, in company with his unrivalled lady, has thus far proved a continuous triumph. Let us hope that it may thus continue unto the end ; neither retarded by physical causes, nor lessened by the diminished exercise of a cultivated and disciplined taste.

A VISIT TO THE GRAVE OF BYRON. — To the same competent hand whence we derived the '*Visit to the Grave of Gray in his Country Church-Yard*' we are indebted for the following interesting account of a similar visit to the former residence and present tomb of the greatest of England's modern bards. Like its predecessor, the ensuing sketch will soon enlist and well repay the attention of the reader: ' Nottingham is a pretty town, noted for its manufactories of lace and hosiery ; it is also celebrated for its ale, which I tasted, and pronounce *good ;* and it is remarkable for wind-mills, great numbers of which are seen closely huddled together on one side of the town, fanning themselves with marvellous pertinacity. And it has an historical interest too, connected with the lives of Queen ISABELLA and ROGER MORTIMER, in the fourteenth century ; with the ' Reform' riots of 1831, traces of which are still visible in the black and dismantled walls of the castle ; and finally, it stands upon a hill which, as you approach from Derby, through the rich meadows of the beautiful Trent, appears like a large fortress. Its market-square is one of the largest and finest in England ; and there are many objects of interest in and about Nottingham to render a visit both profitable and pleasant ; and those familiar with the poetry of the present age will not fail to recollect that here was born HENRY KIRK WHITE :

> ' UNHAPPY WHITE ! while life was in its spring,
> And thy young muse just waved her joyous wing,
> The spoiler came, and all thy promise fair
> Has sought the grave, to sleep for ever there.
> Oh ! what a noble heart was here undone,
> When Science' self-destroyed her favorite son !
>   .   .   .   .
> 'T was thine own genius gave the final blow,
> And help'd to plant the wound that laid thee low :
> So the struck eagle stretched upon the plain,
> No more through rolling clouds to soar again,
> View'd his own feather on the fatal dart,
> And winged the shaft that quivered in his heart.
> Keen were his pangs, but keener far to feel
> He nursed the pinion which impell'd the steel,
> While the same plumage that had warmed his nest
> Drank the last life-drop of his bleeding breast.'

' It is honorable to our country, that the tablet to the memory of WHITE by

CHANTREY should have been erected at the cost of an American gentleman, a citizen of Boston. The inscription is in good taste, and concludes thus:

> "'FAR o'er the Atlantic wave
> A wanderer came, and sought the poet's grave;
> On yon low stone he saw his lonely name,
> And raised this fond memorial to his fame.'

' In the suburbs of Nottingham are great numbers of small gardens, cultivated by mechanics and tradesmen, who thus employ their leisure hours, finding an agreeable recreation in a profitable pursuit; while the beautiful and picturesque view, extending for many miles along the course of the Trent, is scarcely surpassed for quiet beauty in any part of England. Eight miles distant is Hucknall, or as it is more commonly and truly called, ' *dirty* Hucknall;' a collection of huts wretched in appearance; the people idle and ignorant; and the country around rough and uncultivated. A small church crowns the summit of a little hill, with no trees or hedges to relieve the barrenness of the spot; making it altogether as uninviting to the eye, as desolate to the heart, as any misanthrope could desire. We were quickly followed to the church, the object of our visit, by a lad with the keys; and on entering, soon found that the interior corresponded with its outward seeming. It was rude, cheerless and cold; and yet how many generations yet unborn will seek that church, will tread that aisle, and gaze upon the spot which contains the ashes of one who ' twined his hopes of being remembered in his line with his land's language!' A small white Grecian tablet, inserted in the wall immediately over the sepulchre, told us: ' In the vault beneath, where many of his ancestors and his mother are buried, lie the remains of GEORGE GORDON NOEL BYRON, the author of ' Childe Harold's Pilgrimage.' What stranger uninformed of the fact would have supposed that the remains of BYRON were entombed in so obscure a sanctuary! I could not but feel however that it was well ordered in the fitness of things that they should repose there; that the place, church, vault and inscription were in good keeping with the character of him who boasted that he ' stood and should stand alone, remembered or forgot;' and he might have added too with great propriety, 'should sleep alone.' The fierce sun may beat upon that house and the cold winds of winter sigh through its casements; ' but after life's fitful fever he sleeps well;' as calmly, as quietly, as undisturbed in his dark and dreary chamber as the author of the ' Elegy' in his almost perennial daisy-blooming garden. I left, after some delay, but cast no longing lingering look behind.

' Three miles farther on is Newstead Abbey. ' The Hut,' a small inn on the confines of the estate, and just opposite the celebrated ' Oak-Tree,' where we left our carriage, is about a mile from the Abbey. The walk thence is through a rabbit-warren; and thousands of these little creatures were seen skipping from hole to hole: we were told six thousand pairs were yearly sent to market, and the revenue to the proprietor from this source amounted to some five hundred pounds per annum. There were no trees to shade the road; and except a gate or two, which seemed to dispute our passage, the country might have been taken for what we call in America ' a common.' After proceeding nearly a mile through this monotonous scene, a sharp curve around the base of a hill brought us in view of the lake, on which were floating miniature brigs and schooners: catching its hue from the dark clouds which presaged a shower, it was perfectly black. In an instant more the Abbey itself appeared, with its lawns, gravelly paths and beautiful trees. The transition is instantaneous from the dull and dreary scene through which we had been walking. Newstead has been so often described that I shall not encumber my pages with any detail of its features. I must not however omit to remark that the monks of the olden times were men of taste. All the monasteries I have yet visited are situated uniformly by some pleasant lake or running stream, where these self-sacrificing ' holy men' could meditate undisturbed, and — *fish !*'

' Ringing the porter's-bell, and waiting just half the time by which every thing in America is measured, namely ' twenty minutes,' we were admitted into the vestibule of the cloisters, or more properly galleries of the Abbey. Another ten minutes, and a smart, neat and affected piece of vanity, yet perfectly civil, bade us inscribe our names in the register, and follow her. We did so; and after passing through the suite of apartments occupied by the present proprietor, Col. WILDMAN, (son-in-law of the late Duke of Sussex,) which display great taste and splendor, we stepped into those occupied by BYRON when residing at Newstead. Col. WILDMAN has preserved them in the same state as when tenanted by him. There are the bed, wash-stand, towels, soap, table, chairs, carpet — every thing precisely the same as when he left ; and one might imagine from the evident care manifested in their keeping, that the occupant had but just stepped out and would presently return : so also of the apartment adjoining, where slept his ' little page.' The same consideration and care are observed in the library. The chair in which he used to sit, the table on which he wrote, the couch on which he reclined, all are there. I could not but feel that his spirit was still lingering about the scene. The window of the library looks out upon the lake, and affords a charming prospect of water, wood and vale. Our conductress unlocked a door in a side-closet and handed us a human skull. It was the same that was exhumed when BYRON was in possession of the Abbey, and which he caused to be mounted with silver, and converted into a wine-goblet ; and upon which he inscribed the lines beginning, ' Start not, nor deem my spirit fled,' etc. On descending into the lower apartments we were shown the marble sarcophagus in which the skull was discovered, the portrait of the dog ' Boatswain,' and in the garden the pompous and foolish monument erected over his carcass, riven by the lightning and hastening to ruin. It was a circular cone, of large diameter at the base, and surmounted at the top by a shaft on which is the inscription. A walk through the gardens, which are modern, and the grove in which is still to be seen his own and his sister's name carved by himself on the bark of a tree in 1814, and a detention of ' twenty minutes' by one of the most rabid and unmitigated rain storms ever let down from the heavens, terminated our visit to Newstead Abbey.'

MESSRS. COOLEY, KEESE AND HILL, at their new auction-room, Number 157 Broadway, seem to have formed a party with no antagonist side — an anomaly in the history of parties. The ' Universal Public,' if one may judge from the best expositor of its collective opinions, the press, seems to have *adopted* the firm in question. And no marvel ; for Mr. COOLEY is an old and experienced book-seller ; of Mr. KEESE the same may be said, for he both makes clever books and sells them ; and Mr. HILL, although on the sunny side of thirty-five, has had so much to do with them that he is himself a walking catalogue of ancient and modern, foreign and domestic literature. More than all, each member of the firm is a capital *business* man ; so that our friends the publishers, whose ' ventures' sometimes contribute to the trade-sales, now so common, will be sure to find their way to Messrs. COOLEY, KEESE AND HILL.

GOSSIP WITH READERS AND CORRESPONDENTS. — The annexed interesting sketch, sent us under the *nom de plume* of 'ROSE STANDISH,' will be deemed by every true American an appropriate offering at the moment when we are celebrating the seventieth anniversary of our beloved country's independence: ' The following note was found among the papers of the late Lord ERSKINE:

'To GENERAL WASHINGTON: SIR — I have taken the liberty to introduce your august and immortal name in a short sentence, which is to be found in the book I send to you.

'I have a large acquaintance among the most valuable and exalted class of men; but you are the only human being for whom I ever felt an awful reverence. I sincerely pray to GOD to grant a long and serene evening to a life so gloriously devoted to the happiness of the world.
                                                                              'T. ERSKINE.'

' In the year of our LORD 1790 I stood upon the door-step of the counting-house of which I was then but the youngest clerk, when the companion beside me hurriedly said: 'There he comes! — *there comes Washington!*' I looked up Pearl-street and saw approaching, with stately tread and open brow, the Father of my country. His hat was off, for the day was sultry, and he was accompanied by Col. PAGE and JAMES MADISON. Never have I forgotten, nor shall I forget to my dying day, the serene, the benign, the GOD-like expression of the countenance of that MAN of Men. His lofty mien and commanding figure, set-off to advantage by an elegant dress, consisting of blue coat, buff small-clothes, silver knee and shoe-buckles, and white vest; his powdered locks and powerful, vigorous look, for he was then in the prime and strength of his manhood, have never faded from my mind during the many years, with all their chances and changes, which have rolled between! As WASHINGTON passed the place near where I stood, his mild, clear blue eye fell upon me, and it seemed as though his very glance was a benediction. Though high deeds and noble acts — fame, death, a nation's worship and tears — have since in the deep places of my heart consecrated *his* name above every other name of earth, yet even then, boy as I was, the glance thrilled me through and through; my eyes fell beneath it, and my hand was involuntarily raised to uncover my head, as an august being passed by. The aspect of the outer man alone was calculated to enforce respect — to *compel* awe and reverence. But there is that in the sight and presence of a being we revere; a being whose name we have been taught to lisp in infancy with grateful affection; have had held up to us in boyhood as worthy of all honor and imitation, which stirs feelings that lie far down in the depths of the soul, and inspires faith and trust in GOD and in human goodness. Oh! heaven-taught, heaven-endowed man, ordained of thy MAKER to be thy country's deliverer!

'Once again I saw *the* President. He was riding, the carriage being drawn by four beautiful bays. I remember well its silver plate and yellow pannels, which has ever since seemed to me a proper and aristocratic color (forgive me, shade of WASHINGTON!) for a vehicle of this kind. Mrs. or Lady WASHINGTON, as she was always called, sat by his side. She was of a' comely and pleasant countenance, and appeared to be chatting in a lively manner to her noble lord and master, whose usual gravity, if my recollection serves me, was a little relaxed. He turned his face toward her — I think he smiled.

> ' ' Be not too familiar, lest men see thine infirmities and learn to cavil at thy teaching.'

' This WASHINGTON appears to have understood ; or rather, the property was innate in his character; and yet no man had fewer infirmities; none less need to dread a close inspection than he. The most conspicuous trait in his character, and one of the rarest virtue, was *moderation*. In every act of his life this was exemplified. Temperance shone in all ; it was the guide of his conduct, the key to the great success of his life. Ambition, fame, military glory, in themselves considered, seem never to have had entrance into his clear, conscientious mind. With him all the ' pomp and circumstance of glorious war' was never dreamed of. Human oppression, 'the right' and freedom nerved his arm. He drew only the sword of defence. Though his courage was undaunted, enthusiasm formed no part of his character. The loud clarion and the spirit-stirring drum never drowned in his ear the cry of despair, the shriek of the dying. He never for a moment forgot that the fall of the meanest soldier on the battle-field carried desolation, wailing, and often destitution into a household. But to return : The gaily-prancing steeds soon rolled the carriage out of my sight, and left me standing in the crowded street, an enthusiastic boy-dreamer, with wondering gaze and crowding thoughts.

' Once more was he borne along. The steeds not now prancing and gay, but one — the old war-horse — led before his master's body, saddle and stirrup empty, and cloth of black covering him. Mournfully the dumb animal seemed to walk. How mutely eloquent it was ! The scene is now before me ; the solemn procession, slowly moving, marked through all its length with the sad trappings of wo ! The unutterably solemn strain of music, the march for the dead, rings now in my ear! I seem to see again the serious, down-cast faces of the men who followed after ; again I hear the sobs and weeping of the women, and the wondering and affrighted look of little children is present with me. Each one mourned as with a personal grief. Earth will never again behold such a spectacle — *a nation* dissolved in tears ! *Why* were they shed ? What trait of our beloved WASHINGTON do we most gratefully reverence ? Is it not his transcendent goodness, his unsullied integrity, his purest patriotism ? Yes, we *love* while we *honor* his memory. In life we reposed trust in him as in an ark of safety, a shield of defence. A GOD-fearing man, HE prospered him, and blessed his life. Favored of Heaven, he enjoyed the confidence of men. No, I repeat, *never* shall I forget the words which wrought wonder, consternation and fear in my mind, and which was depicted on every face : ' *Washington is dead !*' They were spoken in a whisper, but how full of wo ! · · · For many years I dwelt in the very house in which the Great Defender lived ; I slept in the very room in which he slumbered. Sometimes an ancient friend of the family would point out with irrepressible pleasure and honorable pride the very spot where 'The General' stood, and where his 'Lady,' on grand reception-days; how they were attired; what gracious words they spake; how kindly and how hospitable. And then the old man, sighing, said to my mother, with the ever-retrospective glance of age, 'Ah! Madam, those were palmy days!' There was one article in the house which had belonged to the WASHINGTON family, and only one. It was an old mirror. It fitted over the mantel-piece, underneath the wainscotting, and was never removed. Well do I remember, when I was a mere child, being told this by an old servant; and of my gazing upon it with veneration because it had often reflected the face and form of the beloved WASHINGTON. It was held sacred as a relic of him. Many a weary night, when I have lain sleepless on my couch, the wind (' mournfully, oh ! mournfully') whistling without, a lonely feeling would creep over me as I looked upon the wainscotted walls of 'The Great Room ;' the old blue tiles of the large fire-place ; the deep embrasured windows ; and felt the stillness so profound within that I could almost hear the beating of my heart ; then the dark vision of a fearful imagination has been exorcised, and the words of my mother seemed to whisper me again : ' When vain fears disturb thee, remember the good man who once lay where thou liest, and be thankful ; the dark visions will be dispelled.' Then I have thought, ' *His* eyes have rested on the same objects I now behold ;' I have fancied the thoughts that might have filled his mind, as he lay on a sometime sleepless pillow ; thoughts pure, thankful, self-sacrificing, noble. A vivid picture too of the illustrious man ; his countenance uplifted and lustrous with heavenly peace and hope ; his hands upraised, and his lips moving with words of prayer and praise, has been before me ; for I had been told that he was ' a man of prayer,' and in this I had been taught to believe lay his strength. And then (easy transition !) a yet more glorious vision passed before me ; a beatific vision. I have seen him one of the throng of those who ' walk in white' beneath the shadow of the eternal throne ; his face radiant with light, and a crown of joy encircling his brow; yet wearing the same serene, majestic look which he wore on earth ! Spirit of WASHINGTON ! mild, wise, merciful, temperate, just — we evoke thee ! Influence, guide, rule thy countrymen !' It is a most remarkable fact, that all who ever saw WASHINGTON are unanimous in their accounts of the impression which his personal presence made upon every beholder. · · · THE reader will find not a little wholesome satire in '*The Way they do Things in New-York*,' in preceding pages. The affectation of using French terms when plain English would better serve the speaker's purpose, alluded to by our correspondent, is well ridiculed by ' PUNCH' in a late number of that amusing journal. It is proposed that the French shall reciprocate a compliment so largely paid them by the English, in the adoption of cant terms borrowed from their language by British journalists in order to denote the things and transactions of high life. As, by calling the most fashionable sort of people the *élite* of *ton*, and speaking of a dancing tea-party as a *thé dansant;* whereas it is the party that dances, not the HYSON ; and the tea is quite distinct from the caper ; also, by describing a person of dignified demeanor as *distingué* instead of dignified, a rout as a *soirée*, and a meat breakfast as a *dejeuner a la fourchette*. If we, out of admiration for the French language, says ' PUNCH,' employ it when we might full as well talk plain English, the French ought surely to reciprocate the civility, particularly since we go out of our way in deference to them, often using a phraseology which is at the same time Frenchified and nonsensical.

Accordingly, in their fashionable journals, we shall expect to find such announcements as the following:

'HIER au soir *came off*, a sa maison, dans la Rue St. Honore, le grand *hop* de Madame la Comtesse de VANILLE. La compagnie etait ornée par presque tous les *swells* les plus *tip-top*.
'Aujord'hui, M. de FRICANDEAU donnera, a son hotel, un *spread* magnifique; on plusieurs *nobs* de la premiere distinction se trouveront autour de son *mahogany*.
'On dit qu'l y a sur le *Kidderminster* une aliance nuptiale entre un Marquis bien connu parmi les *crack* cercles, et une demoiselle de *tus*. heritiere a un millionaire Anglais.
'Au plein *tog* et *fancy ball* de Madame de PAPILLOTE, assisterent une foule de *first-rate* gens. L'affaire etait extremement *spicy*.'

Touching the heraldic movement of our Russian contributor, we remain for the present entirely neutral. There will be food for thought, perhaps for anger, in our correspondent's series. Thus far however his sarcasm is as good-natured as it is cutting. . . . 'THERE is some poetry so bad,' writes 'PAUL MARTINDALE,' 'that it's good. Whether the following has that negative quality, you may judge. It is certainly much worse than mediocrity. It was procured by a friend of mine from the author, whose poetic frenzy had probably been fired with golden dreams of an inheritance in the acres of Old Trinity:

'TO THE HEIRS OF ANNEKE JANS BOGARDUS.

—

' BY MRS. T . . . . , ONE OF THE HEIRS.'

—

'HAIL! brothers and sisters and kindred folks are we,
Since we are all descended from one family;
From the fourth King of Holland, King WILLIAM we hear,
And in his royal bounties we all have a share;
By the grants that he has given his children, we find,
And we are their descendants — we are all of his line:
So whate'er be our fortune, whate'er be our fate,
We are the descendants of WILLIAM the Great!

'But some of us come in a second noble claim,
Being the heirs of WYNTIE SYBRANTS BOGARDUS by name;
There is wealth still in Holland, there is treasure, we find,
For the heirs of WYNTIE SYBRANTS, who was of noble line:
She was a great lady, from Holland she came,
She married a relation, BOGARDUS by name:
He too had descended from King WILLIAM's golden line,
Being the son of ANNEKE JANS BOGARDUS, we find.
ANNEKE JANS was King WILLIAM's great-grand-child, we hear,
And ANNEKE WEBBER her grandmother, was his own daughter dear.
So whate'er be our fortune, whate'er be our fate,
We are the descendants of WILLIAM the Great;
Of WILLIAM the Fourth of old Holland, we hear,
And in his royal bounties we all have a share.

'We also are related to VICTORIA the Queen,
Since we all have descended from WILLIAM the King;
Then scorn us not, VICTORIA, thou great and noble Queen,
For we are thy dear relations, as is plain to be seen!
Though thy honors we claim not, thy name we still own,
Since we are thy dear relations, all descended from the throne:
From the fourth King of Holland, King WILLIAM, we hear,
And in his royal bounties we all have a share.
So whate'er be our fortune, whate'er be our fate
We are the descendants of WILLIAM the Great!

'Now AMERICA is our home, where we are happy and free;
Americans we are — yes, Americans we be!
Though we are the descendants of honor and fame,
From the fourth King of Holland, King WILLIAM, we hear,
And in his royal bounties we all have a share,
So whate'er be our fortune, whate'er be our lot
May the name of King WILLIAM be never forgot!'

'Where all is so beautiful, particular references are unnecessary; yet it strikes me that the patronizing tone of the first part of the third stanza, and the patriotic burst contained in the first two lines of the last, are worthy of especial commendation.' Poor parvenu 'poetry.' . . . THE following graphic sketch we derive from a young and talented friend recently returned from Mexico and Texas. The hopeful subject of it reminds us not a little of a kindred 'artist' once described to us by a country gentleman. He was in the habit of speaking of every person who had submitted to his operations as 'a job' of his; and while walking with our correspondent in the streets of the village in which he resided, he would suddenly exclaim: 'There comes one of my jobs — about as difficult a job as I ever had.' The 'job' was a recent widower, and his countenance was sad; but when the dentist met him face to face, he said: 'Won't you be so good as to smile a little? I want to show my friend what I call a very difficult and neat job!' The bereaved husband and father however declined, and went on his way, leaving our operator in a state of surprise and disappointment at his churlishness. But to our new correspondent 'TEJANO:'

'As I returned last week from a turkey-hunt in the Colorado Bottom, I found our little village in an unusual state of excitement at the announcement that 'the celebrated Dr. JOHNSTON, of Virginia, Professor of Dental Surgery,' would that evening deliver an address on a professional subject, 'at J. CRONKRAM'S tavern, on the Square; admittance gratis.' I had been surprised on my return from the 'Bottom' by meeting on the road a very stylish light barouche with silver-plated lamps, drawn by two bob-tail sorrel trotters, and driven by a negro in livery. I now learned that this was the travelling equipage of Dr. JOHNSTON, who having acquired by the exercise of his profession a splendid fortune was now on a tour of pleasure through Texas, accompanied by his lady. Out of compassion however to the citizens of L——e, who had not seen a real live dentist for several years, he graciously condescended to tarry for a time among them, and to torture the nervous system of any unfortunate individual who might require his services. At seven o'clock the lecture began in a large upper room, where a few rough boards for seats contrasted agreeably with the naked rafters of the roof. A row of tallow candles with large wicks were stuck round the walls in little tin holders, affording light to the assembly. This room was in fact the town-hall of L——e. Here the courts were held, and divers important cases of stolen pigs, assaults and batteries and runaway negroes summarily disposed of. Here also were given the concerts of the 'Ethiopian Singers;' the forensic displays of Fourth-of-July orators, and the discourses of any religious professors who might wish to hold forth to the good citizens of L——e; Mormons, Universalists and Shaking-Quakers included. I had been seated for some time, amusing myself in looking around upon the mass of hunting-shirts, home-made cotton coats, of all shapes and colors; buckskin leggings; cocked beaver hats, such as were used in the days of WASHINGTON; cow-hide boots and Indian moccasins; and contrasting them with the more civilized garb of some young lawyer friends of mine from Tennessee, when I was startled by a loud crash, caused by the sudden disappearance of one of the plank-seats, which gave way under its interesting load, consisting chiefly of the gentler sex of L——e. There was (as an old planter near me observed,) for a few moments 'a considerable smart chance of a scramble,' and a confused pile of bonnets, shawls and female forms, with occasional shrieks from a stout lady who had been turned wrong side up, and only regained her equilibrium at the expense of sundry crushed bonnets and prostrated ladies, who served as stepping-stones. At length however order being restored, a cry arose among the negroes (of whom some thirty or forty were collected round the door, of all ages, sizes and shades,) of 'Dar he come!' 'Dar 's Massa Doctor JOHNSTON!' and the doctor appeared, with his lady on his arm. He was a man of the middle size, hard-featured, with a bushy head of gray hair, an immense pair of gold spectacles pushed back on his forehead, from beneath which his cunning-looking yellowish-grey eyes twinkled forth. A white neck-cloth enveloped his scraggy brown neck, and his costume was a full suit of black. As he advanced into the room, he held his wife by the tips of the fingers, making sliding bows to the right and left. After handing her 'trippingly' to a seat, he took his station behind the rostrum, which in this case consisted of a small pine table, grievously cut and scratched, having been whittled upon by the judges, lawyers and politicians of L——e for the last three years: of course, like their speeches, it was rather a hackneyed affair. On this table lay several rolls of paper of different sizes, to be used as occasion might serve, according to the custom of public speakers. The doctor, arranging his rolls, made a bow and commenced as follows:

'Gentlemen and ladies — ladies and gentlemen: I arrived here to-day at your little town for the first time — which are a fact. I 've saw larger places and I 've saw smaller; but it 's a pretty considerable *peart* little place for all that. It requires, gentlemen and ladies, if I may so 'spress myself, a mighty natural genus for to be a good dentistry — which there are no doubt of that; none at all. (A look of inquiry around the audience, to see if any one dissented from this self-evident proposition.) Four year I follered the butcherin' trade, and two year I driv' pill; but I ollers had a genus for the dentistry line; and notwithstandin' the difficulty, I will try to explain the subject so that even a lady can onderstand it. I shall ondertake it from the first progress of disease in the fangs to the formation of the tartarish matter in the little blue veins under the tongue, which are the cause of decay in the enammil — which are ondoubtedly so, gentlemen and ladies; that the decomposition of the teeth affects the systum, and the decomposition of the systum affects the teeth. I shall now proceed to the operation of pluggin' the teeth, which is very simple. You only dig a hole in the tooth a little larger at the bottom than the top, and stuff in a bit of gold-leaf. This is called stuffin' or pluggin'. Two year hev I been a-tryin' to get here, an' could n't do it; my services was wanted in all the cities of the Southern states. There was no denyin' people; they would have Dr. JOHN- STON at any price. I do n't doubt but what you have seen here some of them impostures, which we dentistries krackterize as jack-leg dentistries; but I, gentlemen and ladies, are a rale Scientificky! I an't none of your jack-legs. When you see a man travellin' in his own barootch and his own hosses, you say to yourselves, ' Dr. JOHNSTON ain't no imposture; he 's a Scientificky, and no mistake !' Ninety dollars monthly per annum it costs me to keep my barootch — ninety dollars! — and if it was n't for my 'spenses bein' so great, I should like to distract all the teeth of all the gentlemen and ladies free gratis.. But there is two nearves: the one nearve is of the teeth, and the other is of the pawket; and the nearve of the pawket is fully as sensible as the nearve of the teeth. Here in my jaws, (opening his mouth with a horrid grin, and showing a couple of semi-transparent false teeth as big as pumpkin-seeds,) is two of the famous incorruptible patent plate teeth, which is the monarch-teeth of all others. Fourteen year has these teeth been in my jaws, and yet (giving a can- nibalistic look around him, and grinding together his formidable teeth,) I think I could bite off any body's finger with 'em now. If any gentleman or lady wants to try, just step for'ard and put your finger in my mouth and feel 'em.' Here he held his mouth open for some time; but no one appear- ing to care about having their fingers bitten off just then, he shut it again. It may be well imagined there was a good deal of laughter at this extraordinary address, which the doctor attributed solely to his own facetiousness, and received as a well-merited tribute to his oratorical powers. After some concluding remarks, he informed the audience that he would be ready to receive the calls of the af- flicted at seven o'clock the next morning; when the audience dispersed, not however without a pro- position to duck him in the Colorado from the sturdy backwoodsmen whom he had attempted to impose upon. It was finally decided to let him go scot-free for his wife's sake and in consideration of the amusement he had afforded. The doctor proceeded to San Antonio, where he had an applica- tion from one of Col. HAYS' rangers to extract from his head the iron of an Indian arrow, which he had received in a skirmish two years before. The doctor, after examining the scar, put on his spec- tacles, took them off again, and setting his head on one side with an air of oracular wisdom, gave his opinion as follows: ' I can 't 'stract that 'ere, bekase it would kill you; but I 'll give you some pills that 'll *melt it in your head !'*

' T. P.'s *'Ballad,'* to make out the necessary rhythm, in the ' chorus-line,' would read somewhat like the affecting old ballad of *'Lord Lovel and Lady Nancy,'* as sung by vocalists who understand the requirements of poetical feet:

> ' THEY buried her in St. MARY's church-yard,
>   And they buried him close by her,
> And out of her buzzum there grew a red rose,
>   And out of hizzen a brier-ri-ri-er,
>   And out of hizzen a brier.

> ' And they growed and growed to the steeple-top,
>   Till they could n't grow no higher,
> And there they formed a true loveyer's knot,
>   All true loveyers for to admire-rire-ri-rire,
>   All true loveyers for to admire !'

' T. P.' must excuse us; we have little leisure and less inclination to ' alter or amend' his verse. . . . GILBERT ABBOTT A BECKETT, who writes *'The Comic Blackstone'* in ' PUNCH,' has much of the peculiar humor of the late ever-to-be-lamented THOMAS HOOD. Some of his burlesque illustrations of legal requirements overflow with wit and trenchant satire. Speaking of the act of ' distraining,' he says : ' A bullock walking through a hedge into a stranger's field, may find himself in custody for the rent; and the animal has nothing to do but toss up with the sheriff's officer, if he is desirous of settling the matter without remaining a prisoner. Tools used in trade cannot be distrained, and a shoemaker may hold out to the last ; a carpenter need not consent to be chiseled out of his chisel; and a tailor may defy his landlord to take his measures.' Under the head of ' Wrongs and their Remedies' we have some important information, especially in relation to the law of libel : ' Injuries affecting a man's reputation include slanderous words and written libels. Though it is actionable to print that which may injure a man's reputation, it does not seem that a printer can have an action brought against him for printing a book whereby the reputation of the author is seriously damaged. To call a man a rogue or a rascal in words, is said to be no ground for an action, though it would be very good ground for the action of knocking him down, without going any farther into the merits. Reputation may also be destroyed by malicious indictments or prosecution; as if BROWN out of spite indicts SMITH for forgery, and it turns out that SMITH is a blacksmith, and has forged nothing but horse-shoes and other articles, in the way of his trade, then SMITH has a very good action against BROWN, who has been guilty of a very bad one.' In treating of actions of *detinue*, the author incidentally mentions this fact : ' Detaining of goods may be illegal where the original taking was lawful ; as, if a bull walks into my preserves, I may distrain him *damage feasant* while he is damaging my pheasants. Now, though it is lawful for me to take the bull by the horns, or even to seize him in tail, yet if his owner tenders me amends, I have no right to detain the brute, but must throw him up or be liable to an action.' He gives us also a good idea of debt. ' A debt is a sum of money due ; but as we are not anxious to go very deeply into debt, we shall not attempt a minute description of what every one must be more or less acquainted with.' Here is a specimen of what constitutes a legal ' discontinuance :' ' If A opens a theatre, and lets B a box for three months, and the landlord not being able to get any rent, takes possession of the house, which closes in six weeks, and B absolutely insists on sitting in his box, it is termed a discontinuance.' We have ourselves, in this department, had ' our say' in relation to the ridiculous character of the forms of action in cases of ejectment, but we ' give in' to the comic BLACKSTONE :

' IT is necessary first for the claimant to make a formal entry on the premises, and remain on them till he is turned off; but as he might sit in a field all night, without any one taking any notice of him, it is provided that he may have a friend in readiness to come up and walk him away ; and this friend is called the casual ejector. An action is then commenced against the casual ejector, who writes in a friendly way to the tenant in possession, advising him to come forward and defend his title, for he, the casual ejector, being only in fun, intends letting Judgment go by default if the matter should be proceeded with. The tenant in possession, not relishing the joke, comes forward to defend the action, and then the question is decided as between the parties who are really at issue. After possession is recovered, an action may be brought for mesne profits ; but if the profits have been very mean they are hardly worth incurring the expense of action for.'

WE are glad to perceive by the English journals that Mr. FORREST, our distinguished American actor, has been received in the principal towns of Scotland, Ireland and England with marked enthusiasm by crowded audiences. This success is the more gratifying, since it establishes the fact that talent and genius, which are of no country, will always be appreciated by the people, all private or public cliques to the contrary notwithstanding. Mr. FORREST, we learn, after a journey through Spain with his family, will return to the United States. He will be warmly welcomed. After a professional tour through the Union, he will take his final leave of the stage, and retire to private life. . . . WE were glad to reëncounter recently the following admirable lines, which appeared in BLACKWOOD'S Magazine nearly thirty years ago. They were suggested by a description, in the writings of a French author, of an Egyptian funeral procession on its way to the cemetery, which paused before certain houses, and sometimes receded a few steps. The dead thus stopped before the doors of their friends to bid them a last farewell, and before those of their enemies, to effect a reconciliation before they parted forever :

'SLOWLY, with measured tread,
Onward we bear the dead
  To his lone home :
Short grows the homeward road,
On with your mortal load,
  Oh, Grave! we come.

'Yet, yet — ah! hasten not
Past each remembered spot
  Where he hath been ;
Where late he walked in glee,
There from henceforth to be
  Never more seen.

'Rest ye — set down the bier ;
One he loved dwelleth here ;
  Let the dead lie
A moment that door beside,
Wont to fly open wide
  Ere he drew nigh.

'Hearken ! — he speaketh yet —
'Oh, friend ! wilt thou forget
  (Friend more than brother !)
How hand in hand we 've gone,
Heart with heart linked in one —
  All to each other ?

'Oh, friend ! I go from thee,
Where the worm feasteth free,
  Darkly to dwell ;
Giv'st thou no parting kiss !
Friend ! is it come to this ?
  Oh, friend, farewell !'

'Uplift your load again ;
Take up the mourning strain,
  Pour the deep wail !
Lo! the expected one
To his place passeth on —
  Grave! bid him hail !

'Yet, yet — ah! slowly move,
Bear not the form we love
  Fast from our sight ;
Let the air breathe on him,
And the sun beam on him
  Last looks of light.

'Here dwells his mortal foe ;
Lay the departed low,
  Even at his gate —
Will the dead speak again ?
Utt'ring proud boasts and vain,
  Last words of hate ?

'Lo! the cold lips unclose !
List ! list ! what sounds are those;
  Plaintive and low ?
'Oh, thou, mine enemy ;
Come forth and look on me,
  Ere hence I go !

'Curse not thy foeman now —
Mark ! on his pallid brow
  Whose seal is set !
Pard'ning, I pass thy way ;
Then, wage not war with clay :
  Pardon — forget !'

THERE is n't ' a chance' for you, respected ' TOM BOWLING,' unless you greatly improve upon the two 'experiments' before us. A blind negro with a blown-out candle looking at midnight in a dark cellar for a black cat has a better 'look' for success, 'aperiently.' Still, 'TOM,' do n't let us discourage you from 'trying again,' because you have not succeeded in your first efforts.' '*Three* times, and out.' . . . THERE is not a single word of praise in the annexed notice of ' *Hazen's Grammatic Reader,*' which we take from one of the well-filled columns of the ' *Evening Gazette and Times*' daily journal, in which we do not cordially concur: ' Mr. J. S. REDFIELD, Clinton-Hall, has just published the *Grammatic Reader*, by EDWARD HAZEN, A. M., and we conceive it to be the most elegant book of juvenile instruction ever issued in this or any other country. The author's ability and qualifications for the task he has undertaken have been already shown in '*Hazen's Speller and Reader,*' and a most satisfactory farther development of his system of imparting an accurate knowledge of the elements of our vernacular will be found in the book under notice. It is however to its typographical and illustrated character to which we referred when speaking of the unsurpassed ' elegance' of this little school-book. It is printed on firm thick paper, with handsome open type, and contains sixty-eight engravings from original drawings by CHAPMAN, which are among the most spirited sketches that ever came from the pencil of that accomplished artist ; and these are engraved with a degree of skill and high finish that would befit an illustrated edition of GRAY or GOLDSMITH. Compared with the miserable wood-cuts with which young folks have hitherto been obliged to be content in the volumes published whether for their amusement or instruction, they mark a new era in publications addressed chiefly to the young. *Taste*, that delicate quality of the trained intellect, (and which, with its twin-brother discrimination, makes a *feeler* to the mind as important to some of its operations as is the trunk of the elephant to the purveyance of 'he creature's proper food) true taste is ministered to in these drawings, at the season of life when it is most susceptible of gentle and unconscious training. Boston, which we believe has hitherto been the most famous city for its juvenile books, will doubtless, with its readiness to appreciate a good thing, instantly acknowledge that the enterprise of Mr. REDFIELD has given New-York so much the lead that it will require great efforts to rival her in this department of book-making.' If our readers would see for themselves how entirely just is the praise here bestowed upon the engravings of this beautiful book, let them turn to the cut at the head of our 'Gossip' in the present number, which has been kindly loaned us by the publisher. . . . IT is really amusing to observe how much the meaning of a person may be changed by the mere transposition of words. A friend informs us of an African church in this town which is called ' The Church of the *Colored* Messiah.' He dropped into it one day, he says, and the first sentence he heard from the officiating ' colored pusson' was in a prayer, which commenced with : O ! LORD-ah ! at thy *great feet* we bow-ah !' · · · A RECENT ' *New-Bedford Mercury*' mentions the arrival of the ' *Sarah*' whale-ship at that port, having on board a harpoon which was found in the body of a large whale. The harpoon was marked ' *Lyra*,' and belonged to a New-Bedford vessel of that name, which was lost in 1828 on a reef near Oahu, Sandwich Islands. Our readers will remember the sketch of ' *Mocha Dick, of the Pacific*,' published in the KNICKERBOCKER many years ago ; a huge mountain-whale, that rises like an island every now and then from the bosom of the Pacific, trailing from his sides hundreds of green slimy ropes, that stream like ' horrid hair' upon the waters. He will be a treasure when his time comes, not only to oil-men but to ' workers in iron.' · · · THERE are important facts set forth and enforced in the article on ' *Causes of Early Consumption*,' by Professor MAPES, in preceding pages. The benefits of mountain air in diseases of the lungs are becoming every year more and more apparent. We had the pleasure recently to encounter at that admirably kept and charmingly situated establishment, the '*Weehawken House*,' by Col. JESSUP, a gentleman who had entirely recovered his health at that moderately high altitude, although his case had been pronounced incurable by the physicians who attended him. . . . THE first paper in the present number well deserves the place of honor which it occupies. It is from the pen of a talented contributor, of whom we shall perhaps have more to say hereafter, and from whom we are certain our readers will always be well pleased to hear. . . . '*Charades*' are not accessible, as a general thing, to these pages. We have not the slightest objection however to oblige ' M. D.' by asking, ' What relation is your uncle's sister to you, if she is not your aunt ?' . . . WE appreciate the kind advice of ' OBSERVER,' and shall profit by it, so far as we can, without stretching the writer referred to upon a Procrustean bed. We have ourselves objected to several of the condemned passages from his pen ; but are assured and believe that his ultimate purposes are good, and that if peradventure he may *seem* to do evil, it is only that ' good may come.' ' You shall see anon.'

We are indebted to an obliging friend for the subjoined spirited translation of 'The Midnight Review,' from the German of Baron ZEDLITZ, (no relation of Prince DE ZEIDLITZPOUDRES, once described in these pages by Mr. WASHINGTON IRVING,) which illustrates a popular belief among some of the old soldiers of NAPOLEON, that the Emperor reäppears and holds reviews at midnight. Is there not something awfully weird and grand in the various shadowy pictures here presented?

'WHEN Midnight's hour is come,
    The Drummer forsakes his tomb,
And marches, beating his phantom-drum
    To and fro through the ghastly gloom.

'He plies the drumsticks twain,
    With fleshless fingers pale,
And beats, and beats again and again,
    A long and dreary Reveil!

'Like the voice of abysmal waves
    Resounds its unearthly tone,
Till the dead old soldiers, long in their graves,
    Awaken through every zone.

'And the Slain in the land of the Hun,
    And the Frozen in the icy North,
And those who under the burning sun
    Of Italy sleep, come forth.

'And they whose bones longwhile
    Lie bleaching in Syrian sands,
And the slumberers under the reeds of the Nile,
    Arise, with arms in their hands.

'At midnight, in his shroud,
    The Trumpeter leaves his tomb,
And blows a blast, long, deep and loud,
    As he rides through the ghastly gloom.

'And the yellow moon-light shines
    On the old Imperial Dragoons;
And the Cuirassiers form in lines,
    And the Carbineers in platoons.

'At a signal the ranks unsheathe
    Their weapons in rear and van;
But they scarcely appear to speak or breathe,
    And their features are sad and wan.

'And when Midnight robes the sky,
    The EMPEROR leaves his tomb,
And rides along, surrounded by
    His shadowy Staff, through the gloom.

'A silver star so bright
    Is glittering on his breast;
In an uniform of blue and white
    And a grey camp-frock he is dressed.

'The moonbeams shine afar
    On the various marshalled groups,
As the Man with the glittering silver star
    Proceeds to review his troops.

'And the dead battalions all
    Go again through their exercise,
Till the moon withdraws, and a gloomier pall
    Of blackness wraps the skies.

'Then around their Chief once more
    The Generals and Marshals throng;
And he whispers a word oft heard before
    In the ear of his Aid-de-camp.

'In files the troops advance,
    And then are no longer seen:
The challenging watchword given is 'France!'
    The answer is 'St. Helene!''

MR. C. G. FOSTER, every 'item' concerning whom is well known to the every-morning readers of the 'Tribune' daily journal, has recently issued a prospectus of 'The Apollo, a Journal of Music and the Fine Arts.' It will supply full and impartial musical intelligence from every city in the United States, and from Havana, Mexico, and the principal cities of South America. No requisite expense will be spared to make it a true and watchful exponent of the interests and conditions of music in the new world; keeping pace with its progress and faithfully interpreting its wise and beneficent teachings. Painting, sculpture, architecture, the drama, etc., will receive regularly such attention as their real progress requires. The work will be published weekly, in a large quarto form, on the very best quality of paper and in the most modern and exquisite style of printing, itself one of the Fine Arts. The terms of subscription will be three dollars per annum, always in advance, and no single copies of the paper will ever be sold. We have no doubt of the success of 'THE APOLLO,' because we are quite sure that Mr. FOSTER will make such a journal as will command it. · · · WE had a few remarks upon 'George Downing's Establishment of Good Things' for visitors at Newport, Rhode Island, and (strange juxtaposition!) Mumford's new Translation of Homer. But both being too good to spoil by delay, they are deferred until our next, together with notices of four or five new publications, and some other words to correspondents.

LITERARY RECORD. — 'Consuelo,' by GEORGE SAND, (the *nom de plume* of Madame DUDEVANT,) is the title of two handsomely-printed volumes from the press of Messrs. WILLIAM D. TICKNOR AND COMPANY, Boston. The work was originally translated for 'The Harbinger,' a Boston periodical, whose criticisms we have generally found to be discriminating and just. The name, 'Consuelo,' is that of the heroine, which in Spanish means 'consolation.' 'No word,' says the 'Harbinger,' 'could better describe the peculiar influence of the book. It is consoling to the depths of every tired and weary soul. As sure as you read, you are in a clearer and more loving mood. It throws around you the sphere of an ideal person, a character so truly conceived and so thoroughly sustained that almost you are persuaded it has bodily existence, and that a 'Consuelo' lives for you too.' This is very high praise. · · · WE have received from Messrs. JAMES MUNROE AND COMPANY, Boston, 'The Works of Henry Ware, Jr.,' and cannot resist the inclination to say that these spirited and persevering publishers are most indefatigably supplying us with a succession of excellent works. Their valuable and entertaining Biography of HENRY WARE has been followed by two volumes of the writings of that eminent Unitarian divine. Our opinion of HENRY WARE was greatly heightened by his brother's admirable biography. His own published productions detract nothing from our estimation of his talents. He was more of a man, more of a theologian, more of a right-hearted thinker and more of a poet, than even his fame as a preacher authorized us to believe. Of the talented WARE family, if not the most gifted, he was the most equally versatile. The same degree of merit seems to have prevailed in every faculty of his mind which shone conspicuously. If not possessed of the deep science and close philosophy of his brother, the physician; or if less imbued with the tone and spirit of antiquity which pervade the eloquent 'Letters from Palmyra,' by his brother WILLIAM, (first given to the public in these pages,) he manifests a more varied talent, of the same degree of merit in each department; less perhaps in each particular kind, but in the aggregate of his genius, *more*. The Reverend CHANDLER ROBBINS, of Boston, one of the best men that breathes upon this side the Azores, has with great skill and critical ability selected from HENRY WARE'S writings, in prose and verse, enough to assure us, and posterity too, of the truth of these remarks. Mr. ROBBINS tells us that he has selected the most valuable and suitable of Mr. WARE'S writings under the close restriction as to *quantity* which the author's delicacy of feeling and soundness of judgment somewhat severely imposed. Were there not so much to read that abbreviation has become a requisite virtue, we might tax Mr. WARE'S modesty with too chary a consideration for the public desire; but a glance at our library-table, and the reflection that other good men are yet to be born, (as we trust,) confirm our assent to the good sense of his scruples. Mr. ROBBINS will himself need a biographer one of these days, and many more, it is to be hoped, resembling him. But may that necessity be prolonged far beyond our span:

——— 'diuque
Lætus intersit populo!'

The merit of Mr. WARE'S prose writings is very great; greater than can usually be assigned to the 'taking' compositions of a popular preacher. His more worldly essays well repay the perusal; and all who shall read his lecture upon the 'Poetry of Mathematics,' will acknowledge that it contains observation and argument which must secure for it permanent praise. But to leave the theological and philosophical portion of the volumes for a branch better adapted to a magazine like the KNICKERBOCKER, we would call attention to the merits of Mr. WARE'S poetry. Almost at random, we transcribe the following proofs of his power in verse. The first is a sonnet on the country church of his friend, the beloved Doctor FOLLEN, at East Lexington, (Mass.):

'THE FOLLEN Church — how beautiful it stands,
  Graceful and calm in that sequestered nook!
  How doth a blessing from its placid look
Flow o'er the hamlet and its fertile lands!
Fit monument to him who placed it there;
  Whose soul, all truth, benignity and grace,
  Beamed forth in benedictions, from a face
Where might and sweetness met in union rare.
O light of love, too early quenched in death!
  Yet as that fane, though crumbled to the ground,
  Would still survive, in sacred influence round,
So flows, and shall, from him a quickening breath:
Death to the good man is but life's extension;
Earth mourns his loss; Heaven joys in his ascension.'

There are touches of quiet nature and humor in this ' *Thanksgiving Song*,' written in 1831. It quite makes one's mouth water to read it:

'I REMEMBER, I remember, when I was a little boy,
How the last week in November always filled my heart with joy;
For then Thanksgiving always came. with every kind of pie,
And I for once could eat my fill, though father *did* sit by.

'I remember, I remember. how on Monday they began
With rolling paste, and chopping meat, and buttering patty-pan;
And proud was I to pound the crackers, or to stone the plums,
Or crack the shagbarks with flat-irons that often cracked my thumbs.

'I remember, I remember. how the two next busy days
Kept the kitchen in an uproar and the oven in a blaze;
'Till all was done and cleared away by Wednesday's evening skies,
And the proud tea-table smoked with four premonitory pies.

'I remember, I remember. when the morning came at last,
How joyfully at breakfast I perceived it was not fast;
But loaded plates and smoking bowls assailed our winking sight,
With ' Johnny-cakes' and chocolate hot, to whet the appetite.

'I remember, I remember, when the dinner came at last,
How, like the kings of BANQUO's race, the dishes came and passed:
The exhaustless line seemed threatening to run on till crack of doom,
While still a voice from every stomach cried, 'There yet is room.'

'I remember, I remember, how those lessons in gastronomy
Were sometimes mixed with questions upon Latin and astronomy;
And in geography how JOHN did once, in accents murky,
Reply that Canaan was in Ham, and Paradise in Turkey.

'I remember, I remember, then how tight my jacket grew,
As if 't would burst a button off with every breath I drew ;
And so, to settle all, we boys kicked foot-ball down in town,
Or went to see the marksmen *try* to shoot the tied hens down.

'I remember, I remember — *not* what happened after tea,
For we had then no grandfather whom we could go and see ;
I only know we went to bed when nine o'clock was rung,
And you had better do the same now that my song is sung.'

There is of equal and higher cleverness a collection of poetry sufficient to make a two hundred-paged volume comprised within this series. For the religious or the more serious class of readers there are few books that can with more candor be confidently commended. Messrs. MUNROE AND COMPANY have also published a ' *Life of Fichte*,' a neat little duodecimo, which will be interesting to those who admire one of the most conspicuous of modern German thinkers; aptly characterized by an eminent writer in our kindred tongue as ' a colossal, adamantine spirit, standing erect and clear like a CATO Major among degenerate men ; fit to have been the teacher of the Stoa, and to have discoursed of beauty and virtue in the groves of Academe.' A ' *Memoir of Henry A. Ingalls*,' put forth by the same house, will be found by the friends of the subject to be a gratifying sketch of one who appears — by his picture — to have been a very worthy young man. · · · WE have before us two little volumes of verse from two new candidates for the poet's wreath. The first, ' *A Retrospect, and other Poems*,' reaches us from the press of Messrs. JAMES MUNROE AND COMPANY, Boston. The contents leave little record upon the mind of the reader. Their characteristic is a combination of trite but incontrovertible facts with a kind of rhythmical debility, not capable of precise description. In the blank verse on ' Death,' one of the best of several weak passages is a very bad paraphrase of an eloquent paragraph in Dr. DEWEY's sermon on ' The Natural Dread of Death.' There is throughout the book an equal lack of originality and force. Our next book is called ' *The Indian Gallows, and other Poems*,' by W. H. RHODES. We have read it through, and have found it to contain, in its varied verse, many lines and even passages of very decided excellence. But we assure our young author that he has much to learn, and some things to unlearn. We like for example his tribute to Carolina, and her noble natural features; but such sentences as ' Narrate thy fortunes,' ' squander blood and thousands,' etc., and such ekings-out of poetic feet as ' dash their pow-ers down,' ' flow-ers dot the vale,' ' en-crimson,' Spitzberg-en's,' and the like, we should advise our author forever to eschew. Mr. EDWARD WALKER, the publisher, has done ample justice to the externals of the little volume. · · · FROM the BROTHERS HARPER we have two very ' excellent and approved good works;' the one is the thirteenth Number of the ' New Miscellany,' containing ' *The Voyages of Discovery and Research in the Arctic Regions,'* from the year 1818 to the present time ; under the command of the several naval officers employed by sea and land in search of a north-west passage from the Atlantic to the Pacific ; with two attempts to reach the North Pole ; the whole abridged and arranged from official narratives. The other is entitled '*The Novitiate, or a Year among the English Jesuits,*' a personal narrative ; with an essay on the constitutions, the confessional morality, and history of the Jesuits ; by ANDREW STEINMETZ. The same publishers have given us, complete in one beautiful volume, at the low price of fifty cents, the '*Poems of Henry Wadsworth Longfellow.*' The repeated editions of LONGFELLOW'S poems sufficiently controvert the idea that *good* poetry is unsaleable. The same remark will apply with similar force to the writings of our own BRYANT and HALLECK. Among the serials of the HARPERS we have Number Two of the beautiful '*Pictorial History of England,*' and LEE'S '*Copeland's Dictionary of Practical Medicine.*' . . THE last two issues of Messrs. CAREY AND HART'S excellent 'Library for the People' contains the '*Achievements of the Knights of Malta,*' by ALEXANDER SUTHERLAND, Esq. The author has united the broken links of a very brilliant and extraordinary chain of historical facts, connected with the achievements of one of the most illustrious institutions that originated in knightly daring and pious zeal. . . . SOME of the numbers of Messrs. WILEY AND PUTNAM'S 'Library of American Books' we have not been enabled conscientiously to praise, while one or two of the volumes were so little noteworthy as to demand no remark ; but the two latest issues of the series, '*Mosses from an old Manse,*' by NATHANIEL HAWTHORNE, we can most cordially commend. Refined imagination, purity of thought, and force and felicity of language, are the characteristics of the tales which make up these volumes, and which will not be the less acceptable to the public because they have before been published ; for such productions command the interest of 'once-readers' as well as new ones. From the same popular publishers we have a small neat volume, giving the '*Results of Hydropathy,*' in cases of indigestion and constipation, with an account of the cases cured at a celebrated hydrophathic establishment in England, by EDWARD JOHNSON, M. D., author of the '*Theory and Principles of Hydropathy,*' etc. . . . MESSRS. LEA AND BLANCHARD, Philadelphia, have published the first volume of '*Roscoe's Lives of the Kings of England,*' from the Norman Conquest, with anecdotes of their courts, etc.; now first published from efficient records and other authentic documents — a very interesting and reliable work. . . . '*The History of St. Giles and St. James,*' by DOUGLAS JERROLD, Esq., continues to be published in regular issues by the established and enterprising house of BURGESS, STRINGER AND COMPANY. It is replete with the deepest interest, and its inculcations are of the best tendency. It is deservedly acquiring a very extensive sale. . . . WE have received and read with much pleasure '*An Address delivered before the Was-ah Ho-de-no son-ne, or New Confederacy of the Iroquois,*' by HENRY R. SCHOOLCRAFT, Esq., together with a spirited poem by WILLIAM H. C. HOSMER, Esq., '*Genundewah, a Legend of Canandaigua Lake,*' delivered on the same occasion with the 'Address.' . . . WE would call the attention of our readers to a well conducted journal for seamen, entitled '*The Light-Ship,*' published in this city. We have read several numbers of it. It is an instructive, entertaining and useful sheet, and its wide circulation must be productive of good. . . . MESSRS. BURGESS, STRINGER AND COMPANY have published in a pamphlet which does credit to the care of the printer, Mr. WILLIAM OSBORN, '*An Account of a Journey to Niagara, Montreal and Quebec, in 1765, or 'T is Eighty Years Since.*' We have heretofore alluded, in the editorial department of the KNICKERBOCKER, to this instructive and entertaining *brochure,* giving at the same time several interesting extracts from the original manuscript. The excellent lady who gives the work to the public, remarks in the preface, that as 'the time has arrived when hundreds and thousands will be gliding smoothly and swiftly along to view the most magnificent of Nature's works, it may not be uninteresting to read the journal of an intelligent gentleman when on the same pilgrimage in the year 1765, and to mark the difference of the undertaking then and now. While some, no doubt, will rejoice in being able to obtain so grand a sight at so small a cost of time and trouble, others (perhaps many) will regret that the facilities afforded to travellers in these days should have deprived the enterprise of all its romance, and wish that they too had lived when indeed it was *something* to have seen the Falls of Niagara.' . . . '*The Island City*' is the title of a spirited metropolitan Saturday journal, edited with good taste and tact by Mr. BUCKINGHAM, author of '*Harry Burnham, the Young Continental,*' (a patriotic novel, full of stirring incident and illustrated with excellent wood-engravings,) which appears in weekly numbers in the 'City.'. . . WE find in the '*Evening Mirror,*' (one of the most spirited and various of our daily journals, let us add in passing,) a commendatory notice of the new and rare book-store of Mr. KERNOT, in Broadway, above Bleecker-street. We know the praise bestowed to be well deserved ; and have no doubt that Mr. KERNOT'S intimate acquaintance with ancient and modern English literature, and the best editions of all known works, will secure him a liberal share of the public patronage.

ORIGINAL PAPERS.

1. A 'remembreable' Trout-fishing Excursion; being a 'Full and Particular Account' of Two Day's Sport in the Callicoon and Mongaup Streams. 2. The National and Social Changes in Great-Britain. 3. Messrs. Bangs, Richards and Platt's Catalogue of the New-York Book-Trade Sale. 4. Scottish Song: 'When the Kye come Hame.' 5. The Genus Bore: The 'Sensible Bore.' 6. The Age of Fun: The forth-coming 'Daily Gazette of Wit and Good Nature.' 'The Comic Almanack,' with 'Specimens.' 7. 'The True Lover to his Business.' 8. 'The Red-Skins,' by J. Fenimore Cooper: Mr. Cooper's Reputation Abroad: Oriental Correspondence. 9. 'Gentle Willie,' Etc. 10. The Finger-Whittler: 'P'izen Sarpents.' 11. Mr. Fowler the Bust-er's 'Phrenology:' Lying for a 'Burst.' 12. The Trying Trick of Transposition. 13. The Model of New-York. 14. Writings of Hugh Swinton Legare. 15. 'Foolscap Scribblings:' Mr. James' Jameseries. 16. A Word to 'The Doctor.' 17. Our 'Legal Papers,' Etc. 18. Response to 'Emilie Sphynx.' 19. An Adroit Trickster. 20. Our Troy Friend: Anecdote of Charles Lamb. 21. Prof. Mapes' Theory of the 'Causes of Early Consumption:' Tit for Tat, or a Lawyer Rebuked. 22. 'X. Y. Z.' 23. 'Thoughts on the Magnetic Telegraph.' 24. The Long Island Wives and Wife-Stealers: the 'Thunder-and-Lightning Rod.' 25. An Eloquent Scene: a Primitive Christian. 26. A Quaker Lemonade. 27. 'Greater and Lesser Stars:' Pen-men 'and Pen-women, too.' 28. The 'Gentleman in Black' in Wall-street: the 'Old Masters.' 29. The 'Howard Athenæum,' Boston, by Mr. Hackett: Mr. Hamblin. 30. Reunion of the Chapters of the 'Delta Phi Society.' 31. The 'Alleghanian' Minstrels. 32. 'The Escape, a Tale of the Sea:' Ocean Technicals. 33. Deferred Matters, Etc.

THE KNICKERBOCKER.

Vol. XXVIII.   AUGUST, 1846.   No. 2.

THE MYSTERIOUS DUTCHMAN.

A SKETCH IN ANCIENT GOTHAM

My good old Dutch grandmother! relict of the olden times, reve-
rence to thy memory! Peace to thy ashes, venerable lady and true
christian! Thou wert, despite a few human foibles that made us
love thee all the better, a noble and honored specimen of humanity.
I think I see the old lady just as she used to sit in her gay-colored
chintz-covered easy-chair, for she disdained rockers as a 'Yankee
notion,' and indeed was so attached to all old fashions that she seemed
to regard each new invention as a direct insult to the past. When
she saw new fashions take precedence of old customs, she would
primly bridle up with a stately air, and say as ironically as her good
nature would allow : 'Change, change — all change ; but I cannot
understand any of these new fangles !'

It would indeed seem as if there never had been a wise genera-
tion until the present. My ancestors, and they were true gentry of
the best blood in Holland — for they were the Barnevelts and De
Witts, well-tried friends, and noble martyrs to the good House of
Orange — my ancesters, I say, did without these new-fashioned fan-
cies ; and so will I, their unworthy descendant, who have always en-
deavored as nearly as possible to walk in their footsteps, and God
willing, will so persevere to the end, though all others should adopt
the degenerate innovations of these modern days.' Nothing raised
my grandmother's ire to such a degree as when she heard any one
say, in a deprecatory manner, 'Oh, we are Dutch, you know.' 'And
what is there that you ought to be so proud of ?' the old lady would
reply, with a sparkling eye. 'The world at large is greatly a debtor
to Holland. She first in Europe pronounced the never-to-be-for-
gotten words 'Civil and Religious Liberty.' She first offered on
the altar of Freedom the lives and property of her children for the
regeneration of oppressed mankind ; and in this prolonged and

heroic struggle against a tyrannical monarchy that commanded ten times her wealth and strength, she hoped against hope and conquered almost against possibility. 'Liberty or death' was their firm determination; and they resolved that Holland should be the patriot's grave or the freeman's home. The noble and disinterested WILLIAM of Orange, might with unblushing cheek call our own WASHINGTON brother. Remember that your countrymen first set the example in all that has made Europe prosperous, for the last two centuries; and actually achieved more with small means than any other country has ever attempted. So, my dear young friends, when you own to a fault, nobly acknowledge and endeavor to overcome it as an individual one, but never lay it off on your country.'

We used to joke the old lady on her 'pilgrimage,' as she called it; for every summer she travelled to Schenectady on purpose to worship one Sunday in a little church built with bricks that had been brought all the way from Holland. She knew the names of every family that she considered true gentle-folks in the state, and I believe with but one exception they all had a Dutch sound. If the good lady heard of any of them, for the sake of euphony or convenience, dropping a letter or syllable, she mourned over it as a sign of modern degeneracy, and pronounced them unworthy sons of good fathers. Our grandmother was our kindest and most venerated friend. She it was who pronounced upon and prescribed for all the ailments of the nursery; and if any of the small fry committed a worse fault than usual, she censured with a grave kindness that melted the heart of the young offender, who resolved rather to die than again hurt the feelings of one by whom they were so dearly beloved. And in sickness, whose hand felt so soft and cool on the fevered forehead? — whose eye watched with such unwearied vigilance, and whose voice soothed with such a sympathizing tone, as those of our dear good, loved old grandmother? And who hung on the New-Year's tree such elegant and appropriate presents? On spying hers, each of us used to exclaim : 'Just the very thing I wanted! I am sure that is grandmother's!' Then flying to the old lady, she would enfold us in her aged arms, and amid kisses and joyful tears, pray that GOD's grace might make us good men and women.

She frequently used to tell us tales of other days, particularly of those times when the 'British red-coats' had possession of New-York. But her favorite theme was a little mysterious old gentleman, who hired and occupied a house contiguous to her own, which stood on the identical spot now called Hanover-Square. My grandmother pictured him as having a sallow thin oval face, with a nose and expression of countenance decidedly Dutch. He always appeared in an antiquated suit of black, the coat frogged and braided, with wide skirts, and broad lapelles; the amplitude of these latter being more conspicuous, owing to his diminutive size, and the then prevailing fashion of small-clothes. He wore massive gold knee-buckles, embossed with Oriental characters, considered by many people at the time as cabalistic charms. His feet were neatly-shaped, and encased in thick shining square-toed leather shoes, decorated with a rosette of black ribbon, about the size of a small tea-cup; his well-worn and rather rusty shovel-hat was fastened up with three diminished rosettes of the same material. He used powder, and wore his hair tied in a long thick queue; and my grandmother observed that if any lurking pride could be detected in the little man, it was in his affection and admiration of this appendage. He kept but one aged domestic, who represented him as always engaged in writing; and it was generally supposed, from the minute inquiries that he made from every individual engaged in the late war, and also from frequent letters that passed to and fro between him and the celebrated military officers and civilians of distinction, that he was collecting materials for a history of the Revolution, and had visited the United States for the express purpose.

It was at first supposed, from his well-worn and carefully-preserved apparel, great literary attainments and unostentatious manner of living, that he might be poor, or in circumstances that demanded strict economy. This idea however was soon contradicted; for where money could advance human happiness, the purse of the little man was always open, and his lavish expenditure upon objects of charity stood in strong contrast with his personal economy. His unequalled learning and profound research upon all subjects could only have been the result of a life devoted to ardent and constant study; yet it seemed that no spot on the globe could be mentioned that he had not visited, and from personal inspection acquired a knowledge of the habits, customs and opinions of all nations. He often mentioned his having been detained by sickness on Mount Athos, and dwelt with grateful recollection on the kindness of the good Greek monks who treated the wayfarer as a friend, and ministered to his wants as to those of a brother. He lingered with delight upon the prospect of unsurpassed and ravishing beauty that enraptured the sense of every beholder who looked abroad from its precipitous ascent; he represented the exhilaration produced by the delicious purity of the atmosphere, the glorious recollections inspired by the past, and the profound impression caused by the divine scenery, as superior to every other earthly feeling of delight that he had ever experienced; and to his imperfect conception, it seemed as if Heaven could not bestow a greater joy; and he would add, so inexpressible was his ecstacy, that he could not forbear ejaculating aloud thanks and praises to his LORD and MAKER for such bountiful manifestation to unworthy man of HIS infinite power and goodness. Here, my grandmother said, the little man would feelingly observe: 'It was a wondrous scene, a wondrous scene, my dear Madam; and one that produced a strange struggle and commingling of exaltation and humility, which made the scales to fall from human eyes.'

The old gentleman often spoke of some Greek manuscripts which the monks had presented to him, and remarked, that although without name or date, he yet considered them of great antiquity. On the day previous to his leaving New-York, he requested my grandmother, as a favor, to take charge of a small dark-painted tin box, fastened with a brass padlock, which he informed her contained the identical manuscripts in question.   He observed that he was going to the wildest parts of South America, and as it was uncertain what risks he might there encounter, he should be glad to deposite them with her for safe-keeping, until he appeared in person to reclaim what he considered highly valuable and truly ancient productions. The fate of the old gentleman could not be ascertained, but he was never again seen in New-York.   To all entreaties my grandmother would reply, that the box should never be opened during her life, for she ever after would feel as if she had committed a breach of trust; but at her death it should be considered as my property, when I might examine the contents, and give them to the world, if they should be deemed worthy of publication.

On opening the box, we found several papers neatly arranged and tied with narrow black ribbon.   In each of these was a Greek manuscript, written in extremely old characters, folded within a translation, labelled ' LEAVES FROM MOUNT ATHOS.'   They were chiefly dramatic fragments.   No one who has yet seen them has suggested any doubts with regard to their antiquity.   Indeed many scholars have assured me that the utter absence of artifice, both in style and plan, stamps them as genuine productions of a very early period.

Leaves from Mount Athos.

ISLAND OF ICONIA : TWO OLD MEN MEET ON A HILL WHICH OVERLOOKS THE ISLAND : AT THE FOOT OF THE HILL LIES A BEAUTIFUL AND FLOURISHING TOWN.

FIRST OLD MAN. — This is a sweet place, stranger, and one that makes my old heart feel young again to look on.   Often when a boy I have climbed its rugged sides and steep ascents, and in wrestling with my fellows have had many a trip on this sweet-smelling hill thyme, the odor of which recalls the long-forgotten scenes of youth. I see perched on its rocks the old hives, the self-same colonies of bees, and tending their buzzing swarms the same saucy little rascals, half clad in the ragged sheep-skins that they wore five-and-sixty years ago.   But the city and plain below, O old man! show the work of many hands.   The gods must have showered blessings on this land, and the people have used them wisely ; for how stately, magnificent and numerous have grown the temples ; how enlarged the city's boundary ; and how beautiful and inviting are the groves and gardens that decorate the plain!   Oh JOVE, all-seeing, grant that my family be likewise prosperous !

SECOND OLD MAN. — Stranger, your words and looks denote a time-honored age, which requires rest and friendly tendance ; but I fear that adverse fortune with unfriendly foot has followed your declining years.   Has your old age no son to lean on ? or pious daughter, with ready hand, to administer household cares, so needful to the aged?   Your worn apparel and travel-stained wallet would bespeak a long and lonesome journey.

FIRST OLD MAN. — Ah, friend! to me the fates decreed a long

and lonesome life. But grant, all-powerful Jove! the light of hope to shine on these my latter days! that children's eyes may watch my failing strength, and weep over a father's parting breath; that pious hand of fond son or daughter may decently compose these aged limbs, and carefully perform those funereal rites so grateful to the gods and so necessary to man's repose. Oh, stranger! inform me if you can, and glad a desolate infirm old man with tidings of his long-lost children! Know you aught of Charmion, the son of Glycine and Ageus, whose father many years long passed was forced away by cruel pirates and sold a slave in distant lands?—or of the little Glycine, named after her blooming mother? For I, their most ill-fortuned father, stand here before you asking for my children.

SECOND OLD MAN.—Ageus, old man! are you Ageus? And remember you not young Lyrenus, the son of Eon?—whose father, neighbor next to thine, won a wreath of pine leaves for wrestling at the Isturian games? and how we two striplings used to practice, with firm grip and laced limbs, in the hope when men to do the same?

FIRST OLD MAN.—Thanks to the gods, oh Lyrenus!—and I accept it as a most propitious omen, that in my native country these aged eyes first fell on thee, my boyhood's dearest friend. Tell me, I pray thee, if aught that owed life to me is yet among the living? But if all have descended to Pluto's dark abode, let silence speak the dreaded truth.

SECOND OLD MAN.—Old man, *one* loved one, the good Glycine, still lives to call thee father, the proud mother of six noble, duteous sons, each one of whom will be to thee a Charmion, and multiply the love of one six-fold. The tiny hands of prattling children will climb thine aged knees, and fondly lisp a warm welcome to their grand-dame's venerable sire. Oh! may the fates decree thee a few happy years on earth, thou good old man; and then thou wilt lie down loved and full of years among thy children and thy children's children, honored and beloved of all.

FIRST OLD MAN.—Bitter and sweet, O friend! It is ever thus the gods have mixed the cup of life. But hearty thanks, most joyful thanks, for all that's spared. Oh! thou good Lyrenus! quickly lead me to my child; the father so rushes to my heart that it will burst if I enfold not soon my daughter.

SECOND OLD MAN.—Oh! my Ageus! joy shakes thine aged limbs; thy breath comes short and quick. Sit down beneath this olive shade, close by the bubbling spring, and I will lave your heated head and throbbing breast with its cool waters, and relate your daughter's fortune. Though well and happy, she dwells not on this island. With her husband she joined a colony that settled on the shores of Afric; with a fair wind, but two day's sail from hence. I have a vessel freighted with merchandise that sails for there to-morrow, with Neptune's and the wind's good will, that will afford you a passage most opportune. But my impatience burns to know what lands the fates have led you to; whether among a people barbarous and cruel, who practice impious rites and hate the stranger, or those who, ruled by milder deities and civil polity, are kind and just to all.'

FIRST OLD MAN.—A few short words, O friend! will tell you all; for though joys are quickly forgotten and griefs are remembered long, yet he who has suffered acutely and painfully is loth to paint the past, and shade it in all the dark and dismal colors which have lowered upon his fate; small sorrows, which hope and time can cure, we dilate and dwell upon, and ask for sympathy from those we love; but there are woes unutterable, incurable, which we dare not think on, and that would make us mad to tell; woes that the gods can only know and only death can heal. You, my Lyrenus, knew me a happy husband and father, disporting midst the joys of life, which grew in such a thick profusion round my path that I forgot the world was mutable, and in my dreams filled up the future with the same pleasant, fortunate life that had smiled upon the past; blindly forgetting — oh, short-sighted being! — that Fate has graved on fortune's wheel man's destiny, and chained with iron hand each mortal to the inevitable track. Self-gratulating man, untaught by wise adversity, considers himself the architect of his own fortune, and proudly sitting on the apex of prosperity, swells with vain conceit; when suddenly the pile of happiness dissolves, down falls the stricken wretch, loud crying on the gods that they are greater far than he, and demanding succor for helpless man from numerous deities whose names were quite forgotten when he needed not assistance. Misfortune proves to man his utter insufficiency, and so convinces him of JOVE's all-powerful might, that like a submissive child with mingled reverence and fear he bends before high Heaven, and all his nature kindles with a new-born and enlightened love, that cries out, 'Father! O, my father! give me strength!' and thus, my Lyrenus, through weakness I found greater might.

SECOND OLD MAN. — Wise are the lessons of adversity and safe the counsels guided by experience. Our state at present has need of such. But before we talk of public matters, and I lay out our numerous grievances for your inspection, tell me what peoples you have sojourned with, and where your fortunes led.

FIRST OLD MAN. — It might be such an eve as this fine day will leave, when earth, sky and ocean, wrapped in peace, looked smilingly on each other; it was a most holy eve, so sanctified by love and beauty that you would never have thought a deed of violence had ever stalked abroad or sullied the fair earth; when suddenly, from behind the covert of a rugged rock, four ruffians swiftly rushed and quickly dragged me into a boat; when there, they thrust me down and tightly bound my hands and feet; then threw over me a mat, upon the edges of which they sat, and rowed away with all their force, until we reached a larger vessel. They then unbound my torpid limbs and bade me mount its sides. When there, full soon I read my hopeless fate, for all around stood fierce Corcyrean pirates, who greeted with a fierce inhuman joy another captive. They took me down beneath the deck, and there I met with many other wretched

Greeks, reserved for slavery.   Nine days they pent us in this watery prison; on the tenth we entered the dark and savage Euxine, where they feared pursuit no longer, and escape was scarcely possible. Then they bade us come on deck and bathe and eat, and clad us in such attire as they thought would best please barbarian masters. Day by day some miserable one they bartered, exchanging for the skins of beasts and fleecy wool much-suffering men.   Me they reserved until we reached the southern and most sterile verge of this black sea, where they sold me to the wild Heniochi.   Five-and-fifty years was I—I, a civilized man, knowing and loving a freeman's rights—a slave to these barbarians; long the sport of their uncurbed and fitful whims.   But a firm reliance on paternal Jove, and a most assured confidence that however dark, he never forgets his children's fate, enabled me to meet misfortune with unruffled temper and look on insult with serene composure.   I tried to bear with cheerfulness the savage passions of untamed men, and taught the children many useful arts and sciences, that as they grew waked milder feelings in their young hearts, and inspired them with a new humanity.   They became aware of many wants which their fathers never knew, and gained a sense of beauty and of order that neutralized the savage in their breasts.   These new feelings found vent in words novel and delightful to their untutored ears, creating a social and improving communion.   I also taught them that by planting grain and pulse they might with light labor raise food, which hunting yields with weary toil and most uncertain luck.   Thus, O my friend! by almost imperceptible degrees a great change was effected: the children, as they grew to strong manhood, looked on me with a filial love, and said I had returned them good for evil; and that I was a prophet, or some god who had brought them knowledge and a sense of goodness from a better world.   But I told them, My children, I am a man weak and much-suffering like yourselves, but by the cultivation of our common nature, and early planting seeds of knowledge that have blossomed since, you take me for a higher being; there are some of you with like advantages who might perhaps be wiser far than I.   Then I told them of my country's arts and sciences, religion, polity, and all that makes man honorable, humane and civilized.   After many years, worn and old, I begged them to spare me farther labor, and devise some means whereby I might return and die in mine own country.   This they consented to; with many tears and amid sad embraces they scraped the dust from beneath my feet and laid it on their heads in token of submissive reverence.   Six young men, most beloved, rowed me eight days in a boat until we met a certain galley; then leaving many valuables, they took a sorrowful leave.   But on the dread Chalcidian shore we suffered shipwreck and lost all our cargo; when some Euboean fishermen took pity on a poor old man and offered him a passage home.   On our approach the unfriendly wind and tide set strong against the harbor; this forced them to land me on the northern shore, and this mountain I must needs climb before I could reach the city's bounds.

SECOND OLD MAN.—O, ever-changing Life, how many sides hast thou!—and he who would be truly wise, (sad lesson!) must learn them all. We must be scholars in Affliction's school, and to her sharp chastisements bow, before we can know our own nature and through that knowledge govern others. O, my Ageus, when we were young, Experience was most honored, and on the prudence of the old the youth relied; but now Discretion, that necessary regulator of all virtues, has fled our city, and loud-tongued Zeal, unproved by deeds, has sown dissension through the land.

FIRST OLD MAN.—I see no marks of foreign foes nor still more dreaded civil war. Destruction sits not howling over a desert, nor do I see famished Death, with wide-extended hungry jaws, ready to swallow a nation's life. But happy Peace, twin-born with glad Prosperity, walks smiling, scattering from Plenty's horn rich fruits and flowers over all the land; unarmed Industry reaps with sturdy strength the yellow harvest, nor pauses from the patient toil to look around for open foe or ambushed enemy. Women and little children glean up most carefully the scattered grain, as if War's horrid trump had never pealed its deadly blast in their affrighted ears, nor waked up pale Discord, who with savage joy seizes her whip of flames, and drives over all humanity Hell's fire-breathing hounds!

SECOND OLD MAN.—No, friend; dread Bellona thunders from afar; War's lightning strikes not yet our state. I pray the gods avert the evil! But we have fallen on contentious times; strange, snarling, contradictory times; when men in their high wisdom have discovered, nay proved, that shedding of human blood for the acquisition of larger territory, or to gratify uncurbed ambition, is sinful in the extreme; they also say that persecution for opinion's sake is most unwise, unjust, and fails signally of its intent. Yet before the echo of these words is off their lips, and another inspiration drawn, they tell you that all who differ from them in politics are fools or knaves, too ignorant to know their country's good, or else, subservient to gold or place, they care not for its welfare. If the populace shout for one who squares not with their opinion, they shrug their shoulders, show indifference, and drawl, with affected pity, ' Poor fools! when lank sides come together, and there are no beans or garlic to put between, they will then return to me.' But if intolerant in politics, in religion they are more rigid; and stranger still, O Ageus, to you who have passed your life with savages, it would be incomprehensible how much we hate each other on the gods' account!

FIRST OLD MAN.—Let not such blasphemy fall upon my ears! Men deify their own base violent passions and baptize them in Religion's holy name; thus impiously imposing on their followers a juggle and a cheat as Heaven's divinest will. Oh no, my friend; religion drives out of man all evil passions, and in the place of these, plants every virtue that can benefit his kind; long-suffering patience, meekness, charity, hatred of sin but pity for the sinner, and a deep sense of human frailty; for the good man knows that none are entirely wise or perfect. Oh, my Lyrenus, it must be that you have not quite forgotten your boyish tricks, and make a sport of my credulity; for it is incredible that man, blind though he be, should so far wander from the truth as to distort religion's pact, heaven's most holy bond of love, which binds earth to the gods, man to his CREATOR, and all human beings in deeds of kindness one to the other, into an instrument of hatred. It is most monstrous! Surely such a baleful evil cannot have lighted on Greece.

SECOND OLD MAN.—Would it were otherwise, oh Ageus! but on reaching yonder city, you will find it far too true. Ten years ago rich Myron breathed his last, and on that breath blew countless evils over our land. Some time before he employed the cunning hand of Agenor to form two golden horses with flowing manes and tails; this he performed with such creative skill that they apparently were instinct with life. You would have sworn they champed the bit, and that you saw their nostrils proudly inflate with living breath. These he intended for Apollo's shrine; but taking some angry pique at the priest, he kept them till his death; then said, ' The priest who could prove his god the mightiest should have his horses for a gift.' Each, to do this, incautiously assailed the others' deities, and in their angry eagerness forgot to defend their own; but thought, oh foolish men! that by proving the rest all false, their's would stand as the true. The atheists and sophists opened wide their hungry ears, and listened with delighted sneers; they eagerly caught up the separate arguments, and wove them into one entire negation, denying all, with a more plausible show of reason than they had ever before known how to use. The unwary and wicked rushed into this net of nooses, until all morals are nearly choked; the really good, almost bewildered, pass quietly by unheeded; while Hypocrisy rears aloft her snaky crest, ready to coil round any shrine where Interest leads, or change to any color that Fashion wears. But, my friend, this is the time of day when our citizens take offerings to the temples, and also when orators and clients meet for the discussion of public business. If we walk round and listen among the various groups, their words will best inform you of the city's state. *Exit.*

THE KLEPHT'S LAST FAREWELL.

FROM THE MODERN GREEK.

Down to yonder bank descend;
O, delay not, trusty friend!
Go—and use your hands as oars,
If you 'd touch the farther shores;
As a rudder work your breast,
If on yonder bank you 'd rest;
Make your slender body, too,
Like a ship—so prosper you!
And if to the other side
Through the waves you safely glide,
By the aid of GOD all-wise,
And the VIRGIN of the skies;
And if to our nest you pass,

Where our councils meet, alas!
Where the goats are roasted, too,
PHLORAS, TOMBRAS, which we slew;
And if our companions say,
' What has made the Klepht delay?'
Do not answer that I 'm fled
To the regions of the dead;
But that I have married, say,
In the stranger-land away:
For the wife that I have ta'en
Is the dark Earth's wide domain;
And for kinsmen now I own
Every little pebble-stone.

STANZAS: ON SUNSET.

BY A LADY CONTRIBUTOR.

'T was sunset: and I watch'd the sky
Just as the evening draweth nigh,
   As down he sinks to rest ;
Cloud after cloud was ting'd with gold,
Brighter and brighter to behold,
   Through all the crimson'd west.

How beautiful the landscape o'er,
Now made more smiling than before,
   With his enliv'ning rays ;
The very birds on glittering wing
Seem to select this time to sing
   Their evening song of praise.

The little insects as they fly,
Appear like spangles to the eye,
   As in its beams they move ;
All Nature looks so bright and gay,
Well pleas'd she almost seems to say,
   ' Behold our God is love.'

But as I gaz'd with fond delight,
A cloud just hid it from my sight,
   Though still its rays were seen :
Fit emblem of that love divine,
Which through affliction still doth shine,
   And brighten ev'ry scene.

I watch'd it till it seem'd to go
Farther and farther still below
   The clear blue vault of heav'n ;
Its beauteous pencillings soon did fade,
Cloud after cloud was darker made,
   As evening shades were giv'n.

Just so the Christian's course, when run,
Sinks calmly as the setting sun,
   And enters into rest ;
A heavenly halo spreads around,
He seems with greater glories crown'd —
   His last scene is his best.

Yet lo ! to-morrow's sun shall rise
And tread the circuit of the skies,
   And send its light abroad ;
But now, the Christian's labors o'er,
He too shall rise, but set no more —
   His spirit rests with God !

L. V. C.

New-York, June 6, 1846.

C I T Y   A R T I C L E S,

NUMBER TWO.

The Chatham.

NATURALISTS who go poking through the world, scrutinizing dung-hills and investigating the contents of decayed logs while in pursuit of bugs and spiders, are honored as philosophers and distinguished by grand titles implying learning in their possessors ; but we who venture into crypts and mansards in search of new varieties of our own species, must be sneered at and contemned for our trifling pursuits and vulgar tastes.   Heaven give us patience !   Is a spider then, even though it may have a dozen legs, of greater importance than a man, or must a worm, though it be a glow-worm, take precedence of a woman ?   It may be to gain consideration that learned men call themselves book-*worms*, and that the importance of entomology leads mankind to pay greater respect to hum-*bugs* than to any others of their own species.   We have been compelled into these ill-natured remarks by the imbecile snarlings of the Zoïlus of a Milliner's Magazine, who the other day accused us of vulgarity and a Flemish taste, and because we mean to offend all such delicate monsters in this article by introducing them into low-lived vulgar company.   If they prefer the society of Arachnidæ and Chrysomelidæ to that of beings a little lower than the angels, and can derive more pleasure from a Scarabæus than from a Scaramouch, they would do well to proceed no farther with us.   For our own individual tastes we prefer the lowest order of men to the highest order of insects, and should never choose a bug for the hero of a story, even though it were a gold-bug.   But tastes differ, and we are entirely willing, friend, to allow you the indulgence of your tastes, only we claim the privilege of indulging our own.   It is not our fault, but your own, that you differ from us ; therefore do not quarrel with us because you will not agree with us.

Among all city articles there is none so emphatically an article of city growth as the theatre.   GOD made the country but man made the town, and the town made the theatre.   There is nothing in the world so purely artificial ; even the men and women who make a part of it must be completely unnaturalized before they can harmonize with its other parts.   Their gestures are mechanical, their voices feigned, their dress extravagant, and even the natural outlines of the face are inverted by the light shining on them from below and casting their shadows upward instead of downward.   Such is the necessity for a reversal of nature on the stage, that the drama has continued to decline in popular esteem ever since the practice of substituting men for women was abandoned.   Every approximation which has been made in the theatre toward nature has tended to

destroy its attractions. The Puritans never did half as much to-
ward ruining the stage as the Kembles; and Macready ruined him-
self, and the theatre which he managed, by foolishly giving represen-
tations of natural objects in a natural manner, turning the stage of
Drury Lane into a real forest of Arden. His successor, Alfred Bunn,
understands the secret of dramatic success better, and is giving new
life to the theatre by departing as widely as possible from Nature,
for which he is ridiculed by Punch and patronized by the people.
The English stage was at no time so popular as during the dramatic
reign of Dryden, when Shakspeare was hardly ever presented, and
rhyme had banished blank verse. A manager who perfectly com-
prehended the secrets of dramatic art would study never to offend
the taste of his audience by the introduction of a natural object, or
allowing a natural expression of passion in his actors. It should
be constantly borne in mind that the theatre is essentially an artifice,
and that men do not frequent it to see nature, for that they can see
elsewhere, but to see nature represented. Ignorant artists some-
times put gold-leaf upon their pictures to impart a more striking effect
of gilding than could be done by paint, and destroy their pictures en-
tirely. The effect of a real horse, real furniture, or real water upon
the stage, is equally disastrous. They destroy the tone of the coloring.
It causes no feeling of incongruousness when we see a forest of
oaks growing out of a soil of pine boards, nor when a whole street
of marble palaces is suddenly drawn up into an atmosphere of can-
vass clouds; neither did it ever appear at all absurd to see Lady
Macbeth invite her guests to a banquet of tin pine-apples and paste-
board oranges, nor to see an actor whose salary you know does not
much exceed twenty shillings a week, pull a purse out of his pocket
bursting with pewter guineas; but if Lady Macbeth should point
to a dish of sodden deer on her table, which would be a probable
approximation to the scene intended to be represented, or the profli-
gate hero of the stage should fling about golden guineas, the reality
of the thing would produce feelings of disgust, because you do not
want to see realities, but realities represented. It is generally the
custom to introduce limbs of trees to represent the forest of Birnam
wood, and the scene is always spoiled by them.

The whole action of the *dramatis personæ*, to seem natural and
be acceptable to the spectators, must be a reversal of nature. They
must die with a set speech in their mouths, and without any of the
actualities of the close of life; if they happen to be run through
the body, they must not spill a drop of blood; if they have any secret
thoughts they must speak them out in a loud voice; if they have any
thing tender to say they must sing it, and let their impatience and
ardor be ever so fiery they must wait for two or three dozen fiddles
to play a prelude first, and if they sing particularly well, the chances
are that they will be compelled to stop in the midst of dying, or fight-
ing, or dancing, and repeat their song. A lady who should lift one
leg (pardon the word) to a horizontal position and turn herself round
on the other ' in a ball-room' would probably be tossed out of the
window; but ladies do so on the stage and receive showers of bou-

quets and puffs in the news-papers as rewards for their agility. There is nothing absurd in such things; they are evidences of consummate art, and the most artificial agents will always produce the most natural effects on the spectator. In the days of Æschylus, when the stage had no scenery and the actors wore masks, men swooned and women miscarried at the representation of a tragedy, but no body swoons in the theatre now except tight-laced ladies, and there are no miscarriages but on the stage.

[Although the taste for the theatre is almost universal, it is not a natural taste, as no artificial enjoyment can be. The mind must be educated to appreciate dramatic art as well as any other kind of art.] The meaning of stage signs must be learned before they can be enjoyed. Those who never go to the theatre until late in life never acquire a taste for it. All its shows appear ridiculous to them because they have no key to their meaning. Even to old theatregoers, after a long absence, the stage seems absurd until they recover the lost tone of the mind. Theatres are probably more numerous in New-York than in any other city in the world with the same population. This does not arise from any greater love for spectacles among the people, nor from any particular attraction of the theatres, but from the great number of strangers constantly in the city whose evenings are unemployed, and from the ease with which the poor classes earn their money, the cheapness of living and the certainty of employment. [The wealthy classes are not the supporters of the theatre; they have abundant sources of amusement in their own houses, and are only attracted to the theatre by some foreign celebrity whom they go to see, and not to see the play. In the days of the artificial comedy, when Wycherly, Congreve and Vanbrugh held possession of the stage, the case was reversed; then the playhouse was the resort of the upper classes, who went to see themselves represented. Comedy then presented pictures of high life to suit the tastes of those who patronized her; they were the days of her glory; she died with Sheridan, and it is not likely that she will ever reäppear. What would be the use of putting wits and fine ladies and gentlemen on the stage when there is nobody to see them? Men, like monkies, are fond of seeing themselves reflected, and the mirror which holds itself up to nature must reflect the nature that presents itself. An entirely new class of personages people the stage now; heroic apprentices, the villains of the counter, and the wits of the oyster cellar; Yankees, negroes, pedlars and melodramatic boys, together with a few traditional highwaymen and Italian bandits. Learning, wit, high-breeding and gentility are all banished from the stage: every new play must be essentially low in its tone or it cannot succeed. The most popular play that has been produced the past twenty years is the 'Lady of Lyons,' which has two qualifications essential to success; it is highly artificial and thoroughly vulgar. It would be impossible for an educated audience to endure it. Claude Melnotte is a very ordinary bully, and Pauline is a whining simpleton, while the other personages, to speak as mildly as we can of them, are no gentlemen. But the Lady of Lyons

is played night after night to audiences who could derive no plea-
sure from 'As you Like It,' or the 'Beaux' Stratagem.'

No amusement, no institution of any kind indeed, can flourish if it
is opposed by the religious sense of the community. The religion of
a people is the type of their highest nature, and whatever their priests
disapprove will fail to secure the support of the highest classes, not
because it is forbidden by their religion, but because their will is the
religion of their priests. It is not the priests that make the religion,
nor the religion the people, but the people make both. The priest-
hood of this country disapprove neither of war nor slavery; they
bless the banners of our armies and go to battle with our soldiers;
they hold slaves themselves and prove from the Bible that it is law-
ful; but they denounce the theatre; they will neither enter its walls,
nor associate with its members; they will pronounce no blessings
upon it; they will serve as chaplains to an arsenal, and like M.
Michelet, implore Heaven's light to guard our sacred bayonets, but
they cannot be hired to ask a blessing upon the theatres. Yet the
theatre, like the Ordinary's punch in Jonathan Wild, is no where
spoken against in Scripture, while the sword is forbidden in every
page of it. The reason of this is that the theatre has become dis-
tasteful to the higher orders, because they have devised more refined
modes of entertainment, but the sword is still an instrument of profit
in their hands. Introduce the spirit of democracy into the army,
equalize the pay and honors of its officers and privates, and the pro-
fession of arms will become as irreligious as that of the stage, and
you will get no clergyman to pronounce blessings upon the sword
and the bayonet.

But this is rambling a long way from the Chatham, which we have
selected as a type of the theatre because it is nothing but a theatre.
People go to the Chatham neither for the stars, the scenery, the
music, the dancing, nor because it is fashionable, but because it is a
theatre. It is most favorably situated in the heart of a highly dra-
matic neighborhood, where every thing is essentially theatrical, and
Art has entirely banished Nature. Dealers in second-hand finery,
merchants who trade in copper jewelry, warehouses of painted
window-shades; auctions on the side walk, and a great variety of
showy and eloquent merchandisers surround the Chatham. There is
always the scent of roasted pea-nuts in the air, and bits of orange
peel on the pavement. A great number of foreign-looking gentle-
men with heavy black eyes and aquiline noses, who seem to be
ready dressed for a part, may be seen; and if you happen to pass by
with a coat on your arm, or any thing like a bundle in your hand,
ask you in a mysterious manner if you want to dispose of any thing?
There is so much glare and glitter in the street that you are hardly
sensible of a change when you enter the theatre and see the re-
markable picture of West Point on the drop-curtain suspended from
a proscenium of Egyptian architecture copied from the Tombs in
Centre-street. The stage of the Chatham being small, the manage-
ment confines itself solely to legitimate business, the illegitimate
drama requiring greater room for display. Prices are on the most

reasonable scale, the entrance to the dress-circle being but two shillings, while the pit is free for a shilling. The best of liquors may be had at the bar of the pit saloon for three cents per glass, and a relish of soused pigs'-feet or of pickled clams for a sixpence; so we were informed by a transparency illuminated by a tallow-candle. This is all legitimate, and strictly in accordance with dramatic usages.

The audience at the Chatham enter into the spirit of the scene with a hearty relish, which must be a great comfort to the performers. The dress-circle is mainly filled with the *elite* of Chatham-Square and the supreme bon ton of Catharine-street ladies, who have never spent a season in Paris, and who do not consequently annoy the audience by talking in a loud voice of the merits of Tallbeer and Greasy. Among them may be seen an occasional Hebraic countenance, surmounted by a gauze turban, such as are worn by the princesses of an oriental melo-drama, and by way of antithesis there are young ladies from the neighborhood of Rye and Mamaroneck, looking as fresh and clear as pinks with the dew on them. But the real audience of the Chatham will be found in the pit. The assembly here is both homogeneous and indigenous; those premature philosophers, the news-boys, form the greater part; there are young men in red shirts who belong to the Sound packets in James'-slip, and who make it a point to shout ' physic!' whenever the orchestra stops playing; there are apprentices who have about them a strong flavor of Catharine-market, and pale-faced young men, the most melancholy objects there, who are clerks in dry-goods stores in the Bowery and Grand-street; sometimes there is an inexperienced adventurer from Westchester, who having indulged in too many three cent glasses falls asleep as soon as he sits down, and when he wakes discovers that he has not only lost the play but his pocket-book also.

These are the true patrons of the drama; it is by their loose shillings that the Theatre lives. The stage presents them a better life, a better-looking one at least, than they see in their daily walks. It is true that the scenery is not quite equal to that which they might see if they would open their eyes, but it is high art to them, and satisfies their longings. The language they hear is fine, and the sentiments superfine. The best things of Sheridan Knowles and Bulwer are represented, and are admirably adapted to the understandings of the auditory. Shakspeare would hardly go down with the habitués of the Chatham; he would not be fine enough for them; his tragedies are not sufficiently theatrical; they are wanting in poetical justice. Virtue must be rewarded and vice punished on the stage, and every mystery must be cleared up before the curtain falls. The villain of the piece must always meet with his deserts. This is an important lesson to impress upon the minds of the young. If this could be remembered always, who would be a villain? Men of Dr. Cheever's turn of mind, who insist that rogues shall be hung in this world, lest they escape punishment in the next, must take great delight in the morality of the stage, which never allows a villain to escape. Such tragedies as

'George Barnwell,' where there is a gallows and a hanging in the
last act; or 'Don Giovanni,' where the devil himself bears off the
offender in a flame of blue fire, must be highly attractive to the
friends of the gallows. 'Measure for Measure' is not often put upon
the stage, but if Mr. Duvernay would bring it out at the Chatham
he might count upon a large audience of the coadjutors of Tayler
Lewis, who, we cannot help thinking, would crowd there to hear
the jailer call so lustily to Master Barnardine to get up and be
hanged. The 'Beggar's Opera' has a most tragic ending for the ama-
teurs of the cord and cross-tree. The reprieve of Macheath is said
to have drawn tears from Lord Thurlow, who was never known to
weep before. This play has fallen into disrepute with play-goers,
mainly, we believe, because the catastrophe violates the require-
ments of dramatic justice; and if Dr. Cheever, or some other friend
of the gallows, would alter the catastrophe by hanging Macheath,
we have no doubt that it would revive its popularity, at least among
a certain class of religious people.

Rich people who live in the fashionable avenues and worship
once a week in luxurious churches, can well afford to renounce the
theatre and look with magnificent contempt upon such places as
the little Chatham. They have no need of the drama; they play
parts themselves. They can hire singers to amuse them in their
own parlors, and get up *tableaux vivant* at home. But the habitués
of the Chatham are denied entrance into fashionable houses; they
know that there is another and a better world than their's, even in
this life, and a longing to have a glimpse of it sends them to the
theatre. There they see the insides of palaces, and listen to the
talk of kings and statesmen. They learn how things are done in
the upper circles, and hear royal lovers make love, and meet in
cabinets with prime ministers and statesmen. And, O! most glorious
privilege! the ragged boy who has sold penny papers all day, and
eaten his dinner by the side of a fire-plug for the convenience of
water, may at night see a queen in a blue satin robe curtesy to him,
and hear her thank him for his applause. Sir Lytton and Sheridan
Knowles may have imparted refined delight to many of the aspiring
spirits of Catharine-street, who, after retailing cheap muslins all
day, rise superior to their condition at night, and indulge in cheap
sentiments at the Chatham. There may be better ways of spend-
ing an evening than by listening to romantic sentiments at the thea-
tre; but there are certainly much worse which might be fallen into
by those who patronize the Chatham if that Thespian temple were
closed.

It is not easy to fathom the opposition which professedly religious
people in this country make to such places of rational amusement
as the Chatham. The same men who parade our streets in military
uniforms would feel themselves degraded in associating with a
stage-player, and a colonel of the regular army, who hires himself
to butcher human beings for the privilege of wearing a pair of
epaulettes, is received into company which would not tolerate the
presence of an actor. The Chatham is not the place that we should

select for our own amusement, but it is well adapted for the amusement of other human beings who have quite as good a title to their way of enjoyment as ourselves. We frequently hear people talk of the *élite* of society ; we do not know where they are to be seen, but doubtless some of the choicest spirits on the east side of Broadway may be found at the Chatham ; genteel dealers in feather-beds and auctioneers of second-hand furniture. Very refined people who snuff the air of the Park, whose drawing-rooms open into marble conservatories, where tiny fountains spout from gilded swans among oranges and rhododendrons, may well afford to do without the Chatham. With them it would be descending to a lower position even to enter its dress-circle ; but not so to the denizens of Cherry-street and Cheapside ; for there is a Cheapside in New-York, though you may never have heard of it. Probably none of your acquaintances live there. What of that ? somebody's acquaintances live there : mothers, daughters, sisters ; little prattling boys, the delight of grand-parents, and real living men, whom you may some time meet in heaven, do actually inhabit these unknown parts of the city. It is necessary sometimes to mix among the people and study their habits if you would benefit them. There was once a good caliph, of whom we have all read or heard, who used to go among his people without any of the marks of his royalty, and many an important lesson he learned while so doing, both for his own good and that of his people. Clergymen, philanthropists, and students of human nature ; all in short who have the good of their fellow beings at heart, should look into the amusements of—we must say it, for want of a better term—the lower orders.

It is not long since we heard an eloquent Churchman preach a begging sermon before a fashionable congregation in behalf of a society whose object was the sending of proper reading books to Turkey. The preacher showed himself quite familiar with the necessities of the poor Turcomans, and lamented in set phrases, which we observed had a potent effect upon the purses of his hearers, the debasing effects of their literature. Doubtless there is not a preacher in this great city capable of enlightening his congregation on the subject of the amusements which are nightly offered to thousands of young minds at the Chatham. But why should it be so ? Are these youths of less consequence than Turcomans ? Does familiarity with their condition breed contempt ? Or is it essential to wear a turban to excite the sympathies of benevolent christians ? Suppose instead of sending two thousand dollars' worth of books to Constantinople for free distribution among the subjects of the Grand Turk, that the half of that amount were expended in putting a proper play on the boards of the Chatham ? Can any one doubt which outlay would produce the greatest harvest of good fruits ? We think not. Is it not better to make entire christians of the half-christianized youths of our back-streets than to make half-christians of the pagan Karens ? There is a small province in India which contains but a hundred and twenty thousands souls, where the American churches support six missionaries, at an annual expense of twenty thousand dollars, and their efforts are nearly paralyzed by the reports which reach the people among whom they labor, of the unchristianlike conduct of the churches that send them; at least so the missionaries themselves report. GOD forbid that we should utter a syllable against the noble enthusiasm that sends missionaries to heathen countries. Let the system be good or bad, we cannot but reverence the spirit which animates the people who support it. But do not let us be forever looking abroad. Let us bring our eyes to a focus near home. [St. Paul did not disdain to enter the theatre at Corinth. Any of our clergymen may enter the Chatham without raising the tumult which the presence of the apostle caused among the worshippers of Diana.]

[The Bishop of London recently made a voyage of discovery among some of the meanest haunts of the meanest members of his diocese, and great good resulted from it. Our godly men must not be outdone by a cockney bishop. Doff your canonicals for one night only, and come with us to the Chatham. See what kind of food the young men about town are living upon.] Laugh with them if you can, or weep with them if you prefer it. See how they applaud a fine sentiment, and with what appreciating gusto they clap their hands at the punishment of vice and the reward of virtue. It may disgust you to see women with painted faces; natural rouge is better than artificial, every body will allow. But are you positive, Doctor, that there is no liquid rouge ever seen in your church? are you sure that all those ringlets which you see of a Sunday morning, enough to make St. Anthony forget himself, are the natural products of the heads whereon they dangle? Is every thing pure and spotless in those costly pews? Come, now; do n't be too severe upon the rouge; it may be one of the means of procuring bread for an old mother or a helpless sister. Remember again that there are very few complexions, excepting very rummy ones, that can be seen to advantage in the glare of gas lights, which unnaturally illuminate the face from below and deprive it of its natural shadows.

It is one of the most unprofitable debates in the world to argue about the morality of the stage or the necessity of it. It is enough for you to know that it exists, that a portion of the people will have it, and that many good people approve of it. It is an unprofitable way of spending time, but is there none more so? Are militia trainings better? Are balls and parties, where you sometimes act parts yourselves, better? All the elements of which plays are made up are singly approved by you; why are they more objectionable for being combined? You do not denounce pictures, poetry, music, declamation or costumery. The theatre offers nothing more. You read Shakspeare and Schiller; why not listen to their verses when fitly spoken? Your daughter spends months and years in practising on the piano; you hire choristers to sing hymns for you on Sundays; why do you object to the same music in a theatre which is profitable to you in church? But you will not go to the little Chatham. The news-boys and pawnbrokers' wives will have it all to themselves. Mr. Morris will run through his range of business and not a soul of you will be the wiser for it. Pauline will extract no tears from your eyes, and fat Jack shall raise no smiles upon your faces. By and by the curtain will fall, and the little Chatham and the Gothic churches will be blotted out together.

THE PROUD BEAUTY'S BRIDAL.

BY ANNA BLACKWELL.

A POET sat in his Lady's bower ;
There lay on his heart a withered flower
She had given to him in a vanished hour.

The poet knelt to the Lady fair ;
To him she was 'lovely, beyond compare ;'
' I 'll do for thee all that a mortal may dare !'

The Lady carelessly shook her head :
' My wealthiest suitor will I wed !'
Oh! what cared *she* for hearts that bled?

The glance of her eye was proud and cold ;
She had pledged her hand for shining gold
To a creature lustful and shrunken and old !

He rose from the feet of the Lady fair,
He folded his arms with a lordly air :
' Thou art neither worthy my love nor care !'

The Lady curled her lip in scorn ;
Was ever so haughty a beauty born ?
' You shall see me wed at to-morrow's morn !'

The sun shone out on the bridal gay ;
The poet was there with a princely array,
And a star on his breast as bright as the day !

He greeted the bride with a scornful smile,
As he placed 'mid the velvet's snowy pile
A withered flower on her bosom the while.

' I bow,' quoth he, ' to the mighty power
That offers to Beauty a *golden* flower !
I give you joy of your bridal bower !'

Then lightly he leapt on his charger gay,
And laughed aloud as he rode away :
The Lady glanced on her bridegroom gray !

A F R I E N D I N D E E D.

BY JAMES KENNARD, JR.

A NURSE more tender, friend more true,
  Man never saw, man never can see,
Than ever unto me has been,
Through many a dark and painful scene,
  The good, warm-hearted NANCY !

Her kind attention never flags,
  She faileth in no exigency ;
No mother to her child could be
Devoted more than she to me :
  The generous-hearted NANCY !

When sorely crippled in each limb,
  As one may feel, but none can fancy,
She lifts me then, with gentle care,
From chair to couch, from couch to chair
  The dear, kind-hearted NANCY !

When racked with pain in every joint,
  She practiseth true necromancy ;
And by her soothing kindness then
Drives pain away, brings ease again :
  A true physician, NANCY !

When melancholy fills my mind
  With many a dark and dreary fancy,
With cheerful voice and laughter gay
She drives my gloomy thoughts away :
  A true consoler, NANCY !

Of a large portion of my heart
  She hath the rightful occupancy ;
And there, while life and sense remain,
Her image shall its place retain ;
  The noble-hearted NANCY !

When I am gone, O may it prove
  No idle and unfounded fancy,
That, whether in her joy or wo,
She 'll think of him who lieth low ;
  I know thou wilt, dear NANCY !

And when I reach the ' better land,'
  Where sorrow hath no occupancy,
My joy can never be complete
Till in those realms of bliss I meet
  With thee again, dear NANCY !

Portsmouth, N. H.

LIGHTS AND SHADOWS OF FASHIONABLE LIFE.

BY PATER SCHFMI

'ICH habe geschen, was (Ich weiss das) ich nicht würde geglaubt haben auf ihre Erzählung.'
TREVIRANUS, TO COLERIDGE.

'I have seen what I am certain I would not have believed on your telling.'

CHAPTER SIXTH.

In WHICH MRS. SMITH REQUESTS THE GENTLEMAN IN BLACK TO RELATE SOME OF THE INCI-
DENTS OF HIS LIFE: HER REASONS ARE GIVEN: THE GENTLEMAN IN BLACK STATES THAT
HE IS IN PURSUIT OF PETER SCHEMIL:* CAUSES WHICH COMPELLED HIM TO RECOVER HIS
PURSE: THE GENTLEMAN IN BLACK ELECTED UNANIMOUSLY INTO THE BOARD OF BROKERS:
HIS OPERATIONS: 'OLD NICH.' AND HIMSELF RIVALS IN 'THE STREET;' THE CAUSES WHICH
LED TO THE DESTRUCTION OF THE GREAT BANK — TO THE LATE WAR WITH ENGLAND:
FAILURES OF THE FRIENDS OF THE GENTLEMAN IN BLACK: SETTLES WITH HIS FRIENDS, ETC.

THE Gentleman in Black now rose, and proposed to Mrs. Smith
returning to the saloon, to which she readily acceded ; and resuming
her seat before the mirror, with a look of gentle entreaty, she asked
the Gentleman in Black ' if she was not to be told something re-
lating to his own adventures, and which she had rather know than
any of the scenes he might present her in the glass.'

The Gentleman in Black was really embarrassed by the request,
and reluctantly took his seat on the lounge, with the air of one quite
at a loss how to meet the request which had been made of him.
His air of embarrassment only tended to incite the lady's curiosity,
and to make her gaze the more inquiring and earnest.   The Gentle-
man in Black looked up smiling, and said :

' The interest you have so kindly expressed in my fortunes is every
way gratifying, and the only difficulty I find in the matter is to select
from among the incidents of my life some one or more which may
give you pleasure.'

* NOTE BY THE EDITOR. — ' The Wonderful History of PETER SCHEMIL,' or ' SCHLEMIHL,' has
been variously related by several authors, who have taken the usual liberty of historians of telling
the story in the way best suited for their own purposes. The most popular, and that best known, is
related by ADELBERT VAN CHAMISSO, and was first introduced to English readers in 1824, illustrated
by the plates of CRUIKSHANK.   The story thus told was in those days ascribed to LA MOTTE
FOUQUÉ, and for a while attracted great attention.   From that time, PETER has been invisible, until
he was recalled to the world's regard by the translation of WILLIAM HOWITT, two years since. But
as there may be many of our readers to whom this ' Wonderful History' is unknown, and as we have
every reason to believe that the veritable PETER is on this side of the Atlantic, it may not be amiss to
give the reader some outline of his wonderful history, corrected in such manner as to present what
we are assured are the real facts in the case, and which the license of authorship has in some points
varied from the verities as existing in the life and adventures of our real PETER SCHEMIL.   CHA-
MISSO relates with great beauty and grace the interview of our PETER with the rich Mr. THOMAS
JOHN; the reception of the poor student by that *millionaire* ; his meeting in the train of his friends,
and servitors, the GENTLEMAN IN BLACK, who is caricatured as ' still, thin, lanky, longish, oldish
man, dressed in an old French grey taffety coat.' Now that the GENTLEMAN IN BLACK may be
somewhat given to masquerades of various sorts, we may well imagine, but we do not believe in any
such sort of descriptions as that given by CHAMISSO.   The wonderful pocket of the GENTLEMAN IN
BLACK is very justly described as being singularly capacious; but though we can readily believe it
may have contained English plasters, if need be, to apply to a lady's finger, wounded accidentally by
a thorn, or of a telescopic glass to help the vision of Mr. THOMAS JOHN's guests, we yet find ourselves
compelled to pause and hesitate as to the possibility of its capacity, when we are asked to believe
CHAMISSO'S narrative that the GENTLEMAN IN BLACK really did draw from his pocket, in compliance
with the request of the lovely girl who asked him ' whether he had not, perchance, a tent by him,'
' canvass, poles, cordage, iron work, in short every thing which belongs to the most splendid pleasure-

' If that be all,' said Mrs. Smith, ' I will at once relieve you by requesting you to tell me how long you have been in town, and what may have brought you here ?   I 'm half ashamed of my curiosity, but then it is the custom of the country, and as I shall desire to introduce you to the circles of my friends, they will of course expect me to inform them as to all these particulars ; so you will see it is no mere curiosity that impels me, but the desire to make you at home with us.'

' You are indeed very kind — *very* kind,' answered the Gentleman in Black, with an air of the greatest courtesy and respect.   ' I shall be most happy to become more intimately acquainted with each and all of your friends, but of all and above all, my dear Madam, with yourself.'

' Oh indeed, I think,' replied Mrs. Smith, gaily, ' we may as well write ourselves down as old friends and familiar acquaintance ; no one need know that it is not so ; but that it may be so, you see I must needs know who my old friend and familiar acquaintance is, and what has brought him to the city.'

'Certainly ; and I will at once tell you.   You have doubtless heard of PETER SCHEMIL ?'

' What, poor PETER SCHEMIL who sold his shadow for a purse of gold ?   Yes, I have heard of him many years since ; but what of him ?'

' Well, my dear Madam, I have come to this country to seek him out, and to punish him for his many acts of inconceivable injustice toward me ; a more base and desperately wicked fellow is not to be found : through his mischievous agency I have been all but ruined and disgraced in all the countries of Europe ; represented as a mere shadow myself, dressed in a garb of poverty, and the slave of an upstart *millionaire* whom he calls Thomas John.   And what is the charge he has preferred against me ?   Why, that I exchanged my purse of Fortunatus for this miserable shadow !'   So saying, the Gen-

tent; and our power of credence is altogether surpassed when he is represented as pulling 'three beautiful great black horses with saddle and caparison — three saddled horses ! — out of the same pocket from which already a pocket-book, a telescope, an embroidered carpet twenty paces long and ten broad, a pleasure-tent of equal dimensions, and all the requisite poles and irons, had come forth !' We are assured by *our* PETER that the facts of his private history as stated by CHAMISSO are in the outline fairly given ; that he did sell his shadow to the GENTLEMAN IN BLACK for the purse of FORTUNATUS, but that when he did so he had not a single stiver in his pocket, and his last hope of employment had failed him in the arrogancy with which Mr. THOMAS JOHN had treated him ; that the purse is fittingly described as 'a tolerably large, well-sewed Corduan leather purse, with two stout strings,' into which as often as he plunged his hand gold pieces could be drawn out in any number that might be desired ; that the loss of his shadow caused him all the inquietudes, and far more, than are sketched by CHAMISSO ; that his admiration of FANNY and love for MINA are but poor portraitures of the power of grace, over his own unhappy destinies ; that the desire of the GENTLEMAN IN BLACK to get the *substance*, having possessed himself of his *shadow*, is all very judiciously narrated ; but that he, PETER, should throw into a deep well the Corduan purse which had cost him so much, is altogether a mistake, or a poetical license, as the reader will hereafter see. Indeed, nothing could have been more absurd than such a course of conduct; for what is a man without money ? The method by which our PETER became *invisible* is related by CHAMISSO in a way more improbable than need have been ; but the buying of the seven-league boots is perfectly true, and also the surprise attending his first essay at the use of them. It may be necessary hereafter to make some extracts from CHAMISSO, in explanation of a few things, which will be found stated by the GENTLEMAN IN BLACK in his conversations with Mrs. SMITH ; and these will be inserted as notes at the foot of the page, where they may be required. With this introductory note, we shall now let the series proceed, simply stating, that the GENTLEMAN IN BLACK is still seeking to secure the body of the now invisible PETER, whose presence among us will, we hope, be a matter of very general interest.

tleman in Black put his hand into his pocket and taking out what
seemed like a roll of very delicate tissue paper or fine silk, shook
out the very shadow of the poor miserable Peter, which at the re-
quest of Mrs. Smith, who handed him some pins, which must have
been taken from some covert part of her own dress, the Gentleman
in Black pinned up on the drapery of the window, which, as has
been already stated, hung loose by the rings.

'And that is the very shadow!' said Mrs. Smith.

'Yes Madam, the identical shadow.'

'After all, it is not much of a shadow; and you gave him an in-
exhaustible purse for that shadow?'

'No, Madam, that is one of Peter's lies — his rascally frauds. I
loaned him the purse for a stipulated period, and he, not content
with the use of the purse for the time specified, ran off with it,
Madam — absconded! And more than that, he has by some ras-
cally process which I do not understand possessed himself of *invis-
ibility*, and having no shadow, you may guess the trouble I have
had in seeking him and of recovering my purse; a matter of the
utmost importance to me, as you may guess; and as it is desirable
you should know of the causes which led me to this country at this
time, it may be well to tell you the misfortunes which made it ne-
cessary for me to chase this fugitive, who with his seven-league
boots has thus far eluded my pursuit; but his flight is somewhat re-
tarded by the loss of his boots.'

'And has he lost his boots?'

'Yes, Madam; they were by a happy accident, stolen from him.
But I am anticipating my story.'

'I beg you will not, but tell me it in due order. I am sure it
must be very surprising — seeking a man without a shadow or a
body, endowed with seven-league boots, too; it must be to you no
common task.'

'My dear Madam, you make a mistake. He has a *body*, but not
visibility.'

'Well, it is wonderful; and I beg you will tell me all about it.'

'I am fearful,' said the Gentleman in Black, 'that I shall weary
you with my story, and that it will rob you of your repose, which
you must need after so much fatigue of body and mind as you have
gone through with this day.'

'I thank you, my dear Sir, for your kind consideration of my
comfort; but the fact is it would be utterly impossible for me to
sleep after so much nervous excitement, and it will be quite a re-
lief to me to be amused and interested, as I am sure to be, by the
relation you have promised me.'

The Gentleman in Black commenced by saying: 'I met Peter
Schemil a poor fellow, in the depths of poverty and despair; and
touched by sympathy for his extreme melancholy, I offered him the
use of my purse for the slender shadow you see there,' pointing to
the curtain, 'which shows the effects of poor fare and hard study;
and though he has always denied the fact, it was well understood at
the time that for the use of the purse so given, the shadow was but
the pledge of the body, to be surrendered at some future period.'

'What could he do for you, that he was so desirable to you?'

'I wanted him to be my *amanuensis*, as he is very remarkable for the rapidity of his hand-writing, though it requires some scholarship to make it out; but the especial reason why I have been compelled to seek him I will now state to you, and you will see that, however worthless he may be, my purse which he held has lost none of its value.'

'It is now some twenty years since I came to this city, merely to pass the winter and spring, and to return to Europe in June following. I had not been in the country for some years, and wishing to be as quiet as possible, I took private rooms at the 'Star Hotel,' and entered my name as THOMAS JONES, and for a while was perfectly secure in my *incognito ;* but accidentally meeting with some old friends, who had become the conspicuous operators in Change Alley, I was drawn out from my retreat and almost compelled to accept their earnest and most hospitable invitations to their several houses. I assure you I was not at all prepared for the astonishing changes I found in their circumstances. Men whom I had left dealing in merchandise and stocks, in small sums, living in modest houses at a rent of four or five hundred dollars a year, now received me in splendid mansions, costing in themselves a fortune, and these were filled with the finest furniture, and adorned with mirrors of surpassing size and beauty. Their walls were covered with pictures, more remarkable for their antiquity than any beauty I could discern in them, but which they assured me were from the pencils of the old masters. One of them even showed a '*Madonna in the Chair,*' of which he had a smoky certificate pasted on the back, stating it to be a duplicate of that wonder of the art in the Pitti palace; and another had a '*Fornarini,*' which he convinced me was genuine, though I was somewhat skeptical at first, but of which I could no longer doubt when he showed me in the depth of the coloring of the shadow of her *dress,* the monogram of RAPHAEL himself. There was one picture to which my especial attention was called, and upon which I was specially requested to pass my opinion. It seemed to me a mere mass of black paint, relieved by some few white spots; but what it was designed to represent was altogether beyond my skill to discover; and finding myself so perfectly at a loss, and not daring to venture a guess, I candidly confessed the embarrassment in which I was placed. My friends, for it was at a dinner party, all cried out, it 'was capital,' 'a most admirable criticism,' there was 'nothing but black paint to be seen,' etc.; but our host, not at all disconcerted, said that 'the picture was a '*Salvator Rosa,*' and we should see it to be so, and he should enjoy our surprise.' So he directed all the shutters to be closed save a single half window; and to be sure, there was discernible some armed men at the entrance of what we were told was a cave, in the act of throwing dice, and in the foreground some pieces of plate. 'There,' said he, 'there 's *the triumph of art !*' He looked for applause, and it was given; for who could resist to applaud the taste of a gentleman who gave good dinners, and whose wines were faultless? To be sure, the merits of a picture so plastered with dark brown and black paint as to be undistin-guishable, was not so much to my taste as his dinners and wines were ; yet as he assured us it was a genuine ' Salvator Rosa,' having swallowed his wines I must needs do the same with his pictures. I assure you, my dear Madam, this is no exaggeration of the ' old masters' which I have had exhibited to me in this country. But whatever may have been my misgivings as to the genuineness of the particular ' old masters,' I had no doubt as to the sums paid for them, of which they showed me the receipted bills in order to make ' assurance doubly sure.' And though even then I might have had some lurking suspicions that in these matters my friends may have taken the copy for the original, I could not be mistaken as to the solidity and costliness of the rich plate with which their tables were literally covered. I have visited merchants of other countries, but none whose riches were more *apparent* than that of my friends in Babylon. It seemed as if the lamp of Aladdin had come into their possession, and that the wealth I saw in all their houses was created by some process purely magical.

' Nor was my surprise limited by these exhibitions of taste and luxury. Their entertainments were varied and costly, their wines unsurpassed, except in the palaces of some of the princes of the German Empire. 'T is true they had no Johannisberg in their bot-tles, but the labels were in their proper places on the outside of them ; and I was assured, and had no reason to doubt, that every bottle cost as much as the Johannisberg would have done had Prince Metternich brought his few hundred pipes into the wine market, instead of supplying only the tables of kings and emperors, as he is accustomed to do. The wine was indeed admirable, and was drank with a gusto, and the glass was held up to the eye before drinking with that knowing air which few have any knowledge of, and which distinguishes men who know what they drink and how to drink.

' Our conversation I found took a uniform turn to stocks ; to grand systems of improvement of the country; digging canals, laying down rail-roads, and establishing new lines of packets, with some peculiarity of terms as to making a good ' corner' on this stock, and ' hammering down' another stock, and ' bursting a bank' now and then; all of which I was told were ' fair business transactions.' They sometimes held a long talk as to getting up a ' *leader*' for the organs of the party for a particular purpose; and on such occa-sions two or more would retire to a side-table to prepare the arti-cle, which was to be read and approved by the assembled party; or it might be to get up a set of patriotic resolves for congress, for their legislature, or for a ward committee. Indeed, there were few things these friends of mine did not take in hand; and so varied and multiform were their movements, that I was perfectly at a loss to conceive to what all these things tended. I was indeed charmed by the frankness with which they alluded to these matters before me, almost a stranger as I was to some of them; and seeing that they spoke of their monied affairs as being so prosperous, of which indeed I had the most marked and beautiful manifestations in every thing that surrounded me, I ventured to mention, with no little diffidence, and as one hazarding a very great request, to a compliance with which I had no claims whatever, that I had some spare capital in foreign stocks which paid very low interest, and if they could point out a way of a better investment of this money it would be conferring on me a very great favor to let me take some small amount of their stocks, which seemed so safe and lucrative. With a frankness and cordiality altogether irresistible, they at once told me it would gratify them all to make me a partner in their plans, all of which were sure to succeed. Nothing could have been more hearty than their several expressions of their readiness to aid and serve me; and although I have had some acquaintance with men, I assure you I was for once perfectly disarmed of all suspicion of guile in these capitalists and financiers.

'They asked me what amount of capital I had at command; and when I told them that the amount of funds invested in stocks of the Bank of Amsterdam, which was then paying me but two and a half per cent., was some fifteen hundred thousand dollars, but that in the French funds I had some six millions of francs, beside other stocks in the English funds, all of which I would willingly transfer to stocks paying six and seven per cent. per annum. The looks of pleasure and surprise with which they received this announcement should have excited in me some suspicion and watchfulness; but I must confess their expressions of pleasure at being able to serve me were so natural, and had so much of frank and noble bearing in them, and were seasoned with so many agreeable things complimentary to myself, that I confess to you, my dear Madam, I became the dupe of my own vanity.

' The next week or two passed as the previous weeks had done; dinners almost every day; concerts, the opera or the churches; soirées, evening parties, with glorious suppers, followed in unbroken succession. There were no more nor less attentions on the part of my friends, but somehow I found myself every day more and more in the society of two or three of these friends, who were either more assiduous in their attentions, or that, by a concert of action on the part of the others, these, more adroit than the others, were appointed to manipulate me ready for the general use of the set. From these friends I first received the idea of settling in Babylon the Less for a few years, in which I was assured I could double my capital; and although at first the idea did not present itself to me in an attractive form, yet by degrees it was made to wear a very bright and cheerful aspect; so that at length I consented to entertain the idea as one which might possibly be adopted.

' One day, after a dinner of more than ordinary excellence, I found myself seated with these especial friends in a saloon emptied of the company, who were all attracted into the other rooms to hear a splendid pianist who had been invited to the feast; and in a tone of whispering confidence one of the three said, ' They had been thinking of the various ways in which the wish I had expressed of investing my funds in Babylonian stocks could be best carried into effect ; but the sum was so large and the responsibility so great, that with all the friendship they so sincerely entertained for me, they were compelled to say they felt it too great a responsibility for them to assume.' This was said with tones of voice truly touching; indeed, I verily believe there were tears in his eyes as he uttered these words. What could I say ? So far from seeking the control of my monies, they really seemed to shun the trust they feared I was too ready to impart. How could I distrust such generous, devoted and dear friends ? In fact all suspicion was at an end, and I was ready to adopt any advice they had to offer. They told me they had agreed to advise me to become a member of the Board of Brokers in Change-Alley, and then I could make my own investments ; in doing which they were always at hand to help me, and with my permission they would at once propose my name at the next session of the Board.

'Although I had but little idea of the honorable fraternity of brokers, whose sessions are all secret, yet as my friends were members I was ready to consent, though I could not but express my fears that I should be ' black-balled;' a method of ostracism which is very much practised in this city by gentlemen, who have adopted this plan for preserving their union clubs, boards of directors, and other select and *distingué* associations, from any admixture with those whose claims to membership in the *haut-monde* have been jeoparded by their occupations and employments, and which serve for gentlemen the same purpose as the *Virtuous Indignation Societies*, of which you have told me, do for the ladies. Indeed I was told, so very scrupulous had their clubs become, that the grandsons, and sons even, of those who had, to use the expression of Mrs. Trippe, ' cut candles,' had mercilessly rejected all applicants whose callings had led them to *cut broadcloth* in any lines but those at right angles, whatever might be their standing in society on the score of wealth. All deviations from a straight line was like a *bar-sinister* on their escutcheons, and forever excluded them from admission into those palaces of red sand-stone into which they sought the right of *entrée*.'

'That seems a strange decision,' exclaimed Mrs. Smith ; ' why should curve lines be considered so disreputable ?'

'It is hard to say, and yet mankind have ever had these freaks of fancy. The two great sects of Omar and Ali of Persia, for example, have been created out of the differences in the manner of performing their ablutions. The point in dispute is simply this ; whether the water shall be poured on at the wrist and so run to the elbow, or poured on at the elbow so as to run down to the wrist. And too the great schism of the eastern and western churches arose on the mere question as to the proper day on which EASTER was to be celebrated.'

' Pardon me for interrupting you : but is this the only difference existing between the Greek and Roman churches ?'

' This was the point of divergence ; they differ too somewhat after the manner of the Persians, as to the mode of applying water in their religious rites; the Greek Church, with the Emperor Nicholas for its champion, stoutly contending that the infant shall be wholly immersed three times when baptized, and the Catholic are content with pouring the water on the face; a difference quite sufficient to spill blood about.'

'You speak as though men had a particular love for spilling each other's blood about trifles,' said Mrs. Smith; 'nothing of the sort happily now exists.'

. 'The rack and the stake are to be sure somewhat out of fashion, and the present state of civilization is unfriendly to such obvious manifestations of a principle still vigorous and active. My dear Mrs. Smith, can you tell me the difference between 'excommunication' and the fashionable phrase of 'excision,' adopted so recently in this country, when hundreds of churches of one school *excinded* hundreds of churches of another school, all claiming to be the real Simon Pures? and this too about a question so inexplicable as to puzzle Duns Scotus and the 'old school' men of his day?'

'Pray can you tell me what was the *gist* of that great controversy?—Do you know?'

The Gentleman in Black shrugged his shoulders and said: 'Yes, I had the honor of a seat as a corresponding member in the General Assembly. I took no part in the discussion, though I have been blamed by both parties; so hard it is to please every body. The question in dispute wore various phases, and became at last a division of the south against the north.'

'How very strange! But it must have been based upon some sort of doctrine, was it not?'

'Yes, it was affirmed by the leader of the old school that its 'pivotal,' as the *Fourierists* would say, was the reply to the question in the celebrated Westminster Catechism: 'What is sin?' The old school contending that it should stand as it now reads: 'Sin is any want of conformity to, or transgression of, the law of God.' The new school were for the last clause only.'

'Well, this is a nice distinction, truly!—quite equal to the sects of ALI and OMAR. I shall not puzzle my head about which is right. Pray let me ask the question, now it occurs to me, do you attend the coming 'World's Convention'?'

''A burnt child dreads the fire!'' replied the Gentleman in Black, smiling. 'After all the experience I have had, I am done with councils and convocations and general assemblies of all sorts, especially of this last; for whatever course I should adopt I should be sure to be misconstrued. If I advised adherence to the standards and confessions of faith, then I should be charged with sowing discord; and if I should counsel the relinquishment of all these, and propose some *stand-point* which all could adopt, then it would be said I counselled the giving up the old foundations of the faith, and would bring about a union more disastrous than a deluge of fire and brimstone, and which would finally engulph the churches in a *dead sea* of lifeless uniformity. So I have concluded to stay away.'

'I beg your pardon for leading you away from your story. What were you about to say?'

'Indeed, I do n't know what I might have said; perhaps it was, that this splitting of hairs is based upon the love of power, which lies deep in the human heart; and the more arbitrary the distinction, the more certain is the evidence of conformity to the governing will. If you please, I will go on with my story.'

'I beg you will; and I will promise not again to interrupt your narrative.'

'With the knowledge of these facts I have mentioned, I could not refrain to express my fears of being myself black-balled, when my assiduous friends told me that they had taken the liberty of sounding the leading members of the Honorable Board who had, as they assured me, responded to the suggestion with the greatest cordiality and kindness; so my wish to double my money getting the better of my fears, I consented to be proposed the next day.

'About noon of that day one of my friends called upon me to show me Change-Alley, which was destined to be the theatre of my operations as a stock-broker. As we walked down the street I saw on every side splendid buildings, all of which bore the signs of banks and brokers'-offices, and gave evidence of its being the centre of the monetary world. While I was thus leisurely gazing at the buildings on both sides of the street, I was startled by the sight of a sign painted to the life, of *a pelican in the act of swallowing a golden fish*, the tip of whose tail was only to be seen; the thought was instantly presented to my mind that this was ominous of the fate of those who adventured into 'the street.' Seeing me pause before it, and doubtless reading my misgivings in my countenance, my friend begged me to observe, 'that the pelican was not swallowing *a pelican*, but a *fish*, and that the art and mystery of the trade consisted in bringing into such critical conjunctures the golden fish which came in schools into that narrow inlet, and which fed the fat pelicans who, as in the picture before me, knew how and where to dispose of their prey.' This happy turn not only amused me but entirely dispelled all my forebodings.

'While we were standing conversing about this picture, a crowd of well-dressed gentlemen issued out of a great building, in the merriest mood, and my especial friend seeing me, ran over and shaking me by the hand, congratulated me on my good fortune. They told me 'I had been *unanimously* elected; that though there were upward of two hundred balls cast, not a black-ball was among them all; a piece of good fortune never known but once before since the Board was organized, when one of the most honest and true of all honest men, who had been compelled to withdraw from the Board in consequences of great losses he had met with from a desolating fire which had spread ruin in that section of the city upon hundreds of the first houses, had been, unsought by himself, unanimously reëlected into the Board; an expression of his high standing and of their confidence and respect, as unexpected as it was gratifying.' All I can say of the matter is this, that if he should be hereafter '*done* BROWN' as I have been, he has little reason to rejoice in the distinction so conferred.'

'My operations commenced very quietly, and these good friends of mine found me a plenty of golden fish, whom, like the pelican on the sign, I had no difficulty in swallowing; and in a short time I acquired, to use a familiar phrase, 'the tricks of the trade,' and by and by distinguished myself for some bold and successful operations. The fame of my wealth soon gained for me that consideration which money always commands, especially in Change-Alley. I had my 'hammers' to knock down a stock, or my 'bulls' to cry it up, as by turns it suited my purpose; and many a 'fat goose' was transformed into a 'lame duck' after passing through my magical manipulations. This was all very well for a time; but growing weary of these small matters I ventured upon regulating the cause of exchange. Now this was trenching upon the business of certain capitalists, and soon I found myself the 'observed of all observers,' and the courtesy and smiles and homage paid to me was only equalled by that which awaited on the celebrated 'OLD NICH.' whenever he came into Change-Alley, as he frequently did on visits from his Great Bank, over which he presided with the sway of an autocrat.

'It was truly amusing to see the aspect which some men wore when we both met on the same pavement. The monetary world no more than the physical world will bear two suns at the same time. As a matter of necessity therefore we were understood to be great rivals in all money affairs, and my compeers were somewhat at a loss how to conduct themselves when we stood on opposite sides of the street. It was hard for them so to shape their movements as to stand well with us both, and it was only such men as Van Zandt, and a few others equally dexterous, who could skip from side to side, and cry 'Good Lord!' and 'Good Devil!' in the same breath. It furnished us food for mirth, when 'Old Nich.' and myself met at night, as we were in the habit of doing, at the houses of some favorite and fair friends of his, with whom we supped, and amused ourselves, by talking over the incidents of the day, and repeating the dreadfully severe sayings which had been whispered to each other by the same set, which if they did not convince us that we were two of the most unscrupulous sharpers, satisfied us that they were the paragons of toadyism.

'These were the days of sunshine in the monied world of the Great Republic. In an evil day there came on a contest as to which city should be the centre of banking operations of the country. The aristocracy of Babylon could not brook the rule of 'Old Nich:' they determined that the central power should be removed from Chestnut-street to Change-Alley. And the stupid obstinacy of a pig secured to them what, but for his aid, would have been unattainable.

'A pig! what sort of a pig?' exclaimed Mrs. Smith.

'A very fine fat pampered pig, on four feet, with his tail done up as nicely as any lady's hair could be curled,' replied the Gentleman in Black.

' You do not mean what you say, I am sure,' replied Mrs. Smith, surprised at the unchanging gravity of the Gentleman in Black.

' I certainly do; I can demonstrate this to you beyond all manner of question; that but for the pig in question the monied relations of this country would have remained unchanged, and that the marble palace in which ' OLD NICH.' held his uncontrollable sway, instead of being what it now is, a mere office for the receipt of customs, would still have remained the throne of the monied men of the country.'

' You are speaking enigmas, which I fear no Œdipus can solve,' replied Mrs. Smith. ' Won't you be pleased to let me into the secret ?'

' With all pleasure, if it will not weary you to listen to it.'

' You need not fear any thing but failing to make good your assertions.'

' That I have no fear of. Then, to begin at the beginning. Had the administration of the republic been continued in the hands of the venerable son of Braintree, it cannot, in my opinion, be questioned that the charter of the Great Bank would have been extended and its seat perpetuated in Chesnut-street; that he failed in his reëlection I shall now trace to the pig in question; and you will see how nicely adjusted are the affairs of this great world, and on what slender pivots the destinies of a nation turn. Had a certain gentleman in the city of Providentio never been possessed of this obstinate pig, or had he kept him in a better built stye, ' the HERO of two wars' would have only been distinguished as a famous fighter of men and Indians, and gone to the grave in the humble obscurity of a western farmer; but for this pig, he would never have been elevated to the elective throne of Babylonia; and all the consequences resulting from his election would have been saved to the world.'

' My dear Sir, are you serious ?' inquired Mrs. Smith, who seemed more and more perplexed at the grave and severe tone of the Gentleman in Black.

' Never more truly so in my life; *but for that event I should not now be in Babylon.*'

' May I again beg you will explain what seems to me altogether inexplicable,' replied Mrs. Smith, with some slight expression of impatience, as if teased by his delay.

The Gentleman in Black proceeded in his usual calm and quiet tone to say :

' It is common for historians to spend no little time in tracing to their causes important events which change the current of a nation's history, and in doing so, from ignorance or inadvertence, they overlook incidents seemingly so trivial as to be utterly unworthy of the task they have assumed ; and though I do not undertake to state all the causes which had their separate influence in bringing about the conjuncture of affairs which made it possible for a pig to play so prominent a part, yet I feel certain of tracing to him the catastrophe.'

' There were two neighbors, both of the old Federal school of politics, who had lived for many years in the utmost harmony in the city of Providentio; one of whom was the owner of the pig, and the other possessed a fine garden, in the cultivation of which he took especial pains.　One fine spring morning the pig, waking hungry from a sound sleep, set up a squeal which expressed in the clearest manner his impatience for his breakfast, but as the family were at that time busy and occupied with making their own meal, he was left to wait; becoming restless, and as a lawyer would express it, if he were drafting a bill of indictment, 'being set on end by the devil,' regardless and reckless of all consequences, he clambered over the imperfectly-constructed stye and set out in quest of what he could find ' on his own hook.'　Now he had done this frequently before, and had amused himself in perambulating over the nicely-made beds in the neighbor's garden, into which he had found no difficulty of access from the condition of the fence.　There had been many friendly remonstrances as to this pig's familiar habits; and the one neighbor had urged the other to build a new stye, and to the other it had been kindly suggested that his fence was out of repair.　So matters stood; when the proprietor of the garden discovered the pig in the very act of rooting up and eating some choice bulbous roots, which were very valuable, and had been procured at great expense.　This was ' the last feather which broke the camel's back;' transported with passion, he put a pitchfork he chanced to find at hand into the sleek and tender sides of the pig, and threw him yelling into his neighbor's yard.　His cries though not the most musical were in so moving a tone, that the pig-proprietor and his family were disturbed at their breakfast table and came out in breathless haste to witness the last flourish of their pig's-tail, to hear his last squeal and to see him die.　That, my dear Madam, was the beginning of that bloodshed which was continued by the best blood of the great republic.'

' In consequence of this quarrel, at the coming election then about to take place, the proprietor of the pig voted against his neighbor, and his vote elected a democrat to the general assembly of that state. At the election of a senator to the Great Council of the Senate of the nation, a man devoted to the then Administration of affairs was elected by one vote; and in the year 1812 an act declaring war passed the Senate by one vote; the vote of the Senate elected by the vote of the representative, who was elected by the owner of the pig in question.　Now have I not shown the chain of causes thus far ?'

' Yes, you have ; but what has all this to do with the charter of the Great Bank ?'

' Oh that is readily seen.　The war which ensued terminated with a glorious victory which immortalized the ' Hero of two wars ;' he was made President by the leaders of the great people's party, who found no other way of defeating the election of the son of BRAIN-TREE, believing that when he was elected by their exertions and influence he would suffer himself to be guided by their councils.　But men who set a ball in motion are not always able to resist, when in motion, that which a single arm could have kept at rest. Unfortunately for me, and thousands of others, the first act of resistance to the indomitable will of the 'Old Hero' came from my worthy compeer and associate ' Old Nich.' This was his resistance to the appointment of an officer in one of his branch banks ; and if, instead of trying the strength of their several powers, 'Old Nich.' had submitted to this exercise of power, or made some quiet conciliatory explanations to the 'Old Hero,' who in all probability had ignorantly exceeded his administrative powers, all would have been well. But the habit of uncontrolled sway had been fostered in the heart of ' Old Nich.' by the submissive acts of brokers and bankers, whom he had taught to perform the prescribed *kow-tow*, when admitted into his presence, with an alacrity and skill only to be excelled by the courtiers of the Chinese empire. The hostility which grew out of this conflict in the exercise of appointing powers was fanned and fostered by the Jonathans and the Goodyears and their cliques in this city who saw in this reason for hope that if the charter of the bank should be rejected, a new bank, which they deemed indispensable, would be chartered, and which they felt certain would have its centre in Babylon. But it is easier to pull down than to build up ; and a power arose, unlooked for by them, greater than their own. The iron will of the ' Old Hero' was directed by this power behind the throne with a despotism they could not resist. The consequence was, a revulsion, which brought ruin to the homes and fire-sides of those whose whole scope of policy was limited to the increase of their own fortunes and the up-building of their own city.

' The outcry against the course of policy which struck at all chartered banking associations, and whose war-cry was ' perish credit, perish commerce,' perish every thing, that stands in the way of ' the will of the democracy,' and which for a time seemed to seek to bring every chartered corporation into jeopardy, at length came from those who had made him the god of the people's idolatry.

' Among these was a worthy citizen of this city, who had carried his devotion so far as to have the old hero's bust beautifully chiselled in Parian marble, and which was placed over his mantel-piece as its chief ornament. Here he was caressed, from time to time, by many pleasant love-pats, as one blow after another of his merciless policy struck down the heads of the monied hydra, whose ruin was so earnestly desired ; but when the same club reached other monied interests, and stock after stock declined, bank after bank gave way, and when ruin reached the worthy partisan, from the very idol of his creation and worship, with a feeling not unlike the poor Africans who flog their gods when their wishes are not complied with, coming home to his dinner, for which alas ! he had no appetite, and seeing this ' Architect of Ruin' sitting with his characteristic composure, all unconcerned amid the carnage he was making of the fortunes of his followers, as well as of his enemies, transported with rage, our citizen seized upon the bust and cast it down into an oblivion of shame and everlasting contempt; but Accident or Destiny, which ever made him great, took care of his Image. Through the zealous labors of a society who have done much to enrich the country by their antiquarian researches, the bust of the hero was recovered, and sold by them, heedless of the treasure, with a heap of rubbish. The purchaser, who told me the anecdote, kept his good fortune to himself, and the Old Hero was brought to light transformed into an old Roman, The alkalies of earth have given the Old Hero's face quite an ancient aspect, and there remained little else than the general contour of his face and bust, and the inscription, which had once been 'THE OLD ROMAN,' had become all but defaced. The bust, well washed, was put into the hands of a dealer in pictures of the '*old masters*,' which are annually imported into this market and sold at prices miraculously low, and there it soon attracted the attention of the *pseudo* iconographists of the city, who after mature examination determined it to be the bust of ROMULUS, and this question so decided, it was instantly purchased at a great price by an admirer of the antique, and now holds a conspicuous place in his cabinet, where he is venerated still, as the *oldest* if not the '*noblest Roman of them all*.'

'Pardon this digression, my dear Madam, from my own story, which I fear has already become to you wearisome ' as the twice-told-tale vexing the dull ear of a drowsy man.'

'By no means !' replied Mrs. Smith, with great vivacity. 'I am at a loss to know how this revulsion in the monetary world has connected itself with you, and compelled you to assume so hopeless a task as the finding of PETER SCHEMIL.'

'Not so hopeless as you may at first be led to think it; but all this by and by,' replied the Gentleman in Black, who resumed his narrative by saying:

'After I had fairly established myself in Change-Alley, and in doing so, had necessarily become connected very largely with the stock exchange, to which I exclusively confined my attention, though my kind friends were exceedingly anxious that I should share with them in their speculations in canals and stocks of various kinds, but my grasp of mind I found was too limited to keep sight of so many dissimilar speculations, and as I was succeeding to the utmost of my wishes, I declined their friendly offers, and as they found a plenty ready to unite with them, I was after a while left by them to quietly manage my business in my own way. Unhappily I was recalled by urgent business connected with my Eastern estates; a whole village had gone over to the Abolitionists, and my agents feared a general breaking up of all the ties in which they had been held to servitude ; and having the utmost confidence in my friends, who had won upon my regards by their hospitality and unceasing friendship, I thought it would be safe for me to place my monied securities in their hands to wind up.'

'But was it not a great trust to bestow ? Six or seven millions of dollars is too large a sum to be secured in the usual way, was it not ?' inquired Mrs. Smith.

'It was; but what better could I do? And beside, I had every reason to rely on these good friends, as I deemed them to be; and many little incidents calculated to win upon my unsuspecting confidence had arisen which had had their due weight with me; for example: one of them, a man of great amenity of manners, hearing accidentally from me in conversation that my people were destitute of the 'stated preaching of the gospel,' was extremely desirous of procuring the establishment of a mission among them; indeed, I found it very difficult to satisfy him that I thought they could get on without one. Another proposed some admirable plans 'for the colonization and gradual emancipation of my slaves;' and another swore 'I should go into a grand speculation he had in view for the purchase of coal lands which would never be exhausted while the world should stand.' I mention these among the many like manifestations of their active friendship; and receiving fresh despatches begging me to return at once and at all hazards, I called my friends together and gave into their hands all my books, bonds and bills, for which they jointly and severally receipted to me; and pledging themselves to obey my instructions, which were explicit, to invest my monies as they fell due in such undoubted monied stocks as they thought safest and best.

'Having done this, they gave me a magnificent entertainment, and the next day most of them went down as far as the Narrows, where they took leave of me with many earnest entreaties to take good care of myself, to which I responded very heartily, begging them not to forget me or my affairs.

'I was absent four years, and never so much as received a single stroke of a pen from any one of them. I felt some surprise at this, and on arriving in London, I was thunderstruck at hearing that my friend 'Old Nich.' had deserted his palace; that there had been a general suspension of specie payments in this country, and that a wide-spread bankruptcy had gone over the length and the breadth of the land. As you may well imagine, I felt there was no time to lose in coming to this country, and to see how far my own funds were jeoparded by this revulsion of the affairs of Babylonia, and Babylon in particular.'

'On my arrival I took my old rooms, and the same evening sent my cards to each of my friends, expecting they would at once come to see me. I sat up quite late, but not one of them called. This was rather ominous, I thought. The next day I remained at home till past twelve, and no one calling, I took a walk down Change-Alley. I met the members of the Honorable Fraternity as busy as ever; nearly all had failed, but as this was a general calamity, no one seemed to feel the pressure to be pinching him harder than his neighbor; and as 'misery loves company,' they seemed well content. 'Times,' they said, 'were mending rapidly;' 'hoped I had come back to 'the street;' they wanted some one who had plenty of money to regulate matters;' 'I was the very person they were all looking for;' and they really seemed to express their honest sentiments, and I believe they did; but when I told them all my means were in the hands of my friends in Change-Alley, they looked surprised; some thrust their tongues into one side of their cheeks, others whistled a little, but the most of them said, 'Come and see me; I am just now very busy;' and on they went.

'You may guess I had now very strong convictions that my affairs were in what they technically term 'weak hands;' by which is understood hands so strong that there 's no getting back what you have given them to hold. After looking into one old haunt and another, I stumbled upon one of my trustees; he certainly put the best face upon the matter, and said he had been seeking me; that he had a little party of our old set, and as they all wished to see me, he had on receiving my card sent out his invitations to meet me at his house at dinner at six precisely. His engagements, like all the others, were very pressing, and shaking me by the hand, he shook me off; and finding myself somewhat less important in 'the street' than I once was, I returned to my hotel to prepare myself for the 'entertainment' I had every reason to believe had been prepared for me a long time before my arrival.

'At six precisely I entered the mansion of my trusty trustee. The house was unchanged; the same servants, the same gorgeous furniture, and the same finely-dressed ladies, somewhat fuller and broader to be sure than when I left them, but this was doubtless owing to their style of dress, and the same circle of active and enterprising friends; all looking finely, a little wider over the waistband and somewhat care-worn about the eyes; but their laugh was hearty, while they assured me 'they were ruined past all redemption;' 'burst up;' 'not a figment left;' all owing to the malignant influences of that ' *Sheeted Ghost*,' and of Oliver Dane, by whom the deposites were removed from the banks, without letting them know in time to take in sail, or throw overboard some of the heavy stocks; and when the whirlwind took them aback they went down all sails standing; and there they were, escaped with their lives and wives, and that was all.'

'Was there ever such a sad and summary method of accounting for six millions of the best bills and stocks of the country!

'Dinner was announced, and I thought if I had lost all my money I had better not let my appetite go with it; and so I said no more about money matters, and you would have never guessed that we were all ruined men and women, or that the young ladies had shared in the common disasters of their families. Our conversation as usual was buoyant and spirited; weddings and balls, and operas and diamonds, all shone and sparkled in unison with the rich wines we drank like water; and I thought really, from the excessive gayety of the young ladies in particular, that being ruined was one of the most amusing and delightful things in the world; and though I endeavored to take the same cheerful view of matters, yet whenever the recollection of my good bills and stocks would recur, it did not seem possible I could think of being ruined with the same complacency with which it was regarded by these giddy daughters of my friends.

'The next day they said they would be prepared to render me an account of their stewardship; and one of them candidly confessed it was indeed 'a most beggarly account of an empty exchequer, but it should be as honest as daylight;' and with this assurance I took my leave.

'About twelve o'clock they came with their papers all nicely folded and labelled, with large abstracts beautifully prepared, and ruled with the utmost of clerical skill and beauty. What could I expect more? I had witnessed during my career in Change-Alley many very decided explosions, and I had looked on with calmness, and sometimes with pleasure, as after some deep plotting and counter-plotting I had witnessed the sport 'of seeing the engineer hoisted with his own petard;' but now that I found myself in the air, making the same species of gyrations, I did not find the fun so exceedingly attractive as it had appeared to me when but a looker-on at the misfortunes of others. Dean Swift tells us ' he never knew a man who could not bear the misfortunes of other people with Christian resignation;' but to bear our own is a stern task of soul.

'I will not detain you with all these and other thoughts which rose in my mind as I saw in the abstracts of assets, ready to be turned over to me in full discharge of all my claims, certificates of state stock purchased at an advance of from ten to twenty-five per cent., now merely nominal at ten and fifteen dollars the share; shares of stocks in rail-roads, for which not a rail had as yet been laid down; in canals not yet dug; a variety of stocks, the merest creations of fancy and fraud; heavy loans on coal lands; swamps lying around and about Babylon; cities of the west, drawn on beautifully-colored maps, showing where the public buildings and squares were to be, but the sites of which remained to be cleared of their primeval forests; pine lands in Eastern townships, which they told me had proved to be a congregation of swamps and stones—such were the results of their management, all of which they said would have been in good credit but for the removal of the deposits. That I had some reason to complain of the removal of the deposits they all conceded, but comforted me by saying that every body was ruined; not a good house left—all gone to the devil! I had good reason to guess that this last statement was not true, though I thought it not unlikely it might become so.

To make an end of my long story, I was swallowed up by my pelican friends; and though a fish of somewhat larger size than usual, they had found no difficulty in making me go down, leaving as the undigested tail these miserable certificates of stock, the remnant of all my monies placed in their custody. To me these stocks were utterly worthless, and I at once made them an offer to draw drafts on them at a long date, payable with interest, which they cheerfully accepted; and here they are,' said the Gentleman in Black, with a sneering smile of satisfaction, as he pulled out of his pocket a bundle of papers, carefully done up and labelled.

'And are you not fearful of their defrauding you by taking the benefit of some general act of bankruptcy?' inquired Mrs. Smith, in tones of tender sympathy for the misfortunes of her guest.

'Oh no, my dear Madam,' replied the Gentleman in Black, in a tone of the utmost confidence; 'they will doubtless avail themselves of all manner of 'stay-laws,' but they must come to it at *last ;* these stay-laws will soon be exhausted, and if payment be not then made, I have a summary process, known in law as the writ '*ca-sa*,' which empowers me *to take the body ;* and you may rely upon it, my dear Madam, there's no dodging! They will find no Portia who can, by a quibble of the law, save them from their bonds—the money or the body! As there are no ZACCHEUS's among them, *that* they never will repay; so I have booked their bodies as my own years ago !'

STANZAS: THE RETURN.

BY J. HONEYWELL.

LONG weary years have flown since last
    I stood where I now musing stand;
And, lost amid the teeming Past,
    Thought over-peoples Memory's land.

In Life's warm morning, when the boy
    Knew not of manhood's darker night,
At this same portal, youth and joy
    Blessed me with vigils of delight.

But now the scene with change is fraught;
    The house I dwelt in I mistook,
As, gazing long, I vainly sought
    For its old, quaint, familiar look.

The very room where midnight's chimes
    Once sent me tired from book to bed;
The room that heard my boyhood's rhymes,
    When angel light seemed round me shed;

Now reeks with fumes of smoke and wine,
    And echoes to the sound of trade,
While many a gay and glittering sign
    Is on the dingy walls displayed.

The street, too, lacks its ancient air,
    Its undisturbed and quiet mood,
And has become a thoroughfare,
    Thronged with the jostling multitude.

The old stone church across the street
   Stands where it stood in other days ;
But ah ! my eyes sad changes meet,
   As on its time-worn front I gaze.

Still on its spire the moonlight falls,
   And the old clock-face shines as fair,
But from its desecrated walls
   Ascends no more the voice of prayer.

And manly hearts are in the mould,
   That once these sacred precincts prized ;
Men whose degenerate sons have sold
   The shrine at which they were baptized.

Your fathers' graves, ye cold of heart !
   Are trodden on by heedless men ;
And ye have made a public mart
   Of what was GOD's own temple then.

Thought, lingering, clings to other days,
   Borne back on waking Memory's wing,
While gently falls upon my heart
   The dew of life's remembered spring.

The labors of the day are o'er,
   The cares of business, and its din,
And sweetly through the windows pour
   The silver streams of moonlight in.

Through leaves all tremulous with bliss
   The night-wind like a lover steals,
And its low, soft, and hallowed kiss
   A welcome presence there reveals.

My soul with thought's excess is faint,
   My gaze is on yon starry crowds,
Where the pale moon, like some fair saint,
   Veils half her charms behind the clouds.

This silent hour—its influence sinks
   With power resistless on my soul,
And the hushed present backward shrinks,
   In its majestic, calm control.

My vision dims, as wanes the night,
   The blessed night that brought my dream,
And as I gaze, the holy light
   Falls in a faint and fainter gleam.

Like as the moon is shut between
   The folds of yon swift-rolling cloud,
So 'twixt me and that fancied scene
   The unwelcome Real lifts its shroud.

My heart responds to spoken words,
   As its quick pulses come and go,
And answers with vibrating chords,
   'Change waits on all things here below !'

SPRINGTIME AT IDLEBERG.

'For lo! the winter is past, the rain is over and gone; the flowers appear on the earth; the time of the singing of birds is come, and the voice of the turtle is heard in the land.'

In all the labyrinth of Nature's mysteries, there is no wonder so great to the untutored mind as the periodical advent of springtime. It is by easy and natural gradations, illustrated as they are by man's changing destiny on earth, that we trace from the opening bud the full-blown flower, the ripened harvest, the fall of the leaf, and the dreary desolation of winter; but there is no analogy in man's visible history for the return of that genial season which springs from the very bosom of decay, and restores to us all the pomp and beauty of springtime. It is only by penetrating within the unknown and invisible — by lifting the veil which obscures the future from our vision, and realizing the freshness of a spiritual existence beyond the grave, that we can find the similitude we seek.

One of the poets in a picture of Eden takes occasion to conjecture the emotions with which the father and mother of our race witnessed the first storm that passed over the garden. How eagerly they watched the first, dim shadowy cloud as it floated along like a spirit of light, upheld by the breath of Omnipotence! How their admiration was changed to wonder and alarm as the fair cloud-spirit grew darker and darker, until the heavens were black and terrible! How the dear mother of us all leaned with tremulous anxiety on her protector, while amid the wildness of the storm paradise itself seemed dark and gloomy; and how eagerly at length they watched the first gleam of the blue sky, until the clouds were gone, and Nature, from the genial rain, shone brighter than before, and the terrors of the tempest were forgotten!

Something like these we may imagine would be the emotions of the ardent boy who should for the first time witness the succession of the seasons. Each dropping petal, each falling leaf, each wintry blast would suggest the melancholy thought that Nature had exhausted her resources, and must hereafter accommodate herself to frost and snow and storm-clouds, and thermometers below zero. But at once, as by magic, he beholds a serener blue in the sky, and a breath of warm air sends quick pulsations to his heart. Then as he roams over some cultivated wild, by streams whose mossy banks seem like old and long-lost friends, a violet, the first of springtime, peeps out by the waterfall, and gives pleasant assurance that the seasons have renewed their harmonious career, to pause not until their destiny shall be accomplished.

I saw the beautiful spring first in the sky. A deeper blue in Heaven; light floating clouds, bearing rich treasures for the famished earth; bright-winged birds, fresh from their native south; these were the harbingers of her coming. Clothed with light vestments, crowned with a garland of early flowers, and radiant with the hues of health, the fairy-footed goddess leaped like Minerva full-armed from the helmet of Eternal Wisdom, and standing on the mountain-top, sent forth her fabulous retinue over the earth, until every hill and valley and stream owned its appropriate divinity.

How truly at such a season do we appreciate the sentiment that there are some things — as trees and flowers and birds and running brooks — that remind us of a better and brighter world than this, and seem indeed like captives, stolen and prisoned here from the happier land of their birth! How desolate would earth appear if no verdure bloomed along its barren heaths — if no voices of Nature were heard resounding through its silent forests! How many charms are thrown around the names of home and country by these eloquent though often unobserved companions! The flowers that spring so abundantly in our path-way are not needed in the utilitarian economy of nature; and yet if these were wanting we should miss many a lesson of humility and gratitude. Gentle reader, love the flowers! Wear them near thy heart, and bind them around thy brow; train them about thy lattice, that the way-side traveller may breathe their fragrance and bless thee for the gift. Plant them near thy homestead, however humble, and as they uplift their tiny cups to drink the morning dew, or glow and brighten in the summer sunshine, let them teach thee a lesson of gratitude to HIM who nurtures thee and the flowers.

There are few metaphors in any language more beautiful than that employed by the poet to illustrate the awakening life of a clouded heart, at the first presence of a kindred spirit:

'THOU mad'st me happy with thine eyes,
And gentle feelings, long forgot,
Looked up and *oped their eyes,*
Like violets when they see a spot
Of summer in the skies.'

And not to violets alone is the dawn of summer a talisman wherewith to unlock the hidden treasures of the heart. The denizen of crowded streets, whose barren stones know no change of season, suddenly hies to the forest, whose boughs are beginning to rejoice in their robes of budding green. Go too, thou mistress of that torpid canary, that with cracked voice and moulting feathers is but a lean apology for a bird, and when thy heart shall be filled with the melody that is singing from every tree-top, return and set the prisoner free! And thou of 'sweet seventeen,' away to the fields yet moist with dew, and gather flowers to match thine own freshness and purity! And thou, fond watcher by the bed-side of her whose gentle spirit shall soon claim kindred with its native skies; throw open that lattice, and as she breathes the fresh air and sees the green fields she loved long ago, she will sink to rest with a heart full of gratitude that she has been permitted to die in springtime!

And yet, with all its present delights, how have the prismatic colors of spring-time faded since we first learned to love its gentle airs, its balmy sunshine, its bright and dewy flowers! How often, at such a season, steal over the heart the memories of boyhood and vain longings for its return! To know no thought of the morrow; to remember nought of the past, save that we were blessed; to roam barefoot the world over—the little world that bounded our daily rambles; to have no dream of fame, no goading of ambition, no visions but of angel-wings overshadowing us; to know no light of love but the fond eyes that watched our infancy; to chase gay butterflies with footsteps as light and fleeting as our hopes, with no thought that such was the weary race of many an older leg than ours; to make our beds in green fields and amid the new-mown hay; to lie down when weary of our vain pursuits, to be lulled by 'bird and bee and flowing water;' to be the same glad, thoughtless creature all the day long and every day, let the world wag as it might—these are the pictures of boyhood which the presence of spring-time recalls.

And yet there is much of sadness mingled with all these reminiscences of pleasure. There are memories of bubbles that burst when their rainbow hues were brightest; of flowers that withered when we most enjoyed their fragrance; of cares that came too soon to mingle with the cup of boyhood's happiness; of hearts that once beat in unison with ours, whose pulsations have ceased; of graves whose turf is gay with the verdure of many a spring-time. And thus shall the cup of life be mingled forever!

Spring-time at Idleberg! No longer wrapped in wintry habiliments, but clothed in the freshest garb of spring, with her pleasant streams, her well-tilled gardens, her rural streets, her Sabbath bells, she seems the fairest of all villages.

First of all there is 'Afton,' flowing on as merrily as of yore. It will be the scene of our first ramble on this glorious morning of springtime. Though I have long since become a more ambitious angler than for the minnows that gleam through its transparent depths, its quiet borders are still a favorite resort to me. Morning, noon and night it is ever the same, reflecting from its placid bosom the glory, the azure, or the storm-clouds of the sky. When the broad shadows are lying athwart the landscape it is pleasant to recline at ease along its margin, half hidden by the tall grass beneath and the world of forest-leaves above. Now and then a squirrel barks saucily overhead; now flights of wild-fowl scud along the margin of the stream; and not unfrequently a solitary crane stalks proudly through its depths, to survey the reflection of his fair proportions.

Our 'Afton' hath its legends also. Far down the stream a little bubbling brook empties therein, and a narrow unfrequented path alongside will lead us into the valley where it has its source. That fountain with the rude stone house, now almost a ruin, built about it, supplies the family at 'Dovedale' with the purest water that ever gushed from mother Earth's prolific bosom. Hard-by is the cottage we seek.

It is, as you perceive, simple and neat, yet quaint and old-fashioned in the extreme. There are few signs of animation about the place; if there be any children, they must be gone to school. A solitary brindle-cow is chewing the cud in the shade of that tall poplar. Troops of meddlesome pigs are prying about, with their snouts deep buried in the turf, and a large flock of geese are wading the 'branch,' fanning the air with their swan-like wings, and hissing contemptuously at the intrusive grunters.

The dwelling is nearly hidden beneath the foliage of overhanging tree-tops, and yet you can perceive how neatly it is white-washed, and how gracefully the creeper is trailed over the front-door. A few clustered rose-bushes, chiefly of the cabbage variety, dot the yard, which is enclosed by a paling of dazzling whiteness. It is altogether a spot which with some slight cultivation might be converted into a beautiful retreat; but its appearance evinces an effort to maintain about it the aspect of antiquity, as if its old proprietor had died long ago and left a solemn injunction with his heirs never to touch shrub or timber about the old homestead, until it should rot where it stood. And yet, with all its old and forsaken look, you could not easily find a home better suited in any respect to the tastes of its present occupant; a maiden lady, whose presence adds a becoming zest to the antiquity of the place.

There were originally five Misses C——'s, the elder and younger of whom were respectively Miss Betsey and Miss Sally. In early life they were all left in joint-tenancy of the estate, and secluded as they were from the busy world about them, their deep affection gradually strengthened into feelings of entire mutual dependence. The most beautiful harmony was observed in their domestic economy. To one was conceded the general control of the little estate; another had charge of the dairy; another of the garden. So that each separate interest was well protected by means of this division of labor. The garden, with its many choice vegetables and flowers, was the neatest and prettiest in the neighborhood; their fields were always the first to whiten with the harvest; and it was a pleasant sight to see their sleek flocks and herds basking on the hill-side or browsing on the plain.

Although so blessed in each other and their pleasant home, the sisters at Dovedale soon learned that the chief happiness of life consists, not in a selfish appropriation of the good gifts of Providence, but in the felicity of doing good to others. Their dwelling was always open to the claims of charity or hospitality. The poor never passed by without receiving some substantial gift and a blessing to enhance its value. The young people of the village were always welcome to hold their pic-nics in the shade of their venerable trees. There were no strawberries-and-cream so sweet as those at Dovedale; and very often, years ago, the old dwelling now so silent and deserted has rung with the merry shouts of those who shared its hospitality, while the sisters watched their sports with demure satisfaction, nor ever sighed to be young again.

Very soon each revolving year began to impair the virgin charms of the sisters at Dovedale. They were growing old, though in the

freshness of their hearts they knew it not. After a while, the neat
muslin cap and silver-rimmed spectacles, worn unblushingly at
home and abroad, betrayed the story that the frost was beginning
to mingle with their raven ringlets, and age was coming on apace.
And yet, though endowed with every noble quality of heart and
mind, they never married; though Miss Sally once made a narrow
escape—I will tell you how. They say she was forty then—but
it matters not.

Every body at Idleberg knows good Dr. F——, and always did.
Every body had good reason to know him, for he was every body's
physician, from the cradle to the grave. His appearance was any
thing but prepossessing, his eyes being dreadfully crossed and his
form any thing but erect; but then he had a heart so full of sun-
shine and affection for the whole world, that every body loved him.
He was incessantly on the move with his bob-tailed pony along
the streets of the village or some of the highways or lanes there-
about. There must have been quite as much virtue in his personal
appearance to his patients as in his drugs; for the only prescription
he was ever known to administer, whether for a tooth-ache or a
bilious fever, was the emphatic sentence, ' Give him jalap and bleed
him !' So successful and incessant however were his professional
occupations, that he never had leisure for any such thing as falling
in love, much less marrying; and thus he lived on to the full term
of three score years of single blessedness, which evinced a self-
sacrificing spirit quite in keeping with his whole nature; and every
body always said that if ever any human being laid up treasures in
heaven by means of charities done on earth, that man was good
Dr. F——.

He was of course the family physician at Dovedale, though fresh
air and cheerful labor brought such health to the sisters that they
seldom had need either for the jalap or the lancet. It happened
however that Miss Sally at length stood in especial need of his pro-
fessional services. There was a poor widow living in a cottage just
over the hill, who had been left with many helpless children in a
destitute condition, and very often shared the generous charities of
the sisters at Dovedale. It was on Miss Sally's return on a cold
winter evening from the home of the widow, where she had gone
on an errand of kindness, that she contracted the illness which
called the doctor so frequently to Dovedale.

The illness became more serious than had been anticipated. The
sisters trembled for the fate of their favorite, and felt their first ap-
prehensions of that long and last separation which sooner or later
awaited them. The doctor was most assiduous in his attentions.
He came early and remained late about the bed-side. His skill at
last mastered the disease; and it was there, while observing the
anxious and unwearying solicitude of the elder sisters, and the calm
resignation of the invalid, that his heart was first touched—though
his reason had often been—with a just appreciation of ' woman's
priceless worth.'

By and by the patient grew convalescent, and her first walk out of doors were directed to the garden at Dovedale, her own peculiar department in the economy of the farm.   Here, in the tender care of her flowers, she soon became alive to the cheerful aspect of nature and all the warm impulses of the heart.   It was observed that the doctor did not cease his visits to Dovedale upon the restoration of his fair patient, and for the first time in all his life complaints began to be made of his want of attention to some of the many claims upon his time and skill.   Meantime he improved wonderfully in his exterior; donned a new wig, and exchanged his favorite pony for a charger of higher mettle and more gallant bearing.   Why did he and Miss Sally walk so often together in the garden, as though he were none too old to undertake to study the philosophy of plants?   Why in his absence did she fill the flower-pots in the parlor with such choice bouquets?   Why did she read so assiduously that stray volume of poems, unburied from the dust in his little library; and why tune again the chords of that heir-loom guitar, that had so long lain voiceless and neglected?   Was it true of these old hearts that like dry and withered boughs they were consumed more rapidly than they would have been even in their younger and tenderer days? So it was that the good Doctor, for the first time in all his life, took leisure to reflect that in his declining years he should need a helpmate; and so he dwelt upon the charms of Dovedale and the pure devotion of the sisters, and especially upon the many estimable qualities of Miss Sally, until he could but ' propose.'

The proposal, so startling, and yet not altogether unexpected, was received in trembling silence.   After due hesitation she replied: ' She had the highest regard for the good doctor; she did not know' — bless her dear heart! — ' but that she *loved him;* but she could not decide so important a question without the judgment of her sisters, and would abide their decision.'

It would be difficult to portray the feelings of the elder sisters on receiving the timid announcement, some days thereafter, from the lips of their youngest and best-beloved.   There were surely more tears shed at Dovedale than for many a day previous.   They felt deeply their obligations to the suitor for his personal and professional kindness; but Sally was their favorite; their idol.   What would become of Dovedale without her?   They could not possibly spare her; and after a painful struggle, Miss Betsey announced their unanimous decision: ' After all, Sally, I think we had best not get married.   We are all living very quietly and happily together; perhaps it is best not to break our little circle.   And just think, my child, of marrying *a man!*   Let's not get married, Sally; let's not get married!'

She who was most deeply interested in this decision received it without a murmur.   Submission to the will of her sisters had become a religious duty with her; and this feeling gave her a seeming composure.   When upon the appointed day her suitor returned to learn his fate, she received him alone.   He heard her decision with entire submission; though even then she seemed almost to relent.

She exacted from him a promise, however, that he would continue to visit Dovedale, as though nothing unpleasant had occurred.

I have heard that the separation of these old lovers on that day was truly affecting. That grasp of the hand was almost too affectionate for mere civility; and as he passed through the door-way and across the front-yard, her eyes followed him eagerly until he had disappeared, and she then sank exhausted to her chair. Why did she languish for years from that day? Why did she grow weary of those household duties that had once given her such pleasure? Why did the grey hairs mingle so rapidly with the dark-brown, and her steps tremble on the threshold until they ceased to move about the cottage and her voice was heard no more? They said it was from a winter's cold; but some imagined the cause lay deeper, and remembered that there are such things as broken hearts.

Since then sad changes have come over Dovedale. Of all the five sisters, the eldest alone remains; and she often wonders why she was left. She has faith that she will know, some day. In the excitement of his professional duties, the worthy doctor soon forgot his first and only disappointment; and has religiously observed his promise to Miss Sally by continuing his visits hither from that day. There is an old adage about talking of Old Nick., which we need not repeat; but there he comes — I mean the doctor — descending the road on his favorite pony, to pay his daily visit to Dovedale; so we will leave it, with a blessing on its delightful retreats, and the hope that it may be long before the pleasant intercourse of the good old man and the last of the five sisters shall be interrupted.

Loitering on our way, reader, through green lanes and pleasant fields, and in the light of this glorious sunset, we reach the village church-yard, that bright, gay, tranquil home of the dead. It is brighter, yet sadder than aught we have seen to-day; with its tall grass, its waving ever-greens and its melancholy willows. It should never be an unwelcome task for the living to steal at times from the busy distractions of life, and draw lessons of wisdom from the voiceless eloquence of those who have gone before. There are no terrors for the well-regulated mind in the calm seclusion of such a spot. There is no fear of unwelcome visitants, wrapped in the ghastly livery of the grave. There are some bright and early flowers; the shades of welcome trees; the rustling of the evening wind; and these are all. Yet as we read inscription after inscription, how do these familiar names grow and expand into the forms of humanity, clothed not in the cerements of the grave but in the identical garments they wore when last we grasped their living hands; until we have gathered about us a cheerful little community of the reäwakened dead; the virgin charms we loved to contemplate; the schoolmates who passed away from our side; the venerable forms of those who led the way in paths of virtue, and bade us follow them forever; each character addressing us in its well-remembered tones, and reacting its allotted part in the drama of life. Such is the spell that Fancy, incited by such a scene, throws around the heart, until suddenly some sound of life recalls us to the reality; form after form disappears from our side ; the graven tablets resume their appropriate places, and we are left alone with the dead.

This winding path will conduct us to a monument whose simple inscription has often been read by the stranger. Gentle reader, this is MARY's grave, and the rudest villager can tell you how fair and gentle she was ; how dear to all who ever knew her ; and how her place in our hearts has never been filled.

It was through years of playful girlhood and riper youth that I knew her well. For years our walks and rides and pastimes were often the same ; and I watched with eager interest the opening of the bud, as day after day increased its loveliness, until it burst into the full-blown flower of dawning womanhood. I know how pure and elevating is the charm of such an association, and that there are friendships in the world which ennoble the heart with lessons of purity that passion could never have taught.

There was one sympathy which more than all else bound up the cords of our friendship, and that was a passionate love for music. She was the centre of a little village coterie of amateurs, and her piano seemed her throne, for there alone in the rich, soul-stirring harmonies of the instrument ; now raving with the thunders of passion, and now subdued to the softest cadences of sentiment ; she found expression for the pure and generous impulses of her heart. The effect was still more imposing when her music became the vehicle of sentiments of devotion ; and when, Sabbath after Sabbath, she presided at the organ of the village church, as its solemn breathing rolled through the aisles of the sanctuary, it would not have been difficult to imagine that a spirit of light had come down to worship GOD in one of the humblest of his earthly temples.

I need not tell the reader how tenderly she loved, or how ardently her affection was returned by the objects of her choice. I had long known and esteemed him, and was glad in the prospect of their mutual happiness when riper years should have strengthened their attachment and formed them more entirely for each other. When an inexorable necessity called him far away from her side, it was to me a pleasure, unmingled with any alloy, to bear to her those tender missives which a confiding prudence had entrusted to me ; to speak as they deserved of his many virtues, and to point her to the day when I trusted the fondest dreams of her youthful fancy would be realized. Was any thing wanting that could have enhanced the pleasures of a friendship so refined, a confidence so entire?

That parting, though they dreamed not of it then, was their last on earth. If I have omitted to say it, the reader has doubtless already imagined that her beauty was of that delicate order which so often marks the victim of premature decline. Already in the heyday of her youth, we sometimes saw fearful symptoms in her thoughtful brow, her languid melancholy gait. Still when in the gay circle of her friends it was often difficult to detect in her joyful demeanor any apprehensions of her early doom. Grave professors of the healing art delivered the usual prescriptions of gay company and cheerful exercise ; but society brought no permanent relief to her malady, and the healthful air imparted no bloom to her pale and wasting cheek.   During all this time her piano was her chief society and solace.   In moments of despondency it revived her drooping spirits, and reminded her, perhaps sadly, of other and happier days. Autumn succeeded summer, and while the dreary winds were howling abroad, we learned that her gentle frame was fast fading away.

On a day, never to be forgotten, in the midst of the gloomy winter, the writer was unexpectedly summoned to her dwelling.   I found the mother alone and in tears; and in a voice that trembled with grief and anxiety, she communicated Mary's last request.   There was a plain gold ring, which she had long worn as the seal of her affection for her distant lover; and despairing of her recovery, she desired to have it returned; and to the writer was deputed the delicate mission.   I was glad that the tenderness of our old friendship was not forgotten by her even in her dark and cheerless sick-chamber, and had the message come from above, I could not have executed it more promptly.   She had not lost a tithe of her old regard for him, but of what value were all earthly affections to her who had given her heart to Heaven?

In the midst of this affecting interview with the mother, I observed that the door which led to Mary's chamber was slightly open.   It was with feelings of mingled pain and pleasure that I soon heard issuing thence the faint tones of the piano.   Another and another harmony of exquisite beauty, and at once I recognized the familiar touch of the player.   A thousand recollections of the forgotten past came over me as the soft symphonies of that favorite air swelled into the apartment.   I could but think of the days and hours that could never return; of the cheerful light that had fled from her eyes forever; of the pale cheek, and the trembling voice, and the gentle heart, beating, oh! how feebly and fitfully!   A moment more, and with exhausted strength she rose fom the instrument, and all was silent.   It was, indeed, the ' Last Lay of the Minstrel.'

And this is her grave.   We buried her here in spring-time, years ago, and ever since that day there has been another angel in Heaven. It would have been beautiful if the flowers she loved so well on earth could have blossomed from above the uncovered turf.   A single rose-tree, planted by a mother's hand, grows near; and that is the fittest emblem for the radiant beauty and premature decay of her who sleeps beneath.

Patient reader, we have passed an hour — not a sad one, altogether, I trust — within the precincts of the church-yard at Idleberg. The moon has risen mean time, and is shedding her mellow radiance upon the scene of our communings; and while those graven tablets brighten in her beams, and the leaves quiver overhead in the rustling wind, and the flowers close their petals for the night, we will part with the sweet influences of the scene and the hour resting on our hearts, and with a cheerful hope that we may meet again in spring-time.

Philadelphia, June, 1846.

WILLIE'S GRAVE.

No costly monument is reared above the humble spot
Where WILLIE sleeps more tranquilly than erewhile in his cot,
But on a small and snow-white stone the stranger reads his name,
And feels how far the spell of Love exceeds the power of Fame.

He may have stood where sculptured piles proclaim the mighty dead,
He may have gazed with wondering eye on royalty's last bed;
But all the mausoleums of earth would move his spirit less
Than that small tablet, raised by Love, to tell its hopelessness!

Its hopelessness! nay, Love and Hope can ne'er divided be,
Twin-born of Heaven, they shall endure to all eternity:
And when our hearts surrender up some idol that they love,
They bleed in anguish until Hope leads them to look above.

That lowly grave where WILLIE sleeps beneath the summer sod
Speaks to my heart in solemn tones, as 't were the voice of GOD;
It speaks to me, while mournfully I stand anear and weep,
To think how never more on earth he'll waken from his sleep.

And thus it seemeth to my heart most tenderly to say:
'Though I have hidden from thine eyes their light of life away,
Though buried in my bosom deep thy treasure must remain,
Yet should thy tears give place to smiles, and joy succeed to pain.

'For in the world, where thou dost dwell, full many snares are laid,
By which the ardent soul of youth to Error is betrayed;
And many a cup of bitterness to human lips is pressed,
The poison-draughts of Sin, that leave dark sorrows in the breast.

'These are the lot of human life, from these thy child is free;
He died among the thornless flowers of guileless infancy:
He might have lived to drain the cup of Evil to its lees,
And plant thy bosom with those pangs which Death alone can ease.

'He died in his first loveliness, as flowers do sometimes die,
Broke from their parent stem while yet their leaves half-folded lie:
Thou grievest that the buds so fair were nipt before their bloom,
Unmindful that a wasting blight might be their later doom.

'He passed away from thy glad eye, a vision of delight,
He might have lived to cloud thy soul with shadows dark as night;
His memory to thy heart will now a joy perpetual be —
It might have been in after time a lasting misery!

'Oh, he is blessèd, he is pure; an angel in the skies;
Look up, look up, and ardent Faith shall see him with her eyes;
His precious dust alone is left within my close embrace,
His spirit shines in glory now, before its MAKER's face.'

O! quiet Grave! thy blessed words have soothed my aching heart;
I'll freely leave to thine embrace my darling's mortal part:
And daily pray that when my dust to thy cold arms is given,
My spirit may soar up and join my angel-child in Heaven!

Athens, Georgia, 1846.   WILLIAM C. RICHARDS.

ADVENTURES OF A YANKEE-DOODLE.

CHAPTER NINTH.

It wanted an hour to the time of the ' lectur,' and the evening being pleasantly cool, the Doctor stood looking over the garden rails when one of the ' seven wise men' of the village passed by. ' I hear,' said he, introducing himself without ceremony, ' that you are to enlighten this neighborhood on the subjeck of animal magnetism to-night.'

' I be,' quoth the Doctor, spitting ; ' see advertisement.'

' Well, in that case let me advise you to step over to the reading-room beforehand. There 's something complimentary about you in the ' Flag of the Union,' published at Slickopolis.'

' I thank you kindly,' said the lecturer ; ' there 'll be time to look at it before early candle-lightin'. . A sound press and religiont goes hand in hand. Is your name Horner ?'

' No.'

' Makes no difference. You 're a squire, aint you ?'

' No.'

' I see you on a load of hay day before yesterday. I thought you looked like a squire — kind-of. How 's the cause of justice advancin' ? Look-a-here, I want you should come early to-night, and tell all the public to come early, that they may all get a good seat. But what *is* your name ?'

' What say ?'

' What's your name, my Christian friend ?'

' Name ? oh — ah ! Adjutant-General Hanes.'

' Hanes ? Hanes ? Appears to me there was a man by that name *hung* in the revolutionary war.'

' Die easy ?'

' Why ? — why ? Any relation o' yourn ?'

' Doctor —— '

' Squar' —— '

' My worthy Doctor, I *will* come early. Good night — good night. Do n't forget the ' Flag of the Union.' '

' I wont,' said Dobbs, turning on his heel, and hastening over to the bar-room, which contained newspapers. ' That puff goes into my port-folio. I 'll request the secretary of the meeting to read it out loud. The Flag of the Union ! The Flag of the Union !'

The Doctor was intensely curious to know what the Slickopolis paper had been saying about him. How eagerly in fact do we all spread our sails to catch the slightest breath of approbation ! He would give twenty-five cents to get hold of that paper without an instant's delay. The chance seemed fair. Of seven or eight files ranged along the wall, not one was engaged. This spoke ill for the

cause of information at Jigtown. He ran his eye hurriedly over the
heads : Brattleboro', Bennington, Woodville, and-so-forth, but no
Slickopolis. Tut! Tut! what a vexation! Torn up, no doubt.
Just because he wanted it! Every paper there but just the one!
So it is usually. Just then he saw an old man reading intently in a
corner. He looked over his shoulder. That was it:
'THE FLAG OF OUR UNION: Slickopolis, Friday, June 10: ANI-
MAL MAGNETISM! DE-BUTT of DOCTOR DOBBS!!'
Out of breath, the Doctor relapsed into a chair to abide his turn.
Every second seemed minutes. The reader was at the bottom of
the third page, and he soon turned over to the fourth, which con-
tained advertisements. Still his eye lingered there not without in-
terest. This is the most delightfully suggestive part of a whole
newspaper. The advices from the Rio Grande may thrill the soul
for a moment, but the excitement is unhealthy, unsatisfactory, soon
dispensed. But think of a contract for rails, fifteen thousand rails!
There 's food for three minutes' reflection ; and then you wander on
to Mr. John Smith's advertisement whose customers are invited to
'give him a call.' Fine man, John Smith! Well-to-do in the world
now. Began business on a mere pittance, but by dint of rising
early and retiring late, now placed out of harm's way. 'The ladies
are requested to call there before purchasing any where else.' 'The
Sons of Temperance will hold their next celebration to-morrow,
wind and weather permitting, in the Grove. An oration may be
expected, and root-beer and music provided gratis. A new inven-
tion called lemon-sugar will be exhibited for the approbation of the
audience. A mild, pleasant and agreeable article of cheap sweet-
enin'. A. 28, tf. 9 s. m.'
         'House to let on the edge of a small swamp ; also a few acres
    of land. Enquire within.'
The Doctor pretended to be reading another paper, but his eye
was snatching continually a stolen glance at the 'Flag of the Union.'
The reader finished the fourth page, but O! patience of Job! he
has turned back to the first, and thinks he discovers something inte-
resting in a sketch of 'charming Fanny Forrester!'
'Well, if he is going to read that long article ——— '
The Doctor's face began to assume an expression actually dia-
bolical. He scrutinized his adversary's countenance. Ugh! said
he, what an ugly nose! Red as fire! Better go and sign the pledge!
That will do him more good than to be sittin' here monopolizing a
newspaper. The old cus!'
A twinge of pain shot over the face of the incumbent, which cor-
rugated his countenance into twenty whirlpools, but it relapsed again
into an expression of delightful calm, and he went on reading. 'I
wish it was an attackt of the cholic,' said the Doctor. 'No danger.
Old red-noses live for ever. Oh! Great guns! what a flap of the
ear he's got! Chalky-lookin' forehead! Erysipelas has swept
over his constitution. If it kills him, who 'll cry? Nobody.'
It is impossible to describe the satisfaction which this subject of
internal obloquy seemed to take in his newspaper. He made seve-

ral movements, but they were only for reädjustment.   At last he put it down.   The Doctor approached, his eyes speaking volumes.

'Not yet,' said the reader, quietly wiping his spectacles, and coughing as he spoke: 'I–hi–hi–hi! I been looking over the Haunted Ho–house! Something like it occurred many years a–(a–cho!) a-go!'

'Take a *se*–gar?' said Dobbs.

'No, thank you; I do n't smoke, but I drink.'

'So I thought. I do n't drink, but I smoke.'

'Well, *you* smoke. I 'll *read*. Reading wont interrupt your smoking.'

'In course not; smoking wont interrupt your reading,' said Dobbs, rolling out the most prodigious clouds of smoke.   The tobacco was execrable, and in a few seconds assafœtida was pine-apple to the atmosphere of the room.

'My patriarchal friend!' proceeded the Doctor, 'Reverend and dear Sir, would you obleege me with that 'ere paper only one minute? I wish to see an advertisement about a pinfactory.'

'There 's nothing of the kind here, young man. Noth–ing of the kind — noth–ing of the kind.'

'May be not, but ——'

'Wal, wal; we 'll look for it together.   Let us see what there is: 'Animal magnetism! One 'Doctor Dobbs,' as he calls himself, delivered a lecture last evening on this humbug science.   The Doctor is an arrant impostor, and current report states that he once graced the penitentiary for a misdemeanor.   Let our cotemporaries look out for him.'   Wal, that — that —— Put a pin there; upon me so-o-ul, the very same individual!' said the newspaper-reader, lifting his eyes to a conspicuous advertisement upon the wall.

The Doctor's face was suffused with a transient glory which passed away and left it as before.

'Sir,' said he, looking up at the same placard, 'a licentious press is the curse of any country.   Admittance twenty-five cents.   Let 's go and hear the individooal.'   •

'Oh, I–I never go out at night,' said the old gentleman.

'I 'm glad of that,' said the Doctor to himself; and with that they parted at sunset, never to meet again on the threshold of 'The Rising Sun' Tavern.

——

CHAPTER TENTH.

Stubbs went to hear Dobbs.   On approaching, he saw by the moisture on the window-panes that his new friend was doing a 'living business.'   'Better than school-teaching,' said he; 'an ungrateful trade that.   If it warn't for the fifteen-year-old-girls that I instruct, I should have left it, and don' know but what I shall as it is. I 'm goin' to Mobile.   There 's want of Yankee instruction in that neighborhood.'

As he entered the room, he saw the Doctor sitting on a rostrum, looking about, as if he were casting up figures in his mind.   The latter was indeed gratified with the prospect of the evening 'job,' and making remarks to himself as each new-comer entered the door. As a facetious barber, by an inverse personification, looks upon every customer as a fresh six-pence, so he said to himself, on the arrival of each Jigtonian, 'There comes a wooden bowl;' and when the mayor and his daughters arrived, he said 'There comes *three* wooden bowls.'

At last the room was full. 'My respected countrymen!' rising with much dignity. 'How's that?' said he, turning to some one who interrupted him; ' 'requested to read this notice at commencement of lectur'? In course, I'll do it — with pleasure : '*The audience is respectfully informed that they can be provided at the door, on retiring from the room, for only twelve-and-a-half-cents, with a cake of Jones' Patent Chemical*——' 'VESTIMENTAL HUMBUG!' roared Dobbs, stamping the paper beneath his foot. The patentee had just pounced upon one of the selectmen, and was eradicating a huge dusty grease-spot from a short-waisted rusty-black coat. He barely lifted his eye a second from the operation : 'Humbug *yourself!*' said he ; 'there! — see any grease-spot *now?* The Vestimental won't take grease-spots out of *reputations;* otherwise it will do every thing except talk ; *some* folks can't do nothin' *but* talk. See any grease-spot *there?*'

'Since the gentleman has got his grease-spot wiped out,' proceeded the Doctor, grinning, 'we will proceed on, my beloved countrymen, with what we was a-sayin'. The subjeck of Human Magnetism doos seem to be one which should be classed among the moral weaponry of the age. Social and political statistics are and have been approaching their aggrandizement — their acmy, if I may so speak, (and I presume I may.) It has been objected to me, by a highly respectable citizen of this place, that our science breaks down the fences of religiont and lets in the flood-gates of materialism. Materialism! My fellow-countrymen, I would ask what *is* materialism?' It is a figment. We will let this objection pass for the present. I trust we shall be able to show that it doos not possess the scintilla of a foundation. It is the dream of a disordered stomach! (*Applause.*) It is in fact preju-dice. The human mind is so constituted that the grandest truths make their way slowly through the mists of preju-dice. Religiont, geography, science, and the use of the globes, together with the application of art, bears witness to the fact; and shallow Ignorance is loud in her opposition in proportion as that ignorance is deep and abiding.' Here the schoolmaster winked his eye to the seller of vestimental soap.

'Now to proceed with our argument; however, I guess we will take that for granted; but before coming here this evening I found upon my table certain queries proposed by an intelligent citizen of this place with reference to magnetism, which I shall get rid of before I proceed. Now about electrical currents being the medium of sound. You say *air* is. I deny it *in toto cœlo.* True, this has been the dogma of ages. So they used to say the sun stood still, when it has been proved by Euclid's Emblems that he goes round the earth and stars, and for this Gamaliel was guillotined. Come,

I 'll make myself understood. You put your ear down to one end of a·block of granite and scratch the other with a small pin. You hear it distinctly. What conveys the sound there? The oscilla-tions of the air? What in the name of goodness gracious is air a-doin' into a block of granite? (*Applause.*) So much for that query,' said the Doctor, tearing the paper into small pieces, and dropping them upon the floor. 'Now to come to the next; 'the consenta-neity of mind and matter.' You wish to have your fears settled on that p'int. Do n't let that trouble you one minute. I 'm now coming to that. When I shall show you what kind of matter it is, you 'll say, no matter. (*Applause.*) Why, my friend, the particles of mag-netism is as much finer than rarified air, as the particles of air are than Paixham shot. A million of 'em would n't take up the p'int of a cambric needle. See here. Let me be simplicit. You· see we have a series of *straty* of different densities. First we have the solider straty and rocks deep down in the earth; higher up we have limestone, pumice-stone, rotten-stone and chalk; above that we come to sand; above that we have water; then we have air of great density; higher up we have very thin air; then we come to gasses; but the subtlest, finest, most imperceptible of all particles is magnet-ism, of which the objection has been alleged on the score of con-sentaneity. If you call that matter, when its so fine, why I say, it's *no* matter. (*Immense applause.*)

'Hallo!' exclaimed a spectator, 'them 's the very objections that this man said were put to him on the night when he lectured at Slickopolis.'

'Yes, Sir,' exclaimed the doctor, triumphantly; 'they were the same objections; and I trust whenever they are put to me I shall be ready with the same answers. *(Much applause.)* Now we 've got rid of this and cleared the way handsomely, we come to the subjeck-matter. I s'pose you do n't want to hear a lot of stuff; we 'll go right into the practice. App'int six of your most respect-able men for a committee, and let them put on their spectacles and see whether I play fair. Fair-play 's a jewel; so 's honesty; so 's teetotalism, *(applause;)* so 's religiont.'

The doctor sat down. A committee of six skeptics was appointed, and there seemed to be trouble ahead.

'Now,' said he, 'my clairvoyant has unexpectedly arrived. I see him by the door; let him step this way.'

A fair-haired young man, of sanguine complexion, approached, took his seat and had his eyes bandaged, after being put into the magnetic sleep by the requisite passes.

'Now,' said the doctor, standing behind his chair and holding a lead-pencil, 'what do I have in my hand? Is it black——or white?'

'White.'

'Is it long or——short?'

'Short.'

'Is it used for spelling, reading, arithmetic or——writing?'

'Writing.'

'What is it?'

'A lead-pencil.' *(Much surprise.)*

The same experiment was gone through with, substituting different things; spectacles, knives, and so forth, always with a correct result. One of the committee now presented a small brick-bat. The doctor objected. The object must be one of which the patient must have a clear conception, and to that end the magnetizer himself must have a clear conception. Now for his part he could form no clear idea of a brick-bat, so as to convey it; he therefore threw it down in disgust, and asked whether the committee-man meant to insult him. A second committee-man requested to be put himself into communication with the patient, and then he would believe. The doctor stated distinctly that that was contrary to his practice; that he had done so heretofore and advantage had been taken of it; he was therefore compelled to set it down as a fixed principle, from which he could never depart—no, not for an instant.

'Now,' said he, 'I shall proceed to magnetize his left arm. In that state it is insensible and rigid. It may be cut to the bone, and he won't feel it; may be laid hold of by the strongest man, and cannot be bent. One of the committee will please feel it.'

He did so, and found it stiff as a dead man's from the elbow down.

'Can you bend it?' says the doctor.

'Yes, I can,' replied the other.

'You can 't,' said the doctor; 'hallo! do n't *break* it! He 's a wallable youth. I made him a solemn promise that his bones should n't be broke when he did n't know nothin' about it.'

'Why, you won't consent to any thing,' exclaimed the committee-man.

'Any thing reasonable,' replied the doctor.

'We 're satisfied there 's collusion,' exclaimed several.

'Collision!' roared the magnetizer, in a towering passion; 'If I know what the word means, it 's equal to petit-larceny. I thought I was coming here among gentlemen. But if my motives is to be misconstrued, my character assailed by the eggs of contumely and suspicion, I will withdraw, Sir; I will not go on with the lectur'.'

'Go on! go on!' roared a hundred voices.

'My sympathizing friends, I thank you for your support. I think I know whom I have to thank for this.'

'It 's the Baptist minister,' exclaimed the tavern-keeper, with intense hatred.

Adjutant-General Hanes arose. 'Gentlemen,' said he, 'you perceive that this man is a humbug—an impostor. Nay, more than that, I hold in my hand the Slickopolis 'Flag of the Union,' which lets the cat out of the bag that he has been in the penitentiary!'

Great confusion arose. 'Order! order!' 'go on! go on!' 'let him alone!' 'fair-play!' 'gentlemen of the committee!' 'hustle him out!' 'hurrah!' 'ride him on a rail!' 'sit down! sit down!' 'silence!' 'order!' 'down with him!' 'let him speak!' 'fair-play!' 'hear him out!' 'go on!—go on!—go on!——go on!'

'I had some interesting experiments,' said the doctor; 'if the committee will let me alone till I. get through, I shall be happy to go on; otherwise I shall appeal to the protection of my friends against a colleague of skeptics formed by the Baptist minister of this place.'

'Hustle him out!' 'silence!' 'order!' 'go on! go on! go on! go on!'

'Gentlemen, this experiment shall be not one of curiosity alone, but for the substantial benefit of this community. If any sick man will come for'ard, we 'll examine into his ailments and see what 's to be done for him.'

Applause, in the midst of which a large pale-faced man approached, but the Jig-town doctor left the room in disgust. The patient sat down. He was put into communication with the clairvoyant. A silence ensued, during which every part of him within and without was scrutinized, and the oracle spoke :

'Doctor,' said he, 'this old fellow looks fat and lazy, and he 's got the credit for it. But he 's more; he 's railly sick — sicker than what folks thinks he is. He must have had a hurt at some time or other. There 's a sore place about as big as a dollar over his hip joint.'

'Was that so ?'

The patient replied, 'It was a fact; that he had also received a hurt there when he was young.'

Then, 'his liver was out of order, and there was an obstruction which sometimes nearly shut off his breath.'

'Was that so ?'

'Yes, it was.'

'Doctor, the difficulty is about here,' said he, placing his hand upon the spot. 'Then beside this, he 's got some other complaints, which I should have to think about a leetle longer before I could tell for certain. But the main difficulty is with his breath. If he could get his breath put into shape he would n't care about the rest.'

The patient avowed that his case had been described exactly. This gave a triumphant turn to the exhibition of the evening. Gentlemen were requested to write the name of any animal on a piece of paper. The doctor stood ten feet off from the patient and merely pointed at him with his finger : 'What does it look like ?'

'Why, it do n't look like any thing but itself. It 's got a knowin' look; a sharp nose, wonderful lively eyes. They use it at whig meetin's.'

'What is it ?'

'Why, it 's a coon.'

'Gentlemen, there is written on this paper the word 'coon!'' (*Applause.*)

A correct result was in like manner attained with respect to a great number of animals, bears, snakes, babboons and lizards. A sound tooth was also drawn from a poor woman by mistake. Professor Stubbs looked on in perfect amazement; also the patentee of the 'Vestimental Soap.' The doctor called them both to his side when the lecture was over. 'You have seen the method of procedure,' said he; 'are you now ready for a *lusus naturæ*? We 'll go and dig one up to-night at Lazy Hollow. After that, I guess we 'd better go South. Gentlemen,' said he, turning to some persons who lingered near, 'thanks for your patronage; won't you come and drink—— (checking himself) some ——*water ?*'

S T A N Z A S

WRITTEN ON HEARING A FRIEND SAY 'I 'M GROWING OLD.'

BY A NEW CONTRIBUTOR.

I.

THE soul can ne'er grow old, can wither never,
  It will but flourish in perennial youth,
If thou dost watch the priceless treasure ever,
  With unabated constancy and truth.

II.

Then weep not, as the years, past all returning,
  Come hasting on with never-varying pace;
Weep not as daily, hourly thou art learning,
  Time wastes thy strength and mars thy youthful grace.

III.

His hand the roses of thy cheek may wither,
  But O! the spirit's rose he cannot blight;
The brightness of thine eye may quench forever,
  But can he darken e'er the spirit's light?

IV.

'The rainbow of the soul'—can it e'er languish?
  Say, pure affection, can it e'er grow cold?
Feeling's 'bright wild-flower wreath,' 'mid joy or anguish,
  Can it e'er wither? — *can the soul grow old ?*

V.

Oh, no! no change shall visit the pure-hearted,
  Save that more clear and bright the flame shall glow,
When years have come and silently departed;
  This, *this* the change the pure in heart shall know.

VI.

Then weep not, as the years, past all returning,
  Still bear thee onward to that glorious time,
When hope no more shall cheat the spirit's yearning,
  And youth shall flourish in immortal prime.

THE SAINT LEGER PAPERS.

NUMBER THIRTEEN

'DING-DONG! — one, two; ding-dong! — three, four; ding-dong! five, six; ding-dong! — seven, *eight!* Yes, eight was the hour. And there I stood before a massive, gloomy old building, which presented a most forbidding aspect. There was not the slightest sign of its being inhabited. Not a solitary light gleamed from any one of the numerous apartments. It bore the appearance of desertion and decay. The entrance to the court-yard was open, but no porter was in attendance in the lodge; though I could read by the uncertain glimmering of a lamp suspended across the street the half-effaced words, '*Parlez au concierge.*' I had stood but a moment, anxiously scrutinizing every thing within my observation, when a figure, muffled in a large cloak, approached from the court, came hastily up to me, and exclaimed:

''You are punctual — come with me.'

'I followed my conductor across the court, up two flights of stairs and through several narrow passages and corridors, first turning one way, then another, till I was bewildered. The house was unfurnished so far as I could perceive, and the air was close and noisome. My companion at last stopped before a door, which he opened, and ushered me into a room of moderate size, but exquisitely furnished. It was also brilliantly lighted. A small table of beautiful workmanship stood in the centre, upon which was laid a choice supper, flanked by wines of every variety and flavor. A cheerful fire of large logs blazed in the fire-place, for the evening was cool, and every thing gave token of good taste in the occupant and abundant means to improve it.

''Welcome, welcome, my son!' exclaimed my father, throwing off his disguise and warmly embracing me; 'and may GOD bless you for obeying the summons, though I feared it was too late. Why, Wilfred, you have grown up to be a man almost. Yet I would have known my child among a thousand!'

'I was struck with the affectionate and subdued tone of my parent. The seven years which had made so great an alteration in me had scarcely changed him, as he was in the prime of manhood, and had not begun the melancholy descent upon the other side of the scale of life. Yet there was a seriousness in his aspect, a something terribly calm and determined in his countenance, quite unlike my father, which filled me with apprehension.

''Come, come,' continued he, 'you must be faint and weary; sit down. You see I have been expecting you. We have much to do this very night; so fortify yourself with a hearty supper.'

'We sat down together. My father made some show of joining

me, but only as I believe to persuade me to partake freely. It must be a serious matter which will prevent a youth of seventeen, after a day's exercise and abstinence, from doing justice to an alluring table. The healthful calls of determined hunger are rarely disregarded by the young. GOD forgive me the satisfaction I took that evening at that same table! As soon as I had finished, my father bade me sit down near him.

' ' Wilfred,' said he, ' would that I might now tell you to seek repose after your journey; but time presses, and the case is urgent. Can you listen to me ?'

' I trembled, I know not why, but I answered unhesitatingly that I could.

' ' 'T is well,' he continued; ' you are in time. Had you delayed another day, you might have found no one to have called father !'

' I begged an explanation. ' Listen then,' was the reply, ' and mark my words. You yourself remember, or at least you have heard of, Julian Moncrieff?' I assented. ' Julian Moncrieff, whose fate has been linked with mine for the last twenty years. To-morrow morning, when the sun shall redden yon towers of Notre-Dame, it will shine insensibly to one of us !'

' ' For heaven's sake, what mean you ?' I exclaimed.

' ' Silence !' continued my parent, ' and interrupt me not. Twenty years ago this night, Julian Moncrieff, with your father and his young and beautiful bride — thy mother, thy injured mother, boy — arrived here in this accursed city; nay, came here to this very mansion; entered here into this very room. See you that couch ? On it she reclined — the lovely, the confiding, the virtuous one ! There she sat and smiled, and loved and smiled again. Wilfred, my boy, if I could summon all that is held enviable and precious on this round earth and in heaven above, and add to that the price of my soul's salvation, I would give all, *all*, ALL to recall that scene once more, and see my Isabella for one little moment, as I saw her then, and hear once, just *once* again, the sound of her sweet, sweet voice ! But she is gone — lost to me forever ! Have not years, years passed by since *then?* No; it is not so; else I had not this fresh grief. When have I grieved before ? Do not people lose their wives ? Is it then so dreadful ? Tell me, Wilfred, that there is yet hope !'

' I saw that my father's brain was wandering, but I knew not what to reply.

' ' Wretch that I am !' he continued, without waiting for an answer; ' the bitterness of this moment is more than I can bear !' He went on more calmly : ' This now gloomy mansion we selected because there belonged to it a large and delightful garden, and it was quiet and secluded. A brief year we made this our home. With my young wife's fortune added to my own, we were rich — for Paris, very rich. We took another hotel in Rue Montmartre, where we entertained our visitors and gave fêtes and parties. But here were we most happy, because we lived most within ourselves. I have not time, nay, I have not resolution, to tell my history. You will find all that I have thought necessary to reveal among my papers. Search for nothing which you find not there,' pointing to a small box; 'every thing else has been destroyed. You know that your mother sickened, and then she—yes, she—died! O! she died, Wilfred, but not *here!* No, no; not here—not here. She was happy here, Wilfred! she was happy here! Well, I was a lost being, and I gave myself up to sin—ay, *utterly* gave myself to it!

"This same Julian Moncrieff—he, my companion in iniquity, my sworn confederate and ally, between whom and myself there is an oath which neither dare break—this same Julian Moncrieff has cause for deadly quarrel with me; long has had cause. Ask no more. Every thing is arranged; to-morrow morning at break of day we meet in yonder garden, near my Isabella's bower. The place I selected, for there I will yield myself up a sacrifice, after so many years of criminal neglect. Her memory shall be honored: we meet to-morrow—our weapons the rapier—the combat to cease only with the death of one of us—*and I am that one!*'

"Never!' exclaimed I, starting up, ' never shall so barbarous a conflict take place! I have heard enough; I am a boy no longer. If I have not the power to stop it—I will apply to the authorities; I will go to the police. Father, father, I implore you recall your senses. Speak to me rationally, and not with such portentous calmness.'

'Wilfred,' said my parent, 'let me beg you to sit down and be calm yourself. You cannot prevent this meeting, for I have determined that it SHALL take place. You are too young to understand me. GOD grant that you may never come to do so by experience! I am not a lunatic, nor have I lost my senses. But one thing I say; and think not, my boy, that I am lost to parental feeling. Oh no, my son; had it been so, I would not have sent for thee that I might once more behold my own flesh and blood, once more look upon *her* child. But this I say: that I *will not* live longer on the earth, and I prefer rather to fall by the hand of my antagonist than by my own; and most of all would I fall by the hand of Julian Moncrieff.'

'What could I say? what could I do? Was I unmanly or pusillanimous in yielding to my father? Ought I to have resisted at all hazards? You would think so, doubtless; yet it seemed as if the avenging angel stood before me, and as he frowned fearfully upon me, uttered the word '*Forbear!*' I was silent.

"Now, my son, to business,' continued my father, calmly, at the same time opening a large case of papers. 'I must give you such information as will enable you to act understandingly.'

'So saying, he proceeded to give me a detail of all his estate, with the most minute particulars; directing me whose advice to take in Paris, what to do under this state of things, etc. The bulk of his fortune and of my mother's was in England and Scotland; but a very considerable sum had been invested in French securities, in the name of his friend and solicitor, Monsieur Coulanges. I was then informed that every precaution had been taken, so that the cause of his decease should not be known, and that the funeral was arranged to take place on the second day from the combat. My father made me promise sacredly that I would not attempt to revenge his death, nor harbor malice against his foe.

'It seemed my father's desire to prolong this interview to day-break. This was a relief to me. I would not have dared to retire to rest. I might have been overpowered by fatigue and slumbered. My father would not have called me, and I should have awoke and found him *gone*. I sat the whole night giving a horribly calm attention to all that was said to me. At length the first gray streaks of dawn began to light up the sky, until it was apparent day. Presently the step of some one in the passage-way was heard.

'' *It is time !*' said my father, quickly. ' Wilfred, my son, remember what I have told you. And now, farewell !'

' He took me in his arms and kissed me many times with great earnestness. I was unmanned; I wept like a child. My father stood calm.

'' This is not right, my son. This is not like a St. Leger.'

' As soon as I could speak, I begged my father to allow me to accompany him. He hesitated a moment.

'' Will you promise to be composed ?' said he.

' I bowed my head.

'' It is best so,' he added; ' the sacrifice should be in your presence. Once more, farewell !'

' He then took two rapiers from a side-table, and going to the couch, he knelt before it, and drew a miniature from his bosom.

'' Here, here,' he murmured, ' my sweet and sainted wife, do I expiate my sins against you! At last, oh! at last, I see you as of yore !— at last we are reünited !'

' He started, beckoned me to follow, and left the room. We proceeded from one passage-way to another, down several flights of stairs, to the garden. I had no time to look about me, but followed close after my father into a very secluded part of the garden, until we came to a beautiful bower, the entrance of which was entirely overgrown with vines and evergreens. I could discern the figure of a man pacing impatiently up and down the walk. This figure attracted my whole attention, for I knew it was Julian Moncrieff. As we came up he started on seeing me, made a slight inclination to my father, and hastily exclaimed :

'' How is this ? There were to be no witnesses.'

'' There are none,' said my father, sternly; ' this is my son; he understands our arrangement. He desires to be present, and I have consented.'

'' It shall not be !' said the other, hastily.

'' Nay, but it shall !' replied my father; ' if you wish, go summon your daughter; it will delay us but a moment, and then both will be represented.'

'' Have it as you will,' said Moncrieff; ' we are losing time.'

' I had during this short conversation an opportunity to examine my father's opponent. I had seen him often when a boy, and I knew his character. He was tall, well-made, and in one way handsome; but there was a sinister expression about his countenance which experience and intercourse with the world seemed to have increased rather than diminished. I looked upon him and shuddered. He also brought two rapiers, one of which was laid aside, and the parties, without exchanging another word, advanced toward each other. You are aware that the St. Legers were always accomplished swordsmen and masters of fence. The sword-play is, and ever has been, a favorite pastime of the race. In point of skill I had not the slightest fear for my father; but his express determination to fall in the encounter struck me with horror. As the two became engaged in the combat I almost lost sight of the fearful result in admiration of the skill displayed by both combatants. Do you wonder at this?' said the Woedallah, half turning toward me; 'you need not, for the mind of man is strangely constituted. I soon discovered my father's superiority over his antagonist, and hope revived in my heart, and I began to trust that all would yet end well. Mark me, it did not occur to me that, in case Julian Moncrieff should fall, his young daughter would be left without parent or protector. Well, the conflict went on. My father was perfectly calm and unruffled; Moncrieff, on the contrary, began to lose temper. This increased my father's advantage, but he evidently avoided availing himself of it. Once or twice, when Moncrieff rashly exposed his points, my father would coolly remind him of it by a slight touch, but nothing more. This added to his impatience, and he used his weapon with a desperate rashness. 'I could see my father smile calmly as he managed with most admirable skill every stroke of his opponent, entering in spite of himself into the spirit of the combat. Suddenly his countenance changed; it assumed a deadly, fearful, fatal expression. As he turned aside one of Moncrieff's thrusts, he suddenly struck at the left arm of the latter. The stroke told, for the red blood followed swiftly from the wound. Smarting with pain, Moncrieff made a furious lunge at my father's breast. It was a stroke most easily parried, and when parried, would unavoidably expose the party to a fatal charge in return. What was my horror on seeing my father, instead of taking so open an advantage, deliberately throw his arms up and receive his enemy's sword through his body. He fell prostrate to the earth, directly in front of the bower of his ill-fated Isabella. I rushed forward and knelt by his side, and endeavored to stanch the fatal wound. Moncrieff appeared almost in a frenzy.

' 'Oh, God!' he exclaimed, 'what have I done!'

'He approached to bend over the prostrate body. I repulsed him rudely.

' 'Wretch!' I exclaimed, 'dare not to come near the one you have so foully murdered; if you attempt it, you will find a St. Leger who not only knows his weapon, but has also the disposition to use it.'

' 'Young man,' said Moncrieff, in a subdued tone, 'I blame not your passionate feelings, but I pray you calm them. In the name of your dying parent I adjure you to be calm, and to allow me to assist you. See,' he continued, eagerly, 'he still lives; (my father uttered a slight groan;) let us haste to do something. The wound may not be mortal.'

'I resisted no longer, but with the aid of Moncrieff conveyed my father to the apartment we had left but a few moments previous, and laid him upon the very couch at which he knelt before going to the combat. Moncrieff proceeded to examine the wound with the skill of an experienced surgeon, and with all a woman's gentleness; but soon shook his head despairingly. My father had swooned without uttering a word; still we knew that life was not extinct. After administering a slight stimulant with my own hands, he faintly opened his eyes; and although he looked upon no one, I am confident he knew where he was. He spoke not, save in broken whispers; and as I knelt to catch their meaning, I could only hear faintly articulated: '*My precious wife! — my Isabella! — receive the sacrifice!*'

'My father survived not quite an hour. All of the time he lay almost insensible, he feebly held my hand in his, and occasionally gave it a slight pressure. Suddenly he gave a convulsive start, and his lips moved feebly. I strained every sense to catch what he said. '*My Isabella, come nearer to me! I am happy now!*' were the words that died away upon his lips as his spirit parted from his body.'

Again the Wœdallah paused. I dared not trust myself to look toward him, but waited until he should proceed.

'Three months after I awoke in a sick room. At last my brain was clear and sensible. Of nothing was I conscious during that time save that I was in friendly hands. I remember that there was a still silence that wearied me; noiseless steps and low whispers occasionally relieved it, but it was dreadfully oppressive. At last I awoke. I was reduced to the lowest point, but still I lived. My mind, under the strong and conflicting excitements which had been brought to bear upon it, had at the last moment yielded to their force; delirium ensued; then fever — then convalescence.

'I recovered. Would not my first steps be directed to England, eagerly, rapidly directed thither, to escape from the country which had proved the ruin of my sire?' One would naturally suppose so; yet delay succeeded delay. I was still in Paris. I had first to see Monsieur Coulanges. That certainly was necessary; then the friends of my father called to offer their condolences (for all supposed he had died a natural death) and invited me to visit them in proper time. Although you would hardly suppose an Englishman could find much favor at such a time in France, when all Europe was convulsed with wars in which France and England were always enemies, still you must remember that intrigue was after all the great weapon of the day; that I was born in France, and had powerful friends in Scotland, many of whom kept up a constant correspondence with the French court. Thus I was admitted there without suspicion; and — shall I say it? — after a short time abandoned myself entirely to its influence. Need I tell you how, when I say it was at the profligate court of Louis XV., with youth and wealth and a fair advantage of person? So it was that I did evil in the sight of the LORD, even as my father had done. Oh! what abyss so deep that it can overwhelm the horrible ministers of damnation who waited on that court! Yet the fortune of the young St. Leger was envied, and he was pronounced the most blissful of mortals. Yet what a hell reigned in my bosom! Ten thousand avenging furies were shrieking hourly in my ears, yet I went on, went on my journey to the deep perdition of the damned. I had become a wretched voluptuary; and Pleasure, which retired farther and farther in the distance as I wooed her most, began to pall upon my senses.

'I was at a masked ball given by the Duchess of ——. I had no less than six appointments there, and how to manage all, tasked my skill to the utmost. It was in the midst of the revel that a tall female figure in a plain mask approached me, and with a dignified, commanding air, beckoned me to follow her. As adventures of this sort were by no means uncommon, I followed the retreating form of the lady out of the magnificent *salon* through one apartment after another till we arrived at a small door, to which my guide applied a key and we entered.

'I found myself, not as I had anticipated in an exquisite boudoir fragrant with flowers and perfumes, to add to the voluptuousness of the scene, but in a small gloomy, narrow room, without a single article of furniture except a faint light glimmering on the mantel. I gave a hasty glance over this scene of ill-omen, but fear is not the foible of the St. Leger. I thought I was betrayed by the intrigue of a rival; but I was armed, and the struggle for life would be desperate. While these thoughts were passing through my mind, the lady had advanced into the middle of the room, after bolting the door, and stood regarding me in silence.

' 'This is not exactly as you expected,' said the Unknown, addressing me at length in pure English. 'Not quite so alluring as an interview with the Comptess ——, to which at this hour you were invited.'

I made no reply to the announcement of a secret known as I supposed only to the two interested; but simply asked, in a quiet nonchalant way:

'Pray, what is your wish?'

' 'Nay,' said the mask, in an angry impatient tone; ' ask me not what is my *wish*, but what is my WILL, for by Heaven it shall be obeyed! I have brought thee hither to hear my commands, thou renegade Englishman! Thou shame of a manly house! *Thou* a St. Leger! Go, take the name of one of the strange women who make you their slave; follow on your path even as the ox goeth to the slaughter, or as a fool to the correction of the stocks; go now to their bed which is covered with coverings of tapestry, with carved works and fine linen of Egypt, and perfumed with myrrh, aloes and cinnamon, and take your fill of love until the morning; but by the Supreme Power above, if you do this, and dare again to call yourself a St. Leger, I will plunge this dagger to your heart!'

So saying, the mask half unsheathed a small poniard which she wore at her belt, and went on before I had time to speak :

'You have still another course left. Leave this place of abominations before the iniquity of the Ammonites is yet full. The days of the Jezebels and the Athaliahs and the Delilahs are numbered. In the portion of Jezreel shall dogs eat their flesh. Return to England ; go where you will ; stay here if you have strength to do it ; but I warn you, forget not again that you are a St. Leger ! Sell not your manhood at this debauched and infamous court : if you disobey,' (again touching the dagger,) you know the penalty !'

'The rebuke which these words conveyed, its truth, severe though it was, rendered me for a moment incapable of speaking. I stood discovered, stripped of the miserable dross and tinsel of unhallowed pleasure, in all the ugly and rude deformity of detected guilt. Yes, I stood

'AND felt how awful goodness is, and saw
Virtue in her shape how lovely ; saw and pined
His loss.'

I felt piqued, nevertheless, at the threat of the Unknown ; for man will often listen to persuasion, when he will not be moved by force ; and the idea of abandoning even a course of sin, through fear of my life, struck at my pride. I wished from my heart that such an argument had been omitted.

'Have you nothing to say ?' continued the mask, impatiently, as I was hesitating what to reply.

' 'Nothing,' said I, coldly, ' to one who under an assumed disguise seeks to frighten me by threats into measures which a sense of right alone can ever make effectual or sincere.'

'Spoken like a man indeed !' said the figure, removing her mask, and disclosing to me the clear, penetrating gray eyes, the lofty brow and the haughty mien of the *Lady Alice St. Leger !* 'Kinsman,' said she, 'I have come to save you from shame and ruin !' I did not suppose that threats would accomplish this ; but I wished to show my own determination to preserve our name from farther disgrace. 'Let,' she continued reverently, 'let the dead rest in peace ; with the living there is hope. I come not to reproach nor to direct, but solemnly to warn !'

'The warning shall be heeded,' said I, emphatically, and —— '

'Enough,' said the Lady Alice, with dignity ; 'I believe you.' So saying, she replaced her mask, and notwithstanding my entreaties that she would remain a few moments, she unbolted the door and disappeared. Scarcely sensible whether this was not all a dream, I proceeded to find my way out. The thought of returning to the gay scene I had so lately left, filled me with disgust. I soon discovered a private entrance into the court-yard, and throwing myself into a carriage, was conveyed to my hotel. I went home a repentant man.

'The morning after the first commission of a sin, or after the first resolution to reform, is generally remarkable for severe struggles with ones'-self ; and I had no small share of these. I rose as from a fearful dream. I was not certain that all I had remembered of the previous evening was not an illusion. By degrees it all çame back to me with distinctness. I summoned my valet; he brought me a score of perfumed *billets-doux*, done up in exquisite taste. The moment had arrived which should decide my fate: my hand was on the seal of one which I knew to be from the Comptesse. I hesitated; I called for a taper. If I opened the billets, I was lost — and I knew it. One by one I took them up and deliberately held each over the taper until it was consumed. Somehow, although the Comptesse's billet was first in my hand it still remained there when all the rest were destroyed. 'Surely,' said the Tempter, 'there can be no harm in opening this one — this last one, as I have resolved not to answer it. It was too late : by a tremendous effort I brought the doomed thing across the flame. It turned and twisted into a thousand contortions as if determined to escape. As the heat caused the leaves to open, it gave a vividness to the delicately-traced lines, and I could distinctly read expressions of tender reproach. I turned away my head by a sort of nightmare effort, but held the billet steadily in the flame, nor did I move, nor scarcely breathe, till the subtle element, creeping to my fingers, as if for a farther sacrifice, told me that it was all over, and that I was saved. I started up and ordered horses ready for Bloissy. This was a small and beautiful chateau, about twenty leagues from Paris, which my father had occupied, though it had been very rarely resorted to by him. Once I had been there since his decease to find some papers which were deposited there. Report I knew had said that the place was procured by my father for the purpose of having a secluded retreat for his young wife far enough away from Paris to prevent rumors of his infidelity ever reaching her. Alas ! it was a pitiable device ; as if a husband's dereliction can be long concealed from the trusting heart which has yielded all to him ! Well, at night I arrived at this retired spot. How happy I was ! The battle had been fought, and a victory, a glorious victory over myself, obtained. I determined upon a course of self-examination. I took possession of the chamber which had been my mother's; I invoked her presence to enable me to preserve my purpose. I prayed *God* — yes, I could pray then — to give me strength. I have told you that my father destroyed all his private papers. In searching, however, an old bureau in my mother's room, I found sticking to the end of the drawer one of her letters to her husband. It was written during the second year of her marriage, and as I presume, upon the occasion of their first separation, when my father, representing that his business called him to Paris, and would detain him there for a considerable time, forgot the wife of his bosom, and left her to suffer alone. At this time she was still trustful and unsuspicious. 'Here is the letter,' continued the Wœdallah, holding it out to me. I took it from his hands. It was written in a delicate female hand, and was blurred and blotted apparently by tears, 'precious signs,' the Wœdallah continued, 'of his wretched father's repentance.' I begged the Wœdallah to allow me to take the letter that I might again peruse it, and as it may lend an interest to the narrative, I will give some extracts from it here :

' DEAR, DEAR WILFRED : I cannot realize that you are gone, and to stay from me so long ; but oh ! my heart wants something in your absence ; nay, it wants you, my Wilfred, at this moment to be at my side ; to clasp your arm around me and kiss me, and tell me over and over again that you love me. Do you miss your poor Belle, even now, dear husband, and are you almost tempted to turn back and bring her with you ?' How dependant upon you I have been since we were married ; but I must rely upon myself now, and it is well ; I feel that it is for our good that we are parted, and this reconciles me.' · · · ·

' Oh, gentle loving, trustful wife ! Oh, base perfidious, deceitful husband ! But let me continue the extracts :'

. ' Do you know, dearest Wilfred, that I feel more like staying here, quietly *thinking of you*, than mingling in the gayeties of Paris ? Somehow I cannot feel that I am a mother in yon strange city ; and shall I confess it, dear, dear Wilfred, I have almost thought that you did not love your Isabella so much when surrounded by its attractions. Now, dearest, forgive me, for you know that I do not believe this ; the whole wide world could not make me believe it ; only I love to have you reässure me, Wilfred, and then how confident I grow again !

'*Six o'clock.*

' My precious love, I am home-sick to see you. The day has been lovely thus far, but now it rains. All nature is so beautiful about me that I cannot but be cheerful ; and yet methinks this very loveliness of scenery, which so cheers and gladdens us in bright day-light, lends a saddening influence in sweet melancholy twilight ; sweet when we are together, dearest, melancholy when we are parted.

' My chief solace is our sweet babe ; all is new to him here, and he looks at every thing with great surprised eyes, wondering what it means. He has just gone to his rosy rest. Heaven make his slumbers peaceful ; for troubled waters sweep even over the bosom of infancy.

'*Eleven o'clock.*

' I am going now, my dear husband, to my solitary bed. I have been talking this evening with old Hannah. She has entertained me sweetly by telling me of your childhood. I culled a fresh bouquet of roses for my table this morning, but an instinct of love led me to preserve in my chamber those *we* gathered yesterday. Where is the rose I gave you ? And now love, my precious love, with a sweet, sweet kiss — good night !'

'*Tuesday,* 3 *o'clock.*

' Oh, my Wilfred, I have been so agonized ! How have I been tortured ! What shall I say or do ? To-day Count Davrainville called. He was just from Paris ; and do you think the wretch had the audacity to speak of you as —— Oh, no ; I will not insult my

Wilfred by naming it; but the Count spoke of it so as a matter of course, that it seemed as if I should sink, although I knew every word was false. I assure you I left the room without waiting for a repetition of such despicable slander. Oh Wilfred, Wilfred! what a load is on my heart! If I could only come *now* and creep into your bosom, and have you soothe me like a poor grieved child! Ah! were it not for my precious babe, how quick would I fly to you !'

.   .   .   .

' This letter,' continued the Wœdallah, ' this letter written by my sainted mother completed my reform. I knelt down by the side of the bed where she expired, and made a vow before my GOD to live thenceforth a virtuous life. I shuddered at the narrow escape I had had, and could hardly believe that it was real. Meanwhile my absence from Paris caused a thousand reports to be set in circulation. I abstained as far as possible from listening to them, and finally I was left in peace.'

Here the Wœdallah paused again. He continued silent so long that I turned toward him as before, and as before perceived that he was suffering from extreme agony. As he did not seem inclined to go on, I said to him :

' This cannot be the end of your narrative ; excuse me, but I am painfully interested to know all.'

' I will proceed,' said he, hesitatingly; ' and yet I would pass briefly over the remainder of my life. One cannot well bear to look back upon opportunities of happiness unimproved, nay trifled with, thrown away, and which are lost forever ; especially when wretchedness and despair come in their place. But I wish the history of my life to make you wiser and better ; and this effect might not be produced should I stop here. I had sworn to live a virtuous life, and I kept my vow ; but let me tell you, my son, that man escapes not easily from the consequences of an evil course, notwithstanding he may have altogether reformed, as I did. The remainder of my history conveys that single moral; therefore ponder it well. As for myself, I will say in brief how, continuing in my retirement, I became enamoured with the only daughter of an old French Count, whose château was near my own ; How lovely and innocent the young Leila ! (I started) — De Soisson appeared; how lovely and innocent she was ; how I sought her, wooed and wedded her, and brought her to Paris in triumph as my bride ; how, *in consequence of my previous irregularities,* I became unreasonably jealous of my wife, who had all the freedom and gayety of manner of her nation ; how I believed that I had proof most damning of her guilt; and how when calling her to my presence I accused her of it, I was met with indignant denial and retort. Ah, now my ' pleasant vices' began to be my scourge! I was not satisfied, but swore I would forsake a world which virtue had deserted. I made ample provision for my wife, and after warning her that I should have strict watch kept upon her conduct, took our young daughter, whom I had already began to hate - because she resembled her mother, placed her at a nunnery to be educated, and sailed for Scotland. Here, without making myself known to any one, I proceeded to the Highlands, and having arranged to keep up a constant communication with the main land, I came hither. Here I resolved to do what good I might. I became interested in this simple-hearted honest people. My heart was not yet quite stone. My daughter I frequently sent for, for I could not bear that she should quite forget her father, though he could not *love* his child. You have no doubt heard how I was forced to leave this island and take up my abode in a neighboring one. I acted through the whole conscientiously for the good of this poor people. When the new steward took control, instead of returning myself I went to Paris, in consequence of what I had heard from my correspondent of the conduct of my wife. I went to Paris, but she was not there, but lived, as my agent informed me, at my château at Bloissy, in order, as he said, to enjoy still greater freedom. I determined to stop this dishonor to my name at all hazards. I repaired to the château. I sent for my wife without announcing myself. She came in, and on seeing me threw herself into my arms and fainted. I placed her upon a couch until she should recover. Had I found my wife pale and thin I should have believed her innocent, but although dressed with great simplicity, she looked as rosy and as beautiful as ever.

'She soon recovered from her swoon. ' Oh, my Wilfred!' said she, faintly, ' have you returned to me at last?'

' ' Hypocrite!' said I, sternly, ' cease such abominable, base deceit! I know all; nothing is concealed. Your guilt has been discovered to me.'

' Perhaps you have some time in your life,' continued the Wœdallah, ' unfortunately bruised a young and beautiful flower, and as you turned to view the ruin you had effected, it would seem as if the tender petals, so full of rich and variegated life and beauty and freshness, strove to convey, by their very crushed and shrinking appearance, a deep reproach for your wanton carelessness. So it was with Leila. Oh! what a look!—so subdued, so crushed, yet so reproachful! God! God! how can I bear to think of it!' exclaimed the Wœdallah, starting up and stamping his foot in frenzy, and then reseating himself. ' Yet she said nothing; she would deny nothing; she would acknowledge nothing. So the fiend was busy with me, and I still believed her guilty. I told her to be ready to accompany me, and that she should never return to France. The good old count her father was dead years before, and the count's wife had long preceded him. Leila seemed not at all distressed at the idea of leaving, and the next day we set out for Bordeaux, and sailed thence to Scotland; and then *we came here*. My wife had an apartment appropriated to her exclusive use, and a single female attendant. Books she had, and every thing necessary to her outward comfort. But I never allowed her to converse with me. I never spoke to her. Sometimes her pride would give way to her love, and I could hear her address me tenderly. ' Wilfred! oh, Wilfred!' she would say, ' this is not such severe punishment to be ever near you, under the same roof, and to feel that you are near me, even if you will not speak to your unfortunate Leila.' But she never alluded to her crime—never denied her guilt. My own heart was by degrees wearing away within me. I held communication with no one ; it was a dreadful situation. One morning Sarah, our old attendant, told me her mistress was very ill. I hardly knew what to do, but I bade her go and ascertain the symptoms. As she opened the door of my wife's apartment, I heard my name called most earnestly by some one in extreme agony. It was my wife's voice. I hesitated. At that moment she saw me, and shrieked to me to come to her.

' ' Oh ! Wilfred ! if you do not come,' she exclaimed, ' you will be fearfully judged, forever and forever ! Oh ! come, *come*, COME to me !'

' I rushed into the room, threw myself into her arms, and burst into tears.

' ' GOD be praised !' exclaimed my Leila, ' GOD be praised for this last mercy-drop ! Dearest husband, before my MAKER, before HIM in whose presence I shall so soon appear, I swear that I am innocent of any crime toward you ! My pride, my sinful, foolish pride is all I have to repent of. You have been treacherously dealt by, my husband. Do you not believe me ? Do you not believe your Leila, now that she is dying ?'

' ' Oh, yes ! oh, yes !' I sobbed ; ' Yes, I do ; I *do* believe you. Forgive me, my injured wife ! I ask not GOD's forgiveness, but yours, *yours* I must have !'

' I cannot dwell upon this scene. My wife's days were numbered ; yet we lived a life-time in those few brief hours. And then for the first time I learnt how, for fiendish purposes of his own, which he could not accomplish, my correspondent had foully deceived and lied to me ; and how a noble pride in my traduced and suffering Leila prevented her from affording me an explanation. My Leila died praying for blessings upon the wretch who had embittered her life almost to its latest moment. She rests gently beside my mother, under the shade of her own favorite evergreens at Bloissy. And here am I, the stricken of GOD, before you !'

M A N N E R S.

FROM ' THE CHILDREN'S DANCE,' BY JOHN WILSON.

DEEM not to gilded roofs alone confined
The magic charm of MANNERS mild and free ;
Attendant mostly they on peace of mind,
Best cherished by the breath of purity.
Yes, oft in scenes of lifeful, rustic glee,
Where youth and joy and innocence resort,
The MANNERS gladly rule the revelry ;
Unseen they mingle in the quickening sport,
Well pleased mid village hinds to hold their homely court.

IRISH BALLADS: 'THE BALLAD POETRY OF IRELAND.' Edited by CHARLES GAVAN DUFFY. Fifth Edition. Dublin, 1845.

IRISH LITERATURE! The very words fall strangely on the ear; nor rightly consi-dered, are the thoughts they suggest less strange to the mind. That a nation emi-nently fraught with all the elements of genius should exist for so many hundred years, witnessing the successive development of the other peoples of Europe, and yet remain with scarcely the basis of a national literature, seems almost incredible. Even their unprecedented and unnatural political history can scarcely explain it. Tumult, contention, the fierce passions of revenge, hatred, exultation and despair, aroused by such struggles, seem naturally calculated rather to create a nationality in poetry than to restrain it; and yet Ireland can hardly point to a single name on her annals that will enable her to take her place among the nations. The fact too that England has always been rather loath to receive any thing from Ireland (except lands and money,) would have apparently forced such Irishmen as possessed the power to become intensely patriotic in their spirit. And yet, except the bards, of whom more hereafter, who is there, from DUNS SCOTUS* to SWIFT, GOLDSMITH, BURKE or SHERIDAN, that has turned to place on the brow of his country a single leaf of that wreath which they were all so well able to weave? Ireland has been unfortu-nate in her eminent men, as in every other phase of her most unhappy history. Think what WELLINGTON might have done for her!† MOORE may be regarded as the com-mencement of a new order of things, of the development of which the little volume under consideration forms an important epoch. Irishmen have begun to see that Ireland wants a literature of her own; a literature that shall not consist of the rude ballads of the native bards, unintelligible to the largest part of the intellectual por-tion of the nation, or a cluster of a few bright names, Irish indeed by birth, but Eng-

---

* CLAIMED as an Irishman on the slender ground of a chance expression: ' As in the definition of St. FRANCIS or St. Patrick, man is necessarily presupposed.' He said 'St. FRANCIS' because he was a Franciscan; and therefore it follows from his mentioning 'St. PATRICK' that he was an Irish-man.

† 'THAT chief so coldly great,' to adopt the words of MOORE, ' whom Fame unwillingly shines upon:'

'WHOSE name is one of th' ill-omened words
They link with hate on his native plains;
And why? They lent him hearts and swords,
And he in return gave scoffs and chains.'

lish in thought, feeling and expression. They see that Scotland, having relatively to England many points in common with themselves, yet possesses a literature as national as any in Europe ; a literature which, having adopted the language of England, changed it till it became sufficiently distinct for national purposes ; breathing the very instinct of Scotland, and finding an echo in the heart of every Scot. Such a literature as this they wish to found ; embracing all parties, all sects in the common denomination of Irishman, and giving a new spirit and concentration to the efforts of the nation. It is a worthy cause, and if it succeed may bear fruit beyond the present computations of man. There is more in these disregarded springs of human action than is dreamed of in the philosophy of shrewd statesmen and subtle diplomatists. Ireland has not now a single rallying point.

The book before us is in itself a proof of how much it was needed. With about a dozen or twenty really good ballads, the rest vary from the mediocre to the bad. And yet, such as it is, it has met with great popularity. Five editions have been disposed of in about six months. It forms a part of a series, each one of which is sold at the low price of one shilling ; thus designed to spread rapidly among the people, and well calculated to raise in them the spirit of nationality and union among themselves which is the great necessity of Ireland. In a long preface the editor gives us a somewhat disconnected sketch of his purpose in compiling the work, and the sources from which he has drawn his materials. These he appears to divide into three classes, viz: Translations from the old Gaelic Ballads ; Political Songs written from time to time on both sides, with the Street Ballads recited and sung through the cities and agricultural districts ; and what he terms Anglo-Irish Ballads, a class of but recent origin, English in language but Irish in thought, feeling and expression. This latter division naturally includes the best part of the volume, and is that which this publication seeks to improve and extend. In making his selection the editor has very properly excluded every thing not written by Irishmen, and every thing that did not strike him as being truly national in its manner and matter. He very justly repudiates ' the gibberish of bulls and broken English ; the ' TEDDY my jewels' and ' PADDY my joys' which abound in the caricatures of Irish songs; seeking for a higher standard by which to distinguish the cosmopolitan from the national. This distinction also excludes the exquisite productions of MOORE. National as they are in spirit, they are yet cast into a form too English to fulfil the purposes of such a volume ; and indeed we scarcely see why the two that *are* here, O'RUARK, Prince of Breffni, and ' The Song of the DESMOND,' beautiful as they are, should have been admitted in a collection that has to reject ' Avenging and Bright,' ' Let Erin Remember,' and indeed nearly half of what MOORE has written. In thus selecting, we regret that Mr. DUFFY has not succeeded better, but we trust that the very lack of this peculiar *matériel*, as displayed here, may eventually supply the desideratum.

With the translations from the old Irish ballads we confess ourselves disappointed. We had always imagined them akin to the fine old trumpet-tongued reliques of England, or still more, of Scotland. Yet here we have them, selected by competent scholars, and translated in a manner ' singularly racy and characteristic,' as our editor informs us, ' having caught the spirit and idiomatic character of the language in a wonderful manner,' and being ' more Irish than the Irish itself.' Under these circumstances it is not unfair to presume that we have most favorable specimens of the powers of the native bards, rendered by persons who really write well, and are competent to do them justice ; and yet, with all this, we find but one or two in the whole collection that are really good, and none that will bear the slightest comparison with the similar compositions of the sister island. The following, translated by CLARENCE MANGAN, is almost an exception to these remarks. It is one of the best things in the book, and if all were like it we should not have a word to say against the bards. Its recommendations are its perfect plainness and simplicity and its rough native force. It was written, as tradition goes, to quiet the overbearing pride of a country dame, whose extensive property, consisting of three cows, had caused her to carry her head too high. Its popularity in Munster is demonstrated by a common saying among the peasantry there, ' Aisy, oh, Woman of the Three Cows!' when they wish to lower some consequential individual:

'THE WOMAN OF THREE COWS.

'O. WOMAN of Three Cows, *agragh !* do n't let your tongue thus rattle!
O! do n't be saucy, do n't be stiff, because you may have cattle :
I have seen — and here 's my hand to you, I only say what 's true —
A many a one with twice your stock not half so proud as you.

'Good luck to you, do n't scorn the poor, and do n't be their despiser,
For worldly wealth soon melts away, and cheats the very miser ;
And death soon strips the proudest wreath from haughty human brows;
Then do n't be stiff and do n't be proud, good Woman of Three Cows!

'See where Mœmomia's heroes lie, proud OWEN MOORE's descendants,
'T is they that won the glorious name and had the grand attendants !
If *they* were forced to bow to Fate, as every mortal bows,
Can *you* be proud, can *you* be stiff, my Woman of Three Cows ?

' The brave sons of the LORD OF CLARE, they left the land to mourning;
Mavrone ! for they were banished, with no hope of their returning :
Who knows in what abodes of want those youths were driven to house ?
Yet *you* can give yourself these airs, O ! Woman of Three Cows !

'O ! think of DONNELL of the Ships, the Chief whom nothing daunted ;
See how he fell in distant Spain, unchronicled, unchaunted !
He sleeps, the great O'SULLIVAN, where thunder cannot rouse —
Then ask yourself, should *you* be proud, good Woman of Three Cows ?

'O'RUARK, MAGUIRE, those souls of fire, whose names are shrined in story,
Think how their high achievements once made Erin's greatest glory ;
Yet now their bones lie mouldering under weeds and cypress boughs,
And so, for all your pride, will yours, O ! Woman of Three Cows!

' Th' O'CARROLL's, also, famed when fame was only for the boldest,
Rest in forgotten sepulchres, with Erin's best and oldest ;
Yet who so great as they of old, in battle or carouse ?
Just think of that, and hide your head, good Woman of Three Cows!

'Your neighbor 's poor, and you, it seems, are big with vain ideas,
Because, *inagh !* you 've got three cows, one more I see than *she* has;
That tongue of your's wags more at times than Charity allows,
But if you 're strong, be merciful, great Woman of Three Cows !

'THE SUMMING UP.

' Now, there you go! You still of course keep up your scornful bearing,
And I 'm too poor to hinder you ; but, by the cloak I 'm wearing,
If I had but *four* cows myself, o'en though you were my spouse,
I 'd thwack you well to cure your pride, my Woman of Three Cows !'

The ' County of Mayo,' p. 125, translated by FERGUSON, is tolerable, and its quiet simplicity brings it home to the reader; but we can give but one more specimen of these versions. The following, rendered by CALLANAN, is characteristic, and may be regarded as a favorable example. As the editor remarks, from various and evident reasons, convicts have long been objects of especial sympathy in Ireland :

THE CONVICT OF CLONMELL.

' How hard is my fortune,
   And vain my repining !
The strong rope of fate
   For this young neck is twining.
My strength is departed,
   My cheek sunk and sallow,
While I languish in chains
   In the gaol of Clonmala.

' No boy in the village
   Was ever yet milder,
I 'd play with a child,
   And my sport would be wilder:
I 'd dance without tiring
   From morning till even,
And the goal-ball I 'd strike
   To the lightning of Heaven.

' At my bed-foot decaying,
   My hurl-bat is lying,
Through the boys of the village
   My goal-ball is flying;
My horse, 'mong the neighbors'
   Neglected may fallow,
While I pine in my chains
   In the gaol of Clonmala.

' Next Sunday the patron
   At home will be keeping;
The active young hurlers
   The field will be sweeping;
With the dance of fair maidens
   The evening they 'll hallow,
While this heart, once so gay,
   Shall be cold in Clonmala!'*

Taking them as a whole, these relics of the Gaelic seem to have very little poetry in them.

The next class of ballads to which we have alluded need not detain us long. The political songs of any country are rarely worth much, except as valuable assistance to the philosophic student of history, indicating contemporaneous views and opinions more strikingly than any other records. The details of Irish faction however can possess but little interest for the stranger: that history has no great names or brilliant actions to arrest the attention of any but an Irishman. A mixture of oppression and revolt, each debasing the other; conspiracy countermining conspiracy, and atrocity revenging atrocity, is nearly all we meet in that sullied page of the world's archives. It is altogether too dark a phase of human nature to attract us by its songs and ballads. The ferocious and frenzied of these effusions have not been admitted into this collection: of those that are here, we may mention one by Colonel BLACKER, 'OLIVER's Advice,'† p. 83, with 'Shule Aroon,' p. 130, and perhaps one or two others as being passable, yet not worth quoting. We have been struck with the exceeding poverty of the 'Battle of the Boyne,' a world-renowned ballad, that is about on a par with the poorest of our own political songs. But we turn to the Anglo-Irish class, on which we raise our hopes of something better to come. One or two of these are excellent. Spirited and peculiar, they seem to be the beginning of a new school of writing, which may some day render Irish literature more than a mere name. There are several here by BARRIN, with much rough force. His 'Soggarth Aroon' ('Priest, dear,') p. 68, is strong and impressive, with more character than marks the greater number in this volume. Take the annexed stanzas as an example :

' WHO, in the winter's night,
   Saggarth aroon,
When the could blast did bite,
   Saggarth aroon,
Came to my cabin-door,
And on my earthen-flure
Knelt by me, sick and poor,
   Saggarth aroon ?

' Who, on the marriage-day,
   Saggarth aroon,
Made the poor cabin gay,
   Saggarth aroon ?
And did both laugh and sing,
Making our hearts to ring
At the poor christening,
   Saggarth aroon ?

---

* ONE of the improvements which this little book attempts is the restoration of the Irish names from the barbarous pronunciation of the Saxon. As we see above, Clonmell becomes Clonmala; Erin, it seems, should be Ierne. Many of the changes are singular. Who would recognise MARGARET KELLY in MARGREAD NI CHEALLEADH, or TYRONE in TIR-EOGHAN? HUGH is not much like AODH, nor does M'CARTY retain much semblance of M'CAURA.

† ' PUT your trust in GOD, my boys, and keep your powder dry !'

'Who, as friend only met,
    Saggarth aroon,
Never did flout me yet,
    Saggarth aroon ;
And, when my heart was dim,
Gave, while his eye did brim,
What I should give to him,
    Saggarth aroon?

'Och! you, and only you,
    Saggarth aroon,
And for this I was true to you,
    Saggarth aroon ;
In love they 'll never shake,
When, for ould Ireland's sake,
We a true part did take,
    Saggarth aroon!'

'O'BRIEN of Arra,' p. 188, by the lamented THOMAS DAVIS, is a good national lyric, making up in savage force and fierceness what it lacks by reason of its ruggedness. It takes us back completely, by its striking vraisemblance, to the wild times it pictures so vividly:

O'BRIEN OF ARRA.

'TALL are the towers of O'KENNEDY,
    Broad are the lands of M'CARHA,
DESMOND feeds five hundred men a day,
    Yet, here 's to O'BRIEN of Arra!

Up from the castle of Drumineer,
Down from the top of Camailte,
Clansmen and kinsmen are coming here,
    To give him the CEAD MILE FAILTE."

'See you the mountains look huge at eve?
    So is our chieftain in battle;
Welcome he has for the fugitive,
Usquebaugh, fighting and cattle !

Up from the castle of Drumineer,
Down from the top of Camailte,
Gossip and ally are coming here,
    To give him the CEAD MILE FAILTE.

'Horses the valleys are tramping o'er,
    Sleek from the Sassenach manger ;
CREAGHTS the hills are encamping o'er,
Empty the bawns of the stranger!

Up from the castle of Drumineer,
Down from the top of Camailte,
KERN and CONAGHT are coming here,
    To give him the CEAD MILE FAILTE.

'He has black silver from Killaloe,
    RYAN and CARROLL are neighbors;
NENAGH submits with a pillalou —
    BUTLER is meet for our sabres!

Up from the castle of Drumineer,
Down from the top of Camailte,
RYAN and CARROLL are coming here,
    To give him the CEAD MILE FAILTE.

''T is scarce a week since through Ossary,
    Chased he the Baron of Durrow ;
Forced him five rivers to cross, or he
    Had died by the sword of Red MURROUGH!

Up from the castle of Drumineer,
Down from the top of Camailte,
All the O'BRIENS are coming here,
    To give him the CEAD MILE FAILTE.

'Tall are the towers of O'KENNEDY,
    Broad are the lands of M'CARHA ;
DESMOND feeds five hundred men a day,
    Yet, here 's to O'BRIEN of Arra!

Up from the castle of Drumineer,
Down from the top of Camailte,
Kinsmen and clansmen are coming here,
    To give him the CEAD MILE FAITE.'

Unfortunately, Mr. DUFFY has not been able to collect many like these two last. 'MARGREAD NI CHEALLEADH,' p. 75, and 'EMMELINE TALBOT,' p. 210, are very passable ballads, but scarcely Irish, beyond the cheap nationality of a few local words and phrases. Change these, and they would answer as well for England. 'Fontenoy,' p. 215, a song for the Irish Brigade at that battle, is strong and stirring, but is too close an imitation of the 'Lays of Ancient Rome' to claim much, save its subject, as truly national. 'The Drunkard,' p. 158, is an excellent specimen of the homely ballad ; true, impressive, and withal as minute as a Dutch painting. We would quote it as perfectly Irish in spirit and texture, were not its length impracticable.

We find many ballads very good in themselves, but too cosmopolitan in idea and expression to satisfy us in a collection of this kind. 'The Forester's Complaint,' p. 77, 'The Fairy Thorn,' p. 147, 'Willy Gilliland,' p. 181, 'The Sack of Baltimore,' p. 232, are excellent in their way, but their way is scarcely Irish. Perhaps we can best explain our meaning by an example. 'The Battle of Callan,' p. 194, is a tolerable ballad, but it shows how a piece can be written on a subject wholly national, thickly strown with names and phrases purely local, and yet have in it no spirit of national peculiarity. Its style and manner are the same as those of English ballads

* 'A HUNDRED thousand welcomes.'

on similar subjects, and it might have been written by an Englishman and a by changing a few sectional names:

THE BATTLE OF CALLAN.

'FITZ-THOMAS went forth to the slaughter all burning,
And the dame by Tra-leigh waits the robber's returning,
With the deep-lowing *creach*, with the rich plunder laden,
The altar's best gold, the rare pearls of the maiden!

'Winding down by Ruachta his lances were gleaming;
Floating, wild as a meteor, his banners were streaming;
He rode with the spoils of all DESMOND around him,
But the wrath of the Gael in its red vengeance found him!

'More swift than the eagle from Skellig's high eyrie,
Than whirlwinds of Corrin in hostings of Faëry,
Dark as storm o'er Dun-Mor to the ocean-tried toiler,
Burst M'CARTIE'S fierce wrath on the path of the spoiler!

'O'SULLIVAN MOR, of the mountain and valley,
O'CONNOR, the chief of the tall-masted galley,
O'DRISCOLL, the curse of the *Sassenach* sailor,
Left COGAN'S proud daughter a desolate wailer.

.   .   .   .   .   .

'Chaunt the deeds of the warrior in chivalry vying,
The doom of the Rievers, all prostrate or flying;
The false Saxon's fear, as rejoicing thou lavest
The blood-gouts that burst from the breast of his bravest!'

Compare this for one moment with O'BRIEN of Arra,' and the difference felt and perceived more clearly than it could from pages of analysis.

But what strikes us most strongly and unfavorably in this collection is the poverty of what may be called the national songs; that is, those which are for and sung by the people. Men of cultivated minds may be expected to tolerable verse, but the songs of the people constitute a severer touchston Scotland we find that ballads written by peasants, and read and enjoyed lower classes throughout the country, are such as can give pleasure to the mo vated and intellectual minds. This is a great advantage to any people. It vating to the peasantry, and forms a bond of union, a common feeling be them and those above them. The specimens given by Mr. DUFFY of the and street ballads of Ireland are mournful. We have a right to conclude, a deed he so tells us, that they are favorable examples. If so, what must the r 'WILLY REILLY,' p. 244, spoken of in the highest terms by the editor and Mr. C TON, is remarkably dull. 'The Lamentation of HUGH REYNOLDS,' p. 152, ca lar subject, the editor terms 'the best of its bad class.' It begins:

'MY name it is HUGH REYNOLDS, I come of honest parents,
Near Cavan I was born, as plainly you may see;
By loving of a maid, one CATHARINE M'CABE,
My life has been betrayed; she's a dear maid to me,' etc.

We see thus that Irish literature is not unlike our own, with a few bright but few that savor of the soil. Our position is easily explained; and perhaps Ireland may be resolved by the unfortunate peculiarity of her two languages, di the people with a broad line. We have proved our power of acquiring whate will, as a nation; that they are not without the ability, their peculiarly national would convince the most skeptical. We are both improving, and ere long, wi blessing of Heaven, we may show of what we are capable; but in the mean Ireland should no longer leave unemployed a power, the might of which sh scarcely calculate.

THE BIBLE, THE KORAN AND THE TALMUD: OR BIBLICAL LEGENDS OF THE MUSSULMANS. Compiled from Arabic sources and compared with Jewish traditions. From the German of Dr. C. WEIL, with occasional Notes. In one volume. pp. 264. New-York: HARPER AND BROTHERS.

ANOTHER interesting volume of Messrs. HARPERS' beautifully-executed ' *New Miscellany,*' for which the public are already so largely indebted to them. The leading ideas of these Mohammedan legends, their prominent historical narratives, and the doctrines and precepts which they either state expressly or imply, are contained in the Koran. In some instances it gives their minutest particulars. Indeed, it would seem as if these legends formed part at least of what the founder of the Mohammedan faith terms ' the mother of the book,' indicating that they preceded his Koran in order of time, and embodied the germ of that faith which he subsequently developed. Their leading ideas being found in the Koran invests them with divine authority to the faithful Moslem, since it is a primary article of his creed that every thing contained in the Koran is of ALLAH. They form therefore a valuable acquisition, as an epitome of Mohammedan theology and morals. And their peculiar character, their constant allusion to scriptural facts, with which most Bible readers strongly identify themselves, their novel and gorgeous and often sublime inventions, investing them at once with the fidelity of historical detail and the freshness and fascination of Oriental fiction, seem to fit them especially for popular instruction. ' If it be asked,' says the translator, ' what benefit may be derived from promulgating the tenets of a professedly erroneous system, it is replied that a distinction ought to be observed between the false systems that have ceased to be believed, and those which are still maintained as divine truths by any portion of mankind. The exhibition of a false religion, in which, as in the case before us, one hundred and twenty millions of our immortal race are at this moment staking their all, cannot but be important, at once to awaken within us feelings of deep and active charity for these benighted multitudes, and to furnish us with the requisite intelligence for effectually combating their grievous errors with the weapons of truth.'

SHORES OF THE MEDITERRANEAN, WITH SKETCHES OF TRAVEL. BY FRANCIS SCHROEDER. In two volumes. New-York: HARPER AND BROTHERS.

THOSE who pass by these volumes as being simply the repetition of a thrice-told tale, will lose the perusal of one of the most pleasant and readable books of the season. The author has not attempted to discover novelties, nor to present striking and original reflections, in lands so frequently described as those through which his journey lay. But he has given us, in his free, off-hand, yet most tasteful sketches, glimpses of the scenes among which he wandered, with the natural remarks which would occur to a polished and cultivated mind. He avoids, with an admirable instinct, every thing that could weary or repel, and gives us only those pictures which will please and attract. We have met no book of travels for a long time more admirably adapted to the wants of the reading public than this. It is tasteful, lively and instructive, and deserves, as we doubt not it will receive, a very wide popularity. The neat and even elegant style in which the volumes are published must still farther recommend them to public favor. They contain a large number of very beautiful engravings upon steel and wood, and are among the handsomest as well as pleasantest issues of the press. We commend them to general favor.

WILLIAM R. DEMPSTER, ESQ., THE VOCALIST: WITH A PORTRAIT.—The portrait which accompanies the present number of the KNICKERBOCKER is of WILLIAM R. DEMPSTER, Esq., the popular composer and vocalist. It is engraved by Mr. CHARLES BURT, from a daguerreotype by PLUMBE ; and although, like almost all daguerreotypes, representing the subject as appearing older than he really is, may be regarded in other respects as an excellent likeness. We have made some exertion to procure the following facts connected with the personal history and professional career of Mr. DEMPSTER, which may be relied on as entirely authentic. Mr. DEMPSTER was born at Keith, Banffshire, in the north of Scotland, in the year 1810. He inherited his voice and his talent for music from his father, JAMES DEMPSTER, a man of great respectability, who filled the double capacity of precentor (leader of the singing) and ruling elder in the secession-kirk for upward of sixteen years, when he removed to Aberdeen with his family. His habits were such that his household furnished a complete exemplification of the picture of BURNS' ' Cotter's Saturday Night.' Every morning and night a chapter from the ' big ha' Bible, ance his father's pride,' heralded the heart-felt prayer of a good husband, a kind father and an exemplary christian. This service was usually preceded by singing, in his sweet and plaintive voice, a portion of a psalm, in which he was accompanied by his wife and family of six children, all of whom ' came honestly by' good voices and pleasing execution. The mother of our subject (who was her especial favorite) was the most amiable and affectionate of parents, from whom he derived lessons of the highest value. Young DEMPSTER, from his earliest years, had a strong passion for music ; his taste always leading him to the plaintive and pathetic. At as early an age as five years he attracted the attention of every one within the family circle ; and he remembers that even then those around him were sometimes moved to tears by the pathos and melody of his voice. From this period up to ten years of age he was frequently carried about among the friends of the family, that he might delight them with his pleasant voice and felicitous execution. After the removal of the elder DEMPSTER with his family to Aberdeen, not wishing to gratify WILLIAM's propensity for music, he placed him at a trade ; but the ' ruling passion' would not be repressed. All the young man's leisure hours were devoted to the study of his favorite science, and the development of his powers for music ; until at length he placed himself under the guidance of a competent master, who first initiated him into the mysteries and immutable laws of harmony, and the study of music as a theory. Here a new life began to dawn upon his existence: he now began to see the true meaning and beauty of music, and his soul, he has assured us, drank largely at the fountain which was opened to him. He soon began to entertain a strong desire to try his hand at *musical composition*, and in this new field he at once discovered his forte. After composing the music for one or two songs, (his first attempt was a song of BURNS', entitled ' *My Mary 's No More,*') he conceived the idea of visiting London, in order farther to prosecute his studies in his favorite science. After the death of his father and mother, in 1832, Mr. DEMP-STER repaired to the Great Metropolis, where he found encouragement to try his fortune on the stage as a singer in opera. About this time, however, he visited several portions of England and Wales, with the intention of returning to London and ' coming out ;' but from what he had seen of the stage, our subject conceived a dislike to it and all its associations, and he therefore wisely abandoned the idea of revisiting London. In the spring of 1835 he determined to visit America, and try his fortunes in the New World. He arrived in this city toward the end of July of that year.

Mr. DEMPSTER's first appearance in America was at NIBLO's Concerts, which were at that time ' all the rage ;' the first talent that could be found being engaged there. His first appearance was at Mrs. WATSON's Benefit, in August ; the concerts then being under the direction of Mr. WATSON, of PAGANINI notoriety. His success was complete, and secured him an engagement for the remainder of the season. Here he remained two summers ; and the songs he then sung are still remembered with pleasure by many visitors to this delightful Garden, a favorite place of resort of people from all parts of the United States ; among them, we remember, were ' Erin is my Home' and ' I 'll remember Thee.' At the close of his engagement at NIBLO's, Mr. DEMPSTER formed an arrangement to travel with Mr. WATSON and his family, giving concerts, etc. Owing to a disagreement upon some minor points, he separated from them and proceeded through the United States, giving musical entertainments alone ; and in this way he slowly but steadily worked himself upward to the enviable position which he now occupies. We believe he has visited every State in the Union, for we have seen his performances commended from one end of the country to the other. He is the author of numerous songs and ballads, and is universally known as the composer of that most touching and beautiful of all ballads, the ' *Lament of the Irish Emigrant.*' ' Sound and sense' are in this song so nicely blended that it is now impossible to separate the one from the other.* And here let us observe, that it is a

---

* APROPOS of the ' Lament :' here is an admirable anecdote concerning it, which was contained in a letter from our friend CHANDLER, addressed to the Arm-chair of his popular *United States Gazette.* He is speaking of the parades of the regiment of Highlanders at Montreal : ' As the battalions marched, I noticed that the only being that ventured upon the military ground, beside the military themselves, was a large black dog. He seemed to understand the orders of the colonel, and though he could neither aid in ' taking open order' with the ' rear rank,' nor in wheeling into columns with the whole, yet he evinced much tact in avoiding the tread of the soldiery in their rapid movements, and that without evincing any of that haste which is unbecoming a gentlemanly dog. When the music joined the regiment, the dog took up his march with the band and seemed pleased with the rich Scotch airs to which the battalions marched. He evidently understood them, and evinced both taste and politeness by making no sign of approval until the musicians had completed a tune. The dog had completely got into the spirit of the time and place, and was enjoying the parade and music with special gusto. There was a place in the rank of the musicians unfilled, and the dog took his position there and completed the square as they marched in column. At length there was a halt, and almost immediately the band struck up that plaintive air to which DEMPSTER sings his words of the ' *Irish Emigrant.*' It was exquisitely performed. The poor dog, however, left the ranks, walked slowly the distance of a rod or two, sat quietly down, throwing his head a little on one side, as if to catch every note of the tune, and evincing a sort of melancholy pleasure in the performance. At length the music ceased, and the dog rose slowly, and with a sort of measured step, left the parade. Poor dog ! he had been the property of one of the musicians ; his master, whose place was vacant in the band, had brought him across the Atlantic, and during the sickness which had ultimately laid him in the grave, was wont to play the tune which the band had just performed. The dog had learned to love music, for the sake of his master first, and then for music alone ; but that tune awoke the memory of other days as clearly as you and I recall to the memory of each other some kind and heart-broken friend whom fate has brought to an early grave.'

characteristic excellence of Mr. DEMPSTER's musical compositions, as of his execution, that he rarely if ever fails to give true expression and deep feeling to tender and holy thoughts. He embodies the poet's conception, and thus elevates the affections and increases the religious feeling of his audiences. Clergymen, we have observed, always attend his concerts. Dr. CHANNING, we have heard, never missed being an auditor ; and of Dr. BETHUNE, who addressed to Mr. DEMPSTER some very admirable verses, the same remark may be made. He fully understands the *elocution* of singing. He gives a distinct enunciation to all the vowels, an art which he has acquired by incessant practice. Hence it is, that beautiful and forcible as are the words he has uniformly chosen, he heightens their effect by his execution of them ; for his music is always in sympathy with them.

Almost every thing which Mr. DEMPSTER has composed has become popular. We name such of his pieces as are most familiar to us : ' The Blind Boy ;' ' The Lonely Auld Wife ;' ' Death of WARREN ;' ' JEANIE MORRISON ;' ' I 'm with You once Again ;' ' When the Night-wind Bewaileth ;' ' A Home in the Heart ;' ' The Loved One was not There ;' ' Let us Love One Another ;' ' Bird of the Wilderness ;' ' I 'm Alone, all Alone,' etc., etc. But we think his greatest effort to be his cantata, ' *The May Queen*,' the poetry by ALFRED TENNYSON. The happy and joyous emotions of the young and beautiful child on the eve of May-day, her only thought being of the happy morrow, when she is to be crowned ' Queen of May,' are most felicitously expressed in the enlivening pastoral symphony which opens this cantata. Each note seems to portray the irrepressible joy of a young and innocent heart. The ' Second Part,' representing the dying girl on New-Year's eve asking her mother to call her early that she may ' see the sun rise upon the glad New-Year,' the last that she is ever to see, shows us at once that the composer has entered into the very spirit of the scene before him. The music, although of a subdued and plaintive cast, yet retains a portion of the opening melody, so that it seems like the dying echo of the young girl's first ' happy song.' We defy the veriest stoic to listen to this portion of the song without tears. The ' Third Part,' representing the return of spring, and the dying girl still alive, is in the ' minor mode,' corresponding with the key the composer has just left, and is solemn and impressive. The key at length changes into the ' major mode,' and the idea it conveys is at once grand and inspiring. The dying girl is about to tell of a vision of angels, whom she fancies she hears in ' the wild March morning,' in a mingled sound of music on the wind, which she says comes to the window three times, and then ' goes up to Heaven and dies among the stars.' The mind is relieved from the oppression and sorrow produced by the second part by the assurance which the child now has of going to Heaven :

> ' THE blessed music went that way
> My soul will have to go.'

All thoughts of earth seem now lost in the joy of going ' where the wicked cease from troubling and the weary are at rest.' The music of this part carries the hearer along with the words to the close ; and he at last draws a long breath and says : ' It 's all over ! — and what a happy close !'

We have great pleasure in the thought that Mr. DEMPSTER must share with the EDITOR of this Magazine the credit of introducing this noble composition to the American public. Well do we remember the pleasant October evening, in OLD KNICK.'s sanctum, when thoughtfully tinkling our spoons against our glasses, bereft of their

Glenlivet, we spoke of the touching character of the music of the ' *Emigrant's La-ment,*' then known to us for the first time as Mr. DEMPSTER's; and calling to mind ' The May-Queen,' so kindred in its touching pathos, we took TENNYSON from the library and read it to our friend ; dwelling perhaps upon those passages which had especially impressed us. When we had finished reading it we looked up to Mr. DEMPSTER's face, which always reflects every shade of thought and feeling, ' and therewithal,' as honest JOHN BUNYAN says, ' the water stood in his eyes.' We suggested that he should set it to music ; but he objected that ' it was beyond his reach ;' that ' people could never be brought to listen to so long a piece ;' that ' he could never make it sufficiently effective to cause an audience to sit it out,' and the like ; but upon again urging it upon his attention, he promised to ' see what he could do with it.' On re-turning to town from his residence in the country, some four weeks after this inter-view, Mr. DEMPSTER sent for us to call at his lodgings to hear his music of the ' May-Queen.' We heard it — and from that moment have had only one opinion of it ; an opinion which has been confirmed by the mingled tears and applauses of crowded audiences in every quarter of the Union. ' The May-Queen' is a copyright publica-tion ; and some idea of its great popularity may be inferred from the fact that a thousand dollars have been offered for it by the publishers. Upward of twenty-five thousand copies of Mr. DEMPSTER's various musical compositions are called for every year ; a degree of success altogether unequalled in this country.

His songs have from the commencement been silently and gradually working their way into public favor. They neither astonish nor dazzle at first ; there is ' nothing of the sort' about them ; indeed one is seldom struck with them at first ; but when the ear thoroughly hears them, ' then it blesses them ;' they make a deep impression on the heart and linger long in the memory. When we look back and think of those who have come and gone, and see what songs are now popular, we find that Mr. DEMPSTER's maintain a distinguished place ; they remain undiminished in popularity ; indeed, they are increasing in public favor, being at this moment the most popular compositions in this country. They may be deemed too the production of our soil ; we certainly claim for them an American paternity. This country has been the field of Mr. DEMPSTER's successful labors, and we know that he regards it with gratitude for having nourished and encouraged him in his profession. He is about to revisit his native country, and we cannot better convey to our readers his thoughts at leaving us than by quoting the address which he delivered at NIBLO's saloon on the occasion of his farewell entertainment in this city :

' LADIES AND GENTLEMEN : I appear before you this evening for the last time; and I take this opportunity to thank you from my heart for your kindness, as well at the present as on former occa-sions. Like a guest that lingers in the hall of his benefactor when the feast is over, I reluctantly but respectfully take my leave. It is my intention soon to return to my native country, and I antici-pate a happy meeting with my friends there ; but I must confess that my heart lingers with you, for nourished by your kind indulgence, I have been enabled to pursue with success the exercise of my profession. When I first appeared among you, ten years ago, I was young and inexperienced, but not without hope; that hope you cherished, and enabled me to realize my most sanguine expecta-tions. My songs, with two exceptions, have all been composed and published under your kind and fostering care ; and I trust I am not overstepping the rules of good taste when I say, that they are en-titled to the appellation of *American Melodies.* Those songs have been a source of pleasure to myself; and if they have been the means of beguiling a weary hour, or of contributing to your hap-piness in the domestic circle, when the cares and labors of the day were done, the highest ambition of my professional life is attained. I have several engagements at the South and West to fulfil before I leave the country ; but as this is the last time I shall have the honor of appearing before a New-York audience, I now take my leave, wishing you all health and prosperity; and in the hope that at some future day I shall have the happiness of appearing before you again, I most respectfully bid you *Farewell!'*

Pleasant vocalist! pleasant companion! 'take with you gentle winds your sails to swell!' — and when in the fulness of time you return again among us, may you find as many friends glad to meet as there are now sorry to part with you!

GOSSIP WITH READERS AND CORRESPONDENTS. — It was exceedingly pleasant the other day — pleasant to 'OLD KNICK.,' so long in 'populous city pent' — to find himself on board the 'Eureka' steamer, bound to the trout-fishing grounds of Sullivan county, *via* the Erie rail-road. '*Pleasant*' indeed! — it was something *more*. The country to which we tended, from 'the like o' which' it took so many years to wean us, and toward which, in many a sultry summer day and howling winter-night, our revived boyish fancy had gone forth from the man-made town — *the country was* our's for four days; and to give the true zest to our enjoyment of such a prospect, of early thoughts and early associations, an old and most congenial metropolitan friend, a certain boyishness of heart still fresh as ever in his cheerful bosom, with an agreeable associate, kindred in most things save a slight difference in years — these were our companions. The noble Hudson had scarcely ever seemed so wide to us, nor the shores on either side so picturesque and beautiful, nor the towering Palisades so vast in their shadowy extent; and as the fresh breeze fanned us, and the steamer sped on its swift course, we could well comprehend what OLLAPOD used to designate as the 'juiciness of a young heart.' And so it was, that with pleasant thoughts and pleasant chat, it seemed but a few moments before we were seated in the spacious cars of the Erie Rail-road, and flying to the West as on the wings of the wind; the glorious country opening around us in verdant cultivated valleys and ranges of minor mountains near or far, now towering almost over us and anon taking, in the blue distance, the farewell beams of the declining sun. Streams too, and 'lakelets,' and busy little villages nestled among the hills, slept quietly in the same mellow light. A few stoppages, a few supernatural 'sreex,' as JEAMES DE LA PLUCHE would term them, from the locomotive — that whistles as it runs, apparently not 'for want of thought' in itself, but to stimulate thought in the tardy or the expectant — and we were at Middletown; and after a good supper, somewhere in the neighborhood of ten o'clock on that bright moonlight night we were packed in a lumbering vehicle, called by courtesy a 'stage-coach,' and sent on our way rejoicing toward the blooming village of Bloomingburgh. Do you know of any thing more inspiring, town-reader, than to rise the next morning after the evening you have left the great metropolis, and find yourself in a charming country village which you had reached in the night, shut in by blue receding mountains, extending on every side into the dim distance, the contented green and yellow fields of grass and grain stretching almost to their summits and basking in the early day-beams? To L—— and 'this deponent,' in our morning walk, before the sun had 'climbed the eastern hills,' it seemed, whatever others might have thought of it, a landscape more lovely than the vale of 'Avoca. But scenes like these should be beheld and enjoyed; they can hardly be described: do us the favor to remark therefore that in a tumble-downish sort of two-horse vehicle 'we three' are on our way over 'The Barrens,' in crossing which, we saw on either hand what appeared to be several stones! It might have been deception; and JIM, our accomplished driver, was so engaged with a compressed narrative of his Don-Juanish amours that he 'stayed no question' as to the face of the country through which we were passing. At length, 'replete with chat,' we came in sight of Monti-cello, gleaming in the westering sunlight on the far-off hill-side; a cordon of blue mountains stretching far around the 'rolling country' which it overlooks. Arrived at 'HAMILTON'S,' we were soon rejoined by a brace of *avant-couriers*, two gentlemen who were as much alike as '*two P —— s*;' in fact they *were* 'nothing else.' They had been fishing successfully for trout in a considerable stream that runs out of that gem of the first water, White Lake; and while the obliging mistress of the 'White Lake House' is cooking the fish for our supper, we will cross the way, mount to the top of that newly-raised dwelling, and 'see what we shall see.' Verily it is a beautiful sight! How the blue mountains roll upon the eye in all the visible horizon; deep blue and pale blue; and like faintly-seen clouds, the Kaätskills, eighty miles in the north-eastern distance, bound the view; while in the immediate foreground, lake and grove and stream, studded with the most luxuriant foliage, complete the picture. We can scarcely remember whittling a pine shingle with more delight than we did on the upper piazza-roof of that unfinished building, with this view before us. But 'supper's ready!' cries L ——; and in three minutes we are sitting in the best room of the 'Lake House,' opening upon the lake, which sleeps in silence and shadow almost under the window, the heavy foliage of its borders reflected in its glassy bosom; and before us are *the trout,* 'created best that swim the silver streams;' brown and unc-tuous, and filling the room with a sweet-smelling savor. Whitest bread, sweetest butter, thickest cream, most delicious of Hysons, a noiseless female attendant — what could we wish more? 'I will trouble you, gentlemen,' said L ——, for *another* of those trout,' and he received upon his plate the nineteenth fish; when that had disappeared, '*One* more, gentlemen, and I'll not trouble you again!' And he did n't; for after securing and devouring it, he looked wistfully at the general receptacle, and reaching over, slid a handsome specimen upon his plate, with the ingenuous remark: 'I said I'd trouble *you* for no more, gentlemen, but I did n't say I would n't *help myself!*' Shame-less special pleading! — but any thing is justifiable, to our conception, that secures more trout. But let us hasten on to ROPER'S, hard by the Callicoon; for in that stream, made famous by the charming daguerreotype pictures of our friend STREET, there lurk scores of the aristocracy of brook-fish, which are to dangle upon our lines to-morrow. After a delightful ride, we reach ROPER'S; a glass of milk-punch, and to bed. In the morning, we dig bait; hoes, shovels, spades in requisition — *one* man (the huge feeder) giving *directions*, with great nonchalance; smoking his cigar the while. Rising from a 'hasty plate of mutton,' we are off to the Callicoon. And now, having passed raspberry - 'preserves' sufficiently numerous to supply the New-York markets for ten years, summer-fallows, Pickerel-Pond and the settlement adjacent, behold us taking the very 'forest-walk' that STREET has so beautifully described, on our way to the Callicoon. A picturesque-looking set we are, with our fishing-dresses and gear, a combination of Indian, 'white man' and Yankee-Doodle. And this is the Callicoon! — this clear wide-and-narrow brawling brook, whirling in eddies, rush-ing in straitened channels, boiling in rocky nooks — this is the Callicon? 'It an't nothing else!' Well then, let the two P —— 's and L —— the elder scatter along the west branch, while RANCHERO and 'OLD KNICK.' drop line along down the eastern. We are in the middle of the stream, waist-deep, and there is silence — an 'audible still-

ness,' illustrated rather than disturbed by the faint voices of the wood. There
would have been compunction in screwing a wriggling worm upon the hook, but for
the lucky thought that Providence must have *designed* it for bait. But 'let us drop
the subject' of this remark. Snap! — a quick bite, and as pretty a trout as you could
find of a summer's day! 'First blood' for 'OLD KNICK!' Four more out of that very
eddy; farther down, RANCHERO has pocketed as many more, and 'the cry is still they
come!' Silently we stand, the sunlight shimmering down through the interlacing
boughs and flecking the murmuring waters below. 'RANCHERO!' (in a whisper) 'what
is that!' 'Good Ev'ings!' a deer, a gentle doe, is wading directly toward us in the
middle of the stream; lifting up her long slender fore-legs, and dropping her little
pointed hoofs almost noiselessly into the water; her face absolutely *beaming* with ani-
mal enjoyment! RANCHERO with his finger beckons silence; takes from his pouch a
pistol that he had borne loaded and capped from the city of Mexico through Texas
even unto Gotham, and deliberately cocks it. *Maledetto!* — the cap has been re-
moved, at the instance of a timid friend; the doe is within fifteen yards of us; she
has heard the click of the pistol; she lifts her silken ears, opens wide, after a slow wink,
her great lustrous black eyes, and with a snort of surprise, and three or four bounds of
infinite grace, is up and over the bank, and away to rejoin her companions in the denser
woods! She was a transient vision of grace and beauty, that OLD KNICK. can never
cease to remember ' unto thylke day i' the which he crepes into his sepulchre.' Well,
we have a score of trout apiece, it is high-noon, and — let us lunch; for lo! there
comes the man with the covered-basket, whose contents, potable and edible, have been
prepared by the careful hand of kind considerate Woman. RANCHERO

> 'TOOK a whistle frae his pouch,
> And blew both loud and shrill,
> When four-and-twenty belted knights
> Came skipping o'er the hill!'

Not exactly; but a *human* whistle was given, most like a yell, which brought the
two P——'s, the two L——'s and the one C —— together; and on the rocks, under
the shadow of a rustic bridge, by the side of the gurgling stream, we spread our nice
repast, which we discussed with good appetites, interspersing our operations with
much agreeable chat upon a great variety of subjects. Then we separated and re-
sumed our rods and lines, drawing up the trout until the sun no longer threw any
shadows across the water. But 'something too much of this,' the reader may ex-
claim. Suffice it then to say, that after our return to ROPER's we added together
the amount of two day's fishing in the Mongaup and Callicoon; and four hundred
and fifty trout (*several* of which would weigh half a pound, and a *great many* a
pound!) was found to be the result. What a repast, sweetened by the day's toil,
was the trout-supper that ROPER gave us that evening! — and what a ride was that
which transported us on that lovely moon-lit night to the 'Lake-House!' And oh!
goodness gracious! what a bed-room that was, and what a bed, in which we were
'kept' that night! The architect had made a slight mistake in the construction of
the apartment; he had arranged it so that two persons could *get in*, but he had not
calculated for their *turning round* after they had *got in*! An acute angle of the hot
roof received the person of L——, his head resting upon a Lilliputian pillow, crushed
down endwise, and his feet almost projecting through a sort of loop-hole window
that looked toward the east, and the only one in the room; while 'OLD KNICK.'
sank sweltering into a soft thin billow of feathers, that wanted but two or three more

to make it seem like *a pillow*. (Never mind your pillow; get back to town.') 'Well, then:' In the morning, on to Monticello; climbed the board-fence on the high ground by the court-house, and ' surveyed the landscape o'er ;' thinking mean time how often our friend STREET had looked abroad upon the same grand and beautiful scene ; and thereupon too of ' SLOW-WATER TIM,' whom he has immortalized, who went away from ROPER's ' stoop' before we left, with a gait like that of a kangaroo with a touch of the lumbago, and a mouth like — ' nothing else !' On to Bloomingburg in a stage-coach, and on that ' Hot Friday' too, a day not to be forgotten ; not a breath of air stirring, save the little that Whip was driving away from. On to Middletown, (after waiting two mortal hours,) just in time to be ' ten minutes too late' for the cars. 'Cause why ?' The proprietor of the stage has a ' Rail-road Hotel' at the end of the route, and if you do n't get in in time for the cars, it ' makes it bad' for you, but ' good' for him ; since you must (if you are foolish enough) sup, stay with him all night and breakfast the next morning. KNICK. however sought another house ; and when seated in the cars next morning, moving homeward, remembered him of no *désagre-mens*. What a glorious county is Orange ! The mowers were swinging the scythe or turning the fragrant hay in the lily-sprinkled verdant meadows; on the rounded hills the cradlers were laying the golden grain in regular semi-circular rows, like the rece-ding tide-marks on some crescent sea-beach ; the reaper ' stood musing by gathered sheaves' as the iron horse snorted by with his train; within, sweet farmers' daughters, happy in the prospect of visiting the Great Metropolis, were busy chatting with trim full-bodied young fellows, with chequered linen shirts, handsome whiskers, twinkling eyes and dare-devil airs, who ever and anon rushed out to do duty on the train, and then returned to renew their gossip with the fair milk-maids. Milk ! milk ! milk ! how at every stopping-place by scores and scores the cans clatter in ! — from all the ' Valleys' and ' Kills' in the region round about, until the cars have the mingled odor of a country buttery-and-pantry. But here we are at Piermont ; at the land's end of a most delightful excursion, with no thoughts of regret, no remembrances save of unalloyed enjoyment. Two hours of delightful sailing, and we are seated in our pleasant sanctum. · · · CAN any republican fail to see the inevitable tendency of the important changes slowly but surely taking place in Great-Britain ? Sir ROBERT PEEL's late noble speech, and the ' protocol' of the new minister, Lord JOHN RUSSELL, are full of striking portents. ' I shall leave office, I fear,' says the former, ' with a name severely censured by many honorable gentlemen, who deeply regret the sever-ance of party ties ; I shall leave a name execrated by every monopolist, who main-tains protection for his individual benefit ; but it may be that I shall leave a name sometimes remembered with expressions of good-will in those places which are the abodes of men whose lot it is to labor, and to earn their daily bread by the sweat of their brows ; a name remembered with expressions of good-will when they shall re-create their exhausted strength with abundant and untaxed food, the sweeter because it is no longer leavened by a sense of injustice,' Cheer up ! ye toiling masses of Bri-tain ! there is a better era approaching :

'THERE 's a good time coming, boys,
  A good time coming :
And a poor man's family
  Shall not be his misery,
  In the good time coming.
Every child shall be a help,
  To make his right arm stronger ;
The happier he, the more he has :
  Wait a little longer.

' There 's a good time coming, boys,
  A good time coming :
Little children shall not toil
Under or above the soil,
  In the good time coming ;
But shall play in healthful fields,
  Till limbs and mind grow stronger ;
And every one shall read and write :
  Wait a little longer. '

To FORM any thing like an adequate conception of the casual wholesale trade in books in this metropolis, one should look over the catalogue of the *New-York Book Trade Sale*, to commence at the sales-room of Messrs. BANGS, RICHARDS AND PLATT, the oldest establishment of its kind in the metropolis, on Monday the 24th instant. These sales are held semi-annually, on the last week of March and August, and are attended by the representatives at least of all the book-sellers in the United States. The catalogue before us is by far the largest ever issued to the trade in this country. It contains one hundred and ninety-three closely-printed pages, of the largest size of kindred publications, and embraces upward of two-hundred contributors, including all the leading publishers in the United States, from Portland, Maine, to Saint Louis, Missouri. But it is not only the largest catalogue ever issued to the trade; it contains a far richer and much more attractive stock than has been offered · at any previous sale. · · · WE have alluded on two or three occasions heretofore to the charming pastoral of ' *When the Kye come Hame*,' by JAMES HOGG, the ' Ettrick Shepherd,' and to the delightful Scottish music to which it is wedded, and which was the author's favorite air, as indeed it is of every body who hears it well executed, as we did. We consider ourselves fortunate in securing an authentic copy of the poem for the gratification of our readers. Observe that the refrain,

> ' WHEN the kye come hame,
> When the kye come hame,
> 'Tween the gloaming and the mirk,
> When the kye come hame,'

is to be repeated, in the singing, at the end of every stanza:

' COME, all ye jolly shepherds
  That wander through the glen,
I 'll tell ye o' a secret
  That courtiers dinna ken.
What is the greatest pleasure
  That the heart o' man can frame ?
'T is to meet a bonny lassie
  When the kye come hame !

' T is not beneath the coronet
  Nòr canopy o' state,
'T is not on couch of velvet
  Nor arbor of the great ;
'T is beneath the spreading birk
  In the glen without a name,
To meet your bonny lassie
  When the kye come hame!

' The black-bird builds its nest,
  ' For the mate he lo'es to see,
And on the tapmost bough
  O ! a happy bird is he!
Then he pours his melting ditty,
  An' love is a' the theme,
And he woos his bonny lassie
  When the kye come hame !

' When the blewart bears a pearl,
  And the daisy turns a pea,
An' the bonny luckan gowan
  Has faulded up her ee ;
And the laverock frae the blue lift
  Draps down and thinks nae shame,
To woo his bonny lassie
  When the kye come hame !

' See yonder pauky shepherd
  That wanders on the hill,
His ewes are in the fauld
  And his lambs are lying still ;
Yet he downa gang to bed,
  For his heart is in a flame,
To meet his bonny lassie
  When the kye come hame !

' Then since a' nature joins
  In this love without alloy,
O, wha would prove a traitor
  To nature's dearest joy ?
Or wha would choose a crown,
  Wi' its perils and its fame,
And miss his bonny lassie
  When the kye come hame ?'

A RIGHT clever man is he who in that cleverest of papers, ' *The Spirit of the Times*' literary and sporting journal, discourseth of the genus '*Bore*,' in all its human varieties. He thus paints ' *The Sensible Bore*,' the object of his special detestation:

' I HAVE been subjected to many gross indignities in my time; introduced as a ' promising' young man ; announced to a party in Division-street as ' a man of talent ;' trotted out as a small lion at a gathering in the country, where the ' honest yeomanry' examined me as if they expected to see a tail rise from my coat-skirts *à la Caffre*, or music emanate from my nostrils *à la Memnon*; I have even been spoken of as a ' desirable match' for a girl with a flat chest, large feet, a piano and a fortune. These insults I could endure; but I am grateful that no one ever yet called me ' sensible.'

To see a fellow at a dinner-table, with a face like a mute at a funeral, looking as if the ordinary support of life by eating were too vulgar for his sublimity; turning away abstractedly at times to let you know that his mind is busy on grave and distant subjects; and then to have the villain, when he hears a right good story, start out a lame smile from the corner of his mouth, which hobbling slowly over his arrogant features, returns in his lips about the time they curl up to signify that on the whole he can hardly justify himself for having been amused. When one engages in the chat which best promotes digestion, he drums with his finger-nails on the edge of a plate; when a casual ocurrence is related to him, he interrupts it with 'ah!' and 'indeed!' uttered as if he thought you considered your salvation to depend on his belief. This is the Sensible Bore. Heaven deliver me from such a varlet!'

SIDNEY SMITH called his age the age of *persiflage;* BYRON's was the age of bronze; there was once an age of iron; and Tradition says, but for ourselves we have no great faith in her, that there was once, in the remote ages, a long, long while before the birth of chronology, and as we may easily believe, before writing was invented, an age of silver and of gold. We do not like to envy even our ancestors, but if any of them lived in the age of gold we would like to have stood in their shoes. The present age is not an age of any kind of metal, but of mettle. It is emphatically the Age of Fun. Every body deals in jokes, and all wisdom is inculcated in a paraphrase of humor. In Paris they have the *Charivari,* a daily gazette of broad grins; in London they have *Punch,* in Göttingen they have *Die Fliegende Bläter,* and in this blessed city, where the 'rock-king's dove-eyed daughter,' the good humored Croton, gushes out laughter at the corner of every street, we are to have '*The Daguerreotype,*' a daily gazette of wit and good-nature. We can say nothing more on the subject just now. Among the cockneys, Fun is the only saleable article in the market; and when people talk of a good property, they liken it to PUNCH. The Arch-bishop of the new church, the Prior of the new Paraclete, is GILBERT ABBOT A BECKET, who has already given the Londoners and the rest of the world a ' Comic BLACK-STONE' and a ' Comic Grammar,' and will soon be out with a ' Comic Old Testament.' He is publishing just now a ' Comic Almanack of the Month,' which is as full of fun as an egg is of meat; abounding in important literary, dramatic and legal *on-dits* and information. Among the new books announced for 'the month' are the following : ' The Adventures of a Moustache, being the continuation of the Tale of a Wig ;' ' Five Minutes in China, by the author of ' An Afternoon in Kamschatka ;' and ' The Whole Globe Scoured in Two Days, by an American Traveller.' Here is a clever ' Epigram on a Hard-hearted Parson :'

> ' THE truth that 'sermons are in stones,'
> On any one must quickly dart,
> When told that SMITH or BROWN or JONES
> Preaches directly from the heart.'

The 'Almanack' has a good many rather troublesome correspondents, we are led to infer, from the notices which some of them receive. In answer to one who expresses a desire to know 'why it is that an attendant walks at each side of the elephant at ASTLEY's circus, during the performance of the colossal animal on the tight-rope, ('*credat Judæus!*') the editor says: ' We have ascertained that the men are placed below to inspire the sagacious creature with confidence; for the elephant naturally feels less timidity when he knows that if he should happen to fall there are two supernumeraries underneath ready to catch him !' Notwithstanding the large consumption of fun in his own journals, Mr. A BECKET announces in an advertisement of his 'Almanack' that he has opened a joke-manufactory for the writers of burlesque. He supplies a single pun at wholesale prices, and every facetious article not approved may be exchanged within three nights after it has been tried upon a British audience. 'Gentlemen burlesque-writers wishing their own materials made up can receive back their subject in a thoroughly joked-up condition within four-and-twenty hours.' All the jokes supplied from his establishment are warranted, ' for none but the best workmen are employed, and the highest wages are given.' Instruction is given in joking between the hours of ten and four, and ' punning on the Hamiltonian system may be acquired in six easy lessons. A few old conundrums, in good order, to bo had cheap.' Our lamented friend and correspondent SANDERSON says in his 'American in Paris' that there is a joint-stock joking company in the French capital, for supplying jokes to playwrights, and that so profitable a business is it, that some wits derive a pleasant yearly income from the eighth of a joke ! There is not a little satire, and an implied reproof which is most applicable on this side the water, in the lines addressed by 'The true Lover to his Business.' Read it and think of it :

SWEET BUSINESS! idol of my soul!
  Oh! pardon me, if other charms
Had o'er my bosom the control
  Awhile to tear me from thine arms.
Would thou couldst know, from thee apart,
  How keen hath been that bosom's pain!
What joy returning gives my heart,
  My BUSINESS! unto thee again!

'T were vain to tell thee all I felt
  While breathing vows in Beauty's ear,
And how, while at her feet I knelt,
  I thought of thee, my BUSINESS dear;
How fearfully I viewed the risk,
  The consequences there might be,
My snug, my lucrative, my brisk,
  My BUSINESS ! of neglecting thee !

Oh! not a moment by the side
  (At breakfast, dinner, or at tea,)
Of her who is to be my bride,
  Didst thou escape my memory :
Oh! never in the pleasant walk,
  Through sunlit mead or shady grove,
On other themes though I might talk,
  Ceased I to think of thee, my love !

And though, in roving far away,
  I 've sacrificed a little gain,
Yet, dearest BUSINESS ! thou wilt say
  I have not wronged thee in the main:
For she is rich, that maiden fair,
  For whom I heave the tender sigh :
Thus e'en in courtship I may swear
  On BUSINESS still I've kept an eye.

'The Red-Skins, or Indian and Ingin,' Mr. J. FENIMORE COOPER'S latest work, has just been issued by Messrs. BURGESS, STRINGER AND COMPANY. Its design we take to be not so much that of a novel-proper as an exemplification of practical argument against the anti-rent spirit of the day, which in certain counties of this State has proved so disastrous in its consequences. We receive the volumes at too late an hour to report upon them authoritatively in the present number. SPEAKING of Mr. COOPER, by-the-by, reminds us of a tribute recently paid to his genius by a distinguished foreign Prince, to which, having been in some sort accessory, we shall be pardoned we trust for alluding. A few months since, it will be remembered, we mentioned in these pages a request made by the then Russian ambassador at Constantinople, Prince DOLGOROUKI, (now his Imperial Majesty's plenipotentiary at Tehran, Persia,) through our excellent correspondent, the American representative at the Sublime Porte, for a specimen of the hand-writing of the ' great and good WASHINGTON,' and of ' the distinguished American novelist, COOPER.' Through the kindness of His Honor, then Recorder TALLMADGE, we were enabled to send to our correspondent, for the PRINCE, an interesting original letter of WASHINGTON, in excellent preservation, addressed to Gen. TALLMADGE, of the Revolution, the honored father of the gentleman from whom we received it. A copy of this letter appeared at the time in the KNICKERBOCKER. Mr. COOPER also enclosed us a brief note to be sent to the PRINCE, in compliance with his request, in which he took occasion to express the lively sense he entertained of the liberal and kind feelings generally manifested in Europe by Russians toward Americans. His own introduction at Paris into European society, he remarked in effect, was first owing to the kind attentions of a polished circle of Russians, including the names of various members of the family of GALITZIN ; whom, with other Russians of breeding and intelligence, he still remembered with pleasure. The same kind disposition toward Americans he had found manifested in Rome by the amiable and intelligent Princess Volhouski, Prince Gargazin, and others of a kindred class. Wherever he went indeed and met with Russians he met with friends, and the same was true of other Americans. Mr. Cooper added, we remember, that ever since the noble interference of the just-minded Alexander at the treaty of Ghent, Russia had proved herself the friend of America; and that for his part he was one of those who wished his nation to manifest a public preference for those who treat their country and countrymen, in or out of our hemisphere, with liberality and justice. We have lately received a pacquet from our esteemed correspondent at Constantinople, covering a letter to Mr. Cooper from Prince Dolgorouki, and another acknowledging in grateful terms the receipt of the two autograph letters which we had been enabled to forward him. 'Thanks to your goodness,' he observes, 'I am at last in possession of the hand-writing of the greatest man of modern times; and it is with full reason of justice that you call him the 'Father of your Country.' Certainly I did not expect that your celebrated novelist, Mr. Fenimore Cooper, would give himself the trouble to write to me the few lines which I have received from him, so full of kindly and obliging expressions.' Our correspondent remarks in his note to us: 'I beg you to offer to Mr. Cooper an expression of what I naturally feel for the very courteous and gentlemanly manner in which he sent his autograph. The civility thus shown to the Prince, a distinguished Russian minister, by Americans, will leave an impression which may be of service to such of our countrymen as may hereafter fall in his way; and thus it should ever be with American gentlemen in their intercourse with gentlemen of the Old World.' He adds: 'The Prince possesses one of the richest collections of autographs extant, which he purposes presenting at some future period to His Imperial Majesty, the Emperor Nicholas. I do not doubt (and it would be agreeable to be at his side at the time) but that when the collection is offered to His Majesty, and his eye is attracted by the autographs of the many great and celebrated names which it contains, it will rest with more than ordinary interest upon that of Washington, the Father of our Country.' Mr. Cooper, at our request, has kindly favored us with the perusal of a translation of the Prince's letter to himself; and although not designed for publication, we may perhaps without an infraction of propriety affirm that it is alike honorable to the Prince and to our distinguished chief novelist. He observes, that notwithstanding the pleasure Mr. Cooper's letter has afforded him, he is obliged to confess that it has entirely missed its end; since instead of increasing the number of his valuable autographs it shall remain forever among his family archives, as a precious testimonial of the writer's goodness. 'If my personal admiration can add nothing to the just tribute of homage rendered by two hemispheres to your great and noble talent, I shall at least reserve for myself the privilege of assuring you that the sentiments of esteem with which the two nations whose future is most brilliant have inspired each other, belong exclusively to the relations between Russia and the United States of America.' The entire letter is couched in language equally amiable. . . . '*Gentle Willie*' is neither lost nor mislaid. It 'bides it's time,' and will appear when space and *circumstances* shall serve. We have articles in prose and verse awaiting insertion which were accepted nearly two years ago. . . . A correspondent inquires if it was not the same 'Yankee-Doodle' whose 'adventures' are being recorded in our pages, who while exhibiting some rattle-snakes in a big box at the west, some weeks since, was bit upon a finger of his left hand by one of them, whereupon he took the 'eternal jackknife' which he happened

to have in his hand and whittled his finger down to the bone, and while it was bleed-
ing, tried to 'swap' his remaining reptiles for a jackass belonging to a man who had
stopped to see the 'p'ison sarpents.' . . . Mr. FOWLER, 'practical phrenologist,' has
issued an elaborate work on his 'science.' It contains the engraved busts of a good
many men remarkable for their bumps. *We* once 'lay' for our plaster-portrait to Mr.
FOWLER, and kept a very sober face in our coffin-like box until he had piled the liquid
matériel around our smoothly-greased head and face, to within a half an inch of the
mouth; but when he began to feed the adjacent features with a spoon, and we saw only
a nose sticking out of the warm white hasty-pudding, 'human natur'' could n't stand
it; and just as far as those features *could* laugh they *did;* the muscles below however
were 'stuck;' and the result in the cast was a face solemn as an owl's up to the outer
line of a small circle embracing the mouth and muscles immediately adjacent, which
were themselves 'full of mirth.' 'Picture it, think of it,' reader! And yet Mr.
FOWLER had the audacity to exhibit that bust in his window (PETER ROBINSON the
murderer on one side and our friend Colonel WEBB on the other!) until we extracted
a promise from him to remove it and break the mould which had been worse than an
'iron mask' to us. . . . AN artist-friend has amused himself by seeing how many
different readings can be given, by transposition, to the line of GRAY's,

> 'The ploughman homeward plods his weary way,'

without altering the meaning. He reached the number of *sixty* without the least
embarrassment, beginning thus:

> 'THE ploughman homeward weary plods his way,
> The homeward ploughman plods his weary way,
> The weary homeward ploughman plods his way,' etc.

'T is a singular exercitation altogether. · · · WE regret that we have not space and
leisure adequately to describe the '*Model of New-York,*' and its capacious pictured
canopy, now exhibiting at the Apollo in Broadway. Think of this entire metropolis,
and a part of Brooklyn, represented by the individual street, lane, alley, house, open
lot, tree — *every thing* in short which the city is and which it contains; the whole
perfect in its proportions, and every part entirely correct in its scale! It is truly a
wonderful exhibition, and reflects great credit upon its enterprising proprietor, T. POR-
TER BELDEN, Esq. · · · '*The Writings of Hugh Swinton Legare,*' on sale by the
APPLETONS, demand the attention of the press and the public. Such writers as LE-
GARE and GRIMKE are the true representatives of the literature and scholarship of
the South, and their high claims should not be overlooked. · · · THERE is a very
facile hand engaged in the '*Foolscap Scribblings*' of that spirited diurnal, '*The
Gazette and Times.*' The writer in the following passage informs us of his success
in trying to divert the ennui of ship-board by reading: 'I took up one of JAMES's
novels, and went resolutely on till I came to the part where the sun and the April
clouds are chasing each other over the fields; and where the powerfully-built young
man with the broad and deep chest finds that the sun and the April clouds are
chasing each other also over his heart; I forget exactly where Mr. JAMES generally
places this passage, but I think that in most of his books it occurs somewhere near
the beginning of the second chapter; at all events, it was just here that my patience
broke down, and fearing that an effort to proceed might bring on a relapse of sea-
sickness, I was forced to change my book.' This passage embodies stringent satire,
well applied. · · · THANKS to our old and good friend '*The Doctor !*' Pray con-
tinue your sketches. 'GOD save the Poor and the Humble!' is our aspiration, as

fervent as the prayer ' GOD save the QUEEN !' from a loyal ' British-man.' · · · WE have several ' *Legal Papers*,' including anecdotes of various sorts, which we shall discuss in our next. ' BOOTES' (what ' boots' the delay ?) shall hear from us, and our readers from him, at the same time ; no connection with ' *Conversations with an Old Negro*,' yet *he* too is ' booked ;' together with others, ' as shall more particularly appear hereafter.' · · · DEAR ' *Emilie Sphynx ?*' would that we could gratify your curiosity ; but the most intimate friend that we ever had on earth did not reveal the secret to us. It was a frequent thought to *ask* what it meant ; but in our correspondence, or when we met, we had too much to *write*, too much to *say*, to think of the ' Puzzle.' · · · OUR Tinnecum friend and correspondent saw an adroit trick ' done and performed' the other day in the vicinity of Washington-market. A fellow loaned a countryish-looking man a gold watch for ten dollars, with the privilege of redeeming it in two days, for a dollar premium. ' It was worth sixty ;' ' belonged to his father,' etc. ; but then he *must* have the ten dollars. He took it from his pocket, wrapped a paper round it, gave it to the countryman, and got his ten dollars. ' Hallo! stranger !' said an accomplice over the way, after the fellow had gone off with the money, ' what 'll you bet that ain't a stone you 've just bought ?' ' I 'll bet you tew dollars 't ain't. Did n't I seen him wrop it up ?' ' I 'll stand you !' said the accomplice ; ' money down.' The money was deposited in the hands of. a by-stander, the package was unrolled, and a flat rounded stone was all its contents ! The countryman staid about the market for several days — but he has gone home now ! · · · OUR Troy friend's excuse is more ingenious than satisfactory. It reminds us of CHARLES LAMB's reply to the President of the East India House : ' I have remarked, Mr. LAMB, that you come to your duties very late in the morning.' ' Yes,' answered LAMB, ' I do ; but then I go away very early in the afternoon !' The excuse it seems was considered a valid one, for the President went away laughing. · · · A WAGGISH contributor agrees with all the arguments of Professor MAPES upon the ' *Causes and Cure of Early Consumption*,' but his illustrations are somewhat novel. The fundamental principle of ' *getting high*' to avoid early consumption he considers a correct one ; indeed he thinks with BURNS that getting ' high' makes one ' o'er *all* the ills o' life victorious.' He admits the argument too of enlarged lungs in birds ; he himself shot a large number of *High-ho's* last summer, and did n't notice a single diseased lung among them ;' whereas pulmonary complaints are quite common among wrens and other birds incapable from weak wings of an extended flight ;, the ' *blue*'-*bird* alone constituting an exception. The assertion that Mexicans ' rarely have narrow chests' he disputes ; and quotes from the letter of an American officer at Matamoras a passage describing the bringing into camp of a small party of Mexicans, having several long, narrow chests, which on being broken open were found to contain,' etc. There are other illustrations of the Professor's article, ' a gentleman,' says our amusing commentator, whose opinions I always regard with interest, and whose versatility of talent excites the surprise of all who know him.' Exactly ; and his greatest merit is that in scientific matters he knows how to ' make things plain,' and according to DRYDEN it ' needs all one knows' to do that :

> ' HIS learning savors not the school-like gloss
> That most consists in echoing words and terms,
> And soonest wins a man an empty name :
> Nor any long or far fetched circumstance,
> Wrapt in the curious general'ties of arts ;
> But a direct and analytic sum
> Of all the worth and first effects of arts.'

By-the-way, here is a thrust of the Professor at an inquisitive, impatient, and by no means beautiful lawyer, who was 'worriting' him on the witness-stand, in a case of personal identity: 'What sort of a looking person was he? Was he long or short? Was he heavy or light? Was he young or old? Was he good-looking or ill-looking? Did he look like *me*, Sir, or did he look like somebody else? Now Sir, see if you can answer these questions directly and without equivocation.' The witness replied: 'He was a good-looking man ; he did *not* look at all like you, Sir !' 'If he had had a blister-plaster on his face the night before,' said the Professor, ' powerful enough to draw a prize in a lottery, his countenance could n't have been redder.' The laugh was fairly against him. · · · 'X. Y. Z.' is 'pardoned,' as he requests. His poetry is well-intended, but it is not ' up to the mark.' We are led to think that if he can write poetry at all, he can write better than the specimen before us. 'Unpleasant, but true,' Mr. 'X. Y. Z.' · · · '*Thoughts on the Magnetic Telegraph*' possess a certain vague sublimity, but the literary execution of the lines is beneath their theme. The writer gets into the ' high sentimental latitudes' with some difficulty, and out of them with more. Is it true, that by putting one's ear to a telegraph-post the vibration of sound upon the wire which it supports will indicate the passage of a rail-road car on the line twenty miles distant? This is a singular fact, if it be one. Speaking of magnetic telegraphs, s'pose an' you read this extract from a private note touching the Hempstead (L. I.) wife-stealers and their stolen goods: 'The runaway parties passed through this village the other day. You would have been amused. The men were hand-cuffed ; the women had the freedom of the cars. A great crowd was collected, brutally curious. One fellow chucks the poor lady, who holds her head down to escape the gaze, under the chin: ' Hul' up your head, Sis ; I wan' to see yer.' The barbarian brought to a focus a pair of indignant orbs, which touched him to the very gizzard. It was a curious affair. Two men ran away with two wives, taking advantage of a good head of steam. Before they reached Rochester, a full-length description of them was pasted up in Buffalo ! ' I should ha' got clear off to Wisconsin, and no mistake,' said the disappointed lowyer, ' if it 'a had n't a been for that ere d — d thunder-and-lightnin' rod !' How great must have been his re — *Morse !* — how curious for such sparks to have been outwitted by a spark !' · · · THAT was an affecting conclusion of a speech by a venerable Methodist clergyman at one of our late religious anniversaries. He had been depicting the sufferings of his youth and manhood in proclaiming the ' glad tidings' of CHRIST in the western wilds ; often riding in storm and tempest through the forest, when it was so dark that he could not see the beast on which he rode, and frequently sleeping in the dense woods ; his own hands mean time ministering unto his necessities. He was a poor wayfaring man, he said, with no cottage in the wilderness, but wandering like the Israelite, and lodging awhile in tents, till he should reach the heavenly Canaan. The fervor with which the following lines were given from the lips of the speaker brought tears to many an eye:

'NOTHING on earth I call my own :	'There is my home and portion fair,
A stranger to the world unknown,	My treasure and my heart is there,
I all their goods despise :	And my abiding home ,
I trample on their whole delight,	For me my elder brethren stay,
I seek a city out of sight,	And angels beckon me away,
A city in the skies.	And JESUS bids me come.'

' YOUTHFUL friend,' said a venerable broad-brimmed Quaker to a lad at the bar of a country inn,' ' will thee make me a lemonade ?' The boy squeezed in a half-lemon, put in his sugar, and was about filling it with water, when the Quaker arrested him with, 'Stay, child ; what is that near thy right hand ?'   'Rum, Sir.'   'Pour in a large spoonful of that.'   The boy did so.   'Stay yet again,' said our Friend ; 'what is in that bottle nearest thee ?'   'Brandy,' replied the lad.   'Well, thee may pour in a large spoonful of that, and then fill it up with ice-water.'   The Quaker raised it to his mouth ; and after three swallows, said, with an approving smack of the lips, ' Thee is a *little* lad, but thee makes a *great* lemonade !'   Does our objector, ' P. C.' see the application ? . . .   THAT was what is called a 'politic' man, who in an eulogium at the funeral of a member of a college faculty, spoke of him as ' a star of *pretty considerable* magnitude,' having discovered, when about to say ' *first* magnitude,' that the President of the college was present, and that this star differed from the other star in glory.   A friend tells us that this reminds him of a compliment paid by a writing-master to his pupils : ' If you go on improving like this,' said he, ' you 'll make first-rate penmen ;' but seeing that this compliment did not include his female scholars, he added, ' and *pen-women* too !' . . .   Mr. J. C. KING, of Boston, a sculptor of fine genius, whose busts of ROBERT BURNS and JOHN QUINCY ADAMS have excited so much admiration, has sent us a couple of exquisite cameo-medalions of WASHINGTON and of AUDUBON. The former, as a matter of course, could by no means be mistaken, and the latter is as surely a gem of art.   It is in all respects a correct and most felicitous likeness of our friend, the renowned artist-traveller.   Mr. KING is fast winning for himself a name which the world will not ' willingly let die.'   By-the-by, a few of our metropolitan readers have enjoyed the pleasure of surveying our townsman KNEELAND's model of a horse, designed for his equestrian statue of WASHINGTON, which when finished is to be taken to Berlin and perpetuated in enduring iron.   Even in its present unfinished condition it is a miracle of life and action. . . .   PETER SCHEMIL serves up ' The Street' and certain of the multitudes who traffic therein, with a very trenchant pen in the present number.   The lovers of the ' Old Masters' too, are not particularly spared.   Has PETER ever heard of the connoisseur who invited a friend to visit one of these veritable antiques ?   ' Come up and dine with me and look at it,' said he ; ' I want your candid opinion of it.   A friend of mine was up to see it a day or two ago, and he had the impudence to say that it was a copy.'   ' A copy !'   I should like to hear *another* man say that it was ' *a copy !*'   But pray come up and see it, and tell me exactly what you think of it !'   There was ' a smart chance' for a ' candid opinion,' was n't there ?' . . .   WE are well pleased to hear that Mr. HACKETT, whose merits as a man are well calculated to enhance, in the minds of those who best know him, his acknowledged merits as a various, cultivated and successful actor, has taken the ' *Howard Athenæum*,' a new capacious and splendid architectural structure of granite, now near its completion in Boston.   We have good reason to believe that the ' Athenæum' will constitute one of the best-regulated theatres in the United States.   Speaking of theatres, we desire to ask why it is that Mr. THOS. S. HAMBLIN, for so many years the distinguished and successful proprietor and manager of the ' American Theatre,' Bowery, should not have an establishment of a similar character under his command ?   Who is there in this whole community who from long and successful experience is so well calculated to make such an enterprise a preëminently safe and profitable investment ?   Mr. HAMBLIN requires but the opportunity to make the fortunes alike of himself and his stock-holders.   That opportunity we hope will not long remain a desideratum. . . .   THAT was a very agreeable reünion we had recently of the members of the *Delta Phi Society*, and very creditable were the literary performances at the University.   The oration by Mr. CROSBY was a sound and able paper, delivered in excellent taste ; while the poem of Mr. DELAFIELD SMITH drew down deserved acclamations of applause at its many telling points. The different 'chapters' of the ' Delta Phi,' from metropolitan and neighboring colleges, assembled in the evening at the new and spacious hotel of Mr. J. B. CURTIS, Courtlandt-street, and over a sumptuous repast, regaled each other with intellectual dainties, of every variety. Verily, it was a season to be remembered. We noticed a singular arrangement of the army of black servants in attendance. They came in with the different courses in single file, and with an ostentatious tramping of many feet, like nothing so much as the step by which the state-prisoners at Sing-Sing march to and from their cells. By-the-by, we perceive that one of the sable troop of that night has, for offence ' done and committed,' gone to a larger mansion, where the same lock-step will bring him to viands quite different from the savory dishes he assisted to bear on the evening referred to. . . . A HURRIED note from our old friend CORBYN, contains the following passage. We commend '*The Alleghanians*' to our readers every where : ' I have engaged a quartette of vocalists, who gave three concerts in this city last month, under the title of '*Alleghanians*,' and have added to them a lady who possesses three qualities, likely to win favor with the ' pensive public,' viz. a rich contralto voice, good looks, and an ardent desire to please. Thus my band of ' Alleghanians' will now consist of three male and two female voices, to wit : alto, tenor and bass, soprano and contralto ; each and every one a musician — American, and undeniably respectable. We have also a pianist of considerable talent, who accompanies us. At present we have daily rehearsals, and shall commence our regular tour on Monday the third of August. During two journeys through and around the States, I have noticed the constantly and rapidly-increasing taste for vocal music, of that pure style which touches the heart through the ear ; and knowing that for one who was *really* pleased with the artistic skill of OLE BULL or DE MEYER, a thousand were *actually* amused, delighted, ay, and improved, by listening to simple melodies well performed or sung, I have made up my mind to offer them ' music for the million ;' melodies that every man, woman or child that ' hath music in his (or her) soul' may delight to listen to, even though they do not know sharps from flats, or major from minor ; in short, we shall endeavor to *please*, not to *astonish*.' Success to you, native ' Alleghanians !' . . . '*The Escape, a Tale of the Sea*,' we suspect to be from the pen of a ' land-lubber.' The writer's technical terms remind us of the burlesque directions lately given in one of PUNCH's nautical plays, '*The Seaman's Pipe, or the Battle and the Breeze :* ' ' The Gouger, with all her canvass set, her bowlines gaffed, and her maintop-halyards reefed N. S. by S. N., stands out of the harbor ; and passes under the bows of the ' Blazes :' distant music of ' Yankee-Doodle,' etc. In the next scene, ' the ' Blazes' is seen in full chase, with her dead-eyes reefed, her caboose set, and her try-sail scuppers clewed fore and aft !' . . . WE do not affect amateur *imitations* of ' Transcendentalism' proper. They may be ' startling,' to adopt the words of ' JUNIPER HEDGEHOG,' but just in the way that any man would be very startling, if he walked about the world with a speaking-trumpet to his mouth, making a row with ' How d'ye do ?' ' It 's a fine day !' ' What's o'clock ?' — things common-place enough when uttered like a Christian, but to some folks very startling, when turned inside out, and bellowed as though every syllable had been fished up from the well of truth, and was as great a discovery as North and South America.' . . . ☞ BY a most provoking accident we are compelled to omit an extended '*Literary Record*,' and several subsections of ' Gossip,' which were in type, embracing many things which we desired to say, and several which we had promised to say. We shall make the *amende* in our next.

ORIGINAL PAPERS.

NOTICE.

COUNTRY SUBSCRIBERS who are in arrears should recollect to make returns for what we send them. Remittances to be made to
                              JOHN ALLEN,
                                        139 Nassau-street,
                                                New-York.

MR. T. P. WILLIAMS is our Agent to receive the names of Subscribers in the West and South. Editors and others kindly interested in the circulation of this Magazine, will oblige us by facilitating his designs.

THE KNICKERBOCKER.

Vol. XXVIII. SEPTEMBER, 1846. No. 3.

THE LEGEND OF BABEL.

CHAPTER ONE.

On the broad plain of Shinar spread a prospect of surpassing luxuriance. Sprung from the rank fertility of a soil yet moist and slimy from the universal flood, there arose vast forests of giant trees, rearing their foliant heads to the fleecy summer clouds; rich, profuse verdure, that vied in height with man, and covered the maternal bosom with a thick and matted mantle; flowers of every form and hue, strewn with an unsparing hand, loading the air with fragrance, and reposing in beautiful relief upon the ground-work of dark-green. Throughout the vast expanse the view was on all sides relieved by the scattered marks of cultivation; the yellow grain, the newly-ploughed earth, the shady vineyard, the rustic cottage; while through the midst wound a mighty but placid river, its course marked by a silver sheen as far as the eye could reach. In the distance, upon its banks, rose a great city, whose towering walls in vain strove to hide the golden domes and spires within, that flashed back the sunlight in a blaze of glory. The hum of a dense and busy crowd was borne upon the ear. The clangor of a thousand hammers invaded the stillness, and the smoke of a hundred furnaces rose in dark unbroken columns that pierced the blue sky above, and spread into brooding clouds along its surface. Without the city gates the eye was arrested by an enormous tower, whose base of vast dimensions supported a structure that in its massive strength seemed to surpass the art and power of man. It stood like a giant sentinel guarding a broad domain, which the spirits of beauty and grandeur seemed to have united in creating as the most impressive scene of earth.

From one of the forests, that formed striking features of this landscape, there emerged a man seated on a powerful and fiery horse. A middle age had not yet weakened the iron frame of the rider, although it had sown some silver hairs among his dark flowing locks. His brown features were clothed with an imperious expression, and from his large black eye there beamed a fire which few could steadfastly endure. The habit of command was displayed in every movement, and the intelligence that sat upon his massive brow, the energy revealed in his angular jaw and in the lines of his well-formed mouth and chin, plainly entitled him to the station he possessed. A belt of leather crossed his broad chest, which supported at his back a bow and quiver of arrows. In his right hand he carried a heavy hunting-spear, while his left had deserted the bridle for an arrow, on the barb of which was transfixed a beautiful bird. A deer hung before him across his steed; for he was a mighty hunter, who returned not empty from the chase.

As the monarch left the wood he dismounted, and by the stronger light spent some moments in admiring the plumage of the bird he held upon the arrow. This occupation seemed to be connected in his mind with some distant object; for a shade of tender feeling crossed his features, and he raised his head to gaze at the distant city. The thought that caused this movement was presently diverted by a new idea; for as he gazed at the splendid spectacle, his eye brightened and his form dilated with the pride of power. Then as his look at last rested on the mighty though yet unfinished tower, the proud and elated bearing forsook him, and a shadow of mingled irritation and thoughtfulness flitted hastily over his brow.

At this moment his horse neighed wildly; and as he turned his head, he saw the noble animal standing with erect ears and distended nostrils, trembling under the influence of some sudden terror. At the same instant he heard a crackling in the brushwood at a short distance, and saw by the motion of the grass that some beast of prey was approaching to the attack. Nimrod grasped his spear and advanced to meet the intruder. They encountered, and surveyed each other for a single moment in silence. Here stood the ruler of men, his strong frame thrown into the attitude of defence; his spear advanced and firmly grasped to receive the assailant, and his countenance composed as if quietly seated on his throne. There crouched the king of beasts—an enormous lion; his tail lashing his tawny sides, his mane erect, and his eyes flashing a fearful fire. A terrible roar is heard, and the fatal bound impaled the forest king through the heart upon the strong lance of his foe. A yell of mingled rage and anguish followed, and the death-struggle was ended by the plunge of the hunting-knife, whose home thrust brought the life-blood gushing from the neck of the dying brute. The hunter rose, and a convulsive effort, succeeded by the mortal shudder, announced that all danger was past. A momentary gleam of triumph shone from the eyes of the conqueror as he surveyed his victim, and then mounting his steed he rode away from the scene of bloody strife.

As he approached the city the sun was sinking in the western sky. The noise of toil had ceased, and the swarming laborers thronged the highways and paths, each seeking his home and his

nightly rest.   All who met him bowed the knee; and the monarch
had a familiar nod and smile for each.   The cottage matrons held
up their lisping infants at their doors to point out the great king;
and the sportive urchins left their games to greet him as he passed,
and cry, ' Let Nimrod live forever !'

At the city gate a band of soldiers were drawn up on each side
to receive him; and as he passed under the lofty portal and emer-
ged into the broad, hoof-beaten street, they formed an escort round
his person, and marched forward with him to force a passage through
the crowd and protect him from its pressure.   Here, as he slowly
paced his horse through the busy thoroughfare, his active eye tra-
versed the numberless monuments of art that graced and benefitted
the city.   Here and there he passed a public square, with its ambi-
tious fountain, its luxurious, verdant carpeting, and its immense
primeval trees, preserved from the original forest unharmed through
all the vicissitudes of the city's growth.   Around him stood spa-
cious and elegant mansions, the abode of the chief men of his king-
dom, themselves heads of thousands, but all acknowledging him as
their sovereign lord.   On every side spread broad flights of marble
steps leading into the sacred temples, and surmounted by stupen-
dous monuments, representing the various tutelar deities worship-
ped by the multitude.   Upon vast pedestals of stone stood here an
elephant, there a lion, there again a human form of brass or mar-
ble, wonderful to look upon in their gigantic proportions and lofty
elevation.   Wares and provisions of every kind in the utmost pro-
fusion were displayed at the entrance of shops to attract the eye of
the purchaser, while in other places were heard the sounds of music
and dancing, or of boisterous revelry.

Through the momentary changes of this panorama the monarch
slowly passed; and as from time to time, when he was noticed, the
increasing din of the throng would swell into the air-rending shout
of ' Hail to the mighty Nimrod !' his proud head bent in graceful
acknowledgment, and his winning smile found its home in every
heart upon whose owner that thrilling glance might fall.   At length
he reached the palace; an extensive pile, on whose innumerable
columns and porticos and stately steps the eye might gaze till weary
of beholding.   The vast area surrounding it was guarded from in-
trusion by a numerous soldiery; and far extending along its front
spread a spacious lake, upon whose bosom a modern city might
have found ample room to rest.   Here he rode alone, till reaching
an immense flight of steps whose distant extremities were formed
by square pedestals, crowned each with a colossal elephant of brass,
he dismounted and laid his hand upon the glossy neck of his horse.
' And wert thou frightened, noble Salah, when my face was turned
from thee ?' he said, addressing the affectionate animal; 'thou dost
never tremble while thy master bestrides thy back.'   He stroked
the soft skin of the favorite, and giving some directions to a servant
who drew near, mounted the broad flight and disappeared under
the lofty arch that opened into the royal palace.

CHAPTER SECOND.

THE bright full moon had risen, and now poured her rays upon the brazen dome of the palace and upon the vast expanse of water in whose calm depths its grandeur was reflected. At the casement of a chamber whose white and purple hangings were withdrawn, stood two youthful forms rapt in the enchantment of scenery and the perfume of flowers. Here might a sculptor have found models for immortalizing the perfections of form and feature that belong to either sex. The maiden's face, of a clear and transparent olive, was animated by a pair of eyes that poured from their dark orbs the radiant intelligence of a gifted mind. Her raven hair was bound by a light golden chain-work, and her graceful form was but half concealed beneath the robe of pure white that hung from her rounded shoulders and was confined beneath her bosom by a girdle of crimson, whose ends reached the ground and mingled with the train that swept behind her as she walked. Upon her countenance sat the calm and lofty confidence of virtue and moral strength. In her form was revealed the majesty of royal blood, and she was indeed the daughter of a noble and kingly parent.

And he whose eye was fondly bent upon her was worthy of such a presence. Towering in height above his fellow-men, clothed with a strength of body and grace of form that may have given rise to the ideal creations of a Hercules and an Apollo in after times, these were but the outward adornings of a giant intellect that made its home there. He was born to be a leader of men. The studies in which common minds wore out the prime of life had been to him the mere pastime of youth. Science in its most abstruse mysteries, arts in their extended variety, were at his command. History shed its light upon his mind; government and laws were his familiar study; and this treasury of knowledge beamed in wisdom from his eye, and flowed in convincing accents from his eloquent tongue. And as true wisdom is ever the companion of true religion, his soul was deeply imbued with its light. Far above the blind idol-worship of his day, he brooked no sensible impediment between his soul-worship and the CREATOR of all, who was the immediate object of his love and reverence. Regardless of the priest-craft and ceremonial which diverted instead of directing the multitude to the true object of worship, he offered his praise direct to the prime source of wisdom, and sought direct from HIM the power to concentrate his energies, and the proper path for their exertion.

Adumah was the only daughter of the monarch, and Sadoc the son of his deceased brother. They had been reared together from childhood, and growing up in constant observation of each other's superior character, it was not strange that the intimacy of youth had grown into the deepest love. The king had noticed with pleasure and encouraged their mutual preference; for beside the fondness he entertained for his young relative, he had no son, and was gratified at the prospect of leaving his empire in the hands of one whom he considered in all respects worthy to be his successor. Yet though every thing seemed thus to smile upon the lovers, there was an obstacle which both Nimrod and Sadoc had long viewed with gloomy apprehensions. And at the time of our narrative the crisis had arrived which was to decide the question of life's happiness or misery. What it was and how it resulted we shall endeavor to disclose in the progress of this sketch.

As the lovers stood thus locked in each other's embrace, the silence of their meditations was at length broken by Sadoc.

' Dearest,' said he, ' the heavens and the earth are full of poetry to-night. Is it not fitting that we should breathe the prevailing spirit ?'

Thus speaking, he brought forward to the casement her harp ; and placing a seat, she drew from its chords a wild yet pleasing air, both of them accompanying it with their voices in words which we have literally rendered thus :

> ' The holy law that governs the world is love ;
> And love is the surest, strongest bond among men.
> The moon beams love, upon her sister earth,
> And the stars sing together its sacred song.
> The dew weeps love upon the verdant field,
> And its spirit gladdens the flowers of the plain,
> For the holy law that governs the worlds is love.
> The Deity is the source and the spirit of love ;
> Through it His creatures find their way to Him.
> Music and poetry are the voice of love,
> The eloquent voice that charms the heart of man.
> Let its frequent voice then pour its breathings forth
> Till they reach the ear and the lofty throne of God !
> For the holy law that governs the worlds is love.'

The music ceased, but in a few minutes was resumed :

> ' Sing to the faithful flower of the sun
> The flower that loves the glorious king of day :
> ' Oh ! constant flower, that longs for his approach,
> And follows his ceaseless progress through the sky.
> Oh ! beauteous flower, why art thou mournful and sad ?
> And why is thy head sunk down in silent grief?'
> ' It is night, and my loved one is gone away ;
> I grieve for him, but he comes not back to me.'
> ' Ah ! mournful flower, why dost thou lift thy head,
> And why is thy beautiful face grown bright again ?'
> ' The loved one is mounting above the eastern sky,
> And I feel his warm breath on my dew-wet face ;
> And all the day I shall live in his joyful beams,
> And gaze on his brightness while his chariot flies.'
> ' But what is the hope of thy love, oh ! faithful flower ?
> Dost think the sun rewards thy constancy ?'
> ' True love dies not for want of a return :
> Its hopelessness may rend the aching heart,
> Yet lives it on, in the midst of ruin and death.
> The trammels of earth forever will bind me here,
> But still I shall joy in the glorious light of his eyes,
> And mourn when he hides from me his radiant face.'
> ' But the sun sheds not his light on thee alone ;
> His smiles are meant for flowers more fair than thou.'
> ' Am I worthy the love of one so lofty and bright ?
> And is he not the joy of all he smiles upon ?
> True love hath little pride of self-esteem ;
> Its only pride is in the loved one.'
> ' Well said, oh ! beautiful and constant flower,
> Thou hast a lesson for the sons of men.' '

The song ceased, and steps were heard along the hall without. The hangings of the apartment were withdrawn, and Nimrod entered. His hunting dress was replaced by the royal purple, and his

to her memory. The Ile du Prêtre, or Priest's Island, recalls too a holy legend. It was inhabited by a priest named Andrew, celebrated far and wide for many virtues. His poverty was such however that he possessed only one penny, which he sent, when in need of any thing, to some merchant or laborer, and which was always returned, accompanied by the object of his wishes. The island still retains its name, but the priest and the penny are no more.

On another of the Baltic borders stood in ancient times a church, which was profaned by bachannals and engulfed in the ocean. At night, it is said, may be distinctly heard the miserable victims chaunting with many groans the psalms of penitence ; and when the sea is calm, one can discover through the clear water the candles still burning before the altar.

At Falstar there resided formerly a woman of immense wealth, who unfortunately had no heir to inherit it. Desiring therefore to apply her riches to religious purposes, she used a portion in the construction of a church. On the completion of the edifice she considered herself entitled to some recompense from Heaven for her pious efforts. She prayed therefore that her life might be prolonged during the duration of her church, and the boon was granted. Death passed before her doors but entered not, and though mowing down on all sides friends and relations, left her still untouched. She lived on and on through bloody wars, famine, pestilence, and all the scourges which afflict humanity, until so lengthened was her life that she could find no one whose company was pleasant or desirable. Her conversation was ofttimes so old that none could comprehend her. She had demanded perpetual life, but had forgotten to ask also the additional boon of youth and beauty. Heaven had accorded her exact wishes, but no more. She grew old and feeble, and successively lost her sight, hearing and speech. She then caused herself to be enclosed in an oaken coffin and placed within the church. Each year at Christmas she recovers during one hour the use of her faculties, and at that time a priest approaches to receive her orders ; the unhappy woman, half rising from her resting-place, demands with anxiety : 'Is my church still standing?' 'Yes,' replies the priest. 'Would to God,' she exclaims, 'it were annihilated!' and fainting with the effort, she falls senseless, and the coffin closes over her.

There is still another legend recounted by the poet Œhlenschläger, or rather, as it should be termed, a story from real life. A poor sailor has been rendered crazy by the shipwreck of his daughter. Each day, rowing out his bark upon the ocean, he strikes upon a drum, calling loudly on his child. 'Come,' he exclaims, 'come forth from your retreat. I will place you beside me in my boat, and if you are dead I will give you burial in consecrated ground ; a tomb surrounded with flowers and shading trees, where you shall repose better than amid these wild waves of the ocean.' But alas! the unhappy father calls in vain ; and as night gathers around his way, he returns, saying, 'To-morrow I will go still farther, for my poor child has not heard me !'

business has been the discussion of thine offer of marriage to the princess. Thou knowest how this matter stands. Many, many years will be required to complete this tower, for the difficulties attending the work increase with its progress. My own heart, not less than the hearts of all my nobles, is set on its execution, and as the Destinies may end my reign and my life at any moment, it is essential that my successor shall be prepared to finish the task. I could even give up my wishes in this behalf, for the words I just spoke were the unstudied promptings of irritation; but my word is pledged, and I cannot go back. I could not even bless your union and send you forth to the happiness of private life; for the monarch hath fetters as well as the subject, and a king's faith is not lightly broken.'

'Say no more my father, I beseech thee. It would ill repay a life of kindness if I should suffer my private feelings to thwart the brilliant destiny of the daughter of the kingdom, even were there any hope of success in such a selfish attempt. The council desires my answer; and having heretofore explained my views at large, I can give it in few words. I deem the work a foolish absurdity, and as a ruler, could never give my sanction to an undertaking that will consume in vanity the precious energies of a whole generation; while as an humble worshipper of the God of heaven, I could never encourage an act which I look upon as full of impiety and insult to the great Preserver of men. And now, my father, I prepare with a sinking heart, to leave this my beloved home. My duty to her I love demands that I should tarry here no longer; and my duty to the Creator who bestows man's faculties for usefulness, still more loudly calls on me to leave a spot where I can be no longer useful.'

' Alas! has it come to this!' was all that the emotion of the king permitted him to utter. They fell into each other's arms, and in that long embrace the pent-up fountain of tears was opened. Yes, the strong man whose iron will had moulded into being a powerful and flourishing empire, wept like the weakest child; and he whose aspirations were still more lofty and quenchless, whose faculties were still more vast and potent, even he paid tearful tribute to the emotions that wrung his soul with agony.

The silence, for some time interrupted only by stifled sobs, was at length broken.'

' My father,' exclaimed Sadoc, in a choked and broken voice, 'I will retire to my chamber to spend the night in such preparation as this grave crisis demands. We will not bid our farewell now. On the morrow I prepare for my departure, and the next dawn shall find me on my way. Her parting and mine will be a sad and bitter one. Thou wilt strive to prepare her for it.'

While the monarch stood bewildered and almost stupified, Sadoc reached the door.

'Stay,' cried Nimrod, stretching forth his hands in supplication, " even yet it is not too late. Oh! speak but that one word, and all is well. Think of the happiness, the misery thou leavest. Oh God! is there no hope!'

He bowed his head in agony, and the stormy flood again burst
forth. Sadoc had partly recovered his calmness, and he answered:
' My father, do not thus give way to despair. It cannot be. Thou
and she would scorn me, if at this hour I turned traitor to myself.
It is all over now.'

He was gone, for he dared trust himself no longer. The king
passively heard his footsteps till they grew faint in the distance.
Then he rose and looked wildly round him, as if waking from a ter-
rible dream, and slowly, almost unconscious what he did, he returned
with faltering step and heavy heart to the council hall.

CHAPTER THREE.

THE last sun that shone on the fated city had risen in wonted
splendor. The din of labor had commenced, and swelled in volume
as each new car of burden joined the rumbling throng, and each
new forge opened its deafening clang. The tough clay of the river
bank furnished the endless material for making brick, and its slimy
bed was scraped for the requisite mortar. Outside the city gates,
the open field was a vast highway, thronged with smoky brick-kilns,
crowds of vehicles and beasts of burden, and a restless multitude
of human forms. The ass, the horse, the camel, the elephant, were
made the laborious and serviceable aids of man in this stupendous
and unremitting work. Round the base of the tower vast beds of
mortar and heaps of brick were receiving constant additions ; while
by means of huge cranes planted in the body of the structure, these
additions were as constantly disappearing, hoisted from one stage
to another till they finally reached the dizzy height where they
entered into the composition of the gigantic whole. In vain the
eye might essay to detect the thousands who at that awful eminence
were building themselves still higher into the vault of heaven. Yet
at that height these workmen passed their days and nights ; for the
time they would consume in daily ascent and descent was too great
to be thus sacrificed. Throughout the whole work the utmost sys-
tem and discipline was maintained. Each man had his appointed
work, which was to be exchanged for no other. A chief superin-
tended the labors of each gang, while each set of chiefs reported
progress to their immediate superiors, and these again received their
general directions, and submitted the account of their management
to the king in council.

It was the usual morning occupation of Nimrod to visit the scene
of labor, to inspect the progress of the work, and to encourage by
praise, or stimulate by rebuke, the activity or remissness of those
who had the charge of its various divisions. But this day he did
not appear. Many an eye was often directed to the great gate-way
of the city expecting to see the black horse of the monarch proudly
bear his rider on his wonted tour, but hour after hour passed, till
morning had mounted into noon, and yet he came not. What had
befallen him ? Was he detained by pressing business with the
council ? If so, what was the nature of that business ? Could it

be war? And at this thought the thrill of ardor spurred their hot blood, as they longed to show the readiness and valor of their swords in his behalf. Or again, was the king stretched upon the couch of illness, and was each breath of him they loved and feared drawn with pain and weakness? Ah! how eagerly would they fly to his relief, could they render it, and what dismay was caused by the mere foreboding of his death! These, and a thousand such fanciful speculations agitated the minds of his subjects, all remote from the true cause of his absence.

Yet he was indeed ill, not in body but in mind. To a sleepless night had succeeded a day of anguish. He had broken the tidings to his daughter, and in her heart-rending agony the soul of the father was again pierced with torture. In the first transports of the widowed one she would listen to no words of consolation. Indeed, what consolation could be offered for grief like her's? She would fly to her Sadoc, her husband, her lord. She raved against the cruelty that would sunder them, even for the short hours that remained. She broke through all remonstrance, all restraint, and rushed to the apartments of her lover. Wo upon wo! he was already gone. His chambers were deserted. His parchments, his books lay scattered in disorder; his instruments of music were cold and silent. His weapons, his garments hung upon the abandoned walls. The natural stillness of inanimate matter was tortured into unnatural proofs of his final departure. His servants — ah! call his servants! They are summoned, and their tidings breathe the blessed air of hope. He had sent for his horse and had ridden forth, saying that at sunset he would return.

At sunset! Who can describe the alternate hope and fear, the longing and the anxiety that filled those tardy hours! Now wailing in grief over the irreparable loss, for which even his return brought but a momentary relief; now lost in rapture at the thought of being once more embraced in those arms; thus she passed the sluggish day. The rude shock seemed to have utterly crushed the fortitude of her nature. The daughter of the oak was apparently transformed into the aspen; and she whose self-command seldom suffered her feelings to be betrayed, was unable even to collect her scattered faculties to make the effort at calmness. Oh! how deep into the heart of hearts are twined the tendrils of a woman's love!

At the window that overlooked the path by which the return of Sadoc was expected, Adumah sat the remainder of that day. The sun poured his radiant glory over the scene, but she had no eyes for the beauties of nature. The garden birds warbled their joyous strains, but her ear was lost to all sound, in striving to catch the distant foot-falls of his horse. He would not stay till sunset; oh! no! the next moment would reveal his manly form speeding to her presence. The overstrained senses lost their power, and their office was supplied by fancy. On the distant horizon a phantom of the mind would form a moving speck, and until the illusion vanished, that was he. Each rustling of the wind, or air-borne bubble of the brook, was tortured into the clatter of a horse's hoofs. She would start at hearing, in imagination, the tones of his voice, and relapse into solicitude, to be again visited with the same delusions.

Yet even to hours of watching there is an end. The sun at last did go down, and night without an interval of twilight succeeded. A cloud of ominous darkness shut out the rays of the moon, and its gloomy pall spread upon the sky. Was she again deceived? No; it was a horse; but ah! not his. His steed would not move thus slowly on his return to her. Yes! it was his; for as the sound drew nearer, the rapid pace was detected. It ceased; door's opened and shut; a quick tread was heard, and as Sadoc entered the apartment, Adumah, worn out with mental excitement, fainted in his arms.

. . . .

The father, the daughter and the nephew stood gazing out upon the darkened sky. No star, no moon was visible; all was sad and gloomy as a funeral pall. An unnatural quietude pervaded the atmosphere. Not a breath of air ruffled the water, or stirred the leaf, or could be felt upon the face. The slightest sound fell upon the ear with startling distinctness. The neighing of horses, the howling of dogs, the bleating of sheep were heard, as if instinct presented the brute creation with forbodings of danger. Large birds of prey flapped their wings and screamed as they flew past. The extreme rarity of the air and the unusual heat were painfully oppressive. The city was in commotion, and every face dark with the apprehension of some dreadful impending disaster; but of what nature, or whence to be expected, none could reveal.

The face of Sadoc was calm, but pale and thoughtful. His fears had assumed a definite form, but the proper course of action was yet undecided. While he mused with a heart filled with anxiety, a low tremor passed over the surface of the ground, scarce perceptible, save to one momently expecting it; and on the instant, in the far distance, he caught a glimpse of a dim meteor, so sudden and transient that it almost seemed the creature of an excited fancy. At once he exclaimed, 'My father! my sister! the tempest and the earthquake are upon us! We must escape to the open plain while yet there is time.'

He waited not for an answer, but flew to the court of the palace. Here he met one of his own trusty attendants. ' Go to the stables, Etseo,' he said, 'and bring out to the main entrance the three strongest and surest steeds.' Then collecting the terror-stricken servants, he addressed them in a calm and distinct voice:

' We must leave the city, or the earthquake and the storm will bury us in its ruins. Let each one provide a horse and be prepared to ride forth with the king and the princess by the eastern gate. Away! there is no time to lose.'

The decision and energy of Nimrod had not failed him in this crisis, and in mere bodily peril Adumah was true to her natural firmness. Wrapped in heavy clothing, they stood awaiting the return of Sadoc. Hastily entering, he threw round him the mantle provided by the forethought of affection, and in silence they went forth and descended the broad steps. A large escort was already formed.   They mounted their steeds, and surrounded by the troop of servants, rode fast across the palace enclosure and entered the wide streets of the city.

CHAPTER FOURTH

THE crowds that already choked the avenues were every moment increased by other thousands that streamed from the houses with alarm and amazement depicted on their features.   Apparently without a purpose in view, and almost without consciousness, they hurried to and fro like a nest of ants whose roof-stone has been dislodged.   Fully impressed with the apprehension of sudden and awful danger, fully aware of the necessity of exertion to avoid it, they knew neither where to look for the evil nor how to escape its stroke.   The escort of Nimrod could make scarce any progress through the dense shifting throng.   Every moment was most precious, and yet no speed could be effected.   Then Sadoc, well knowing the influence of a prompt and definite will in moments of panic and confusion, cried out with a clarion voice that was not only heard but *felt* through all the uproar and tumult : ' Escape from the city ! fly by the eastern gate !'

In a moment, moved by a common impulse, the human tide turned itself in that direction.   Again and again that clear loud voice was heard, and the torrent hurried onward with a force that defied all resistance.   The hearts of the fugitives now beat high with hope as they pressed their horses to a greater speed.

The lightning and the thunder now began to act their part in this sublime but terrific spectacle.   The first large drops of the tempest fell and were soon followed by a deluge that seemed to pour rather than rain from the opened clouds.   More vivid and frequent came the blinding flashes, and more loud and deafening waxed the peals of thunder ; while the wind rose, and in violent gusts dashed the drenching rain into the faces of the flying crowd.   The thousand torches of the multitude were extinguished, but the abandoned houses glared forth their light upon the mass, and the lightning each moment illumined the scene with unnatural distinctness.

As they hurried along, every instant added some new element of sublimity to the sight.   The broad and lofty flights of marble that led up to the temples were thronged with suppliants, who, prostrate and with out-stretched arms, called wildly on their gods to save them.   The huge idols that surmounted the lofty columns or pedestals were at times wrapped in the blue flame of the lightning, and again shone as if themselves were fountains of light.   Surrounded by these fearful yet beautiful spectacles, the multitude was borne onward without pause or interruption, each moment adding to its speed, while the gates were now disgorging their ceaseless thousands.

Still the rain and the furious wind, the lightning and the thunder, plied their exhaustless weapons.   The royal fugitives were but a short distance from the gate, when a low distant rumbling was heard, increasing in volume as it approached, till it resembled the flight of an army of chariots and horses over a paved way. The earth trembled, then heaved beneath their feet like the swell of a troubled sea, and the convulsion passed on. The dense column of human beings reeled and wavered, and in another moment would have broken and hurled itself backward in its course. Then again was heard the firm trumpet-voice : ' Onward ! onward to the gate !' and in another moment the escort reached the open plain.

Here new difficulties beset them. All was dense darkness, save when the dazzling flashes darted across the black sky. The ways were choked with fugitives and lumbering vehicles, which made their progress hazardous in the extreme. Yet they struggled on, shaping their course by tacit consent toward a hunting-lodge of the monarch, at the edge of a neighboring forest. Again the jar and tremor of the earth was felt, and the stunning clangor heard. By an irresistible impulse they reined in their horses and looked back. A fearful crash fell upon their ears, and at the moment a broad sheet of flame overspread the heavens. By its light they beheld the city prostrate. Its walls, its palaces, its domes and spires lay levelled with the ground, and a thick murky cloud rose from the ruins.

Amazed and stupified, they stood motionless and silent. Another lingering glare sheeted the sky, and while the sharp, pealing thunder burst forth, a huge globe of fire, hurled by the hand of Omnipotence itself, fell upon the summit of the massive tower, which, as if molten into liquid matter, sank down beneath it to the earth. No crash was heard, no ruins were left, no cloud of smoke arose. The fire of heaven had in the twinkling of an eye utterly consumed from the face of earth the pride and the toil of man !

The divine vengeance was accomplished. The torrents ceased, the wind fell, the lightning came more faint and at longer intervals, and the thunder rolled and muttered in the distance. The gloomy covering of the sky broke in ragged clouds ; and in the patches of deep blue that follow the thunder-storm, the silent, watchful stars were seen. At length the struggling moon escaped from imprisoning clouds, and looked down again upon the earth. Her light revealed a strange spectacle. At the moment when the tower was stricken down, the sentence of dispersion and confusion of tongues went forth ; and now the multitude, no longer in swarming crowds, were scattered in countless groups over the surface of the plain. Of these detached parties, none understood the language of the rest ; and dating as it were a new existence from that moment, they wandered forth to seek new homes and new employments wherever the hand of Providence might direct.

As in that hour of solemn and conflicting thoughts the eye of Nimrod surveyed the ruin of his empire and the dispersion of his subjects, he kneeled down upon the wet earth, and with a chastened and humble heart poured forth to the true GOD the silent homage of his soul. Then rising, he joined the hands of his children, and while tears of penitence and gratitude coursed down his face, he uttered in a faltering voice these words :

' Blessed be the name of the LORD ! He hath stricken, but preserved us. He hath abased the proud, and set at nought the devices of the haughty. He hath also united you, my children, and may His richest blessing rest upon you !'

.   .   .   .

NIMROD was again the founder of a kingdom ; but during a reign of many years he never again forgot the GOD whose power and justice had been thus signally brought home to him. He was succeeded on the throne by Sadoc, who ruled long with wisdom and in peace, happy in the love of his beautiful and noble queen. They were the founders of a line of princes that governed the plain of Shinar for ages; till the tragic history of Babel began to be with them, as it is with us, a scanty narrative, furnishing scope and data for boundless speculation.

LAYS OF A PEDESTRIAN.

BY LUCIUS E. SMITH.

I.

I AM weary, I am weary, and behind the western hill
Lo! the sun is sinking fast, and the dews are falling chill :
Far along the fading landscape evening's lengthened shadows creep,
And the violets are folding up their tiny leaves to sleep.

II.

I am weary, I am weary ; I have wandered far away
From the hill-side where I loitered at the breaking of the day ;
Oh, ye birds! to whose glad voices then I listened joyfully,
While I lingered at your bidding — happy songsters! where are ye ?

III.

Welcome, Night ! thy pall of darkness o'er the earth that hovers now,
Welcome too thy dewy breezes, that refresh my fevered brow ;
Welcome, Silence ! that composes every living thing to rest,
Save the wanderer's languid heart, faintly beating in his breast.

IV.

Stars ! that in your silent courses ever circling, never tire,
Guide me in my onward journey by your own unflickering fire ;
Underneath your gentle radiance seek to pierce the thickening gloom,
Eyes of love that wait my coming — sleepless, anxious eyes at home !

V

Yes ! the light of home is shining ; now it meets my longing gaze !
Weariness and faintness flee from before its kindling rays !
Morning's rising splendors vanish, vanished is the night-fall's gloom,
By the fireside's love-lit flame, in the sacred rest of home !

Williamstown, Mass.

THE   BEAUTIFUL: WHERE   IS   ITS   HOM

—— ' Beauty is still
As beautiful as ever ; still the play
Of light around her lips has every charm
Of childhood in its freshness : Love has there
Stamped his unfading impress, and the hues
Of fancy shine around her, as the sun
Gilds at his setting some decaying tower,
With feathered moss and ivy overgrown.'

WHERE dwells the Beautiful ?
Ask the young mother, when at close of day,
Her infant slumbering on her warm heart lay ;
While the last day-beam, passing to its rest,
Kisses his brow and leaves its last bequest :
Look at that mother, gazing, rapt the while,
And see! she points thee to her infant's smile !

Where dwells the Beautiful ?
Ask him who rides upon the restless wave,
That rolls perchance above his destined grave ;
Who sees the lightning's flash, and hears the moan
From the sea's caverns, dirge-like, sad and lone ;
And he will tell thee that the heaving breast
Of ocean claims it in its wild unrest.

Where dwells the Beautiful ?
Ask him who scans the starry heaven at night,
And reads its pages by its own pale light ;
Who, led by Science o'er bright worlds untrod,
Looks up ' through Nature unto Nature's GOD :'
Will he not answer, rapture in his eye,
The Beautiful ! it dwells alone on high?

Where dwells the Beautiful ?
Ask him who seeks it mid ' the stars of earth,'
Those floral treasures, in whose beauteous birth
We trace Almighty wisdom, and that love
Which like the dew descendeth from above ;
And he will tell thee that the lily's bell
Hideth the treasure in its fragrant cell.

But ask the poet where it hath its home,
If, in the infant's smile, the billows' foam,
The stars' soft radiance, or the petals bright
Of flowers rejoicing in the warm sunlight ;
And he will answer, while his moistened eye
Foretells the rapture of his lip's reply :

That earth hath not so drear, so dark a spot,
Nor heaven a tablet where he finds it not !
Its pathway may be traced the wide world round,
And yet no limit to its home be found :
Not only in the stars of earth and heaven,
The white wave's crest, the smile to mothers given ;

Not only in the rainbow's mingled dye,
The gorgeous drapery of the evening sky;
The clouds that hasten to refresh the earth,
The dew that sparkles o'er each floweret's birth;
Not only in the streamlets, as they glide,
Now smooth now rough, e'en as life's changing tide:

But in the tear that Mercy sheds for those
For whom life's shadowed path yields no repose;
Whose toil finds small reward, while pining care
Sits at the board, and meets them every where!
Oh! when such sorrow hears sweet Mercy's tone,
The Beautiful may claim it for its own!

When human love doth dry the orphan's tear,
And soothe the weeper bending o'er the bier
Of him, her stay, her earthly solace gone,
While she stands widowed, in the world alone;
Oh! there believe the Beautiful hath birth —
That nought more lovely greets thee on the earth.

He sees it when the sire's fond arms are round
The prodigal returned, the lost one found;
When by his penitential tears restored,
The wanderer seeks again his father's board;
Oh! when those lips revered breathe pardoning love,
There's nought more beautiful in heaven above!

He sees it when the maiden turns aside,
From earthly pomp to be the Church's bride;
And loving still the world, which GOD hath blest,
Beholds it now in hallowed brightness dressed;
Her earthly hopes from earthly bonds released,
She bows to taste the eucharistic feast.

And when the mother takes her infant boy,
Her new-born treasure, her young heart's first joy,
And standing by the sacred chancel's side,
Prays that GOD's blessing on his life abide;
When the baptismal water bathes his brow,
Where dwells the Beautiful? — oh! askest thou?

Then grant me, Heaven! the poet's eye to see
The Beautiful where'er its dwelling be;
His ear to hear, when Pity's voice doth bless
The joyless widow or the fatherless;
Nor close it to those notes of sacred love,
' By choirs of angels chanted from above.'

But more than all, the poet's heart, to feel
That every spot some beauty may reveal;
That every human soul doth bear some trace
Of HIM who claims it as HIS dwelling-place;
Some mystic tie, some link unseen, but given
To bind him to his future home in Heaven!

o. w. s.

Portsmouth, (N. H.)

THOUGHTS ON HUMBLE LIFE.

BY 'THE DOCTOR.'

THERE is much beauty in humble life. Could we but enter into the hearts of the lowly and obscure, and see their efforts to compass their little ends; their noble sacrifices for one another; could we but lay our hands on their hearts, and feel the beating there of hopes and fears; vain struggles to rise out of poverty, and honest desires after a more favored place in the world, we should perhaps realize the relationship we have with the poor, the humble, the unknown.

There is no mistake so common as that which judges of a man's nature by his clothes. The lady and her maid have a common nature. What is love to one is love to the other. Analyze the tears that fall from their eyes; you will find them composed of the same elements; open their bodies, and the internal structure is the same. By what rule then do you decide that what is joy to one is not joy to the other? As the inhabitants of distant planets look at our world as a point in infinite space, may it not be that superior intelligences regard humanity and not the individual?—that to them grief is the grief of the world, and joy the happiness of the world; to them, 'when one member suffers all the members suffer with it?'

I heard a little story of love and conjugal affection lately, which touched my feelings deeply. It set me to thinking about the feelings of the humble and the laborious; and I thanked GOD in my heart that, in spite of poverty and reverses, there is in store for every faithful loving heart rich sources of delight, which not even the darkness of poverty can hide.

An Irish laborer left his native country in the hope of improving his condition. He arrived on our shores after a long voyage, which had eaten up his means and left him without a penny. In the same vessel that brought him over there was a pretty Irish girl, who had left her home to lighten the burthen of her parents, perchance assist them in the feeding of their large family and clothing them; educating them was out of the question. An attachment grew up between these poor emigrants on their voyage. They learned to love each other, and before the arrival of the ship at her destined port had plighted heart and hand. The long voyage had also exhausted the small means of the girl.

Strangers and wanderers, they landed on these hospitable shores, full of faith and hope and love. The girl engaged at service in a hotel in the city of New-York; the man met a contractor of some of the rail-roads, and soon was at work with his shovel. Each was so occupied for the first few days that they had no time to communicate together; and by frequent removal here and there, they lost trace of each other. But they labored on, and laid up their means, hoping soon to find an hour of meeting.

The girl proved an excellent housemaid, and was soon advanced from better to better places, until she found a permanent home in the house of a widow, living some few miles out on the island. A month, a year elapsed, and she had no tidings of her lover, whose image was deeply graven on her heart, as the sequel will show. So fine a girl in person, so excellent help, commanding such high wages, was not without offers. The coachman courted her; the butler wooed her; a neighboring farmer was caught in the trap of her shining eyes and tidy waist. Lovers were not wanting, but they all pleaded in vain. Her heart was fixed on the lad that stood by her side in the sunshine and the storm; whose hand she had clasped when the vessel plunged and labored, until there seemed to be danger to life. She often thought too of the bright hours they had passed together, the moon-lit seas, the clear heavens above, when an approving PROVIDENCE seemed to look down and smile upon their happiness. She could not forget all the past, and loved on in hope and trust her Irish boy.

We cannot call names, because our story is true, and our friends may one day be people of consequence in the world; a gentleman and lady, according to conventional sense, perhaps in high office and dignity; and there would be indelicacy in printing their names; but we will print the moral of their constancy and honesty and good sense. For convenience' sake we will call them Charles and Abby.

The fate of Charles was less fortunate. He could not bear his solitary lot so equably and patiently as his mistress. The truth must be told; he drank to drown his sorrow, lost his place, and became an outcast in the land. We will not follow his painful degradation. Could we examine into all the causes, we doubt not we should find him helped along down hill as long as he had any thing that could be of use to any body. But when he was completely beggared of his money and clothes, with barely enough to cover his nakedness, he was kicked out of the low places that had helped to ruin him, and stood degraded and despised, hungry and cold, in the streets of the city.

As you pass along, kind reader, to your place of business in the city, do you not often see some poor wretch who seems to be bewildered and forsaken? and do you not pass him by as you pass a horse or a dog? There stands a man, a brother man, *your* brother, by a common relationship to CHRIST. Do you ever think of helping such an outcast? No; you think it impossible that you can do him any good. You have had no experience in such instances, and you think him a hopeless case, a ruined man. But you are wrong. That form possesses a heart, pride, generous emotion, reverence, affections; and now that you are regarding him, his tears flow; his heart is breaking as he remembers his father, his mother, his home, far off in a foreign land. A word of kindness will be sweeter now to that man than a handful of gold. He is lost, crazed, forsaken, in despair. Only the best, the truest natures are capable of feeling as he feels. The bad prosper by crime; by foul if not by fair means. Only the pure can be broken-hearted.

Abby was riding into the city with her mistress, who treated her with unusual confidence. Her bright eyes saw every object in the street. Was Charles ever absent from her thoughts? Never. She saw a poor object by the side of the way; it could not be—yes, it is—it is like—but oh no! it is impossible. The coach nearly ran over him. His eyes met her's. Yes, it is he!—there is no mistake. She asked leave to get out. She did not hesitate what to do. She saw at a glance how it was; she read with the eye of true love his whole history since their separation. Her mistress had been informed of her secret grief, and divined the cause of her conduct when she saw her, a lady to all appearance, leave the carriage and rush into the arms of her lover. The street passengers said she was crazy. It seemed so strange that two persons, so differently clad, could by any possibility have any affinity. But so it was.

It is only necessary to our moral to say, that from the time of this meeting Charles found a friend. The means Abby had accumulated were freely spent in restoring her lover to his reason and his health. She left her place and watched by his bed-side. As soon as he was well they were married.

These facts came to my knowledge as their physician. They removed to the village where I reside. Abby has a place in a family as cook. Charles is gardener to a gentleman of fortune. That which has pleased me the most in this matter is the deep attachment they seem to feel for each other. They expect soon to go to house-keeping. They tell me that as soon as they have saved a few hundred dollars they shall venture upon this step. They labor in patience, slowly laying up their little fortune cent by cent; and every penny they save is of as much consequence to them as the thousands embarked in speculation by their rich employers. I often talk with them about the future, and I learn to estimate my own good fortune in having a comfortable home by seeing the striving of these poor foreigners barely for a place to live in. The summit of their felicity will be attained when they can rent and furnish a cottage which they can call their home.

Their life is as veritable a romance as Bulwer ever concocted. Their emotions, their hopes and fears, are as real as if they were a gentleman and lady struggling through a fashionable engagement to marriage.

I am sure, Mr. KNICKERBOCKER, if you knew these people you would be interested in them. Your Magazine has ever pleaded the rights of man; you have pledged yourself to respect honest effort. I have been thinking what power you have, as Editor of so popular a work, to breathe heart and hope into the humble; how much you have it in your power to do for the obscure and ignorant, by exciting in the hearts of your rich readers—those who can afford to enjoy the luxury of a Monthly—an interest in the struggles of the

Poor. There is no pleasure like it — like benevolence. I am a poor doctor, in a country town; I get fifty cents a visit from the rich; nothing from the poor. I am called up at night in all weathers, to ride miles perhaps; and even if I get no money for my visit, I am always paid in feeling that I relieve the suffering.

I have been in your great city, and been shocked with the machinery of vice there. Why do not the people of the city take some action for the poor? Shut up those low grog-shops and establish public baths, and use other means to elevate the poor to comfortable habits and better morals? Are you blind to your duty as Christians, or do you only go to church to hear the music and see the ladies' feathers? I can't understand the indifference of the proud cities of a free nation to the low vice in them. Is it a necessary evil? No one will say so.

I see by a late article in your Magazine that you have a valuable contributor, of my profession, who has considered consumption in its causes and cure. He speaks of the air. I would say a word about the vice that produces it. Intemperance makes more consumptive cases than low situation. It is low habits, not low rooms alone. Excuse my bluntness. I have written to you the exact truth, as it seems to me; and am very truly your obedient servant,

'THE DOCTOR.'

STANZAS.

I.

BRIGHTLY the moonlight is gilding the river,
Stars are all dreaming serenely on high,
Leaves full of mystery witchingly quiver,
Night with her spirits bears rule in the sky.

II.

Come to the trysting place! Spirits are calling,
Beauty and Purity hallow the air;
Love has a holiness, now so enthralling,
We shall grow fonder and truer while there.

III.

Dewy and mystic, the hill-side is gleaming,
Silence seems bathing in moonbeamy mist,
Rose-buds with beauty all stainless are teeming,
Beauty no wantoning zephyr has kissed.

IV.

Come to the trysting-place, dearest! and kneeling
Reverently there at our love-lighted shrine,
Earnestly, truly, we 'll worship there, feeling
Love that brings worship so pure is divine.

J. D. B.

only by the obscure hints of a few faithful domestics, who without betraying their comrades warned their masters of their danger.

The fearful question will intrude : ' In the event of invasion, war without or dissension within our own borders, would the down-trodden, heavy-laden, ignorant beings in bondage among us turn at last and rend their oppressors ?   Paying off at one fell stroke the long score of stripes, cruel sundering of heart-ties, unnoticed wailing and tears, unregarded complaints and prayers ?   It is a question of fearful import.   There might amid the mighty mass be found a few faithful ones, who in the love which responds to kind treatment, would at all risk, warn off the impending danger.   But with the thousands, we fear the iron has entered the soul as well as seared the skin.   The exasperated feelings, hatred, revenge, and every evil passion, though stifled and hid beneath a smooth surface, may, like the long slumbering volcano, with the grass growing green at its edge and the peaceful village at its feet, at length burst forth to wither, to overwhelm, to consume.

The explosion at St. Domingo was sudden and terrible ; all the beautiful plains in an hour were covered with fire, and the labor of a century was devoured in a night ; while the negroes, like unchained tigers, precipitated themselves on their masters, seized their arms, massacred them without pity, or threw them into the flames.   Those who escaped from this scene of horror on board of ships were lighted in their passage over the deep by their burning habitations.   They almost all took refuge with us and were welcomed with generous sympathy and kind hospitality.   To their misfortunes alone we owe the arduous and successful efforts of some of the most accomplished teachers and professors among us.   The frigate ' La Fine' foundered, and five hundred of the survivors from the flames perished in the waves !

The subsequent history of this beautiful island forms another melancholy attestation to the truth that they are least fitted to rule who cannot be ruled ; self-government and justice in the governors being no less essential than subordination, order and respect for superiors in the governed ; the bondage from which they emerged being light in comparison to the bondage to vice, indolence and anarchy into which they rushed.   The champions of liberty are looking on with sad interest in her fate, and may well weep at her unhappy state.

During the massacre of Cape-Town, when thirty thousand wretched beings perished, with atrocities unparalleled even in the long catalogue of European crime, a gentleman of standing and wealth was walking in the out-skirts of the town, where he had placed his little family for safety, when suddenly two negroes turned an angle of the street and stood before him.   They were armed with huge clubs, and their aspect was ferocious and dreadful.   They held but a short parley, when they commenced to strip the prisoner of every article of value, using all the while great swelling words of liberty and equality, right and freedom ; desecrating them at every breath !

Their unresisting victim pleaded at length for life ; his little ones ; aged parents.   All in vain!   With dew-eyed Pity what had *they* to do ?

At two o'clock, the usual dinner hour of Germany, heaven only knows how many are the long discussions on the occurrences of this eventful day; the sage conjecture as to that fair lady who passed the streets 'with the large and curiously-fashioned sleeves,' or that gentleman who 'sported the gold-headed cane and wore the star of diamonds.' Terrible indeed is the confusion, if amid the numerous arrivals there should be found any one demanding particular attention; as for instance, the stall-master of some petty prince, some counsellor or baron, and still more anxious the gossip as to his business, connexions and whereabouts.

It is thus that this memorable Saturday passes in a state of constant pleasurable excitement, each hour adding something to the stock of interest destined for a week's consumption. But alas! time fleets away, and the hour of departure is at hand. Already is the smoke ascending from the chimneys of the crowded steamer, and the Danish flag floating at its mast-head. The inhabitants of Kiel, true to the promptings of their curiosity, have assembled at the harbor, and arranged themselves along the quay. The time has arrived for a quick eye and a ready ear, for soon this little world of strangers will have passed away and nothing remain but the remembrance of this active and exciting day.

It is now seven! Already has the canon uttered its farewell salute to the village, and the little vessel swam like a bee-hive with its multitude of occupants, as it glides swiftly out upon the ocean. Many are the neat white 'kerchiefs waved in token of adieu, and still more numerous the blue eyes glistening with tears of sadness, falling like pearls on many a rosy countenance. Alas! happy indeed are those who weep! The far wanderer from his native land has no such consolation. He quits each foreign shore without regret, with scarce sensation; for there are none to tender him the hand of friendship nor to breathe farewell! *His* friends, alas! are elsewhere, and how knows he in that moment that they think of him!

But the busy, living machine is now in motion. The waves ripple around the wheels that break their surfaces of crystal, and the vessel speeds her course right onward like a bird. Already all of Kiel has disappeared save her Gothic steeples, and her house-tops, lessening in the distance. The sea is calm, and the sky most beautiful, while the setting sun just visible above the leafless height of Dunsterbrook is gilding with its rays the bay and all surrounding objects. It is now the stillness and repose of nature! Why, mingling as I do mid such sweet scenes, was there not granted me a poet's nature! With what enthusiasm could I then describe this holy hour of peace; this seeming withdrawal from the world, where one beholds above and around him nothing but the heavens, glowing with the last rays of the departed sun, and overhanging this vast silver ocean! With what rapture might I then speak of this beautiful Baltic; this sea, chaunted by the ancient Scalds and traversed by the Vikings!

But alas! I claim to be no poet, nor is the appearance of a steamer even in mid-ocean aught else than prosaic. Look for instance at that column of smoke, creeping stealthily and slowly upward; that machine graduating its movements with mathematical precision; that vane, lazily pointing out the changes of the wind, and those wheels which have usurped the place of the ancient full-oar battery! It has gone now, this once sweet poetry of the sea! All is busy, bustling reality. Adieu forever to those beautiful evolutions of better times, commanded in high tones and executed with inconceivable rapidity! Adieu to those snow-white sails, gracefully rising above each other, now swelling as it were with conscious pride, and anon drooping lifeless along the mast, as if mourning their departed energies. Adieu to all those excitements and uncertainties, those joys and deceptions, which once constituted the beauty and the romance of the sailor-life!

Yes! ploughing through it, as one does at present, the sea must be regarded as prosaic. Who could imagine Byron gazing on the tar-besmeared chimney of a steamer, and inditing those verses of Childe Harold:

'He who hath sailed upon the dark blue sea,
Hath viewed at times, I ween, a full fair sight!'

Or think you that the actors in 'Othello' would have uttered the joyful cry of 'A sail! a sail!' when gazing upon the vessel bearing the gentle Desdemona, had they only to announce an oily, smoky steam-boat?

No! the steamer is emphatically the vessel of the merchant; and one lives there as within a counting-house. Every thing is neat, polished, distributed with reference to the strictest economy, and arranged in perfect order. The passengers all pay in advance. They depart precisel at the time appointed, and arrive with equal regularity. During the continuance of the voyage, they must prove themselves sociable men and good companions. No one has the right to withdraw in melancholy moodiness nor to dream apart. Your fellow prisoners come to you; they claim the right to know your birth-place and the story of your travels. In return they give you their own history and projects. They bid you good-night affectionately and greet you in the morning as a friend.

Even those who seek to escape this intimacy, will fall the victims of sea-sickness which may be pronounced the perfection of democracy, perfectly annihilating all distinctions and humbling human vanity. The powerful noble, struggling beneath its influence, thinks little of his chateau or his titles, but stretches himself at full length on the deck, beside the common peasant. The haughty dame too seems to forget her dignity with each movement of the vessel. The proprietors of steamers are great lovers of sea-sickness. They count upon it, and it rarely deceives their calculations. In passing for instance from Kiel to Copenhagen, dinner must be paid for in advance, at least by those who are sufficiently fool-hardy to consider any such meal an act of prudence. It is always served however under the worst possible circumstances; that is to say, on one's arrival opposite Kioge, in a narrow strait where the wind has its full force and the sea is most outrageous. It is hardly to be wondered at then that the miserable passengers receive all invitations to their places with evident reluctance, or that the beef-steaks literally walk over the tables, finding no consumers. To all this may be added another notable invention, that of endeavoring to cover the beds of the unlucky occupants with two miserable apologies for sheet and blanket. In this way one is employed during 'the first portion of the night in vain endeavors to enclose himself in a sheet, whose two sides seem to have sworn eternal opposition, and the other half in constant clutchings at a coverlid, which following the laws of gravity is continually gliding to the floor. The result is, as the sheet obstinately refuses all attempts at its enlargement, and the coverlid with equal pertinacity resumes its downward tendency, that every one is ready to hurry on deck with the first dawn of daylight, heartily blessing his stars that he has not another night to pass in this foul place of misery.

Happily on escaping from this scene of suffering one finds himself enjoying the freshness of the morning air, and surrounded by innumerable charms of Nature; for she at least has formed no alliance with the steam-proprietors of Copenhagen to mete out the happiness of travellers by the gingle of a few miserable shillings.

At sunrise the vessel doubles the point of Falstar, passing between Seeland and a great number of small islands, floating like flowers upon the water. It is on these isolated spots that the peasant-fisherman lives as in a life-boat, with the waves leaping and revelling around the very door-steps of his miserable cabin. The sea however is his element; the source of his joys and griefs; his world and barrier. It is here that he pursues his daily occupation. Sometimes the smiling surface of the water seems to call him forth upon its bosom, gently undulating beneath the dippings of his active oar, while the cloudless heavens lie spread out above, resembling clear blue plains that storms have never visited; and the whispered murmurs of the forest winds are not more pleasant than the gentle rippling of the waves parting before his gliding boat, to close again in arrowy lines of foam, resembling silver ribbands. It is then that the water-spirits seem to chant wild sea-songs in their grottoes, and the mermaid rising to the summit of the wave, charms the deluded voyager.

But anon this sea so calm is irritated into sudden fury, and howls around these desolate islands, enchaining them with its mad sweep of waters like a zealous and despairing lover. The hardy fisherman knows well these caprices of his mistress, and he loves her alike in her gentleness and her wrath.

It is asserted by tradition that these islands are the work of powerful enchanters, who placed them as so many stepping-stones to aid their progress; thus establishing convenient stations along their route. In some instances they approach so near to each other that the intermediate space of water loses altogether the appearance of a sea, and more resembles such rivers as the Rhine and Scheld. The opposite shores are distinctly visible, and one can easily count the houses which adorn them, or on Sundays, when the steamer passes abreast of Falstar, can hear the sound of its numerous bells, and almost respond to the religious services of its cathedral.

A little farther on, and the inhabitants of the place, taking you to the bows of the vessel, point out with pride an immense mass of gray rock, running up into arrow-like summits and crowned with scanty trees. One should not however be deceived in its appearance, for though a geologist would place it amid the calcareous formations, yet far different is its origin; nor are those real trees which seem to crown the summit. It is in fact the residence of a young and beautiful fairy who reigns over the islands and adjoining sea. This apparently naked rock is her robe descending in ample folds to the water, and colored by the sun-beam, while these needle-like summits form her sceptre, and these trees her crown. It is here she presides in state, seated on the highest pinnacle, called the Drouning's-stol,* and watching over her empire, guards alike the vessel of the merchant and the frail bark of the fisherman. Often too the most harmonious sounds are heard floating from the coast, sung by no mortal voices, and resembling not the music of the world. It is the melody of the young fairies chaunting as they dance around their gentle Queen, who regards their sports with pleasure. Is it not true that the common people are the greatest of all poets? In their hands imagination becomes most active. It analyzes and discusses, invents and bestows life on inanimate objects, finding vigorous existence where mere philosophy dreams only of inert matter. It passes along the border of some lake and peoples it with spirits; it wanders beneath a mountain precipice, and discovering it to be the castle of some youthful sovereign, calls it 'Monsklint.†'

At Monsklint the sea resumes its usual open appearance, and the coast of Kioge seems to recede suddenly as if to give place to the numberless vessels which pass along its shores. From this point to Copenhagen the ocean is literally alive with barks of all description, some flying before favorable winds, and others beating up against rebellious waves. If there ever is a time when the commander of our little steamer may feel justly proud, it is while passing rapidly through this forest of masts, many a schooner famed for its swiftness, many a staunch brig, now struggling for a passage, or some proud frigate with its cloud of sails and army of seamen. One sees before him on the right the coast of Sweden, and the towering spires of Lund; on the left, the shores of Denmark, the fortress which defends the capital, and the harbor filled with vessels of all nations. At noon we were off Monsklint; at two we anchor in the bay of Copenhagen.

The shores of the Baltic teem with innumerable traditions. Some bearing the impress of a true religious sentiment, and others equally strong characteristics of a pagan origin. The former are touching

---

* Queen's Seat.   † The Rock of the Young Beauty.

and simple as an elegy; the latter, wild and impassioned as some
fairy tale. The sailor of the Baltic is proverbially superstitious.
His adventurous life, and the vicissitudes and dangers to which he
is subjected, seem to nourish a love for the wild and marvellous.
Surprised as he often is by sudden tempests on that fickle sea, and
wholly unacquainted with the laws regulating the great changes in
temperature to which he is daily subjected, he is prone to attribute
each new effect to supernatural causes. He believes in evil genii
and unlucky days, in fate and earthly penances. These traditions
seem to be perpetuated among the Islands of the North by the lone-
liness of their position. They originate as it were in the very soil,
and are transmitted by successive generations. The mariner learns
them in his childhood, recounts them in his numerous voyages, and
brings them back uninjured by the lapse of time to be re-told beside
the hearth of his family. In these islands, as in the northern coun-
tries of Germany, every one knows the history of elfs and giants,
of magic swords and treasures guarded by dragons. They tell you
of old men of the sea, with green beards, whose falling hair resem-
bles water-lilies; who sing at evening from the wave-tops, calling
the young Queen of the Ocean, that they may conduct her to the
crystal grottoes. They have dark tales too of sorcerers who are
able by enchantment to produce tempests and huge waves, destroy-
ing the barks of the fishermen. They believe also (as is general
with the inhabitants of the rocky countries of Europe,) in ' Chas-
seurs' who in expiation of offences are condemned to wander eter-
nally through tangled underwood and marshes. The inhabitants
of Sternsklint declare that they often hear at night the deep baying
of the hunting dogs of Grôngette, and behold the hunter following
with lance in hand; and they often scatter oats before their dwell-
ings, as food for the unearthly coursers, that their owners may not
trample down the harvest fields in their wild chase. Here too they
believe in the existence of a Dwarf-King, who reigns at the same
time over the islands of Stern, Mô and Rüger; that he has a chariot
drawn by four black horses, as he passes through the air from one
possession to another. When the neighing of his courser is dis-
tinctly heard, the sea is overspread with darkness. This king has a
numerous army at command, and his soldiers are the trees that stud
the islands. During the day-time they are condemned to wear the
appearance of trees, but at night retake their real forms, and armed
with sword and helmet, march proudly in the moonlight. In periods
of war they assemble for battle, and wo to the enemy who meditates
an invasion of their country !

We have said that some of these traditions owe their origin to a
religious sentiment. The great law of charity, the dogma of pe-
nance and the mysticism of the middle ages are often found con-
cealed beneath the garb of fiction, and shadowed forth in symbols.
The very name of Maribo, for instance, suggests the residence of
Mary. It is said that the Virgin announced by celestial tokens her
choice of this spot as an abode, and caused a chapel to be erected

to her memory. The Ile du Prêtre, or Priest's Island, recalls too a holy legend. It was inhabited by a priest named Andrew, celebrated far and wide for many virtues. His poverty was such however that he possessed only one penny, which he sent, when in need of any thing, to some merchant or laborer, and which was always returned, accompanied by the object of his wishes. The island still retains its name, but the priest and the penny are no more.

On another of the Baltic borders stood in ancient times a church, which was profaned by bachannals and engulfed in the ocean. At night, it is said, may be distinctly heard the miserable victims chaunting with many groans the psalms of penitence; and when the sea is calm, one can discover through the clear water the candles still burning before the altar.

At Falstar there resided formerly a woman of immense wealth, who unfortunately had no heir to inherit it. Desiring therefore to apply her riches to religious purposes, she used a portion in the construction of a church. On the completion of the edifice she considered herself entitled to some recompense from Heaven for her pious efforts. She prayed therefore that her life might be prolonged during the duration of her church, and the boon was granted. Death passed before her doors but entered not, and though mowing down on all sides friends and relations, left her still untouched. She lived on and on through bloody wars, famine, pestilence, and all the scourges which afflict humanity, until so lengthened was her life that she could find no one whose company was pleasant or desirable. Her conversation was ofttimes so old that none could comprehend her. She had demanded perpetual life, but had forgotten to ask also the additional boon of youth and beauty. Heaven had accorded her exact wishes, but no more. She grew old and feeble, and successively lost her sight, hearing and speech. She then caused herself to be enclosed in an oaken coffin and placed within the church. Each year at Christmas she recovers during one hour the use of her faculties, and at that time a priest approaches to receive her orders; the unhappy woman, half rising from her resting-place, demands with anxiety: 'Is my church still standing?' 'Yes,' replies the priest. 'Would to God,' she exclaims, 'it were annihilated!' and fainting with the effort, she falls senseless, and the coffin closes over her.

There is still another legend recounted by the poet Œhlenschläger, or rather, as it should be termed, a story from real life. A poor sailor has been rendered crazy by the shipwreck of his daughter. Each day, rowing out his bark upon the ocean, he strikes upon a drum, calling loudly on his child. 'Come,' he exclaims, 'come forth from your retreat. I will place you beside me in my boat, and if you are dead I will give you burial in consecrated ground; a tomb surrounded with flowers and shading trees, where you shall repose better than amid these wild waves of the ocean.' But alas! the unhappy father calls in vain; and as night gathers around his way, he returns, saying, 'To-morrow I will go still farther, for my poor child has not heard me!'

LITTLE MARY: A LIFE-SKETCH.

PART FIRST.

WITHIN a vale, a cottage white,
   From out its nest of vines and trees,
Stole picture-like upon the sight,
   And spoke of simple life and peace.

And there each morn the dewy air,
   With many-scented fragrance fraught,
To hearts that felt no heavy care
   A fresher life of joyance brought.

There dwelt a pair, whose daily strife
   Of mutual love and careful duty
Kept always fresh, around their life,
   The rarest charms of quiet beauty.

Their life, that far from panting noon,
   In morning freshness round them lay,
First felt complete its richest boon
   When little MARY came with May.

Then all their inmost being gushed
   With music that had slept before,
And light whose radiance all things flushed,
   Till earth and sky their gladness wore.

In all the pure delicious claims
   That round a parent's spirits coil,
The baby brought them gladder aims,
   And firmer strength for daily toil.

In bliss they watched its waking gaze
   Of curious wonder, vague and dim,
And smiles, the spirit's dawning rays,
   Till oft their eyes would overbrim.

And when at length in utterance broken
   They heard the little creature's voice,
No angel's song could so have spoken
   To wake the answering choir of joys.

She grew a beauteous sybil-flower,
   From whose unfolding breast it seemed
Some blessed spirit's eyes, each hour,
   In fuller, brighter beauty gleamed.

Five years she grew, and ever made
   Their home with bosom-fragrance rife ;
It seemed with them an angel stayed
   To move the sweetest founts of life.

Joys grew; with daily deepening glow
　Around them fell the morning light;
Days went with more melodious flow,
　And wearying toil was rich delight.

Their life appeared a wondrous song,
　That spoke response to all things fair,
Whose mystic tones, the air along,
　Came gushing soft from every where.

————

PART SECOND.

BUT we are blind, and fail to see
　The holiest things, until appears
(When Joy's delicious trances flee,)
　The sacred ministry of tears.

No human soul on earth may spend
　Entranced in bliss its force divine,
Or leave its awful task, and bend
　Unscourged before an idol's shrine.

Oh, no!　They woke in stunned surprise,
　For MARY's music-breathing lips,
Her frolic hands and pleading eyes,
　Were cold and still in Death's eclipse!

How still in waxen beauty lay,
　With faded rose-buds on its breast,
The little form, when borne away
　And laid alone in earth to rest!

They felt a darkness in the sky,
　The summer winds all sang of sorrow,
The flowers for *something* seemed to sigh,
　That could not come again to morrow.

Oh GOD! the aching heart was sent
　To give divinest Wisdom birth,
And wake Thy truth in soul's intent
　To build a Paradise on earth.

—————

PART THIRD.

STILL MARY's name, a holy thing
　Kept warm by many a long caress,
Has undiminished power to bring
　The pangs of hallowed tenderness.

Her little garments, books and toys,
　Preserved like things a saint reveres,
Remembrance often still employs
　To make them tremulous with tears.

THE· ST. DOMINICAN REFUGEE.

BY ROSE STANDISH.

Not many days since, a history of a romantic nature came to my knowledge, which I recorded, as being interesting and remarkable, if not instructive.   It grew out of the Revolution at St. Domingo. But let me first refresh the reader's memory as to the existing state of public affairs at the time of the narrative.

The cry of liberty and equality which resounded in revolutionary France was responded to nowhere more warmly and vehemently than in the beautiful and hitherto peaceful island of St. Domingo. The slave population, which exceeded that of the white by more than ten-fold, were quickly imbued by revolutionary agents and emissaries, who poured into the minds of this benighted yet ardent people the new-born ideas of perfect equality and ' largest liberty,' which prevailed at home.

The French Revolution was hailed by the friends of freedom and humanity over the whole world as an event portending rich blessings to mankind.   In a deep and true sense so it proved,

' From evil still educing good.'

It taught indeed many a deep and solemn lesson; lessons which will not soon be forgotten.   Barriers were broken down, prejudices weakened, distinctions removed.   The foundations of society were broken up, and an edifice more grand and simple in its proportions has·arisen, in place of the one encrusted with decorations, crowded and cumbered with ornament, yet wholly inconvenient and without utility.   Still, the heart of ' millions yet unborn' will sicken at the recital of those sanguinary and heart-rending scenes, when the names of Reason and Philosophy were desecrated, and their light quenched in passion, brutality and blasphemy.   Many an eye unused to weep will shed pitying tears over the history and bitter fate of the beautiful Queen and her children, and the amiable monarch, of whom a generous poet has said :

' Jamais tant de respect n'admittant de pitié.'

The planters of St. Domingo took part with the popular party, and blindly aided in the propagation of principles destined erelong to fall in retributive justice on their own heads.   On the night of the twenty-second of August, 1791, the negro revolt, long and secretly organized, broke forth, and wrapt the whole northern part of the colony in flames !

So inviolable was the secresy, says Alison, so general the dissimulation of the slaves, that this awful catastrophe was no wise apprehended by the European proprietors ; and a conspiracy, which embraced nearly the whole negro population of the island, was revealed only by the obscure hints of a few faithful domestics, who without betraying their comrades warned their masters of their danger.

The fearful question will intrude : ' In the event of invasion, war without or dissension within our own borders, would the down-trodden, heavy-laden, ignorant beings in bondage among us turn at last and rend their oppressors ? Paying off at one fell stroke the long score of stripes, cruel sundering of heart-ties, unnoticed wailing and tears, unregarded complaints and prayers ? It is a question of fearful import. Theré might amid the mighty mass be found a few faithful ones, who in the love which responds to kind treatment, would at all risk, warn off the impending danger. But with the thousands, we fear the iron has entered the soul as well as seared the skin. The exasperated feelings, hatred, revenge, and every evil passion, though stifled and hid beneath a smooth surface, may, like the long slumbering volcano, with the grass growing green at its edge and the peaceful village at its feet, at length burst forth to wither, to overwhelm, to consume.

The explosion at St. Domingo was sudden and terrible ; all the beautiful plains in an hour were covered with fire, and the labor of a century was devoured in a night ; while the negroes, like unchained tigers, precipitated themselves on their masters, seized their arms, massacred them without pity, or threw them into the flames. Those who escaped from this scene of horror on board of ships were lighted in their passage over the deep by their burning habitations. They almost all took refuge with us and were welcomed with generous sympathy and kind hospitality. To their misfortunes alone we owe the arduous and successful efforts of some of the most accomplished teachers and professors among us. The frigate ' La Fine' foundered, and five hundred of the survivors from the flames perished in the waves !

The subsequent history of this beautiful island forms another melancholy attestation to the truth that they are least fitted to rule who cannot be ruled ; self-government and justice in the governors being no less essential than subordination, order and respect for superiors in the governed ; the bondage from which they emerged being light in comparison to the bondage to vice, indolence and anarchy into which they rushed. The champions of liberty are looking on with sad interest in her fate, and may well weep at her unhappy state.

During the massacre of Cape-Town, when thirty thousand wretched beings perished, with atrocities unparalleled even in the long catalogue of European crime, a gentleman of standing and wealth was walking in the out-skirts of the town, where he had placed his little family for safety, when suddenly two negroes turned an angle of the street and stood before him. They were armed with huge clubs, and their aspect was ferocious and dreadful. They held but a short parley, when they commenced to strip the prisoner of every article of value, using all the while great swelling words of liberty and equality, right and freedom ; desecrating them at every breath !

Their unresisting victim pleaded at length for life ; his little ones ; aged parents. All in vain! With dew-eyed Pity what had *they* to do ?

They laugh — a fiendish laugh! The hand of the most savage, if there could be such distinction, was raised to do the murderous deed; it was about to fall, when a piercing cry rent the air. It issued from a neighboring balcony, and arrested the uplifted arm. In a moment the utterer of that cry of despair rushed toward them. The lady had heard the pleading words, had seen the murderous arm upraised. Horror-struck and agonized, she was impelled to attempt a rescue, although she knew not the victim. Personal safety was unthought of. Precious fruit of humanity!

She took from her finger a jewel of great value. It flashed in the sun, and soon caught the cupidity of the dusky band. Contrasted with their dark skin, it shone as a star amid the night, and they smiled in unholy pleasure. They gave up their wretched captive, on the condition of his immediately fleeing from the island. Hurried to the sea-side, he was made to embark in a ship setting sail for the 'Home of the Free.'

We may imagine but cannot describe the feelings of a parent, in leaving to the tender mercy of rebel-slaves — in blood-thirstiness, cruelty and revenge, fiends incarnate — his little innocent children, dear as his heart's-blood, and the 'light of his eyes!' As he leaned against the vessel's side, and watched the shores of the island fast receding from his sight, their soft endearments and winning ways, so fresh in his memory; their helplessness, baffled inquiry and fruitless search for *him;* wrought so powerfully upon his frame, that his limbs refused to bear him up; all resolution was taken away; and the 'strong man and mighty' wept as a child! The ship was swiftly bearing him away from all that made life dear; its sweetest tie was rent. For what had he fled?

He landed on these happy shores, but went about a heavy-hearted man in a strange land. Its fields were green, its skies clear, its waters pure; its freedom was peaceful: open doors welcomed the exile, and warm hearts received, cherished, and essayed to comfort; but the 'hunger of the soul' would not be appeased. He thirsted for tidings of his little ones, and the sight of a pebble from the shore of his ill-fated island-home would cause his heart to swell with anguish, and wring the tears from his eyes!

Scarcely a week after the embarkation of the vessel above-named a ship bound for a northern port of the United States stood off the shores of Cape St. Francois. The fearful work of destruction was going on within the town, and hundreds of poor creatures had sought refuge from death and outrage in this floating sanctuary. They are about to draw anchor, when the captain espies from the deck of the vessel two very little boys on shore. They are gazing seaward with streaming eyes and wistful faces. Anon, they run up and down the beach; stop, and gaze again. At length one, in childish innocence, begins sportively to tumble in the sand, to build sand-houses, and dig little pools for the ocean-waves to fill, as they advance higher and higher, while the elder sat down and wept.

It was a touching sight. The captain was a humane man; he knew the insurgents would soon be upon them; that they had slender chance for life; yet he determined to make an effort to save them.

There was no time to be lost, and he quickly ordered out
they were brought safely on shipboard.   He questioned th
they only knew 'that their father had gone to sea, and the
he would never, never come back.'   So the captain broug
to a northern port ; caring for them as for his own, and soothin
tenderly all the way.   On his arrival he placed them with
family, with whom they shared equally in attention and kind

Meanwhile the disheartened Eugene —— entered the ar
subsequently distinguished himself at the battle of New-Orlea
had learned that his boys were rescued, but to the name of the
or the port to which she sailed, he could obtain not the slighte

After the passage of weary days, months, years, ever
yet never finding ; travelling north and south, to and fro, h
to this city, knowing it to have been the asylum of a great
of the St. Dominican Refugees.   On inquiry among his old
whom he was transported to greet, he discovered the long-l
wept-over, the fondly yearned-for children of his love !   Of
of such a meeting it is vain to speak.   From the lips of one o
little boys, rescued from the beach, snatched amid the pitiless
of the storm by the humane captain, now a man venerable ii
a beloved and respected resident among us, came the foregoi
tal.   His father died recently at a very advanced age ; and tl
now but few remaining survivors of the St. Dominican Refu

·

DREAMS OF FAME.

I was a child ; had gathered not
  The wisdom of a longer life,
And far away had been my lot
  From all the stirring scenes of strife ;
But oft I heard the noise of war
In other lands and climes afar ;
And learned of fame brave men had won
Who led the strong in battle on,
And sought beside a foe as brave
The glory of a soldier's grave.

I was a child when first I learned
  To dream of glory and of fame ;
And then awhile my head was turned
  To hope and struggle for a name :
I thirsted in my youthful heart
For fame that never would depart :
I begged a name which men would love
To list and learn the story of ;
And glory that would never die
Till perished earth and sea and sky.

My dreams were of the battle-ground ;
  I saw the ranks of foemen come,
I heard the bugle's thrilling sound
  And the loud thunder of the drum :

I heard the tramp of man and horse,
The onset of contending force ;
I saw the warrior fall and die,
I heard the victor's battle-cry,
And vowed to be, while dreaming then,
A hero in this strife of men !

Now years have fled, nor years alone ;
  The idle hopes of youth are gone,
Ideal dreams afar have flown,
  And manhood's earnest toil comes on :
This have I learned, that to my hand
Is given the labor of the land ;
My foot must tread the furrowed ground,
And stand when harvest-time comes round ;
To me is given the laborer's care,
In autumn, mine the laborer's share.

I seek no more the warrior's fame ;
  But covet honor with the good,
And not with him whose fearful name
  Is written in a foeman's blood ;
Let me be known as one whose hand
Hath brought a blessing to his land :
Whose heart is filled with something more
Than longings for 'he golden ore ;
Whose prayer has been not all in vain
To love man more than earthly gain.

And what is this which I have sought
  In childhood ? — this the world calls ' fame ?'
Hath it to the needy brought
  Food and raiment when it came ?
Nay, thou who should have been the pride
Of nations, ere they meanly died ;
Whose deathless words have borne along
Their country's glory in their song ;
Though honored as the mighty dead,
Have lived in rags, and wanted bread.

Ah ! this is fame ! to toil and live
  Through hours of hope and years of dread ;
Awaiting honors men will give
  When we have been for ages dead !
To live unknown and struggle on
Till courage, hope and life are gone,
And with the marble o'er our bed
Sleep with the broken-hearted dead !
This is the glory of a name,
All man may reap of earthly fame !

No more a child, devoid of fears,
  The perilous seas of life beside
I stand, but feel the rolling years
  Uplift me like an ocean's tide :
O ! hopes heroic that arise
Serene in manhood's morning skies,
Like stars belated till the day,
In fairer light to fade away,
O ! veil the splendor that ye wear,
As hides the star its radiance there !

A. M. Ide, Jr.

VENUS AND HER CESTUS.

BY A NEW CONTRIBUTOR.

A HUNDRED miles round Mount Olympus is to me hallowed ground. In spite of all the bold and chilling superstitions that have had their origin there, an overwhelming feeling of veneration forbids me to desecrate its solitudes even in thought. The majesty of the many conceptions that have there sprung from the ideal almost into actual life, is more than a match for the puerility of their kindred follies. I have not the heart to tear the veil from off the ambrosial mountain, or piece the dreamy mystery which invests it. In the airy freshness of a solitary ramble, or in the substantial comfort of a brown study, I can bring myself to an almost perfect belief in the bodily existence and mental attributes of the royal council of Jove and Juno. Doubtless there are many absurdities and contradictions which no art can reconcile; many glaring sophisms and paltry conceits; but in the beautiful construction of the whole, the want of harmony in some of the parts melts and fades away. In fact I am not sure that the general effect of the structure is not heightened by these occasional flaws; in the same way as a cheek indented with dimples is more highly prized by the ladies than one undiversified with these love-provoking valleys; though anatomically, a dimple is a disfigurement, caused by some nervous contraction. At any rate, I have learned to be credulous and lenient in regard to all that remains of heathen mythology. The story of Narcissus will drag me headlong from the society of the blue devils; and the bare recollection of the fauns and dryads will infuse new life and force a quicker circulation into my gouty toe. I sometimes freeze up with morose thoughts and gloomy despondency; but the heat of Vulcan's forge, or the flame on the altar of the Vestal Virgins, is at any time able to thaw me into great good humor. Dulness and stupidity, begotten over the pages of some profound disquisition and learned argument, are easily dissipated by a glance at Lempriere. I hold a classical dictionary to be an antidote for Hallam's Middle Ages, and the Glossary of Classical Terms to be a specific against the Universal Gazetteer.

But still there must be some limits even to credulity. There is a story in point, of an individual of the Jeremy Diddler school, who posted himself at the steam-boat landing in New-York, in quest of high-soul'd adventure and pecuniary profit. As the puffing monster came slowly to the quay, our adventurer singled out a person upon the lower deck, who offered, as he thought, a safe investment for any stock of impudence and cunning which might be lying unemployed in his hands. With a nonchalant air of having done the same thing unnumbered times before, and of a readiness to continue the performance upon the other passengers, he extracted from the Vermonter one dollar for the privilege of entering the city. Simplicity did not feel itself outraged at this first trial of its good nature, and even paid with undaunted willingness a toll of seventy-five cents on entering the Park. The same man, presuming upon his first success, had dodged him along the streets, and with some slight change in voice and appearance, to which his roving habits had accustomed him, cajoled his unsuspicious victim a second time. Have a care, friend! — simplicity and credulity have served your turn thus far; but another attempt, and they rise in revolt. But the blood of the walking gentleman is up, and hurries him on to his own defeat. He boldly meets the stranger on the threshold of the Astor House, and levies a contribution of half-a-dollar for admittance to the premises. Here suspicion was aroused; Simplicity felt itself insulted and good humor was annihilated; the enraged New-Englander dashed by the self-appointed ticket-taker, and sought refuge in the bar. Like the Green Mountain boy, I have a limit beyond which my willingness to believe and repose undaunted faith cannot carry me. Like Charles Lamb, who in the extremity of his generosity still would not give *every thing*, so I, in the fulness and plethora of my confidence, will not *believe* every thing. Elia took his stand upon burnt pig; that savory dish called up all his latent selfishness, and made him look with an evil eye upon all who were hungry and disposed to make a meal. I take *my* stand upon Venus and her Cestus.

Ransack your Grecian story-books and your genealogical tables of heathen mythology; pick out all the enormities, prodigies and monstrosities of tale-telling; get together every horror and abomination found upon the classic page; select all the awful barbarities, the dreadful depravities and shocking cruelties; gather into one overwhelming mass of argument the most diabolical incidents in the life of the gods, the most unfeminine, indecorous actions on the part of the goddesses, and the most sottish outbreaks of debauchery laid to the door of the demi-gods; in short, make Mount Olympus a brothel, a gambling-house, a den of thieves, a school of deception, cheatery and lying, and install the deities as president and chief directors of crime, and you will have shown nothing so difficult of belief as the fable of Venus and her Cestus. It is not in the power of a polysyllabical adjective, coupled with the most significant noun substantive, to call up any idea so beyond the power of my mental digestion to accommodate as this extravagant exaggeration. Every thing else from the mint of Grecian mythology I can read of and speak of without a show of incredulity. The springing of Minerva from the head of Jove; the rising of Venus from the foam of the sea; the metamorphosis of the stones by Deucalion and Pyrrha into human beings; the sowing of the dragon's teeth and the reaping of the harvest of armed warriors — instances of the order of nature being broken in upon and of a miraculous birth — I pass over with no such contemptuous sneer as I bestow upon Venus and her Cestus. The yawning of the camel's back and the closing again upon the hunted Daphne; the hospitable reception of the sisters of

Phæton by the poplar-trees; the sudden dropping away of Narcissus the man into Narcissus the flower; the change of the coy nymph Arethusa into the chilling Sicilian fount, of Atalanta into the lioness, and Adonis into the anemone, modes of death neither supported by our own notions of dissolution, nor by the dreamy trio over which Atropos presided, call for no such stretch of the imagination as is required by the story of Venus and her Cestus. Mr. Swiveller's doubtful piece of furniture, bedstead by night and book-case by day; the Talmud, the Koran, the Arabian Nights, Baron Munchausen and Mendez Pinto, may all be reached by an easy flight of the imagination; Venus and her Cestus are beyond the reach of wings.

'Sappho,' says a late writer, 'was a brunette and a widow; for none but a brunette could have loved so deeply, and none but a widow could have told it so candidly.'

The Lesbian poetess is acknowledged by a world's acclamation to have been more desperately touched by the passion of love than any other inhabitant of earth. But the sacrilegious hand of modern innovation has spared not even Sappho : the prying spirit of the present age pronounces unhesitatingly upon the shade of her complexion and entwines a widow's weeds with her flowing robes. I feel less delicacy in mangling the time-hallowed associations that cluster round the memory of Venus the *Olympic* queen, after so presumptuous an attack upon Sappho, the *earthly* love-regent.

Venus, then, apart from the influence of the Cestus, whatever it was, was a goddess of very respectable appearance, with undeniable evidences about her of being beyond the teens and somewhere in the twenties. A sublunary lady resembling her would have been stamped twenty-six. But age appertaineth not to the society of heaven. With the same eagerness that Hercules the demigod pressed forward to title and investiture as King of Clubs, did she yearn for coronation and worship as Queen of Hearts. But alas! her natural graces gave her no prescriptive right to captivate and tyrannize; her whole commingled beauties of body and soul were equal to but little more than the occasional capture of a blear-eyed bachelor or unsophisticated youth. She saw, as she bent over the side of some woodland stream, that though she might entice her regal sisters Diana, Pallas and the rest, many a laundress on the banks of the Tiber, many a shepherdess on the plains of Arcadia, might dispute with her the prize of beauty. With all a goddess' foresight, she saw that she must make an effort for the golden apple. Her only refuge from despair, her only chance of success, she found in a thorough knowledge of the MYSTERIES OF DRESS; the application of the science of dress-making and millinery to the art of making one's-self agreeable. Here was the universal catholicon first discovered.

The phantom of the Cestus, then, is easily explained. It was not an airy filament of gauze, whose touch endued with magic grace and beauty, but some well-fitting stomacher and gently-flowing skirt. No hardly palpable strip of lace with just sufficient body for its owner to discern when it was on and when off, but a substantial

And I knew what a capital chance
    That fellow would have to make love ;
I fancied I saw in each glance
    A look that said plainly, ' My dove !'

It half drove me mad to reflect
    That *I* might have gone with you too,
But my sorrow for this was soon checked,
    For *he* would have been in full view !

Oh ! still, still the memory lingers
    Of that saddest hour's parting pang,
As you gracefully kissed your white fingers,
    When the third and the last bell rang !

A GHOST-STORY BY A GHOST.

AN EXTRACT FROM AN OLD MANUSCRIPT MARKED AS FOLLOWS : ' HOW THAT MANY GHOSTS DID ONCE
HOLD SOLEMN SERVICE IN A CHURCH.'

BY J. HYATT SMITH.

'ONE after another the grave-stones began
To heave and to open, and woman and man
Rose up in their ghastly apparel.'   GOETHE.

As I have said, we had no longer any reason to doubt that the stranger who had joined our company in the bar-room of the ' Red Tavern' that night, and who had just commenced a ghost story, was himself a ghost.

It was the traveller who many years ago was found murdered not far from the tavern, and who was buried down in the ' Beech Wood.' People speak of it as the ' Beech Wood Murder.' The place where they made his grave is near the road-side, midway in the wood ; a dark, still place, entangled round with bushes and brambles. There can be no doubt of the fact that the wood is haunted. Men are now living, who having to pass along the road by night, have heard groans sounding from among the bushes, and have seen a blue light shining above the grave. Deacon Morris, one Sunday morning, when on his way to church, stopped and cut a twig from a small tree which grew there, and whose roots were supposed to bind around the tra-veller's coffin. Now when he had cut off the branch, blood oozed out and trickled down the tree. When he reached the church, a short distance, the stick bled afresh. Every leaf too gave a faint sigh, rising and falling like the breast of a sobbing child. There never has been any doubt that the Beech Wood was haunted.

Some six years previous to the night on which the story was told, the traveller's ghost made its appearance. One dark, restless night, when a club of young men were making merry, myself among the rest, he stood suddenly and silently in the bar-room. His eyes were

ing hopeless cancers upon her unoffending cheeks.   She is no longer
an artless, confiding, guileless being, with a Cestus for a god-mother,
but a decidedly worldly, sophisticated creature, with more art than
beauty and more beauty than heart.

There is a fault-finding critic looking over my shoulder, who
thinks it a miserable begging of the question to assume the propo-
sition that Venus was not perfectly handsome.

'She was the goddess of love and queen of beauty,' he sneeringly
remarks ; 'and of course was as beautiful as tradition represents
her.   She is universally acknowledged to be the empress of loveli-
ness, and to suit your own ends, you drag her features and form
down to the standard 'moderate,' and ascribe all her conquests to
her unequalled taste in dress.'

The argument from analogy will refute the skeptic.   None of the
gods and goddesses were perfect in their way.   Jupiter, the Thun-
derer, the All-powerful, shook in his sandals at the audacity of
Prometheus, and trembled for his safety when the Titans climbed
the skies.   Apollo, the successful roué, found Daphne proof to all
his fascinations.   Vulcan, his majesty's blacksmith, had many thun-
derbolts returned upon his hands as unskilfully welded.   Diana, the
virgin huntress, the goddess of chastity, pleads guilty to at least one
lapse — blushes at one 'soft impeachment;' ask Endymion.   If
Venus, then, *were* supereminently beautiful, it was an elevation and
overtopping in her own line of attributes not enjoyed by the other
members of the aristocracy of Olympus.

THE PARTING.

Dear Mary ! when last we parted,
  (It occurred at the end of the dock,)
On board of the steam-boat you started,
  Leaving me fixed there as firm as a rock.

And far up the river you wended,
  While your handkerchief faded from view;
Then with head on my breast sadly bended,
  I trotted home, thinking of you !

As the Astor-House windows I passed,
  I sought for your figure in vain,
And I strode away ' tolerably' fast,
  Looking backward again and again.

I swallowed mint-juleps all night,
  Cigars I smoked all the next day,
To see if in *that* way I might
  Drive my sad recollections away.

But still the remembrance returned
  Of each gesture and look that you wore,
And still my beating heart burned
  With the thought, ' She will be here no more !'

fixed on the landlord for more than three whole minutes, and then extending his bony arm from the shroud that hung about him, he slowly raised his finger until it pointed directly at the landlord, and with one deep groan, he vanished. The landlord looked like a corpse; he said he was not well, and left the room. Sometimes a person about to drink at the bar has discovered a face like that of a dead man at the bottom of the glass. At another time, each decanter which the landlord would attempt to take down from the shelf with his *right hand*, would seem instantly filled with blood. There is an axe-helve kept in the bar-room, and it is said by truthful witnesses that as often as the twenty-second of June comes around, precisely at seven minutes of eleven on the night of that day the head of the axe-helve seems to drip with blood.

There are great many strange sights and sounds in and around the 'Red Tavern.' Some folks think the traveller was murdered in the bar-room and then carried down into the wood. No one seems to *know* any thing of the matter, farther than the fact that his body was found not far from the tavern, near where it is buried, dreadfully mangled. It is said, that as the people were standing around the corpse, the landlord came up to look, and that just as he bent over the body, the warm blood gushed out afresh from every wound. Some say that is a sign against the tavern-keeper, but I make no charges against any man.

'I tell you,' continued the ghost, 'that old church in the village where I was born has a history quite surpassing that of any other in the world. The edifice has stood a century and a half; I don't know but more. A thunder-bolt once struck the building, and spent its fury harmlessly; for the whole pile, from the foundation up to the topmost stone that crowns the tower, had been separately blessed and fully consecrated. The lightning only removed some of the moss that grew upon the top of the tower, making the church to remind one of some old patriarch with a bald head. A blessed place was our little village because that hospital of souls was there. Its influence was good, and that continually. Few can tell the power exerted by one true church. Like some venerable old man, whose words are wisdom, whose counsel is safe to follow, and whose very presence among men as he walks in silence, moves those around him to good thoughts and good deeds. So stands the church. It is a place to learn wisdom and forget sorrow. And when men are driving furiously after the things that perish, and forget higher interests and a better world, the silent church, with its tower ever pointing up to Heaven, and its congregation of dead slumbering by its side, preaches a sermon audible to the soul.

'Well, many years ago an assembly of Christians worshipped in our church, and all were very old. The officers were white with age. The pastor had reached his eighty-ninth year — a venerable old father in Israel. The ground where he rests is watched always by guardian angels. We have not many like him in our congregation.

'Years passed, and each in its flight could boast of having seen one or more of those good men gathered to his fathers. At length, the great reaper bore away the shock of corn that stood ripest in Heaven's harvest-field. The good old preacher rested from his labors. The sexton soon followed, and was buried near the gate. He had long served faithfully, safely passing one after another of his aged brethren into the house of death; and with the burial of the pastor his work was accomplished, and he laid himself down to sleep at the door. And now the old church was silent. The last words of admonition had been given; the last song of praise had gone up to Heaven; and the last prayer had found acceptance at the mercy-seat. Silent, all silent!

' At the head of the grave-yard was buried the pastor, as if he still watched his flock. Directly in front was the chorister; and in a semi-circle around him were the officers. The remaining portion of the ground was occupied by graves corresponding with the form observed in the arrangement of the pews in the church.

' The grave-yard was adorned with a quiet beauty. Willows were bending around the place, and flowers blossomed on every grave. A clear stream, from an unfailing spring, ran near the graves, gently murmuring; and pinks and violets bloomed in rich profusion along the path that led from gate to gate. There was a holy worship there. Choirs of birds sung praise, and every bud and blossom-altar daily sent up its morning incense. It was the prayer of the flowers, breathed silently to Heaven, and the answer came in the sun-light and the dew.

' Well, there slept that congregation, year after year, year after year; and the tomb-stones began to lean forward like old men, and the inscriptions upon them grew dim, as eye-sight fails. The bier that stood near the gate had silently rotted down upon the ground, and rank grass had entwined a shroud for its covering. The sexton's spade was rusting beside his grave; the grave-yard had itself grown old; but still there sparkled the brook, emblem of the eternal stream. The flowers grew old and died in the fall, repeating the story of those who slept beneath them; and they came forth in new beauty in the Spring, silently speaking, as they lifted their buds and blossoms toward Heaven, of a glorious resurrection.

' I noticed these things, for I had a mind fitted to enjoy that grave-yard scene. The dead! the dead!' exclaimed the ghost, ' do you not suppose the dead are pleased or troubled like other men ? If I were to tear away that fleshly tabernacle of thine,' continued he, addressing himself to me, ' why, you would fly out like an uncaged bird. But I would not; no, it would be unkind to suddenly break down that beautiful temple in which you dwell. Do you know it is strange to be quickly driven out into the spirit-world by one rude blow, like a sleeper dashed from his bed by a thunder-bolt, amid glare and tempest? Those who go down into the sea are many months, as men measure, before they reach the surface. They linger there, working the coral in its thousand beautiful forms, and painting the shells that adorn the halls of the ocean. Then for months more they haunt the surface of the water. They ride the crested wave in the moonlight, as it speeds to the shore, a billow of silver. On the backs of dolphins they dart through the sea; and when the storm draws nigh, they sigh in the rigging of the ships.

'The grave-yard was growing old, and so was the church. All within was left as when the last sermon was preached, for the good villagers feared to disturb the quiet of the old building. The bell was rusting in the tower; the pews were decaying, the cushions were rotting. Silently as the fall of autumn-leaves, the glory of the inner temple was departing. The Bible was upon the pulpit desk; *that* was undisturbed by Time. A record for eternity, there was no decay among its precious leaves. It was the soul of the old church; and like the spirit of him who once taught from its sacred pages, it remained unimpaired amid the ruin of the tabernacle. Think of the silence of a half a century! Fifty years of dumb time! At morning, mid-day, evening; spring, autumn, winter; silent, all silent!

'There was a stir once in the grave-yard and in the church. Not always silent there. I recollect it was one still moonlight night, about the middle of June, a great many years ago, when the silence of the old church was disturbed, and the grave-yard was full of strange life. It was such a night as spirits most like for their visiting; very late, when every stir and sound of noisy life was quieted. The still moon bathed the old church tower and the grave-yard in a flood of dreamy light. Beautiful, very beautiful!—a kind of solemn gladness reigned among the tombs. Every tiny grass-blade had clad itself in a moon-beam, and stood adorned with a diamond. The rays were busy in beautifying the grave-yard; and each flower slept with its closed leaves sealed with a dew-drop, like a child slumbering with a tear just resting on the fringe of its eye-lids. The stream as it rippled along was all of glancing silver. One could plainly read the inscriptions on the tomb-stones, the night was so bright. How much of Sabbath there is among the graves, in a still moonlight night! How holy!

'As I have said, it is on such nights that good spirits leave their graves. And each one has his own errand of mercy to perform. They do not loiter around the habitations of men as idle spectators, gratifying mere curiosity. No idleness among spirits!—none any where throughout the CREATOR's realm, save among men. One visits the mourner's couch, and as he whispers in his ear, the tears are dried away, and the mourner smiles in his sleep, and hopes, and dreams of Heaven. Another flies to the bed of the hungry, the thirsty and houseless, and bids him eat of the bread that cometh from above, and tells him of the eternal fountain, and of a building not made with hands.

'Well, that night was to be a time of visiting and of solemn service for the dwellers in the old grave-yard. It was about eleven, when the turf on the sexton's grave seemed moving; not fast at first, but slow, as the growth of a thrifty plant. The long grass gently parted on either side, a rich drapery of living green, fringed with violets. Then could be heard the dull rattling of the earth as it moved on every part at once, and fell in a heap beside the empty grave. A moment passed, and a dry skeleton stood erect on the ground, with a white garment loosely hanging about his shoulders, and tied at the neck with a worm. It was no one else than James Owens, the sexton. Slowly and solemnly he walked toward the entrance of the yard ; and as he drew near the gate, like that of Jerusalem before the liberated Apostle and his angel-guide, it opened of its own accord. From thence he glided noiselessly on, until he reached and entered the church. Then all was still again ; and were it not for the open grave, one would have observed nothing calculated to disturb the quiet of the place. Soon there was heard a dull, faint clang, away up in the tower ; another and another followed, clear and more clear, and then the old bell tolled out full and strong, as it did when calling the living congregation to worship years before. It was heard for many miles around. It awoke the sleeping villagers, and they drew near the church trembling. That solemn tolling was heard by the dead congregation ; and now all was action in the grave-yard. Every where the grass was parting and the fresh earth up-heaving. The graves opened, and the dead arose. First, the old pastor came forth, and walked slowly down the path ; the chorister and the officers next, followed by the whole assembly : and in that order they passed out from the yard and entered the church. That was their manner of proceeding when living. The shepherd led his flock, walking before ; he did not drive them, walking behind. The preacher went up to his place in the pulpit. The singer sat in front with the officers before him. There was a dry clattering as the congregation took their seats.

' The bell ceased tolling, and the sexton stood by the door. Among the graves, beside each, stood an angel, keeping watch until the worshippers should return, for evil spirits often intrude on the graves of the good ; desiring their place of rest, that they may be numbered with the forgiven at the resurrection. So those angels who minister to the elect always guard their open graves.

' The church again heard the voice of prayer and praise. It was a strange sight to see that ghastly congregation as they sat in the seats they occupied more than fifty years before ; each one clad in the night-dress of the death-chamber ; each one worshipping. But that was a service that gave a better report above than much that bears the holy name among the living. There was no desire for display ; no flowing robe there, but the winding-sheet ; no pride of form and feature in that skeleton assembly. Not an unholy thought nor an impure desire ; and when they bowed, it was prayer. The supplication was an acceptable offering, which, like that of righteous Abel, rose peaceful and pure to Heaven. Their prayers were for the living ; themselves had no need of prayer. It was an earnest service in the church that night. Fifty years before that time, and they were gathered in the same temple, a venerable assembly of worshippers ; and when they stood in prayer, moved by one holy impulse, they bowed their heads, facing the pulpit ; as the field of ripened grain, white unto the harvest, bends to the gentle breeze : they remembered those days of worship, as they bowed that night.

Then the service began. When they sung a hymn, the angel-guard among the graves joined the song. Now your service is not always so solemn nor so sincere as the worship of that night; and it is not much liked above. I say many a praise-offering that goes up from the living worshipper does not rise above the church, but falls a blasting mildew on the soul.

'Well, after the hymn then came the sermon. The Bible was as when the last sermon was preached. It was open, and the book was Matthew. The text the pastor chose was not inappropriate for the occasion : 'And the graves were opened, and many bodies of saints which slept arose and came out of the graves after his resurrection, and went into the holy city, and appeared unto many.' '

'Did he preach a sermon, Sir?' asked one of our wondering circle, venturing for the first time to interrupt the strange narrator. As the ghost paused and fixed his cold, glassy eyes on the presumptuous questioner, we all shook with fear, while our friend turned deadly pale, and looked anxiously toward the door. [He told me afterward that the fearful glance of that ghost made him to feel numb and deadly ill. He was probably faint.] 'A sermon!' he exclaimed, after the lapse of many painful seconds ; 'yes, he *preached* a *sermon ;* he did not *read* an *essay.* In the dignity of his office as an ambassador, he stood up before men and spoke plain words of truth. As the energy of the mind shook the feeble frame, his sermon waxed stronger and more earnest ; and the congregation received much precious knowledge. So a tree, bending with its golden burden, when shaken by the wind, sheds down the fulness of its fruit in rich profusion upon the ground. Could you have heard that sermon you would have received much wisdom. He told of all the dead who ever rose; he traced the path of that company spoken of in the text, who sought Jerusalem ; their errand and their return. Then he dwelt with great earnestness and strength on the missions from the dead ; the duty of those spirit-missionaries ; their power, their labor, and their reward.

'All the while he preached, the villagers stood without, filled with fear and wonder. The sermon was long, and yet it seemed too short. But time had passed rapidly away, and it was wearing very late. The moonlight struggled faintly through the stained windows, and the shadows of the tomb-stones stretched far along the graveyard. The sermon was ended ; the last words of the closing hymn had died away ; and in the order of their entering, the congregation moved slowly and silently out. The conscious gate opened wide to receive them, and the sexton stood in his place until pastor and people had gone in to their graves. Then the angels who had kept watch arose with their wings extended, and as they hovered above the graves, they joined in a hymn of holy music. Birds that were dreaming among the willows, swayed by the heavenly melody, half warbled their songs as they slept. When the last grave was wrapped in its green covering, the angel-choir raised a higher note of music, and as it rose, they floated up to Heaven.

'All was again quiet among the graves. It was said by some

that in the still night one could hear the benediction of the old pastor sounding solemnly in the church; and that the 'Amen!' first heard from near the pulpit, and then repeated fainter and fainter as it swept along the building, finally whispered out from the top of the gray tower. Still! in that church and that grave-yard — all still!

'Did I not say with truth that the history of our village church was a strange one? I could tell you much more; but not now. I cannot stay here; I have no room. Years ago a landlord hurried me to my chamber, which is alone among the trees. It is a dark silent place, and its windows will know no light until the resurrection morning.

'THE SIXTH! OF ALL, OF ALL OF THEM THE SIXTH, THE SIXTH COMMANDMENT!'

No door opened, nor window, but instantly he was not.

You may well guess our bar-room frolic was not renewed. We felt no heart for mirth. So lately had that mysterious being stood among us, that there seemed to be an awful presence still in our midst. For many minutes we all remained silently looking at the place where he had stood; while that unearthly voice yet sounded in the bar-room, and through every room in the tavern, 'THE SIXTH COMMANDMENT!'

We remained at the tavern the rest of the night, for we greatly feared.

The landlord, having left the bar on the entrance of the ghost, did not return during the three hours in which he stayed, but remained in his room the whole time. He was very ill, and his mind strayed sadly. At one time he supposed himself to be pleading his own cause in court, having been arraigned for murder. He said his property was willed to him; that he came innocently by it; and that he murdered no man for money. He said the traveller was a very poor man, and was in debt to him for board at the 'Red Tavern.' Then he appealed to the sympathies of the jurors; addressing himself to those who stood near his bed, and begged them to think of his wife, his children, and his feeble old father. He said that if the law required his death, and if they had a right to decide against him, they had no right to crush the heart of an innocent woman and rob his children of their bread, and break the staff on which a tottering parent leaned for support; that he expected to die, but not yet, for his death would ruin those who were so feeble and so innocent. As the by-standers wept to hear the poor man talk so wildly, he took courage at the sight of their tears, and pleaded with renewed earnestness. He ceased speaking, and turning toward me, as he stood on his knees in the bed, he bowed his head very low, and with his hands clasped and his whole frame quivering, he awaited sentence of death. Then all the energies of his body suddenly failed, and he sank down upon the bed, sighing and grieving like a child. As he looked toward the door, that stood ajar, he asked that it might be closed, for he saw a pale finger pointing from there, and feared that some one was coming. The bed-clothes were winding-sheets, and from every part of the wall wild eyes were staring upon him.

When the parting ghost gave that last fearful cry, a shudde
went through all his frame, and drops of cold sweat started out ₁
his brow.   Again he darted up from his bed, and repeated his
before the jury, begging that his wife and children and his old fa
might be saved from disgrace and death by the preservation o:
own life.   And then he thought he was riding to the place of
cution, sitting upon his coffin; and he marked time with the m
striking his clenched fist upon the bedstead.   He implored the
cutioner not to kill him with an axe-helve; and then, shrinking p
down for an instant with his eyes closed, and his bleeding lips ₍
ering in a half-articulated prayer or curse, he awaited the blow
was but a moment, and he swooned and sunk back upon the pil

We all thought he would die, but he quite recovered after a
weeks of illness.   He sold the tavern, and with his family left
village.   Some thought of gathering up the evidence that migl
found and bringing him to trial.   But his mind never was right
that sickness: he was a miserable man, and no one laid any ol
cle in the way of his going; but we all pitied him, and let him l
a village which he had troubled too long by his presence.   I b
no more of the landlord of the 'Red Tavern' until many years a
ward, when reading an account of a fearful wreck at sea, I fi
his name in the list of the dead!

<hr />

L I N E S

ON A BEAUTIFUL IMAGE OF A SLEEPING MAIDEN.

PROMETHEAN ART, what matchless skill
Thus moulds the marble to thy will,
Each glance some hidden grace revealing,
So faultless is the lovely form,
O'er which the life stream pure and warm
In silent waves seems softly stealing.

How tranquilly the eyelids close,
In all the languor of repose!
So balmy and so beauty-breathing,
To life the semblance is so true,
We pause, upon a nearer view,
To see the snowy bosom heaving.

And musing think that dreams of love
Might e'en the stony bosom move,
Which, though the tongue hath ne'er confessed,
Breathe in her ear the one loved name,
Would not the flush of maiden shame
And conscious blushes tell the rest?

We thus behold with mute surprise
What dangers dwell in slumbering eyes,
Whose fatal spells in hours of waking
Are reck'd not of; the charmers sleep,
Nor dream of those who suffering weep —
How many hearts despair is breaking!

A SCENE AT SEA.

FROM THE 'RIME OF THE TRANSPORT MARINER' AN UNPUBLISHED POEM.

I.

THE morn was quite remarkable
  On board the Mariposa ;
For in addition to the dawn
  So golden-hued and rosy,
We had a treat of rarities
  Beyond our fondest hopes,
All coming, as misfortunes do,
  Not singly, but in troops.

II.

And first, a 'school' of whales we saw,
  A 'school' I think they spell it,
Though if you ask the reason why,
  I really cannot tell it ;
Unless it be because all day,
  Like school-boys playing truant,
They love to frolic time away,
  Of fun alone pursuant:

III.

We saw, I say, a school of whales,
  All swimming on together,
See-sawing with their heads and tails,
  Up one and down the other ;
And showing now and then their backs,
  And every time they rose
Their engines working like a club
  Of firemen with their hose.

IV

And as I watched these creatures huge,
  These noble spermaceti,
So brimming full of life and glee,
  It seemed a burning pity
That this our world so dark should be,
  That man's especial lighting
Requires of all this buoyant life
  So merciless a blighting !

V.

Yet had our ship a whaler been,
  And sent her boats among them,
And on the points of their harpoons
  Our gallant tars had strung them,
'T is ten to one that at the sight,
  While Sympathy lay sleeping,
My eyes had watched the cruel fun
  With very little weeping.

VI.

The whales with all their water-works
  Were still on exhibition,
When a school of shining porpoises
  Appeared in opposition ;
Around our bows the nimble fry
  Came circling like a comet,
Now under water shooting by,
  Now briskly leaping from it.

VII.

Our sailors soon with barbed harpoon
  Complete their preparation
To pay these new aquatic friends
  A New-Year's salutation.
So just beneath the vessel's prow
  A shrewd harpooner standing,
The task politely undertakes
  These guests on deck of handing.

VIII.

And when a porpoise he discerns
  Within his reach below him,
To help him up, a keen harpoon
  He instantly doth throw him ;
In vain the creature struggling tries
  To quit the scene of slaughter ;
A dozen hands a bowline seize
  And lift him from the water.

IX.

Three several times a writhing fish
  Was thus in air suspended,
When breaking from the iron fluke,
  He down again descended;
But spreading round a bloody wake,
  Worse fate was soon to meet him,
For when a wound a porpoise gets,
  They say his comrades eat him !

X.

Just as it happens oft among
  Perambulating fishes,
Where crafty Slander, when with ease
  She'd carry out her wishes,
A character has but to wound
  With her unerring hatchet,
And, porpoise-like, the world around
  Fall on and soon despatch it !

THE SAINT LEGER PAPERS.

NUMBER FOURTEEN.

THE Wœdallah had concluded. I felt no way disposed to break the solemn silence that ensued. The shades of evening had begun to gather; the waves grew black in the twilight; the roar of ocean resounded with a more ominous distinctness; until 'darkness covered the face of the deep.' The elements, the situation, the spot itself, combined to produce a solemn effect upon the spirit.

And there they sat; the gloomy meditator upon what had been, and the eager expectant upon that which was to be — a singular companionship! There they sat; and while they lived upon the past and the future, both forgot the eternal *present;* the everlasting, never-ending Now, for which only man exists; for in it are embraced yesterday, to-day and forever! Alas! vain mortal! to feed upon dim recollections, or upon the unsubstantial frame-work of false hopes, forgetful of that *which is !*

But must faith, must hope be banished? Ah, no! 'Does not the earnest expectation of the creature wait for the manifestation of the sons of GoD?' Assuredly. But it must be such faith, such hope, such expectation, as will make the Now important. Tell me of a faith that bids me forget the *present*, and I will brand it *'false.'* Show me a hope that connects not with *what is*, and I will mark it *'vain.'* Summon me an expectation that refers not to what I *now am*, and I will stamp it *'futile.'* And yet man sits and waits, and hopes and expects, and waits again, while nothing comes of it; and he murmurs, but still expects, and still the river runs full flowing by, and the current will not diminish. Still the wheel goes round, but nothing is accomplished. And what has his faith or his hope or his expectation done for him? Therefore, oh! being, created by Almighty GoD, when unquiet and dissatisfied thou busiest thyself with vain imaginings, know that thou neglectest the *present*, and if thou neglectest IT, thou art lost!

The Wœdallah had concluded; but it was evident that he had given a very brief outline of his history: farther I could not ask. Yet how I longed to question him about the young Leila! Here was a mystery still unexplained. Not love that beautiful creature! not love the only child of his unfortunate and deeply-wronged wife! But the Wœdallah had not said that he loved not his child. True, Leila had confessed that she could not love her parent. Perhaps — perhaps—— But it was idle to conjecture; so I was consoled with the hope that time would explain all. I now went back to myself. I was adrift again. The narrative of my kinsman made me tremble at the resolution I had taken a little before. Like a successful ambuscade, it found me at unawares, and put to flight my fancied security. Pleasure! — what *was* pleasure? It seemed to me like some accursed fiend, whose end was to accomplish my destruction. My heart acknowledged to itself an incipient guilt, which waited only for temptation to be developed. In vain I determined to adhere to my resolution. My resolution had vanished; I could not grasp it:

> 'Ter frustra comprensa manus effugit imago,
> Par levibus ventis volucrique simillima somno.'

Every thing was gone save one absorbing idea, and that idea was LEILA! I say 'idea,' for I had as yet no notion of the ideal. Oh! beautiful and holy IDEAL! thou belongest not in thy perfection to youth, for youth is attracted too much by earth to worship thee. The dross must be first expelled; the flame of life must burn clear and pure, not fed rankly by the fever-heat of too young blood. How few possess thee, lovely IDEAL! And how, alas! do the many, led away by mimic Fancy,

> —— 'which, misgiving shapes,
> Wild work produces,'

create for themselves a world of ecstatic dreams, fed with unhealthy excitements, which consume the young heart by their false fire, and wither up for ever the well-springs of life; leaving the fountain which should flow with perpetual freshness, scorched and arid and desolate!

But who can *realize* thee, sacred IDEAL! They only upon whom true imagination waits; who live in the momentous Present; who yield not to Fancy's airy nothings — *they* shall enjoy thee, heavenly IDEAL! for to such Heaven has already begun!

.   .   .   .

I MUST not farther digress. When at length I parted from the Woedallah, and proceeded toward the village, my mind was in a whirl of excitement. I saw in my fancy nothing but Leila; I thought of nothing but Leila; I gave myself up entirely to Leila. She was the all-absorbing idea. Why, for what, to what end, I did not ask — I did not care — I would not think. If I could only have one more interview, that was all I would demand; all the happiness I required; *one* more interview! I accused myself of rudeness, of heartlessness, of every thing that was unkind. I thought of every word she said; I remembered every step, every gesture. How I dreaded to think of any thing else! how I loved that night! how I hated the thought of the morrow, with its dull routine of common-place incidents!

With my bosom full of these emotions, I reached the habitation of the worthy minister. I paused upon the threshold. I turned and looked up at the still heavens. How quiet and how awful they appeared! The stars which lighted the 'dark-robed night' glittered with unusual brilliancy. Perhaps Leila was at that moment gazing upon the same scene. *I felt that she was.* My soul drank in a world of bliss, of rapture, of indescribable ecstacy. Were we not both regarding the rolling heavens? Were we not both gazing at yon sparkling stars? Were not those stars 'charged with destiny — revealers of every fate ? Could the transport have been greater were we gazing into each other's eyes ? ' Glorious stars ! truthful stars !' I exclaimed aloud, and I repeated with enthusiasm a favorite passage from the ' Orphic Hymns :'

Ἀστέρες οὐράνιοι, Νυκτὸς φίλα τέκνα μελαίνης
Ἐγκυκλίοις δίνῃσι περιθρόνιοι κυλίοντεσ
Μοιρίδιοι, πάσης μοίρης σημάντορες ὄντες
Ἐπταφαεῖς ζώνας ἐφορώμενοι, μερόπλαγκτοι
Αὐγάζοντες ἀεὶ νυκτος ζοφοειδέα πέπλον!

Were these feelings true ? Did my heart beat with a healthful excitement ? Was I experiencing what writers of romance delight to describe in terms so rapturous—'*first love ?*' We shall see.

The next day a great hunt for birds and birds'-eggs was to take place. So remarkable is this affair, that I cannot resist giving a brief account of it. As the St. Kildans subsist chiefly on wild fowl and the eggs of the wild fowl, it follows of course that enterprise, courage and alertness in securing these necessary articles of subsistence, form the highest accomplishments of the male sex. The bold adventurer who by feats of extraordinary hazard captures the Solan goose as the creature sits upon a shelving rock a thousand feet from the toppling crags above, or secures the eggs of the Lavie, deposited midway between the top of some fearful precipice and the foaming sea below, is regarded as a hero in the island, and his praises are chaunted by the St. Kilda maidens in songs remarkably descriptive and full of fancy. The heroic actions of the men; their disregard of peril and fatigue; their success in these enterprises, and sometimes their untimely fate, form the main topics of St. Kildan song.

All the rocks in the island which overhang the sea are divided among the inhabitants in the same way as the land, and any infringement upon the right of possession is regarded as heinous as theft itself, and punished accordingly. Every family who can afford it owns a '*rope*,' which is absolutely necessary as a means of subsistence. This rope is made out of cow's-hide and cut into three thongs, which are plaited together, after having been thoroughly salted. This 'three-fold cord' is remarkably strong, and with proper care will last for two generations. It always descends to the eldest son, and is considered equal in value to two good cows.

The St. Kildans seemed desirous to afford us a fair exhibition of their skill. The hunting party consisted of the boldest adventurers of the island; the most dangerous crags were selected, and the sport commenced. Two of the party, having made fast to each other, began the perilous descent. First one would take the lead, throwing himself carelessly from rock to rock, then darting away from his precarious foothold, he would hang suspended in the air, his partner supporting him by bracing against some sharp angle in the rocks. It was next the turn of his companion, who pursuing a similar course did all he could to surpass his comrade, by exposing himself to the most extraordinary perils. After spending some time in this way, the two returned, each having secured a fine string of birds and a large quantity of eggs. Another couple succeeded these, with exploits still more hazardous, and thus the afternoon passed away; some ten or twelve St. Kildans engaging in the hunt. In the evening it was resolved to invade the territory of the Solan goose. These creatures engage so industriously during the day in fishing that they are content to sleep soundly at night. They select some large rock where hundreds of them herd together, and after placing a sentinel to keep guard, abandon themselves to repose. The fowler, having a large white napkin tied across his breast, to deceive the sentinel, approaches cautiously. Too late the unsuspecting bird finds an enemy in the camp. The sentinel is despatched. The fowler takes him and lays him among his comrades, who by this time waking up, gather round the unfortunate bird, bemoaning his death and uttering cries of sorrow; nor do they think of flight till a large number of their company are killed by the active fowlers, who take this cruel advantage of the ill-timed lamentations of the flock.

Much sport was expected the present evening, as it was discovered that an immense number of these birds had settled upon a well-known rock on the east side of the island, inaccessible to ordinary pursuit, but presenting no insurmountable difficulty to a St. Kildan. I had watched the whole proceedings during the day, accompanied by Hubert, who entered fully into the excitement. As we were about starting for the scene of the new adventure, the latter said to me :

'St. Leger, have a care; Vautrey is somewhere near us!'

'Indeed !' said I; 'have you seen him ?'

'I have been watching him,' continued Hubert, 'all the afternoon. His body-guard are with him; his foreign servant and that peculiar imp of Satan whom you saw at the glen. They are apparently spectators of the hunt; but let us be watchful during the evening.'

We both agreed to this, and proceeded to join the party. But two couples undertook the perilous descent to the spot where the birds were congregated. At one time hanging over dizzy heights, at another resting upon the edge of some slippery rock, so narrow that there seemed no place even for the slightest foot-hold, the daring adventurers proceeded on their perilous descent. Below, at a distance of some thousand feet, the sea raged and foamed and lashed itself into a resistless fury; while the sharp projections of rugged rock, protruding here and there from the different cliffs, indicated with a fearful certainty the fate of the wretch who should miss his uncertain foothold.

All eyes were turned toward these intrepid fowlers. Now the heart quailed at the fearful risks they ran; now admiration for their extraordinary daring was paramount. In the midst of the excitement, and when all were watching the adventurers with breathless interest, I perceived a person coming cautiously toward me, along the side of the cliff. I knew the stranger to be Vautrey. He was, as I thought, alone; but on looking more carefully I fancied that I could detect some one following him in the distance. The Count was apparently getting a position to see the fowlers to the best advantage; at any rate he paused at the place where one of the couple had descended, and leaned over as if watching their movements. My own attention was soon directed to the same object and when I again glanced toward the Count, I was surprised to see that the figure which I had before observed had approached near him, and that it was his attendant, the wild savage. There was something so treacherous and stealthy in the manner of this hideous-looking creature, that I at once suspected something hostile to myself; but on closer scrutiny it seemed as if the savage was attempting to come up with Vautrey unobserved. He certainly did not seem aware that I was near. So extraordinary did this appear, that I ceased longer to look at the fowlers, and turned my attention entirely toward the Count and his attendant. The latter approached nearer and nearer to his master; now he would pause and glance hastily around, or skulk behind a rough projection of rock, and then resume his stealthy, cat-paced course. He came nearer and nearer; I rose instinctively to warn Vautrey of something, I knew not what; but I felt that there was danger. At the same instant the savage started up, ran swiftly toward the Count, and rushing upon him with a sudden desperate fury, seized him in his grasp, and by a tremendous effort hurled him over the precipice — clear over into the frightful chasm below!

It was too horrible, and I shrieked in spite of myself. In a moment the savage was by my side. I was upon my guard, yet he attempted no violence; but throwing off a quantity of coarse hair from his head, I recognized the wild Highland follower of the young Glenfinglas, *Donacha McIan!* The eyes of the savage gleamed with malignant fire; his soul seemed completely abandoned to the furies. Pointing with exultation toward the cliff, and then to himself, as if glorying in the act, he turned, uttered a fierce Highland cry, and disappeared in the darkness. This was the work almost of a second. The alarm was given; the whole party were in confusion.

But Count Laurent de Vautrey was not thus to perish. Strange, nay incredible as it may appear, although he was cast by the sudden attack of Donacha completely clear of the cliff, still, after falling several feet, he caught the projecting point of a rock, which, although it wounded him severely, served to arrest his fall. But he could not hang by it a moment; it only gave him an instant longer to think upon his fate. It will be remembered that the Count had chosen a place for his observation where one of the fowlers had descended. This choice saved his life; for only a few feet below, the same fowler was cautiously ensconced upon a narrow shelf of rock, braced up continually to meet any emergency of his partner, who was linked to him, and who was pursuing his way toward his eyrie, some hundred feet below. The fowler, as I have said, was braced up, on guard, ready for any emergency; and as the miserable Vautrey caught upon the point of rock, the former saw him, and accustomed to such fearful accidents, he prepared to do what he could. The next instant Vautrey fell heavily down. What a fearful abyss was below! He fell heavily down, but not into that abyss. The intrepid St. Kildan watched him as his hold loosened on the crag, and by an extraordinary effort caught and held him in his descent. His partner was called to; the rope was tied round the Count, and he was drawn up to the top of the cliff, lacerated and bleeding to be sure, but not having met with any mortal injury.

The Count was conveyed to the house of the minister. Hubert and myself at once yielded up our bed to him, and sought accommodations elsewhere. As I was the only eye-witness of the attack made by Donacha, I hesitated to state that I recognized in him the follower of Glenfinglas. I finally concluded to speak of it to Hubert only, and leave it for him to make farther mention of it, if he chose to do so. The latter heard me in silence; walked up and down for a moment with a serious air; then stopping short, he exclaimed:

'St. Leger, mark my words, 'Vautrey is a dead man!''

'What do you mean!' said I. 'A dead man!' continued Hubert; 'Donacha is as sure of him as if his dirk was now through his heart. I know the race; but I did not know that Donacha, being a captive, acknowledged fealty to Glenfinglas. Dead!—yes, if he escaped for seven times seven! Never did a McIan lose sight of his victim, when revenge sharpened the pursuit. The blood-hound has not a surer scent; the fox is not more subtle, nor the tiger more fierce, nor the cat more stealthy, nor the tortoise more patient, than a McIan of the Black Cloud when pursuing his enemy!'

'Nonsense!' said I; 'Vautrey will be on the continent in less than three weeks, beyond the reach of all the thieving caterans 'twixt this and Ben Nevis.'

'You will see,' said my cousin; 'and as for telling Vautrey who his enemy is, it will only give him cause for alarm without in the least assisting to prevent the danger. No, no; let him imagine that the savage undertook this as a revenge for some supposed affront while in his service, and let it pass. I'll not put *my* finger in a dish of the devil's cooking, at any rate. If Vautrey does not like the entertainment, he must cater better next time.'

I saw that Hubert had a full share of Highland prejudice, which I did not care to interfere with; so I left the matter with him altogether.

I thought much about it, nevertheless. It was quite time for us to get away. I went once more to the glen to make my parting salutations to my kinsman. He received me with a composure I had not before witnessed in him. He was evidently calmer and happier. We conversed for some time, and I rose to leave. 'My son,' said he, 'I thank you for this visit. It may eventuate in good. I will make your adieu to Leila. (I had asked for her.) She is not well, poor child! Perhaps you will see her when she leaves this. (I started and changed color.) Speak of me to the Lady Alice. I remember her token; and, my son, forget not my farewell admonition : ' *At the parting of the ways mistake not ; seek no pleasure which satisfies not ; be self-denying and be great. Adieu !*'

Much affected, I turned from the Wœdallah. I took my last look at the stone grotto, at the delightful little valley, and the scene beyond. I hastened to the village ; all was ready for our departure, and we set sail. Soon the threatening cliffs of Hirta receded ; and after a quick passage, we made the coast, and sailed up the loch to Glencoe. Then came parting with my dear friends there ; and then, ' Ho ! for merry England !'

WAS the WILLIAM HENRY ST. LEGER who started in the spring-time upon his tour, the same WILLIAM HENRY ST. LEGER whom the early autumn had returned in safety to his home ?

END OF PART FIRST.

THE DYING GRAHAMITE.

BY ONE OF THE VICTIMS

UNLIKE the fox, whose was the dire mishap,
    As through the lonely wilderness he came,
To lose one luckless member in a trap,
    And then advised his friends to do the same,
And e'en affirmed, though some have dared to doubt it,
That for his part he'd rather be without it :

Now, though I am a sad, unlucky wight,
    Yet lend an ear, while I attempt to show
What brought me into this most awful plight,
    And shun what I by sad experience know.
I'll not conceal my knowledge like a miser,
For when I die, the world shall be the wiser.

Once I could boast a round and ruddy cheek,
    The like of which could put the moon to shame :
The lily and the rose you there might seek,
    Nor vain the search ; but ah ! the assassin came !
He bade me starve, in hope of getting stronger,
And kill myself, that I might live the longer.

O ! how my helpless hands incessant tremble !
    How my poor feeble knees each other smite !
Behold my face ; what does it most resemble ?
    Alas ! the fruits of turning GRAHAMITE !
E'en gentlemen avoid me ; as for ladies,
They shun me like a ghost sprung out of Hades.

In vain, to heal the ailments that I feel,
  I make my bread and puddings all of bran,
Perform ablutions with an Arab's zeal,
  And walk each day much farther than I can.
My abstinence from coffee and from tea,
And fastings oft, would shame a Pharisee.

In vain a mattress bears my weary limbs ;
  In vain I rise at four, and oft before it,
And put in practice endless, nameless whims ;
  I 'm in ' a fix,' and ever must deplore it !
Oh, GRAHAM ! is it thus thy system strengthens,
And life beyond three-score and upward lengthens ?

Now, if I fall a victim to my folly,
  My blind devotion to bran-bread and water,
Cold baths, straw mattresses, and melancholy,
  By which I 'm led like oxen to the slaughter,
My pale sepulchral ghost shall ever haunt thee,
And with thy meagre system ever taunt thee.

Before I sink to premature decay,
  Ere one short hour shall close my little span,
Before the passing wind shall blow away
  The little left of what was once a man,
Fain would I consecrate each passing breath
To speak the name of her I love in death.

Thee I invoke, unkindest of thy sex !
  Who thus hast dared to fill my heart with grief,
And my already tortured soul to vex,
  Because I eat brown bread instead of beef ;
Because (for this my other sins surpasses)
Because I left off butter for molasses !

Anon, when I am numbered with the dead,
  Mark what I say : for all thy scorn and pride,
A frightful ghost I 'll hover o'er thy bed,
  And say, but for thy scorn I ne'er had died :
But oh, my stammering tongue ! be still and quiet,
'T was not her scorn ; 't was GRAHAM's meagre diet !

I wish thee well ; and be thy happy lot
  Where dietetic lecturers are rare ;
Where butter is, and GRAHAM-bread is not ;
  Go live on things more tangible than air !
Go sip thy tea, while I lie cold and moulder,
And shun cold water lest thou shouldst be colder !

But ah ! my time is short ! I feel the chill
  Of death come o'er me, ere my pen can trace
The lines with which I fondly hoped to fill,
  Though sad the task, my sheet's unlettered space :
I faint ! — I fall ! — the painful strife is over ;
Thus perish all who will not live in clover !   C.

A DREAM THAT WAS NOT ALL A DREAM.

A TRUE YARN OF THE MEXICAN COAST.

IN 1834, when I was yet a youngster before the mast, I took a trip to Tampico in a little trading schooner called 'THE ELLA,' commanded by a jolly skipper from Florida, one MAT MARIN, a dark-skinned Spanish creole, who '*for short*' was by his friends always termed 'NIG.' The schooner generally carried out dry-goods and provisions on her owners' account; but I always had an idea, (which I kept to myself,) that she 'tonned' more than her register made her responsible for, and that her hold always contained more goods than could be found on her manifest.

But to return. We were only nine days on our run from New-York out to the mouth of Tampico river; and about noon on the tenth day we stretched in over the bar, with a leading wind, that would easily have carried us with a flowing sheet up to the town, which was nearly twelve miles above; but for reasons best known to himself, the captain anchored as soon as we passed the fort and rounded Point Tañupeco, just above and out of reach of its guns. The revenue-boot from the *guarda-costa* came on board before our sails were furled, and the custom-house officers overhauled our papers and manifest. They seemed a little suspicious, and one of the officers was left on board to watch us, while the rest went aboard of their own craft, which lay nearly half a mile farther down the river, under the guns of the fort. As soon as dinner was ready the captain invited the revenue-officer down in the cabin to dine with him; and as they went below, the former winked his large laughing eye at the mate, and I knew well that there was fun in the wind. As soon as the captain and Mexican had got below, the mate slipped into the small-boat and sculled ashore. I saw no more of him until after dark that night. In the mean time I could tell by the lively voices in the cabin that the officer and captain were getting along very well together; and once in a while the tinkle of meeting glasses and a jolly song spoke of a 'spirit potential' that was playing upon the hearts and senses of both parties.

As night came on, more hilarious were the tones and more varied the sounds which arose from the cabin; and it appeared that while twilight began to get blue above, they were fast getting 'blue' below. First I could hear our Mexican spluttering out a Spanish bacchanalian glee; then Captain Marin would give a touch from a sea-song, or a specimen of a 'nigger-melody.' At last, a little after dark, with a real Havana in each of their mouths, they came on deck, the skipper and the watcher. Both were decidedly and unequivocally drunk, if one might judge from their 'walk and conversation;' but I could see at a single glance that the captain was shamming, although the 'spiritual reality' was visible in the Mexican. 'He seemed however to retain some shrewd notions of his duty, and to know that as night was over us, if we intended to smuggle, it was necessary for him to keep his eyes open. So he seated himself on the taffrail with an air of drunken dignity; and as he hummed a Spanish barcarole, kept watch over the movements of the crew about the deck, glancing now and then up and down the still river.

As the night advanced, I saw that Captain Marin began to look uneasy and anxious, although he pretended to be even more drunk than his guest and spy. At last, when it was near midnight, the Mexican became less frequent in his snatches of song, and the 'liquor-drowse' seemed to be coming over him. He would all unwillingly close his eyes, and then his head would make a long slow bow toward some being, imaginary or invisible, until the chin rested on his breast, when up it would fly, as if a bee had stung it, and slowly, drowsily the eyes would open to the accustomed watch.

Captain Marin now lay down beside the Mexican, and pretended to fall into a sound sleep, attesting the same by a long, loud and regular snore. This threw the Mexican completely off his guard; and wrapping his watch-coat closer around him, he followed suit; and then the twain seemed to be trying which could snore the loudest. When the Señor Mexicana had got fairly under headway the captain arose lightly from the deck, and passing forward, took the lanthorn from the binnacle and held it for a minute over the bows. Presently I saw several dark objects coming out from under the shadow of the land, and in a few moments more six large native canoes were alongside of us. In the first one that boarded us was the mate and a merchant whom I well knew to belong to one of the first houses in Tampico. The boats came noiselessly alongside, and their crews crept stealthily on board. Without a sound the hatches were raised, and package after package of rich dry-goods was passed up from the hold and over the side into the boats, by the tawny, half-naked rascals.

The boats were nearly all loaded, when I, who had been placed to watch over the sleeping revenue-officer, saw him open his eyes; and before I could move or speak, he saw and comprehended all that was going on. Springing to his feet, he shouted :

'*Guarda costa ! — contrabandistas !*'

One bound from where he stood by the main-hatchway to the taffrail, and our captain was by the side of the officer, with his brawny hands encircling the wind-pipe from which proceeded so much noise. The Mexican tried to draw his sword, and struggled manfully to get free from the choking grip; but Captain Marin knew that the entire loss of his vessel and cargo would follow detection, and he was not disposed to trifle. Raising the Mexican, in spite of his kicks and writhings, in his strong arms, he coolly pitched him overboard! It was quite dark, and as the tide was ebbing swiftly downward, he passed out of sight instantly; but for minutes we could hear him splashing and gurgling in the water, and trying to shout.

Then all was still again. We knew not whether he had sunk or gained the shore; nor, to tell the truth, did we much care.

'Bear a hand, boys!' said the captain; 'tumble in these packages; get the rest of the goods into the boats, and let them get ashore. If that *diego* has n't drank too much water, he may give us some trouble about this matter yet.'

In a few moments the last package to be smuggled was passed into the boats; the 'patron,' who had made the purchase, counted out the pay in doubloons; the canoes pushed off, and soon vanished up the river. In a few minutes our hatches were replaced, the decks cleared up as before, and the crew retired to their berths, with orders to be sound asleep and not to wake up on any account.

All this was scarcely arranged, when the dash of oars coming hastily up the river was heard, and in another moment an armed boat from the *guarda-costa* was alongside. At the first sound of the approaching boat, Captain Marin had lain down where he first pretended to go to sleep, and he was now snoring louder than ever. Even the curses, many, loud and deep, of the angry Mexicans, failed to arouse him from his deep slumber. The officer who had been thrown overboard, still dripping from his involuntary bath, rushed aft, and with no gentle means tried to arouse the sleeper. At last the captain, gaping and stretching, slowly opened his eyes, and as he yawned and scratched his head, coolly asked what was the matter and what was wanted. Then came a *scene!* All the Mexicans cursing and swearing and threatening and carrahooing at once, pointing to the officer who had been taking a midnight swim all alone by himself, who, with voice louder than all the rest, swore that he should have been drowned if St. Antonio had n't made the sentinels hear his voice aboard the guarda-costa, and caused them to send him a boat. The captain could not be made to understand what was the matter; and when he was charged with having thrown the revenue-officer overboard, and with having smuggling-boats alongside, he raised his hands in holy horror toward the stars, and indignantly replied: 'It 's all a d——d lie! Why,' said he to the other officers of the guarda-costa, 'that gentleman dined with me; we drank pretty freely, and then came up *from* the cabin. when both of us lay down here to sleep. I did not wake up until now: he must have been dreaming, and have fallen overboard in his sleep! You all saw that *I* was sound asleep when you came aboard; how then could I have thrown him overboard? The idea is absurd, nonsensical; the whole story improbable—yes, *impossible!* See, my hatches are all battened down, just as they were when you were on board, when I came in from sea to-day; nothing has been moved; my crew are all asleep. He must have been dreaming; and while he dreamed of smugglers, and the like of such, he must have fallen overboard. He knows very well that he was ' as. drunk as a lord.'

The story of the captain was well conceived, and told with still better effect among all the revenue-officers, save the victim himself, who called upon every saint in the calendar to come down and swear that his story was true. But the perfect order and quietude of our vessel; the crew all sound asleep; the hatches battened

n, just as they were in the morning ; the honest indignation of
sleepy captain, and the acknowledgment of the victim that he
been very drunk, compared badly with his own story, and the
ı of Captain Marin was believed.   The 'soaked' official was
ɩn back to his own vessel, to be tried and punished for sleeping
ɩis watch, while another officer was left in his place to keep us
ɩ smuggling.   When day-light came, we weighed anchor and
ıd up to the town, where we honestly discharged the cargo per
ɩifest, paying honorably all charges and duties thereon.
aptain Marin *only* cleared five thousand dollars by that trip ; and
have often laughed since at the scene I have described, espe-
ly the Mexican's *Dream, which was not all a Dream.*

NED BUNTLINE.

LINES ON A PiCTURE OF AN INDIAN GIRL.

BY E. GALLAUDET.

WHAT sees she as she gazes there alone
Out on the wide, wide ocean ?   Is there aught
Her sight descries of moving thing ; a bark
That but a speck in the far distance seems,
And which she hopes will bear to her fond arms
Him who has vowed to her unchanging love ?
Or, as the vast expanse her eye surveys,
All vainly does she look for his canoe ?
And are thick-coming fancies troubling her ?
Is Passion's host at strife within that breast ?
Is Jealousy inflicting her keen pang,
And picturing to this simple native's mind
Him, whom she loves, who is her all on earth,
Wooing, while yet he waits, some other maid ?
Say, is her soul thus tortured ; and does Death
Look up inviting through the glassy sea ?
And hesitates she whether still to live,
Or plunge beneath the tide and end her woes ?

Far, far from this the truth.   No torment's her's,
No doubts of love, no maddening jealousy ;
No warm expectant she of one to come,
Who in her ear will breathe Love's magic tones ;
For as upon that water-circled rock
She peacefully reposes, friends and foes,
Her lover and her rivals, from before
Her mind's eye fade away ; and of the past
And future now she has no troubled thoughts.
The still smooth water and the tranquil air
Have filled her soul with calmness ; and that bow
She sees upon the disappearing cloud,
Though why GOD placed it there she knows not yet :
So full of promise of the clear blue sky,
And beautiful it is, that as she looks,
Her spirit, though untaught, rises to HIM
Who made that bow, the earth and all she sees,
And the GREAT SPIRIT worships as she kneels.

LITERARY NOTICES.

HOMER'S ILIAD: TRANSLATED BY WILLIAM MUNFORD. In two volumes. Boston: CHARLES LITTLE AND JAMES BROWN.

A NEW translation of HOMER'S ILIAD, by a VIRGINIAN, written in 'our English heroic verse, without rhyme,' and issued with all the luxury of the Boston press, is an event in literature. Such a work, if accomplished with a spirit equal to that which dictated the attempt, cannot fail to be a matter of pride and congratulation to our own country, nor to command the attention of scholars abroad. An examination of its pages has convinced us that it will confer lasting honor on the memory of its author, who only lived to bring it to a completion. Mr. WILLIAM MUNFORD died at his residence in the city of Richmond, (Va.,) in 1825. The work on which he had spent the intervals of a life devoted to many responsible labors is now first published by his executors. The completion of such a task is almost of itself a sufficient argument for the requisite qualities of the translator. It must be confessed that the inducement was small, beyond pure love and admiration, and the illustration of genius for its own sake. It was laborious, intrinsically difficult, and might not be appreciated, at least in this hemisphere. POPE wearied of his labors before he had accomplished the many books of HOMER. COWPER flagged according to the variations of his unequal spirit. Both failed; not from want of genius in either, but the impossible nature of the thing. A translation is the divorce of a spirit from the body which was born with it, informed by it, and which was the outward, visible image of itself. The two are inseparable. We always confound them together; we never think of one without the other. The difficulty is inherent, and ever will stand out against the complete success of any attempt of this kind. Why is it that little phrases in French, for example, are often in request, which may be translated, and yet for which there is no translation? — which somehow or other signify nothing when analyzed, and yet taken as they are, are provokingly apt and piquant? The fact is, the body and soul of such things are born together. '*Stimultuaneousness*' is the western phrase, which expresses the concurrence of original ideas with the language in which they may be expressed. In vain do we seek an adequate converse with the noble spirits of antiquity, if we strive to bring them back to our times, to make them dwell in our habitations, if through our ignorance we make the language in which they are enshrined the grave in which they lie dead, rather than the bright adornment which only illus-

r beauty. We 'may go to them, but they cannot return to us.' What
, however executed, can give us an idea of that strength of pinion

> 'WHICH the Theban eagle bare,
> Sailing with supreme dominion
> Through the azure deep of air?'

eader of PHILIPS has possessed the wealth of golden SAPPHO, though he
heart that musical ode,

> 'BLEST as the immortal gods is he
> The youth who fondly sits by thee?'

en we come to HOMER, where the marriage of the lofty thought with its
iful language is most holy and inseparable, consecrate by age, and ever-
hopes of a translator become in proportion faint and his task doubtful. We
e remarks not to discourage a perusal of the work before us, nor to lessen
of the author, but to show that his execution of it, in the face of inherent
, amounts as far as can be to an actual triumph. Would that we could see
a refreshing tokens of a love for classical studies! What so calculated to
taste, improve the judgment, and shed a charm over the common pursuits
We are far from saying that those who cannot read HOMER in the Greek had
attempt him in a translation; and we are sure that the scholar will take in-
sure in the comparison of this version with those which have gone before,
with the great original. We shall present some passages selected from
ortions of the Iliad, and not with a view of showing the best parts of this
The first may be referred to in the Fifth Book, and were marked with an
y ancient critics, to denote their transcendent beauty. They describe
arming herself for battle:

> 'MEANWHILE MINERVA of the thundering god
> Dread daughter, on her father's floor threw off
> Her flowing robe with various ornament
> Elaborate by herself with hands divine,
> Assuming then of cloud-compelling JOVE
> The cuirass, for the mournful war she girds
> His armor on; she takes his dreadful shield,
> The shaggy ægis which throughout its orb
> With terror was emblazoned! Discord there
> Was seen; there valor stern; there swift pursuit
> Bloody and fierce; there too the Gorgon's head
> Tremendous monster, horrible and dire,
> Portentous prodigy of awful JOVE.
> Next on her head she placed his helmet crown,
> With four bright crests, adorn'd with radiant stars
> And fram'd of gold; so large it would suffice
> For all the warriors of an hundred states.
> She mounts the fiery car and takes the lance
> Huge, heavy, strong, with which she prostrates hosts
> Of heroes against whom her anger burns
> Resistless in her father's boundless might:
> JUNO, impatient, lashed the flying steeds;
> Opening spontaneous rang the gates of heaven,
> Kept by the Hours, who the wide expanse
> Of Heaven, and Olympus have in charge
> To roll away the cloudy barrier dense,
> Or to replace it. Through these gates the steeds
> Were by the scourge impelled They found on high,
> Sitting apart from other powers divine,
> Saturnian JOVE upon the topmost cliff
> Of all the summits of immense Olympus.'

ry first sentence in the above version will serve to illustrate some of the
remarks, by showing the difficulty of translation. While the whole pas-

sage in the Greek has been admired, we do not remember that any critic has pointed out the exquisite beauty of that expression for disrobing:

Πέπλον μεν κατέχευεν.

It is true our translator has ' flowing robes,' but to to find another *verb* for κατέχευεν in our language, in such a connexion, would be difficult. COWPER has it thus:

> ' Meantime MINERVA, progeny of JOVE,
>   On the adamantine floor of his abode,
>   *Let fall profuse* her variegated robe.'

Mr. COLERIDGE very truly remarks that there is *that* about the Greek which has no name, but which is of so fine and ethereal a subtilty that it can only be *felt* in the original, and is lost in an attempt to transfuse it into another language.' How hard to give an idea of the unbroken power of verse which rolls on through those wonderful rhapsodies in which HECTOR bursts through the gates of the Greek fortifications and fights his way to the ship of AJAX! How is it possible to convey the whole of that tender pathos which marks the interview of HECTOR and ANDROMACHE? Or the lamentations of ANDROMACHE and HELEN over the corpse of the departed hero? But we come to that grand picture of ACHILLES struggling in the surges of SCAMANDER.* How does the verse roll on full and sonorous as the torrent; the fall of the elm, the tearing up of the bank, the rustling of the branches in the water, all put into such words that almost every letter corresponds with the sound! Would that we could find room for our author's correct and excellent version of the whole of this unequalled picture:

> ' THE wrathful river, rolling billows huge,
>   Pursued him rapidly with all his floods
>   Foaming and furious. Many of the dead,
>   Which lay in heaps by stern ACHILLES slain,
>   He raised aloft and floating threw them forth,
>   Roaring and bellowing like a bull enraged
>   Upon the land; but in his beauteous stream
>   Sheltered and saved the living Trojans, hidden
>   In eddies deep and wide. Around the chief
>   A turbid surge, enormous, horrible,
>   Swelled high. The weight of waters on his shield
>   Falling, pressed hard; nor could his slidd'ring feet
>   Support him. With his hands a stately elm
>   Growing luxurious on the river's brink
>   He grasp'd; the tree gave way with all its roots
>   Bore down the bursting bank, and falling sheer
>   Within the flood, with branches broad and dense
>   Obstructing, bridg'd it. To the shore he sprang:
> 　　　.　　　.　　　.　　　the potent god
>   Ceased not, but more enraged behind him poured:
>   PELIDES with prodigious effort sprang
>   At every leap as far as flies a spear
>   Thrown with strong impulse, darting rapidly
>   Like the black eagle. Upon his breast
>   The brazen armor rang with clanging loud
>   And terrible; endeavoring to escape,
>   He fled, obliquely turning: XANTHUS still
>   Pursued him every way with deaf'ning roar.
>   Whene'er again the chief indignant stopped
>   To try the contest.　　.　　　.　　　.
>   So often did the river sprung from JOVE
>   His neck and shoulders bathe, and o'er him swell
>   With overwhelming waters.'

Wearied and slipping from the ground, ACHILLES now implores the gods that he might not perish by so ignoble a fate:

> ———' MEANLY to be swept away,
>   Drowned in a river, like a swine-herd boy:
>   He said, and instantly beside him stood
>   The god of ocean and the martial maid.

---

* BOOK XXI.

> · · · He with strength
> And speed renewed, encouraged thus from Heaven,
> Rush'd to the plain which then was covered deep
> With outpoured waters. Many splendid arms
> Were floating, many ghastly carcasses
> Of youths in battle slain. His vigorous knees
> Sprang upward right against the rushing stream;
> For not the potent river in its strength
> Restrained him now, such energy divine
> MINERVA gave him, nor SCAMANDER yet
> Relax'd his efforts; with augmented rage
> Against PELIDES, high his boiling surge
> He rolled a torrent flood, *calling for aid*
> *To Simois also.*'

We commend this translation of HOMER as one which challenges a comparison with any that has yet been made, and as in many respects better than them all, as might be shown by the collation of passages, and as deserving a place on the shelves of every scholar and in every public library in the country. By the way, what has become of that promised translation by the author of ' Oberon,' (Mr. SOTHEBY,) which was to be more faithful than POPE's, and more harmonious than COWPER's? Until that appears, we shall consider the present version as holding such a position.

THE TREES OF AMERICA: NATIVE AND FOREIGN, PICTORIALLY AND BOTANICALLY DELINEATED, AND SCIENTIFICALLY AND POPULARLY DESCRIBED: being considered principally with reference to the Geography and History, soil and situation, propagation and culture, accidents and diseases, etc. Illustrated by numerous engravings. By D. J. BROWNE, author of 'Sylva Americana.' New-York: HARPER AND BROTHERS.

THIS excellent illustrated work of Mr. BROWNE has strong claims upon the attention of both the general and the scientific reader. The subject is treated of in a popular form, but at the same time with strict regard to scientific accuracy. The author has mostly followed LOUDON in his arrangement, which is admirable; and in this respect the work will not suffer by comparison with the best works of the kind within our knowledge. First we have the genus, with the order in both the natural and LINNÆAN systems; then follow the synonymes, derivation, generic characters, general description, and geographical distribution. Then follow the species, with the synonymes; derivation of the name; a list of works in which the tree is figured; the specific characters; then a general description; varieties; geography and history; soil and situation; propagation and management; insects; properties and uses; and, in short, every thing which is necessary to be known in order to obtain a full knowledge of the subject. The work is abundantly illustrated with engravings; and to make the descriptions easily understood, we have a figure of the general appearance of the tree, and another of the leaf, flower, fruit, etc.; and these are so true to nature, that any one at all familiar with the subject will be able at once to recognize each particular tree wherever he may meet with it. We have only to glance at this outline to perceive that the present volume has been a work of much labor and time, and we take pleasure in bearing our testimony to the care and accuracy with which it has been accomplished. In collecting his matériel, the author travelled into various and distant parts of the world, and thus had an opportunity not only of verifying and correcting the observations of others, but also of examining the trees of the countries visited under a great variety of circumstances, beside having had access to nurseries and the collections of amateurs. In addition to this, he has carefully consulted the most judicious writers on the subject; and as the result of all, he has given us a work which will rank high as a literary performance; and we feel confident that it will take its place among the standard productions of the country. The author's style is characterized by an agreeable simplicity, while at the same time it is sufficiently vigorous and spirited to enlist attention. But the matter and arrangement are of more importance than the style, in a work of this nature, and in this respect its merit is certainly very great. There is one very pleasing feature in the book which we cannot help noticing; we allude to the introduction of legends and historical associations connected with individual trees, which frequently have all the charm of romance, and serve as a relief to what may be called the dryness of scientific detail. The subject naturally affords many poetical allusions and interesting associations, and these are introduced with great good taste. The subject is interesting and important in every point of view, whether we regard trees as subservient to usefulness, ornament, or as performing an important part in the economy of Nature. The cultivation of trees for ornamental purposes has occupied the attention of mankind in nearly every age of the world, although at times the taste for it has been greatly neglected or entirely lost. We find evidence of this in the history of every nation of which any record remains. The Greeks, Romans, Persians and Jews had their ornamental trees and gardens. *Arboriculture* is a comparatively modern art, for we do not read that these nations planted trees for any purpose but that of ornament, if we except the elm and poplar for the support of vines. We are much inclined to the opinion, however, that SOLOMON cultivated the celebrated cedar of Lebanon for useful purposes; and to him belongs the credit of having made the first plantation of which we have any certain account. No doubt that singular people, the Chinese, have had plantations of trees from time immemorial, for they appear to have been in advance of all nations in every thing pertaining to the arts and sciences. In England, the first plantation was made during the reign of HENRY the Eighth. The tree selected was the famous English oak, and the acorns were planted where the trees were intended to stand. We are not aware that arboriculture was much known on the continent of Europe before the age of LOUIS the Fourteenth; but from that time it began to occupy much attention.

But let us come nearer home. Owing to the newness of our country, the great magnitude of our forests, and the almost inexhaustible mines of coal with which a bountiful Nature has veined our land, the attention of our farmers has not been directed to the formation of plantations to any great extent; and yet it is a singular circumstance, that while the pioneer of the west is cutting his way through immense forests to still more distant regions, the inhabitants of the oldest settled portions of the country are beginning to feel the necessity of creating plantations of trees. Coal will answer very well for fuel, but we cannot use it to build ships nor houses, nor for a thousand other purposes. We may build iron ships, brick houses, mud cabins, etc., but yet we cannot do without wood; and the farmer is beginning to feel alarmed at the gradual disappearance of his forests. We might pursue this subject to a great length, had we the leisure to do so. In view of what has been said, however, we cannot help thinking that Mr. BROWNE's work has appeared at an opportune moment. It will be highly useful to the farmer: in it he will find the most minute directions for laying out a plantation; the proper soil for each kind of tree; the best modes of propagation; the properties and uses of trees — in short, every thing necessary to be known to insure success and a profitable return for his labor; and it will also afford him the means of making a judicious selection. These remarks are not confined to forest-trees, but apply equally to fruit-trees, for the work contains ample directions for the cultivation of our choicest kinds of fruits, the best time and the most approved methods of pruning, beside a great deal of other useful information. Doubtless the work will be farther useful in promoting a taste for ornamental trees. We are surprised at the little attention this subject has excited in our large cities ; we have decidedly too few trees, and those that we have, beside being many of them of the wrong kind, are shamefully neglected. Insects are allowed to collect on them in such great numbers that their beauty is entirely destroyed ; and instead of their shade being sought as a grateful protection from the rays of the sun, they are avoided as objects of disgust. Why should this be ? No good reason can be given ; nevertheless this state of things will continue until a proper knowledge of the cultivation and nature of trees has been acquired ; and we look to Mr. Browne's work to impart this knowledge, which will open to its recipient sources of enjoyment of which he never dreamed before. Each tree will wear the aspect of a familiar friend, with whom he may hold silent but sweet converse. We shall never forget with what grateful feelings we have found repose under the cool shade of some wide-spreading tree, after having rambled for hours over parched fields, with the sun pouring its burning rays upon our devoted head. And why should not trees afford a grateful shade to the crowded streets of our cities? We deprive ourselves of a great luxury in overlooking this subject, as well as neglect an important means of promoting health. We know of at least one street in Brooklyn where the branches from the trees on each side meet and form a beautiful arch : it is a pleasure to walk beneath it. The avenue thus formed not only serves as a ventilator, and keeps up a cool current of air, but the trees also purify the air by taking up carbon and giving off oxygen. But perhaps we have said enough. In conclusion, we urgently recommend Mr. Browne's work to the notice of our state and county agricultural societies throughout the country. We know of no more suitable work for a premium ; and we will just venture the remark, that our agricultural societies make a great mistake in offering dollar-and-cent premiums. This remark is based upon considerable experience of the effects of such premiums. We know that committees are frequently embarrassed in making a judicious and suitable selection of books ; but this is often owing to a want of familiarity with the literary world. If books cannot be found, let more medals be given. These remarks are based upon the principle that premiums act as a stimulus, which is effective only as long as the premium lasts ; and every body knows which will last longest, books or money. The money is quickly and often imprudently spent ; the book may always be shown as a matter of pride, and will be of lasting benefit. We deem this matter of so much importance that we would pursue it farther were this the place for an argument. Again we recommend this work to our agricultural societies ; many of them, whose premium-lists are already made out, might still award it as a discretionary premium. We should be sorry indeed to say so much in praise of any work without having it in our power to recommend it also to the ladies. We *know* that they feel a deep interest in the subject, and we have never yet seen an agricultural or horticultural exhibition to which they did not contribute their share, and in which they did not form the most attractive point of beauty ; and we also know that they have frequently been successful competitors in floral exhibitions. We have always taken pleasure in showing them a little partiality when we could do so without manifest injustice to the hardier sex. Now Mr. Browne's work is a very suitable present for ladies, copies of which are elegantly bound, with gilt edges ; and we hope to see it take its place in the ladies' boudoir, where it might very well supersede the ridiculous ' *nouvellettes*' of the day.

PROGRESS: A SATIRICAL POEM. By JOHN G. SAXE. pp. 32. New-York: JOHN ALLEN, 139 Nassau-street.

WE desire the reader at once to understand that he has no *dissertation* to encounter in our notice of this poem. Dissertations, we have had frequent occasion to observe, are called for mainly by those rhythmical compositions miscalled ' poetry,' with which pseudo-bards deceive themselves and astonish their immediate neighborhoods during an immortality of three weeks; and the less one has of extracts, the efforts of this nature, the better is it for the literary reputation of the author and much the better for the reader. We shall unhesitatingly avow in the first place that we have not for many years met with a kindred poetical performance in all respects more felicitous than the one before us. The satire is not less just than trenchant; the wit is as natural as it is keen; and the verse, it is sufficient praise to say, is equally harmonious and terse. But we do not choose to have the reader take our word for the character of the poem; the author can ' speak for himself' in the best meaning of that saying; and it is our present purpose to afford him the opportunity of doing so. Premising therefore that the theme of the poet is the much-vaunted ' Progress' of the age in which it is our happiness to live; ' progress' in all its various shapes and phases; we proceed on the instant to ask the reader's attention to a few passages, skipping by-the-by several spirited extracts which are' more or less intimately connected with three or four brief selections which we had the pleasure to present in a previous number of this Magazine. Can it be that our poet has allusion to the imitative Transcendentalists, the CARLYLEISTS of a ' tertian formation,' and to the half-learned scholars of ' *the day*' instead of ' the time,' in the lines which ensue ? ' Likely as not :'

> ' ROOM for the sages! — hither comes a throng
> Of blooming PLATOS, trippingly along.
> In dress how fitted to beguile the fair!
> What intellectual, stately heads — of hair!
> Hark to the oracle! to Wisdom's tone
> Breathed in a fragrant zephyr of Cologne.
> That boy in gloves, the leader of the van,
> Talks of the ' outer' and the ' inner man;'
> And knits his girlish brow in stout resolve
> Some mountain-sized ' idea' to ' evolve.'
> Delusive toil! — thus in their infant days,
> When children mimic manly deeds in plays,
> Long will they sit and eager ' bob for whale'
> Within the ocean of a water-pail!
> The next, whose looks unluckily reveal
> The ears portentous that his locks conceal,
> Prates of ' the orbs' with such a knowing frown,
> You deem he puffs some lithographic town
> In western wilds; while yet unbroken ranks
> Of thrifty beavers build unchartered ' banks,'
> And prowling panthers occupy the lots
> Adorned with churches on the paper-plots.'

>   .   .   .   .   .   .

> 'TALK not, ye jockies, of the wondrous speed
> That marks your Northern or your Southern steed;
> See Progress fly o'er Education's course!
> Not far-famed Derby owns a fleeter horse!
> On rare Improvement's ' short and easy' road,
> How swift her flight to Learning's blest abode!
> In other times, ('t was many years ago,)
> The scholar's course was toilsome, rough and slow;
> The fair Humanities were sought in tears,
> And came, the trophy of laborious years.
> Now Learning's shrine each idle youth may seek,
> And spending there a shilling and a week,
> (At lightest cost of study, cash and lungs,)
> Come back, like *Rumor*, with ' an hundred tongues!'

We remember reading last winter an exceedingly graphic letter from the national capital, descriptive of the scenes to be witnessed upon the floor of the 'popular' congressional branch; of men who had 'sneaked into greatness' jumping up by scores at a time to 'catch the eye' of the long-suffering Speaker; small craft, each one supposing himself a ship-of-state, and carrying guns so noisy as to be mistaken for 'first-rates;' advancing with an onslaught of terrible adjectives, and putting that glorious bird, the 'American Eagle,' through a series of evolutions such as no bird in his senses would condescend to perform; combining the eternal twang of the 'nasal Northerner,' as the Yankee is called; the pompous BOBADIL-bearing of the 'sunny South' and her 'chivalric sons;' the brilliant scintillations of Western ge-nius, prepared to gouge the British lion, bite off the universal English nose, and des-poil Britain of its aggregate ears; and other the like feasible exploits, the boast whereof was designed for the immediate region of 'Buncombe.' But hear our au-thor on a cognate theme:

'BUT times are changed; a rude degen'rate race
Usurp the seats and shame the sacred place:
Here plotting demagogues with zeal defend
The 'people's rights,' to gain some private end;
Here Southern youths, on Folly's surges tost,
Their fathers' wisdom eloquently boast:
(So dowerless spinsters proudly number o'er
The costly jewels that their grand-dames wore.)
Here would-be TULLY's pompously parade
Their tumid tropes for simple 'Buncombe' made;
Full on the chair the chilling torrent shower,
And work their word-pumps through the allotted hour.
Deluded Buncombe! while with honest praise
She notes each grand and patriotic phrase,
And, much rejoicing in her hopeful son,
Deems all her own the laurels he has won;
She little dreams how brother members fled,
And left the House as vacant as his head!
Here rural CHATHAMS, eager to attest
The 'growing greatness of the mighty West,'
To make the plainest proposition clear,
Crack PRISCIAN's head and 'Mr. SPEAKER's' ear;
Then closing up in one terrific shout,
Pour all their 'wild-cats' furiously out!
Here lawless boors with ruffian bullies vie,
Who last shall give the rude, insulting lie;
While 'Order! order!' loud the chairman calls,
And echoing 'Order!' every member bawls;
Till rising high in rancorous debate,
And higher still in fierce envenom'd hate,
Retorted blows the scene of riot crown,
And big LYCURGUS knocks the lesser down.'

We are compelled to close our extracts with the subjoined passage; and although it is but a 'sample' of many others which might be cited, we cannot forbear to ask the reader's attention to its searching sententiousness. There is more thought in any six of the ensuing lines than can be found in whole pages of certain bardlings who consider their poetical reputation as established; and *it is*, by-the-way, for that matter, such as it is:

'O, MIGHT the Muse prolong her flowing rhyme,
(Too closely cramped by unrelenting Time,
Whose dreadful scythe swings heedlessly along,
And missing speeches, clips the thread of song,)
How would she strive in fitting verse to sing
The wondrous Progress of the Printing King!
Bibles and novels, treatises and songs,
Lectures on 'Rights' and strictures upon wrongs;
Verse in all metres, travels in all clines,
Rhymes without reason, sonnets without rhymes;
'Translations from the French,' so vilely done,
The wheat escaping leaves the chaff alone;

> Lampoons, whose authors strive in vain to throw
> Their headless arrows from a nerveless bow ;
> Poems by youths who, crossing Nature's will,
> Harangue the landscape they were born to till ;
> Huge tomes of law, that lead by rugged routes
> Through ancient dogmas down to modern doubts ;
> Where judges oft, with well-affected ease,
> Give learned reasons for absurd decrees ;
> Or, more ingenious still, contrive to found
> Some just decision on fallacious ground ;
> Smart epigrams, all sadly out of joint,
> And pointless, save the 'exclamation-point,'
> Which stands in state, with vacant wonder fraught,
> The pompous tomb-stone of some pauper-thought ;
> Ingenious systems, based on doubtful facts,
> 'Tracts for the Times,' and most untimely tracts ;
> Polemic pamphlets, literary toys,
> And ' easy lessons' for uneasy boys ;
> Hebdomedal gazettes and daily news,
> Gay magazines and quarterly reviews ;
> Small portion these of all the vast array
> Of darkened leaves that cloud each passing day,
> And pour their tide unceasingly along,
> A gathering, swelling, overwhelming throng!'

We shall say no more of the poem of ' Progress' than to mention that the notes to it are in excellent keeping with the text ; that it is dedicated with great propriety to a kindred poet, OLIVER WENDELL HOLMES ; that it is admirably printed by Mr. WIL-LIAM OSBORN ; and that we desire every one of our readers who can do so to secure a copy for immediate perusal and long preservation.

A PRACTICAL TREATISE ON DYEING AND CALICO-PRINTING : including the latest Inventions and Improvements ; also a Description of the Origin Manufacture, Uses and Chemical Properties of the various Animal, Veg table and Mineral Substances employed in the arts　With an Appendix. By an EXPERIENCED DYER, assisted by several Scientific Gentlemen.　With engravings on steel and wood.　In one volume.　pp. 734.　New-York : HARPER AND BROTHERS.

FEW subjects connected with the arts form a more useful study than that of dyeing ; no one is more immediately connected with human gratification and comfort ; and assuredly no one has its basis in more philosophical and well-defined principles. The great advancement which has been made in latter years in chemistry as a science has contributed much to the permanency as well as the beauty of colors ; and yet, strange to say, BERTHOLLET alone has merited any great distinction in giving to the world a treatise on the subject of dyeing.　Dr. BANCROFT, it is true, has written a book upon this important art, but it is quite too theoretical and immethodical, and is therefore of little use in the dye-house.　The time therefore would seem to have arrived in which the public and parties interested must be anxious to have just such a treatise as the one before us.　The author's object, as stated by himself, is, ' First, to reduce the whole theory of dyeing to the utmost simplicity and accuracy ; secondly, to classify, arrange and define colors, in order to enable those who are pursuing the relative branches of study, as well as the artist, to comprehend more easily the nature of each particular hue, tint and shade, and the relation it bears to the primary elements of light, darkness and color ; thirdly, to elucidate each particular subject in such a manner as to impart substantial knowledge to those seeking it, and at the same time exhibit those shoals toward which so many have been attracted by erroneous deductions and false conclusions ; fourthly, to set forth the active properties, characters and uses of the various animal, vegetable and mineral substances employed in dyeing and the auxiliary arts ; and finally, to define the various chemical and technical terms employed in the dye-house, print-work, etc.

'LOBSCOUSE, OR THE ADVENTURES, YARNS, SONGS, ETC. OF SQUILGEE, HIS MESS-MATES AND SHIPMATES.' — We can scarcely remember when the echoes of our silent sanctum were awakened by more obstreperous laughter than while we were perusing a little manuscript-journal entitled as above, and written by an officer engaged in the floating service of 'UNCLE SAMUEL.' Into it we plunge, *in medias res;* commencing on the first leaf with what SQUILGEE jotted down, being 'hungry at the time,' concerning the poetry of BYRON and other self-excruciating writers; which reminded him forcibly of the *paté de foie gras:* ' Both are unnatural products; goose and poet being tortured, by fires external in the one case and internal in the other, before they are enabled to furnish the delicacies so much craved respectively by gourmand and sentimentalist. Goose, being under influence of the flames, sings — at least so says Mr. BULWER LYTTON ; poet, burning almost to spontaneous combustion, sings likewise. The resemblance is apparent, although not perfect ; for the poet's song is all we have of him, whereas the goose yields the equally delicious and more substantial residuum of the *paté.*' We have read in our time a good many sketches descriptive of first going to sea on board a man-of-war ; but we can call to mind nothing more graphic than the following running narrative : ' We were just losing sight of the Capes of Virginia, bound on a cruise of years, and the people had been on deck from an early hour ; first, ' All hands up anchor,' and then ' All hands work ship.' It was past two when the pilot was discharged, and BOREAS the boatswain had just ' piped down.' There was no dinner ready : SQUILGEE, like the rest, had been fasting since dawn ; he was hungry, he was in love, he was nostalgic ; need it be added that he was as cross as the 'Gentleman in Black' when he assumes his most diabolical *rôle;* and this brings on an *exposé* of the cause and a sample of the effect which I flatter myself few writers have ever more connectedly and satisfactorily presented to the understanding of an intelligent reader. I said we had all fasted; alas ! there were many who for long, horrible days were doomed to fast ; men who raised their heavy eyes toward the fading outlines of the land in a despair which knew no hope ; men who in their inmost hearts would have considered it a boon of Heaven's own gift to have been placed on the extremest point of Cape Horn, amid the raging of eternal storms, and would have encountered the perils and hardships of weary wayfaring, inexorable wilds, giant Patagoniahs, cougars, gauchéros and caymans, jungle and yellow fevers, and worse than all, the laugh of jeering acquaintances and friends ; willingly, gladly would they have encountered all these, to get at their late despised homesteads again. Like the elder BRUTUS, the earth to

them was a mother on whom they would have cast themselves and embraced her.
The earth, heave though it may in billowy undulations at rare epochs when the earth-
quake is abroad, for centuries swerves not from her vast stability ; but who ever saw
great 'NEPTUNE's Ocean' still? It is in one everlasting state of rolling, pitching,
dashing, breaking ! In its mildest mood, when the long, dead, heavy swells come one
after another in eternal monotony, it is dreadful ; but when the winds are at work and
the waves come thick and fast and sharp, in the stream of the Florida Gulf, for ex-
ample, it is absolutely *awfully horrible* to the sea-sick ! They eat? Pah ! the very
idea is disgust itself. 'Grub,' a word of vulgar sound, conveys to their disordered
brains the idea of a monstrousness undefinable. They ' will none of it !'

'We were just losing sight of the Capes, or rather of the Cape, for it was Cape
Henry, which in the time we could write it disappeared ; its last dim line of tree-
tops dropped below the western sky. Dismal Cape Henry ! — a dreary beach of
unvaried sands and gloomy pines is all that is presented to the ocean-tossed ; false
outward show of the happy homes and teeming hospitality for which the margin of
the noble Chesapeake is noted far and wide. Who that unknowing had come and
looked upon that low line of verdant sterility, and then turned his prow, re-seeking
other lands, would dream of the thousand spires shooting up from rising cities; of
the banks of great rivers adorned with smiling habitations ; of the wealth, the beauty,
the capitol of a great nation, that lay beyond? But deceiver as thou art, old Cape ! to
us the extremest point of Fatherland, GOD grant us no worse fate than to fall in with
thee again, safe and sound and soon !

' My native land, good night !'

'During the night, running off with a dashing breeze from the south'ard and west-
'ard, we found ourselves, by the high temperature of the water, some ten degrees
above the air, in the Gulf Stream. And now commenced a series of petty conflicts.
As if provoked because there was no regular storm on hand to be let loose upon us,
the Spirit of the Winds, who rules the track of that mighty ocean-river, came whiz-
zing along, scattering dirty squalls of wind and rain, sometimes tolerably heavy, at
others light as vapor. 'Shorten sail!' one instant, 'Make sail !' the next, are the
orders of the day ; for although it will not do to trust the squalls, no one wishes to
lose a moment in crossing, if the course permits. Very 'tricky' is the weather in
the Gulf. You shall see the clouds gathering on the horizon ; they begin to look
black ; they rise rapidly ; the rain comes on with them, shortening and shortening
the range of sight. 'In top-gallant-sails !' 'Up main-sail and spanker !' 'Stand
by to clew down the top-sails !' Poh ! it 's nothing but rain, or as JACK calls it, 'a
paddy's hurricane, right up and down.' Once, twice, thrice, a half dozen times
this occurs. But lull yourself to security, and trust it the next time. Over goes
your ship, lee-guns in the water ; whang ! bang ! crack ! goes your light spars ; pop !
ter-r-r-r ! away go some of your sails, as a heavy gust passes over you and leaves a
job of clearing away the wreck. We had, as I before observed, a south-westerly
wind, which runs along with and soothes the current. Lucky for us ! Had there
been a north-wester or a north-easter roughing its surface and opposing its way, then
there would have been seen the anger, the fury of the mighty stream ; leaping in
wild rage toward the skies, flashing in raging spray, tumbling in mad phalanxes of
waves toward us, as if arrayed expressly for the destruction of our devoted bark.
Oh ! a wild, a fearful scene is the Florida Gulf, chafed by opposing storms ! For-
tunately it does not take long to cross, and we were soon over. The water began

to cool; the gulf-weed was seen ranged in long wind-rows; the breeze became steady; the rain-squalls ceased; the sky became clear. We are on the fair open sea! Let us make the most of it. Clear of the influence of land and of shoals, there is an honesty, a decorum about an ocean, that is highly to be respected. One can easily fancy that NEPTUNE in all the dignity of his personal presence is presiding there. Along-shore the regulation of affairs is entrusted to his understrappers, and they sometimes play the very devil in a tricky way; but when it 's himself who has hold of you, you know him and esteem him, I assure you. It is a testy, headstrong old official who has charge of the tepid, hissing, snake-gliding portion of his dominions which we have just left. However, let us not get back to it.

'DUMP had got over his sea-sickness, and had 'stowed away' a meal; he felt that something had been achieved; in short, he felt well; and like most green-horns in this stage of their voyagings, he was determined to appreciate the romance of his situation. It is only once, and alas! for a very short period *then*, that people who follow the sea are able to indulge in such an hallucination. DUMP was having his turn. He looked upon the heaving expanse of waters; cast his eyes along the well-defined edge, where sky and water meet, and muttered to himself sentiments which two days before it would have nauseated him barely to have thought of: 'There is something grand,' said he, 'in these mighty billows; something sublime in this immensity of uninterrupted space!' Something grand in Lynnhaven oysters, sublime in a Norfolk green goose!' said BOGEE, who was at his elbow. 'I 'll tell you what, Mr. DUMP, by the time you 've seen as many of these 'mighty billows,' as much of this 'immensity of uninterrupted space' as I have; by the time you 've left your home for as many three years' cruises; been borne here and carried there; frozen with cold and melted with heat; tossed in a calm and blown out of your seven senses in a hurricane; you 'll think salt water a very fine place for commerce and fish, and all that sort of thing; and at Pensacola, where the crows take to the sea for a living, very good for *them;* but let me assure you that for a reasonable being it 's one of the most stupid and unprofitable occupations in the world, this going to sea.' 'But, Mr. BOGEE,' said DUMP, in a deprecatory tone, for it was rather a damper on the new-born buoyancy of feeling which was succeeding the settling of his stomach, to hear one of the undoubted denizens of this field of his romance speak in such a matter-of-fact style on a subject upon which he was disposed to be so enthusiastic; 'but, Mr. BOGEE, if it 's so bad, why do n't you resign?' 'Resign the d — l!' ejaculated BOGEE.

. . . . . .

'THAT day, the weather being fair, and a bottle of fine East-India Madeira having gone the rounds, become a marine, and been succeeded by another of the same sort, there was a look of cheerful coziness and satisfaction visible in the countenances of all hands at the mess-table. TODDLINGS had charge of the deck, so that SQUILGEE and BOGEE were below at dinner. 'SQUILGEE,' said BOGEE, sententiously, 'give us a yarn.' 'Oh yes! do, Mr. SQUILGEE,' exclaimed DUMP; 'I 've heard so much about sailor-yarns, I would like to listen to one.' 'Let 's have it,' said the senior PILLS. 'Well, here goes; but, Mr. DUMP, I 'm afraid I can 't gratify your wishes on this occasion; and Mr. BOGEE, as you will figure extensively in what I 'm about to relate, I beg to engage your particular attention to my story, which we will style ' *The Adventures of a Night.*'' 'Never mind your preface,' replied BOGEE; 'drive on with your yarn.' So SQUILGEE commenced: 'It was a calm, clear winter's night in 18 —, that BOGEE and myself crossed the ferry into Brooklyn, with the intention of going on board the receiving-ship, where we were domiciliated at that time. We had just left a dinner-party at the old City-Hotel, where there had been something more than a moderate quantity of wine drank, and quite a number of the convivialists left under the table. Among our party were COTTREL, BOGEE and your humble servant. The former got into one of his obstinate fits, and would not accompany us; so we were obliged to leave him.

'The moonlight was shining upon the beaten snow, and the intense cold caused our ears and noses to tingle again, as we walked toward the yard. Going at a brisk pace we soon came in sight of the gate, having reached that delectable portion of Brooklyn which is known to the naval world under the title of 'Irish-Town.'

''Deuced lucky for us, is n't it, SQUILGEE, that there is no seven-bell regulation on board the Guardo? I often feel a wish to have myself called of a morning, for no other reason but to vent my spleen against the intruder on my repose; to ask him how he *dare* disturb a gentleman at such an unseasonable hour; to curse him heartily, and end by ejecting him; not forcibly, for that would require me to leave my warm bed, a thing not to be done for a light cause on these cold mornings; but I would most vehemently threaten to do so.' 'You are thinking of old 'JINGLE' and his rules,' said I, laughing; 'there was no laying-in after hours on board the Panther. However, let us make the most of our immunities, for this night at least. It must be nearly morning, and there is rather too much dissipation in the idea of playing the owl for two nights in succession. The Colonel and his party may find their prospect of a bed in the city a bad one; it is later than we any of us thought for.'

'What a good joke if they should have their walk for nothing, and be obliged to return, after all! What's the countersign?'

''Hanged if I know! Have n't you got it?'

''I? No; that confounded fellow COTTREL went for it to the first Luff., and d—n him! he has forgotten to give it to us. Little has *he* to care, however, for I suppose that by this time he is warm in bed at the 'City.' LORD, SQUILGEE! how my teeth chatter! What shall we do, now? We can't climb the wall, can we?'

''I had rather not run the risk to-night, for to tell the truth, my breeches are so infernally tight that it would be a clew-up and a furl with them if I were to make the attempt. We had better turn back and try to get into some tavern.'

''I am decidedly for scaling the battlements, breeches or no breeches!' said BOGEE, merrily. 'You may go back, if you like; but *I* go over the wall—that's certain! You had better try it too, man. I know an excellent point for an escalade, at the long shed. There is no sentry posted in that neighborhood; the coast is all clear, and there is a good coal-fire and a comfortable cot awaiting you on board the Guardo. Come on, man!—only think what an uncomfortable walk you 'll have down this dreary street! Come on! Sacrifice your unmentionables to your comfort.'

''Really, BOGEE, I do not feel myself competent to the attempt. You seek your lodgings after your plan, and I after mine. Good night!'

''Well, an obstinate man must have his way. A fine laugh we 'll have at you though, when you come wading through the drift to the ship! Good night!'

'BOGEE walked briskly off for the scene of his intended exploit, and I turned to retrace the dreary road we had just travelled so bootlessly, cursing the carelessness we had exhibited, for both of us knew the utter hopelessness of gaining admission into the Navy-Yard without the 'open sesame.' The jingling of the sleigh-bells had long ceased ; a few dark and dirty-looking houses gloomed at intervals along the unlighted way ; and an old starved horse was the only living creature visible in the whole route. Presently however I heard some one talking behind me ; and looking back, I discovered a solitary individual emerging from a cross-road into the street. A second look told me it was COTTREL ; and as there was no one with him, I at once concluded that the wine he had drunk was at work within him, and that he was conversing with himself for want of better company. He paid no attention to me ; but seeing the half-dead horse I had passed, walked up to him with an air of no small concern. 'Ah! old fellow!' said he, 'you have no doubt been toiling all day in harness, dragging the bloody meat of some equally bloody butcher, or the flour-covered bread of some floury baker; or perhaps you have been carting oysters from the ferry to glut the palates of greedy epicures? A milk-man's horse you are not, for they are sleek and well-fed ; at all events, you are *somebody's* horse ; that I think even *you* will not dispute, indignant as you must feel at the man who, after working you all day, has turned you loose at evening. ' all alone for to die !' '

'This last part he sang in a regular 'forecastle whine ; then seizing the unresisting animal by the mane, he continued: 'But droop not, old friend! — here is one who will devote himself to your comfort, hoping thereby to deface from your memory the many wrongs his race have rendered to your's. I will be your friend ; you shan't suffer any longer, old fellow! You shall go with me ; you shall have lodging, food, raiment and a coal-fire. I'll stick to you like a brother, my old friend! Come with me. Ay, splash away — I will not be angry ; but d — n you! do n't tread on my toes! So, come on ; forgive my harshness ; 'forget and forgive!''

''Who comes there?' shouted the sentry at the gate.

''Friend and company,' was COTTREL's reply.

''Stand, company! Advance friend, and give the countersign!'

''One moment, my dear friend,' said COTTREL, apologetically, to his four-legged companion ; and then advancing, gave the countersign, 'Charity,' so loud that it reached my ears.

''Countersign's correct ; pass, 'friend and company,'' said the sentry, coming to a stiff shoulder-arms ; and the lamp-light showed that he did not move a muscle of his countenance as the singularly-assorted pair entered the gate and passed on ; COTTREL saying to the horse, ''Charity,' you see, is the order of the day here ; 'Charity' lets you in at the gate, and 'Charity' shall furnish you with a bottle of ale and a cold collation.'

'I immediately used the countersign thus oddly thrown in my way, and passing by the building in which were temporarily situated the office of the commodore and an apartment used by the officer of the guard, (who was then in bed in a room above,) I perceived that COTTREL had taken the liberty of entertaining his company in the latter, having no doubt chosen it from an idea of the difficulty of taking his friend over a frigate's gang-way ; beside which, the remains of a coal-fire was burning in the grate, and COTTREL appeared by his subsequent movements to know of several other advantages which this place possessed for the accommodation of the distinguished stranger ; for after replenishing the fire, he produced a candle, and lighting it, went to a small closet and brought forth a loaf of bread, a bottle containing some drinkable or other, several' cold cuts,' and a large boiled lobster ; the neglected lunch of the rightful proprietor of the place. The horse stared sleepily at the light, yet with no sign of dissatisfaction ; he seemed rather to be well pleased with so very superior a specimen of stabling. COTTREL gave him a huge slice of bread, which he munched with infinite gusto.

'Humph! how d' ye like it, old boy? Is n't it prime? Do you use butter Sherry or Madeira? Immaterial, eh? Well enough that it is so, too, for devil the taste of either has old SHAKINGS got here; but here's brandy; a small touch of this won't hurt you after your walk. By-the-by, you must be cold there about your quar ter-galleries, for I see you can't get in, altogether; you ain't good stowage, my friend but here, *this* will serve your turn.' And as he spoke, he took down the watch-offi cer's cloak and placed it gently on the hinder-extremities of his quadrupedal guest There was a split in the back part of the garment, as was the fashion at that time and through this the — the — dorsal termination of the animal protruded, and thus supported it in its place.

'All comfortable and snug now? Take a lobster? No dressing, though; you must excuse *that*, my dear BUCEPHALUS. Cut of veal, eh? Here's more bread Well done! By the ugly phiz on the Jezabel's cat-head!' he exclaimed, in great glee, as the starved creature devoured whatever was handed him; 'who'll say you have n't a a taste for dainties as well as a human ——'

'The harangue was cut short; for the incautious tone which COTTREL had by this time assumed, together with the stamping of his four-legged friend, who liking the treatment he was meeting with began to make himself quite at home, had the effect of breaking the deep slumbers of the tired watch-officer, who was heard hastily de scending the stair-case. His head peered through one door at the same instant the COTTREL, having extinguished the light at the first alarm, made his exit through the other, between the legs of the horse.

'Who's this? — the devil! — hell-o! — what does this mean!' shouted the officer 'get out, you d — d rascal! — out with you!' Then came a sound as of a chair in the act of being broken over some object of tolerable solidity; the heavy irregular stamp of the horse, as he endeavored to back out of the presence, '*sélon les regles de cour;* and presently COTTREL's late guest made his appearance, flying toward the gate with the watch-cloak dangling about his heels. Not caring to be identified in any manner with the affair, I hurried on board, expecting to meet the triumphant BOGEE, but his cot was empty, and he was not in the ward-room which we then occupied as our berth. COTTREL came on board just as I was addressing myself to sleep, and made directly up to me, as I had left a light on a camp-stool near the head of my cot, for the convenience of blowing out.

'Well, SQUILGEE, my man, just turned in? I thought you were fast long ago in the arms of MURPHY, as the Irish mate used to say, on board the Bull-Dog.'

'But what's the matter with you?' I asked; 'you look confoundedly out of sorts Colonel —— thought you were going over to the city to sleep.'

'Yes, but you see I met with a friend, got into a scrape on his account, and had to run for it; so, as you may perceive with half an eye, here I am.'

'I wanted sleep too much to encourage COTTREL's conversational powers by ex plaining how much I had seen, and was therefore silent on the subject. I slept until nearly eleven the next day, notwithstanding the sky-larking of some twenty mid shipmen who had been up in the ward-room two or three hours before, and who, as all first lieutenants in the service will bear me witness, are not the most quiet set of young gentlemen in the world. At the moment I awoke they were around BOGEE and commenting on a narrative he was giving, by immoderate fits of laughter. A soon as I was dressed I joined the group. 'Avoid thee!' exclaimed BOGEE, as I approached, 'thou base deserter of thy comrade in the hour of trial!'

'At all events,' said I, 'I reached the rendezvous before you; but in what particular way did you amuse yourself among the snow-drifts last night?'

'"I am thinking that I was rather more amusing than amused,' he replied. In fact, it came near being any thing but an amusing matter to my old ship-mate; and nothing, to use his own paraphrase of DIBDIN's words, but 'the sweet little cherub that sits up aloft, to keep watch on the fate of bad reefers,' saved him from being reported to the Department. It seemed that after leaving me he made directly for the 'excellent point for an escalade' which he mentioned. All was quiet when he reached it; and without farther ado he mounted the 'long shed,' and was proceeding exultingly to the 'consummation' of a warm bed, 'so devoutly to be wished' for in his case, when the measured tramp of the 'relief' was heard, apparently approaching that part of the yard. 'Strange, too!' thought BOGEE; 'but lie low; they'll be past in a moment.' The fates were against him in this particular, however; for to his utter horror and surprise, a voice directly under where he was crouching gave the challenge and was answered by the relief. A sentry had been but that day posted there. The new man was left to walk his weary round, and the one relieved was marched off on an airy promenade around the yard for the purpose of picking up others who like himself were to be 'relieved.'

'Excellent! beautiful! fine!' internally ejaculated the mid., intending thereby to be sarcastic with himself for his want of foresight; 'but 'faint heart never won fair lady,' and if I give up, may I be d — d!' He thought too of the laugh that would be had at his expense, and this determined him to get into the yard, sentry or no sentry. Creeping cautiously to the edge of the shed, he looked down upon the unconscious soldier. The relief was out of sight; there was not a sound to be heard except the footsteps of the man beneath him; who for his part, as he walked to and fro in the moonlight, little thinking that there was any human eye upon him, cut up a variety of diverting antics. He would hum a short tune, or whistle a stave, and anon would break into a regular shuffle; then he amused himself by kicking the little clumps of snow from his path, in the most disdainful manner; then he would stretch himself with a yawn, and sigh, and effect the most singular contortion of his limbs. At last he leaned his musket against the building, and using his arms as the fabled phœnix was supposed to use her wings, endeavored to infuse warmth into his body. 'Oh!' thought BOGEE, 'if I could but reach that musket!' The musket was out of his reach, however, and the sentry soon resumed it. He thought at first of giving him a trial of the supernatural; but a moment's reflection told him that playing the ghost would bring matters to a crisis just as probable to take a turn against him as in his favor; it would depend altogether on the amount of superstition with which his intended subject might be endowed, and would be certain to call attention to himself; which, if his attempt failed, would as surely defeat farther proceedings. By this time the marine had begun his regular pace, taking the whole length of the shed in his walk. Now at one end of this shed was a tree growing in the yard, but partly concealed by the building, against and over which grew some of its branches. By means of this tree BOGEE had proposed to reach the ground inside; for the shed, although low on the outside, and easily mounted by means of small buildings and fences placed against it, presented in front an elevation of some twenty-five feet, exposed to the view of the sentinel, and possessed of no conveniences for descending. He determined to watch his opportunity, when the man was at the opposite end, and then getting down, run along the wall which for some distance was screened by the projection. If he escaped the notice of the sentry at the first turn, he was quite certain of making good his undertaking ; for a short run would bring him to a set of sheds and the ship-houses, entirely clear of all question. Accordingly, rolling over and over, in order to avoid the creaking of the snow under his foot-steps, and to prevent his shadow from being seen on the ground underneath, he at length reached the desired spot, just as the marine turned to retrace his steps from the same point. 'Now or never !' said he ; and holding on to the branches, he swung into the body of the tree and commenced his descent, 'bear-fashion.' 'Hurra !' said he to himself; 'here goes by the run, like a spanker out-haul in a squall !' and he was slipping down with no easy velocity, when a dry limb, the presence of which he had not observed, or had forgotten, brought him up with a crash.

'' Who comes there !' shouted the sentry, running to the spot, and placing his shining bayonet in close proximity with that portion of the human person which touches the chair when in a sitting posture.

'' Officer,' returned the 'treed' individual, hugging the tree, and looking down as well as he could, to ascertain the situation of matters.

'' Advance, officer, and give the countersign !'

'' Well, take your infernal bayonet from under me, and I will advance ; but really, the countersign is one of those few things in the way of information which I regret to say I can't impart to you.'

'' You see, I thought that by a little coolness and what is termed in the vernacular 'high dick,' it was possible for me to get off; meanwhile I was hugging the tree bear-fashion. The sentry seemed to have a proper conception of my condition, and to be aware that one could not consistently, at least not comfortably, descend while his bayonet held that relative position in regard to one's body ; so he withdrew a short distance, keeping his musket at a charge. As soon as the ground was reached, 'Sentry,' said I, how late is it ?' 'About three, Sir,' he replied. 'Cold.' 'Yes, Sir.' Which do you think is the shortest way to the Guardo ?' 'That way, down by the office ; but I can't let you go till the relief comes round, Sir.' 'The d — l you can't! I 'm going to my own ship, and I'm inside the yard.' 'Yes, Sir ; but I saw you up in the tree.' 'Poh ! that be shot ! I was only roosting there.' 'Ah ! well, Sir ; in course you have a right to roost where you please ; but really I do n't think you could have been very comfortable, playing fowl up there of a cold night like this.' 'Oh ! yes, very ; I like it for the air. Sentry, good night, and be more particular in future about your dancing.' 'Ho ! ho ! ho ! — ha ! ha ! ha ! Good night, Sir !' 'And thus,' said Bogee, ' I got off, though I have scarcely told you half that occurred ' for reasons why.' 'Squilgee' adds in a note to the foregoing : 'It is to be borne in mind, that frolics such as are here described are of rare occurrence now. A different tone prevails in the service at the present day. Those I have attempted to figure forth ' came off,' like ' the days when we went blackberrying, ' a long time ago.' '

—

Thus much for one taste of '*Lobscouse ;*' a term, by-the-by, which it may not be amiss to say, indicates a sort of *Ollapodrida*, made of sea-biscuit, hung-beef, potatoes, etc., a favorite ' stew' with seamen. There is another rich dish in preparation for the palates of our friends, which will be served up ' smoking-hot' hereafter, with all proper condiments and seasoning.

'MY FIRST LOVE:' BY THE LATE WILLIS GAYLORD CLARK. — We little thought ever again to have the pleasure of handing to the printer an unpublished article in the hand-writing of the lamented 'OLLAPOD;' but the following sketch, lately found mislaid in a pacquet of his letters, has never before appeared, and is placed in type from his own manuscript. We can call to mind no prose subsection of the 'Ollapodiana' papers of superior freshness, or more replete with unstudied grace and beauty.

MY FIRST LOVE.

—— 'the thochts of by-gone years
Still fling their shadows o'er my path,
And blind my een wi' tears:
They blind my een wi' saut, saut tears,
And sair and sick I pine,
As memory bringeth to my view
The blithe blinks o' Lang-Syne.'   MOTHERWELL.

GENTLE READER, do n't be frightened. I am not going to inflict upon you a catalogue of sighs and tears, and the everlasting concomitants of 'raven tresses' and 'bright eyes,' and all that forlorn sort of thing, in which your regular tale-wright deals withal. I feel in a retrospective mood this afternoon, as I sit wielding my gray goose quill by an open window near my table, and which looketh toward the west : the sun is rolling down behind the mountains in the distance ; and I can peer over the roofs of the city, beyond the river, and see his radiant smiles quivering above a long sweep of waving foliage, over which, against an amber sky, there are long bars of beautiful clouds, of various shapes and sizes, and in lots to suit observers ; floating along, turning their gay borders to the breeze, and apparently rejoicing in the proud thought that there is nothing so brilliant as they. Never do I look upon such a scene, but I think of the days beyond the flood of time ; of the vernal shores of boyhood and youth, that I have left forever ; and from which even Memory herself, that solemn and sad antiquarian, hath scarcely a flower left in her hand. Many and sober are the reflections which a glance at the evening west can awaken in my mind. Friends that are distant and hopes that are dead, never more to be revived with the freshness wherewith they shone of yore ; ambition that was thwarted, confidence betrayed, impressions changed, fantasies dissolved — these are a few of the associations with which I gaze upon the regions of the setting sun. I think how many visions that were as radiant as that fiery sphere have wrapped themselves in darkness and made the clouds their pavilion ; how the gorgeous creations have disappeared like the golden exhalations of the dawn or the dews of the evening, leaving the thoroughfare over which I was passing more arid and dreary.

Now some clever reader, who fancies that fair words butter no parsnips, and who is fond of incident, will be likely to ask, what all the preceding matter has to do with my first love ? Nothing, in particular, my good friend ; it is only a sort of overture to that delicious symphony of details which I shall soon arrange under thine eye, on these pages. It is my wish to give a prelusive quaver, a delectable cadence or two, before I give way to that narrative flood of reminiscence, which will bear thee *nolens volens* onward over its bosom, and marvellously endanger thy sensibilities, if indeed thou art a christian soul, and thy heart be fashioned of penetrable matériel.

I take it of course, beloved reader, that you have been to school. Did you ever experience any thing, in all your days, so sweet as Saturday afternoon, when the school was kept only half-a-day, and you could go off, with a few boon good friends, gathering strawberries in the fields, or filling your dinner-basket with hedge-blackberries that grew along the borders of the meadows, and which you could take home and eat with white bread and sweetest cream? Oh! delicious are those days to my recollection! I feel at this moment a kind of juiciness about the throat, simply from their remembrance

Well, it was in one of these simple excursions that my *first love* began. It was my last summer at school. I was fifteen; a good-looking boy then, with rosy cheeks, collar open, tied with a black ribbon, and fastened below with a brooch which my father, honest man, gave my mother in *their* first wooing. I was graceful enough for a country lad, and somehow or other had contrived, during the winter previous, to make myself the first among the boys in the estimation of the girls, at the evening weekly spelling-schools; eras in the young scholar's existence, where if he be a wight of parts he cannot fail to make his best qualities known.

It was on one of those very Saturday afternoons I speak of, that I first discovered the power of that blear-eyed urchin CUPID in my soul. JULIA MAY, the companion of my ramble, was one of those sweet capricious creatures that you cannot describe. I know of no word which can express her peculiar loveliness. She was young, and what the Irish call *streelish*, being scarcely fourteen years old. She was *petite* in form; but her hair parted so richly on her forehead, and clung with such bright brown lustre about her downy, fruit-like cheeks; her eyes were of such melting blue, Heaven's own color; her lips so ripe, so freshly red, and her smile so sweet, that my heart was gone into her keeping almost as soon as we knew each other. Our acquaintance began in the winter, at one of those private little costumeless exhibitions of theatricals, with which country teachers sometimes indulge their scholars. The teacher, (he boarded with my father in the district, and I was his favorite,) knew my predilection for JULIA, and he cast us in one of those simple dialogues containing only two interlocutors. It was a wooing piece; we played it to perfection; and there our friendship, cordial and trusting, began. We shared in the triumph which our endeavors produced, and we regarded each other the more fondly that our triumph was in unison.

One Saturday, in June, the school was dismissed at noon; and as it was a granted holiday, and we had the leave of both of our parents, JULIA MAY and I wandered off together, on a visit to my cousin LUCY's, nearly of JULIA's age, who was going to give a strawberry-party; namely, invite a few of her friends, each with his own cup or basket, to stray into some of the broad meadows of her father, and after all had filled their vessels, meet in the middle of the largest meadow, by the side of a clear stream, and underneath the shade of a wide beech along whose fantastic roots it ran. There, as was the custom, the lad and the lass who filled their vessels the soonest were wont to repair, and await the coming together of the bright young company to which they belonged.

I recollect, as if it were but yesterday, the kindling delight with which we set off over the green fields to my cousin's. We were alone, and we strayed along through the verdant grass, her white and soft little hand clasped in the meanwhile in mine. With what pleasure did I let down the bars of every 'lot,' and assist her over the stile! We did not hurry; we felt that the sense of existence in each other's company was pleasure sufficient : hope was swallowed up in present fruition. No stormy desires nor withering passions stained our spontaneous affection : we knew that each loved and was beloved, though no confession had been made. That was a happy time, reader, and I am sure I never shall witness its like again. When you have read my whole story, you will think with me.

We reached my cousin's just as the assembled company of young folks were on the point of setting out *en masse* upon their expedition. These particulars may be dry ; but my good friend, now honoring me with a perusal, we were both children once ; and I have doubts about the purity of his heart who cannot look back with delight upon the dreams of his earlier years. They formed the morning of our endless existence ; they had their griefs, but they were transient ; and they were full-fraught with raptures which no success nor joy of manhood can parallel ; for then the heart was a novel, and its transports were new, although too bright to endure:

> ' WHAT though those days return no more ?
>   Their sweet *remembrance* is not vain,
> For Heaven is waiting to restore
>   The childhood of the soul again !'

And thus ends this little record of the heart. It was but the simple precursor of a story which would have appeared in these pages had not the writer been early called to renew the childhood of his soul in a ' better land.'

THE DRAMA: PARK THEATRE. — This establishment was reöpened for the season on Monday the seventeenth ultimo, with Mr. COLLINS, an Irish actor new to the American boards, but whose reputation had preceded his début in the United States. We hardly ever saw, in any other hands than the lamented POWER, a richer performance than his *McShane* and *Teddy the Tiler*. Both were rendered to the life, and the effect was irresistible. Mr. COLLINS possesses a good gentlemanly brogue, a humorous countenance, and a happy delivery. His characters are portraits, not caricatures ; inferior certainly to those of his great prototype, that consummate comedian, to whom he bears that resemblance which a similarity of genius cannot fail to create. His laugh is infectious, and he always appears in the best possible humor with himself and the audience. Mr. COLLINS too has acquired considerable celebrity as a vocalist, and gives Irish melodies in a most delightful style. He has a fine and flexible voice, with considerable knowledge and execution ; sings strictly in tune ; and his songs are always encored. The success of Mr. COLLINS with the New-York public has been complete ; laughter and enthusiastic applause nightly crown his efforts ; yet a few presses have seemed disposed to treat him with harshness, and we fear injustice. *Unbiassed* criticism is of service both to the actor and the public, and cannot fail of having due weight on all occasions. But it often happens, we apprehend, that under the mask of criticism, personal antipathies are introduced, intended to destroy a man's reputation and prospects in life, by exposing him to the petty shafts of envy and the torture of caprice. An actor like Mr. COLLINS, who from long experience and painful apprenticeship has attained a professional respectability, may feel assured of the protection of the public. The healthy impulse which was given last season toward a wholesome reformation of the drama, we are glad to find is to be carried out with an earnest spirit in the production of ' King John' and ' Macbeth.' Every true lover of the drama must wish the manager success in his arduous undertaking.

GOSSIP WITH READERS AND CORRESPONDENTS. — Looking the other day at MR. BELDEN's extraordinary ' Model of New-York,' (that most faithful ' picture in little' of our great metropolis,) and admiring the admirable proportion which has been so accurately preserved in every feature of the vast miniature city, we were irresistibly led to think of *Gulliver in Lilliput.* Indeed, it required nothing but a thousand or two diminutive ' humans' bustling through the little streets, to have made the illusion complete. And speaking of GULLIVER, reader, did you ever think of the great genius displayed in the history of that veracious gentleman, and the narrative of his adventures in Lilliput and Brobdignag, especially the former ? Could any thing be more felicitous than the accuracy with which all his proportions are preserved, and the manner in which his mind conforms to the dimensions of every thing around him? With what solemnity he talks of the stately trees in His Majesty's park at Lilliput, the tops of some of which he could hardly grasp with his clenched hand ; and with what becoming admiration he celebrates the prodigious leap of one of the imperial huntsmen over his foot, ' shoe and all !' Nothing surely could be more inimitable than the imperceptible mode by which he assimilates our ideas of proportion to those of his little people. Observe the perfection of the scale by which his personal wants are graduated by the Lilliputians. After his measure had been taken by the help of a quadrant, three hundred tailors were ordered to make him a suit of clothes ; he had the tallow of three hundred cows to grease his boots ; and his supply of meat and drink, established by an accurate measurement of his corporeal capacity, was exactly sufficient for the support of seventeen hundred and twenty-four Lilliputians. The beef furnished him, he tells us, was excellent ; and often a sirloin would be so large that he was forced to make three bites of it. The poultry to be sure was ' not much to speak of,' although he once saw a cook plucking a chicken that was considerably larger than a fly. When he first visited the Emperor at his palace, (which was surrounded by an impregnable wall more than two feet in height,) His Majesty had his sword in his hand to defend himself if the ' Man-Mountain' should chance to break loose. It was a terrific blade, nearly three inches in length. The voice of the great potentate who wielded it, although shrill, was yet very clear and articulate, for the ' Man-Mountain' could distinctly hear it when he stood up. What a sensation was created among the little folk, when by means of pullies they drew from the deep Charybdis of his watch-fob the ' prodigious engine,' which made ' a loud and incessant noise like that of a water-mill !' How astounded were they when they climbed by the aid of ladders over the side of his snuff-box, and on descending to the bottom, found themselves ' mid-leg deep in a sort of dust' that made them well-nigh explode with sneezing ! GULLIVER's own impressions, on the other hand, were equally vivid at seeing a daring rope-dancer sporting upon a tight-rope as big as a thread, and full six inches from the floor, and a young girl threading an invisible needle with invisible silk. What *could* be more ridiculous than the manner in which the ' Man-Mountain' repels the slander that he had been guilty of too great familiarity with the Lilliputian treasurer's wife, whom Scandal had reputed as having once come privately to his lodgings ? ' It was not so ; to be sure, he had sometimes had her in his hand, and had frequently lifted her carriage upon his table, around which the coachman had driven while he sat looking at the occupants ; but she had always on such occasions two or three companions with her. No ; he defied any informer to prove that he was ever guilty of any improper conduct with the treasurer's wife !' It must have been rather a difficult matter for SWIFT, when he had brought GULLIVER into Brobdignag, to reverse entirely the order of his narrative ; yet nothing could be more successfully accomplished. The ' Man-Mountain' becomes himself a Lilliputian the moment he sees a Brobdignagian, as tall as an ordinary church-steeple, advancing toward him, ten yards at a stride. Accidentally discovering him, he takes him up by the middle from behind, as if afraid that he would scratch or bite him, and brings him within three yards of his eyes, that he may examine him more closely ; then takes him home ; places him on a table about thirty feet high from the floor, and scrutinizes him minutely. His great captor's features, as he looked up at him at a distance of sixty feet, appeared very well proportioned. He was much amused with a little dim-sighted old man, scarcely more than forty feet high, who put on spectacles to examine him critically. 'His eyes appeared like a full moon shining into a chamber at two great round windows.' The ladies of the court were much delighted with him, and one of them carried him around to exhibit to her friends, covering him up, to prevent his escape, with a fine white handkerchief, ' larger and coarser than the main-sail of a ship.' The habits of the Brobdignagians were very disgusting to him. He could not ' abide' to see them eat ; craunching with a loud noise the wings of larks that were nine times larger than English turkeys, bolting huge pieces of bread containing at least three twelve-penny loaves, and drinking out of large vessels more than a hogshead at a draught. The knives were twice as long as a scythe, and set strait upon the handle, and the forks, spoons, etc., were in proportion. When ten or a dozen of these enormous knives and forks were lifted up together, by ranks of voracious eaters at a table, it was a sight terrible to behold. The annoyances of the reduced ' Man-Mountain' were neither few nor small. Flies, larger than ravens, alighted upon his food and face, leaving behind them that viscous matter which naturalists tell us enable them to walk with their feet upward upon a coiling ; the children plagued him ; one little boy, not more than twenty feet high, came near knocking his brains out with a hazel-nut as large as a pumpkin ; another mischievously dropped him into a silver bowl or circular vat of cream, where if he had not been an expert swimmer he must inevitably have perished ; moreover, on one occasion a dog, to his great terror, took him up in his mouth while walking in the garden, and ran with him strait to his master, wagging his tail all the way ; fortunately the animal bore him between his teeth so gently that he neither hurt him nor tore his clothes. It is evident however that these *désegramens* must have soured the ci-devant ' Man-Mountain' against Brobdignag, and caused him to underrate its attractions. Something of this feeling no doubt induced his depreciating estimate of the tower of the chief temple : ' It greatly disappointed me. It was not above three thousand feet high, at the outside ; and this is not equal in proportion to Salisbury steeple.' It requires a ' trusting spirit' to read GULLIVER aright. He seems himself to have been aware of the necessity of this ; for he tells us distinctly that a ' severe critic of his pages might think that he had enlarged a little, as travellers are often suspected to do ;' but he repels the imputation in his own case with becoming indignation. · · · THE sadly self-contemplated death of the late WILLIAM M. PRICE has created a profound sensation in this community. A lawyer of eminence, widely known for so many years not only for his rare legal endowments and especially for his distinguished eloquence, but also for the surpassing urbanity of his manners ; an urbanity which sprung from the natural kindness of a warm heart ; he has passed from among us, leaving behind him the regretful remembrances of all who best knew

him and his eventful history.   Those who have heard in past years the eloquent ex-
ordium fall in silvery tones from his lips at the bar ; who have seen him in better
days the chief adornment of the social board ; who have known his genius and
tested his heart ; while they lament his loss, will look with a lenient eye upon his sur-
render at last to a resistless despair.   With his mental powers frozen to indifference,
his heart ossified with melancholy forebodings, his soul shrouded in clouds of gloom,
no consolation could break the death-like calm, no love warm the pent-up heart ; no
sunbeam dispel the cloud.   Think of this, all ye who condemn, and drop a tear to
the memory of one whose own heart was seldom untouched by the wants or the
afflictions of his fellow-men. . . .   WE recognize in the following the hand-writing of
the correspondent who favored us with a pleasant poetical epistle from the same wa-
tering-place last season :

THE LAY OF VAN DAWDLE.

WHERE SHARON'S bubbling waters
  In sulphurous streams arise,
And Gotham's fair-haired daughters
  Employ their witching eyes ;
Where Messrs. LANDONS cater
  For country appetites,
Their omelettes and their batter
  Puddings and other bites ;
Where on the long piazza
  Beaux and their loved ones walk,
And every couple has a
  Most sentimental talk ;
Where Mr. HARRIS drives the
  Canajoharie stage,
And wholesome air revives the
  Vitality of age ;
Where tambourine and jaw-bones
  At eve invite to dance,
And BOWEN'S ancient raw-bones
  At morn are wont to prance ;

Where every ancient sinner
  And every time-worn dame,
In brimstone before dinner
  Renews life's flickering flame ;
Where maidens seek for husbands,
  And bachelors for wives,
And the lover of the picturesque
  To Cherry Valley drives ;
Where easy indolence maintains
  Its undisputed sway,
And the gouty man regains
  His trotters for a day ;
Where the bowling-alley's balls
  And the billiard table's cue,
And strolling to the falls
  Employ the restless few ;
There may I meet again
  With thee, my CAROLINE,
And pouring forth my sweetest strain,
  Essay to make thee mine !

THAT most 'reverend' satirist, DEAN SWIFT, in the following passage has hit off,
even better than ' PUNCH' in ' The Seaman's Pipe, or the Battle and the Breeze,' the
minute accounts of storms and naval manœuvres, so common in the writings of lite-
rary 'land-lubbers' in our own day.   ' The sea-terms,' says his editor, ' are put to-
gether at random, but in such accurate imitation of the technicalities of the art, that
seamen have been known to work hard to attain the proper meaning of them :'

'FINDING it was likely to overblow, we took in our sprit-sail and stood by to hand the fore-sail ;
but making foul weather, we looked the guns were all fast, and handed the mizzen.   The ship lay
very broad off, so we thought it better spooning before the sea than trying or hulling.   We reefed
the fore-sail and set him, and hauled aft the fore-sheet ; the helm was hard a-weather, for the ship
was making a little water.   But she wore bravely.   We belayed the fore down-haul ; but the sail was
split, and we handed down the yard and got the sail into the ship and unbound all the things clear of
it.   It was a very fierce storm ; the sea broke strange and dangerous.   We hauled off upon the lan-
iard of the whip-staff and helped the man at the helm.   We would not get down our top-mast, but let
all stand, because she scudded before the sea very well ; and we knew that the top-mast being aloft
the ship was wholesomer, and made better way through the sea, seeing we had sea-room.   When the
storm was over, we set fore-sail and main-sail, and brought the ship to.   Then we set the mizzen,
main-top-sail, and the fore-top-sail.   Our course was east-north-east, the wind was at south-west.
We got the starboard-tacks aboard, and cast off our weather-braces and lifts ; we set-in the lee-
braces, and hauled forward by the weather-bowlings, and hauled them tight, and belayed them, and
hauled over the mizzen-tack to windward, and kept her full and by as near as she would lie.'

This description.is as vivid and clear as any thing that could be picked out of any
one of ' Professor' INGRAHAM's weekly ' novels' for the last five years. · · ·   MUCH
praise has been awarded by the press to the ' *City Article*' in our last number.   The
truth is, the public *will* have amusements, and all *classes* of the public, too ; and well-
conducted theatres are not objectionable on the score of morals.   Hear the late Rev.

SYDNEY SMITH on this very point : ' There is something in the word play-house which seems so closely connected in the minds of some people with sin and Satan, that it stands in their vocabulary for every species of abomination.   And yet why?   Where is every feeling more roused in favor of virtue, than at a good play?   Where is goodness so feelingly, so enthusiastically learned?   What so solemn as to see the excellent passions of the human heart called forth by a good actor, animated by a great poet? To hear SIDDONS repeat what SHAKSPEARE wrote!   To behold the child and his mother, the noble and the poor artisan, the monarch and his subjects, all ages and all ranks convulsed in one common passion, wrung with one common anguish, and with loud sobs and cries doing involuntary homage to the GOD that made their hearts! What wretched infatuation to interdict such amusements as these!   What a blessing that mankind can be allured from sensual gratification, and find relaxation and pleasure in such pursuits !   As to the spectacles of impropriety which are sometimes witnessed in parts of the theatre, such reasons apply in a much stronger degree to not driving along any of the great public streets of London after dark ; and if the virtue of well-educated young persons is made of such very frail materials, their best resource is a nunnery at once.   It is a very bad rule, however, never to quit a house for fear of catching cold.'   Would that the spirit which dictated the above was more prevalent on this side the Atlantic !   We should then hear less denunciation in certain quarters of the innocent exercise of dancing, and of the occasional perusal of entertaining works of fiction.   Who has not felt his frame invigorated and his spirits enlivened by hearty trippings on the 'light fantastic toe' to the pleasant airs of Scotland and Ireland, or our own African refrains?   ' Who does not derive a more distinct idea of the state of society and manners in Scotland from the Waverley novels than from the best of its historians? — of the condition of the Middle Ages from the single novel of ' Ivanhoe' than from all the volumes of HUME or HALLAM?'   And yet there are thousands of carpers among us, brim 'full of piety, go to,' who would never permit a dancing-step to be taken nor a novel to be read by a member of their families.   The reign of CANT is not yet over; but 'there 's a good time coming,' when it *will* be. . . .   ' BOOTES' must have been taking a lesson or two of ' ROSA MATILDA' in 'The Rejected Addresses.'   His ' *Stanzas to* ——' are quite in the sounding and utterly meaningless style of that ' benign cerulean.'   Hear him :

> ' ETERNAL glows the glassy morn,
> The rose is on the wave,
> The deadly dew-drop and the thorn
> To shiver or to save.

> ' Wide o'er the welkin sweeps the west,
> In summer beauty set,
> Impurpling on its azure vest
> That deathless word — forget!

> '' Forget' thee, silent sleeper ! — no!
> Though suns should cease to swell,
> Though raving winds and circling snows
> Their melting murmurs tell.

> ' Ah! blossom of the budding tree,
> Ah! glory of the grove,
> The saddened sinner sets me free,
> And wildly whispers — ' LOVE !'

' I 've had several pieces like the above,' writes the author, ' printed in the Ladies' Magazines ; and one editress told me that the lines I send you were ' very sweet.'   I think they are, myself.' . . . It was a sad thing just now, in the gay and busy Broadway, under a sunny, cloudless sky, with the healthful current of life coursing joyously in our own veins, to relinquish the feverish and wasted hand of a friend at whose door DEATH will call ere long, and walk with him through the Dark Valley. 'I am going,' said he, in a voice scarcely above a whisper; 'I am fast going; I shall leave all this;' and he turned his glassy eyes upward to the calm clear heavens, and waved his hand toward the busy crowds that rolled through the street or pattered with hasty steps upon the pave; 'I shall *soon* leave all this!' 'It is but too true!' thought we, as we turned to watch his slowly-receding footsteps:

> —— 'Yet a few days, and thee
> The all-beholding sun shall see no more
> In all his course; nor yet in the cold ground,
> Where thy pale form was laid, with many tears,
> Nor in the embrace of ocean, shall exist
> Thy image.'

May he be able to say with joy, when the Last Messenger shall await his departure, 'Come DEATH to this frail, failing, dying body! come the immortal life!' . . . THE last number of the London 'United Service Magazine' has a graphic description, from the pen of Sir J. E. ALEXANDER, of '*The Burning of the St. Louis Theatre at Quebec.*' There is an instance of 'the ruling passion' recorded in it which seems almost incredible. While the flames were rolling down from the top to the bottom of the stairs that led into the pit; while every head below seemed on fire, and the swollen tongues of the victims prevented an utterance of their awful agony, a woman was rescued 'who in the midst of her terror called out for her bonnet!' 'Where is my bonnet!' she cried, as the betrothed bride and her lover dropped into the arms of death together, the child sank into the fiery flood, and the aged wife and husband, arm-in-arm as in life's long journey, yielded up their spirits; '*Where is my bonnet?*' Did the lady find her hat? . . . MANY years ago a group of persons were assembled at a private house in a certain town in the northern part of Vermont, for the purpose of holding what they termed a 'religious conference.' The good old parson 'took the lead,' as was his custom, in the 'exercises' of the occasion. After the introductory hymn and prayer, he read the first chapter of the Second Epistle of PETER, and proceeded to expound the same for the edification of the brethren and the instruction of sinners. Having finished his exposition, he remarked, according to custom, that 'opportunity' would then be given to any of the brethren who might have any thing to communicate to the assembly. A long pause following this announcement, and no one offering to speak, the parson gave out a hymn. He then repeated the call upon the brethren to 'free their minds' if they had any thing to say. No one seemed disposed to respond, and the pause at last became not a little embarrassing; for the people were unaccustomed to 'silent meetings,' and considered as wasted all the time that was not employed either in speaking, reading, singing or praying. The parson's face began to exhibit signs of anxiety lest the meeting should come to a dead halt, and 'flat despair' brooded over the minds of the congregation. The good minister at length coaxingly remarked, that possibly his exposition of Scripture had not been altogether clear, and that some of the brethren might perhaps like to interrogate him, with a view to elicit farther explanations. If such were the fact, he hoped there would be no hesitation in putting the necessary questions. Another 'awful pause,' longer and more painful than that which preceded it, followed the parson's hint. Saints and sinners now became decidedly 'fidgety,' and the meeting was on the point of 'breaking up,' when a deacon of the church, who probably felt that the minister had a right in such an emergency to look to him for succor, after some slight bodily twichings indicating his embarrassment, broke the silence thus: 'There is one passage in the chapter read by our minister which his remarks did not make altogether plain to me. Perhaps others understood it, though I did not; but if there is no objection, I would like to ask a question.' The parson hoped he would do so without hesitation. The deacon, who was more remarkable for zeal than for grammatical or exegetical knowledge, being thus encouraged, remarked that the passage which he did not quite comprehend was contained in the tenth verse, where the Apostle said, 'Wherefore the rather, brethren, give diligence to make your calling and election sure.' He would ask what class of brethren was referred to by the term 'rather-brethren!' It was now the minister's turn to squirm. It was becoming evident that the gravity of his face could scarcely hold out against the exhibition of such ridiculous ignorance, when he found words to explain that 'he supposed the phrase 'rather' did not designate any particular class of brethren, but was simply an adverb,' etc. We think we should have explained that 'rather-brethren' were a species of 'so-so' religionists, whose stupidity as far exceeded their piety as their zeal was above their knowledge. · · · WE invite the reader's attention to the ' *Ghost-Story told by a Ghost*,' in preceding pages. There is something very mysterious in the manner in which the manuscript came into our possession. It was just at the late twilight of a hot and thundery afternoon, when the clerk was about rising to close the shutters of the publication-office, that a tall, thin man, clad in what seemed a long white linen loose-gown or robe, suddenly stood in the door-way, in strong relief against the fading western light. It was particularly remarked of the strange visitor, that

> —— 'from his cavernous eyes
> Pale flashes seemed to rise,
> As when the northern skies
> Gleam in December;'

and the clerk does not hesitate to aver that a feeling of indefinable awe came over him as the voiceless Figure 'made a long arm,' and extended toward him a manuscript, which he had no sooner taken, than the bearer, 'staying no question,' was gone. The manuscript itself was as remarkable as the manner of its acquisition. The sheets were glued together in several places by map-like patches of brown mould, which had almost obliterated the yellowish-green ink-marks, some of which were only deciphered with great difficulty; and there was an odor exhaled from the decaying leaves like the first cold air that issues from an old vault, newly opened. We have thought it proper to mention these circumstances, although we admit that they have little to do with the merits of the story in question, concerning which we have no desire to forestall 'public opinion.' · · · WHEN we took steamer at Piermont, on our return from the ever-memorable excursion to the trout-streams of Sullivan county, Sing-Sing, across the broad Tappaan-Zee, arrested for a moment our attention. The state-prison gleamed a white speck in the fervid sun; but what a world of sorrow was condensed in that little focus! We thought of the wretched horde there; of the coarse garb of shame and the coarser fare; of the long files, dingy with dust or 'begrimed with black,' sliding with grating step and locked feet to their narrow cells; of men dying in the hospital; the last look of the glazing eye resting upon bolts and bars and armed guards; without hope, without sympathy, without friends. Yet not altogether without friends; for there is a spirit abroad which will not rest until Humanity reigns triumphant in the management of American prisons. The good work has begun at Charlestown and is advancing at Sing-Sing. All honor to those who have engaged in this 'labor of love' for their erring, repentant brother MAN! ··· READER, 'did you ever see a wild-goose a-sailing on the ocean?' That is 'a sight,' no doubt; but it strikes us that the amphibious stalking Flamingos around the fountain at the Bowling-Green are objects even more to be admired. A Transcendental correspondent of ours, who had just been reading a 'chorus of spirits' in a new German play, improvised the following lines the other day, while looking through the rusty iron pickets at that bit of 'chaste practice' in fountain-architecture, the pile of rocks that rises in 'ragged majesty' within the pales:

NATURAL HISTORY: THE FLAMINGO.

FIRST VOICE.

'OH! tell me have you ever seen a long leg'd Flamingo?
Oh! tell me have you ever seen in the water him go?'

SECOND VOICE.

'Oh! yes, at Bowling-Green I've seen a long-leg'd Flamingo,
Oh! yes, at Bowling-Green I've seen in the water him go.'

FIRST VOICE

'Oh! tell me did you ever see a bird so funny stand-o,
When forth he from the water comes, and gets upon the land-o?'

SECOND VOICE.

'No! in my life I ne'er did see a bird so funny stand-o,
When forth he from the water comes and gets upon the land-o.'

FIRST VOICE.

'He has a leg some three feet long, or near it, so they say, Sir,
Stiff upon one alone he stands, t' other he stows away, Sir.'

SECOND VOICE.

'And what an ugly head he's got! I wonder that he'd wear it,
But rather *more* I wonder that his long slim neck can bear it.'

FIRST VOICE

'And think, this length of neck and legs, (no doubt they have their uses,)
Are members of a little frame, much smaller than a goose's!'

BOTH.

'Oh! is n't he a curious bird, that red long-leg'd Flamingo?
A water-bird, a gawky bird, a sing'lar bird, by jingo!'

THE first edition (five thousand copies) of Mr. COOPER's last work, 'The Redskins, or Indian and Injin,' was entirely exhausted before our last number, announcing its current publication, had reached its destination. This is an un-lying 'figury-fact,' which literally 'speaks volumes' in the author's favor; but it is a test which would hardly be applicable to the slow-moving elaborations of certain 'novelists' among us, whom one sometimes hears amusingly enough cited as possessing kindred power and repute. ··· WE regret to be obliged to record the death of Dr. HUGH M'LEAN, one of our oldest and most distinguished medical practitioners. As a physician he was preëminently skilful. He possessed great professional integrity and courtesy; was benevolent and humane; an accomplished musician, an instructive and entertaining companion, and a gentleman, in the best sense of that much-abused term. We had last the pleasure to meet him at a musical soirée, where his critical and appreciative comments gave an added zest to the entertainment. To adopt the language of our friend and correspondent, Dr. Francis, ' by the death of Dr. McLean we are called upon to mourn the loss of an enlightened, eminent and benevolent physician ; and our Knickerbocker associates of the *St. Nicholas Society* will unite in sorrow at the final departure of their senior medical adviser and friend, who lived respected and died lamented.' · · · ' Never go to France,' says Thomas Hood, ' unless you know the lingo ;' and he gives several amusing illustrations of the penalty to be incurred by a disregard of this injunction. The same advice will apply in the case of Italy, according to Dickens: ' There was a travelling party on board our steamer, of whom one member was very ill in the cabin next to mine, and being ill, was cross, and therefore declined to give up the dictionary, which he kept under his pillow ; thereby obliging his companions to come down to him constantly, to ask what was the Italian for a lump of sugar, a glass of brandy-and-water, ' what 's o'clock ?' and so forth ; which he always insisted on looking out, with his own sea-sick eyes, declining to entrust the book to any man alive.' ' Ignorance' was scarcely ' bliss' in this case, howsoever much folly there might have been in being ' wise.' · · · The lines assuming to be ' descriptive' of ' *The Battle of Resaca de la Palma*' are quite too sanguinary. They are revolting. It is not minutely-described horrors that convey the most forcible pictures of a battle-field. Accessories, naturally cited, are far more effective. Does our correspondent remember Campbell's account of his first sight of the 'circumstance' of war ; the returning dragoons wiping their bloody swords on the manes of their panting horses, after a victory ? Or did he ever hear the eloquent Hoffman depict the scene on board the President before her engagement ; when, the guns being ready, and the boldest ' holding his breath,' the saw-dust was spread upon the deck to drink the yet unshed blood ? These are not minutiæ, but ' additaments' of description far more striking and powerful. · · · The summer solstice is generally a period in which our artists disport themselves in the country. We found one of them the other day, Mr. Charles Jarvis, enjoying the pleasant groves and life-giving sea-air of Bath, on Long-Island. He was combining business with pleasure, however ; being engaged in painting several members of the family of a distinguished patroness of his, Mrs. Douglas Cruger. We were glad to learn, from the best source, that he had been very successful. Apropos of paintings : our Boston friends will find in their Athenæum exhibition two or three pictures by our friend Elliott, to which we desire to call their attention. There is a female portrait among them, a fair, sunny face, concerning which we should like to collect their suffrages. · · · The thoughtful reader will remark, in the opening of the present number of the ' St. Leger Papers,' some reflections upon faith, imagination and the ideal, which we commend to their careful consideration. We consider it one of the most important of all spiritual subjects, and one on which most christians seem to us to be astray. While therefore the writer's positions will be likely to attract criticism, they can yet scarcely fail to be sustained by all deeply-reflective minds. · · · The patriot, the accomplished musician, the kind-hearted man, the good Maroncelli is no more. ' After life's fitful fever, he sleeps well,' lamented by all who had the happiness to know him. He has joined his fellow-captive, the long-suffering Pellico, in a land where the ' prisoner rests from his labor, and hears not the voice of the oppressor.' *Requiescat in pace !* · · · There has always seemed to us to be a great deal of pathos in the ensuing stanzas. The lady to whom the writer (whose name was Morton) was attached was married to another. Morton was present at the marriage, and was never seen to smile afterward. He died at Corfu; and a portrait was found in his port-folio wrapped up in these lines:

'I saw thee wedded!—thou didst go
Within the sacred aisle,
Thy young cheek in a blushing glow,
Between a tear and smile:
Thy heart was glad in maiden glee,
But he it loved so fervently
Was faithless all the while!
I hate him for the vow he spoke,
I hate him for the vow he broke!

'I hid the love that could not die,
Its doubts and hopes and fears,
And buried all my misery
In secrecy and tears:
And days passed on, and thou didst prove
The pang of unrequited love
E'en in thy earlier years;
And thou did'st die, so fair and good,
In silence and in solitude!

'While thou wert living, I did hide
Affection's secret pains;
I 'd not have shocked thy modest pride
For all the world contains:
But thou hast perished; and the fire
That often checked, could ne'er expire,
Again unbidden reigns;
It is no crime to speak my vow,
For ah! thou canst not hear it now!

'Thou sleep'st beneath the lonely stone
That dark and dreamless sleep;
And he, thy loved and chosen one,
Why goes he not to weep?
He does not kneel where I have knelt,
He cannot feel what I have felt,
The anguish still and deep:
The painful thought of what has been,
The canker-worm that is not seen.

'But I, as o'er the dark-blue wave
Unconsciously I ride,
My thoughts are hovering o'er thy grave,
My soul is by thy side.
There is one voice that wails thee yet,
One heart that cannot e'er forget
The visions that have died;
And aye thy form is buried there,
A doubt, an anguish, a despair!'

—

THE clever 'City Items' man of the *Tribune* daily journal, alluding to the statement of some medical authority, (probably a steam-doctor,) that if people would keep their mouths shut in time of a steam-boat explosion, they would not be so likely to be fatally scalded, recommends that a notice be conspicuously posted on our steam-boats to '*Keep your mouth shut when the boiler bursts!*' A capital thought; but there should be yet another regulation, that in case of an explosion all stray legs and arms should be landed before the baggage. Passengers have only to 'stick up for their rights' in relation to the final disposition of their limbs, to obtain them. 'Hence we view' the great force of 'associated effort.' · · · WE have many and many a time in the country felt the force of 'M. D. P.'s' '*Noontide-Scene in Summer.*' There is scarcely any thing which so forcibly arrests the attention of the denizen of the city, when after a long interval he revisits the country, as the *audible stillness* which pervades the air around him. Not more perceptible to a country lad on his first visit to a great metropolis is the eternal hum of 'multitudes commercing' and the roaring of

, wheels. We stood lately for an hour overlooking the beautiful scenery that surnds the village of Bloomingburgh, and not the faintest sound reached the ear, save
laintive moan which came from a distant point in the nearer landscape, where a
er

> ——'forgot to graze, and stood
> Leaning his horns into the neighbor-field,
> And lowing to his fellows ;'

l even that faint note in the minor key rather illustrated than broke the silence that
gned around. MILTON could find nothing so like the stillness of death as 'sumr's noontide air.' · · · IF we had not had in these pages so many descriptions of
, ocean, ' in calm or gale or storm,' we would gladly accept the spirited lines of our
idison-county correspondent, ' *The Sea, from the Telegraph-Station.*' We know
l well the ' sensation which a first view of the great deep awakens in the mind of
ioy,' for we have ourselves often

> ——' climbed the lofty mountain-top to view
> From far the cloud-like waste of ocean blue ;'

d we shall never forget the impression that the first glance through a wooded
ta at a lake of fresh water made upon our almost infant mind. Its wavelets sparkle
en now in the sunlight of that clear October day, so long buried in the ' dark backird and abysm of time.' · · · OUR readers have more than once welcomed the
mmunications of the snug and contented bachelor who sends us the annexed picre of his room. He has little envy of those who, having more than much, are yet
sking more, for they are in want, and are therefore poor. Poor are their riches,
:h his poverty ; for ' Content hath all, and who hath all, is rich :'

MANKIND may boast their gathered gear,
  Their honors and their fame,
But for myself, I 'm happy here,
  'Though destitute of name.

This little room my blazing fire
  Makes cheerful with its light ;
My books are friends that never tire
  In th' longest winter's night.

Secluded from the busy throng,
  My hours glide swift away,
Oft ending with a cheerful song
  The labors of the day.

And when, with daily toil oppressed,
  I to my room repair,
In my old working-jacket dressed,
  I feel as free as air.

And sometimes, just to please myself,
  I write — in prose or rhyme ;
Or take a book from yonder shelf,
  And read away the time.

My furniture is very scant,
  To buy I am not able,
I have two chairs, (they 're all I want,)
  A bedstead and a table.

A looking-glass hangs on my wall,
  'T is cracked — a sad disaster !
A book-case too, it is but small,
  A WASHINGTON in plaster.

A bureau stands in snuggest place,
  It holds my scanty linen,
And over it, to fill the space,
  MURILLO's beggars grinning.

Of pictures I have few to boast ;
  A profile or engraving,
So poor they 're dear at any cost,
  And hardly worth the saving.

A razor that would fright a monk,
  A wash-stand and a basin ;
So dull the first, it tries my spunk,
  The last I wash my face in.

A shoe-brush and a box of LEE
  And THOMPSON's ' first-rate blacking ;'
A razor-strop that cost me three
  And sixpence — 't was a ' take-in !'

A sponge, tooth-powder, and a broom,
  (And something I can't mention,)
Complete the trifles of my room,
  My property's extension.

Oft here in quiet and alone,
  I sit in meditation ;
These pleasant hours I call my own,
  Free from the world's temptation.

With books I quietly converse
  In English, French, or German,
And think with them, in prose or verse,
  As Fancy may determine.

Then what is all the world to me,
  When by these things surrounded ?
I now enjoy the liberty
  With curses to confound it !

Then here 's confusion to the strife
  With which the world 's attended !
And like my verses, may my life
  With cheerfulness be ended.

A LESSON in plain English is conveyed in a circumstance recorded in a Cincinnati journal, of a grocer who wrote by the steamer *Simmons* for a ' lot' of cranberries, which word his correspondent could not make out, but ' send a hundred bushels per Simmons' was clear to his perception. He collected all the boys in the neighborhood, and filled the order he had received as near as he could, by despatching *eighty* bushels of *persimmons* to his friend the grocer, with a promise to send the remainder in the very next boat! · · · WE have to return our thanks to the Associated Alumni of Middlebury College, Vermont, and of Lafayette College, Pennsylvania, for the honor they have done us in electing us an honorary member of their association. We shall be glad at any time to be advised how these pages may aid the cause of literature and learning in either of these flourishing institutions. . . . OUR friend CHANDLER, of that pleasantest of diurnals, the ' *United States Gazette*,' says well and truly: ' No man can talk well who has *not* read, but no man can talk well who talks what he *has* read. The pabulum of the mind must be digested ; and we must derive our advantage from the tone and character which good reading has given to the conversation.' Would that certain professional talkers (portentous bores !) whom we could name, understood this gentlemanlike conception of true conversation ! The ' art of conversation' is an unpleasant phrase. The power of conversing well is least agreeable when it assumes the character of an art. To listen well is an accomplishment, and bespeaks a kind and unselfish heart. Some people appear to be in a violent hurry while others speak ; hastening them on, and interrupting them with ' ah,' ' yes,' ' very good,' etc.; others stare like an owl upon the speaker, with whom they seem to have no sympathy. All these vices of manner are avoidable, and are avoided by well-bred people. · · ' S.'s '*Leaf from the Album at Niagara*' reminds us of a kindred measure in the old and well-known song of the ' University of Göttingen.' We take two illustrative stanzas from the ' Leaf :'

' *Nil ad.*' had surely been suppress'd, Had not that pagan HORACE lack'd The privilege, with which we're blessed, To gaze upon this grand majest- Ic cataract !	' Forever may thy waters flow, And rush and fall with vast impact ; Then boil and howl and hiss below, Then speed again, most omnipo- Tent cataract !'

OUR Yankee brethren ' down east' are literally ' supplying pulpits' at the Sand-wich-Islands. The editor of that clever journal, ' *The Polynesian*,' tells us that a huge pine-wood pulpit recently made its appearance, flights of steps and all, in the streets of Hawaii, covered with carved work and faded cushions, whose lustre had somewhat faded through long service at home. ' If an Esquimaux,' says the editor, ' clothed in skins, and redolent with train-oil, had been suddenly dropped into our prin-cipal thoroughfare, he would not have been more astonished at the heat than the recipients of this bounty were at its magnitude. From its tout-ensemble, we are not surprised that its original proprietors were pleased to get it twenty thousand miles from home.' · · · THE ' *Elegiac Stanzas*' of ' G. L. S.,' of Sandusky, have much deep feeling but little melody of rhythm. Nor are they quite original. Take the first four lines of the third stanza, for example, ' G. L. S.,' and tell us whether BURNS did not write something *very* like them, when he penned the following :

> ' O PALE, pale now those rosy lips
> I aft hae kissed sae fondly,
> And closed for aye the sparkling glance
> That dwelt on me sae kindly !'

The *feeling* was original, no doubt, with our correspondent ; the words are his who

gave to the same feeling such matchless expression in his ' Highland MARY.' . . . ' IN
Schoharie county,' writes an obliging friend, ' there lives a man whose addiction to
profanity is such that his name has become a by-word and a reproach ; but by some
internal thermometer he so graduates his oaths as to make them apply to to the pecu-
liar case in hand ; the greater the mishap or cause for anger, the stronger and more
frequent his adjurations. His business is that of a gatherer of ashes, which he collects
in small quantities and transports in an ox-cart. Upon a recent occasion, having by
dint of great labor succeeded in filling his vehicle, he started for the ashery, which
stands upon the brow of a steep hill ; and it was not until he reached the door that he
noticed, winding its tortuous course down the long declivity, a line of white ashes,
while something short of a peck remained in the cart. ' The dwellers by the way-
side and they that tarried there' had assembled in great force, expecting an unusual
anathemal display. Turning however to the crowd, the unfortunate man heaved a
sigh, and simply remarked: ' Neighbors, it 's no use ; *I can't do justice to the sub-
ject !'* · · · LET one who had tested the utter vanity of seeking ' more than was
meet' illustrate this true philosophy : ' I have enjoyed,' says the renowned Earl
CHESTERFIELD, ' all the pleasures of the world, and consequently know their futility,
and do not regret their loss. I appraise them at their true value, which in truth
is very low ; whereas those who have not experienced always overrate them. They
only see their gay outside, and are dazzled with their glare ; but I have been
behind the scenes.' And so he had. · · · WE wish to make you acquainted,
reader, with a couple of advertisers, one of whom is a perfect CALEB QUOTEM, residing
at South Framingham, (Mass.,) and the other a Spanish DON, whose knowledge of
segars is unquestionably greater than his knowledge of the English language. He is
' up' to tobacco in the shape of segars ; he may be equal to a conception of cavendish
for ruminating chewers ; but he is not quite ' up to snuff' in the finer kinds of com-
position :

' A. Fuller

' WOULD respectfully inform the inhabitants of South Framingham and vicinity that he has fitted
up a shop at his house formerly occupied by Mr. F. MASON as a bonnet manufactory, where he will
attend to the manufacture of BLIND FASTS, which for cheapness and convenience and durability,
surpass any in the market; make stuffening and lappet knives for shoe manufacturers; cut figures
on cast-steel for marking boots and shoes, cut brands and stencil work; percussion and repair guns;
fit keys and repair all kinds of locks; manufacture curriers' steels of all descriptions; cement all
kinds of broken earthen, china and glass ware; grind, polish and repair razors, knives, shears, scis-
sors, etc.; repair umbrellas, parasols and sun-shades; also do soldering and brazing; turning done
on wood, brass, iron and steel; file and set saws; gilding and silvering done by the electro-galvanic
battery; clocks cleaned, repaired and warranted, and likewise do all jobs in iron, brass and steel
usually done in a small machine-shop; and should the DOMINIE be sick or absent, will preach when
occasion shall require it. Singing-school will be open every Wednesday and Saturday evenings at
eight P. M.; funerals attended at the shortest notice. Orders respectfully solicited.'

' Spanish Segars.

' NOTICE is given that having been hired the Establishment Dos AMIGOS, where this Segars are
manufactured, by Mrs. PLA, RAMON AND Co., the proprietor now has put himself again to the ad-
ministration; and that the tenants have opened anoter of the Same nature under the sing DOS AMI-
GAS, and as they might be confounded, whilst they only can be distinguished by the masculine termin-
ation of the former and female of the latter, for to prevent all mistake, the boxes and casks of the
mark; DOS AMIGOS wil henceforth bear on their inside, besides the aver user countermark, this no-
tice in the English, French and Spanish, sucribed by my son Mr. DOMINGO HERNANDEZ ABREU,
without the verification of whom they are not genuine.'

<hr/>

MR. J. S. REDFIELD, Clinton-Hall, has issued, in a very handsome miniature vol-
ume, the ' *Complete Poetical Writings of the late Willis Gaylord Clark.*' We
shall add nothing to the announcement of the fact of its publication. · · · EVERY
body will recollect SWIFT's ' reading Latin into English,' as thus : ' *Lætus peco fit,*'

etc., for ' *Let us pack off*,' etc. A Scottish friend of ours, who admits that he re-
members ' small Latin and less Greek,' sends us the following from the latter :

Ιον Καμερον Καμερτο πλαιονθέ φιδελτς θελασσις ;

' *Ion Cameron camerto plaionthe fidelto thelassis ;*'

which he translates thus : ' JOHN CAMERON came here to play on the fiddle to the
lasse's ! · · · WE can say but little for the long tale of our Galena correspondent.
Although there is ' a good deal therein that ought to be thereout,' yet no amount of
' cutting out' or ' pruning' would make it acceptable to our readers. ' Sorry ; but
so it is.' · · · ' JEAMES DE LA PLUCHE, Exquire' evinces in the decoration of his
dining-room a sort of pictorial loyalty, which we have often had occasion to admire
in the British subject on this side the water : ' Portricks of my favorite great men de-
corats the wall ; namely, the DUKE OF WELLINGTON. There 's four of His Grace.
For I 've remarked, that if you wish to pass for a man of weight and consideration
you should holways praise and quote him ; I have a valluble one lickwise of my
QUEEND, and two of PRINCE HALBERT — has a Field Martail and halso as a private
Gent. I despise the vulgar *snears* that are daily hurlled aginst that Igsolted Pot-
tentat. Betwigxt the Prins and the Duke, hangs me.' · · · OUR friend and corres-
pondent, Mr. PHILIP HONE, who seldom meets us that he has not some pleasant
thing for our pages, hands us the following : ' The Commercial Bank of Albany re-
ceived lately one of their own notes with these lines endorsed upon the face of it :

' BANK-notes, it is said, once gold guineas defied
To swim in the current of Trade's swolling tide ;
But ere they arrived at the opposite brink,
The notes loudly cried, ' Help, cash us ! we sink !'

' That paper should sink and that guineas should swim
May appear to some folks a ridiculous whim ;
But ere they condemn, let them hear this suggestion,
In pun-making, gravity 's out of the question.'

—

THE love of money has been the root of great evil in a local case which has lately
come to our knowledge. One of our wealthy citizens (who was so fond of merely
handling money that he would always take his seat at the far-end of an omnibus
that he might have the pleasure of scrutinizing and fingering the coin of the pas-
sengers before passing it up to the driver,) has recently become insane from anxiety
in relation to a very large fortune ; from the sheer excitement of ' buying and selling
and getting gain.' He is now at the Lunatic Asylum on BLACKWELL's Island, where
he was adroitly induced to go to look at a ' piece of property' there that was to be
purchased at a bargain. The ruling passion is strong upon him ; so that he is quite
contented in his new position. He has been negotiating with the keeper for several
weeks for the purchase of the Asylum and the adjacent grounds ; but owing to a
point on which the cunning superintendent higgles a good deal, the papers still re-
main unsigned. · · · WHO ever conceived a more beautiful illustration of a sub-
lime text than the following by Bishop BEVERIGE ? ' I AM.' ' HE doth not say, I
AM their light, their guide, their strength, or tower, but only ' I AM.' HE sets as it
were his hand to a blank, that his people may write under it what they please that
is good for them. As if he should say, ' Are they weak ? I AM strength. Are they
poor ? I AM riches. Are they in trouble ? I AM comfort. Are they sick ? I AM
health. Are they dying ? I AM life. Have they nothing ? I AM all things. I AM
wisdom and power ; I AM justice and mercy ; I AM grace and goodness ; I AM glory,

beauty, holiness, eminency, super-eminency, perfection, all-sufficiency, eternity! JEHOVAH, I AM! Whatsoever is amiable in itself, or desirable unto them, that I AM. Whatsoever is pure and holy ; whatsoever is great and pleasant ; whatsoever is good or needful to make men happy, that I AM.' · · · IF there be ' any friend that loves us,' let him take our advice, and when he visits Philadelphia, repair at once to the ' *Franklin-House*,' kept as none but Mr. D. K. MINOR (so long and so honorably known in Gotham,) and SANDERSON the Younger *can* keep a ' house of entertainment.' Large and airy parlors, spacious dining-rooms, clean bed-rooms, whitest linen, courteous hosts, and *such* a cuisine ! ―― *go to the Franklin !* · · · READING in the journals every day or two of the arrest of EPES, the Virginia murderer, and again of his being still at large, we have been led to think what the sensations of the guilty man must be. Are they not well described in the BOOK of books ? ' And thy life shall hang in doubt before thee ; and thou shalt fear day and night, and shalt have none assurance of thy life. In the morning thou shalt say, ' Would GOD it were even !' and at even, thou shalt say, ' Would GOD it were morning !' for the fear of thine heart wherewith thou shalt fear, and for the sight of thine eyes which thou shalt see !' · · · THERE was quite a little pimple broke out this season on the face of the sun. The spot however was but seven thousand miles in diameter, and soon passed off. It was a mere trifle, occupying with its fellow-eruptions only five times the size of the number of square miles on the surface of the globe, as near as we can ' calculate.' · · · ' *The Storm-King*' commences well, and that is all :

'THE Storm-King rages on the land,
  He dashes down the rugged steep,
Nor rocks nor trees behind him stand,
  And frighted waves before him leap !'

These are very good lines ; but for the rest, it is nothing more than

――' a kind of hobbling prose,
Which limps along, and tinkles in its close.'

' J. D.'s' poetry, from ' Old Pocumtuck,' contains ' things both new and old, but the old are the best ; although this compoundly-descriptive couplet is not amiss :

'His education was complete,
He was six feet high in his stocking-feet !'

' J. D.'s' anecdote is better than his ' poetry.' Par example : ' At the time the small-pox was raging in New-England, many years ago, a town-meeting was called in the town of D――, in the southern part of Vermont, to consider the expediency of establishing a pest-house, and anticipating the arrival of the disease by inoculation. After grave deliberation, it was '*Voted*, That we will not admit the small-pox into town by inoculation or any *other way*.' This was a ' scarlet decree,' and the pit-marked monster has duly ' respected' it to this day.' · · · WE quite agree with our Charleston (S. C.) correspondent in his ' *Thoughts on the Affinities of Man with Nature*.' Without doubt,

――'there radiates from our own
A soul that lives in every shape we see ;
There is a voice, to other ears unknown,
Like echoed music answering to its key.'

The cause of this secret affinity ' we know not now, but we shall know hereafter.' In the meantime, ' away with every saddening memento ; away with sombre colors and gloomy hues, and let us surround ourselves with all that is gay and cheerful, bright, beaming and happy, in order that our associations may be of a sympathetic quality ; for the mind, like the chameleon, takes the hue of that which environs it.'

LITERARY RECORD. — WE have already noticed at large and in advance, Col. M'KENNEY'S new work, '*Sketches of Travels among the Northern and Southern Indians ;*' and it remains only to add, that the volume, admirably printed and profusely illustrated, has appeared, and is on sale at PAINE AND BURGESS'S in John-street. . . . WE welcome with sincerest pleasure two beautiful volumes from the press of Messrs. WILLIAM D. TICKNOR AND COMPANY, Boston, containing '*Minstrelsy, Ancient and Modern, with an Introduction and Historical Notes, by William Motherwell.* We shall have more to say of this most desirable work in our next number. . . . MESSRS. HENRY M. ONDER-DONK AND COMPANY, John-street, have published, with improvements and additions, the '*Eaton Latin Grammar,*' from the twentieth London edition. . . . FROM the Messrs. HARPERS we have two excellent volumes, in their 'New Miscellany,'*Keppel's 'Expedition to Borneo,*' and '*The Modern British Plutarch.*' Both works demand farther notice. '*Draper's Text-Book of Chemistry,*' for the use of schools and colleges, with nearly three hundred illustrations, is also extant from the same house. . . . THE last two issues of Messrs. APPLETON's 'Literary Miscellany' are devoted to *M. Guizot's 'History of Civilization,*' which has excited so much attention in the original. . . '*The Preludes,*' a collection of very clever poems by EUGENE LIES, U. S. N., '*War Songs and Ballads,*' from the Old Testament, by WILLIAM PLUMMER, Jr., '*The Probe,*' by L. CARROLL JUDSON, Esq., and '*Chambers' Information for the People,*' will receive speedy attention. . . . MESSRS. LEA AND BLANCHARD, Philadelphia, are publishing a series of '*Small Books on Great Subjects,*' at twenty-five cents per number. The issues before us are upon '*The Connection between Physiology and Intellectual Science ;*' '*The Principles of Criminal Law ;*' '*A Brief View of Greek Philosophy, up to the Age of PERICLES ;*' '*Man's Power over Himself to Prevent or Control Insanity ;*' and '*An Introduction to Practical Organic Chemistry.*' These little tomes are well printed, upon fair paper. . . . WE have from the press of Messrs. GREELEY AND McELRATH an excellent little volume, from the pen of S. S. RANDALL, Esq., our capable State Superintendent of Common Schools, containing '*Incentives to the Cultivation of the Science of Geology,*' designed and every way well calculated for the use of the young. It is a work likely to meet with a wide diffusion. The same publishers have issued, in two large and handsome volumes, LARDNER's popular '*Lectures on Science and Art.*' . . . WE have alluded to the new up-town book establishment of Mr. HENRY KERNOT, late with Messrs. WILEY AND PUTNAM. He has associated with himself Mr. SILVANUS MILLER, Jr., a gentleman likewise of thorough knowledge in every department of his business; and the first fruits of their union is an admirably-arranged catalogue of a large and valuable collection of English and American books, making altogether a most copious '*Dictionary of Literary and Scientific Wants,*' for the use of the 'several' people in this 'great country.' · · · MR. EDWARD WALKER, 114 Fulton-street, deserves the thanks and patronage of all Americans for the two large and well-executed volumes which he has recently issued, containing the '*Addresses and Messages of the Presidents of the United States,*' inaugural, annual and special, from 1789 to 1846, with a memoir of each of the Presidents, and a history of their administrations ; also, the constitution of the United States, and a selection of important documents and statistical information, compiled from official sources by that indefatigable statist, EDWIN WILLIAMS. The work is embellished with engraved portraits of all the American Presidents and the arms of the several states · · · AT the late hour at which we received '*Dolores: a Novel by Harro-Harring,*' (a work which, owing to a recent literary controversy, has excited considerable attention,) we were only enabled to dip into it here and there, and cannot therefore pronounce definitively upon its merits. It seems to us, from a very imperfect perusal, to indicate deep feeling and sensibility, and powers of description of no common order. We may take another occasion to refer to the work. · · · '*The New-York Mirror*' is publishing a powerfully-written tale, entitled '*Eighteen Hundred and Forty-Four, or the Power of the S. F.*' Its purpose is to develope the secret action of parties in the late exciting election canvass ; and without siding with either of the great national divisions, we have reason to think the author will make the ears of both (to adopt a catachrestical personification) to tingle before he is through with his subject. We shall see. · · · THE last three numbers of Messrs. C. S. FRANCIS AND COMPANY's 'Cabinet Library' are devoted to Mr. WARE's '*Zenobia, or the Fall of Palmyra,*' (two volumes concerning the merits of which our readers do not need to be advised, since their contents originally appeared in these pages,) and '*The Epicurean,*' by THOMAS MOORE. Both works are well printed on good paper. · · · MESSRS. BARTLETT AND WELFORD's '*Catalogue of Books for July and August,* 1846,' has appeared. It embraces all the recent importations of rare and valuable books for which this house has established a high reputation. MESSRS. BARTLETT AND WELFORD will hereafter publish gratuitously a quarterly catalogue.

ORIGINAL PAPERS.

NOTICE.

COUNTRY SUBSCRIBERS who are in arrears should recollect to make returns for what we send them. Remittances to be made to

JOHN ALLEN,

139 Nassau-street,

New-York.

MR. T. P. WILLIAMS is our Agent to receive the names of Subscribers in the West and South. Editors and others kindly interested in the circulation of this Magazine, will oblige us by facilitating his designs.

O. D. DAVIS and JOHN STOUGHTON, Jr., are canvassing for subscribers to this work in the state of New-York.

THE KNICKERBOCKER.

Vol. XXVIII.   OCTOBER, 1846.   No. 4.

A DAY AT RHODOS.

'Deinde Rhodum appropinquamus, ubi tanta est viriditas arborum atque amœnitas locorum, quod est mirabile ad videndum et prosortim Paradisum a Florentius factum.

CHRIST BUODELMONTE, FLORENT/

HAVING been dismissed from the Greek service in consequence of the revolution at Athens on the third-fifteenth of September, 1843, I went to Smyrna, where I joined a party of travellers, who in the spring of 1844 intended to undertake a voyage to Syria and celebrate the Easter festival in Jerusalem. On the 29th of February, 1844, we embarked on board the fine Austrian steamer 'Count of Kollowrath,' commanded by the polite Dalmatian gentleman, Captain Ventile Flanowitch. The tumult and disorder on deck occasioned by the hurried arrival of quite a number of Turkish officers with their harems and domestics departing for Syria, and a still larger crowd of Greek and Armenian Pilgrims, was highly interesting. The continual shouts and clamors, in the most different dialects, and the general hurly-burly, did not terminate until the signal for departure was given, the anchors heaved, and we, at three o'clock in the afternoon, left the beautiful roadstead of Smyrna.

Running close up to the castle of St. Giacomo, commanding the narrow channel for ships of larger burden, we passed the batteries and stood away westward for the green and hilly Durlachs islands, beautifully studding the large gulf of Vurlá. The Greeks call them νησιά τὰ ἀγγλέσικα, or the English islands, because the English fleet had its principal station here during the revolutionary war, and the ships generally lie-to and water at the plentiful fountain gushing forth from the rocks near the shore. These little conical islands, forming a group by themselves, are covered with copse-wood and fragrant shrubs. They present a different picture from the rocky, barren and sun-burnt cliffs of the Cyclades in the Ægean, and remind one of the verdant tropical islands of the West-Indies. At some distance from the coast the white domes and minarets of Vurlá are seen rising above the olive groves. The ancient city of Clazomenæ was situated farther down in the innermost part of the bay, and was united by a bridge to a small island off the shore. Few ruins are now to be found, the exuberant fertility of the soil and the foundation of the modern town of Vurlá having caused them to disappear in the course of so many centuries.

At sunset we doubled the high and eminently picturesque promontory of Kará-Burnú (Black Cape,) the ancient Melæna Acra, with many Turkish villages peeping forth from the woods covering the steep offsets of the mountain, and steered south between the island of Chios and the Ionian coast. Night was already setting in, when we arrived on the height of Chios, but the many lights, shining over to us from the shore, indicated that we were just passing the city of Chios, once so happy and beautiful, until it was destroyed during the last war of independence in 1822, by the barbarity of the Turks. More than twenty thousand Christians were butchered by the Asiatic hordes, and the fairest city of the Levant suffered a destruction from which it never will be able to revive beneath the tyrannic sway of the Turks.

Although I have undertaken many voyages on the Mediterranean, still I have never met with any company on board so singularly diversified by nations and tongues, so eminently picturesque, and therefore so highly interesting to an occidental traveller, as on this Syrian pilgrimage. The passengers in the first cabin, consisting of twenty-five ladies and gentlemen, formed almost a society by themselves; although among the number were two young French Lazarists, going to their convent in Beyroot, in order to study the Arabic language, and get promoted as teachers at the French Schools on the Lebanon. A Turkish colonel from Stambul, Mohammed Said-Bek, who spoke a few words in French, had likewise his berth in our cabin; but he of course did not dine along with us, and was served by his black slaves on deck, where all the Mahommedan families were quartered. The Turkish ladies with their black girls were sitting in large wooden cages, built for that purpose, and carefully closed with curtains, while their jealous husbands with their tiresome countenances and long pipes kept the most severe watch over them.

Although the Turks had been disarmed at their arrival on board, still a bearded old gentleman, of high standing, who brought three pretty young Turkesses along with him, had obtained the permission from the obliging Captain, Flanowitch, to place his armed *Tshibouksis*, or pipe-bearer, before the virgin-bower. But it happened, during the slumbers of the old gray-beard, that a young Frank traveller approached the harem, and the wind just blowing aside the curtain and showing the beauties unveiled, the mischievous eunuch, with a scream of horror, instantly snatched his pistol from its belt, when a tumult ensued which did not subside until the captain, hurrying to the spot, had ordered the black to be disarmed and brought off to the main-deck.

Here a number of Greek pilgrims, among whom were many priests and monks from the kingdom of Greece, had their quarter.

Some forty Russians, Cosacks from Bessarabia on the Danube, in their sheep-skins and fur-caps, attracted the attention of all the travellers on board. These good-natured nomades, who appeared to be sufficiently furnished with money, would sometimes during the bright moonshiny nights entertain the company with their pretty songs, the religious melodies of which indicated the particular care of the Russian government to promote a general instruction. in a melodious church-music. From the four parts of the world travellers belonging to more than thirty different nations were united on board this Austrian steamer, among whom almost all the Christians had made the sepulchre of our SAVIOUR the object of their pilgrimage.

Next morning at sunrise we sailed through the extensive bay of Ephesos. Ancient Ionia, renowned for the mildness of its climate, the wealth and beauty of its flourishing cities and its early civilization, now lay stretched out before our view, a dreary and solitary plain, bounded on the east by distant mountains. The clear, dark-blue sky is still the same ; but where in days of old Lebedos, Klaros, Ephesos and the other thriving Greek colonies arose in the beautiful plain of the Kaystros, no villages, nor hardly any human being, is now to be seen. We kept on, close to the shore, because the brisk · south-western breeze, setting in motion the hollow surge of the Icarian Sea, forced the captain to steer his course through the Samian straight. The coast all along appeared a perfect desert. At noon, on approaching the island of Samos, we distinguished a miserable village, Giaour-Kioi, inhabited by poor Christians, who may have forgotten their native tongue, like their brethren in the interior of Asia-Minor. The wood-clad heights of Mycale now arose on our sight, and in the distance appeared to melt away with the lofty ridges of Samos. We passed close to the mountain villages of Agios Constantinos, Carlovasi, and others almost hid in the far-spreading forests, which· cover in part the precipitous eastern shore of the island, the impregnable bulwark of the independent Samiotes against their Asiatic tyrants.

Quite near to the promontory of Mycale, now called Santa Maria, the ancient Trogylium, we discovered the straight Kutschuk Bogazi, or small entry which divides the continent of Asia Minor from the island of Samos, and which since the days of the Persian wars has been the theatre of so many interesting events in Greek history. Its breadth is only seven stadia, or half a mile, but it appears to be more narrow on account of the· high peaked mountains skirting it on both sides. We then passed close by the little rocky island Trogylia, now called Lerina, and doubled the projecting cape, the south side of which sinks less precipitously and in several offsets down on the low and sandy coast of Miletos. Yonder, at the foot of the promontory, the battle was fought, wherein the Spartan King Leotychides and the Athenian Xanthippos vanquished the fleet and army of the Persians on the same day in which the united Hellenes at Platæa in Bœotia destroyed the large invading army of Xerxes, in September, 479 before CHRIST, (Olymp. 75. 1.) It is evident from the relation of Herodotus, that the battle was fought on the south side of the mountain, the Persians having despatched their Milesian auxiliaries to the heights of Mycale in order to secure their retreat to Sardis in Lydia in case of a defeat. But the Milesians turning their arms against the Persians flying from the field of battle, a dreadful slaughter ensued, and only a few dispersed detachments of retreating Persians were able to force the mountain passes and open their way back to Lydia.

On the northern descent of the promontory stood the famous Panionion temple, consecrated to the Helian Neptune, where the Ionic confederation celebrated their annual assemblies and games. The large southern bay of Samos extends westward; and at a distance of eight miles we were able to distinguish the gigantic column of the ancient temple of Juno close to the shore. This is the most fertile part of the island, and several beautiful villages are seen on the slope of the high mountains, embosomed in groves of olive trees and charming vineyards, descending all along the terraces down to the plain. Opposite to Mycale arises the Posidonian promontory of Samos, which has attained a historical name by the valor of the Samiotes during the last war of independence.

The Turks having assembled a large camp near Mycale, in the year 1821, the Admiral Kara-Ali attempted to land his army here on a place called Odondia, (the teeth,) by the Greeks. The Samians awaited quietly on the mountains the descent of the Asiatics, and then rushed sword in hand down upon them, and after a bloody conflict, forced them to fly to their boats. The Turkish Capitan Bey now mustered his fleet along the strait, and cannonaded with all his might the barren rocks of Samos, to the great delight of the Greeks, as he was expending in vain his powder and balls; when all at once the appearance of the vanguard of the Greek fleet forced him hastily to heave his anchors and stand out for the open sea.

This attack and another unsuccessful attempt in June, 1825, when the brave Constantin Canaris with his fire-ships destroyed a large Turkish frigate, were the only undertakings of the Turks against Samos during the last war. The brave islanders now live quietly beneath the sway of their governor, Prince Vogorides, and every where in the Levant is seen their blue-and-red flag with the white cross.

South of Mycale the coast again appears so low that although the steamer passed very near, we did not recognize the site of Priene, nor the mouth of the river Mæander. The only prominent point is a Turkish village, with a mosque situated on a hillock near the shore, where several high antique marble columns, still united by an architrave, present themselves as the only remains of the splendid temple of the Dìdymæan Apollo at Branchidæ.

Again turning off from the continent, and leaving the high peak of Patmos on our right, we struck across the picturesque gulf of Iasos, studded with many rocky islands, in the back-ground of which the high inland-peaks of Caria, towering in three or four ridges, one above the other, now glittered in all the rosy hues of the setting

sun. Twilight was setting in when we reached the height of Bu-
druni, the ancient Halicarnassos, and we continued our course dur-
ing the night along the eastern coast of Cos. At dawn of day, on
the second of March, we hurried away past Cap Crio, on the Dorian
peninsula, and steering in an easterly direction among the small
islands of Syme, Telos and Nisyros, we speedily approached the
desert and sandy northern shore of Rhodos.

At eight o'clock we doubled Cum-Burnû, or Sandy Cape, and
the delightful city of Rhodes, with its walls, towers, minarets and
straggling palm-trees; and then all at once the charming environs
with the numerous villages, vineyards and groves opened upon us,
just as we passed the batteries of the tower of St. Nicolaos, which
protect the entrance of the old galley-harbor, Darsena, and came
to anchor in the large harbor, the ' Porto di Mandracchio' of the
Knights, between the two prominent towers of St. Michael and St.
John.

The city of Rhodos is situated on the north-north-east coast of
the island, facing the high mountains of Caria, at a distance of
twenty miles, and arises gently from the shore, forming a crescent,
enclosing the largest of the harbors. The old bastion of St. Pietro,
formerly armed with immense guns, but now lying in ruins, and the
high square tower of St. Michel separate this eastern harbor from
the northern galley-port. The upper town *(la haute ville)* ascends
westward to the Palace of the Grand Masters, which by its treble
walls and bastions in its high situation formed the castle or citadel
of the city. It is still separated by a transverse wall with round
towers from the lower town, *(la ville casse,)* where in the times of
the Order of St. John, the Greek subjects, the Jews, and all the mar-
ried citizens and retainers of the order, lived. Even to this day, the
Jews have their quarter in the eastern part of the city, toward the
Baazar and the large inner harbor, while the whole Greek popu-
lation, together with the foreign consuls, inhabit the pretty villages
at a distance of a mile encircling the fortress. The Christians have
permission to enter the castle only after sunrise, and on penalty of
the bastinado are obliged to leave it again at sunset.

The Turkish commandant occupies the ruinous palace of the
grand-masters and the adjacent buildings. Hassan Pasha, the go-
vernor of the island, has his residence outside the gates on the gal-
ley-harbor, in a large irregular Turkish seraï.

The general view of Rhodos, as it is seen from the port where
we anchored, is highly picturesque; nay, you would suppose your-
self suddenly transported back to the times of the Knights of St.
John; the whole line of walls and fortifications extending along the
inner harbor being preserved almost in the same state wherein
the city three centuries ago surrendered to the victorious arms of
Sultan Suleiman the Second, on the twenty-fifth of December,
1522.

This harbor, ' Il Porto di Mandracchio,' has the form of a horse-
shoe, and is divided by a small mole for boats and the roadstead for
ships of larger burden. The galley-port is smaller, but better pro-

tected. It is formed by an immense mole, constructed with extra-ordinary expense and solidity by the ancient Rhodiens, and is now termed Molo di San Niccolò. The entrance is obstructed by a barrier of rocks, so as to admit the entry of only one ship at a time, but it offers perfect safety against wind and waves. If it were kept in good repair it would still be an excellent refuge for the light ships of the Archipelago; but the fatal indifference of the Turks has suffered the sands to accumulate until the mouth has been gra-dually choked up; and now-a-days merchant vessels can only enter after being obliged previously to unload their cargoes. Barks and small vessels enter without any difficulty, and anchor opposite the palace of the Pasha.

The other harbor is larger: within the two projecting turrets even frigates of thirty guns find a convenient anchorage ground, although they are sometimes exposed to the violent north-east storms, and then are in danger of being dashed against the walls of the city or the rocky coast. During the sway of the Order of St. John, both harbors were shut with huge chains in time of war, and the Grand-master Zacosta imposed in the year 1462 a tax on all goods and merchant-men, which was called 'chain-money,' (diritto di ca-tena,) and was employed to augment the fortifications of the har-bors. One of these strong chains, more than a hundred fathoms in length, is still shown to the traveller in the vaults of the ancient Hospitium.

The walls surrounding the large harbor in the form of a bow, are built of fine squared free-stone. They have strong and well-se-cured battlements, projecting parapets and round flanking towers. Between the largest of these is situated the ancient gate, (Porta di Santa Caterina,) now walled up. It is ornamented with the armo-rial bearings of the order, and the Grand Master Emeri d'Amboise, with the date A. D. 1512. The present entrance into the city is through a postern near the Turkish custom-house.

The Saracens of Egypt having obtained possession of the king-dom of Jerusalem in consequence of the destruction of Acre or Ptolemais in the year 1291, the Knights of St. John or Hospitali-ters sought a refuge on Cyprus, where the Knights Templars had already obtained large estates, and King Henry the Second of Lu-signan, now likewise invested them with the town and castle of Li-misso. There the order erected a new convent, armed a fleet, and escorting the pilgrims to the holy land, carried on a successful war-fare with the Saracens.

Still the enterprising warriors were dissatisfied on the island, be-ing involved in the feudal dissensions between the king and the Latin barons; moreover, they found their sphere of activity too circum-scribed, and desired to establish an independent dominion, which they shortly afterward effected, when the Grand Master Fulco de Villaret, with the assistance of the Pope and the King of France, conquered the beautiful island of Rhodos. The richness of its soil and the purity and salubrity of its climate caused it to be considered in antiquity as consecrated to Phœbus Apollo, and as the birth-place of the Heliades. During the thirteenth century it had remained in the possession of the noble Genoese family of Gavala, and then devolved on the Greek empire of Constantinople. But during the weak and turbulent reign of Andronicus the Younger, Turkish and Saracenic corsairs from the coast of Asia Minor and Syria established themselves in the island, united with the Greek inhabitants, and extended their piratical expeditions over all the adjacent islands of the Ægean.

In the mean time Pope Clement the Fifth proclaimed a new crusade in Europe, with the pretext of conquering Jerusalem and the holy land from the hands of the Saracens; and in the spring of the year 1310 large bands of warlike noblemen, particularly numerous German knights, assembled at Brindisi, in southern Italy, whence a Neapolitan fleet transported the crusading army to Cyprus. There they united with the Knights of St. John and unexpectedly landed at Rhodos. Defeating the Saracens in several naval combats, they laid siege to the city; but the Crusaders, being disappointed in their hopes of conquest in Syria, now abandoned the Knights of St. John, who were thus obliged on their own part to sustain a fierce contest with the Greeks. At last, on the Day of the Virgin, August 15th, 1310, they stormed and took the city of Rhodos. With the holy banner of the order in his hand, the brave old Fulco de Villaret was the first knight who ascended the wall; and after the conquest of the capital soon followed the surrender of the strong fortress of Lindos, on the eastern shore of the island; but it was not until after an obstinate warfare of four years with the Greeks that the knights obtained the quiet possession of the whole island. They then extended their conquests to the surrounding Archipelago of Syme, Chalkis, Nisyros, Cos and the strong fortress of Halicarnassos, on the main land of Caria, fortified then with castles and garrisons, and thus laid the foundation of the glorious dominion of the Order of Rhodos, which for more than two centuries held the sway in this part of the Archipelago, and formed the bulwark of Christianity in the Levant against the rising power of the Osmanlis.

During the first years subsequent to the conquest, the harbors of Rhodos were only defended by the ancient Saracenic tower, in a later period called 'Tower of St. Michel;' but in the year 1353, the brave Grand Master Deodat de Gozon, the renowned champion of the Dragon, constructed the extensive fortifications along the interior harbor, uniting the city with the ancient mole; and the subsequent erection of the strong tower of St. Nicolaos at the mouth of the galley-port in the year 1461, perfectly secured the harbors from every attack on the sea-side. The defence of these maritime walls was entrusted to the care of the Castilian knights by an order of the Grand Master Zacosta;* and still many Spanish coats of arms are seen on the towers, among which I remarked the escutcheon of Don Hernando de Heredia.

The city of Rhodos, generally so dull and silent, presented on

---

* CORONELLI Isola di Rodi Venezia, 1688, p. 119.

that day a scene of unusual life and bustle. In the morning three
Hydriote vessels arrived with full cargoes of pilgrims for the Holy
Land. Having obtained permission of the Pasha to buy provisions
in the city, hundreds of men, women and children were now seen
to row on shore, shouting and singing.

After breakfast, our own party of ladies and gentlemen followed
the example, and went on shore, where we suddenly found our-
selves in a press of Turks, Christians and Jews, crowding about
the Bazaar. Shops and tents had been pitched on the outside of
the walls, where the vociferous Greeks were exhibiting the delici-
ous fruits and productions of the island, while all the coffee-houses
were occupied by taciturn Turks gravely smoking their long pipes.

At the gate we enjoyed the ridiculous sight of a Turkish guard
of regular infantry in European regimentals, sitting cross-legged at
the entrance, their muskets leaning against the wall, while their
lieutenant seemed to take a comfortable nap in the shade. Nothing
looks more unwarlike and awkward than these poor Turkish re-
cruits, in their slight dresses and misshapen trowsers, with bare feet
stuck in their down-trodden slippers. How often have I seen offi-
cers on service in Constantinople sitting before the guard-houses
knitting stockings! A 'progress,' certainly, in modern Turkish
civilization.

Inside the gate we arrived at a fine square, surrounded by chival-
resque buildings and high shadowy plantains. On the right stands
the well-preserved hospital for sick and wounded knights, which the
Grand Master Anton de la Rivière built in the year 1436 from his
own private fortune. Opposite is seen the large convent of the
order, highly ornamented in the Gothic style, with two front sides
facing the square and the Street of the Cavaliers. The marble stair-
case is still in good repair, but an entry was not permitted, both
buildings serving at present as barracks for the Turkish garrison.
From this square the famous Street of the Knights, (la Rue des
Chevaliers,) leads westward to the Palace of the Grand Masters.
It runs on four hundred paces in a straight line, having fourteen
paces breadth, and being paved very neatly with a mosaic of small
black-and-white stones. Elevated foot-paths run along the sides.
In this street arise the dwellings of the principal knights and the
auberges of the eight nations or tongues wherein the order was
divided.*

It proved to be a happy circumstance that we found in our own
company a knight of the modern order of Malta, a British captain,
who being deeply versed in the science of blazonry and the history
of the Middle Ages, explained to us every coat of arms still orna-
menting the ancient palaces. The noble, venerable-looking street,
with its well-preserved Gothic buildings, seemed to be quite solitary
and deserted; not a single human being was to be seen, and with-
out any great stretch of fancy one might have imagined that the

---

* THE seven ancient tongues were those of France, Germany, Auvergne, Aragon, England. Pro-
vence and Italy. In the year 1462, during the dissensions in the order, the eighth tongue, Castile-
Portugal was created.

city had just been surrendered and abandoned by its brave de-
fenders.

All the houses are solidly built of square lime-stones.   The cor-
nices, architraves and high oral windows are richly embellished with
festoons, wreaths of flowers, leaves, and other arabesques or
Gothic decorations.   The coat of arms, neatly carved in white mar-
ble bas-reliefs, in the very best style of the *cinque cento,* stand every
where above the principal gate-way or beneath the windows on the
front side.   They are admirably preserved, owing to the profound
respect with which the 'Turks still observe the command of the
magnanimous Sultan Soleiman on the capitulation of the city, ex-
pressing his admiration of the heroic.defence of the knights, and
ordering his pashas carefully to preserve the city in the same state
in which it was surrendered, as a glorious memorial of the invinci-
ble strength of his arms.

The windows are now closed up with boards or shut with Turk-
ish verandahs, indicating that the buildings are still inhabited by
Turkish families.   The interior of the halls and apartments is said
to present many interesting traces of the olden time, such as gilt
mosaic ceilings, wainscotted walls, inlaid pavements, Gothic chim-
ney-pieces and niches ; but the Turks did not permit us any where
to penetrate into their sombre retreats to make inquiries ourselves.

ADDRESS TO THE IDEAL.

BY GEORGE L. RING.

HAST thou stores of gold from the darken'd mine,
   Hast thou pearls from the deep blue sea ?
Where the jewels shine 'mid the ocean brine,
   Hast thou culled a gem for me ?
Canst thou call a star from its orbit far
   In the azure vault of Heaven,
And send it back in its flaming track
   To the source whence its glory 's given ?

Canst thou people this ancient earth once more
With the mouldered forms of the days of yore,
   The sage and the hoary seer,
Who walked the earth in its early prime,
Who looked through time with a faith sublime,
And pointed its sons to a cloudless clime,
   A holy and happy sphere ?

Canst thou journey swiftly and far and wide,
   Where mortals have never trod,
Where light never dims with the eventide,
Where beings too pure for this earth abide,
   The unmarred work of GOD ?

Canst thou follow the trail of the shooting star,
　Canst thou dip thy brush in the hues of even?
Canst thou paint the sun in his chariot-car,
　As he gleams afar in the upper heaven?
Canst thou call from the dim and shadowy land
　The early loved and the early lost?
Canst thou gather again the household band,
　And breathe new life in the sleeping dust?

Canst thou kindle afresh the holy fire
　That burnt on the ancient altar's shrine?
Canst thou breathe again o'er the slumb'ring lyre,
　And waken once more the tones divine?
Canst thou read the Present; survey the Past,
　From what hath been, to what shall be?
Canst thou rival Time in his flight, and cast
　A glance o'er his vast Eternity?

I asked, and a spirit thus answered me,
With a voice like the wind o'er a summer sea:

' I dwell with men, and a power is mine
　To soothe the soul in its low despair,
To raise from depression to light divine,
　And cancel each trace of corroding care :
Though the body languish in captive chains,
　"T is mine to set the spirit free,
And send it abroad where freedom reigns,
　Unchecked by the minions of tyranny !

' In the poet's mind and the poet's dreams
　I give the rein to his fancy's flight,
And I cull for him holy and rapturous themes,
　Till his vision teems with a new delight;
And he looks on Nature with other eyes,
　And I haunt him with visions of future praise,
And he sighs for a place in the memories
　Of those who shall live in the after days.

' O'er that which the spirit hath darkly scanned,
　Where the light of the mental eye grows dim,
O'er the mists which darken the spirit-land
　Where the harp is struck by the seraphim ;
I wave my wand, and a light appears
That pierces the gloom of the coming years.

' I teach the wings of Faith to rise,
　And bear them on in their upward flight,
Till she can gaze with unquailing eyes
　On the fount of Heaven's pellucid light.

' I point the worn and weary one
　To a place of final rest on high,
Where the light dies not with the setting sun,
　And the stars fade not from the evening sky ;
Where pure, immortal joys abide,
　Such joys as the spirit may only know,
In its radiant form, all purified
　From the crimes that darken the world below.'

OLD AGE.

Thou art coming, art coming, old Age! old Age!
  Thou art coming, old Dot-and-go-one!
I see thee now, with thy fixed look, so sage —
Thy thin, shrivelled cheek, like a parchment page,
  Where time hath recorded the cares that are gone.

Thou art coming, aye coming, old Age! old Age!
  Thou art coming, old Picture of Fun!
Thy white locks are tossing along the rude blast,
Thy gait is a stumble; and yet comest thou fast!
  Thou art coming, fast coming, old Dot-and-go-one!

But an angel floats o'er thee, old Age! old Age!
  All tranquil, all gentle, all changeless, her air —
She smiles at thy turmoil, and wondereth to see
All the fright that thou causest the world too and me —
Hark! hark now! one soundeth! 'ETERNITY!'
  'T is a name for this angel, thus changeless, thus fair!—OLD ALBUM.

IRENE travelled to Epidaurus, to visit Esculapius in his proper temple, and there consult him in person as to the nature and cure of the various maladies that afflicted her.

'Son of Apollo!' said she, 'I am most heartily fatigued; I am tired, even unto death.'

The oracle politely intimated to her, that she had accomplished a long and arduous journey, which had probably overtasked her strength and spirits.

'You are very good,' replied the Lady, 'but indeed it is not the journey. I have complaints that seriously affect my enjoyment; and that produce an overwhelming lassitude of mind and body. When I rise in the morning for example, I have no appetite whatever for my breakfast.'

'Eat less supper,' said the God.

'And then at night, I am quite troubled for want of sleep. O I cannot tell you how very restless and discomposed I am! how often I turn and turn again in my bed, endeavouring, but ineffectually, to lose myself in the delicious slumber that I once enjoyed; that came so lightly over me, and dwelt so sweetly, and that used to refresh me so much. Those nights are gone from me!'

'You must pass your waking hours in gentle and benevolent occupation. Let it be useful and regular. Dismiss from your mind all anxious and all ambitious thoughts, and never under any presence suffer yourself during the day to nod in your chair; nor loll for a moment upon your couch.'

'Ah! but then,' said she, 'I am become so excessively languid; and, may it please your worship, heavier, and heavier, alas! every day; sometimes do you know I think, every hour!'

'You should force yourself to get up before noon, my lady; and often employ those pretty limbs of yours in moving about from place to place. Perhaps you may not know it, but they were given to you for this purpose.'

'Wine hurts me,' said the belle. 'Drink water,' said the oracle.

'And my sight fails me !'—'Use spectacles.' 'And then as for my digestion, good GOD, my digestion!' cried she, in an accent of despair——'Diet yourself; never eat unless you are hungry, and then less always than you desire.'

'No, but I wish you fully to understand,' replied the fair patient, 'that I find myself altogether weaker than I used to be ; that I am no longer by any means so healthful, and vigorous, and fresh in the enjoyment of my time, and of the pleasures that wait now almost unoccupied, around me ! Life itself in short wears no longer for me the gay, and the elastick charm that it was wont to possess !'

'*You grow old, my friend,*' answered the God, in a low tone of voice.

'Old ! certainly ! bless me, yes ! we all do that !' exclaimed the Lady : 'but I have come now to ask you how I am to get rid of this languor and stiffness and heaviness and incapacity for active enjoyment that harasses me thus ?'

'The shortest, and indeed the only sure method that you can re- sort to, O beautiful IRENE, is to follow the example of your mother, and of your grandmother.'

'Ah indeed !' said the Lady ; 'and pray if you please, tell me, what *was* that ?' 'To DIE,' returned the God.

'To. DIE ! to DIE !' repeated she ; 'and is this the counsel that you give me ! Is this the result of all that vast reputation for science which is associated with your name throughout the world ? which men delight to publish and rehearse, and to which I have listened in admiration both at Athens and in Rome ! What single word have you now told me that is either oracular or even novel to me ? Did I not myself know every one of the remedies you have pre- scribed before I had stirred a foot beyond the borders of Attica ?'

'Why did you not then avail of them ?' answered the God, 'and spare yourself the inconvenience of travelling so far from your comforts ; abridging as you have done the short remainder of life by so long and fruitless a journey ? A person of your accomplish- ments and discernment ought to know, that for Old Age there is no other remedy than DEATH.'

This story of Irene is a recollection from La Bruyère ; who has himself taken it from Theophrastus, the 'man of divine words ;' of whom Cicero has written : 'Who is there in language more abun- dant and rich than Plato ; more solid and vigorous than Aristotle ; or than Theophrastus more delightful and sweet ?' 'Quis uberior in dicendo Platone ? Quis Aristotele nervosior ? Theophrasto dulcior ?'

I often advert to it in my thoughts ; often speak to myself in the low tones of the oracle at Epidaurus, 'You grow old, my friend ;' and generally with much the same effect as that impressed upon the mind of Irene. I admit the fact ; indeed I feel that I cannot con- test it ; while the inference that follows it still rests inconceivable to my apprehension. There is no delusion about the melancholy state itself ; the difficulty is to submit gracefully to its fatal conse- quences, and to realize, uncomplainingly, that it has at last come over me.

'Old!'——the sad, sad word! 'There goes JOHN WATERS the old man!' what a melancholy, what an uncourtly phrase! how much preferable that. which Shakspere makes Benedict to fear; and yet Benedict was a brave man. It is absurd to say that I am old only in judgment and understanding. 'That which was brown has become grey, while that which was foolish remains foolish still.' Alas! that a change so obvious should have been wrought in this physical organization, and the ethereal structure that abides within it bear so slight an indication of the approach of the life to come! that the march of Death with all its 'pomp and circumstance' should be palpable to every sense — and Immortality remain a calm conception only of the soul!

O who that examines his heart can ever doubt the strong necessity of the Revealed Word; or fail to see, in this necessity, an argument, upon this ground almost incontrovertible, of the truth of its Existence!

But it is not in the order of my vocation to attempt a sermon, and no one should permit himself to assail the world with a lament. I had it merely in my thoughts, when I sat down, to describe a vivacious gentleman of a certain age who without visiting Epidaurus in person, had cheerfully and contentedly listened to the whispering expression of the God, and who now beheld the approach of age without a sigh.

But as I sat in my nice fauteuil imagining the scene in the Temple, and picturing gently again and again the delicious repose enjoyed in her youth by the beautiful Irene, I anticipated thee, dear Reader, by sinking fast asleep over this my own Essay, and I shall now close it by imparting to thee the vision that ensued. I have only to express the hope that thine own dream — if what I write shall have the merit of inspiring thee one — may be a thousand times the happier of the two.

Methought then, that emancipated from all the remaining ties of Earth, my spirit stood upon the Southern side of the base of the mountain of LIFE; into which a huge part of the world had risen up before me in the form of a cone.

Methought, while I gazed upon the vast acclivity, that the mountain-side grew covered over with myriads of my own race, of both sexes, and of every age under ripe manhood; all climbing diligently upward, over barren passages of earth, over wild extended coverings of heather, or through flowers and shrubs and groves of endless variety of leaf and fruit; or beside rocks and along precipices that were quick with the numbers that were falling over them.

At every step, for every step was upward, some change took place in the appearance of each Individual in form in height in beauty or in grace. Infants became young girls, and girls were belles, and belles grew matrons. And boys who escaped the dangers by which they had been surrounded in like manner became youths, young men, and men.

The destruction of the race appeared to my spiritual sense to be by no means whatever limited to those who like samphire-gatherers

come down and pray and sing a verse or two, and we shall expect all that do n't want to be written damned forever to come forward while we are doing it, and kneel down in the altar. Half an hour's waiting will make it too late; come at once, all that will come. Mercy can't wait longer for sinners that deserve damnation for every day and hour of their lives, (advancing to the steps and still rubbing his hands.) We are coming down now.' After this regal announcement, he stepped down, walked out in the centre of the altar, and imperatively commanded one of the sisters, who had dropped in to share the labors, to pray. While this was being done, he promenaded the inclosure, still rubbing his hands, smiling on those whom he wished to draw within the circle; and contemplating those who, alarmed and excited, rushed in from time to time and buried their faces in the seats, with a look which I could liken to nothing but that with which an amateur butcher regards a fine lamb. When the prayer ceased, the verse or two were performed; always by himself in a most execrable style; a short exhortation was then delivered, generally in the following style :

' Well, we have prayed and sung, and some of you that want to be saved have come in; but you have n't all come. We 'll give you a little longer time to escape from hell, and then if you won't, you must be damned. We 'll sing a verse or two more, and we shall expect you all to come in. Do n't wait to think what other folks will say to see you come in, but think how all hell will roar with laughter for every one that stays away. Now then, while we sing, come in.' There was one redeeming feature in these blasphemous exhortations. The daring wretch who uttered them seldom named the name of GOD. He could join in the exultations of fiends over lost souls, but never in the joys of purer spirits.

The exercises thus introduced were termed prayer rings. They were scenes of confusion of which the most powerful language would convey but a faint description. I expressed something like this in the hearing of a brother.

' Oh,' said he, ' this is no account, nohow; wait till after night, if you want to see the meeting awake.'

I did so, and found the good brother had not exaggerated. At dark candles were lighted, and placed in the trees, on the posts around the stand, and along the tent doors. As soon as this was done, Brother Damall rose on the stand, and announced that a prayer ring would be formed in the altar for the salvation of lost souls. After the usual blasphemous harangue, he advanced to the steps, and said, ' We are coming down now to pray for you lost and damned sinners, and if you do n't come in you will go to hell in spite of us.' In the altar were a few seats and scattered chairs, across which several women and a few men were already kneeling. I recognised Sister Blowoph's scanty skirt under one of the dropping candles; but whether she was kneeling or not it was impossible to tell. When Brother Damall had advanced near the centre of the altar, he turned abruptly, looked sharply at one of the kneeling figures, and speaking in the most peremptory tone, ordered Sister Harris to pray. She

Upward, upward, all clomb upward! and the heart of every crea-
ture occupied the expressions of his face! Some gazed in the air
with wild extatick fervour, imagining that which was not yet re-
vealed; some watched the ever-varying colours of the sky and
Earth, and GOD loved them for the unmeasured joy with which
they read HIS language; some occupied themselves with motes
that floated in the sunbeams; and not a few, especially among the
un-paired climbers of my own sex, fastened their observations upon
the soil, and every now and then dug and picked up and encumbered
themselves with valueless pebbles, which they falsely esteemed to
be the richest treasure that the mountain afforded.

Upward, upward, all clomb upward! And now when they had
attained the full maturity of all their faculties, the few that survived
the countless dangers of the way had reached the apex of the moun-
tain; and by far the larger portion of these few crossed it to de-
scend upon the northern side. They were wedded to Earth; and
to them it appeared as if nothing had been accomplished while any
thing remained to be gained or acquired. They had become pos-
sessed by habits of accumulation, by habits of surmounting difficul-
ties and dangers; and they preferred that mode of life, and to pur-
sue it, even alone, than to retrace their course by gentle paths to
the tranquil vale of years that extended itself along the southern
base of this vast mountain.

The choice to return was freely at the option of all who had
reached the height of land, but it was generally refused, and by
those who afterward perished miserably in the descent upon the
northern side, haunted as it is by the thousand Demons of avarice, of
malice, of ambition, hatred, sensuality and wordly love, who enticed
this wretched portion of our race into the frightful caverns of Hy-
pochondria and Madness or Despair, where their lives were ex-
hausted in the severest imaginable grief and sufferance.

It was a pleasure to me to turn from such a fate to the few who
had chosen ' that better part,' and were descending downward on the
sunny side of life. Few indeed were they in number; and scat-
tered as they were amidst the vast ascending multitudes, I was not
for some time conscious of the paths by which they threaded their
way against the upward tide; and I had falsely imagined that all were
going with it.

But now it was given me to behold them, and to watch, with a
serene joy, the gentle spirit that seemed to actuate their movements,
as they accosted, or for a moment paused to converse with the young
ascending couples, or with the unpaired climbers of either sex.

Step after step, they took every step downward, some thought-
lessly; some heedlessly; some reluctantly; none gladly. For the
most part they wore ' a longing, lingering look' as the bright eye,
the youthful complexion, the fair form, the elastick footstep, or the
gallant and resolved bearing of the young and ardent upward-tra-
veller caught their attention upon all sides and gave joy to existence:
and some among those who were thus descending alone were un-
wise enough to make instant love to the young faces they encoun-

tered, and tried in vain to retrace the upward path with those they had thus incautiously engaged. But nothing could be shewn to be more absurd than an attempt of this nature between individuals who were obviously journeying in opposite directions; and often at the moment that they joined hands, the air was filled with a laughing pleasantry of musick that rang to the following words:

> ' CRABBED Age and Youth
>   Cannot live together;
> Youth is full of pleasance,
>   Age is full of care:
> Youth like Summer Morn,
>   Age like Winter Weather;
> Youth like Summer brave,
>   Age like Winter bare.
> Youth is full of sport,
> Age's breath is short;
>   Youth is nimble, Age is lame;
> Youth is hot and bold,
> Age is weak and cold,
>   Youth is wild, and Age is tame.
> Crabbed Age and Youth
> Cannot, cannot live together.'

While I stood for a moment regarding these idle, misjudging, frivolous old fellows, a LADY whose large dark contemplative eyes will never fade from my memory, descended with a movement of exquisite grace and gentleness, and yet withal a fixed determined step, upon her lonely way.

Time, the Restorer, had calmed the griefs of earlier life, and quieted the one great disappointment of her youth, which had deprived her of that wider sphere of usefulness that sometimes surrounds the wife and mother. But usefulness of the highest order was still hers, and every duty was fulfilled. Tranquillity, surpassing pleasure, was enshrined in her face; order, propriety and meekness marked every act. The old were comforted by her. The sick were solaced, and the heart was cured. Eyes was she to the blind, and strength to the weak, and, to the dying, Hope in prayer! The young hailed her and blessed her as they ascended and drew near, and listened to the gracious words, and watched the sainted upward look, with which she awakened in their spirits a holy joy 'while life itself was new.' They called her ' a Sister of Mercy;' but it was given me to know that her style in Heaven is to be ' an Angel of the Little Ones,' such as stand before THE THRONE!

I know not how much longer I should have gazed at her, but my attention was at the moment irresistibly attracted by the appearance of a half-jovial, half-sentimental old fellow who drew a double allotment of pleasure and pain from every thing that was going on. I saw at a glance that he was endued with a quick and nice perception, a profound love and veneration for the beautiful and the good, and a gentle incalescence toward those charms of social life, the table and the glass.

He seemed to have a share, beside his own, in the happiness and in the cares of half of his acquaintance; and he strictly followed, of his own natural bias, the injunction to mourn with those who weep, and particularly to rejoice with them that rejoice. His chief desire, so far as his own concerns were in question, seemed to be to take his steps downward with a certain gentility and nicety of tact, but his proprieties were sometimes interrupted in the ardour of his temperament.

His own affairs he took for the most part easily, and reconciled himself with an adjusting sort of philosophy to those events which were beyond his controul, or which happened diversely to his expectations : like the judicious person we read of who threw a stone at a dog and hit his cruel stepmother and yet soon consoled himself by the reflection, that although he certainly had failed of his aim, the stone was not altogether lost.

Now among the young faces who were coming upward, and upon whom his eye rested with an unspeakable joy, was one of surprising brilliancy and sweetness, not unaccompanied with an air of much archness and espieglerie, that revealed a half-disposition to make game and sport of his predilections ; and I was just prepared to listen to the song I have recited of ' Crabbed Age and Youth,' when, happily for his reputation, he sank into the earth upon a bed of roses while his look was yet fastened on her and he was thus lost to the mountain forever !   When she saw that he was disappearing from her sight, she threw toward him a wreath of laurel which even while sinking he caught to his heart, and valued, chiefly because of the affinity it bore to her charming name.

I was so shocked at his fate, that I started and awoke ; and it was not till I had repeated glass after glass of my best sherry, which happened fortunately to be at hand, that my mouth was relieved of a fancied taste of rose-leaves and garden-gravel —— so effectual had been my sympathy for this poor light-hearted old fellow, whose fate even while I write I cannot but think an hard one, though I laugh too when I dwell upon the fun that sparkled in her bright face, and that hung enamoured around the most beautiful mouth in the world. I will go muse upon it.   JOHN WATERS.

THE TRANSIENT: FROM THE GERMAN.

SAY, where is the violet seen,
  Summer's joys pursuing ;
And the flowers' gentle queen,
  Her path with wild flowers strewing ?
Youth, the flow'ret's spring, is fled ;
And the violet is dead !

Say, whither has the bright rose flown,
  We singing pluck'd at morn ;
As shepherdess and lover prone,
  Their breast and brow adorn ?
Maiden, summer's warmth is fled,
And the rose lies scentless — dead !

Where 's the brook flows wild along,
  And violets did drink ?
Let me hear its murmuring song,
  Ere in the vale it sink !
Air and sun are heated sore,
And that brook is now no more !

Take me to the leaflet's shade,
  Once with roses strew'd ;
There the lover sought his maid,
  Found her — and there woo'd !
Wind and hail are storming sore,
And the leaflet is no more !

Say, where has the maiden fled ?
  Her resting-place reveal ;
I mark'd her bow her humble head,
  And to the violet kneel :
Youth, that beauty all has fled,
And the maiden fair is dead !

Where 's the singer in his bower,
  Who singeth rural lays ;
Who sang the shepherdess, the flower,
  The leaf, the rivulet's praise ?
Maiden, swiftly life's hours fly ;
And the singer too must die !   L. A. B.

THE LAST OF THE RED MEN.

BY MISS M. R. GARDINER.

I saw him in vision — the last of that race
Who were destined to vanish before the pale-face,
As the dews of the evening from mountain and vale,
When Night from the sunbeam flies stricken and pale ;
Alone, mid the wrecks that rise great in decay,
Gigantic, sublime, in their mantles of gray,
Though Nature has leagued with the Spaniard to throw
A veil o'er the records of might and of wo ;
Alone with the Past and the Future's chill breath,
Like a soul that has entered the Valley of Death !

He stood where of old from the Fane of the Sun,
While cycles unnumbered their centuries run,
Never quenched, never fading and mocking at Time,
Blazed the fire sacerdotal far o'er the fair clime ;
Where the temples o'ershadow the Mexican plain,
And the hosts of the Aztec were conquered and slain ;
Where the *Red Hand* still glows on pilaster and wall,
And the serpent keeps watch o'er the desolate hall.
He stood like the lightning-scath'd oak in its pride,
All leafless and hoar on the bleak mountain side ;
But stately in death and refusing to bend,
To the blast that ere long must its frail branches rend ;
With the ruin around him unwept in his fall,
And gazing alike on the sunshine and pall ;
With coldness and courage confronting Life's care,
But the coldness, the courage that 's born of Despair.

I marked him where winding through harvests of gold,
The ' Father of Rivers' in majesty rolled ;
Where the dark mounds in silence and loneliness stand,
And the wrecks of the red man are strewn o'er the land.
The forests were levelled that erst were his home,
O'er the fields of his sires glittered city and dome ;
The chieftain no longer in green wood and glade,
With trophies of fame wooed the dusky-haired maid,
And the voice of the hunter had died on the air,
With the victor's defiance and captive's low prayer.
But the winds and the waves and the firmament's scroll
With divinity still were instinct to his soul ;
At midnight the war-horse still cleaved the blue sky,
As it bore the departed to mansions on high :
Still dwelt in the rock, and the shell, and the tide,
A tutelar angel, invisible guide ;
Still heard he the tread of the Deity nigh,
When the lightning's wild pinion gleamed bright on the eye,
And saw in the Northern-Lights flashing and red,
The shades of his fathers, *the Dance of the Dead !*
And scorning the works and abode of his foe,
The pilgrim turned far from that valley of wo,
His dark eagle gaze to the sun-gilded West,
Where the fair land of shadows lies viewless and blessed.

Again I beheld him where swift on its way,
Leaped the cataract, foaming with thunder and spray,
To the whirlpool below from the dark ledge on high,
While the surge of its waters commixed with the sky,
And the Iris celestial arched bright o'er the swell,
Like a vision of heaven descending to hell.
The dense earth thrilled deep to the voice of its roar ;
With the ' Thunder of Waters' shook forest and shore ;
As he steered his frail bark to the horrible verge,
And chanting his death song went down with the surge :

On ! on! mighty Spirit !
  I welcome thy spray ;
As the prairie-bound hunter
  The dawning of day ;
No shackles have bound thee,
  No tyrant imprest,
The hand of the pale-race
  On torrent and crest.

Their banners are waving,
  O'er hill top and plain ;
·The stripes of oppression
  Blood-red with our slain ;
The stars of their glory
  And greatness and fame ;
The signs of our weakness,
  The signs of our shame.

The green woods no longer
  In majesty rise,
To sport with the lightning,
  The God of the skies :
There are chains on the meadow
  And chains on the stream,
And our hunting grounds pass
  Like the shades of a dream.

The hatchet is broken,
  The bow is unstrung ;
The bell peals afar,
  Where the shrill war-whoop rung ;
The council fires burn
  But in thoughts of the Past,
And their ashes are strewn
  To the merciless blast.

But though we have perished
  Like leaves in their fall,
Unhonored with trophies,
  Unmarked by a pall ;
When our names have gone out
  Like a flame in the sea,
Pale-Faced shall our curse
  Cling forever to ye !

On ! on ! mighty Spirit !
  Unchecked in thy way ;
I smile on thine anger
  And sport with thy spray ;
The soul that has wrestled
  With Life's darkest form,
Shall baffle thy madness,
  And pass in the storm.

eyes were deep-set, and half-shaded by brows that pointed downward from all directions, giving an expression of indescribable villany to the little black, shining, restless balls that glared from these hairy caverns. The forehead was low, compressed, and covered with a yellow skin drawn like parchment over it. Immediately below, the face expanded laterally to an enormous width, from which it tapered again to a wedgelike point in the long, projecting chin. But his smile was repulsive, chilling; it froze every genial spring in the bosom, and made you feel that humanity was degraded in being linked to such a face and nature. I studied this smile afterward, and am bound to say that it grew more and more diabolical at every change. I was so lost in contemplating the extraordinary character of the face, that I paid no attention to the words which issued from it. When therefore an elderly sister, who had observed my earnest look, congratulated me on having arrived early enough to hear Brother Damall, and requested the favor of my opinion, I was obliged to solicit a longer time to make it up. I took the liberty, however, of suggesting that if good doctrines came out of that face, it was one of the greatest paradoxes I had ever seen.

'Pair o' does,' she replied. 'I do n't know nothing about them, but we all know Brother Damall is the powerfulest preacher we 've ever had, and there 's been a heap on 'em, first and last.'

'But his face, Madam. If he were as eloquent as Gabriel, his face would ruin him any where.'

'Brother Gabriel never has preached here, I reckon; I do n't recollect him. But if he did, I do n't think he could be smarter than Brother Damall, nohow. His face ain't handsome, I know; but if you know'd him as well as we do, he would n't look bad to you.'

'Is he so good a man, then, as to make you love him by his deeds?'

'Yes, he is that. I never know'd a man that was so quick to see any thing that 's wrong, and he 'd tell his best friend the next minute; he don't mince it either I can tell you; but let's you know mighty quick where you 'll go to if you do n't stop.'

'Indeed, he must be a very valuable man in your neighborhood. Does he ever do any thing wrong himself?'

'Not often, I calculate; but he will call himself a sinner, because all men are; and he says he feels sometimes as if he was the greatest one living'.'

It was plain that Brother Damall wished his people to believe him a sinner in the abstract only; an unwilling, but helpless victim to the depravity which shackles the purest, as well as the vilest of his race. I was strongly inclined to think he spoke the truth, and that he was really one of the greatest of sinners.

·Soon after this sermon closed, the signal for dinner was given, and about half the congregation retired, in good order, without the long line of tents to the tables. They were spread with the greatest abundance, and were really tempting, to appetites sharpened by a long ride and the fresh air of the grove. While we were eating, a brother and sister near me took up a lamentation over the smallness of the meeting, and the coldness of those present.

'They do n't git the spirit yet, nohow,' said the sister.

'No, they do n't,' replied the brother. 'I calculate we shan't get very warm afore to-morrow. We always have to wait till Sister Blowoph comes: she 'll start a meetin' better than a dozen preachers.'

'Oh yes, she 's a host herself. I remember two years ago there war n't a convert made till Sunday noon. Then she come, and there was mor'n twenty converted that night, and a right smart of 'em afore the meetin' broke up.'

From these remarks I concluded this sister must be very efficient in the good work; and felt no little curiosity to see her. About two hours after our return to the meeting, while a quiet and very honest man was preaching in the place recently occupied by Brother Damall, there was a considerable bustle for a few moments around the main entrance, and a woman was ushered into the assemblage, who, I felt assured, could be no other than Sister Blowoph. She was really a striking personage, to figure on such an occasion. She was about four feet two inches in height, and of a uniform width of three feet, from the shoulders downward. The outlines of her person had not the slighest visible curve. A straight sack, of her height and circumference, stuffed and dressed, would have been as symmetrical. She wore a dark brown dress of coarse circassian. The sleeves, very slightly enlarged at the top, were placed above the shoulder, and rose in a smart, ambitious little puff on each side of her small head. The latter, wearied apparently with a fruitless endeavor to sustain itself against the encroachments of 'the flesh' had abandoned the contest, and settled down quietly, just in time to preserve the organs of hearing against the rapacious enemy. The skirt of her dress was briefer even than the figure of the wearer; and revealed in all their glory the tops of a pair of cowskin boots, and the middle latitude of a pair of home-knit woollen hose. But its brevity was by no means a striking peculiarity, compared with its narrowness; and each was more distinctly exhibited from opposite points of view: the latter when the wearer's face was turned from you, the former when this position was reversed. The shoulders were partially covered with a very small cape of light blue calico, and the head was honored with an ancient 'straw scoop.' This extraordinary figure rolled across the camp-ground, its little head bobbing and smiling in a charming manner, and at length seated itself on a chair, which was vacated by a nimble little woman on its approach. Several significant nods and smiles exchanged between the more zealous, convinced me that my first conjecture was true. This was Sister Blowoph, the woman who had been so graphically described as a host in herself. It yet remained to ascertain in what her efficiency consisted. She was still panting from the recent effort, and could not have been reasonably expected to commence her labors till she had enjoyed a brief period of repose. But Sister B. was not subject to the mortal weakness of resting, though she appeared to be to that of eating. The most bitter and distressing groans were soon heard to issue from her panting form; her face, instead of fading, grew redder every moment; her eyes became suffused; her chest heaved, and she appeared, although the discourse then in progress was a very quiet one, to be laboring under a high degree of excitement. Her groans were soon responded to; her wailings and ejaculations seemed to harrow every bosom; and when the sermon closed, and she fell on her knees, there was a general outburst, and response of prayers, shrieks, and lamentations.

Sister Blowoph enjoyed no undeserved reputation. Her industry was great, her zeal greater, and her power and readiness surpassed them both. Her energies seemed to be perfectly kindled by the short exercise which she led, after the sermon; and she rose from her humble position, evidently prepared for any thing that might be demanded of her.

Brother Damall led the meeting; preaching frequently himself, and always dictating from the stand, at the close of every sermon, the order to be observed till the horn was blown to summon the audience to another. One of his favorite injunctions on these occasions was to gather in the tents to prayer. He usually delivered it smiling and rubbing his hands. He exhorted the brethren and sisters to remember that nothing could be done without prayer; that he and his colleagues might preach from the stand till doomsday, but they could never convert a soul without the prayers of all. He generally added, it was more convenient and fitting for the sisters to assemble on one side and the brethren on the other, and he hoped his brother ministers would distribute themselves among the tents, and remember that their hope of converting souls lay in prayer. I watched this villain's steps and deeds closely, in order to ascertain whether or not his face libelled his heart; and became convinced that it did not tell half the truth. He never entered the tents in which the men were assembled for prayer; but he could be seen standing over the kneeling form of some trembling girl, and looking upon her with a fiendish smile that chilled the heart of the beholder.

He descanted much and often on the efficacy and want of prayer, but never opened his own lips to utter a petition during the whole time that we witnessed his proceedings. I pondered much over the cause of this singular conduct. He was evidently a rank impostor. But he either had too much moral sense left to dare approach his Maker in that most sacred of all attitudes; or else he was too indolent to perform a duty which must have been extremely onerous to a nature like his under any circumstances; but more especially so there, where so much fire and zeal were demanded by the feelings of the listeners. Invariably when the season of devotion came, he called on some honest brother or sister. His wishes were always uttered as commands. When a ' prayer ring' was to be formed, he announced it at the close of a sermon, in something like the following style, rubbing his hands, and wearing all the time his diabolical smile.

' We are coming down now to pray in the altar for the conversion of souls whose damnation is just going into the record books of heaven. We are going to offer them one more chance. We shall come down and pray and sing a verse or two, and we shall expect all that do n't want to be written damned forever to come forward while we are doing it, and kneel down in the altar. Half an hour's waiting will make it too late; come at once, all that will come. Mercy can't wait longer for sinners that deserve damnation for every day and hour of their lives, (advancing to the steps and still rubbing his hands.) We are coming down now.' After this regal announcement, he stepped down, walked out in the centre of the altar, and imperatively commanded one of the sisters, who had dropped in to share the labors, to pray. While this was being done, he promenaded the inclosure, still rubbing his hands, smiling on those whom he wished to draw within the circle; and contemplating those who, alarmed and excited, rushed in from time to time and buried their faces in the seats, with a look which I could liken to nothing but that with which an amateur butcher regards a fine lamb. When the prayer ceased, the verse or two were performed; always by himself in a most execrable style; a short exhortation was then delivered, generally in the following style :

' Well, we have prayed and sung, and some of you that want to be saved have come in; but you have n't all come. We 'll give you a little longer time to escape from hell, and then if you won't, you must be damned. We 'll sing a verse or two more, and we shall ·expect you all to come in. Do n't wait to think what other folks will say to see you come in, but think how all hell will roar with laughter for every one that stays away. Now then, while we sing, come in.' There was one redeeming feature in these blasphemous exhortations. The daring wretch who uttered them seldom named the name of God. He could join in the exultations of fiends over lost souls, but never in the joys of purer spirits.

Tho exercises thus introduced were termed prayer rings. They were scenes of confusion of which the most powerful language would convey but a faint description. I expressed something like this in the hearing of a brother.

' Oh,' said he, ' this is no account, nohow; wait till after night, if you want to see the meeting awake.'

I did so, and found the good brother had not exaggerated. At dark candles were lighted, and placed in the trees, on the posts around the stand, and along the tent doors. As soon as this was done, Brother Damall rose on the stand, and announced that a prayer ring would be formed in the altar for the salvation of lost souls. After the usual blasphemous harangue, he advanced to the steps, and said, ' We are coming down now to pray for you lost and damned sinners, and if you do n't come in you will go to hell in spite of us.' In the altar were a few seats and scattered chairs, across which several women and a few men were already kneeling. I recognised Sister Blowoph's scanty skirt under one of the dropping candles; but whether she was kneeling or not it was impossible to tell. When Brother Damall had advanced near the centre of the altar, he turned abruptly, looked sharply at one of the kneeling figures, and speaking in the most peremptory tone, ordered Sister Harris to pray. She opened her petition with a few words which were inaudible, amid the half suppressed groans, and the bustle of people hurrying in from their seats outside. But her voice soon rose; the groans and ejaculations increased; shrieks were heard, hands were clapped; many joined in with the leading prayer, others took up short pithy sentences uttered by their neighbors, and repeated them with great rapidity. One man prayed that they might be 'led out of the captivity of sin.' His next neighbor took up the sentence, and shouted as loudly as his broken breath and high excitement would permit, 'lead us out! lead us out! lead us out!' Another prayed that they might 'be held up in their trials and difficulties.' This was seized upon by a person near the first one, and they shouted alternately, 'Hold us up,' 'lead us out,' 'hold us up,' 'lead us out,' as long as I was within hearing. All this time others were praying, singing, shouting, clapping hands, swinging to and fro upon their knees, groaning, shrieking, screaming.

The altar was crowded. The voice of Sister Harris was lost; and indeed, no words were intelligible save those uttered by persons directly at your side. The crowd pressed up against the railing, and the situation was becoming very uncomfortable. But our little party maintained its union, and we concluded to linger a few minutes longer, to see if any new feature could be added to a scene that already beggared all description. We felt some interest, also, to learn how Brother Damall was employed during this extraordinary period. I was satisfied that, if any convenient opportunity presented, he would throw off the assumed character, and indulge in the luxury of a natural manifestation. After some effort, my friend discovered him kneeling across a chair, at the opposite side of the altar; his hands clasped, and his face wearing an expression of the most devout entreaty. It was worth some effort to discover whether he was really engaged as he appeared to be, or not. But, as all sounds were becoming more indistinct in the general Babel, it was impossible to ascertain this without placing ourselves close beside him. Accordingly, keeping the inside of the curious and excited crowd, we made our way around till we came opposite him. His lips moved, but the sounds, if any came forth, were inaudible, till one of us bent toward him, and found him uttering the words, 'Oh, thunder! thunder! thunder!' in a tone expressive of a satisfaction and triumph that were irrepressible! His imposture was completely unmasked. The confusion had favored his desire to have a little confidential intercourse with himself, and he was enjoying it in the elegant terms just stated!

Shocked and disgusted, beyond measure, with the whole scene, we went to a little cabin near the camp ground, where we had been very hospitably invited to take beds for the night, and attempted to sleep. The noise increased, and the deep wood echoed to sounds more frightful and abhorrent than the war-whoop and death-song of the Indian, till past midnight, when our wearied senses were lost in sleep.

At early sunrise a horn was blown from the stand, and in a few

moments the whole camp-ground presented a lively scene of pre-
paration for the day. The breakfast fires sent their light blue smoke
curling through the dewy tree-tops; white cloths were spread about
on the turf. Forms were glancing to and fro among the tents; little
children who had forgotten where they went to sleep were gazing
delightedly about, and endeavoring to recollect how they came in
such a fairy place. A few tidy maidens were sweeping the stand
with bough brooms; careful matrons were depositing articles of
dress in safe places; those who cooked were compounding dodgers,
biscuits, etc.; coffee-kettles were bubbling; ' chicken fixens' were
smoking; and every thing indicated that a lively day was opening
upon us.

Brother Damall delivered a short discourse before breakfast, in
which he more than suggested that it seemed advisable to him to
change somewhat their mode of proceeding. And as prayer had
not been very efficacious in awakening the damned, he thought it
best to exhort and sing more. He would recommend less public
and more private prayer; and expressed himself decidedly confi-
dent that the secret petitions of the brethren and sisters, seconded
by singing and exhortation, would be more efficient than the means
they had previously adopted.

He was evidently clearing the field for himself. After preaching,
singing and exhortation were his only resources. In the former he
enjoyed some celebrity. One of the sisters had predicted at the
close of his sermon on the previous day, that when he sang I would
say I had never heard such a singer open his mouth. The good
lady's words were literally true, though not in the sense which she
meant to convey. He sang wretchedly. There were a hundred
persons on the ground whose singing was infinitely superior to his,
and yet he had contrived so to master the affections and even the
senses of these people, that their very ears refused to do their
duty.

When his discourse, which was very brief, closed, the breakfast
signal was given, and we were just stepping out to the tables, when
Sister Blowoph emerged from one of the tents, like a morning cloud
from the palace of the young day. She was clad in a sky-blue silk,
briefer in front than the brown dress of yesterday, and if possible,
a trifle narrower on the opposite side. The cow-skin boots were
still the same, rejoicing only in the additional lustre of a new coat
of tallow; the butternut hose still looked out between; the straw
scoop was still fresh and shady; and the blue calico cape had
been replaced by a bright orange bandanna handkerchief. Sister
Blowoph was evidently to be the distinguished personage of the
day—and a most ethereal-looking one she was, saving the boots,
hose and kerchief. The effect of her costume was at times exceed-
ingly picturesque. She was a moveable back-ground of cloud, rising
up frequently in the most unexpected quarters, and disappearing
as suddenly.

Seats at the tables were under no regulations. People sat down
wherever they chose as long as there were any vacant places. And

I could not forbear embracing this delightful liberty, to fall into the wake of Sister Blowoph, and seat myself by her side. When our plates were filled and the coffee served, she looked sharply out of her fat little eyes at my tumbler of water, and addressing me very abruptly, said, 'Young woman, do you love the LORD?'

What connection there was between the use of the pure element which seemed to have excited her disgust and the moral duty on which she interrogated me, did not clearly appear; but I replied that such different ideas were entertained as to what constituted love to GOD, that it might be difficult to answer her question.

'Have you ever been convicted of sin?'

'Oh yes! every day of my life.'

'Do n't you tremble when you think what a sinner you are before the LORD?'

'If I do,' I replied, 'it will not be more apparent to HIM that I confess it to you.'

This placed the good woman on her favorite ground. 'Oh, the pride of the carnal heart!' she exclaimed, in a tone which drew all eyes toward us. 'Oh, the wickedness of the nateral sperit! Ashamed of JESUS, that died on the cross for your sins! The carnal appetite (here she paused to introduce the limb of a fowl to her masticating organs,) is inemy against the good sperit! Oh, the sinfulness of the nateral heart! Young woman, if you do n't repent and confess your sins, you 'll be lost! I feel as if I should have to answer for you at the day of judgment! You must come to the SAVIOUR while he 's got marcy for you!'

By this time she had set into the rocking motion and whining tone which seemed to constitute much of the essential efficacy of her exhortations; and I took advantage of a short pause to stop the malicious laugh of my friends, who were seated in enviable security at a little distance, and the distressful groans that began to be poured forth on every side over the sinner.

'But, my good Madam,' said I, 'not so loud. If you mean to remonstrate with me upon my sins, it is a little indelicate, not to say unfriendly, to call the whole company to witness my condition and your reproof. Beside, I have a slight preference for enjoying the liberty which has been bestowed on me of confessing my sins to my MAKER alone; and still more, how should I know that you, who summon me to this duty, are not a greater sinner than I am?'

'Me a sinner!' she exclaimed, trembling with indignation, and speaking in her shrillest key; 'me a sinner!' But suddenly recollecting that Brother Damall taught that all men, and women too, were sinners, she assumed an air of the deepest humility, and added, 'Ah, yes! we 're all sinners! As St. Job says, 'we 're all strayed away and come short;' there ain't none that does good; no, not one.'

'Very well then, Madam, I call on you to confess your sins, or expect the fate which you do not hesitate to pronounce on me. Wicked woman,' I added, assuming her own style, 'how do you know that you are not waited for at this instant?' She groaned.

' How do you know but your fate is recorded, and you are sentenced to eternal perdition! And if you are, what can save you but the mercy which you deny to others? Does not St. Job, whom you have just cited, enjoin us to eschew ornament, and avoid all decoration of the person?—and here are you, an elderly woman, who ought to be a mother in Israel, and a pattern for the younger members of the flock, dressed in a sky-blue silk, with an orange shawl! How can you reprove me, who wear a garb so much more consistent with Christian plainness? Does not the same saint prohibit the indulgence of the carnal appetite? yet you have consumed five cups of coffee, while I have taken but half a tumbler of pure water. But sinful as these things are, I forbear calling the attention of the company to them; and only exhort you to think on them and mend your ways before the days come in which mercy will not be found of you.'

Here I paused in my exhortation. I had spoken in the gentlest tones, but my neighbor's face was nevertheless purple with rage.

' Young woman,' she replied, her small head shaking with passion, ' Brother Damall shall talk to you. He 'll let you know who 's a sinner, I reckon, afore he 's done with you.'

' I shall be exceedingly obliged to him for such information, Ma'am,' I replied; and our meal being over, the cloud departed in a tempest, and I rose and rejoined my friends.

The proceedings of this day were very similar to those of the previous one. Sister Blowoph's half-buried eyes twinkled daggers once or twice, when they rested on our party; and Brother Damall more than once made a demonstration of approaching; an event most ardently desired by each of us. But he never consummated his purpose.

In the afternoon we fell into conversation with an elderly gentleman and his wife, who were also zealous leaders in the good work, but of a very different stamp from those already introduced. The husband had come from Virginia, long years ago, and had moved from place to place at different times to escape the Yankees. The woman, then by his side, had been his companion in all his wanderings; and now, when the heads of both were whitened with age, they were living in a little cabin about five miles distant; their home as new as if both had just brought from paternal firesides the vigor and hopes of youth wherewith to build themselves up among men.

This I learned in a few words from the honest, unassuming wife, whose strong, dark face beamed goodness and intelligence. Her language, rough and unpolished though it was, was filled with meaning, and bespoke a soul that neither sought nor needed disguise.

Her husband was an open-browed, noble-looking man, slightly bent, but hale, and still athletic and sprightly. He was one of the true noblemen of these primitive regions, strong in mind, generous in spirit, fearless and prompt in action. He had been many years a member of the church; his house had been the home of the clergy until Mr. Damall came among them. He did not like him, he said, at the first, and had found no occasion to change his mind. He was right sorry; some of the brethren and sisters thought a heap of him, but he always seemed to him a mighty mean man. And his preachin' he did n't think was much account. He liked to hear a man say a pleasant thing sometimes, and he never did hear that yet from him. 'And I calculate,' said he, ' that he,'ll put for tall timber one of these days, and our folks 'll find they 've been barking up the wrong tree.'

I asked his opinion of camp-meetings in general. He looked at me with some surprise, and then said,

' Oh, I reckon a power of good may be done by 'em when they 're well led. I 've know'd a heap of folks to be converted at camp-meetings that would never have heer'd a sarmont any where else.'

' And are these conversions,' I asked, ' as likely to prove permanent as those which take place under less excitement ?'

' Why, I reckon that 's pretty much as folks choose for themselves,' said the sensible old man. ' I 've know'd a right smart of men, and women too, in my time, that have lived and died good Christians, that got their first religion at a camp-meeting. But it was n't under such preachin' as we are going to have now,' pointing to the stand where Brother Damall was already stationed, book in hand, ready for another onslaught upon his fellow-sinners.

' My text this afternoon, brethren,' said he, ' is in the words following, viz : ' And the wicked shall go away into everlasting punishment, prepared for the devil and his angels.' '

Disgusted with the grossness of his imposture and the unmitigated hate displayed in his discourses, we wandered out into the grove to enjoy the quiet and beauty that lay around us, until this vulgar reservoir of anathema should be exhausted. We had to walk some distance to place ourselves beyond the reach of his voice, but were amply repaid by the deep repose to which nature invited us in those deep recesses. It was near the close of summer. Vegetation had nearly perfected itself, and was awaiting the touch of decay with a resignation indicative of the success of its mission. There were a silence and rest in the deep wood which contrasted powerfully with the stir and hum we had just left. No one was abroad in the direction we had chosen. The very leaves hung motionless upon their stems. The intense sunlight poured over the forest and shot through the dense foliage upon the herbage below, in beams as changeless to the eye as if eternal day had come and the fountain of light were never again to be closed. The very birds had sought rest in the shade, and the only sound that broke the deep stillness was the soft murmur of the little brook as it bubbled over the roots and broken branches that crossed its bed. It had wrought a small basin at the foot of a stately oak, whose roots struck across into the opposite bank ; and here, embraced with piled moss and fringed with graceful flower-stems, whose petals had long since floated down its tiny current, the waters rested on their way, nestling and whispering softly to the wood.

While we lingered on its bank, two or three gray squirrels glanced along beneath a nut-tree on our right.   They were evidently reconnoitring for the approaching harvest, which the bending boughs promised should be very abundant.   As we were contemplating their movements the leaves began to shake and the sunny spots to dance upon the turf.   The spirit of motion had come abroad over the wood.   Sounds from the distant crowd swelled faintly on the wind; the shadows began to lengthen, and at intervals disappear altogether, and there was a hollowness in the air which indicated an approaching conflict of the elements.

We bent our steps to the camp-ground.   When we arrived Brother Damall had finished his discourse.   It was pronounced by an elderly brother near us to be ' *a peeler for sinners.*'

A shower was rising in the south-west.   Heavy masses of black cloud had already mounted half-way to the zenith.   The wind came in gusts, and the tops of the trees bent and rose under it like the heaving of the ocean.   Every thing was gathered hastily beneath the tents, and the people sat within them waiting the tempest.   The sun went down.   A few candles were lighted, but they were more quickly extinguished; and the camp-ground without was soon involved in profound darkness.   Here and there a straggling light shone dimly through the cloth tent, whose inmates sat huddled in silence; and occasionally the voice of prayer or the singing of a hymn greeted the ear.

We left the camp-ground early, grateful that a secure shelter from the impending storm awaited us.   It was long before we slept. The gusty wind, the booming thunder, the lightning glare, coupled with the thought of the helpless crowd who were awaiting the drenching rain, banished sleep.   The sublime, the sympathetic and the ludicrous were never more strongly mingled.   Contrasted with the warring of the elements was the image of Sister Blowoph, the glories of the ' sky-blue' violated by the ruthless storm; the upright scoop soaked and drooping from its fair proportions; the ribbons dishevelled, the orange kerchief wrinkled and lustreless; nothing left of all the brilliancy which had shone on the morning but the cow-skin boots and butternut hose.   The catastrophe deserved graver treatment than the peals of laughter which its bare anticipation drew from us.

But while we were thus indulging in half-ludicrous, half-painful fancies, the shower lingered strangely.   The lightning played over the black heavens, the thunder rolled fearfully, and the wind rushed through the grove as if all were acting in concert for the detection of some evil spirit lurking in the wood.   A little after midnight the rain began to fall; at first in large and distant drops, then by smaller ones, so close upon each other that the whole atmosphere seemed a falling ocean.   The shower was one of the heaviest that ever falls, even in this country of heavy showers.   It drenched our little cabin, and drove many of the sleepers, who were lying on their cloaks in the next room, to a frequent change of place.   What then, we thought, would be the condition of the crowds gathered n those frail tents? But morning came at last to tell us. The rain had ceased about three o'clock, and the sun rose clear over the sparkling grove. Where the branches were thickly woven the light seemed struggling through a vault of flashing gems. The grass and numerous plants bent beneath the weight of the large drops that hung upon them; and the leaves, as their burthens fell from one to another, resumed their natural positions with a slight and lively motion, that formed one of the most charming features of the scene. The birds rejoiced in the fragrant air, the bright sun and the glittering leaves, and hopped from branch to branch, twittering and uttering songs, broken into fragments by the deep joy of the hour.

We wandered toward the camp-ground. The fire-places were drenched and the ashes beaten into little pools that were now drained. The charred logs shone coldly in the morning sun, and the cooking vessels were half filled with the water that had fallen into them. Two or three forlorn figures had strolled from the tents and were looking dismally over the scene. The faculties of one seemed to be quite arrested; for he stood against the slab wall of a shanty, balanced on one foot, the other placed against the boards behind him. He was making an effort to adapt his eyes to the strong light of the sun, which shone directly in his face. One hand shaded his half-closed organs of sight, the other had dropped into his pocket and was buried nearly to the elbow. He was soliloquizing upon the violence of the storm :

'Well, this is the houdaciousest bust-up *I* ever seed, any how! Who 'd a calculated yesterday mornin' that we 'd been in this fix now? I reckon we shall have to put out to-day, for there ain't a dry rag among us, and the straw 's as wet as Mississippi sawyers. There 's no chance for another night here, no how! The truck 's all soaked, and there can 't nobody stay here to save souls without some kind of *roughness* to keep up natur'.'

His saturated garments smoked in the warmth of the sun, and the drooping rim of his sea-weed hat began to curl back in its heated rays. We passed on into the camp-ground. The scene was just opening here. Men, women and children crept cautiously from beneath the tents, and occasionally a dishevelled head was thrust forth, and a view of the scene taken, to be deliberated upon, before the body belonging to it was raised from its recumbent posture. There were men with cotton and linen coats, the skirts of which were thoroughly wet, while the remainder was dry; some had both legs wet to the knee, while others had preserved the whole of one limb dry at the expense of its fellow, which was thoroughly drenched. Some were soaked from head to foot on one side, some on the other; some on the back, indicating the choice of position in sleep; for nearly all had addressed themselves to sleep after the shower was over. The ground enclosed by each tent had been covered with straw, which answered the three-fold purpose of floor, seat and bed. This was saturated, or as the soliloquist outside had more happily expressed it, ' wet as Mississippi sawyers;' and now

began to send up volumes of vapor, which crowded through the
seams and burst out when the cloth door was drawn aside, as if each
tent had for the time been converted into a smoke-house.   Some of
the females had their skirts wet half a yard from the bottom; some
were drenched throughout, and some appeared in borrowed ones,
a world too wide, or too long, or too short; but still preferable to
their own dripping garments.

As they came forth they greeted each other with all the variety
of expression and sentiment that would be naturally called into
being by the occasion.

'Good mornin', Sister S.   You got a smart sprinklin' last night,
I reckon.'

'I calculate we did!   The water ran over us like a spring fresh.
My gown was wringin' when I got up, and the gals' is jest as bad.
But the sun 'll soon dry us off.   My old man wanted to gear up and
put right out; but I allowed we·'d better stay till arternoon, and I
told him one sprinklin' wan't of no account.'

'Well, I reckon you're right.   If we can't stand as much as that
to sarve the Lord, we need n't count ourselves much, nohow; an'
I told Brother Damall, when he allowed the meetin' would break
up this mornin', that I did n't think he know'd our sperit!'

'But I reckon,' said Sister S., 'some of 'em 'll have to put out,
any how.   There 's old man B.'s team gearin' up a'ready; but
they 're right bad off.   Sister B. has a baby, you know, only four
weeks old, and they was all soaked through.   It 'll be a massy if
the baby do n't die by it.   But I must go and see her afore she
goes; it 's like I can lend her something to wear home.'

Just as she returned to the spot where we were standing, a small
shrill voice from the second or third door called out, 'Mammy!
mammy! John has got all my wheat-doin's away from me!'

'I must go to the young ones,' said the vivacious woman, turning
quickly away.

We advanced a few steps and met an elderly brother, who was
limping from his tent, apparently all the worse for his involuntary
bath.   As we approached he was met by a young man, who accosted
him with the compliments of the hour, and inquired how he found
himself after the rain.

'It 's been mighty bad for me,' he replied.   'I reckon it 'll fetch
back the embargo I got in my back last summer; it 's full of misery
now.   Do you know any body going our road, that could tote me
home?'

'No, I do n't rightly; but I reckon there 'll be enough afore long.
There 's plenty of teams gearin' up.'

Leaving the old gentleman whose back was under an 'embargo,'
we turned our steps in another direction.   By this time the people
were pouring rapidly from their little steam-rooms, wet, wrinkled,
soiled and disconsolate.   One or two faint wreaths of smoke curled
lazily up beyond the tents, indicating some activity on the breakfast-
ground; but the life and joyousness of the previous morning were
all gone.

We looked anxiously about for Sister Blowoph; but she was no where visible. Brother Damall had mounted the stand and blown one or two blasts on the long tin horn; but even his fiery zeal was essentially cooled, and he sat turning over the leaves of a well-thumbed hymn-book as tamely as if there were not a sinner within the sound of his voice. An irrepressible burst of laughter and a jog of the elbow drew my attention from him, and turning in the direction of my friend's finger, I beheld the sky-blue suspended to the lower branch of a large elm, which swept the farther end of the camp-ground. It was inflated with the wind, and at the first glance looked as if Sister Blowoph were ascending bodily toward the cerulean; but a second look showed the absence of the boots and hose beneath, and the scoop above, and left the mind relieved of its painful anticipations. But the sky-blue, filled to its utmost capacities by the free wind, danced incontinently about before the eyes of the astonished spectators. While we were enjoying its graceful evolutions, the corporeal form with which it had before been identified appeared beneath it; so that she looked as if she had dropped out of her outer self, and there was one woman of flesh and bone and another ethereal copy; a sort of improved daguerreotype on a large scale. This time her efforts were put forth in behalf of the scoop, which had been suspended by the strings from the roof of her tent for greater safety than could be found elsewhere. While in this position it had been ingloriously filled with water; the crown was swelled out at the top to a sharp pyramidal form, and several enlargements at the side marred its former fair proportions. Every attempt which the afflicted woman made to restore it, only caused the hills to sink into alarming hollows; and from the forlorn expression with which she turned from it to her dress, I feared that hope had forsaken her afflicted heart.

Thinking that some bits of milliner-knowledge, therefore, might be so acceptable as to procure my pardon for the offence of the previous day, and if the truth must be told, desirous of enjoying the good woman's trepidation, I sauntered carelessly around toward the tree. By the time I reached it she had been to her tent and returned with some other bits of soiled finery, which she was exposing to the morning sun. It was a delicate matter, considering the rage in which she had parted from me and the ridiculous spectacle before us, to approach her; but the vein of her love for ornament was a rich one, and I felt safe in relying upon it. She was so busy as scarcely to heed my approach, until I accosted her with a 'Good morning, Ma'am.' 'Good morning, young woman,' she replied, glancing coldly at me.

'This is a delightful morning after the shower.'

'You may well say that, and be thankful for it too. I do n't know what 'ud 'a become on us if the LORD had n't sent this sun!'

'Now your dress and hat would have been seriously injured I fear, if you could not have dried them here.'

'That dress,' she replied looking affectionately upon it, 'I 've had this twenty-five year, and it never got such a wettin afore; I 'll be ruined and undone forever, I am afraid,' she added, taking hold of the linen and looking at its lustre, dimmed by the water and earth which had washed through her tent. 'I 've wore it to camp-meeting every year since we come from Indianny; and this bonnet too; and they have never been so much damaged afore. But LORD be praised, 't aint no wuss as it mought ha' been.'

'But if you could restore the hat to its proper shape,' said I ——

'Why I 'd be right glad to do it, young woman, and that I tell you ;' but I do n't know nothin' about doin' such jobs.'

All this time the distressed woman was smoothing the silk, patting the ribbons, and endeavoring to level the unsightly elevations that maimed the proportions of her much-loved hat. Groans and ejaculations of gratitude that it was no worse, interlarded these employments, and broke her conversation into fragments, so that it ran very much as follows : 'I reckon it never will come right again; but massy, 'taint a soul lost if it do n't. LORD be praised, if I know'd any body that could make 'em look smart again, I 'd give a heap. But 'taint no 'count for a Christian woman that's got a soul to save to be spendin' her time with sich vanities. But, young woman, if you happen to know any body can do it for me, I 'll pay 'em well. I reckon you 're from the East; and Miss Shippen told me t'other day that the eastern folks knew how to make new bonnets out o' old. It must be mighty handy. But LORD bless us, 'taint worth thinkin' about when any body's got a soul to save from eternel ruin.'

'I can tell you, Madam,' I at length said, 'how to restore your hat so that it will be none the worse for the rain.'

'Can you ? LORD bless you ! how can I do it. The Yankees know a heap more than we about all sich things. I reckon you 'll know how to fix my gown too. But they aint hardly worth a Christian's thought. But how shall I do it ? Tell me that, an' I shall be mighty obleeged to you.'

'It will be so trifling an object for a Christian woman,' I said, 'that you might not choose to do it after I had told you. The hat will shelter you just as well now, soiled and bent as it is, and it is sinful to want more, is it not ?'

'Now do n't be so tough,' said she, in a delightfully confidential manner. 'I reckon I 'm as good a Christian as most that 's goin', but I aint so nigh heaven that I want to wear such a bonnet when I can just as well have it better. There 's proper ways in every thing, young woman, and I do n't think 't would be improper for me to make my hat look as well as I can ; so, as I said afore, if you know any way to do it you 'll obleege me by tellin' it.'

I accordingly enlightened the old lady in the mysteries of pressing damp braid, advised her to dye her silk gown, and to abate some of her zeal with which she attacked strangers in their religion, and bidding her good morning, rejoined my friends, who were now preparing to return home.

As we passed the stand, Brother Damall was delivering some hints to the brethren on the care of their horses. What they were, we did not stop to ascertain. The breakfast-tables were not yet laid, and every thing about the fire looked cheerless enough to make us think with pleasure of the cheerful cabin and the social little home table where so many delights had been shared.   We hastened down to the room where we had slept, put our baskets, etc., in order ; and were soon riding merrily off over the prairie.

REASON AND FANCY.

BY SUSAN PINDAR.

A boy once launched a little skiff
  Upon the summer sea,
And with him two companions took,
  To bear him company.

First Reason came, with sober mien,
  And clear and steady light,
Then Fancy, with her golden wings,
  And changing colors bright ;

And as they left the verdant shore,
  And floated down the tide,
The boy exclaimed, in gleeful tones,
  ' Let Fancy be my guide !'

The Goddess shook her glittering plumes,
  And steered the little bark,
While Reason's light waned pale and dim,
  And faded to a spark.

Where'er the eddies brightest danced
  Beneath the sunbeam's ray,
With rapid and unskilful stroke
  Gay Fancy led the way.

And oft they lingered near the shore
  To cull the blushing flowers,
Nor heeded in their wild delight
  The swiftly-passing hours.

But soon a threatening cloud arose,
  And veiled the sunny sky ;
The angry waves, in hasty strife,
  Rose fearfully and high:

And darker still the storm-cloud grew,
  Their mirth was lost in fear ;
Poor Fancy, 'wildered and dismayed,
  Was all unfit to steer.

And tempest-tossed, their little skiff
  Rocked wildly on the wave,
When Reason calmly took the helm,
  To succor and to save.

While with a steady hand she steered,
  Her lamp shone clear and bright,
And o'er the water's dark expanse
  Shed forth a cheerful light.

And when the sun smiled gaily down,
  With glances kind and warm,
The little bark, by Reason's skill,
  Had weathered out the storm.

Then Fancy plumed her golden wings
  And sung a joyous strain,
But Reason kept the helm, for fear
  A storm should rise again !

Her mellow light with Fancy's glow
  Harmoniously blended,
And evermore their pleasant course
  With safety was attended.

And thus, when youth first spreads his sail
  Upon Life's changing sea,
He dreams not how o'ercast with clouds
  His future course may be.

But blest, if Reason's steady light,
  His little boat doth steer,
While brilliant Fancy sits beside,
  The fleeting hours to cheer.

For life, how smooth soe'er its sea,
  Hath many a wintry season,
And Fancy is a fickle guest
  If guided not by Reason.

M A N :   A   R H A P S O D Y .

BY THE LATE MRS RIGGS.

'How poor, how rich, how abject, how august,
How complicate, how wonderful is man!'— YOUNG.

'WHAT a piece of work is man!'— SHAKSPEARE.

So MUCH has been said and written upon woman, and her influence upon the world, that one would be led to conclude that men were in fact the human race ; and that woman was a sort of afterthought, an addenda no way essential to the existence of things, but which really proved so convenient and agreeable as to call forth a continuous stream of wondering gratitude. We have been looked at in every possible point of view, morally, physically and intellectually. We have been analyzed, criticized and eulogized ; not a trait nor peculiarity about us but what has again and again been held up to an admiring world. We have been called ' a delightful puzzle,' ' an enigma,' ' a conundrum ;' and have been thanked in the warmest manner for existing, as if it were wholly gratuitous on our part, and simply from an amiable wish to oblige.

Now, to bring a little common sense to bear upon this subject, it seems scarcely worthy of all the ado that has been made about it, that exactly one-half of the human race should be of some consequence to the other half, or should have qualities to fit them for the station for which they were designed! But while we cannot but laugh in our sleeves at being so terribly ' bepraised,' it must be admitted that in one point of view it is wholly disinterested ; since no female writer has ever risen up to pay them in kind by going into extacies with *Men*, and the influence *they* exert upon society! The reproach of insensibility shall no longer rest upon the female sex. Be mine the privilege to give them a *quid pro quo ;* and would that I could bring to the task talents commensurate with the magnitude of the subject!

Let us look at him, reader, in every point of view. And first, as to his terrestrial frame. He is taller, stronger, and has more matériel in him than we have. He is better adapted for gloves and roundabouts—at least so say our neighbors the French, and they know ; for during their memorable revolution they beguiled the horrors of the scene by little useful and curious arts, such as tanning the skins of the victims ;* and while that of men was found to be truly excellent and serviceable, that of women was weak and tender—absolutely good for nothing. Now this is a tangible proof of their superiority, and is worth volumes of abstract reasoning. What symmetry of form does he possess! And then his com-

_____

* CARLYLE.

plexion! — I *could* liken it to the rind of a common tropical fruit, or the outside of a necessary article in equestrian exercises; but not for the world would I have my refinement or good taste called in question; therefore I say nothing. His dress too is so calculated to please the eye and set off any natural advantages he may possess! To a sensitive mind it might seem somewhat trying to exhibit to a critical and unthankful world any peculiarities of shape or gait; but I am not sure that it is not an advantage. If his contour reminds you of a parenthesis, or a pair of walking dividers, there is no harm done. It relieves the sameness of life; it gives a variety. Women seem all run in the same mould, and there is no distinguishing nature from art; but with the sterner sex it is otherwise. If they are corpulent or emaciated, crooked or straight, the whole world is aware of the fact, and nobody the worse for it.

Where all are excellent it may seem invidious to give one class the preëminence; but if I have a preference, it is for men a *little* inclined to corpulency! What dignity does it impart, and what an outline! And then what husbands and fathers they make; for, knowing 'the ills that *flesh* is heir to,' they are prepared to meet them. And as to you, ye little *tom-tits*, parading about as if it were no manner of consequence that your nearest female relative was ignorant of your whereabout, although I would fain avoid bearing too hard upon you, yet let me whisper to you in confidence that if you desire to be honored, respected and craved, *grow!* GROW! But this is a digression.

In expatiating upon the physical perfections of the lords of the creation, let me not forget their mental superiority. Such powerful and commanding intellects as they possess; all of them too; it shows itself from the highest literary effort down to the sitting for a daguerrean portrait! Yes, humbling as it may be to us, never is their surpassing greatness more plainly evinced than in this; for while they can keep their eyes wide open by sheer force of intellect, we wink and blink, and thus almost lose the benefit of the invention. This may be said to be a weak argument, but nothing can be considered trifling that tends to elucidate my point.

But let us look at them in their social relations. And to begin with their boyhood: what spectacle can be more pleasing to a refined and benevolent mind than a lovely family of boys, ranging from the age of five to eighteen? How amiable; how fond of each other; how observant of all the little proprieties and courtesies of life! Sedulously attentive to all the minor virtues, such as neatness, etc., what a deference they show to the feelings and opinions of others! No noise, no kicking, no fighting! (ah me! I grow inelegant; 'no tumult, no confusion,' I should have said;) naught but peace and serenity; a little circle of angelic tempers! And as they advance in years, no conceit, no doggedness, no selfishness; nothing but those traits which adorn and dignify human nature! And then comes glorious Manhood, with all its hopes and fears so deeply, so tenderly interesting! They see us, they adore us, they marry us! They permit us to bear their names; to labor in their families; to spend their money, (a little of it;) to repair their ancient vestments; to sustain the maternal relation; to have the care of their children; the undivided care, night and day, year in and year out; to devote ourselves, in short, body and soul to their service during our natural lives; and when wearied and worn out with the task, we drop into our graves, we have the consolation of reflecting that another will be quickly installed in our places, to be equally valued and equally loved.

'But you forget your '*thirds !*' ' No; let me do them all justice. With a generosity that reaches beyond the grave, they provide that, if forced to go before us, we shall be comforted and consoled by our 'thirds'—and it *is* a comfort.

Who, in view of these privileges, can avoid being filled with love to such a benefactor ? And if he is dear to us in health, how much more so when illness has invaded his mortal frame ! Enter with me the chamber of sickness. Ah! how becoming is the snowy drapery to his bronzed and elongated visage ! Who does not feel the force of the temptation to clasp that 'mutton-fist,' as it lies in bold relief upon his couch, even at the risk of its being called into action! But if the outward man is so touching, what is it to the inner ? *So* patient, *so* gentle, *so* uncomplaining ! With what lamb-like sub- mission does he yield to the various remedies prescribed for him; and what gratifying proof of affection does he give in insisting that you and you alone shall watch his pillow, arrange his straggling locks, ablute his countenance, and perform a thousand offices equally tender and endearing, repaying you by gentle smiles and more gen- tle words! Ah, ye wives ! let not such ineffable sweetness, such superhuman patience, convert your love into idolatry, lest he be taken from you! Who, who in passing through such a scene can avoid exclaiming with the great poet of nature, '*What* a piece of work is man !'

To estimate them truly, we should consider what we should be without them. Bear with me, my sister, while I for one moment indulge this hypothesis. No balls, no parties, no moonlight walks; no serenades, no flirting, no marrying; no plaguing (I mean pleas- ing) your husband; and to use the words of an enthusiastic young creature, carried away by the vehemence of her feelings, 'no no- thing !'

For myself, I am free to admit my own inferiority. I love to lie at their feet and look up. It suits well with the emotions of a ten- der and confiding spirit. But though happy and satisfied with my lot, there are moments when I confess a touch of human weakness. When the cry is ' To the polls !' and the meanest article ' in hose and doublet' takes precedence of the fairest daughter of Eve, then I feel a drop of bitterness rise in my heart. I seem to realize and take in, as it were, that after all that has been said and sung, I am nothing but ' a poor female woman;' or as a friend more truthfully than elegantly remarked, ' Women are very well in their place, but they *an't men !*' I feel it too on those days when the ' pride, pomp and circumstance of glorious war' are faintly shadowed forth. Behold that manly form, arrayed in gold and scarlet, mounting his prancing charger! Anxious to reach the goal, his plumed head far in advance of his steed, he careers across the field, cutting and thrusting the innocent air with his dread-inspiring falchion. Who can stifle a secret wish in the heart that ' Heaven had made her such a man ?' But be comforted, ye hapless ones! It is *our* privilege to sacrifice ourselves to such a being; and though many a weary year may have been spent in vain repinings, yet the time will come, *must* come, SHALL come! But I forbear.

Dear married sisters! if these general remarks have not convinced you of the debt of gratitude you owe to your ' liege lord,' I will be more personal. Let me figure it out to you. In these United States there are upward of seventeen millions of inhabitants; half of them are of our sex. You have been selected, extracted, absolutely fished up, so to speak, from more than eight millions of females! The obligation becomes still greater when you take in the whole world, but the idea is too overpowering. It is enough that you alone out of eight millions could make him happy; that you alone out of such a vast assemblage should be permitted to share his sorrows and salary. And yet there are those, strange as it may seem, and only to be accounted for on the principle of total depravity, who speak lightly of this precious privilege, and deny the self-evident proposition that matrimony and perfect felicity are synonymous terms. There are some beings who would be dissatisfied in Paradise; but to such I have nothing to say. I scoff at them; I repudiate them.

I have now, my sisters, completed my task. I am sensible I have but poorly performed it; for, enraptured with my subject, and carried away by the ardor of my emotions, I could little attend to the graces of composition. This must be my excuse for its imperfect fulfilment; and in your heart I trust I shall find a ready apology. To do justice to such a theme would require an angel's pen:

' COME then, expressive Silence, muse his praise !'

THE MANIAC MAID.

BY J. CLEMENT.

HER face is fair, her form erect;
  Her motions full of grace,
But not a gleam of reason 's light
  Within her eye we trace.

The bright blue sky above her spreads,
  The gay green earth around;
And myriad voices, sweetly tuned,
  Wake every pleasant sound.

And yet to her there 's nothing fair
  In all that GOD has made;
And not a harp could thrill her soul
  Though by an angel played.

The beauteous world of thought, to us
  So full of heavenly light,
To her is but a dark morass,
  Where reigns primeval night.

The smile on Friendship's face is dim,
  The glow of Love concealed,
And all the woman in her heart
  Is like a fount congealed.

It here seems strange that GOD should hide
  A ray of His own light;
But Heaven will yet illume the page,
  And all will there be bright.

THE ALBATROSS.

FROM ' THE RIME OF THE TRANSIENT MARINER,' AN UNPUBLISHED POEM.

OF dappled wing, and snowy breast,
  And dark, undaunted eye,
No fairer bird, be it confessed,
  Or nobler, cleaves the sky ;
Ay, noblest of all birds is she,
  That e'er the ocean cross,
So bold, so beautiful, so free,
  The queenly Albatross.
A mighty bird, a queenly bird,
  A bird of high renown,
The Eagle's true competitor
  For diadem and crown ;
For, if the title 'King of Birds'
  Suit well his royal mien,
By equal right, to her belongs
  The title of their ' Queen.'

Her graceful majesty — the ease
  And 'poetry' of motion,
With which she soars upon the breeze,
  Or skims along the ocean ;
Her queenly bearing, as she takes,
  On long and level pinions,
Her flight thus o'er the waves, and makes
  The tour of her dominions ;
Her fay-like floating on the air,
  Moving, yet scarce the mover,
As float we, seemingly, when o'er
  Some gulf in dreams we hover ;
All these the Albatross proclaim
  A bird of noble mien,
And worthiest of birds to bear
  The title of their queen.

Those curving lines of symmetry
  That mark her graceful form,
Her snowy-white and mottled robes
  Of plumage thick and warm ;
The dignity and easy air,
  With which along the water
She seems to glide, as if she were
  The very ocean's daughter ;
The bearing too, of conscious pride,
  With which, unawed, approaching
' Creation's lord,' she seems to chide
  His arrogant encroaching ;
All these, in sooth, the Albatross
  Proclaim of noble mien,
And worthiest of birds to bear
  The title of their queen.

And then, when from her native realm
  By cruel man betrayed,
A captive that no ills o'erwhelm,
  Alone, but undismayed,
Amid her foes on deck she stands,
  And with a keen, calm eye,
Seems, monarch-like, e'en in their hands,
  Her captors to defy ;
Ay, then the queenly dignity,
  With which she meets the knife,
And yields, at length, without a sigh,
  Her undefended life,
Proclaims her still a peerless bird,
  A bird of royal mien,
And worthiest of birds to bear
  The title of their queen.

Oh ! cruel, cruel, cruel man !
  Such queenliness unheeding,
Thy arts of treachery to plan,
  And basely lay her bleeding !
That form so graceful to despoil,
  That eye to rob of brightness,
To pierce that noble heart, and soil
  Those robes of sunny whiteness !
Ay, cruel man ! that bird to meet
  With such malign atrocities,
All for the sake of wings and feet,
  And beaks for curiosities !
For arrant trifles, thus to slay
  A bird of royal mien,
And worthiest of birds to bear
  The title of their queen !

Ah ! Curiosity ! Thou 'rt still
  The same on land and sea,
Where'er there 's room for working ill
  Thy harpy hand will be.
Thou 'lt bring old mummies from the Nile,
  Strip fanes of bust and banner,
Jove's brazen nose knock off, or file
  A finger from Diana ;
From Bonaparte's or Andre's skull
  Thou 'lt pluck off hair for lockets,
Cut canes in grave-yards, or e'en cull
  Coins from dead soldiers' pockets ?
Ay, e'en for a few relics, here
  Thy cruel hook thou 'lt screen,
And slay the noble Albatross,
  That Bird of birds the Queen.

No wonder then her phantom haunts
  The waste and lonely deep;
No wonder for revenge it pants,
  And vigils long doth keep;
No wonder when the seaman binds
  Sleep's poppies on his brow,
Her spirit wakes the stormy winds
  That o'er the ocean plough;
No wonder, thus in wind and gale, ·
  On stormy nights and dark,
That spectre, with a dismal wail,
  Chasing their fated bark,
Doth haunt for aye the guilty crew
  That erst, with hook so keen,
The *Albatross* profanely slew,
  That bird of birds the Queen!

These verses on the Albatross,
  It may be well to mention,
In order somewhat to enhance
  Your interest and attention,
Were with a pen that I myself
  Plucked from her pinions, written,
And with the hand, (or arm, in truth,)
  That by her beak was bitten:
For bitten was I on the arm —
  To say it, much I grieve;
Not that the bite did any harm,
  Except to tear my sleeve;
But 't is because the fact, I fear,
  May lead you to suppose
That for the bird in rhyme I weep,
  And do not so in prose!

POPULAR AMUSEMENTS.

BY 'THE DOCTOR.'

MANKIND are pliant in their hour of gayety. When the heart is ftened; when the enmities are asleep; when pleasant sounds fill e ears and beautiful objects pass before the eyes; these are the urs to pour into the open heart the claims of Truth; to gain the r and arrest the eye and mould the character to love only virtue d real excellence.

The drama has only succeeded when it had a moral object. The ch comedy of the last century, broad and coarse as it often is, was imed at the sanctimonious restraints which would turn the world to a charnel-house and hang the streets in black. Its objects were ood and noble; and it demands from our judgment a lenient deci- on, from the time in which it had its birth. Its objects were moral; e reäction of puritanical manners and ungraceful costume. Its nsel and levity are satires upon affected plainness and solemn farce; s intrigue and infidelity were introduced to unmask hypocrisy and eep-seated vice; its ready wit and keen repartee kept the audience good nature, while they learned morals and studied nature.

All amusements must have a deeper object than to amuse, or they ill fail. While the palate is tickled, the body must be nourished. bey must be based upon something; must have a bottom. There ust be a substantial liquid beneath the sparkle, to quench the thirst. *ll froth* is too light.

We understand this principle very well when we deal with chil- ren, for whom alone is felt disinterested love. We teach them eography by games, and lure them into the mazes of arithmetical lculations by exciting puzzles; by questions about apples and tops d nuts. Generous conduct and amiable feelings are inculcated pretty stories. The little fellows will wait patiently, looking one steadily in the face, with open mouth and wondering eyes, for the result; and then draw a long breath and smile their thanks. They understand this principle of having a bottom to a thing; be it a tub or a story.

Men now-a-days turn up their noses when one talks about utility, and say: 'Let us have pure pleasure, amusement only; away with your everlasting cant about morals!' And yet these very men will quote sagely the maxim, '*Necessity is the mother of Invention.*' We undertake to say that all amusements had their origin in some actual want of the world; something society could not do without. They were wise men who opened the theatres to cure the plague. The popularity of Bath as a fashionable resort was begun by invalids in search of health; and our own Newport can trace its throngs of gay and light-hearted visitors; its airy castles, built as by enchantment, to a few faint and pale forms, whose last hope was sea-bathing and the air from the ocean. So the theatre was first introduced, travelling about in a cart, to represent ideas to people who could not read — an edition of a book as large as li'e. We say the stage will succeed when it does something for the mind and heart of man, and only then.

Herein lies the reason of a class of plays indigenous to our country. There may be occasional representations of ancient plays and foreign plays, but the stock must be something that tells upon our people. What sympathy have our audiences with gentlemen (in the play, so called) who treat their servants as if they were a different race from themselves? To be a gentleman, on the stage, the master must at some convenient point of the dialogue kick his servant off it; an audience that laugh at and applaud such an act are descending in the scale of manners and morals, and will soon have no theatre to — drink in.

The best play we ever saw, the one that brought down the most applause, that created the greatest number of wet eyes, and hasty recurrences to pocket-handkerchiefs, was one upon which Mr. Tupper may have founded his 'Crock of Gold.' A poor cobbler, happy as a lark, singing at his work all the day long, in the dispensation of Providence becomes suddenly rich, and undertakes to play the fine gentleman. No long time is required to plunge him in difficulties. He nearly breaks the heart of his poor wife; and, in his intemperance and madness, estranges all his acquaintances. Though rich, he is steeped to the lips in misery. Some fortunate accident deprives him of his money, and soon after we see him at his old stand, giving forth his old songs with unusual glee; his wife beside him, all smiles and joy. And they moralize upon their fate, and make a wise and honest confession of the emptiness of human wishes for a state it is not prepared for, by discipline and slow attainment. There seemed to be but one heart in the theatre that night. The play drew the boxes down into the pit, and ascended the pit into the boxes. The upper tier was hushed into silence; and large tears fell glistening in the gas light. The heart of the people was touched. It was all so true, and every body felt it so. 'Here,' thought we, 'is a model play for our nation.' Our philanthropists might expend their capital stock, in giving away tickets in the market-place for such plays. Soon there would be no poor to help; no vice to reform ; no prisoner to visit ; for the theatre would be the school of morals and manners, and carry out on the week-day what the pulpit might recommend on the Sabbath.

We say this is one of the best of plays, if plays are to be judged by their effects upon the audience. We need a set of plays adapted to the genius of our form of government. Our people have no real sympathy with a titled aristocracy. We do not need to have the false notions of monarchies taught to republicans. We are not pleased to see men represented as high and low by birth; to see virtuous Poverty bowing, hat in hand, to titled Vice, as if it were the order of nature and GOD. We believe the *curiosity* of the public is satisfied upon this point; for it is curiosity that has filled the theatre. It is no longer filled ; and the cry is, that the stage is declining; that it has had its day. We hope not. The people of large cities *must* have amusements. This is settled. The mind needs recreation as much as it needs rest.

Our idea is, that the stage, beside giving us the visible history of the past, should embody the ruling powers of the present age; set before the crowds that visit nightly there the great principles that are now animating the world and carrying it forward to virtue and happiness. People love to look in the glass. They love to see themselves as they know they ought to be. Let the stage then but speak the voice of its time ; let it say what the heart of the multitude says to itself; let it hush riot by its majesty, and put lust and sensuality out of mind, by pictures of true affection and honest love; let it quell desire by its purity and block up paths of vice by angel-forms of all the virtues ; let it set forth Truth in form and shape and action as it is spoken in seriousness elsewhere, and the stage will obey the high destiny which poets and scholars have dreamed of her attaining.

Of all humbugs, not intended to be humbugeous, we think the late attempt to substitute dramatic readings for the theatre the most conspicuous. It is a kind of drawn-game, reflecting credit on neither party. It is bowing to a prejudice for the sake of the money. It is opening the door for all sorts and breeds of 'striped pigs.' Where is the harm of aiding words by action and costume ? Why not also add scenery and stage-effect; light and shade ? Why emasculate the theatre, and take from it that which addresses the common mind; the illusion, the show, the burst of light, day and night, thunder and lightning, moonlight and water-falls, thrones and crowns ? Why not let us see for once how a real king looks, instead of putting up Mr. Smith, in a plain suit of black, to stand for majesty. Poor old Jack is indeed now dead, and we shall no more hear the sound of the spade, as it strikes the skull of Yorick in the grave-yard. Ghosts shall in future have 'form as palpable' as living man, and Lady Macbeth shall never look distraught again. Richard shall no more start from his uneasy slumber, but shall cry 'A horse! a horse !' from an easy-chair in a parlor.

Could we have our way, the theatre should be arranged after this manner : They should be but one price for grown persons, throughout the house, which should be large enough to accommodate. well all who might enter it. There should be no bar or refreshment-room about the premises. All persons should be admitted to arrange themselves as they might choose, as in a lecture-room. Any person in a clean garment should pass unquestioned. Proper officers should be in readiness to keep order. The price of admission should be less than it is now, and the house should be larger. Cheap postage and cheap fare on the rail-road pay the best interest on the stock employed there. Why will not this principle apply to the theatre ? All the costume and scenery and music should be continued, as of old, only it should be much improved upon. Why not leave the audience to take care of themselves, as you do in a lecture-room or a church ? Suppose people of bad morals do frequent the place; have the performances so good as to reform them. Let the moral influences be the main object, and not a line here and there, just for the ' saints.' Let the whole tone be high ; let the wit be attic, not Billingsgate. Let it be such a place as Cato would love to visit, and from which religious people might go, with no stains upon their garments or blushes upon their cheeks. Public amusements are well worthy the attention of our citizens ; and if the city would give more heed to establishing them, it might forego much of its trouble about its police

A SUMMER-DAY'S DREAM.

Hither! hither! come to me,
Sunny sprites of gayety!
Come from out the morning-blue,
From the sparkles of the dew,
From the light cloud's lovelinesses,
(Flitting clouds with silver tresses,)
From the frolic breeze that lifteth
Young flow'rs' heads where'er he shifteth,
Peeping in their modest eyes,
Stealing kisses as he flies!
Come from where, through fountains playing,
Diamond-golden gleams are straying;
Where the swan's fair neck doth brightly lave
Its wreath of snow beneath the wave!

Come! the thrush is wildly singing,
On the bending roses swinging,
And the busy bee o'erhead
Hummeth over thymy bed;
Tinkling echoes coming, going,
Where the babbling brook is flowing;
And the merry chapel-bell
Chimes with softened airy swell
Through the pleasant solitude
Of the blithely rustling wood,
As the village wedding passes
Cheerly o'er the nodding grasses!

Weary, weak and sad am I,
Lonely 'neath the summer sky;
Hither come, ah! come to me,
Sunny sprites of gayety!
Hist! I hear the joyous beat
Of their tiny dancing feet;

In the sunlight, in the shade,
Through the dingle, through the glade,
In the meadow, on the hill,
By the willow-bordered rill,
In the whispering of the pines,
Where the wing of wild-bird shines,
On the billow's feathery crest,
In emeralds and foam-beads dressed,
Over land and over sea ;
But they come not unto me,
Sunny sprites of gayety !

Sweetest sprites ! no more round me
Ye 'll weave your frolic ministry !
Never as in days of yore !
Never more, ah ! never more !
Light of heart and bright of eye,
Knowing naught of tear or sigh,
Strung to gladness, tuned to pleasure,
Breathing soft a Lydian measure,
Only these will ye receive
Where your graceful dance ye weave!

I the rosy spell have broken,
Lost the potent fairy-token,
And profaned each blithesome rite
That shapes your airy glancing flight!
For I have dared to sound the deeps
Where the soul in shadow weeps;
Weeps the lost, the loved Ideal,
Weeps the found, unlovely Real;
Heart so learned in Sorrow's lore
Ye will visit never more!

ANNA BLACKWELL.

' D I N N A   F O R G E T .

ing verses were suggested by observing the words ' Dinna Forget' on the seal of a letter
a writer to day for transmission to the United States

I.

Oh! dinna forget, Love,
Each bright happy day,
Of the sweet sunny past, Love,
Now faded away!
In the depths of thy soul
Keep each hope treasured yet,
Oh! dinna forget, Love,
Love, dinna forget!

II.

Thou hast wandered afar, Love,
Beyond the wide sea;
And fond hearts are watching
And praying for thee:
Eyes once beaming brightly,
With sad tears are wet,
Then dinna forget, Love,
Love, dinna forget!

III.

Forget not thy MOTHER!
Her years glide away,
While oft she recalleth
Her heart's hope and stay;
Oh! daily she weepeth
Fond tears of regret,
And seeketh her loved one;
Then dinna forget!

IV.

Forget not thy FATHER!
O'er Time's rugged path
He toileth, and counteth
Each jewel he hath;
But the brightest of all
In life's diadem set,
Is the one who now roveth;
Love! dinna forget!

V.

Forget not thy SISTER!
Thou little hast known
The changeless affection
Her bosom hath borne;
How her eye sweetly glistens
When, some token met,
Tells a tale of the absent:
Love! dinna forget!

VI.

Forget not the MAIDEN
  Thou 'st won for thine own,
The vows thou has spoken
  In days that are gone :
Though the sun of her young love
  On others has set,
Yet it beams bright above *thee*,
  Love ! dinna forget !

VII.

Forget not thy GOD, Love,
  Where'er thou may'st be,
Thy prayers and thy BIBLE,
  That chart of Life's sea.
If no more here on earth
  We may joy to have met,
We shall part not in Heaven,
  Love ! dinna forget !

Sweden, July 16, 1840.   M. W. L.

IS DANCING SINFUL?

BY MRS. WILLIAM TURNER.

BEFORE we pronounce any practice sinful, is it not the duty of
every just man and conscientious Christian fairly to examine *both*
sides of the question, with a mind unbiassed by any preconceived
opinion, or previous teaching, or early impression ? And is it not
also his duty to make the BIBLE only his standard for determining
what is sinful and what is not ? If these two points be conceded,
(and we see not how they can in justice be denied,) we think it can
be fairly proved, not only that dancing in itself is not sinful, but
furthermore, that it is a means of promoting the Christian spirit.
We know that many Christians imagine that an essential of reli-
gion is melancholy ; another name for what perhaps they consider
mere solemnity. Whence arose this conceit ? We have not Holy
Writ for its authority. Must not then religion have first received
its garb of gloom from disappointment and satiety ? — or from sad
old age, which no longer feeling the buoyancy of youth, had for-
gotten that gloominess would be an unnatural exotic in the fresh-
ness of the youthful mind ? The sad and sorrowing, who have
passed their lives in thoughtless levity, may, in despair at the ap-
proach of death, in fear and trembling, imagine that they can make
amends for their having so long forgotten their CREATOR, by adopt-
ing the other extreme in their conduct ; but this is the result of fear,
not of love. A well-regulated mind will perceive that GOD's favor
is not to be thus purchased. He who has a correct conception of
the character of the SUPREME knows that HE looks at the heart, and

:t be right, the external demeanor will be also. A gloomy re-
ι cannot be of celestial origin; for turning to our Bible, we
joyousness and grateful gladness constantly enjoined. We
read : ' Be not as the hypocrites, of a *sad* countenance :' MAT.,
ΐ. We no where see sadness inculcated, but we find the Apostle
pronouncing joy to be one of the traits of the true Christian
er : ' The fruit of the spirit is love, *joy*, peace, long-suffering ;'
ιs, patient suffering ; ' gentleness, goodness, faith, meekness,
erance.' GAL., v., 22. We also read : ' For this is the love
ɔD, that we keep HIS commandments ; and HIS command-
s are *not grievous :*' 1 JOHN, v. 3. But do not the melancholy
onists make them *grievous ?* Are they not imbued with the
spirit which prompted the servant to lay up the pound in a
ιn, and who excused himself by saying : ' For I feared thee
ιse thou art an austere man ; thou takedst up that thou layedst
lown, and reapest that thou didst not sow :' LUKE, XIX., 21.
ιey not, like this servant, look upon GOD as an austere master,
ιd of a kind, indulgent, loving FATHER ? Are they not in a
of fear of punishment for some unreasonable requirement ?
ιey not virtually deny that ' GOD is Love ?' and does not their
ɔf HIM stifle their *love* of HIM ? ' There is no fear in love,
erfect love casteth out fear; because fear hath torment. He
ëareth is not made perfect in love :' 1 JOHN, IV., 18. We may
therefore that that melancholy demeanor which is the offspring
ar is sinful; and that they who would forbid innocent joyous-
nake an assumption of superior holiness and wisdom over the
Word; for in the Bible innocent amusement is not forbidden.
y attentive reader of the Scriptures knows that every sin is
enumerated and condemned ; if then we can prove that dan-
ιs repeatedly mentioned, yet *not once censured,* is it not a fair
ιnce that dancing is not sinful ? Every humble Christian will
ss that the Bible is all-sufficient for Christian practice ; and
it does not deem sinful man has no right to pronounce so.
learn from Goldsmith's ' Manners and Customs of Nations,'
ιlmost all the nations on the face of the globe were from the most
nt time in the practice of rejoicing and showing their glad-
ιnd joyousness of heart by music and dancing. In Robbins'
lines of History' it is said of the Hebrews : ' Their diversions
to have consisted chiefly in social repasts, music and dancing.
:wo latter partook of a religious character. Games were never
Iuced into their commonwealths.' In the Holy Record also,
nd that joy and rejoicing were most commonly evinced by
ι and dancing. If a practice so ancient and of so frequent occur-
ι were really censurable in the eyes of the LORD JESUS CHRIST,
ɪ HE not have taken occasion to make *some* condemnatory re-
upon the subject ? Yet HE does not; HE never once pro-
ɔes it sinful, nor tells them to refrain from it; but rather implies
t is a fitting manifestation of rejoicing and of grateful glad-
ιnd a natural demonstration of the exuberance of lively feel-
for HE himself narrates the mode of rejoicing at the return of

'Familiarity breeds contempt,' even with the art of chopping, and I soon began to look upon it as an irksome duty rather than a pleasure. As I lived entirely alone I was compelled to practice the culinary art, and became quite a cook on a small scale; my experience however in these matters was rather limited, being confined to the different methods of preparing pork and venison which I had bought from the Indians, potatoes and coffee. But I racked my invention to discover the subtlest methods of preparing these dainties, and became a proficient in making that unleavened bread known, *inter sylvas*, as 'shanty cake.' Often when I have produced a *chef d'œuvre* of cunning cookery have I wished that some fastidious gourmand was there to share my feast. My dreams were not even yet all dispelled, and though I sometimes thought that a life in the bush looked better in print than in Canada, still I persuaded myself that a little exertion and a year or two of privation would not fail to produce the glorious results that I had predicted.

That long and dismal winter at last came to an end, and the spring burst upon me in all the sudden beauty of the American season. Myriads of birds of the most exquisite plumage filled the woods, and the earth was covered with flowers; flocks of pigeons flashed across my clearing, the swift messengers of summer; the trees put forth their leaves, and all nature rejoiced in verdant glory. I had little time however to admire the great change, for it was necessary to burn the piles of 'brush' and clear away the fallen timber on my land before I could sow or plant. This was a work not to be done without help, requiring both men and oxen; so I repaired to the 'settlement' in search of assistance. I soon found that this was not easily to be obtained, for every man was in the same predicament as myself; all were in a hurry to 'log' their own chopping, and none were willing to go fifteen miles to help me until their own work was done; which would be too late for my crops. With much ado I prevailed on two men to spare me one day, and I succeeded in getting half an acre cleared.

I was fain to moderate my ambitious views of husbandry for that year, and to devote myself to the culture of a garden. Having a choice supply of 'Shaker's seeds,' procured in the States, I arranged some small beds, and in good season 'committed them to the earth,' together with a small patch of potatoes, which were planted in the firm belief that they would return a hundred-fold. But the thing to which I looked forward with the greatest pleasure was the raising of Indian corn, of which I had a few seeds. Having never seen a field of corn, my curiosity was excited, and I had unlimited faith in its beauty and productiveness as a plant, and its excellence as a luxury. One fine morning in May I had commenced planting my corn, when suddenly, as if by preconcertion, myriads of small insects assailed me. I carelessly brushed them from my face at first, unwilling to believe that such minute creatures could do more harm than annoy one a little. Miserable error!—in less than an hour my eyes were swollen and nearly closed, my ears, neck, face and hands were in the same condition, and I was fairly compelled

we perceive that dancing is expected, and is deemed consistent, at other times. Thus : ' We have piped unto you, and ye have not danced ; we have mourned unto you, and ye have not lamented.' MAT., XI., 17. Evidently reproaching them for not having danced when they were piped unto. Also : ' There is a time to weep and a time to laugh ; a time to mourn and a time to dance.' ECCL., III., 4. It is mentioned as a mark of happiness : ' They send forth their little ones like a flock, and their children dance.' JOB, XXI., 11.

Even in infancy we behold the intuitive exhibition of exuberant health and vivacity in infantile dances. Does it not then seem cruel to magnify so natural an impulse of innocence, into an act of sinfulness, and thus to cramp the healthful elasticity which GOD has given them ? The Scriptures clearly show that rejoicing was most commonly demonstrated by dancing. For it is said : ' And Miriam the prophetess, the sister of Aaron, took a timbrel in her hand ; and all the women went out after her, with timbrels and with dances.' EXOD., XV., 20. ' Jephthah's daughter came out to meet him with timbrels and dances.' JUDGES, XI., 34. ' Is not this David, the king of the land ? Did they not sing one to another of him in dances ?' etc. SAM., XXI., 11. ' Again I will build thee, and thou shalt be built, O virgin of Israel! Thou shalt again be adorned with thy tabrets, and shalt go forth in dances of them that make merry.' JER. XXXI., 4. ' And it came to pass as they came, when David was returned from the slaughter of the Philistines, that the women came out of all the cities of Israel, singing and dancing, to meet King Saul, with tabrets, with joy, and with instruments of music.' 1 SAM., XVIII., 6. ' Thou hast turned my mourning into dancing ; thou hast put off my sackcloth and girded me with gladness.' PSALMS, XXX., 11. ' Let Israel rejoice in HIM that made him. Let the children of Zion be joyful in their King. Let them praise His name in the dance.' PSALMS, CXLIX., 23. ' And they shall not sorrow any more at all. Then shall the virgin rejoice in the dance ; both young men and old together : for I will turn their mourning into joy, and will comfort them, and make them rejoice from their sorrow.' JER., XXXI., 13. ' Therefore they commanded the children of Benjamin, saying, ' Go, and lie in wait in the vineyards ; and see, and behold if the daughters of Shiloh come out to dance in dances ; then come ye out of the vineyards, and catch you every man his wife, of the daughters of Shiloh, and go to the land of Benjamin. And the children of Benjamin did so, and took their wives according to their number of them that danced whom they caught.' JUDGES XXI., 20, 21, 23. ' And David danced before the LORD with all his might. And as the ark of the LORD came into the city of David, Michal, Saul's daughter, looked through a window, and saw King David leaping and dancing before the LORD ; and she despised him in her heart. *Therefore* Michal, the daughter of Saul, had no child unto the day of her death.' 2 SAM., VI., 14, 16, 23. This conduct of Michal's has been quoted as an argument *against* dancing ; whereas, if justice had been done, it would have been quoted in *favor* of it ; for the LORD deemed her despising David worthy of *punishment*. And when

In a short time a thought of profound wisdom struck me, which was, that a man who had resolved upon turning farmer would be none the worse for possessing a little stock, and that my coffee would be all the better for a little milk ; so I resolved at once to purchase a cow. 'T is true I could not milk a cow, and the idea itself was extremely ludicrous, but I overcame my foolish scruples by reasoning that 'where there 's a will there 's a way ;' 'people must adapt themselves,' etc. And after all it would furnish me with an excellent topic of gossip in my next letter home. Away I went one Thursday morning, as I thought, before sunrise, to a Scotch settlement, where I discovered that it was Sunday, and waiting until next day I bought a cow, and also permitted a yoke of oxen to be palmed upon me, and after taking half a dozen lessons in milking, I returned with my three cattle as proud as a plebeian who had suddenly come into possession of a large fortune, and as much perplexed with my acquisition.

I invented a new method of milking with my finger and thumb, and on certain occasions when the cow was unusually patient, and the flies unusually scarce, actually succeeded in obtaining a little milk. But her ladyship took to rambling, and frequently when searching for the cow, I lost myself, and spent whole days in endeavoring to find my small clearing. At length I became weary of this amusement, and she disappeared altogether. I put my oxen through 'all their paces ;' hitched them to logs, and practised 'haw' and 'gee' with the obstinate brutes, until I became a tolerable 'teamster.' But they, like myself and my cow, were given to wandering, and one day basely deserted me. The best temper in the world may be ruined by continued ill-treatment and ingratitude ; and so poignantly did I feel this heartless conduct, that I subsided into a sullen despair, resolving to take no steps for their recovery, but leave them to the fate they deserved for abandoning so excellent a master. I took things very easily in fact. I am afraid I was getting dispirited, and sometimes thought, in spite of myself, that my great scheme would prove a bubble, and that my own society, very *exclusive* though it was, did not possess all the charms with which my imagination or vanity had endowed it.

One day, in default of better employment, I had taken a pocket copy of Virgil in my hand, and after dreaming for half an hour over the name and date written on a blank leaf, when I was a school-boy, and the hundred recollections this slight incident awakened, I commenced to read the first Eclogue : I had got as far as that passage in which Tityrus solemnly vows Olympian honors to his patron, because as he says :

> 'Ille permisit,
> Meas boues errare,'

when my attention was arrested by a loud crash outside, and I instantly went to discover the cause. Oh Virgil! Oh Tityrus and horned cattle! what a sight! My harvest cares were ended ; my year's work was consummated. A drove of stray cows and oxen were in my garden ; my beautiful tomatoes were destroyed, my dar-

characters of those who practice it, and according to the
ıts, intentions and feelings of the dancers. Let *these* be cor-
ıd pure, and the act will be so too, and void of offence, 'toward
nd toward man.' If the children of professing Christians are
: genuine goodness, and true *practical* holiness, we venture to
at there will be no inexpediency in teaching them to dance ;
e evil of dancing consists in its intemperance. This, Scrip-
eems sinful, and this only it forbids. Intemperance therefore
l be shunned in dancing as in every thing else. Let dancing
ıd from immoderation, immodesty and imprudence, and it will
:hing more than a temperate exercise, a stimulator of health,
ı innocent promoter of cheerfulness ; while at the same time
induce and enhance an ease and grace of carriage, which is
inently conducive of feminine and manly beauty.

STANZAS: GREY HAIRS.

BY H. W. ROCKWELL.

Old man! upon whose thoughtful brow
The hairs are gray and scattered now ;
Who sadly, and with many tears,
Hast mourned the loved of other years,
Whom thou in childhood's sunny bloom
Saw'st laid to slumber in the tomb ;
Old man ! I deem it well for thee
That thou hast hairs like those I see !

I deem it well ; for thou at last
The snares of life hast safely past ;
If it hath brought thee years of wo,
If thou hast seen its hopes laid low,
If thou hast got with care and pain
That which in turn thou'st lost again,
It matters not ; but by these hairs
Be warned to penitence and prayers !

Soon, with thy thin hands clasped so cold,
Thou'lt rest beneath the church-yard mould ;
Soon o'er thy head the wintry sleet
And early rains of spring shall beat ;
And Summer, with her cheeks all bloom,
Shall plant her violets 'round thy tomb ;
For this 't is meet thou shouldst prepare,
Thou, on whose head I see grey hair!

Full many a fair and joyous day
On thee hath beamed and past-away ;
Full many a warm kiss thou hast shed
On lips now sealed, and cold and dead ;
But by thy looks, old man, I know
That soon 't will be thy turn to go ;
Nor vainly by those scattered hairs
Shouldst thou be warned to faith and prayers !

RECOLLECTIONS OF THE BACK-WOODS.

WRITTEN BY MYSELF.

WHEN a new writer makes his début before the world, it is but reasonable that the world should inquire who he is; and justice to the world, and mercy toward the world's wife, who has a violent passion for acquiring information, demand that the writer should. ‘ define his position.’ It is particularly necessary also when the said ambitious scribbler, as in the present instance, thrusts himself into the society of his betters without bringing letters of introduction from complaisant editors, or a recommendation from that powerful authority, ‘ Orator Puff.’ It may be said by some far-seeing reader that this writer has done nothing entitling him to the patronage of this latter power. I object to any prejudicial inference being drawn from this premising, inasmuch as his favors have frequently been extended to persons who have done worse than nothing. It is ne- cessary too that the reader, especially the critical reader, should have a proper knowledge of the character, station, etc., of a literary débutant, as otherwise incautious praise might be given to his work for its intrinsic merit, which it would be found expedient to revoke on a nearer acquaintance with perhaps his peculiar idiosyncracy on debateable subjects; his country; his connections; his religion or his poverty. On the other hand, hasty censure might be passed on his production for its individual dulness, when the author himself might be found to be a young gentleman of high standing in society, and of immense riches, or golden expectations. To prevent the occurrence of such annoying mistakes in my case, I have resolved to have no subterfuge, but anonymousness, and to ‘ make a clean breast of it.’

‘ Well, who am I ?’ It is a question, dear reader, that I have asked myself a thousand times. When any thing has occurred to ruffle the equable current of my mind; when I have considered myself neglected by the world, I have frowned at a mirror and asked in- dignantly, ‘Who am I ?’ When a young lady whose person and for- tune had captivated my heart, has slighted my addresses and laughed at my soft speeches, I have retired to a solitary room, and shaking my fist violently at my shadow, have inquired, ‘ Who am I ?’ On vari- ous occasions have I thus interrogated myself; and Myself, who is the best fellow in the world, though some envious people call him vain, has invariably returned most satisfactory answers, which my modesty forbids me to repeat. I may however say, without becom- ing liable to the charge of egotism, that Myself has always assured me that I am a charming young fellow, and though possessing a few back-woods accomplishments, I am, in my rational intervals, upon the whole, rather amiable. I have the height, whiskers and impu- dence necessary to manhood ; although to be candid, I lack the most essential requisite — money. *N'importe;* it may come with the *silvery* hairs of old age.   I may as well state too, as some *may* be interested in this point — who knows ? — that I am a bachelor; and I forgot to say, remarkably handsome.

As it regards the important point of family, I believe few can claim a more ancient pedigree.   Our genealogical tree is completely withered and fallen away with old age.   Our family arms is quite palsied, wrinkled, and shattered with senility ; and the ancient ' supporters' of our heraldric honors are entirely *worm-eaten.*   My grandfather boasted his descent from one Adam, whom he asserted lived before the flood, and my grandmother proved by her actions that she was a lineal descendant of Eve his wife.   Our armorial bearings is a shield with numerous quarterings ; in the principal one of which is the head of a Saracen, which from immemorial time has been afflicted with strabismus, which is nothing improved by age, and which the learned say betokens a bend *sinister.*   The rest are filled with rampant spoons (pewter,) and similar articles of *vertu,* on a field *brass;* the whole of which is exceedingly appropriate, and was devised by some prophetic herald, who knew well that none of the family would have silver spoons in their mouths at their birth, and that their general characteristic in after life would be a brazen one.

But all the glories of my ancient pedigree would not find me bread, nor would a plebeian world supply me with new coats ; therefore my father resolved to give me a profession ; thinking, good old soul! in the fulness of paternal pride, that I was destined to make a figure in the world, and illuminate the family arms with a field *or.* But my dear mother, who was a very learned lady for country parts, had fallen in love with Bruce's travels before I was born ; to which unfortunate circumstance I attribute a rambling propensity which I possess, which effectually marred all my father's stay-at-home schemes of prosperity, and rendered nugatory his oft-repeated maxim, ' A rolling stone gathers no moss.'

I read Rosseau, and therefore fancied I disliked the conventional shackles of society ; my profession proved dull and irksome, and I was seized with a longing after primitive life.   I was not long in determining to seek my fortune abroad ; but where should I go in search of it ?   The West Indies were too hot ; the East Indies were overdone ; Australia was too far ; Timbuctoo would not do ; the United States were too civilized, and I cried in despair, ' Where, oh ! where !'   My situation also was becoming embarrassing, having rashly impaired my small fortune in paying my debts.   Solicitous tradesmen, at whose requests I had signed my name to mysterious pieces of stamped paper, were anxious to become intrusively familiar with me, and I was compelled to lead a solitary misanthropic life, to avoid that vulgar race of beings who salute you in the streets with a tap on the shoulder.   They started up in my path

' Whene'er I took my walks abroad,'

and thrust villanous papers into my hand, purporting to come ' by the grace of GOD,' from ' Victoria, Queen,' etc., etc.   I entertained

serious thoughts of bargaining with some sea-captain to place me
on an uninhabited island, and forsaking a cruel world, take the
Bible and Robinson Crusoe, lead a solitary life, cultivate the ac-
quaintance of intelligent monkeys, devote my energies to the civili-
zation of affectionate goats, and teach paroquets to accompany my
flute in ' I am monarch of all I survey,' to the tune of the dead-
march. But

'Heaven sends relief to the woe-laden breast,'

and I thanked my lucky fate that one morning sent me a pamphlet
issued by the ' Canada Land Company.'

This philanthropic society offered an asylum to all persecuted
people, a refuge to the briefless barrister, a patrimony to the poor
physician, who had been for years alike patient and patientless, es-
tates to the landless, and an Arcady to the rurally-inclined. I flung
my hat to the ceiling in transport, and leaped about the room in
extacy. I rubbed my hands and said to my soul, ' Oh, be joyful!'
' I thank thee, Fortune!' I exclaimed, addressing the invisible god-
dess with vehement gratitude, ' I thank thee that thou has reserved
a retreat for thy successless followers; where duns will not assail,
where bailiffs will not affright, nor visions of writ and ' capias' dis-
turb their slumbers!   ' Farewell, a long farewell,' to all my anxious
cares, my ceaseless searchings for patrons among men whose ' ears
are deaf to the voice of the charmer!'   Oh! ye company of joint-
stock Howards! how shall I thank ye?   Buried in the primeval soli-
tudes of Nature, will I forget my troubles, and elevate my soul in
communion with her in the unbroken silence of her strong-holds.
My farm shall supply my wants; care shall not enter ' in my cot-
tage, near a wood.'   The mighty lakes and rivers shall yield their
' finny tribe' for my food, and my rifle shall supply my table with
luxuries.   I will dress in furs and shear sheep; sing pastorals and
dream dreams!'

When I had thus opened the safety-valve of my excited feelings
I retired to bed, where I dreamed of sagacious oxen and amiable
cows. I found myself in the act of embracing an Indian, who was
suddenly transformed into an interesting fat pig of my own raising;
and the transport of delight I experienced awakened me.

I was never much burthened with what the world calls wisdom,
or calculation; and without having reflected twice on the subject,
I arranged my affairs as quickly as possible, and was almost sur-
prised one morning to find myself on board a New-York packet-
ship. The dulness of a sea-voyage can only be equalled by the
narration of it, which in charity I withhold.

I was delighted of course on entering the New World, of which
I had heard so much, and enraptured with the magnificent bay;
and as we neared the neat white houses I became elated with the
fairy-land appearance the country of my adoption presented in con-
trast with the dingy, smoky look of the towns in the ' old country.'
I was struck on landing with the home-like appearance of every
thing around, and stared like an owl struck marvellous to hear the

same language, to see the same features, the same dress and manners I had left behind.   I confess I felt half disappointed on finding that no *foreign* wonders awaited me.   But ' Onward !' was the word. I-fled up the glorious Hudson by moonlight, from thence to Rochester, wondering at and admiring every thing, and began to be convinced by slow degrees that New-York was larger than even Yorkshire, and that the United States actually possessed towns and cities in the interior of the country ; positively handsomer and better than the thousand year old provincial towns of England.   I had serious thoughts of changing my intention, and tempting fortune in this land of promise ; but dreams of Arcady possessed me and impelled me still onward ; and thus I discovered myself one dark windy night in October, in Coburg, in Canada.

When I looked upon the town next morning and compared it with those through which I had passed on my route, my spirits fell, and I sighed despite myself.   It was a bleak-looking place, which they ostentatiously called a town, and its few inhabitants appeared to have given themselves over to lethargy and dejection.   But what did this matter to me ?   I came to found a Utopia on a small scale ; to make a home in the glorious wilderness ; to hunt and fish and farm, to go wild and free, to sing madrigals and rear sheep.

· I will not bore the reader with an account of my wanderings in search of a situation that suited my romantic notions.   I declined purchasing the most excellent ' mill-sites,' refused tempting ' water privileges,' rejected offers of ' never-failing creeks,' exhaustless ' sugar bushes,' and most unexceptionable ' hard wood' land ; all because they were too near the bounds of civilization, and I had resolved to make my home in the solitudes of the primeval forest. With this view I started for the far West, and after experiencing for a month all the horrors of travelling in that country, its swamps, 'corduroys,' and worse than all, its log-taverns, I arrived at a small town on Lake Huron, purchased land in a newly surveyed township, forty miles farther on, and having laid in a stock of necessaries for the winter, gallantly set out to take possession of my *estate.*

On the second day of our journey we (myself, a teamster and two ' choppers,') had left behind us all marks of civilization.   Not a solitary log-cabin peered out from its nook in the bush ; no occasional sound of an axe was to be heard, and the dull rumble of our solitary wagon along the narrow ' high-road,' or the loud voice of the driver as he urged his horses to greater exertions in some frequent dilemma, which the echoes caught up and mocked as if in fiendish exultation, were the only sounds that broke the oppressive silence.   Our progress was often interrupted by fallen trees lying across the path, which had to be cut through and removed.   At length about night-fall on the second day we reached my ' lot,' very tired, silent, cold and miserable.   A wigwam in the Chippewa fashion was speedily erected, a good fire ' built,' and over our supper of bread, pork and coffee, something like good-humor and hilarity returned.

On the ensuing morning the ground was covered with a foot depth of snow, which had fallen in the night; the trees were hung with white drapery, which would have appeared beautifully fantastic at another time, but only awakened a sensation of desolation and misery now, considerably heightened by the dark appearance of the sky, which had donned a dun robe of clouds. Our driver speedily 'hitched' his horses to the wagon and left us, and I could perceive by the look of pity with which he regarded me that he considered me as an insane monomaniac, whose wilfulness in selecting such an abode was a fool-hardy tempting of Providence.

It was necessary first of all to build a house; and as there was no probability of the snow disappearing before spring, the sooner it was done the better. With this view we proceeded to fell trees of the proper thickness and to cut from them logs of the proper length, then to split bass-wood logs and hollow them into 'scoops' for the roof. This done, my two companions started for the nearest settlement, fifteen miles, to procure a yoke of oxen to haul them, and to request the assistance of my 'neighbors' in raising my future abode. They came cheerfully to the 'bee,' and after the usual amount of eating, drinking, swearing and joking, the house or rather 'shanty' was raised and covered in, while all the time it was snowing as I believe it can snow in no other part of the world; actually tumbling in heavy masses from the clouds, silent and incessant. Our next labor was to hew planks of bass-wood for the floor and door, to make a fire-place and chimney as well as we could, and fill the apertures between the logs with splinters and moss, as the inclemency of the season prevented plastering.

In three weeks after this, the two men I had brought with me having chopped five acres of land according to their engagement, returned to their homes and left me 'alone in my glory.'

When I was left alone the grim reality of my situation dimmed the romantic dreams in which I had indulged. My impressions in these inhospitable solitudes were any thing but cheering. The cold frowning silence of the leafless forest inspired me with feelings of ineffable awe and stupendous loneliness. A chilling austerity seemed to rebuke my intrusion into the untrodden recesses where Nature kept her secrets and brooded in awful grandeur and eternal stillness. Around my small clearing the moss-hoared elms and mighty maples stood like stern and sorrowful guardians of their smaller brethren in the back-ground. Over head now and then would pass a heavy-winged raven, maddened with hunger and moaning for his far-off home, and in the forest the hardy woodpecker would occasionally make the depths ring with his fierce assault on some barkless and rotting trunk. All else was silence; a vast melancholy; an unspeakable sadness of nature. But it is on a moonlight night in mid-winter that the woods assume an aspect of severest majesty; when the heavens pour their beauty across the swell of forest-tops, casting a darker shade below, and look as if in loving sorrow on the glistening snow in the clearing, like Pity upon fruitless Hope; casting their mild charm over torpid nature, cold and beautiful as a smile arrested in its transience, that half

umes the features of young Death.   Then the woods are filled
ith unseen voices, for the great trees are tortured by the frost, and
ack and groan and shout in agony, and the owl sings her night-
ng to the moon, and calls on the clamorous echoes.   Perhaps the
orm will be abroad exulting through the heavens, and veiling the
oon, as he raises his wild outcry and wrestles with the giants of
e forest, which bend and writhe and shriek in the contest, and
ng their mighty arms defiant, as they escape unscathed; while
me, less strong, sink beneath the tyrant's attack, crushing their
ns that stand around, and strewing the woods with ruin in their
ll; while high above the tumult the owl shrieks in fear, and the
rowling and distant wolf yells in horror.

I had often wished for solitude, and I had it now in earnest; be-
g fifteen miles from any human being except a few harmless
hippewas, who had come down to hunt.   I involuntarily began to
k with the poet,

' Oh Solitude ! where are thy charms ?'

I had no books except a few pocket volumes, having left them
ith other things to follow me by way of Quebec; and my only
musement was to chop, which I did daily.   This was excellent ex-
·cise, and I took great delight in it at first.   Although laborious,
has much excitement for a young beginner.   After having calcu-
ted in which position it will be most advantageous for your tree
 fall, you proceed to chop in the direction that in your judgment
ill secure such a result.   After an hour's chopping, which has
ade your blood fly through your veins and your heart leap with
ealth and pleasure, your exertions are rewarded by the tree giv-
g its first crack; being young at the business, you cease to chop,
ok up at the tree-top, and think of making your escape.   The
ee however shows no signs of falling, and you strike a dozen more
ows as fast as possible; then follows two more cracks.   The tree
 evidently showing symptoms of distress, and you retreat with
ste, and watch it from a convenient distance.   At this instant a
ight breeze arises and threatens to carry the tree in the contrary
rection.   You now hold your breath, fearful lest your plan should
 thwarted.   The wind ceases, the tree rights itself, and you ad-
nce and strike more blows, and retreat with great precipitation.
sinks at last, crash ! crash ! and your eyes sparkle to see it taking
e proper direction; now the top becomes entangled with the
anches of another tree; it is an anxious moment, for it threatens
 remain there; you creep toward it and give three or four quick
ows to throw more weight upon it by cutting away its hold on
e stump.   At last it strips off the limbs that interrupt its descent,
ad falls with a mighty crash, flinging up a cloud of snow, and you
out in involuntary gladness.   The next thing you do is to mount
n the trunk of the prostrate giant, and being light-hearted, sing a
erry catch as you walk up and look at its head, as if you expected
 find a treasure there.   Having achieved this great exploit you
aturally fling your axe across your shoulder, and still singing or
whistling, walk into your shanty to congratulate yourself.

'Familiarity breeds contempt,' even with the art of chopping, and I soon began to look upon it as an irksome duty rather than a pleasure. As I lived entirely alone I was compelled to practice the culinary art, and became quite a cook on a small scale; my experience however in these matters was rather limited, being confined to the different methods of preparing pork and venison which I had bought from the Indians, potatoes and coffee. But I racked my invention to discover the subtlest methods of preparing these dainties, and became a proficient in making that unleavened bread known, *inter sylvas*, as 'shanty cake.' Often when I have produced a *chef d'œuvre* of cunning cookery have I wished that some fastidious gourmand was there to share my feast. My dreams were not even yet all dispelled, and though I sometimes thought that a life in the bush looked better in print than in Canada, still I persuaded myself that a little exertion and a year or two of privation would not fail to produce the glorious results that I had predicted.

That long and dismal winter at last came to an end, and the spring burst upon me in all the sudden beauty of the American season. Myriads of birds of the most exquisite plumage filled the woods, and the earth was covered with flowers; flocks of pigeons flashed across my clearing, the swift messengers of summer; the trees put forth their leaves, and all nature rejoiced in verdant glory. I had little time however to admire the great change, for it was necessary to burn the piles of 'brush' and clear away the fallen timber on my land before I could sow or plant. This was a work not to be done without help, requiring both men and oxen; so I repaired to the 'settlement' in search of assistance. I soon found that this was not easily to be obtained, for every man was in the same predicament as myself; all were in a hurry to 'log' their own chopping, and none were willing to go fifteen miles to help me until their own work was done; which would be too late for my crops. With much ado I prevailed on two men to spare me one day, and I succeeded in getting half an acre cleared.

I was fain to moderate my ambitious views of husbandry for that year, and to devote myself to the culture of a garden. Having a choice supply of 'Shaker's seeds,' procured in the States, I arranged some small beds, and in good season 'committed them to the earth,' together with a small patch of potatoes, which were planted in the firm belief that they would return a hundred-fold. But the thing to which I looked forward with the greatest pleasure was the raising of Indian corn, of which I had a few seeds. Having never seen a field of corn, my curiosity was excited, and I had unlimited faith in its beauty and productiveness as a plant, and its excellence as a luxury. One fine morning in May I had commenced planting my corn, when suddenly, as if by preconcertion, myriads of small insects assailed me. I carelessly brushed them from my face at first, unwilling to believe that such minute creatures could do more harm than annoy one a little. Miserable error!—in less than an hour my eyes were swollen and nearly closed, my ears, neck, face and hands were in the same condition, and I was fairly compelled to abandon my work and run into the house, where alone I was free from the enemy. These insects are called 'black flies,' and are exceedingly venomous. The next day, having tied up my head with handkerchiefs, I ventured out again, and by perseverance I at length succeeded in finishing my planting.

These annoying insects disappeared in about a month, but their place was taken by a more formidable enemy, the musquitoe. Surely all the plagues of Egypt combined could cause but trifling misery when compared with this monster 'visitation' as it exists in the back-woods. They are not to be counted by myriads, but clouds, that emerge from the woods night and morning, and during the entire day in cloudy weather, obscuring the view like an animated fog. If you retire to your log-house on a rainy day, and endeavor to dissipate melancholy by reading, half a dozen will pounce upon your nose before you have got half through the first page. Would you write? As soon as you have commenced 'My dear ——' one pounces upon your finger, you fly into a passion and blot the sheet; and if, exhausted with the heat, you fall asleep, are not a dozen of the vampires feasting upon your temples?

You have been out all day, trying to roll together impossible logs, and retire to your shanty at evening tired and disconsolate; you find it full of musquitoes, and a swarm before the door and every crevice, striving to gain admittance; you make a large 'smudge' fire outside that the smoke may drive these away, and another inside in a sugar-kettle which you feed with moss and the fungi from fallen trees, and suffocate yourself in endeavoring to dislodge the intruders. They are gone at last, and you thank heaven. Not a solitary 'hum' is heard; you rid the house of smoke, and become better tempered with the prospect of having one night's uninterrupted repose; for the dew is now falling, and they will not venture from the woods again. You say your prayers, or at least you ought to do so, and go to bed: you cannot sleep at first for listening if one solitary fly is buzzing around; all is still, and you feel grateful. You revolve in your mind the cares of the day, the duties of the morrow, the schemes for the future; an indistinctness pervades your thoughts, unconnected images flit before your mind's eye in quick and vague succession; you abandon yourself to the fulness of lethargic happiness; a swooning pleasure steals through your frame. Then in the wierd phantasma of shadowy images that perplexes you, appear familiar scenes and beloved faces in vivid distinctness; these disappear, and one more beloved than all the rest arises and remains; you are again at home, once more enacting that last farewell scene which has taken ineradicable root in your memory; once more you feel choking as you look upon the tears that bedim *her* eyes; again you bid her be of good cheer, and endeavor to console her by referring to the far-off home in a beauteous land that you go to provide for her; again you utter the last harsh word farewell; the last long burning kiss is on your lips; when buzz, buzz! The spell is broken, and all the tribe of musquitoes is hastily consigned to a nameless personage of doubtful caste.

In a short time a thought of profound wisdom struck me, which was, that a man who had resolved upon turning farmer would be none the worse for possessing a little stock, and that my coffee would be all the better for a little milk ; so I resolved at once to purchase a cow. 'T is true I could not milk a cow, and the idea itself was extremely ludicrous, but I overcame my foolish scruples by reasoning that ' where there 's a will there 's a way ;' ' people must adapt themselves,' etc. And after all it would furnish me with an excellent topic of gossip in my next letter home. Away I went one Thursday morning, as I thought, before sunrise, to a Scotch settlement, where I discovered that it was Sunday, and waiting until next day I bought a cow, and also permitted a yoke of oxen to be palmed upon me, and after taking half a dozen lessons in milking, I returned with my three cattle as proud as a plebeian who had suddenly come into possession of a large fortune, and as much perplexed with my acquisition.

I invented a new method of milking with my finger and thumb, and on certain occasions when the cow was unusually patient, and the flies unusually scarce, actually succeeded in obtaining a little milk. But her ladyship took to rambling, and frequently when searching for the cow, I lost myself, and spent whole days in endeavoring to find my small clearing. At length I became weary of this amusement, and she disappeared altogether. I put my oxen through ' all their paces ;' hitched them to logs, and practised ' haw' and 'gee' with the obstinate brutes, until I became a tolerable 'teamster.' But they, like myself and my cow, were given to wandering, and one day basely deserted me. The best temper in the world may be ruined by continued ill-treatment and ingratitude; and so poignantly did I feel this heartless conduct, that I subsided into a sullen despair, resolving to take no steps for their recovery, but leave them to the fate they deserved for abandoning so excellent a master. I took things very easily in fact. I am afraid I was getting dispirited, and sometimes thought, in spite of myself, that my great scheme would prove a bubble, and that my own society, very *exclusive* though it was, did not possess all the charms with which my imagination or vanity had endowed it.

One day, in default of better employment, I had taken a pocket copy of Virgil in my hand, and after dreaming for half an hour over the name and date written on a blank leaf, when I was a school-boy, and the hundred recollections this slight incident awakened, I commenced to read the first Eclogue : I had got as far as that passage in which Tityrus solemnly vows Olympian honors to his patron, because as he says :

> ' Ille permisit,
> Meas bones errare,'

when my attention was arrested by a loud crash outside, and I instantly went to discover the cause. Oh Virgil ! Oh Tityrus and horned cattle ! what a sight ! My harvest cares were ended ; my year's work was consummated. A drove of stray cows and oxen were in my garden ; my beautiful tomatoes were destroyed, my darling garden plants were ruined, and my cherished corn had disappeared. I gave up all hopes from that hour, and retired into the 'shanty' a broken-hearted and disconsolate man. I had found to my cost that people in the present age permitted their *bones errare* as in Tityrus' time.

I learned shortly that my errant cattle had returned to the 'place from whence they came,' and sallied forth after the unrepentant animals. I found them in excellent preservation, or to speak plainly, 'in the pound.' It appeared that the gentleman from whom I had bought them was a man given to practical jokes, and had sold me a yoke of 'breachy' oxen, notorious for their deeds throughout the settlement. They had obligingly thrown down a farmer's fence, to give easy entrance to themselves and about twenty of their brethren and sisters into his wheat-field. I saw plainly that I was 'done,' and complaint was useless; so I paid about half the value of the three cattle for damages, and in the spirit of forgiveness once more took the graceless prodigals to my home.

I succeeded in the course of the summer and fall to get the whole of my 'chopping' logged and cleared, making six acres of land ready for crops in the ensuing spring. It is needless to say any thing of the next winter. It passed monotonous and melancholy, and all my high-flown notions of romantic happiness and primitive life were effectually dissipated. In the spring I succeeded in sowing my whole clearing with wheat and oats. I erected a small log barn and made my house more comfortable; but alas! the season proved unfavorable, my crops were destroyed by mildew or 'rust,' and were actually not worth gathering. In despair I went to ask the advice of an old friend, who lived about twenty-five miles away, in the same district, an old naval captain, who had retired with his family to Canada. These people, by the way, make the best farmers in the provinces, perhaps from having been accustomed to '*plough* the deep.'

'The only thing that can insure success in the bush,' he said, 'is work, hard and unceasing. Here education will not avail you : the best man is he who has the strongest arm, and has been least accustomed to the refinements of society. To the worn-out mechanic and half-starved artisan the country offers many advantages, but it is essentially the *poor man's* country. For myself I have accomplished what they call success; that is, after five years of work and privation, shared by my wife, my sons and daughters, we can raise a sufficiency of every thing that we absolutely require; this is all you can ever achieve, and to secure this you must devote yourself to a life of laborious industry.' Of exertion and privation I had had enough ; and returning home I packed up my 'traps,' sold my cattle for half their value ; and as I could not get a purchaser for my land, I left it to take care of itself, crops and all.

The last accounts that the friends of this writer heard of him testified that he was in the United States, desperately bent upon making his fortune, but all his efforts up to that period had been characteristically unsuccessful. His life was spent chiefly in dreaming over imaginary widows, disconsolate and rich, young ladies with tender hearts and heavy dowers, and dyspeptic old gentlemen, childless, friendless, but not fortuneless. The Editor of the KNICKERBOCKER, after having listened to his sorrowful story, kindly offered to make his hard case known to the public, in the hope that perhaps some charitable person, of either sex, might feel inclined to alleviate his misfortunes and make his fortune.

STANZAS: TO MY SISTER.

'My sister, my sweet sister! if a name
Purer and holier were, it should be thine.'—BYRON.

THE heart that for so many years
  I knew and felt was wholly mine,
With hopes from which I banish fears
  I now must share, perhaps resign.

From boyhood's up to manhood's hour
  This heart has soothed my every care,
Has wiled me from Temptation's power,
  And shielded me with holiest prayer.

Has had a spell to lure from harm,
  Such as those fabled spells of old,
Which could the yielding spirit charm
  From all that wizard tale has told.

How often to my stricken bed,
  Where I have known whole years of pain,
Thou cam'st, with woman's gentlest tread,
  To give me hope of health again!

With a fond eye that never slept,
  Holding my hand in both of thine,
For me thou hast long vigils kept,
  Until thy health grew frail as mine.

My better angel ever thou!
  Who by my side shall take thy place?
And calm the fever of my brow,
  And plume my spirit for the race?

Now thou art far upon the sea,
  And I am far within the West;
And waves and mountains keep from me
  My loved of all the world the best.

Far, far o'er wave and far o'er wild,
  The storm-tossed of the troubled deep,
Of home the loved and favored child,
  How rough and rude thy ocean-sleep!

Alas! and do the rude winds blow,
  And toss the fierce waves o'er thy path?
O, God! that thou couldst these forego,
  That I might bear the tempest's wrath!

With a firm faith that He above
  Will guard thee to thy destined home,
I would that I could see the dove
  Careering o'er the ocean's foam.

O! blessed be thy marriage-vow!
  Far parted, sister, though we be,
And though the distance lengthens now,
  I send a brother's love to thee.

Then send me back a sister's love,
  While seated by thy husband's side,
And it will to him stronger prove
  The worth of his belovéd bride.

rten, D. C.   F. W Thomas.

THE VISION OF ABD-EL-BENDER.

A LESSON FOR REFORMERS.

10 among the sons and daughters of men sighs not for happi-
  However dark the clouds that hang over him, who does not
1at there is sunshine high above the mists and vapors that dim
orizon? However sad, thorny and weary the path he treads,
loes not crave the beauty of earth? — who does not feel intui-
  that bright sky, flowery meadows, breezy hill-sides, music of
fountains, and shadowy canopy of waving boughs, are all for
1nd belong to him, in virtue of inherent right?
e child's desire is but the germ of the man's aspiration; and
1art filled with unsatisfied cravings, journeys from the cradle
 grave, and goes to seek beyond its shadowy Rubicon the reali-
1 of those visions of something better which have haunted it
the disappointments of earth.
s this yearning for an unattained ideal good, so deep, so uni-
|, so ineradicable, manifesting itself in so many ways, according
 diversities of individual character, which has prompted the
ods, Alexanders, and Napoleons of our race to acquire do-
n; Sybarites to distil the honeyed drops of pleasure; philoso-
to ransack the realms of speculation; astronomers to watch
3h star-lit vigils; Homer to sing, Raphael to idealize form and
 and Beethoven to wring, by the force of indomitable aspiring,
arvellous secrets of harmony from the reluctant tone-spirits.
  seek; yet who are satisfied? Yet can it be that the plastic
 whose mighty working has laid together the foundations of

our being, would implant in the universal soul a useless tendency, an endless aim, a mocking guide-post that should lead no whither ?

. . . .

In ancient days, and in an eastern land, lived ABD-EL-BENDER. Young, of strong and manly beauty, endowed with a powerful mind and a capacious soul, in possession of health, wealth, and friends, he was determined to be happy, He lived in a magnificent house, whose exquisite appointments won the admiration of his guests, and surrounded himself with all that Luxury offers to her votaries. His gardens were adorned with fountains and statuary, and displayed the rarest and most fragrant flowers ; and in their midst, deep whispering groves enclosed a little lake, in whose clear depths the clouds and the stars loved to see themselves ; while an artificial wilderness, rocky and wild, charmed by the force of contrast, and invited to quiet contemplation the wandering worshippers of pleasure.

But this external loveliness did not satisfy him ; he felt that amidst it all the soul of beauty was wanting; and when he went abroad, when he saw the want, the misery, the meanness, the conflict, and the manifold ugliness of life, his spirit sickened, and he could no longer enjoy the luxurious ease of his own privileged estate.

He sold his house, distributed the proceeds among the poor, whose miserable condition had excited his compassion, and gave himself up to Science. Diving into the deep places of Nature, seeking the laws of her wondrous working, and striving to elicit the meaning of her phenomena, he became a wiser but not a happier man. He saw every where around him such a prodigality of latent energies, whose effects might be multiplied into infinite blessings, that he was puzzled and confounded ; for why, amid such rich possibilities, must actual life be so poor, so pitiful ? Glimpses of wide applications, phantoms of far-reaching improvements, succeeded to his former wish of personal gratification, and gave a broader and nobler turn to his desires : but just as he was elaborating a grand scheme for levelling a ridge of mountains to the east of the city, in order to furnish land to all who needed it, and a splendid plan for endowing a college for the education of cats into a higher order of beings, a terrible fire broke out, caused by the drunken revellings of the rabble on whom he had bestowed his ill-advised bounty, which destroyed half the city, and left him in possession of a bare competency.

His grand schemes of improvement thus literally ended in smoke; for it is certain that a very considerable amount of money must be expended before mountains can be lowered to plains, or cats raised to human beings ; and Abd-el-Bender, in his altered circumstances, had recourse to philosophy.

He frequented the schools, and soon exhausted all that their conflicting systems had to offer. Disgusted with their unsubstantial bases, their partial views, and inadequte solutions, he retired into a mountain solitude to meditate alone. Although his studies had failed to bring him peace, they had served to stimulate his mind ; the sublime idea of a supreme controlling First Cause, and consequently of Progress and immortality, had dawned, though faintly, upon his soul; and the feverish ardor with which he had investigated the possibilities of Nature, had softened and risen into an aspiration after a higher spiritual state.   But though every year found him calmer and stronger, as belief in the Invisible sank more and more deeply into his soul, though Nature and Reason united to assure him of the reality of a Central Mind, whose prolific energies created and sustained all things, he yet thirsted for a clearer revelation of the meaning of life.

One evening the sun went down with unusual splendor; the mountain peaks above his dwelling glowed with intense lustre, while shadows gathered over the vales below; and twilight fell so softly, so sweetly upon forest, rock and river, that the heart of the recluse was melted within him.   He fell upon his knees and bowed his head reverently to the fragrant turf; and as he felt the evening wind sweep lightly and lovingly over his brow, and saw the silver-eyed watchers of the night looking out so radiant and so peaceful, his soul went up in intense yearning to the unseen and yet present Divinity, whose love he felt to be infinite and universal.   Gradually the vividness of these emotions subsided; a quiet drowsiness stole over him; and soon the shifting phantasms of a dream flitted before his spirit.

He stood in the midst of a wide flowery plain: the most delicious fragrance filled the air, and hosts of gay-winged creatures fluttered brightly by.   The rich, harmonious contrasts of form, color, motion and odor filled him with admiration; and as he gazed around with rapture, he heard a voice singing near him, so melodious, so full of a beautiful lovingness, that he was quite penetrated by its tones. Soon other voices were heard blending in chorus with it, and ever deeper and higher and wider swelled the song, until it seemed in its triumphant fulness to fill the air, and soar among the stars; which 'in their turn, awakening their silvery lyres, flung back high answering music from the blue depths of space.

Then there shone before him a cloud of soft white light, which, as he gazed into its depths, opening gently and fading away, revealed the form of a young and beautiful maiden, who, smiling upon him, thus addressed him:

'Behold, O Seeker! the open Secret of the Universe!   When human hearts shall unfold themselves to the sunlight and the dews of Heaven, like the beautiful unselfish flowers, which seek not to absorb the blessings of cloud and beam, but accept each its own portion, and grow lovingly and peacefully thereby; when the voices now loud in angry conflict shall cease their dissonance and blend in harmonious concert; when Love, broad, wise and universal, shall rule the world, then will the potent influences which bind together all the realms of universal being, flow down to earth; and the voice of Humanity, mingling with the music of the spheres, shall rise in majestic harmony to the throne of GoD!   Be thou loving, patient, hopeful!   The ages will realize the vision!'

The dream faded and the sleeper awoke.

The lesson sank deep into his spirit. He left his retreat and mingled again in the affairs of men, disciplining himself to love and patience ; and whenever he found a soul who yearned like him for a better life, he counselled him to do the same.

While he lived he blessed by the influence of a beautiful example, and he died at an advanced age, in full faith of that brighter future, when love and peace shall humanize and glorify the earth.

A S O N G F O R S E P T E M B E R :

BUT WILL DO FOR OCTOBER

I.

SEPTEMBER strews the woodland o'er
  With many a brilliant color ;
The world is brighter than before,
  Why should our hearts be duller ?
Sorrow and the scarlet leaf,
  Sad thoughts and sunny weather —
Ah me ! this glory and this grief
  Agree not well together.

II.

This is the parting season, this
  The time when friends are flying ;
And lovers now, with many a kiss,
  Their long farewells are sighing.
Why is earth so gaily dressed ?
  This pomp that autumn beareth
A funeral seems, where every guest
  A bridal garment weareth.

III.

Each one of us may often here,
  On some blue morn hereafter,
Return to view the gaudy year,
  But not with boyish laughter.
We shall then be wrinkled men,
  Our brows with silver laden,
And thou this glen may'st seek again,
  But never more a maiden.

IV.

Nature perhaps foresees that Spring
  Will touch her teeming bosom,
And thinks a few brief months will bring
  The bird — the bee — the blossom.
Ah ! these forests do not know,
  Or would less brightly wither,
The virgin that adorns them so
  Will never more come hither !

                                                    T. W. P.

Leyden Glen, Greenfield.

LITERARY NOTICES.

N: OR INCIDENTS OF LIFE AND ADVENTURES IN THE ROCKY MOUNTAINS. By an AMA-
TRAVELLER. Edited by J. WATSON WEBB. In two volumes. pp. 465. New-York:
R AND BROTHERS.

.LY nine years the EDITOR of these well-written and interesting volumes passed
army of the United States, and during most of that period upon our then
estern frontier; at Green-Bay, Chicago, the Upper Mississippi and M'ssouri;
riod too when the white man was only known to the native of the forest
the army, and the Indian trader and voyageur, who annually passed into
untry, but confined themselves to its principal water-courses. Mr. WEBB
ll claim therefore to be qualified by experience to judge of the faithfulness
lelineation of the aboriginal 'native' character, as displayed in the work for
with little fault of temerity, he stands sponsor. The volumes before us
. us after the notices in this department were in type; and although but five
ave elapsed since their receipt, we have read them through; that is, we have
erused them in detail as to be enabled to say that they not only justify the
y and the encomiums of the EDITOR, but they reflect the highest credit upon
husiasm, the love of manly adventure, and the literary ability of the writer.
lowing account of the author, by Col. WEBB, will be read with interest:

summer of 1832 a British half-pay officer visited this city, and we were accidentally thrown
each other's society. A similarity of tastes and pursuits soon produced an intimacy, gradu-
ing into a friendship, which I trust is destined to continue through life. He was one of the
llows who fought under WELLINGTON at Waterloo, and bore upon his person honorable
his gallantry upon that occasion, and among his insignia the evidence of his country's gra-
The second son of one of the most ancient families in Great Britain, with the blood of
a his veins, and connected by birth and intermarriages with royalty itself, he had retired
f-pay; and in the spirit of adventure, which forms a prominent trait in his character, visited
d States for the sole purpose of penetrating the great wildernesses of the West, and partak-
excitement and adventure which it promised; regardless alike of the privations and dan-
parable from such a life
it period I was probably of all others the person in this city who could best further his views;
the season for his departure arrived, he carried with him the necessary letters of introduc-
y old fellow-soldiers in the West, and to such prominent gentlemen, not in the army, as
their position and advice put him in the way of accomplishing the object of his visit to our
Among those to whom I gave him letters were the late Governor CLARKE, of Missouri, and
ATKINSON and ASHLEY. The latter, though not of the army, went annually into the In-
atry in military array, to receive on the head-waters of the Yellow-Stone the furs and pel-
ch had been collected during the preceding year, and to furnish the next year's supply of
oods to the traders; and it was under his auspices that our author first visited the Rocky
s. When General ASHLEY returned to the haunts of civilization, my friend, accompanied
ll band of hired voyageurs, continued his course to the Pacific; visited the different estab-
s of the Hudson's Bay Company; spent three winters in the Rocky Mountains, in Oregon
or California; and finally. after an absence of three years and a half, returned to St. Louis.
his long sojourn in the wilderness he had literally suffered every thing but death from hos-
s of Indians, from hunger, exposure and fatigue. He had met with 'hair-breadth 'scapes'
kind; but he had hunted and killed the grizzly bear and the buffalo; he had seen and

lived with the North-American Indian in his native wilds; and he had looked upon a country fresh from the hands of the CREATOR, filled with magnificent lakes, lofty mountains and boundless prairies, which spoke the nothingness of man, and involuntarily carried the heart and the mind 'from Nature up to Nature's GOD.'

'On his return to St. Louis he learned that his brother, the head of his ancient house, had died without issue, and that he was the inheritor of the family title and a princely estate. He came and spent some time with me on Long Island preparatory to his return home; but eager as ever for the life of adventure he had been living, he soon abandoned his purpose, and determined to revisit the Great West, accompanied by a large retinue, and an artist of merit to sketch the various scenes which had made an impression upon him during his previous visit. Again was he absent two summers and a winter, devoting his time to hunting, and partaking of all the excitement of that boundless region; and on his return, after spending some time with his earliest friend in America, he sailed for home to take possession of his paternal estates.

'There, in the castle of his ancestors, a venerable pile, erected in 1604, I have since visited him and spent many a happy hour. There he is not only surrounded by a devoted tenantry, whose cares he makes his own, and a large circle of distinguished friends, who honor and appreciate his virtues, but by galleries of magnificent paintings, executed by our countryman MILLER, from sketches by himself, made during the second visit of the author to the Rocky Mountains, Oregon and California. And there too I took our friend INMAN, during his visit to Europe in 1844; and had his life been spared, the present volumes would have been illustrated by drawings of his, taken from sketches in the portfolio of the author. But our departed friend detailed to you the pleasures of that visit, of which 'Salmon-fishing near Birnam Wood,' one of his last works, and so justly admired, is a speaking memento.

'When the author first visited the Great West, I urged him to keep a journal of his travels and adventures for publication; but to this he was greatly averse. He made however a half promise that he would do something in the way of recording the incidents of his travels and describing the countries of his wanderings; and the work I now take pleasure in dedicating to you is the fulfilment of that promise. It was written solely for the eye of my family and for the amusement of my children; and it was only during my last visit to the author, accompanied by INMAN, who promised to prepare the illustrations for the work, that publication was determined upon and promised. 'The sketches of Indian habits, and the incidents of the chase which it contains, are,' he tells us in his notice to the reader, 'taken from life; and the descriptions of the regions where the scene is laid in the Western wilds, are drawn from nature.' This, it is scarcely necessary to say, gives an historical interest to the work; while the reader will find no difficulty in discovering how much of it is fiction, and adopted only to give it additional zest to ' his young friends on Long Island.'

'Oregon and California, the Rocky Mountains and the boundless prairies of the West, have at this time charms for children of a larger growth than this work was designed to amuse. And although, as the author says, 'it was written during voyages over heaving seas, and in moments of idleness in different parts of the world,' it is not the less true to nature; because he had with him the original notes made during his sojourn in the Indian country. Since his first visit to the United States the author has travelled in the inhospitable regions of Northern Russia, and through the more luxurious though scarcely more civilized East; and a portion of the manuscript was forwarded to me from Constantinople. It may not be uninteresting to the young traveller to add, that in 1842 the author again visited our country and the scenes of his former adventures; declaring that it had charms for him which no other land possesses.'

Thus much for a brief but clear and graphic account of the author, indicating somewhat also the character of his work. We take it from a very appropriate dedication to CHARLES FENNO HOFFMAN, Esq., a gentleman, as is well remarked by the EDITOR, whose knowledge and love of woodcraft, and whose ability to appreciate a correct picture of the North-American Indian, sketched from life by the pencil of a master, may well justify the choice of his friend. We are not sorry to be made aware that the EDITOR was limited to a few pages in his introduction; since the result will be, that we shall hereafter have the stirring narrative of personal adventure, here so graphically commenced, continued in a more elaborate work, which cannot fail to prove of deep interest. Mr. WEBB narrates a wonderful instance of instinct in an Indian guide, who piloted his party on a dark and bitter cold night to a distant wood on a prairie; concerning which he remarks:

'Now comes the question, and it is one which has bothered me for twenty-four years; how did the Indian avoid losing his way? Why was he confident that he was going directly to his place of destination? My sergeant, an old woodsman, and myself, had made use of all our experience, judgment and intellects to keep in the right direction, but had failed; had wandered no one can tell where; and yet this child of the forest, without a trail, in a dark night, without a moon, star or wind to guide him, and quite ten miles from the wood, had never for a moment doubted that he was in the right direction; in short, *knew* that he was; and the result demonstrated his *knowledge!* Whence came this knowledge? Was it instinct? or was he indebted for his knowledge and safety to his keener sense of *smelling*? You once said to me, that a critical examination of Indian skulls had led a friend to believe that the orifice through which the olfactory nerve passes is larger than in the white man; that the eye is set differently, so that he may see farther behind him than civilized man; and that the passage for admitting sound into the head is larger. If this be so, the secret of my Indian's knowledge is at once developed; and we cannot but be struck by the wonderful and inscrutable provisions of a kind PROVIDENCE for all His creatures, of whatever condition in life.

Minstrelsy, Ancient and Modern: with an Introduction and Notes, by William Mothers-well. In two volumes. pp. 562. Boston: William D. Ticknor and Company.

We have already cordially welcomed this well-arranged collection of ancient and modern minstrelsy. It embraces a numerous and highly interesting body of short metrical tales, of a tragic complexion, 'which, though possessing all the features of real incident cannot after the lapse of ages be traced to any historical source, public or private ;' ancient songs, which treat of incredible achievements and strange adventures by flood and field, and deal largely with the marvellous ; and narrative songs, which derive their origin from historical facts, such as national or personal conflicts, family feuds, public or domestic transactions, personal adventure, local incidents, etc. We make a single extract from the gloomy and superstitious ballad of ' Sir Ronald.' The story is of a young lady, who on the eve of her marriage invited her lover to a banquet, where she murders him in revenge for some real or fancied neglect. Alarmed for her own safety, she betakes herself to flight ; and in the course of her journey she sees a stranger knight riding slowly before her, whom she at first seeks to shun, by pursuing an opposite direction ; but on finding that wheresoever she turned he still appeared between her and the moonlight, she resolves to overtake him. This however she finds in vain, till of his own accord he stays for her at the brink of a broad river. They agree to cross it ; and when in the mid-stream, she implores his help to save her from drowning. To her horror, she finds her fellow-traveller to be no other than the gaunt apparition of her dead lover:

She has mounted on her true love's steed,
  By the ae light o' the moon ;
She has whipped him and spurred him,
  And roundly she rade frae the toun.

She hadna ridden a mile o' gate,
  Never a mile but ane,
When she was aware of a tall young man,
  Slow riding o'er the plain.

She turned her to the right about,
  Then to the left turn'd she ;
But aye, 'tween her and the wan moonlight
  That tall knight did she see.

And he was riding burd alane,
  On a horse as black as jet ;
But tho' she followed him fast and fell,
  No nearer could she get.

'O stop ! O stop ! young man,' she said,
  'For I in dule am dight ;
O stop, and win a fair lady's luve,
  If you be a leal true knight.'

She whipped her steed, she spurred her steed,
  Till his breast was all a foam ;
But nearer unto that tall young knight,
  By Our Ladye ! she could not come.

' O if you be a gay young knight,
  As well I trow you be,
Pull tight your bridle reins, and stay
  Till I come up to thee !'

But nothing did that tall knight say,
  And no whit did he blin,
Until he reached a broad river's side,
  And there he drew his rein.

' O is this water deep,' he said,
  ' As it is wondrous dun ?
Or is it sic as a saikless maid
  And a leal true knight may swim ?'

' The water it is deep,' she said,
  ' As it is wondrous dun ;
But it is sic as a saikless maid
  And a leal true knight may swim.'

The knight spurred on his tall black steed,
  The lady spurred on her brown ;
And fast they rade unto the flood,
  And fast they baith swam down.

' The water weets my tae,' she said,
  ' The water weets my knee ;
And hold up my bridle reins, Sir Knight,
  For the sake of Our Ladye.'

' If I would help thee now,' he said,
  ' It were a deadly sin ;
For I've sworn neir to trust a fair may's word,
  Till the water weets her chin.'

' O the water weets my waist,' she said,
  ' Sae does it weet my skin ;
And my aching heart rins round about,
  The burn maks sic a din.

' The water is waxing deeper still,
  Sae does it wax mair wide ;
And aye the farther that we ride on,
  Farther off is the other side.

' O help me now, thou false, false knight,
  Have pity on my youth ;
For now the water jawes owre my head,
  And it gurgles in my mouth.'

The knight turned right and round about,
All in the middle stream,
And he stretched out his head to that lady,
But loudly she did scream.

'O this is hallow-morn,' he said,
'And it is your bridal day;
But sad would be that gay wedding,
If bridegroom and bride were away.

'And ride on, ride on, proud MARGARET!
Till the water comes o'er your bree;
For the bride maun ride deep, and deeper yet,
Wha rides this ford wi' me!

'Turn round, turn round, proud MARGARET!
Turn ye round, and look on me;
Thou hast killed a true knight under trust,
And his ghost now links on with thee!'

We should not omit to add that the typography and paper of these volumes are excellent, as is indeed uniformly the case with the issues of the enterprising publishers from whom we receive them.

--- --- --- ---

THE PROBE: OR ONE HUNDRED AND TWO ESSAYS ON THE NATURE OF MEN AND THINGS. By L. CARROLL JUDSON, of the Philadelphia Bar. In one volume. pp. 329. Philadelphia: G. B. ZIEBER AND COMPANY.

THE foregoing is the title of a well-executed volume from the press of ZIEBER AND COMPANY, Philadelphia. The book is really replete with wisdom and good counsel, rendered attractive by a general ease and force of style, and by not infrequent felicitous illustration. The tendency of the volume is to inculcate sterling integrity, unyielding virtue, ardent patriotism, active philanthropy, pure benevolence and universal charity. We subjoin a few sententious passages, taken quite at random from scarcely a moiety of the work:

PEACE-MAKING LAWYERS. — 'If no lawyers were patronized save those who are emphatically peace-makers; who can clearly discern the right and wrong between litigants, and kindly enforce the one and correct the other, by patient and sound reasoning; millions of money would pass through a better channel, and thousands of friendships be saved from dissolution.'

'RELIGIOUS' SECTARIANISM. — ' Different sects of Christians, are like the children of one father; each has a different Christian name, but all belong to the same family; so all Christian churches belong to the household of faith, and should soar above family quarrels.'

PATERNAL ADVICE. — ' If we wish the seed sown to take root, we must mellow the soil by proper cultivation. So in giving advice, we must first gain the confidence of those we deem it a duty to advise.'

CITY vs. COUNTRY LIFE. — 'If multitudes, who are hard run to get bread, would leave our pent-up cities, and occupy and improve the millions of fine land in our country, yet unlocated, it would greatly enhance individual happiness and public good. Try it, ye starved ones; if you are disappointed, then I am no prophet, nor the son of a prophet.'

ANGER AND ITS CURE. — 'Anger, like too much wine, hides us from ourselves, but exposes us to others. If the man who has for years been a confirmed drunkard, can form and religiously keep a resolution to refrain from the fatal poison, the man who has often been intoxicated with anger, should go and do likewise.'

BE NOT CAST DOWN. — 'Never be cast down by trifles. If a spider breaks his thread twenty times in a day, he patiently mends it each time. Make up your mind to do a good thing, it will be done. Fear not troubles, keep up your spirits, the darkness will pass away. If the sun is going down, look at the stars; if they are hid by clouds, still look up to heaven.'

PUNCTUALITY AND DESPATCH. — 'In business, punctuality and despatch make short work. Let friendly calls be short. Twice glad, in formal visits, is coming short of the mark. Let your communications to those who are busy, be short. Hold no man by the button in the street, or in the door; be short. Let your anecdotes and stories be short.'

CONDESCENSION. — ' I have somewhere read of two goats that met midway, on a narrow pass, over a deep gulf. Neither could turn round to go back, without danger of falling off, and one very courteously laid down, and permitted the other to walk, not harshly, but gently over him, and both passed on in safety. This is not the first wise lesson I have learned from brute animals, who act much more consistently than some men, who claim reason for a guide, but seldom follow its directions. In passing over the highway of life, it is often necessary to condescend to accommodate our fellow travellers, and put ourselves to mutual or individual inconvenience, to get along smoothly.'

A TART REPLY TO A CHALLENGE. — I recollect many cutting answers to challenges, that inflicted severer wounds than to be shot with the blue pill. Here is one: 'Sir, your desire to have me shoot you, cannot be complied with. My father taught me, when a boy, never to waste powder on game not worth bringing home.'

PRESENCE OF MIND. — 'An instance occurred in India about thirty years ago, of remarkable presence of mind in a lady. Several ladies and gentlemen went on shore, and had seated themselves near a jungle, the lady in question sitting a few feet farther out than the rest. Suddenly, a huge tiger sprang at her ; she instantly spread an umbrella in his face, which so discomfitted him, that he retreated, and the party escaped unhurt.'

Had we space, we might fill pages with passages of kindred force and interest from the essays and sketches whence these are taken. We have quoted enough however to indicate the terseness of style and variety of theme which characterize ' The Probe.'

LIDDELL AND SCOTT'S GREEK-ENGLISH LEXICON: WITH CORRECTIONS AND ADDITIONS. BY HENRY DRISLER, M. A. New-York: HARPER AND BROTHERS.

THIS Greek Dictionary must inevitably take the place of all others in the classical schools of this country. In England, DONNEGAN, GROVE, SCHREVILIUS, etc., have been entirely discarded since the appearance of LIDDELL and SCOTT's edition of PASSOW. The principles upon which it is prepared; the manner in which they have been carried out; the arrangement, definitions, derivations, usages, etc., of the words are very far superior to those of any other work to which pupils can have access. The American edition is still superior to the English, inasmuch as its Editor, the Adjunct Greek Professor of Columbia College, and one of the ripest scholars in the country, has added to and otherwise improved it very materially. No care or labor has been spared. The task seems indeed Herculean ; but it has been performed, with heroic courage, and in a style that leaves nothing to be desired. Every part of it has been adapted to the wants and necessities of classical students. It is published in a large, heavy and neat substantial octavo volume, of above seventeen hundred pages, clearly and very handsomely printed upon fine, strong, white paper, and in a style throughout which reflects the highest credit upon the house by which it is issued. It is sold for five dollars.

TWO LIVES: OR TO SEEM AND TO BE. By MARIA J. MCINTOSH, Author of ' Conquest and Self-Conquest,' ' Praise and Principle,' etc., etc. In one volume. pp. 318. New-York: D. APPLETON AND COMPANY.

WHENEVER the readers of this Magazine encounter a new work which announces itself as having been written ' by the author of Conquest and Self-Conquest,' our advice to them is, to purchase it and peruse it at once. There is such a vein of strong good common sense running through the productions of this author ; her inculcations are so well calculated to do good, and the naturalness and interest of her illustrations of the various kinds and phases of human character are so preëminent, that no one can rise from her pages without being deeply entertained and as sensibly improved. In the volume before us, the title of which well expresses its scope and design, we have a story in which the one great feature of romance, a love-tale, is certainly predominant ; but while there is enough in the way of illustration to prove that ' the course of true love never did run smooth,' there is an under-current of practical instruction, VANITY teaching by example, which will be lost upon no thoughtful reader. One thing we especially admire in the writings of this gifted lady ; it is the absence of any literary pretence or pomposity. Her descriptions of scenery and the phenomena of the elements are clear and not over-labored ; her conception and discrimination of character are vivid and distinct ; and the beauty and truth of a true woman's heart appear in all her literary productions. The incidents in the story of the ' Two Lives' are too closely interwoven to be segregated and dwelt upon at large in the little space which we have at command. We must content ourselves at present therefore with commending the work to the cordial acceptance of our readers.

ANOTHER DISH OF 'LOBSCOUSE.' — We have the pleasure of presenting our readers with a second dish of '*Lobscouse*,' which we trust may prove as palatable as the first. Indeed we can have but small doubt of that; since the naturalness and simplicity which are the characteristics of these unstudied sketches are qualities that will always insure commendation. But to begin: 'SQUILGEE apostrophiseth the Island of Madeira:' 'Oh, lovely island of Madeira! oh, genial 'South-side!' where the rich clusters of the grape blush on the hills' acclivity, beneath the warm glances of the glowing sun; where products of the temperate and the torrid zone vie in luxuriance, and all is fresh and green; how grateful is the sight thou presentest to the consumers of 'hard tack' and salt junk! — for understand that by some mismanagement our fresh 'grub' had given out a week before. Howbeit, we had potatoes and onions, two necessary ingredients, and were thus enabled to concoct that savory mess, the name whereof, like that of my yarn, is '*Lobscouse*.'' SQUILGEE proceeds to record a spirited account of '*Old Boreas the Boatswain's Courtship and Wedding*,' as taken down from the lips of the 'Old Salt' himself: 'Old BOREAS the Boatswain had a most lugubrious expression on his excessively ugly countenance, one cool afternoon, as SQUILGEE went forward to smoke a 'mild Havana;' (*en passant*, let me add, that that was his style of doing up the sentimental.) 'Mr. BOREAS,' said SQUILGEE, 'what's the matter with you? Your face is as grum as the carving at the end of a cat-head.' Before going any farther, however, let us take a look at the individual. You must know, reader, that the carving on a cat-head is generally designed to represent the flattened face of a ferocious lion or tiger, and is frequently gilded. Take such a face, give it a little more prominency of nose, letting it turn up withal; bring the chin out to a point, backed by a doubling of the 'dew-lap;' color it with a mixture of red and bronze, and you will have what I think all who remember BOREAS will consider a true likeness of that old and faithful servitor of his country. His body too possessed some distinctive features, in the peculiarity of its shortness, roundness, and manner of stepping the legs. Having been for the greater part of his life a boatswain's-mate, he had been during that time confined to the use of a roundabout; but no sooner was the appointment of boatswain conferred on him, than 'long togs' were the order of the day; and as if to make up for the past, he had a coat manufactured with an immensity of flap and a length of tail truly astonishing. Of a Sunday, when after piping 'all hands to muster' he came up to the officer of the deck, in all the dignity of his situation, and reported 'Men all up, Sir,' his appearance reminded one forcibly of a swallow lighted on the ground. Many of my readers have no doubt observed how those birds strut about with their wings folded over their tails; even so looked Boreas on these occasions, with his broad-tailed coat enveloping the rear of his rotund person.

'Ah! Mr. Squilgee,' replied Boreas, in answer to the question, 'What's the matter with you?' 'I was a-thinking of old times, and it makes me sort of solemncholy-like.'

'What on earth can you have to make you sad, Boreas, unless it may be that some of your various little peccadilloes are rising up in your memory? You've certainly done your country good service.'

'Yes, Sir, but 't ain't about the sarvice I was a-thinking. My mind was a-going back to the days when I was young, before I signed a purser's receipt; when Peg Cleaver and me was a-going to be spliced—'married' I used to call it in them days.'

'Have you never been married, Boreas?'

'No, Sir, I never have,' he replied, heaving such a sigh; drawing in his breath and throwing it out with such tremendous force that it could only be compared to the blowing of a porpoise. 'Some folks ashore,' he continued, 'say a sailor has a wife in every port, and that out o' sight's out o' mind; but I can tell 'em a man has feelin's, if he *does* go to sea for a living; and that 'ere matter of Peg Cleaver has been writ down in the log of my memory from that day to this.'

'What prevented your marrying her?'

'Well, Sir, while you are up there a-smoking I will give you the yarn. It ain't very long, and I think I can reel it off by the time you'll get through with your cigar.' Putting an enormous quid of tobacco into his mouth, and seating himself on the gun beneath me, he related the story of what I will venture to say was the only incident of romance and sentiment in the whole course of his long and rugged life.

'Well, Sir, this 'ere turn-up came off about the·time they was fitting out vessels for the Tripolitan war. It was at Philadelphia, where we was both born and lived opposite to each other, that it took place. I was about eighteen; she mayhap was a year or two younger nor me, and a monstrous handsome girl she was. But you must first understand that our grandfathers and fathers was butchers. I was 'most out of my 'prenticeship to the same trade, and she was a pretty good hand a'ready at making sassages. All this made a sort o' good feeling 'twixt the two fam'lies, and Peg and I used to be always a-playing together when we was children; but arter a while, as we grew up, somehow we began to fight shyer and shyer of one another, until at last we knocked off playing altogether; and one day Peg says to me, as I passed and said, 'How d' ye do, Peg?' says she, 'How d' ye do, Mr. Boreas?' That took me all aback. Arter that I always when we met had a kind o' queer feeling, and was 'most afraid to speak to her. She generally spoke first, and when she said 'How d' ye do, Mr. Boreas?' I would say, 'How d 'ye do, Marm?'

'Well, as I was a-tellin' you, I was about eighteen, and she sixteen or seventeen, when one day the old woman came to me, and says she to me, says she, 'Ben,' says she, 'Why do 'nt you go over and see Peg Cleaver?'

''Lor! mother!' says I, 'what's the use?' And I felt my face kind o' sneaking and turning all over red.

''Ben,' says the old woman, 'Mrs. Cleaver and me have made a bargain 'bout marrying you two; the sooner the better, 'specially as that young carpenter, Jack Plane, is fooling around the girl. To tell you the truth, her father and your'n has agreed with us that there shall be a wedding to-morrow; for there 's no telling which is the worst to let run on long, a courtin'-match or a butcher's-bill; and as it 's you and PEG is the ones that 's to be married, and I know you like her and she likes you, you must go right away and see her — right away, now! You 've got on your new clothes, (it was a Sunday,) so you must go.'

'I knew it was no use backing and filling about the matter when the old lady put her foot down, so I made sail for old CLEAVER's. But there was PEG standing at the door, and that made me feel bashful. If she 'd been in the house it would have been something of a stave-off; but to walk upright to her a-standing, I swore, come what would, I would n't do it. She stood in her door and I in our'n, looking up the street and looking down; up at the eaves-trough and down at the pigs in the gutter. Sometimes our eyes met; quick as wink down her's would go, and her face turn scarlet-red. I see at onst they 'd been a-telling her, too. At last she went in. 'Now 's my chance!' said I, and away I went across the street, my ears buzzing, my face burning and my eye-sight clean gone. How I made the door is more nor I can tell. When I first came to my senses, old Marm CLEAVER was a-joking me about falling foul of PEG too soon.

''BEN,' says she, 'if you commence that way in the beginning,' says she, 'there 's no telling how you 'd treat the girl arter a while: but never mind; I know your disposition, my son; you was only a little bashful. You 'll get over *that* 'fore you 're married long.'

'Well, there set PEG, looking as red as a boiled lobster, or a British soger's jacket, and I, I suppose, like a French soger's trowsers, while the old woman was a-telling how happy we 'd be together; how the old folks would set us up in business, hauling off themselves; and how we must be careful and saving for our children as they had been for their'n.' Jist then my old woman came in, and at it *she* goes. Mean time, PEG and I was afraid to let our eyes meet, but we kept 'em a-going like main bunt-ling-blocks; when one pair was up, the other was down. Howsomdever, arter a while my old woman says, 'BEN,' says she, 'kiss your intended, and let 's be off.'

We both stood up; but that 's all; neither of us stirred tack nor sheet; just as if we was hard and fast a-ground, and had n't any purchases to heave off with.

'Fie! for shame!' said both our mothers.

'Then PEG, who was braver about them matters nor I, pitched into me, kissed me very sweet on my lips, and ran out o' the room. We then went home, and such a making of cakes, and custards, and high-seasoned sassages, and cutting off ch'ice j'ints of meats, you never did see. The old woman, soon arter we got back, took me one side and said I 'd have to write some poetry to PEG in course: 'Your father did it before we was married, and I never know'd a decent woman as did n't get a set of varses before her wedding; you may say it's a part of the sarimony.'

'I could n't help bu'sting out a-laughing: 'How can I send PEG any poetry, mother, when I haint got any, and what 's more do n't know where to get any? It's sartain I can't manufacture it myself.'

'You 're a fool!' says the old woman: 'aint DUMPLIN's daughter here? — the one as has been to boarding-school? — and aint she a prime hand at making poetry? Look 'ere, BEN, I know'd how it would turn out, so I got her to write this 'ere for you.' At that she hauled out of her buzzum a sort of young letter. On the inside of it was a couple of hearts, with an arrow through 'em, and a d — l of a fire round 'em a picture of them 'ere hearts is pricked onto my arm, and the varses is fresh in my mind now.'

'Let's have them,' said SQUILGEE. 'Well, Sir, they was quite pretty, and went someway like this:

> 'PEG, my love,
> My turtle-dove !
> To-morrow night,
> If the moon shines bright,
> You and I, though *two* we be,
> Will be made *one* by matrimony !'

'I signed my name, 'Your loving BEN BOREAS,' and sent it over by one of the girls who was a-helping to get ready for the wedding, and she told me, when she came back, that PEG read it and kissed it, and put it in her buzzum.

'Well, I stood it pretty well, Sir, till the time for the wedding came on; but when they told me to go up and dress, I was as scared as a dolphin with the grains in him. I loved PEG worse nor a albatross loves blubber, or yet fat pork ; but when our folks got over there, and I see 'em all seated round the wall, my hair fairly stood on end like the bowsprit-bits. Howsomdever, seeing that carpenter chap, that JACK PLANE I was telling you about, in amongst 'em, in I went, out of spite. The girls was all giggling together, so I walked into the back entry, out of sight. Jist then there was a noise at the front door: it was the parson coming in. After a little talking with the old folks, 'Is all ready?' says he. 'All ready.' 'Bring in the bride!' I looked through the passage ; the back door was open, swinging back'ards and for'ards. I do n't know what it was, praps 't was a *ge-nii*, but *so'think* come over me ; and just as the bed-room door was opened to let PEG in, I shot out the back gate !

'Well, to make matters short, as I see your cigar is a-most out, Sir, I listed on board the frigate Philadelphia, and went to Tripoli, where we was captured, on account of running on some rocks unbeknownst to us, as we was a-going to 'tack the town. They took us ashore, those bloody-minded villains, the Turks, and fastened us up at night, and made us work ; but you know all about that, and how Commodore PREBLE and DECATUR, and some of the gentlemen, fixed 'em off. Well, we got home at last, and as soon as we was paid off, I made sail for Philadelphia ; and when I got there I started with a straight wake for the old man's house. When it hove in sight, the pumps began bringing up water into my eyes faster than the eye-lids could clear themselves. I could not well see, but lost my course, and fetched up on the other side of the street ag'in a woman and two small children.

'My G – D ! BEN BOREAS ! is that *you !*' says she.

'Yes, by G – D ! it is !' says I.

'At this point BOREAS was perfectly overcome with his remniscences. It appeared that the parents of the girl, indignant at his desertion, and bearing in mind the expenses of the wedding-preparation ; BEN's parents unable at the same time to justify him ; PEG being an obedient child ; JACK PLANE likewise being present, and taken into the conference with PEG, CLEAVER and his moiety ; it was agreed upon, on their return into the room, (the BOREASES having retired,) *first*, that BEN was 'a poor stick ;' *secondly*, that it would be a pity to waste so much good 'prog ;' *thirdly*, that as JACK said he had always loved PEG, and PEG said she thought she could love him, now that BEN had sloped ; that therefore they should be married. The proposition was received with universal applause, the ladies appearing to be the most enthusiastic. Accordingly they were married ; and hence the little ones who greeted BEN's sight on his return from Tripoli.'

WILL you take another plate, reader? Do n't be afraid of its 'sitting heavy' upon you; it is light, and easily digested. *Try* another plate:

' ONE day — you know time will pass, so that it is scarcely necessary for me to say that this occurrence took place many years ago, like the rest of this veritable record, the events of which occurred, and were known to SQUILGEE, his messmates and shipmates — one day, as I've said, DUMP being or having been disturbed by a holystoning in the morning, made use of the following expressions to BOGEE:

' Sir, it is perfectly horrible how much one has to suffer, in order to enjoy the pleasures of a sea-life!'

' How so, Mr. DUMP?' inquired BOGEE.

' Why, Sir,' replied the ' respondent,' to use a chancery phrase, 'all this hauling of big stones, this clattering of squilgees, this slapping about of swabs, is perfectly horrible; in fact, Sir, it is a great taxation, and is enforced at an enormous cost to those taxed.'

' Mr. DUMP, do you know any thing about taxation?' said BOGEE, squaring himself up, and looking like one who was about to impart information; although any one who knew him well could have detected a certain twitching of the lips, which indicated something that was not particularly serious in regard to any kind of subject. ' Did you ever hear, Sir, of taxation in its worst form?'

' No, Sir.'

' Then I 'll tell you where you'll find it; it 's in Morocco. The emperor, you must know, Mr. DUMP, cannot call on his subjects for their taxes directly; but he sends an order to the bashaw of a district. The bashaw sends to the sheik, or some other such outlandish sort of character. The sheik calls for the richest men in his villages, and states, that like Mr. YORK, they are wanted. The Jews are generally those most likely to be selected. Well, they are brought into the presence of the man of authority, and ranged according to rank; that is, according to the amount of the ' available' they may be supposed to possess. Those of the highest rank are placed in boxes suited to their dimensions, their heads being left out, in order that they may see what is going on. A grim old Moor, the executioner of the tribe, perhaps, comes forward with a saw in his hand, and at a given signal commences sawing away at the box. ' God is great!' says the sheik, who I might as well say is a perfectly disinterested spectator of the scene, 'GOD is great, and MAHOMET is his prophet!' The great wearer of the parasol, (for you should be informed that the emperor of those regions is the only person who is entitled to wear an umbrella,) is in want of 'the ready,' and it becomes every true son of his father to bring forth that portion which, blessed be ALLAH! it is allowed him to contribute toward the support of our holy religion.'

' ' Most Magnificent!' says the Hebrew capitalist, ' your miserable slave has not wherewithal to feed himself, his wife or his children, his ox or his ass!'

' ' Chee-chaw! chee-chaw!' goes the saw; and the old Moor who is using it does not look the prisoner in the face, neither does he look at the cadi; for he knows there 's to be no sign of mercy from him until the regular or, rather the irregular contribution is made. ' Chee-chaw! chee-chaw!' goes the saw. The old Moor begins to perspire; but he is a robust and athletic man, and will not stop until the cadi tells him so to do. The cadi *looks* on and says not a word, and the old Moor *saws* on, and says just as little; but the man in the box protests that his springs have dried up, his dates have failed, his wives are dead, his slaves are dying; that a piastre is a curiosity to him, and ' Job's turkey' a Crœsus in comparison ; in short, that he cannot produce ' the needful.'

' ' Chee-chaw ! chee-chaw !' is the voice of the saw ; the old Moor goes on, and the saw is entering the wood ; ay, it enters into the very folds of his clothes.

' ' Most Magnificent !' says he, in an agony of fear, ' I will give thee a thousand !' The cadi shakes his head, and the saw enters farther — even into the texture of his under garments.

' ' Five thousand !' exclaims the man in the box — a d — d *bad* box too, you will say.

' ' Fifty thousand !' replies the cadi, unmoved in thought, unmoved in feature.

' ' Chee-chaw ! chee-chaw !' goes on the saw, and the old Moor holds on to his business, for he knows that it is near its end.

' ' Most Magnificent !' screams the boxed, ' fifty thousand ! fifty thousand !' for the saw, you must understand, is eating into his flesh. Well, he always has a friend at hand with the necessary number of purses, which being presented, they rip him, or I should say the box, open, and let him out. A man possessed of more moderate means is ' *squeezed.*' *His* ' taxation' is a rough, angular stone, placed in his closed hand, over which a piece of green hide is tightly sewed. The hand thus enclosed is then exposed to the influence of a Morocco sun. The contracting of the hide-envelope, as you can easily conceive, would bring any reasonable man to terms.'

' I should certainly think so !' remarked Dump.

' But,' continued Bogee, ' the compulsory process adopted with the minor liabilities is the most singular of all. You 've never seen the oriental style of dress, Mr. Dump, have you ? Instead of our fashion of unmentionables, they cover their extremities with a sort of loose bag, with holes in the lower part just large enough to stick their legs through. Well, when they do n't ' come up to taw,' and fork over their one, two, or three hundred, as it may be, several large Thomas-cats are placed in these peculiar kind of breeches ; the individual then has his hands tied in front, and is led through the streets by a grave official with a very long beard, and followed by crowds of the curious, particularly the urchins of the village, all of whom are watching to ascertain what degree of scratching and biting a man can endure ; for you must know that those miniature tigers, when jumbled together in such an unceremonious fashion, are not the most amiable animals in the world. In fine, the poor devil is at length absolutely clawed into fulfilling his national duties by the cats in his capacious trowse'loons.'

' What an embarrassing position to be placed in !' said Dump.

' There are cases where a resort to the *duello* may be absolutely necessary ; but as a general thing, I think the reply of an old sea-dog, a boatswain in the service, to a gunner of the ship he belonged to, on the receipt of a challenge, admirably and sarcastically paints the ridiculous nature of trivial challenges. The gunner — and it must be borne in mind that both the parties belonged to a peculiar class of officers, that is, ' Forward Officers,' from whom a fist-fight might naturally be expected, but never a resort to deadly weapons — the gunner wrote to the boatswain thus :

"Sir : I demand satisfaction of you, on account of what you have done. Please to name time, place and weapons. Yours, G – D d — n you ! till death !'| '— —.'

' To which he of the spun-yarn and junk replied :

"Sir : Not being much acquainted with ' high dick,' I write these few lines to tell you that I 'll meet you ; time, one hundred years from this present ; place, top of Mount Ætna ; weapons, harpoons. Yours, till after we meet, is all that I have to say. No more from your humble servant,   '— —.''

LAW AND LAWYERS: A LEGAL SALMAGUNDI. — We have had our say, as our readers are aware, touching law and lawyers; let us hope too that the members of our State Convention have very *nearly* had their several 'says' on the same general theme. But say what we all may, it cannot be denied that lawyers 'make a great deal of talk' in the community. There is scarcely any class of society concerning whom so much is said, and of whom so many anecdotes are told. In looking over a neglected port-folio this morning, we have found so many sketches and stories connected with the profession, that we incline to throw together a *Legal Salmagundi*, from the original matériel, crude and undigested though it be, which lies before us. We begin with a western correspondent, who writes us that he 'wishes to convey to the readers of the KNICKERBOCKER some of the anecdotes which he has heard in the courts of certain western states,' or from his brother members of the bar. 'It is perhaps generally known,' he continues, 'that in many of the western states the supreme court judges hold the circuit court for the several counties in their district; and the lawyers in travelling round from court to court with the judges, perform what a Methodist minister denominates 'riding the circuit.' Always after the adjournment of court, the attorneys get together in some sitting-room of a tavern, which is very commonly nothing but a pile of log-cabins, and in the company of the supreme court judge and the 'side-judge,' take the opportunity of having a bit of fun in relating original anecdotes, stories, etc., which they have heard on their circuit. I will mention one or two which I heard in some of these log-cabin hotels in the west, during a session or after an adjournment of court. Perhaps no where is there greater sport than among the attorneys at such 'times and places.' When court is over, his honor the judge mounts his horse, or if the roads are good, gets into his 'sulky' or 'buggy,' and lays his course for the court in the next county, and the lawyers in a body all follow him. What they lack in accommodation they make up by having good company, in telling entertaining stories, and 'cracking rough jokes.' Frequently they are obliged to travel through a dense forest for miles, without seeing a house; over causeways, round 'stumps,' over logs and dense brush-heaps. In other counties they have pleasant rides over the prairies, the oak openings, and the wide-extended plains, covered in summer with a great variety of wild flowers. Often they are compelled to ford the streams for want of bridges, not unfrequently swimming their horses across some deep running-brook. If they are so unfortunate as not to reach the county-seat when they expected to, and are compelled to come to a halt in the woods, before reaching a tavern, they all turn into the first good-looking comfortable log-cabin they come to, and there enjoy the hospitalities of the 'Hoosier,' 'Wolverine,' or 'Sucker,' as the case may be. These log-cabins sometimes appear to be a real paradise, and are often the home of the contented and happy. Here, after partaking of a meal of the farmer's very best, viz., venison, prairie-hen, and pork-and-beans, they all retire to rest, having for their beds buffalo robes thrown upon the floor, with carpet-bags for pillows — all in the same room, and where all the family sleep. The next morning they all start for court, in good spirits; the farmer giving them their bills in compensation for a dozen little law-questions with which he had troubled one of the lawyers, for most likely he is or has been a justice of the peace.' . . . 'IN the Wolverine state, on one occasion, Judge M——, a very facetious man, was alone upon the bench, and one of the attorneys had just finished the argument of some cause, and the judge was proceeding in his opinion upon the case, when a large bull-dog came up on the side of the judge, and looked down upon the lawyers with a very judge-like aspect. His honor was so intent upon the question before him that he did not notice the dog, and in a few minutes gave the decision of the question, which chanced to be against the attorney who had last spoken in the case. The latter asked the judge ' if that was the opinion of the court ?' ' Yes,' replied the judge. ' Well then,' replied the discomfitted lawyer, ' I would like the opinion of the *other* member of the court !' When the judge turned around and saw the solemn-faced dog apparently ruminating or deliberating upon the case he had just decided, he burst into a laugh which ran like electricity through the court-room.' . . . ' IN one of the western counties in Michigan a case came up before the court, in which a general demurrer had been interposed by the counsel for the defendant, which had been decided by the court in favor of the defendant, thus ending that case. The defendant was a deaf man, and asked his lawyer how it was that he had beaten the opposite party ; to which he replied, that it had been accomplished by putting in a demurrer. When the defendant was returning from court, overjoyed at his success, some friend of his asked him how the suit had gone ? ' Oh,' said he, ' my lawyer beat 'em.' ' How did he do it ?' asked his friend. ' Why,' said the defendant, ' he pleaded the *murrain-act !*' . . . ' I HEARD an amusing story to-day of a pettifogger who had but lately been admitted to the bar. He had got a smattering of Latin, but had never taken much pains to remember what he had learned. He was employed in a famous ' horse case,' an action brought by a man against another for cheating him in a ' horse-trade.' Our pettifogger was engaged for the defendant, and in his remarks to the jury had occasion to quote ' CHITTY on Contracts,' where he read the following, among other things : ' Gentlemen,' said he, ' CHITTY lays it down that where a man buys a horse with a ' well-known and visible defect,' etc., the rule of ' *caveat emptor*' applies ; which being interpreted, gentlemen of the jury, means ' *contract express*,' etc. Hence, gentlemen, I say that the horse which my client sold had such *visible* defects that a blind man could *see* them.' It is needless to add that the court was convulsed with laughter at this new reading and interpretation of a familiar Latin phrase, and its accompanying Irish bull.' . . . ' L. E. S.,' writing to us lately from Williamstown, Massachusetts, gives us the following, which embodies, we cannot help thinking, a lesson worthy of heedful note : ' You have sometimes, Mr. EDITOR, shown up the injustice perpetrated under forms of law. I take the liberty of subjoining a story, which is a true record of *facts*, going to prove that justice in this glorious clime is sometimes administered in a manner ' 't were pain to hint on.' During a week's ramble in one of the eastern counties of the Empire State, I heard that a justice's court was ' coming off' at a rising village, usually called by the natives '*Gomorrah*.' My friend, with whom I sojourned, was ' summoned' to sit on the jury, and received his statutable shilling ; whereupon, led by my instinctive love of a scrape, I accompanied him to the scene of action. He was excused as a supernumerary. The court was held in a dirty grocery ; the justice, in a fustian jacket and blue checked cravat, sat behind an unpainted table, with a pocket Bible and two law-books before him. The jury sat on a bench without any back, and during the trial freely conversed with the parties and the spectators. A boy, apparently eight or ten years old, was arraigned on a charge of larceny, and the witnesses were sworn ' in manner following, that is to say :' ' You do solemnly swear in the presence of Almighty GOD, that in this traverse between the People of the State of New-York and ABRAHAM DE GROOT, defendant, so help you GOD !' The testimony showed that the said ABRAHAM ' did feloniously steal, take, carry away and convert to his own use the following property, of the goods and chattels of one P. W——, grocer; *videlicet,* one clam and three crackers!' The jury found the little wretch 'guilty in manner and form as in the complaint is alleged,' and he was fined *four dollars and the costs of prosecution!* 'Mein GOTT!' said an old KNICKER-BOCKER Dutchman who was present, 'is dat vat dey calls *justice!*' · · · ANOTHER correspondent sends us this anecdote of a legal wag whom we know well, and who, while he retains the voice and manner which are natural to him, (and he is not the man to retain 'any thing else,') will keep vividly alive the recollection of 'poor POWER' in the minds of all who have the pleasure of his acquaintance: 'An irreverent wag of a lawyer in New-England, who was no respecter of 'the cloth,' having heard that he was to encounter in a witness a sanctimonious personage of the Baptist order, resolved to show him that he knew and appreciated him. As he came upon the stand with a most ' down-trodden' expression of humility upon his face, the lawyer inquired, 'What may be your profession, Sir?' 'Oh! Sir,' sighed the reverend witness, 'I am only a feeble candle in the LORD's sanctuary.' 'Ah!' answered the legal wag, 'a *dipped* candle, I suppose! Well, Sir, can you throw any light on the case before the court? You need not 'flare up' in your examination; for the whole truth must come out.' The laughter which ensued was not checked until the crier had three times called out ' Sila-a-ns!' at the top of his voice. · · · THUS much for the present, touching law and lawyers. There will be an attempt made, however, four weeks from this time, ' at early candle-lighting,' to prove in these pages, by elaborate argument, that a ' Lawyer is not necessarily a Rascal.' ' Heaven defend the right!'

FAMILIAR EPISTLES FROM ABROAD. — A friend of our boyhood, being on his travels abroad, has despatched hitherward three or four hurried epistles, pleasantly descriptive of his voyage over, in the steamer from Boston, and his ' first impressions' of the Cumberland Lakes; fine engravings of which, we may remark in passing, surmount the top of each letter-sheet; thus affording to the cis-Atlantic correspondent a very good idea of Derwentwater and Keswick, from Skiddaw, Windermere, from near Ambleside, Ulleswater, Loweswater, Buttermere, etc. Why would it not be a capital idea for some of our best stationers to prepare similarly engraved letter-paper, representing the finest portions of the scenery in the neighborhood of New-York, views of the city, and on the North and East rivers? Would there not be a continual demand for such paper from the thousands who write to the ' old country' by every sea-steamer and sailing-packet? We ' throw out the hint' merely. But we are keeping our correspondent waiting: consider him therefore to be writing from Keswick, Cumberland, SOUTHEY's old residence, under date of July sixth, as follows: 'On the sixteenth ultimo, at twelve o'clock at noon, we were rolling over the streets of Boston on our way to the steamer, to which we crossed by a ferry-boat which landed us at East Boston, where the Hibernia lay, lashed to the dock; a huge black hull with a scarlet pipe and volumes of thick smoke tumbling heavily from its flue. Passengers and their friends occupied the deck; carts and carriages were unloading on the dock; the escape-pipe emitting steam enough to make a steady noise. It is two o'clock; a wagon loaded high with white bags is driven hurriedly to the wharf; another follows. HER MAJESTY's agent, the master of the mails, (a lieutenant of the navy) orders the tars ashore to lug in the newspapers and letters; sixty or seventy bushels of newspapers and about forty bushels of letters. They are now stowed away. The captain is on the paddle-box with his speaking strumpet. He cries, ' At the larboard hawser! capstan heave — heave away !' A half dozen sailors spring as if they were about to save their lives, and the capstan is turned. The ship is drawn to the larboard ten feet, and lies straight in her slip. The captain beckons to the engineer; the huge wheels revolve ; we sweep out to the middle of the channel ; the captain shouts to the helmsman two or three times ; the bow of the stately vessel swings out toward the sea. The American flag is run up to the fore-top-mast ; three thundering cheers go up from those on shore ! We swing round a little more, and head to the channel ; the captain cries, ' She 's all ready.' He swings his hat to those on shore ; three more thundering cheers from those on ship and those on shore ; a gun to the larboard and one to the starboard ; a wave of the captain's hand to the engineer, and the huge wheels move again, bearing us out to sea, while we wave our 'kerchiefs to our friends on shore. We are out in the wide bay ; a gentle swell rocks us gently ; one after another grows pale, and makes a false excuse to get to the cabin; the ' old 'uns' laugh in their sleeves. Soon we have passed the last light-house ; the wheels have stopped ; the captain is on the paddle-box, with his trumpet again. I ask, ' What is going on ?' ' Parting with the pilot, Sir,' is the reply. I look behind and see a small boat with four oars and six persons dropping astern, toward a rakish little schooner-rigged craft that lies in our wake. The captain beckons to the engineer again, the roar of steam is hushed ; the wheels splash ; and we are fairly off to other lands !' I wish I could describe to you the peculiar excitement of the scene !

' The voyage was propitious. No storm, no adventure ; every thing seemed like a comfortable hotel. Even while looking out on the sea I was disposed to deny our position, and insist that it was but a bay or a lake we were crossing, and that we should land in an hour or two. All were pleased with the ship. For one or two days we had a wind ' right aft' that made the vessel roll like a log, and sickened every one who ever was sick. I kept up however, and was not sick at all. My wife suffered amazingly. On the morning of the twenty-seventh of June, ten and and three-quarter days out, ' Land !' was cried by a tar at the fore-mast. But the cry was not what it has been so often described to be. Our passengers and crew were not worn out by a long voyage ; we had just began to enjoy the ship. These vessels are magnificent. The table is always furnished with the greatest profusion of luxuries; wines and liquors are used to a great extent, and are of prime brands ; cards are played, and chess and backgammon. All who are well enjoy themselves wonderfully. At noon of the twenty-eighth ultimo, we were in the channel of Liverpool harbor. All were on deck, gazing at the cottages and fields. Soon we rounded the little fort, much smaller than Castle-Garden, and were in the river Mersey ; the great commercial city on either side of us. Immense stone docks, forests of masts, and clouds of black smoke on one side, and neat little cottages, with terraced gardens, and closely-clipped lawns, and little steam-boats and small yachts and bathing-tents on the other.' · · · OUR friend gives us a vivid picture of Liverpool, its hotels, public edifices, general appearance, etc.; a sketch of his visit to Chester ; the old Roman walls ; and the ancient cathedral ; Eaton Hall, the seat of the rich Marquis of Westminster, etc. Speaking of the scenery of the Cumberland lakes, he remarks : ' I shall not be so foolish as to attempt to give a description of this delightful scenery. You must *be here*, among the naked peaks and stern defiles and placid waters ; you must breathe the very air, and feel your soul's communion with the superior influences that float in visions and delicious reveries about these altars, fully to understand their grandeur and beauty. I call them altars, for no man of feeling, no one who ever had an impulse of love or a consciousness of the existence of a supreme CREATOR, can stand here without feeling a sentiment of devotion. I believe that no person who discards religious influences can fully comprehend the eloquence of these scenes; and certain I am, that no man who *does* cherish religious emotions can look upon them without adoration of their AUTHOR.' Our correspondent writes us last from 'Auld Reekie,' whither himself and party had arrived, after having made the circuit of the lakes, visited the former residences of COLERIDGE and WORDSWORTH, and the present residence of the latter; and examined in detail the famous old castles of Scotland. Of his farther journeyings our readers may perhaps hear more hereafter.

A REMINISCENCE OF THE PAST: CONVERSATION WITH AN OLD NEGRO. — We have been somewhat forcibly struck with the subjoined '*Conversation with an old Negro,*' for which, as we perceive by the manuscript, we are indebted to an old metropolitan correspondent of this Magazine. We could not help thinking, while reading over the little sketch, how much that is worth preservation might be treasured up by an observant citizen, while remembering every day, with SCOTT, that 'it is difficult to converse for ten minutes with *any* man, not irredeemably stupid, without receiving *some* information which it is worth one's while to remember.' Especially is this the case with 'garrulous Eld.' We have held long conversations with superannuated 'colored brethren' on Long Island, in the vicinity of old revolutionary battle-grounds, that would have possessed interest for the very dullest member of the New-York Historical Society, and which, although coming from a 'darky,' might have thrown light upon important accessories of detail that now rest in obscurity. But listen to our correspondent's hero: ' I do n't know jest where it was I come from; but they stole me when I was very young — when I was a leetle boy; but it was somewhere in this country. They put me on board a ship, and I hollered, and wanted to go back; so they throw'd me overboard; and what become of me I do n't know, but I s'pose they took me aboard again. (There was a yaller girl, bigger than me she was, aboard.) I found it was the *Argus,* lying in New-York harbor, and the British had possession of the city. The Argus ship belonged to old ROBERT NICHOLSON, of Shields, Newcastle. While we lay thar they had a great jollification in New-York and on board the ships. They played the music and danced all night. I do n't know what it was for; but they played the music, and beat the tamborine, and kept singing all the time:

> 'LADY LEE, de Toby LEE,
>   Lady LEE, de Gineral How,
>   Gineral How, de Gineral LEE,
>   Mee-tee, diddle-de, big bow-wow!'
>   [*Sings to the tune of 'Yankee-Doodle.'*

' When I got in Russia, the first tune I heard was the same tune; played by a band of music on board of a great big war-ship. It went jist the same. We went in the Argus to Newcastle, and from there they sent me to King GEORGE the Third, and he sent me over to the Empress CATHARINE, at Archangel. We had a gun-maker on board, named CARLE GASCOIGNE. King GEORGE sent him over to make guns. I was there a great while, and I went every where — I can't tell where; I do n't remember all; but I got back to New-York from France in 1824, and went to look for home, and the old land where I was born, but I could n't find out any thing about it ; I do n't know jist where it was, but I know it was an island, and we had fresh water on one side of the island. I went to Staten-Island and walked twenty miles all round, but could not find the fresh water. They said there was books which would tell ; but I had no money to pay for 'em. They kept the books seven miles up from the dock. BEN SEAMAN, I think it was, lived up there, and there was two churches up there ; but I could n't never find nothing about it. But I s'pose I must try to keep clear from that OLD MAN who makes all the mischief.' 'Who is he ?' said I. 'No matter ; he does every thing ; he made the old war with this country. He is as thin as a wafer ; so thin you can't hardly see him ; but he is too strong for every body. He wants to know whar he 'll go when he dies. But I do n't believe he 'll ever die. But whar can he go ? His soul can't go any whar's but right into h – ll. No, I could n't find any thing about it, and I never shall. But it 's no matter, I s'pose.' There are some octogenarian KNICKERBOCKER citizens among us who will think of other days while perusing this hasty record of a 'Conversation with an old Negro.'

GOSSIP WITH READERS AND CORRESPONDENTS. — 'As I write, I can appreciate the *autumn feeling*; something holy and peculiar, prevailing within me. I can see by the increasing azure of the sky, by the enlarged clearness of the distant landscapes, when the eye greets them from the city, and by the transparent briskness of the air at evening, that the summer has gone and the autumn-time begun. The woodlands stand in calm solemnity, robed in that rainbow coloring, the herald of their fallen honors and the November storm. At such a season the heart goes back as on wings of the dove to departed friends and vanished pleasures, and the sad hours of memory come up in long review.' Thus wrote the departed OLLAPOD, many Octobers ago ; but how perfectly is the season and its associations renewed this beautiful morning ! The sad hours of memory have indeed passed in long review before us while we have sat and meditated; and we have been made sensible by the season's changes, as thousands of our readers will be, of the loved and the gifted who have gone before us into the vale of death ; and therewithal have come thoughts of that last bitter hour which cometh to all, even as the later hoar-frost to the clinging leaf:

> 'NATURE, in simple beauty drest,
> Still dances round the restless year,
> And gazing on her yellow vest,
> I sometimes think my change is near :

> 'Not that my hair with age is gray,
> Not that my heart hath yet grown cold,
> But that remembered friendships say,
> 'Death loves not best the infirm and old !'

> 'As many a bosom knows and feels,
> Left, in the flower of life, alone,
> And many an epitaph reveals
> On the cold monumental stone.'

Well, spring will come again ; daisies and violets will appear upon the renovated earth ; songs will resound in the green woods and sunny fields once more ; and bountiful and loving Nature shall emblem again the glorious resurrection of the loved departed, who have laid them down in the dust and made their beds in ashes. . . . THE reader will agree with us that the subjoined good-natured effusion upon a recent local event is quite in the vein of the most heroic of LOCKHART's Spanish ballads. Quære, by the way: is this ' General SUTHERLAND' the same person whose *will* was so rampant for battle, in the Canadian ' Patriot' war, but whose *bowels* placed him on the peace establishment of a sudden, when he was pretending to cross the river to relieve the brave and unfortunate VON SHULTZ, whom he had inveigled into danger, and basely deserted ? ' We only ask for information :'

THE CONFLICT. A CALIFORNIAN BALLAD.

BY J. HONEYWELL.

I.

THRONGED is the high tribunal,
  The crowd sways to and fro,
And the Judge looks down in grandeur
  On the curious mass below.
Robed in imagined ermine,
  Too pure for our thick sight,
He sits like Rome's Dictator,
  Sole arbiter of right ;
Above stands blindfold Justice,
  Rapt in an endless dream,
Grasping the golden emblem,
  That swings with even beam.

II.

Forth comes the northern warrior,
  The mighty SUTHERLAND,
Holding the precious parchment
  Like a war-club in his hand ;
The writ of Habeus Corpus,
  With words of power and might,
Have brought to the Halls of Justice
  The wronged man for his right.
Protective scroll ! that raises
  The soul from grief to joy,
As now it brings from durance
  The Californian boy.

III.

Gird up your loins, brave soldier !
  To meet the coming fray,
For you must do your devoir
  Right gallantly this day ;
This day are you entrusted
  With business of great weight,
There is on you depending
  An anxious army's fate.
You have sworn the direst vengeance
  Against yon craven COLONEL,
And he who meets your wrath unscathed,
  Must stand on height supernal.

IV.

The crowd looked on with wonder,
  In wonder gaped and gazed,
Wondering if this great pleader
  Were most inspired or crazed ;
Now quoting calf-bound volumes,
  Now subtly arguing thence,
Men doubt which is profoundest,
  His lore or eloquence.
So deep in seas of learning
  At times he seemed to dive,
We marvelled if the actor
  Would o'er come up alive ;
Anon with flight of eagle,
  So high his rapture bore him,
The crowd in admiration
  Were ready to adore him.

V.

With awful voice, His Worship
  Checked him in mid career,
And clipped his fancy's pinions
  With lip and brow severe.
But in that soul was kindled
  A fire he could not quench,
And the intrepid soldier turned,
  In act to beard, nay almost spurned,
  The Judge upon the bench !

VI.

'Hear ye ! Hear ye !' the warning
  Goes forth for a recess,
And what may hap upon the morrow,
  The shrewdest can but guess.

VII.

Calm and sedate, the COLONEL
  Watched his antagonist,
Heard his forensic brilliancy,
  And marked his poised fist ;
Yet his soul within him trembled,
  Quivered his lip as well ;
But it was not at great swelling words
  That his stern visage fell ;
Nor yet at words of learning
  That graced the speaker's lips,
Nor feared he that the verdict
  Would his high hopes eclipse.

VIII.

But time with him was precious —
  The bugle called to go,
And his impatient soldiers
  Were fierce to meet the foe !
So like the fat knight famous,
  Whose face ne'er harbored pallor,
He bethought him that discretion
  Was the better part of valor.
Though duty would have kept him
  To strike th' opponent dumb,
Yet his martial soul could not withstand
  The rousing music of the band ;
And his nerves thrilled, as from the strand
Rolled the wild clangor o'er the land,
  Of trumpet, fife and drum !

IX.

And when the pregnant morning
  Beheld the assembled court,
Were gathered a great multitude
  To see the giant sport ;
But lo ! our sanguine hero
  Stood with bewildered look,
For where a COLONEL should appear
  There only stood a COOK !

As when the crafty Indian,
  Whose prey eludes his grasp,
Stands with dilating nostril,
  His knife within his clasp;
With bloodless lip compressed,
  And eye-balls in a blaze,
So stood that thwarted champion,
  In fury and amaze.

x.

He had reared his legal bulwarks,
  And planted his stockade,
And was ready on the bastion
  For a heavy cannonade;
But when the guns were waiting
  For the match to be applied,

Above the enemy's camp-fires
  Non est was seen inscribed!

xi.

Hail to the gallant soldier!
  Hail to the pleader strong!
And hail to the chief, who yielded,
  Nor did his country wrong.
To SUTHERLAND be glory!
  Let echo's answer swell
With 'Honor to the name of him
  Who fought so long and well!
Who fought so well and bravely,
  With might and eke with main,
But as in former conflicts,
  Who fought alas! in vain.'

A FRIEND of ours records in a recent hasty notelet an amusing anecdote of a trick
which was lately played by a mad wag at a horse-race, not a thousand miles from
Detroit, upon a young friend who had chanced to over-tipple; insomuch indeed that
was quite incapable of locomotion. Our wag carefully removed him to a place
where he could sleep off the fumes of his intoxication, and gently abstracted his
wallet, partly to save him the risk of losing it and partly to complete the wicked
me which he had in view. After due time he returned home. When his friend
woke he found himself minus one hundred dollars, and in spite of every exertion,
could obtain no clue to the perpetrator of the robbery. The Rev. J. N. MAFFITT was
then preaching in Detroit, and creating much religious excitement in all classes of
community. Taking advantage of this circumstance, the wag wrote to his friend
in a disguised hand the following letter:

MY DEAR SIR: I can make you no explanation of the wickedness I was guilty of in robbing you
the money which I herewith enclose to you, other than that I have sincerely repented of my
x, and hope for your forgiveness. I repeat, I sincerely repent the enormity of my transgression,
bless the PROVIDENCE which directed hither that polished, pious and pathetic preacher, Rev.
J. MAFFITT, under whose powerful persuasion my eyes have been opened. Hoping that you your-
' may close in with the offers of mercy before it is everlastingly too late, I remain yours, S. F.'

The cream of the joke is, that overjoyed at recovering his money, the victim
immediately enclosed Rev. J. N. MAFFITT fifteen dollars, with his fervent thanks for
the great good which he had done, and was all the while a-doing!' And this
very case is now going the rounds of the country press, headed '*Power of Con-
science!*' . . . A MOST capable poetical correspondent of this Magazine has copy-
ited a work which we have little doubt will forcibly arrest the attention of the
literary public. It is none other than OSSIAN, divided into the measured but irregu-
lar blank-verse in which it is written, but until now not printed, and illustrated by
various notes, explaining such passages or allusions as are not likely to be quite clear
to the unassisted reader. The plan is an admirable one, and the execution, so far
as we have examined the work, is exceedingly felicitous. It is a task of no small
labor, as the reader can easily ascertain by reducing the following sublime '*Address
to the Sun*' to the rhythmic form in which it was evidently composed:

O THOU that rollest above, round as the shield of my fathers! whence are thy beams, O SUN?
everlasting light? Thou comest forth in thine awful beauty; the stars hide themselves in the
, and the moon, cold and pale, sinks in the western wave. But thou thyself movest alone! Who
be a companion of thy course? The oaks of the mountains fall; the mountains themselves de-
with years; the ocean sinks and grows again; the moon herself is lost in heaven; but thou art
ever the same, rejoicing in the brightness of thy course. When the earth is black with tempests,
in thunder rolls and lightning flies, then thou lookest forth in thy beauty from the clouds, and
phest at the storm!'

Our thanks are due to ' J. G. H.,' of Springfield, (Mass.,) for his communication touching the course and the capabilities of the wretched inebriate whose personalities disgrace a certain Milliner's Magazine in Philadelphia; but bless your heart, man! you can't expect us to publish it.   The jaded hack who runs a broken pace for common hire, upon whom you have wasted powder, might revel in his congenial abuse of this Magazine and its EDITOR from now till next October without disturbing our complacency for a single moment.   He is too mean for hate, and hardly worthy scorn.   In fact there are but two classes of persons who regard him in *any* light — those who despise and those who pity him ; the first for his utter lack of principle, the latter for the infirmities which have overcome and ruined him.   Here is a faithful picture, for which he but recently sat.   We take it from one of our most respectable daily journals:

'IT is melancholy enough to see a man maimed in his limbs, or deprived by nature of his due proportions ; the blind, the deaf, the mute, the lame, the impotent, are all subjects that touch our hearts, at least all whose hearts have not been indurated in the fiery furnace of sin ; but sad, sadder, saddest of all, is the poor wretch whose want of moral rectitude has reduced his mind and person to a condition where indignation for his vices and revenge for his insults are changed into compassion for the poor victim of himself.   When a man has sunk so low that he has lost the power to provoke vengeance, he is the most pitiful of all pitiable objects.   A poor creature of this description called at our office the other day, in a condition of sad imbecility, bearing in his feeble body the evidences of evil living, and betraying by his talk such radical obliquity of sense, that every spark of harsh feeling toward him was extinguished, and we could not even entertain a feeling of contempt for one who was evidently committing a suicide upon his body, as he had already done upon his character. Unhappy man !   He was accompanied by an aged female relative, who was going a weary round in the hot streets, following his steps to prevent his indulging in a love of drink ; but he had eluded her watchful eye by some means, and was already far gone in a state of inebriation.   After listening awhile with painful feelings to his profane ribaldry, he left the office, accompanied by his good genius, to whom he owed the duties which she was discharging for him.'

Now what can one gain by a victory over a person such as this?   If there are some men whose enemies are to be pitied much, there are others whose alleged friends are to be pitied more.   One whom this ' critic' has covered with what *he* deems praise, describes him as ' a literary person of unfortunate peculiarities, who professes to know many to whom he is altogether unknown.'*   Can it then be a matter of the least moment to us, when the *quo animo* of such a writer is made palpable even to his own readers, that he should underrate our circulation by thousands, overrate our age by years, or assign to other pens the departments of this Magazine which we have alone sustained, with such humble ability as we possessed, through nearly twenty-six out of its twenty-eight volumes?   As well might CARLYLE lament that he had called him an ' unmitigated ass,' or LONGFELLOW grieve at being denounced by him as ' a man of no genius, and an inveterate literary thief.'   And as to his literary *opinions*, who would regard *them* as of any importance?— a pen-and-ink writer, whose only ' art' is correctly described by the '*London Athenæum*' to ' consist in conveying plain things after a fashion which makes them hard to be understood, and commonplaces in a sort of mysterious form, which causes them to sound oracular.' ' There are times,' continues the able critical journal from which we quote, ' when

* HE is equally unknown to those whom he abuses.   The EDITOR hereof has no remembrance of ever having seen him save on two occasions.   In the one case, we met him in the street with a gentleman, who apologized the next day, in a note now before us, for having been seen in his company ' while he was laboring under such an ' *excitement ;*' ' in the other, we caught a view of his retiring skirts as he wended his ' winding way,' like a furtive puppy with a considerable kettle to his tail, from the publication-office, whence — having left no other record of his tempestuous visit upon the publisher's mind than the recollection of a coagulum of maudlin and abusive jargon — he had just emerged, bearing with him one of his little narrow rolls of manuscript, which had been previously submitted for insertion in our 'excellent Magazine,' but which, unhappily for his peace, had shared the fate of its equally attractive predecessors.

he probably desires to go no farther than the obscure ; when the utmost extent of his ambition is to be unintelligible ; that he approaches the verge of the childish, and wanders on the confines of the absurd !' We put it to our Massachusetts correspondent, whether such a writer's idea of style is at all satire-worthy ? And are we not excused from declining our friend's kindly-meant but quite unnecessary communication? · · · '*American Progress*' is certainly an ' acceptable *theme ;*' but, good Sir, it is the manner of *treating* a theme, and not the *theme itself*, which should be regarded as especially praiseworthy in a literary composition. Observe how OLIVER WENDELL HOLMES in fourteen lines exhausts the entire matériel of your fourth and fifth pages of long foolscap:

> 'ON other shores, above their mouldering towns,
> In sullen pomp the tall cathedral frowns,
> Pride in its aisles, and paupers at the door,
> Which feeds the beggars whom it fleeced of yore.
> Simple and frail, our lowly temples throw
> Their slender shadows on the paths below ;
> Scarce steal the winds, that sweep his woodland tracks,
> Tho larch's perfume from the settler's axe,
> Ere, like a vision of the morning air,
> His slight-framed steeple marks the house of prayer ;
> *Its planks all reeking, and its paint undried,*
> *Its rafters sprouting on the shady side.*
> *It sheds the raindrops from its shingled eaves,*
> *Ere its green brothers once have changed their leaves.'*

This is ' the vision and the faculty divine,' elaborate ' P. D.' · · · OUR editorial veteran, Major NOAH, speaks of an extremely professional editor of his acquaintance, who upon being asked on one occasion at dinner if he would take some more pudding, replied : ' Owing to the crowd of other matter we are unable to make room for it until a subsequent issue.' This plural style reminds us of a description which the late SUMNER LINCOLN FAIRFIELD once gave of his arrest at the instance of a captain of a Mississippi steamer, for the amount of his fare, his name not being *quite* sufficient at that time to pass him free through a thousand miles transit or so on the western waters. The characteristically tautological ' paper' was served upon him at the principal inn of an isolated village, where the steamer, owing to some defect of her machinery, was tarrying for the night. The officer was imperative — inexorable, even. The ' delinquent' was toasting his feet by a comfortable fire, when he was made aware of his presence and his ultimatum. ' You must come with me, Sir, and at once !' ' We turned to him,' said Mr. FAIRFIELD, ' and with a glance of withering scorn upon our clouded brow, replied : ' Would you place us in duress without our seeing counsel ? Would you remove our person without our hat ? Would you dare, Sir, to take us away in our slippers ?' The officer ' did n't do nothing else,' if we remember rightly. · · · WE have been looking from one of our sanctum-windows this morning at the progress of church-building, almost under our gardenward-eaves ; holding forth the promise that in the fulness of time we shall be under the very droppings of two sanctuaries. From the one, we may hear, sitting by our open windows on the LORD's day, the voice of prayer and praise, and perhaps even the language of that sublime and beautiful Litany, which has fallen from the lips of so many saints who now chant their adorations around the throne of GOD. We have been thinking, while we watched stone after stone rising to its long resting-place in the edifice, of the congregations that will fill the space now open to the day when we shall have gone hence to be here no more. Parents, gazing with a calm and unspeakable delight upon their children, growing up around them in the love of GOD ; children, ripening into youth, glowing with warm affections, and experiencing, almost for the first time, the pulsations of the tenderest of passions; the young and the fresh-hearted who have enjoyed its perfection in the interchange of hearts and the pledge of hands in the holiest of ties; all these will be there; and when the sound of solemn music shall swell from the organ through all the vaulted aisles, their souls will be wrapped in dreams of heaven. Well may such exclaim, with hearts of fervent gratitude to the GIVER of all GOOD, ' How amiable are thy tabernacles, O LORD of Hosts !' . . . THE initial paper of the present number, the theme of which will be concluded in our next, will arrest the attention of the reader. It is from the capable pen of Prof. KOEPEN, who resided for ten years in Greece, chiefly in Athens, in the university of which place he held the professorship of Greek history and literature. In the revolution which took place about two years since, all the foreigners in the employ of the government, as well as the professors in the colleges, were compelled to leave. Professor KOEPEN has since travelled extensively in Asia Minor, Syria and Palestine, visiting the most interesting objects of antiquity, and making scientific observations on certain parts unknown to modern travellers. Several memoirs and letters by him on these countries have been published in Germany and Denmark, and he is now contributing an interesting series of letters to the ' New-York Observer.' His authentic sketches will well reward an attentive perusal. · · · AMONG the pictorial publications which we receive, we consider as among the best the '*Christian Parlor Magazine.*' Its engravings are uniformly excellent; its matériel is entertaining and attractive, as well as religious; it is free from sectarian cant; is edited with decided ability and good taste; and the neatness of its typography, the excellence of its paper, and its prompt publication, leave little to be desired. · · · THACKERAY, better known perhaps as Mr. MICHAEL ANGELO TITMARSH, proposes to Monsieur ALEXANDRE DUMAS, in the last number of FRAZER's Magazine, there being at present a great dearth of novels, whether of the ' fashionable,' the ' historical' or the ' terrific' schools, the heroes and heroines of which are quite exhausted, that he should take up other people's heroes, and give a continuation of *their* lives. ' There are numbers of WALTER SCOTT's novels,' he remarks, ' that I always felt were incomplete. The Master of Ravenswood, for instance, disappears it is true at the end of the ' Bride of Lammermoor.' His hat is found, that is to say, on the sea-shore, and you suppose him drowned; but I have always an idea that he has floated out to sea; and his adventures might recommence, in a maritime novel, say, on board the ship which picked him up. No man can induce me to believe that the adventures of QUENTIN DURWARD ceased the day after he married ISABELLE DE CROYE. People survive even marriage; their sufferings do n't end with that blessed incident in their lives. Do we take leave of our friends, or cease to have an interest in them, the moment they drive off in the chaise and the wedding *dejeune* is over? Surely not ! and it is unfair upon married folks to advance that your bachelors are your only heroes.' Mr. TITMARSH recommends ' the dear old IVANHOE' especially, as admirably calculated for a continuation, by reason of its present unsatisfactory ending. It was impossible to suppose that the disinherited knight could sit down contentedly for life by the side of such a frigid piece of propriety as that icy, faultless, prim, niminy-piminy ROWENA; he therefore calls upon the French novelist to ' complete this fragment of a novel, and to do the real heroine justice;' and he offers a few hints for his consideration :

' WHEN the daughter of ISAAC of York brought her diamonds and rubies — the poor, gentle victim !— and meekly laying them at the feet of the conquering ROWENA, departed into foreign lands to tend the sick of her people, and to brood over the bootless passion which consumed her own pure heart, one would have thought that the heart of the royal lady would have melted before such beauty and humility, and that she would have been generous in the moment of her victory. In fact she *did* say, 'Come and live with me as a sister,' as the last chapter of the history shows; but RE-BECCA knew in her heart that her lady's proposition was what is called *bosh* in that noble Eastern language with which WILFRED the Crusader was familiar, or *fudge* in plain Saxon, and retired with a broken, gentle spirit, neither able to bear the sight of her rival's happiness, nor willing to disturb it by the contrast of her own wretchedness. • ROWENA, like the most high-bred and virtuous of women, never forgave ISAAC'S daughter her beauty nor her 'flirtation' with WILFRED, as the Saxon lady chose to term it, nor above all, her admirable diamonds and jewels, although ROWENA was actually in possession of them. In a word, she was always flinging REBECCA into IVANHOE'S teeth. There was not a day in his life but that unhappy warrior was made to remember that a Jewish maiden had been in love with him, and that a Christian lady of fashion could never forgive the insult.'

It is recommended that IVANHOE shall grow thin under this treatment, lose all appetite for his meals, grow dissipated and keep bad hours, while the lady ROWENA is sitting up for him at home. A chapter descriptive of the siege of Chalus is suggested, which can be spun out to any length to which an enterprising publisher would be disposed to go. Single combats or combats of companies, scaladoes, ambuscadoes, rapid acts of horsemanship, destriers, catapults, mangonels and other properties of the chivalric drama, are at the use of the writer. A chapter about famine in the garrison is especially recommended, in strong contrast with a description of great feasting in the camp of the enemy, with a display of antiquarian cookery; all descriptions of eating being pleasant in works of fiction. Mr. TITMARSH throws off a description of the assault, 'just to show what *might* be done,' which is strikingly IVANHOE-ish, and an uncommonly rich specimen of the burlesque ; abounding in those explosive terms of chivalry, 'Ha! St. RICHARD!' 'Ha! St. GEORGE!' ' Now by St. BARBECUE of Limoges !' said BERTRAND DE GOURDON,' and the like. BERTRAND is flayed alive after RICHARD'S death, and as there is no chapter in any novel extant where a man being skinned alive is described, this incident is suggested as an excellent one for a powerful and picturesque pen. The novel concludes with the death of IVANHOE and ROWENA'S marriage to the stupid ATHELSTANE. · · · · IN reading the account of the eloquent address of JOSEPH R. CHANDLER, Esq., on laying the cap-stone of Girard College, we were led by an ' electric chain' to think of the last time we saw that splendid structure. We stood with W. G. C. upon the broad top of one of the western columns, looking off upon the October landscape, beyond the Schuylkill, when he said, ' L——, I must add another verse to my ' Laurel Hill ;' this will be a very different view in a month's time.' When we got home he added to that poem, which had already been published, the second of the ensuing stanzas:

> ' THERE is an emblem in this peaceful scene ;
> Soon rainbow colors on the woods will fall,
> And autumn gusts bereave the hills of green,
> As sinks the year to meet its cloudy pall.

> ' Then, cold and pale, in distant vistas round,
> Disrobed and tuneless, all the woods will stand,
> Till the chained streams are silent as the ground.
> As Death had numbed them with his icy hand!'

Do n't these lines seem *bleak*, like the scene they depict? · · · THE paper entitled ' *Camp-Meeting in Prairie Land*,' which we are assured is an exact *transcript*, in scene and character, will awaken profitable reflection in the minds of some readers, and perhaps elicit the angry animadversions of others. But it is the *abuses* of the custom of forest-worship; the impious and unchristian language which one hears, at times, in the 'first temples' of GOD, that our correspondent exposes and condemns, and not the worship itself. We have seen, and this journal has not unfrequently depicted, the influence, infectious for good, of well-conducted camp-meetings; yet it cannot be denied that the grossness, the vulgarity, which sometimes characterize the harangues of the over-zealous, the ignorant and the passionate at such assemblages, imperatively demand the whip and the branding-iron. We are credibly informed that at a camp-meeting, not many months since, in the vicinity of New-York, the following almost profane language was made use of by one of the speakers: 'Come up, my brethren-ah! come up-ah, and give in-ah! Come now! come *now-ah!* Do n't have any half-way work about it-ah! Come up to-once, and go the whole hog for CHRIST-ah!' Surely the utterers of such blasphemous rant as this, (and we ourselves have heard language on similar occasions scarcely less profane,) can find no conscientious apologist. . . . . 'CAULD Winter is coming' anon, with its snows and its storms without, and its bright reünions within. The season of festivity and happiness for the fortunate and the beautiful has come, when the circles which the sunshine of summer had scattered are again gathered in all the haunts of fashion; the old to recount their several experiences of success by flood and field, and the young and lovely to perfect the conquests begun amidst the gayeties of the Springs, or those delightful moonlight walks along the sea-shore, so favorable for the inception of tender affections. To our readers the approach of winter we hope is full of recollections of past successes in business, of pleasant excursions and safe returns from distant tours. And now the refitting of their own dear homes is a theme full of cheerful anticipations of coming winter. Our prospects of pleasure, we are assured, were never greater. The PARK and other theatres will present their accustomed attractions; for scores of artists in the departments of the drama, ballet and opera are on their way to our shores. NIBLO'S, phœnix-like, has taken its flight in flame and smoke, and like the phœnix, to reäppear in the spring, we hope, with even added beauty and wider wings; but for the season we must be content to submit to the privations incident to the loss of one of our accustomed haunts of mirth and amusement. If it was its fate to be burned, it could not have taken itself off at a more fitting moment. Now whatever winter evenings may be to the poor — and for them we ask the sympathy and aid of the happy — they are brighter than summer suns to the young, whose eyes rival in brilliancy the stars shining over them. A beautiful girl said to us, as we were sitting in our old arm-chair, talking with her over plans for her second winter's campaign, ' All that repays one for the weariness of preparation for an evening party are the hours after midnight; but for these,' said she, ' I would not stir a step.' ' And why ?' we asked. ' Oh, because all before that time is so formal; the rooms are so crowded till then, and the gentlemen too are so hungry till they get their suppers, that they are like unfed bears; but after supper they become amiable and willing to be amused and to say pleasant things to us ladies. Then they find out that we are well-dressed and look particularly attractive, and are ready to dance to our heart's content. Then it is that we dare to whirl through the waltz, and gaily trip it in the Redowa, the Polka and Mazourka, and so shake out the folds of our dresses; and AUNT STACY has told me,' she said, in a low tone of whispering confidence, laying her beautiful white hand on our knee, ' that when I get ready to do such an act, never to make any attempt at conquest till after midnight; when, she says — and she, you know, has had a large experience in these matters — men are much more *impressible.* And then, if we venture a little pressure of the hand, it is always effective; and then if we look up into a face with some little particularity, it never fails to light up a smile which is very pretty to look at. Do you understand?' asked the sweet girl, with a knowing smile. ' Bless us!' we exclaimed, 'yes; and well provided as we are with wife and weans, are ready to go into the pit-fall of love, head-and-ears over, you little witch!'' Indulge us here, reader, because the thought comes over us in this connection, in a word or two about *light*. Every night we are reminded of the value, luxury and perpetuity of the *Mechanical Lamp*, the only lamp we know which really answers the earnest prayer of Mrs. SMITH, in her colloquy with the 'Gentleman in Black:' 'Oh! for lamps that never burn dim!' And we have thought that had DEMOSTHENES but possessed himself of one of them, how little of the 'smell of the lamp' there would have been perceived by the most delicate of the Athenian noses, so scornfully turned up at the parchment rolls of the orator; for to our best belief, they are without smell or smoke, and as economical as they are brilliant and beautiful. Our lamp! we have good reason to admire it, and to speak its praise. If our articles are ever bright, we owe it to its rays, and any scintil-lations which may be seen in our pages are but its beams concentrated at the point of the metallic pen which tips our long porcupine-quill. So much a favorite with us is the 'French Mechanical Lamp,' that we could well wish all our readers might re-joice in its light; and we have been thinking to-night how much more of cheerfulness there would be around all our firesides, if ' the light that shone,' instead of being ' dim-med and gone' before the witching hour of midnight, (that ' noon of night' as the poets call it, and with as much of truth as poetic license,) could but be as perennial as the *midnight suns* sold by our friend AUGUSTIN DIACON, at Number twenty, Jol.n-street! Honest SANCHO PANZA found it in his heart to exclaim, ' Praise be to !. m who invented sleep!' We would rather say, ' Praise be to him who introduced to our benighted city the splendors of the Parisian Carcel Lamp!' . . . THE cele-brated establishment of Messrs. TIFFANY AND YOUNG, Broadway, opposite the City-Hall, is one of the fixed lions of the metropolis. It is the largest of its kind in Ame-rica; is always crowded with the most *recherché* articles of art and *vertu* that can be found in the cities of the old world; and is always freshly supplied with the very latest attractions; the articles being all of their own importation, made to order, or selected from the best sources, by one of their firm resident in Europe. It is worthy any one's while to spend an hour in examining the beautiful fabrics to be encountered here. One comes away almost ' dazzled and drunk with beauty.' . . . NEW-YORK is blest with a distinguished lecturer, in the person of REV. GEORGE OGLE, who in di-verse suburban quarters ' unfolds to view a retrospective and prospective prospect of tyranny; liberty, honor and dishonor; the ocean; disappointment; superstition and fanaticism; benevolent exertions in favor of literature; scenes in nature; the public press; and a prospective view of America and her prospects!' A ' large and se-lected assortment' of topics. . . . WE announced last October that our ' ency-clopedic friend GOURAUD' would lecture on the application of his system of mne-motechny to the learning of languages; but this was prevented by a severe illness, which kept him on the ' boundary line of the other world' nearly six months. We are glad to have occular proof that the Professor is still in the flesh, and full of energy in carrying out the plans he has in view. He is now in town, ' direct from the ely-sian solitudes of Niagara,' for the purpose of attending the *Phonographic Convention* to be held in this city about the middle of the present month; when he proposes to put *hors de combat* PITMAN's system, as well as any other which may be presented, by his ' American system of *True* Phonography,' which he is now editing. He asserts that by the help of this system all the spoken languages of the world can be written and read, with their exact pronunciation, and that he will soon teach us all how to pronounce in a few hours the French, the Spanish, the Italian, etc., just as well as Louis Phillippe, Queen Isabella, or the new Pope, *è tutti quanti !* Verily, if such power be possessed by the ' True Phonography' which the proposed convention will assemble to examine and decide upon, we predict for Mr. Gouraud a perfect rush to his philological lectures. '*Nous verrons.*' . . . The lines '*To My Sister*' in preceding pages, by F. W. Thomas, Esq., of Washington, were addressed to Mrs. Watt, a most lovely and amiable lady, who, with two beautiful children, was wrecked in April last, in the ship Gentoo, near the Cape of Good Hope. She was on her return from Calcutta, where her husband resided, for the purpose of educating her children in the United States. Previous to her marriage, she was the idol of her relatives, the light and life of the circle in which she moved, and an object of warm regard to all who were fortunate enough to enjoy her intimate friendship. By her most distressing death, the ' dark unfathomed caves of ocean' have had added to them ' a gem of purest ray serene,' and an ' aching void' has been left in many a heart. . . . Messrs. Anthony and Clark, at their spacious National Miniature Gallery, have copies of their magnificent engraving of the *Senate Chamber of the United States*, each member and spectator in which is a portrait ! It is a noble work, and will demand further words from us hereafter. . . . Our readers will be glad to welcome back again to the country which loves and honors him, Mr. Washington Irving, our late distinguished minister to the court of Spain. He is in excellent health. Time seems in passing over him to leave his person unscathed and his equable spirit untouched. ' May he live a a thousand years !' . . . 'T.' wonders why it is that the *Caffres* are enabled to ' bush-fight' as they do at the Cape of Good Hope. ' Judging from the specimens of Caffre-blood at the American Museum,' he thinks ' the contest ought long ago to have been decided.' Bless his heart ! he does n't know the monkey from the native ! . . . Our acknowledgments are due and tendered to Tsow-Chaoong, late of Canton, for his pleasant remembrancer. When he reaches the flower-land, we shall address him in Chinese. Decidedly, we shall do ' nothing else.' A special intention. . . . *Graham's Magazine* for October, the best by far of the Philadelphia monthlies, is a good number. Its engravings are a portrait of Dr. Reynal Coates, one of its contributors, ' The Bride,' a rather hackneyed print, and a well-engraved and colored plate of the fashions. The best papers in the number, to our conception, are ' A Day's Fishing in the Mongaup,' by Alfred B. Street, and a fine poem by William Pitt Palmer, both our constant contributors. . . . It is not a little amusing sometimes to watch the manners of a dare-devil guest from our boundless ' back country' at a public hotel. A friend of ours mentions one of this description, who was sitting by a gentleman at dinner, who sent for a bottle of champaigne, giving to the waiter ' Ninety-five' as the number of his room. No sooner had he turned out a glass, than the stranger-guest did the same. ' That 's first-rate drink !' said he. ' Here, boy, bring me *a bottle of Ninety-five, too !*' The next morning he was seen fuming about the hall in his slippers, calling out, ' Where the d—l is my boots? They've left me nothing but these flat-footed, no-heeled shoes !' ' Boots?' asked the servant; ' what is your number?' ' Number twelve — largest size — pegged heels; bring 'em quick — I want 'em !' It was *rather* supposed, by those who overheard this dialogue, that the servant desired to know the number of the unfortunate stranger's room rather than that of his cowhide boots. . . . Charles F. Daniels, Esq., so long and favorably connected with the New-York daily press, leaves the ' Courier and Enquirer' daily journal on the first instant. It makes us 'feel our years' to remember how long we have been accustomed to read the pleasant paragraphs of our old friend and contemporary ; and we must still hope to recognise his style in some of the daily gazettes with which our good city of Gotham abounds. They will be fortunate gentlemen who succeed in securing his valuable services. . . . MR. FORREST has just concluded a very popular and profitable engagement at the Park-Theatre. 'Old Drury' never before resounded with such long-continued, enthusiastic, tempestuous, *loving* applause, as made our most distinguished American actor *feel* that he was 'welcome home again' on the first night of his appearance. Similar applause has followed him through his entire engagement. Our duties, pressing always at the period of the month in which he was performing, prevented our seeing any of his representations save *Lear ;* that, in bursts of stormy passion, was tremendous, and in the pathetic scenes exceedingly effective. There are others, who have been fortunate in frequent visits to the Park, who pronounce his *Othello* and *Richelieu* superior even to his Lear. We rejoice in his distinguished success. . . . '*A Crack in the Wall for You to take a Peep in if you Choose ; there are some Things in the House,*' is the title of a thin pamphlet which has been sent to us, we suppose for notice. We have taken a 'peep' at it, and find that the principal 'crack' is in the author's head, and that if what remains *in* that receptacle is not better than what has come *out* of it, the 'things' which it contains can hardly be considered '*some :*' the head itself however, as they say at the west, may be 'some punkins'—at least one. . . . 'NED BUNTLINE' intends, at some early day, to issue his '*Life-Yarn*' in a book ; so that our readers must await its continuation and conclusion in that form. . . . NOT one of our town-readers should fail to attend the '*Irish Evenings*' of the accomplished SAMUEL LOVER, one of the most 'variorum' entertainers we have for a long time had among us. We have had the pleasure to witness examples of his delightful powers in society, and can assure the reader that what 'poor POWER' was upon the stage Mr. LOVER is in his songs and other entertainments. They are most admirable. . . . THE Alumni of the Bangor High School must have had a 'good time' at their recent anniversary dinner. Their bill of fare, *literarily* speaking, was capital. But as touching the rest, 'judgment rests.' . . . MR. B. W. CAREY MASSETT, Professor of the Greek, Latin and French languages and English literature, continues to give instruction in private families and schools, and to prepare young gentlemen for college. His references are of the highest order. . . . THE following rather curt epitaph is copied from a tomb-stone in New-Jersey :

'READER, pass on ; ne'er waste your time
On bad biography or bitter rhyme ;
For what I am, this cumbrous clay insures,
And what I was, is no affair of yours!'

In another grave-yard, in the near vicinity, is the following touching inscription :

'HERE lyes JOHN ROSS,
Kicked by a Hoss!'

SEVERAL acceptable communications, among them 'Evening on the Sea-shore,' 'Lines to my Cigar,' and 'Is the Profession of an Advocate consistent with Perfect Integrity?' are filed for insertion in our next. Four or five new publications, including Rev. THOMAS P. TYLER's poem before the Alumni of Trinity College, Hartford, Prof. FORESTI's OLLENDORF's 'New Method of Writing and Speaking Italian,' and the 'Chess Palladium,' will receive attention at our earliest leisure. Three pages of 'Gossip' in type are unavoidably deferred till our next number.

LITERARY RECORD. — We are right well pleased to be enabled to welcome a new and very beautiful edition of LONGFELLOW'S ' *Outre-Mer. a Pilgrimage beyond Sea*,' from the press of Messrs. WILLIAM D. TICKNOR AND COMPANY, Boston. Upon the appearance of the first edition an elaborate notice of the work, with copious extracts, appeared in these pages; and it is only because we do not wish to ' repeat ourselves' to our readers, that we resist the temptation of again quoting largely from this various and entertaining volume. Here is its motto, from from old Sir JOHN MAUNDEVILLE: ' I have passed manye landes and manye yles and coutrees, and cherched manye full straunge places, and have been in manye a fulle gode honourable companye. Now I am comen home to reste. And thus recordynge the tyme passed, I have fulfilled these thynges, and put hem wryten in this boke, as it wolde comen into my minde.' Purchase the book! · · · WE have from Messrs. APPLETON AND COMPANY, in one of the most beautifully-printed volumes of the season, TORQUATO TASSO'S '*Jerusalem Delivered*,' translated into English Spenserian verse, with a life of the author, by J. H. WIFFEN. The volume is illustrated with six fine steel engravings, and is the first American from the last English edition. So distinguished and withal so beautiful a work wi l find no lack of purchasers. · · · THE last issue of the '*Southern Quarterly Review*' is a well-supplied number of this well-conducted work. Its papers are nine in number, including as the last a cluster of sixteen brief 'Critical Notices.' The first paper is upon MUNFORD'S 'HOMER'S Iliad,' which is elaborately considered and its merits well discriminated and warmly commended. 'The Preacher,' the second article, and the third, on 'Travellers in Italy,' we shall have occasion to refer to hereafter. Both are written with spirit, and embody much matter that is provocative of thought. These are all the articles which we have found leisure to read. · · · THE enterprising house of BARTLETT AND WELFORD are publishing '*The Standard Library, a Series of the best English and Classic Authors*,' equally adapted to the library and the fire-side. They are issued monthly, in volumes of about five hundred pages, printed in a clear and elegant type, on fine linen paper, with portraits, indexes, etc and handsomely bound in cloth, at a dollar and twenty-five cents each. The following volumes have already been published: 'Miscellaneous Works and Remains of Rev. ROBERT HALL;' ROSCOE'S 'Life and Pontificate of LEO the Tenth, edited by his Son,' in two volumes; SCHLEGEL'S 'Lectures on the Philosophy of History,' translated by J. B. ROBERTSON; SISMONDI'S 'History of the Literature of the South of Europe,' translated by ROSCOE, in two volumes; ROSCOE'S 'Life of LORENZO DE MEDICI;' SCHLEGEL'S 'Lectures on Dramatic Literature,' translated by Mr. BLACK; BECKMANN'S 'History of Inventions and Discoveries, enlarged and completed by several editors,' to be completed in two volumes; SCHILLER'S 'History of the Thirty Years' War,' and uniform with the 'Standard Library;' and GRAMMONT'S 'Memoirs of the Court of CHARLES the Second, with the Boscobel Narrative.' · · · AMONG the new and attractive publications of the BROTHERS' HARPER are JOHN FOSTER'S '*Statesmen of the Commonwealth of England*,' edited in numbers by that accomplished scholar, Rev. J. O. CHOWLES. The engravings in this work are capital. The fine portrait of CROMWELL makes us 'realize' what the Protector meant when he said to the painter, 'If you leave out a wart or a wrinkle I won't have it!' The nose too will remind the beholder of CARLYLE'S description of CROMWELL'S coming out of the Parliament, mad as the maddest bull, 'from those broad nostrils of his proceeding a kind of *snort*.' Mr. SAUNDERS, the capable and indefatigable superintendent of the 'issuing' department, has given us a catalogue of the valuable standard works in the several branches of general literature, of real bibliographical and literary merit. It is divided into twenty-three chapters, or heads, and fills an hundred closely-printed pages, embracing history, biography, arts and sciences, etc.; an excellent document for every body. · · · Messrs. C. S. FRANCIS AND COMPANY have issued, in a very handsome volume, '*Rev. Orville Dewey's Discourses and Reviews upon Questions in Controversial Theology and Practical Religion*.' The distinguished author avows his purpose in the volume to be, 'in the first place, to offer a very brief summary of the Unitarian Belief; in the next place, to lay down the essential principles of all religious faith; thirdly, to state and defend our construction, as it is generally held among us, of the Christian doctrine; fourthly, to illustrate by analogy our views of practical religion; and finally, to present, somewhat at large, the general views entertained among us of the Scriptures; of the grounds of belief in them; of the nature of their Inspiration; of the New Testament doctrine of Justification by Faith; and of the just Principles of Reasoning in religious inquiry.' · · · WE have received from Messrs. CAREY AND HART, Philadelphia, an elaborately-illustrated work, entitled '*French Cookery: the Modern Cook, a Practical Guide to the Culinary Art in all its Branches*,' adapted as well for large establishments as private families. It will receive farther notice at our hands in a subsequent number.

ORIGINAL PAPERS.

NOTICE.

THE KNICKERBOCKER.

Vol. XXVIII.   NOVEMBER, 1846.   No. 5.

LAW AND LAWYERS.

IS THE PROFESSION OF THE ADVOCATE CONSISTENT WITH PERFECT INTEGRITY?

BY J. P. JACKSON.

IT is one of the dicta of the infallible mob, that the legal profession necessarily involves many practices inconsistent with elevated integrity, or even common honesty. A successful lawyer is a sort of licensed knave, refined perhaps in his mode of cheating, but really little better than a prime minister of Satan, or at least a member of His Majesty's cabinet. To conceal truth, to pervert evidence, to mislead juries and brow-beat judges, are supposed to be the grand attainments of legal ambition.

It needs but little philosophy to account for this prejudice against the votaries of the law. The reasons for the obloquy cast upon the legal profession are numerous. At present we shall notice only two; the expense attending a suit at law, and the delay. The complaints made against the law on account of its expense arise from the fact that men are prone by nature to consider the possession of their property as an indisputable right, and to regard whatever is spent in defending it as lost. The ' law's delay' is undoubtedly a serious evil, which we hope will soon be amended; but the party who suffers from it can rarely blame his lawyer. The fault lies rather at the door of the legislature, or whoever constitute the courts of a state, for not establishing a reasonable number of judicial tribunals; or it is more frequently attributable to the trickery of the other party litigant, who contrives by dishonesty to obtain continuances and raise obstacles to a speedy settlement of a dispute. The advocate is the last person to be held responsible for this great stain upon our legal system. Excellence of any kind has a tendency to produce envy in the minds of some men; and intellectual superiority and eminence in a learned profession are sufficient causes to arouse the bitter feelings of an ignorant rabble, and to incur their upbraidings. The effects of the vulgar and mistaken notion of which we have spoken are as pernicious as its origin is apparent; for men are apt to be virtuous or vicious according as they are considered to possess the one or the other of these qualities. Once let a man know that he is looked upon with suspicion and scorned, and the golden chain which bound him to virtue is severed, and the way paved to all sorts of meanness.

For ourselves, we have no more respect or faith in the cynicism of the modern rabble than we have in that of the ancient philosopher who lived in a wash-tub. We do not believe that a candle in broad daylight is necessary to find a man among the human race, or that any extraordinary means need be resorted to to find honest men in the legal profession. We do not pretend however to deny that the advocate is perhaps exposed to greater temptations to wicked practices than any other person in society. The profession of the advocate is eminently one of confidence, and there is no method of gaining an ascendancy over the minds of others so direct and complete as that of becoming master of their secrets. Many chances also occur in a science so intricate and mysterious as that of the law, to pervert its true object, and in the name of Justice itself to thwart justice. Moreover, by becoming intimately acquainted with the circumstances of his client, the lawyer has better opportunities to defraud him without detection, or even suspicion; but it is certain that to do this the lawyer must boldly commit a sacrilege at the altar of which he is ordained high priest; he must contradict in practice the system to which he is professedly attached; in short, he must ' steal the livery of Heaven to serve the devil in.' But the same can be said of the other liberal professions. Such reflections are by no means peculiar to the legal profession. The physician can be in a family like the serpent in the garden of Eden. Many a pure woman, or hapless husband, has been perfectly convinced, and is daily convinced, of the truth of this remark. These evils all flow from the fact that the medical profession, like the legal, is one of confidence. Noxious doctrines can be promulgated from the pulpit; and in the secret bethel of the homestead the confiding heart may find that the black cloth and the white cravat are but disguises assumed by the traitor to his GOD and to his fellow-man. The politician or the statesman, by wily arts seducing the mass, can introduce false principles into the government of a nation, and thus corrupt the fountains of the happiness of a whole people. Why not argue from this that these professions too are more refined inventions for the practice of villany? Why not change the plan of attack upon the medical profession, and brand physicians as scientific murderers and pompous quacks? Why not call the ministers of the gospel a troop of hypocrites? Why not stigmatize the statesman as a destroyer of human happiness and as an evil genius to the confiding and the trustful? In short, in every profession where mental discipline and superior abilities raise a man above the level of the surrounding crowd, and equip him with extraordinary influence, the avenues of dishonesty and treachery are a thousand-fold increased. ' Let him who standeth take heed lest he fall !' But that there is any thing in the science or the practice of law which necessarily involves a stifling of conscience, the sacrifice of one iota of principle, a support of injustice or inevitable dishonesty, we do most firmly and solemnly deny.

In maintaining our position we shall examine and try to show the groundlessness of some of the chief objections which have been brought against the legal profession. Among other calumnies thrown out against the advocate, it is triumphantly asserted by some wiseacres of the present day that he often enlists in a cause without knowing or even caring which side is in the wrong; that it is impossible when the interests of two parties conflict, as in a case at law, that both can have the right, and therefore the advocate of one at least is of necessity guilty of dishonesty. But on this point the voice of reason and common sense is far different from that of the rabble. To see the fallacy of the charge, it is only necessary to bear in mind that all matters of opinion are not capable of perfect mathematical demonstration; that they are not so obvious as to make it necessary that either party should prosecute his claim at the expense of integrity; that the affairs of mankind are not so nicely adjusted as that one party in a law-suit should be entirely right and the other entirely wrong; and that truth cannot be elicited and justice awarded unless both sides of a case are fairly represented. Consider the intricacies of contracts and commercial relations; the difficulty in many cases of ascertaining the true meaning of the will of testators; and above all, the nice distinctions to be made in determining the degree of criminality. It were palpably absurd for the advocate to prejudge the questions to which these and a thousand other subjects, equally complicated, give rise. Beside, it is not for the advocate to say whether a cause is just or unjust; for him to decide upon the justice or injustice of a case would be to usurp the province of the judge. Many cases which at first seemed to be bad have on examination proved to be good. Nay, it often happens that the advocate is unable to see the justice of his client's cause until it is brought before the court. In short, the advocate is bound to represent his side of the case, *right or wrong*, in the best possible light, and to enforce the strongest arguments he can devise in favor of his client, leaving the validity of those arguments and the true merits of the case to the decision of the judge, whose business alone it is to decide. Let the advocate prejudge a case, and you bar the citizen from seeking redress in a court of justice; you defeat the very object of trials at law; in a word, you introduce mob-law, and make every man his own judge and his own avenger.

It is also charged against the profession that the advocate appears in defence or prosecution of a claim which he believes to be unjust; that he defends the wrong side, knowing it to be wrong. For example, he defends a person whom he knows to be *morally* guilty. Is this consistent with perfect integrity, or is it not? Now there is such a thing as justice to a depraved criminal, and the interests of society demand that justice should be done to him as well as to the offended law and the outraged community; and it is a maxim established since the 'time whereof the memory of man runneth not to the contrary,' that every man shall be presumed innocent until proved guilty.* It is also an important rule of justice that punishment shall be apportioned to crime ; and in order that these fundamental principles of justice may be maintained and their strict application secured, the services of an advocate must, from the very nature of the circumstances, be obtained, that he may expound the law ; suggest every reasonable doubt; insist upon palliating circumstances ; and in short, put the most favorable construction upon the conduct of the accused which the principles of justice will allow. If this be not done, the very objects for which courts exist will be utterly defeated, and trials at law become a mere farce.   It is asserted that the advocate, by appearing in defence of a person whom he knows to be guilty, tacitly acknowledges his belief in his innocence, becomes an abettor in crime, and thus swerves from the path of integrity.   Now actions are moral or immoral according as the motives by which the agent is actuated are good or bad.   And is it not strange that sensible men should say that an advocate defends a criminal from any love of crime ?   Beside, the law under which punishment is inflicted has not the same facilities of information as private individuals; the only way in which it can ascertain crime and award justice is by a fair hearing of both parties.   No matter how certain the community may be of the criminal's guilt, it would be a palpable subversion of law to allow this fact to detract one iota from his privilege of defence.   Without this faithful scrupulousness of the law it would lose its authority and we its protection. And this same glorious caution must also be exercised in determining the degree of guilt; for the *degree* of guilt is as necessary to be ascertained as the fact of the *existence* of the guilt.   It would be palpably absurd to convict a man of murder who had merely committed the crime of manslaughter, or to convict a person of manslaughter who had merely committed a justifiable homicide.   In the majority of instances the shade of difference between the first two crimes is so slight, depends so much upon the color given to the transaction by the witnesses, and a reasonable explanation of the various circumstances of the case, that the learning and ingenuity of counsel are absolutely necessary to make as clear and favorable a definition of legal terms as possible ; to explain the relation of circumstances to each other ; to apply the strict test of cross-examination; to ascertain the credibility of the witnesses, and sift from the evidence the prejudices of those who detail the facts.   Here then, on the immutable principles of justice, do we take our stand, and maintain that *every case, however bad, every criminal, however depraved, has a claim upon the services of the advocate, and that the ad-*

---

* We are aware, however, that there are certain tribunals in some of our colleges before which young men are sometimes arraigned and held guilty until they have proved their innocence.   But this is an exception to the general rule, and there is no need of its being recorded in any system of law, since college faculties are ' a law unto themselves.'

vocate may honestly defend a person whom he knows to be guilty of some crime; and we hold that in attempting to avert from his client a penalty disproportioned to his offence, he is discharging a duty as truly just and noble as if he were holding the shield of his eloquence over the most pure and innocent. It is upon this principle that the humanity of modern law provides, in contradistinction to the barbarism of former ages, that the most abandoned criminal may confront the majesty of the law and the sternness of his accusers through the mediation of an advocate. Those certain wise nobodies who charge the members of the legal profession with dishonesty, seem to forget that there is in the human mind a tendency to imbibe prejudice in favor of the side of a question which it hears first, or for which it has sympathy on account of the relation which it sustains to the person who is intrusted in it, as the relation of client and lawyer. Probably in the majority of cases which turn out unfavorably to the advocate, he really believes himself to be in the right.

Another charge brought against the profession is, that the advocate, knowing his client to be guilty, endeavors to prove him innocent. Is this right ? To answer this question correctly, it will be necessary to glance at the objects of trials at law. Laws are presumed to be so framed as to promote the good of the greatest number by saving the innocent from condemnation and convicting the guilty. For this purpose TECHNICAL RULES have of necessity been adopted. The intricacy of the law, arising from its technicalities, has been and still is the cause of much censure upon the profession of the advocate. Some men seem to regard the law as a mere piece of mechanism ; a form without spirit ; words destitute alike of philosophy and meaning. But every science has its forms. Grammar and mathematics have their rules and figures of demonstration ; and it is only through the technicalities of the law that its spirit can be imparted and the understanding reached. When a man commits some heinous crime, say that of murder ; when he is arraigned before a court of justice ; when the community think he ought to suffer the penalty of death ; when the feelings of men are excited against the offender, if the advocate for the criminal appears and proceeds to show that, owing to some flaw in the indictment, the trial cannot proceed, and thus clears the criminal, it is not strange that superficial reasoners, and even men of sense, should become prejudiced against him who ' made the worse appear the better cause.' But then it is not the advocate who clears the criminal. He only performs his duty to his client, leaving the result of his arguments to the judge and jury. Why not throw the blame, if blame there be, upon them ? Every avenue of escape for the prisoner should be kept open. The learning and ingenuity of skilful and practiced men are absolutely necessary to explain and apply the technicalities of the law in regard to evidence. For if all evidence is to be indiscriminately admitted, then the most perjured villain has the most spotless character completely under his control. On this account, proceeding upon the reasonable doctrine that it is better that many guilty should escape than that one innocent person should be punished, the law

requires that a certain amount of proof shall be necessary to estab-
lish guilt. In short, the evidence must be such as to exclude every
rational doubt. Whatever is less than this, if allowed to be sufficient,
is an injury to society for the sake of avenging a single crime. The
advocate, therefore, may honestly and conscientiously, with a view
to the interests of society and the security of innocent men, labor
with all his might to show that the evidence adduced in a given case
does not justify a conviction. We do not say that he may have re-
course to bribery or trickery, or any other sort of meanness, to gain
a verdict in his favor ; but we do say that it is the advocate's sacred
duty to use all fair means and exert himself to the utmost to make
it appear that the law does not declare his client guilty. ' No matter,'
he might boldly proclaim in the eye of common judgment or common
prejudice, ' how great the moral iniquity of my client may be, if on
this account he can be convicted upon slight evidence, a precedent is
established which controverts the very object of all law, and endan-
gers the purest virtue, the most complete innocence.'

Another objection not unfrequently urged against the profession
of the advocate is, that he keeps within his own bosom facts which
the confidence of his client has entrusted to him, and thus *cheats* the
law out of its proper victim. But it must be remembered that the
advocate stands in the very place of the accused; that he becomes
acquainted with what he would not know upon any other condition.
And we would ask upon what principles of reason or justice can a
man be made to testify against himself; or by what right can the
advocate, standing in the place of the accused, be compelled to do
the same ? Of course a system of law so weak as to require, in
order to sustain itself, the confession of the accused, would be too
contemptible to be dignified with the name of law ; a system founded
upon such inquisitorial tyranny would be too gross to be called the
child of equity and justice ; it would be impracticable ; it would
defeat itself ; in short, it would be wretched lawlessness.

Far be it from us to say that trials at law are never scenes of
dishonest wriggling and palpable falsehood. That the law itself is
defied and mocked and tricked by its own ministers, we do not pre-
tend to dispute. But if a few yield to temptation, and become, in-
stead of lawyers, usurers and gamblers and sharks and thieves, we
would ask by what rule of logic it follows that the whole class must
be stigmatized as rogues unwhipped of justice, unbranded felons,
uncaged wolves ? Of course we do not say that a man is honest
merely because he is a lawyer ; but we do religiously believe that
it is equally ridiculous and absurd to say that because a man is a
lawyer he is therefore a knave. The true lawyer, imbued with les-
sons of wisdom, and accustomed to labor in all that ennobles the
soul and refines the mind and chastens the feelings, is one of the
ornaments of his race. The vindicator of the laws of GOD and
man ; a guardian of morality and conservator of right; the distri-
butor of justice and the protector of the injured and the innocent;
a public sentinel to sound the alarm on the approach of danger;
he is one of the firmest safe-guards of society. His profession is one

of transcendent dignity. Its object is to shield the oppressed from the oppressor; to equalize the disparity which nature has fixed between the weak and the strong; which circumstances have made between the rich and the poor, the favorite of fortune and the beggar-brat of misfortune; to defend the fatherless and the widow; to protect innocence against the wiles of its enemies, and the prejudices of a world which was more ready to crucify CHRIST than Barabbas. Whoever then perverts this object, and commits a sacrilege at the altar of justice at which he is sworn to minister, shame on him! — and equal shame on him who endeavors to convict a class for the vices of a few, and dares attempt to make the law appear, instead of the handmaid of justice, the slave of injustice; and the profession of the advocate, dignified and noble as it is in all its *true* objects, to seem a mere school of refined knavery!

Of LAW, the world's collected wisdom, the good man's defence, the bad man's dread, founded as it is on moral rectitude and the principles of eternal truth, 'no less can be said, than that its seat is the bosom of GOD, its voice the harmony of the world; all things in heaven and earth do it homage; the least as feeling its care, the greatest as not exempt from its power; both angels and men and the creatures of what condition soever, though each in different sort or manner, yet all, all with uniform assent, recognize it as the life of their being, the giver of their peace, the safeguard of their happiness!'

FANNY HALL.

THE sweetest girl of all I know
  Is charming FANNY HALL;
The wildest at a husking,
  The gayest at a ball;
Her cheek is like a Jersey peach,
  Her eye is blue and clear,
And her lip is like the sumac
  In the Autumn of the year.

CANOVA never made a hand
  Like hers, so plump and fair;
Poor RAPHAEL had been crazed with her
  Madonna brow and hair;
And I'm inclined to think if POWERS
  Could see her, he would grieve
To find a romping Yankee girl
  Had beaten Mrs. EVE!

There's not a blemish in her form,
  No fault about her face;
Sit down and gaze from morn till night,
  You'll find her perfect grace;
And then, to finish all, her voice!
  From the sweetest bird's in spring
You couldn't tell its warble; but
  She 'does n't know a thing!'   CHARLES G. EASTMAN.

Montpelier. Vt.

TO MY CIGAR.

COME to my lips, my brown cigar!
   And while, in circling train,
Thy puffs cerulean slowly curl
   Around my busy brain,
Bring to my mind, as thou hast often brought,
     Some pensive thought.

With careful art the maker's hand
   Hath formed and fashioned thee;
' Wrapper' without, ' filler' within,
   A two-fold unity;
And slowly, like an old gray-hooded friar,
     On creeps thy fire.

Not for thyself thy balmy leaves
   Were thus together laid,
Nor was the glowing coal for thee,
   But thou for it wast made;
My breath still draws thy silent fire aright,
     And keeps thee bright.

And as the red slow-moving line
   Creeps up along thy side,
Thy ashes sinking down to earth
   Or mingling with the tide,
Aloft I see thy pure aroma rise,
     To seek the skies!

Yet perish not, my brown cigar,
   Nor end in smoke alone,
But show me, in thy brief career,
   An image of my own:
So shall thy fragrant memory still live on
     When thou art gone.

With wondrous art my MAKER's hand
   Hath formed and fashioned me,
Body without, and soul within,
   A mystic unity;
And in me burns, to purge each gross desire,
     A Holy Fire.

Not for my earthly self was I
   With this my body clad,
Nor was that holy flame for me,
   But I for it, was made;
His breath still draws the sacred fire, His light
     Still keeps it bright.

LORD! while within my mortal part
   Thy heavenly fire is burning;
Ashes to ashes, earth to earth,
   And dust to dust returning;
Still homeward let the ethereal Spirit rise,
     And find the skies!

Burlington, September, 1846.   J. H. BROWN.

𝕮𝖌𝖞𝖕𝖙𝖎𝖆𝖓 𝕷𝖊𝖙𝖙𝖊𝖗𝖘.

ADDRESS.

MANY authors present their works to 'The Reader,' or in softer terms, to 'The Gentle Reader,' to the 'Candid Reader,' others to 'The Public.' I shall not follow this method of making myself known, neither shall I adopt the formal rule of Queen VICTORIA, and say, 'My Lords and Gentlemen;' but I make my approaches by commencing with the terms of

LADIES AND GENTLEMEN:

THESE letters I address to you because you form the public, and the apellations I here give are smoother, besides being more in accordance with the mode of address among us. I desire however you will not imagine that I am about to write a formal dedication; such is not my intention. These letters are derived from you, and in making them public I only render back what you have been pleased to lend. You have freely given the materials, and now that the work is put into shape, the whole is presented in this form that you may behold as in a glass your own thoughts and words. If I do not propose to flatter you by a studied dedication, much less do I intend to inflict upon you a dry preface; but I do mean to converse with you concerning these letters, for which purpose I request you will allow me to talk in the familiar way in which you often indulge me.

Many persons in New-York remember to have seen a foreigner walk leisurely about in the streets with his hands behind him, looking in all directions as if to spy out something new; and this being so novel a sight it did not fail to attract much attention. This same foreigner was clothed in what we call a Turkish dress; but as we give the name of Turk to all people of the East, he might have been an Egyptian or an Arabian, or even an African, saving the color. A flowing robe, a large beard, a turban and a pipe are sufficient to show that this man is not of *this* our world; and as the person in question bore all these external signs, it can hardly be doubted that he was ABD' ALLAH OMAR, the author of these letters. I said this person or some one like him was often seen loitering in the streets; indeed, if he had been properly dressed, and a Christian, we should have viewed him as a 'loafer,' whose company it were best to shun. But it is not in the streets alone so strange a looking being is to be found; a man answering to his description kept a small shop in the upper part of Broadway, near Prince-street, where he might be seen daily, surrounded by essences, pipes, smoking-tobacco and a thousand articles made to give much enjoyment to one individual and much annoyance to many others. But I am far from asserting that this was our man; indeed I feel pretty sure he was not the same. There also appeared occasionally at evening parties, even among the 'upper ten thousand,' another person with an outlandish face and singular costume, who was an object of much attention. He was a sedate personage, more given to listen than to talk, with sandals on his feet, a profusion of beard on his face, and who was looked upon as being altogether very harmless; so that any thing might be said of him and to him without fear of its going farther. The ladies in particular treated him with great regard, not only on account of his well-trimmed beard, which all like to see, but also for his white teeth and bright black eyes. They were pleased with his unassuming manners, never interrupting them in conversation; and then, being from the land of the Pharaohs, his remarks threw so much light on scripture history! Indeed there were those who thought some of the prophecies (I do not recollect which) were fulfilled in his person. They were unreserved in their intercourse for all these reasons; beside, not being a Christian, any thing he should repeat would never be believed, it being a characteristic of Christians alone always to speak truth.

Notwithstanding Abd' Allah (we may as well give the true name) was a close observer and a person of much discernment, he never could have acquired so intimate a knowledge of our manners, social habits and every thing connected with our society, had he not been aided by a friend whom he chooses to call 'the man with a white cravat.' He could not have made choice of a better counsellor; yet why he should address himself to a man with a white cravat and suppose this to be a sign of wisdom, I am unable to imagine; for of the three hundred thousand and upward of bipeds in this great city who lie every night in a horizontal position, with night-caps on their heads, how few there are who, when they rise in the morning, put on white cravats, and of this number, how few of them are wise! I know several who are possessed of very little worldly wisdom. Be this as it may, it appears from the remarks made by this individual in various parts of these letters that he was one well calculated to enlighten Abd' Allah, not only on many points which to him must have seemed dark, but likewise to have had the power of giving much wholesome advice. It was my good fortune to have a slight acquaintance with a person answering to this description; it might be the same, and I may as well, now that I am upon the subject, give out all I know. I will merely observe that the white-cravatted man to whom I allude was a person in years, of a calm temperament, much gifted with the talent of silence, yet willing to talk when necessary; one who had seen much of the world, both at home and abroad; who had tasted of its joys, and had been made to swallow a few of the nauseous drafts administered to human sufferers in the shape of crosses, vicissitudes, reverses and afflictions, which by moral physicians are prescribed as strengthening plasters for character. He was not what is called a 'smart man,' for he meditated too much, and what he had acquired of experience was more directed to regulate his conduct than to increase his fortune. This lowered him in the opinion of the world, but raised him in his own estimation. He was gentle in manners, not quick of speech nor loud when he did speak. He was far from being exempt from faults, some of which were striking; he was capricious; so much so, that when he formed an acquaintance with a person who was not according to his taste, he would shun him, or treat him with so much marked respect as to show he did not respect him at all. This made him at times appear formal, and gave him what the Scotch call a *prigmidenty* air; then he had a good deal of pride; but as this was more hurtful to himself than to others it is not necessary to dwell upon it, especially as he was poor. People said it kept him down; he had a notion it held him up. He was looked upon as a good sort of man, was treated civilly, but as one whose judgment could not be depended upon, being without fortune. I might mention other traits of his character, but it would be taxing too much the patience of my readers to listen to more. Suffice it to say, he was gray-headed, never could be brought to sign a temperance pledge, had a mortal aversion to anthracite coal, contented himself with quietly floating down the stream of time, wore a flannel waistcoat all the year round, beside an outside coat in winter; and when Morris's thermometer marked ninety degrees in the shade, preserved an even temper and perspired freely.

Having given a sketch of the characters of the author and assistant author of these letters, it remains that I say something of the letters themselves, as well as of the manner by which they fell into my hands. They were written at intervals of leisure whenever topics occurred to Abd' Allah's mind. When he came home from a tour of observation it was his custom to make his ablutions, smooth his beard, light his pipe and sit down to meditate on whatever he had seen or heard. After a good deal of hard thinking and much harder smoking, his thoughts would become composed, and he would forthwith indite. If it be asked how he could acquire so intimate a knowledge of our ways, I reply that we are a very social people; that when we see a person, especially if he be a foreigner, who pleases by his appearance, manner and general aspect, we receive him with cordiality, bring him into our family circles, and soon let him into the heart of the mysteries of our domestic life. Several of the letters give an insight into the manner our author was treated, with the facilities afforded him for obtaining as thorough a knowledge of our character as if he had been 'one of the oldest inhabitants.'

An objection may be raised against these letters, that notwithstanding the facilities granted to their author, he could not have lived long enough among us to learn our customs and early training, so as to give him a warrant to cast an indirect censure on our manners and habits. This being done in a pleasant way does not the less sensibly inflict a wound upon our self-love. To this it may be replied, that a looker-on often sees more than those who play the game; and if the faults in question are glaring, and such as on a comparison with the customs of other enlighted countries are at variance with the rule of right as established by long experience, they should be brought to notice in such terms as may best tend to correct them. If he has followed nature in drawing his portraits, we have no right to complain; and if he gives to them too high a coloring, we can only object to his want of taste, but not to his judgment as a painter. Much of this objection is matter of opinion. The picture may not be displeasing to those who are not touched by its application, while those who think they see their own likeness may efface the impression by correcting the faults it is meant to portray. Those who undertake to write should endeavor to instruct; and if our author insinuates truth while he amuses his readers, he performs a meritorious act, and should be thanked for trying to make them better, even although it be done by stealth. While bestowing implied censure, he has not been sparing of praise when praise was merited, well knowing what is said by a learned Englishman : ' Praise is the reflection of virtue, and if it be bestowed by persons of quality and judgment, it filleth all round about and will not easily away; for the odors of ointments are more durable than those of flowers.'

You, my friends, fair and foul, whom I now address, may look upon this reasoning as being more plausible than solid, and may think I have no right thus to screen Abd' Allah from the charge of asserting more than he could possibly know. To speak truth, (to which, by-the-by, I am a perfect slave,) and to have a hold on your favor, I will confess myself not entirely a convert to the arguments I think it advisable to use, and will make amends so far as the case will admit.

The letters are evidently the production of a black-bearded Moslem, aided and abetted by a white cravatted Christian; yet the black beard predominates, as is apparent by the unfair remarks made on certain of our customs and habits. No American, an ardent lover of his country, would ever think of so unjustly accusing us of vanity, a fault unknown among us, or of our fondness for place and titles; two of the last things we ever covet. No Christian would speak so disparagingly of our social intercourse, of our admirable method of bringing up young ladies and young gentlemen. These are clearly the remarks of an observer less careful than he pretends to be, are fully refuted by truth, and should not wound your sensibility, but rather warm you into pity for the ignorance of a stranger and a Mohammedan. I recommend to you to slide over lightly the letters which are so objectionable, and take up others that will make a better return for the labor of perusal. Several others are evidently the production of one who has reflected much; and although you may at first think them dry and prosy, yet they offer good materials for thinking. On the whole they are a novelty; and as we all hunt after new things, or even take old things, provided they are presented to us in a new dress, it is probable they will be read by many, young as well as old.

In order to comprehend the dates Abd' Allah has affixed to his letters, it should be mentioned that the Mohammedan calendar commences at the year of the Hegira, or flight of Mohammed, answering to the year 622 of the Christian era. The Hegira dates from the sixteenth day of July, and the Mohammedan months are lunar;

making three hundred and fifty-four days to the year. This makes a difference of one year in thirty-three; wherefore, to find the corresponding date of the Christian era, substract from the Mohammedan years one for every thirty-three years, and add thereto six hundred and twenty-two years. In this way 1260 of the Hegira gives 1844 of the Christian era, and the moon Regel, the date of the first letter, corresponds with our month of January.

It is in my power to say that the translation is most faithfully done. In the originals the modern Arabic character is preserved, and contrary to custom among Arabian scholars, the vowel points are brought in and distinctly marked. This has greatly facilitated my labor; and having collated the translation with great care, the reader may rely upon the letters which are now presented·as being an exact transcript of the author's thoughts.

I believe every thing has been said that is necessary to make known the real author of these letters, and to induce you to read them. One thing is still needed, however, which is the manner these epistles fell into my hands. This is a matter on which I know your curiosity is greatly excited; and as it is yet a profound secret, I am determined not to divulge it till I write a preface.

I am, Ladies and Gentlemen, with a decided partiality for the one, and a decent respect for the other;

Your faithful friend,

New-York, November, 1846.   —   MATHEW MARKWELL.

Letter First.

FROM ABD'ALLAH OMAR, TO SEYD AHMMAD EL RAJI, CHIEF SECRETARY OF THE OKADEE AT CAIRO.

You, who have been my companion and friend during so many years, know the ardent desire I ever felt to travel into this new country, and may remember that I often expressed to you, while we pursued our studies together, my intention to avail myself of the first occasion that should present, to carry my wishes into effect.

When according to the recently established rule of our Pacha Mohammed Ali, (whose name be praised!) a number of us were selected to be sent to Europe, there to acquire a more profound knowledge of the arts and sciences than is taught at home, I felt my desire revive, with a willingness to forego all the pleasures the society of the old world could bestow, for the novelty of being the first Egyptian who wandered to a region so much talked of and known to him only in story. I besought our ruler to change my destination, and I cannot describe to you how great was my joy when yielding to my earnest entreaties, supported by your active friendship, he gave me permission to visit the far distant land of America. You know that I lost no time in preparation, but commenced the voyage without delay; and, praise be to Allah! I am here in safety, though in the midst of the profane.

How shall I convey to you, my dear Ahhmad, my sensations on finding myself on the unfathomable deep; the broad expanse of waters which seemed to be without bounds! All around was one great circle, in the centre of which we seemed to be placed, and although continually advancing, the end appeared still at the same distance, with no object in view where our laboring ship could find rest. And then the wonderful ocean, ever agitated even when the surface was calm, and when ruffled by winds, how awful, how grand! The voyage from Alexandria to the mouth of the Mediterranean, gave me an idea of the sea, yet how faint was it compared with the reality presented by the broad sheet of the Atlantic! The sight was often beautiful. The white swelling sails, the taper masts towering to the skies, each rope braced to its proper place, every thing about the ship in fair proportion to make her buoyant or aid her speed; all to me was new, and filled me with constant delight.

Even a gale with all the fear it awakens brought with it the charm of a newly-raised emotion, and created in me a mixed feeling of pleasure and awe which our poets liken to the sublime. Our ship might be called a moving dwelling, for it was provided with every article that is seen in an abode on land and furnished with every material that could minister to comfort. The same regularity of meals and hours of rest were observed as on shore, and time was passed in watching the progress of the vessel, in agreeable conversation, or in light games of hazard, where the passengers played only for enough to excite an interest.

In this way the voyage seemed short, yet when the cry of land first broke upon my ear my heart leaped for joy. The sea is not the natural element of man, and every hour passed thereon by one whose habits fix him to the earth is so much taken from the sum of his accustomed enjoyment. Judge then of my delight when I set my foot on land!

I am here among a people who seem kindly disposed, yet their ways are strange; they not only do not follow the precepts of our holy law, but rather contemn them. My first duty on landing was to render thanks to Allah through our holy Prophet (God favor him!) for his watchful care of me while on the deep, accompanied by a humble hope that he would still have me in his holy keeping.

I had learned on ship board the points of the compass, and my pocket dial gave me the time of the *'Asr* (the hour of prayer.) After making my ablutions as our law directs, when with my shoes off I stood on my feet, my face turned toward Ckib'leh, (Mecca) my two hands open and my thumbs touching the lobes of my ears; would you believe it, oh! Ahhmad! they laughed. May our holy prophet enlighten them!

Although I am come at a season of the year when cold gives to the country a withered aspect, yet I see enough even in its wintry dress to convince me it must be lovely in its summer apparel. This is a great city; larger than Cairo or Alexandria, lying at the confluence of two great rivers which are filled with ships, whose forest of masts soar to the heavens, and with smaller craft that are constantly skimming the water like the flight of birds. In the upper part of the town the streets are spacious, and the houses are numerous and of immense size when compared with our dwellings. And then the concourse of people is exceedingly great. What struck me with astonishment was to see a multitude of females gaily dressed, walking to and fro with the utmost freedom without attendants, and unveiled. They greeted me with smiles as I passed. I cannot describe to you the pleasure I felt at being so kindly received, nor how grateful I am that they should take so great pains to adorn their persons with the design of giving welcome to one whose name even they could not know. Many of them possessed dazzling beauty, which forced me to exclaim mentally, if of the seventy-two wives, which as one of the faithful I am to have in Paradise, *one* only should be as lovely as these. I would humbly thank the prophet for his bounty, and relinquish the remaining seventy-one without a murmur.

Flattered as I am by these outward marks of regard, I cannot conceal from you, dear Ahhmad, that I have much anxiety for myself when I think of the immense distance that separates me from my parents, kindred and all I hold most dear, and that I should thus place myself out of reach of their aid in case I should fall into distress. I resign myself to the guidance of Allah, while I cherish as a relief from all earthly troubles the persuasion that your kind sympathy will ever be alive to sooth my pains.

New-York, 13th day of the Moon Regeb,
Year of the Hegira, 1260.

Letter Second.

FROM THE SAME TO THE SAME.

EDUCATION is widely diffused over this country, yet rarely do you meet with what may be called a full educated person, one of deep research, a profound student, in short one of erudition; and of polite belles-lettres scholars the number is still smaller. This is not surprising, for here in a new country all that seems necessary is to give a youth so much instruction as shall enable him to make his way through life; any thing beyond this is left for him to find, as it becomes essential in his progress. He is brought up to depend upon his own exertions, mental or physical, for a livelihood, and on his own merit for performent; consequently polished manners and refined literature are neglected, it being merely sufficient that he know enough to secure the one and give him an equal chance with his fellows to obtain the other. I do not undertake to say that, under the circumstances in which these people are placed, it is not the best course that can be adopted. Men of the closet are not needed where woods are to be cleared, cities to be built and institutions to be formed, but rather those made of coarser materials, who have just knowledge enough to lay the foundation, leaving the superstructure to be embellished by the art and science of their more polished successors. Those whose means of support are derived solely from their own personal labors have not leisure to bestow on the studies requisite to form a learned man, neither can they pass years of foreign travel, to become refined, and wear off those local prejudices, which home keeping youths always retain; still less can they mingle so much with strangers as to strengthen their own minds by bringing them into contact with those of others. There are instances where this is done, but they are few, and the effect is partial.

Farther : the condition of a young man educated to be a person of refined literature, without a profession, is by no means enviable in this country. Admitting that he is possessed of fortune, by which his mind is relieved from the cares of business, and has abundant opportunity to keep up his knowledge of art, science or literature, yet he finds himself an isolated being. In a country like this, where all are employed, and that actively too, he can have no associates, no congenial spirits to commune with ; no exercise for the knowledge he has acquired, for it is not adapted to the society in which his lot is cast. In this state of existence his animal spirits decline from want of excitement, his faculties become sluggish for want of exertion, and he is apt to fall into irregular habits as a relief from ennui. This result is not universal, but yet sufficiently general to cause it to be cited as a rule. Hence America has few learned men, but she has what serves her present purpose better, many wise ones.

In all the large cities schools are numerous, and they are to be found in remote regions where the population is thin and the means of maintaining them very limited ; yet it is not to these alone that the Americans are indebted for their knowledge. These establishments are of the highest utility as a means of developing the faculties, and showing forth the innate qualities which are afterward to be moulded to useful ends. Fertility of soil is not discovered till the earth is moved, and the elements of fruitfulness contained within its bosom are thrown out to give activity to vegetation. In like manner the qualities of the mind lie dormant till they are stimulated; then instruction comes to direct them to proper objects, till at last a harvest is gathered in the enlargement of the understanding.

The elementary knowledge gained in schools is moderate compared with the benefit they impart by training the mind to look into itself, and by teaching it to fix itself on subjects which can be learned only by study.

But the real foundation of the American character is laid in the domestic education children receive from the moment of their birth. This species of education is given here almost exclusively by the mothers, the fathers possessing less of patience, beside being absorbed by their more active duties abroad. Mothers possess a stronger hold on the child's affections, and it is by these the system of moral culture is quickened. They are also able by their position sooner to see the child's early propensities, and for the same reason are more capable of giving them a proper direction. It is moreover not to be doubted that much of mental acuteness is derived from the greater or less degree of physical sensibility with which the child is endowed, and these are soonest made apparent to the one who is nearest and ever on the watch to notice each of the child's habitual motions. And a woman of an ordinary understanding of her own, when attentive to correct whatever is defective in these movements, is unknowingly performing an act which will most effectually discipline her child's intellectual powers.

I read in the Koran of the Christians, that the ancient Hebrews instructed their children solely by the precepts laid down in the written law, and I learn from more modern history that the children of Sparta were taught by a system so purely local as to render advancement impossible, and which kept society always in the same state. These systems would now be found defective ; a proof that they are so, exists in the low state of education in our own country. You know of the attempt making at Cairo to give general knowledge by the teaching at Mosque El-Azhar, yet learning is there so much fettered by religion as to deprive it of much of its real benefit, and much that is there taught is so superficial of its kind as to prevent us having scientific men ; and as to persons of literary acquirements there are none.

Notwithstanding the Arabs gave to the world the first knowledge of mathematics and astronomy, their descendants, the Egyptians, are wholly unskilled in these branches of learning. Alchymy is more studied than chemistry, and astrology more than astronomy ; while those who are so unfortunate as to be afflicted by illness are forced to resort for medical aid to barbers, who are alike ignorant of the healing art and unskilful in practice.

America is not hampered by old systems, but is free to create any new method that may soonest advance her rising generation. Instruction keeps pace with the wants of society; this is evident by seeing persons taken from all classes of the community to fill places of honor or trust, who if they do not rise to distinction, do not bring upon themselves disgrace by ignorance of the duties they are called upon to perform.

The freedom of thought and action which prevails gives a wholesome self-confidence, which is controlled by gentle laws, while the early impressions are invariably good, being derived from the moral culture given by the females, who are ardently fond of their offspring, and who though indulgent, often to excess, yet ever instil into their minds sound precepts, and what is more, hold forth to them a bright example of maternal virtues.

New-York, 16th day of the Moon Regeb, }
   Year of the Hegira, 1206. }

                    Letter Third.

                 FROM THE SAME TO THE SAME.

THEY have in this country a way of disposing of their female offspring which is quite singular, and to us in Cairo would be diverting. The care of bringing up daughters devolves entirely on the mother; the father has merely to pay the bills for the child's tuition, or for the adornment of her person, even if these should sometimes be raised to a point beyond what he can afford to bear. At the age of fourteen or fifteen the child is looked upon as a young lady ; goes to school or makes visits alone ; and, what to all rational people is highly improper, may appear abroad without a *tashmak*, (veil,) particularly if she be pretty. While pursuing her studies she is allowed intercourse with male youths of her own age, for the laudable purpose of early acquiring a practical knowledge of easy manners. This is called ' mutual instruction,' a system of education highly prized in this country. Indeed the advantages derived from it are soon made evident, for the damsel learns from her youthful companion a thousand things not laid down in her books, and avoids injuring her health by too close application to her lessons while at school; beside this, her mind is not so much burdened with learning as to render her pedantic, and remains free to imbibe a great number of new impressions, which fit her to converse without reserve on a variety of topics all at the same time, with like knowledge of each.

When the young lady has passed a certain number of years at school, her education is supposed to be complete, for instruction is measured by time, not by acquirements; she is then what is called *brought out*. This is done by dressing her in rich apparel and carrying her from house to house for the purpose of making her more fully known; when the acquaintances of the family generally make an evening festival out of respect to the parents and as a compliment to the newly-initiated member. This being done, another process is adopted, which is to send the young lady forth alone into the public walks that she may be seen by those who were unbidden to the evening festival. At this period of her career a sudden change takes place in her personal appearance : from being a slender girl with a modest down-cast look, she is at once transformed into a self-confident woman, and by a process I cannot discover, her person becomes suddenly inflated in a manner quite painful to behold. ' Why this should occur at this particular period, when the young lady should appear with all the charms Nature has bestowed upon her, is not easy to say, and I confess my pity is always greatly moved at seeing this unaccountable and sudden disfiguring of a beautiful person. But my pity is thrown away, for I find it in no way affects the lady's health or diminishes her enjoyments. Her animal spirits seem unabated, and she moves and dances with as much vigor as she did before this irruption appeared.

On inquiry of one of my friends, he told me this change of shape was produced by artificial means known only to the mothers, the intention of it being to give an outward sign that the damsel is marriageable. This strikes me as a novel method for the purpose, but I now remember to have read that something of the kind is observable at the Cape of Good Hope, but there the Venuses of the country exhibit the solid flesh they are born with, while the belles of this country use artificial means to produce the same end.

This people are wonderfully inventive, and the beauties that Nature denies are quickly supplied by the skill of art. What increases my wonder is to see the effect this change of shape produces on the other sex. You will hardly believe it, but the young candidates for wives are greatly pleased with the display of this deformity, and from admirers are soon formed into ardent lovers merely by looking, not at the face, but at other parts of the person. This strange custom has exercised my mind not only to discover if possible its origin but its use ; and after much reflection I have arrived at the conclusion that the procedure is attended by many advantages which to strangers do not appear at first view. It renders less essential beauty of countenance or strength of mind, one being seldom viewed, and the other not being requisite to be brought forth. We are all slaves of habit, and in this case the force of it is so great that a lover's passion is ruled by the sight, not by his understanding or heart; and if he perceives that the object of his new flame is ample in dimensions, he need give no scope to his imagination, but yield himself at once to the attraction, not of the countenance, which is the index of the mind, but to the parts of the person developed especially for the purpose of drawing his regard. It appears to me that this must be mainly the motive for changing the female form at a particular period of life, for it will hardly be imagined the mammas would encourage, or the young lady's tolerate, this burden, were it not that the other sex behold it with pleasure, and feel their ardor enkindled by the influence of this newly-discovered magnetic power.

The account here given is derived from my own observation, and from the testimony of a friend on whose knowledge I place the fullest reliance. It will amuse you and our social circle at Cairo, as describing a singular custom of a strange people, and may be added as an interesting note in your elaborate work on human physiology.

I have formerly written on the subject of the dress of females, which is here gorgeous in costly silks and rich ornaments. Yet many things are wanted to increase their personal charms. Some few use cosmetics for the face, and others slightly color the eye-brows, but they do not, like our lovely sisters of Cairo, draw a circle of *khot* beneath the eye, neither are they sufficiently advanced in taste to employ *Hhennah*, which gives so beautiful a yellow tinge to the nails of the hand and feet.

None ever wear the *khizam* (nose-ring) and I have not yet seen a damsel with the *khoolkhal* (anklets), that charming ornament, the sound alone of which awakens so many delightful emotions :

> ' The ringing of thine anklets hath deprived me of my reason, O moon !'

is the ardent exclamation of one of our amatory poets.

I wonder much that both these ornaments are not worn, seeing they made a part of female attire in very ancient times, as is mentioned in many passages of the Hebrew books from which the Christians derive their law ; but custom and taste change with time, and in a new country with a climate differing much from that of the East, it cannot be expected the same fashions will prevail. We are all creatures made variable by many external causes, not only as regards our taste, but also our understanding ; not so the heart, for if I know my own, neither time nor distance can diminish its warmth for you, my dear Ahhmad.

New-York, 21st day of the Moon Regeb,
Year of the Hegira, 1260.

𝕷etter 𝕱ourth.

FROM THE SAME TO THE SAME.

WHEN a stranger in a strange land becomes partially acquainted with the inhabitants, the first object of his attention is the society he is about to associate with, to the end that, studying the manners of the people, he may acquire a knowledge of their character, and learn in what way he shall so conduct himself as to gain their favor. This is done as well to render himself a welcome guest to his new friends, as to observe, in a philosophic spirit, the causes that produce different modes of action in a new country, among a people not strictly new, but with many peculiarities of thought.

The term ' society,' in its enlarged sense, means an association of individuals created for the purpose of self-defence, or of forming a government of laws, or of doing certain things essential to their happiness which can be better done by several persons united toge- ther than it can be by individuals separately; in its limited sense the term means the social intercourse subsisting between individu- als of a community already formed. I believe this is what is called ' society;' yet I desire you would not imagine that because the defi- nition is laid down with so much apparent gravity, I intend to give a treatise on all the stages man passes through from the day he puts on a shirt for the first time to that when he puts on the full dress of a civilized being and congregates with others to form what is called an association or society; far from it. I would as soon undertake to discover the origin of evil or perpetual motion. My purpose at present is to hold converse with you on society in its restricted sense, or in more appropriate terms, on social intercourse, as well as I am able to obtain a view of it in New-York, where I now am. I am however obliged to use the word ' society,' as this is the term em- ployed to designate what I am trying to discover and describe to you.

I should say that in this city society has no special form, no marked tone; nothing to give it a distinguishing characteristic. It may be said to be utilitarian, which in truth here means little more than an inordinate love of money, with never-ceasing endeavors to obtain it. The character of a new people of course takes its hue from that of the original settlers, and this it retains till the number of the new generation has greatly increased, and new modes of thought and action are introduced by the creation of new wants and desires. Where the new settlement increases mainly by its own natural means, society is indigenous, and the original manners long keep their hold; but in a community where, exclusive of the natural in- crease, the number is greatly augmented by an accession of new- comers, society takes a tone less exclusive, less local; each stranger brings a habit or custom which becomes in time amalgamated with those of the country, and fails not by the admixture to give a new cast to social intercourse. The customs of the new country lose some of their stiffness when brought into contact with those of the old; and the latter, to promote harmony of social feeling, conform, in a certain degree at least, to the habits already established in the land where they are introduced.

This is the aspect of society as it is now to be seen in New-York. The primitive state has long since disappeared; indeed, the people have passed more than one state to arrive at the present point. Log-huts have given place to elegant mansions of brick or stone; women comb their hair and put on stockings; men shave oftener than once a week, and not only brush but polish their boots. Refinement has crept in, arts and sciences are held in respect and cultivated, while literature is relished and religion is observed under milder forms. Virtue, if not universally practiced, is yet held in honor, and abilities shine forth by the stimulus given to them by new demands upon intellect.

With this improved condition of things, manners and conversation have not kept pace; not for want of intelligence in individuals, but for want of knowledge of the art of enlivening customary intercourse; of giving animation to the habitual routine of life. People are sober in their mirth; almost sadly gay. They think strength of understanding will enliven the spirits; that when the mind is well stored with knowledge bright thoughts will flow, manners become lively, 'sweet talk' will follow, as a matter of course, and all the sensibilities be awakened. But this is a mistaken idea. Good sense and knowledge should be the foundation of all rational discourse, but these alone do not render social commerce bright and pleasing. So far from it, the man of learning only is often very deficient in conversational powers; his mind wants flexibility; he thinks intensely and is wedded to a formal system. The sum of life is made up of little things, and a man who wants to make himself an agreeable companion must know how to turn these little things to good account. More effect may often be produced, in the way of repressing vice or encouraging virtue, by a pleasing tale or a lively jest than by a serious homily; and he who wishes to improve mankind may frequently do it most effectually by touching the heart through the medium of the imagination. Conversation or small talk is an art to be acquired, and one the people of this city do not possess; the reason is, they do not give encouragement to the sensibilities or learn the science of manners, from which spring ease and grace. A very competent judge in such matters has said : 'Il ne faut pas avoir toujours raison pour plaise; il y a une manière d'avoir tort qui est faite pour réussir.' The Prince de Ligne spoke from experience, and by constant practice retained the spring of life even when octogenarian.

In consequence of these deficiencies, the reünions so common here are for the most part very uninteresting; have nothing in them enlivening. Conversation falls upon the common topics of the day, which have already been discussed in the street, and nothing within the house is generated to enliven the fancy, warm the imagination, elicit wit, or give to the social meeting a charm to make one forget for a time the cares of the world. In an assemblage of persons of both sexes, met together for the purpose of passing a few hours in sprightly converse, no one should enter who is unwilling to sympathize with the reigning feeling. We can listen with close attention to the aphorisms of a learned man when delivered in a lecture-room, or receive with awe from the pulpit a lesson of wisdom or rebuke ; but in the gay saloon we look for that noble part of the mind which seems to dwell more in the heart than in the brain, and whose thoughts are feelings. And herein lies the mistake many persons make ; and the reason is apparent why social reünions formed for the purpose of giving and receiving pleasure are formal, monotonous and dull. All can reason well, many can write, but none can talk. Let me see and read of great men ; but for the companion of a convivial hour let me have one with less of learning and more of open heart, more of frank unreserved conversation untramelled by forms, and with mirth that diffuses gladness to all within reach of its influence. Preserve me from the man who is 'looked up to !'

Thus far I have marked the state of society as it shows itself in places where persons assemble to be themselves pleased and to give pleasure to those that surround them. Let me now speak of it as. it appears in the more undisguised form of the domestic hearth. The fire-side is said to be one of the touch-stones of connubial comfort, and he who is admitted to the sanctuary wherein are enshrined the household gods, has bestowed upon him the privilege of viewing life devoid of the many gauds that disfigure it, and has the power of forming a just estimate of character. When an accidental visitor is received with unstudied ease and made at once to feel that far from being an intruder he is welcomed with cordial frankness, he sees every object with a tranquil mind ; he leaps at a bound the space that separated him from intimacy, and enters at once into the heart of the mystery of social life. Here is the place where men and women are to be best known ; where their private habits are brought to view, their modes of thinking thrown out without reserve, and where may be had a thorough insight into all the elements which go to make up the sum of domestic felicity.

The dwelling-houses in New-York are all built of nearly one size, and apportioned within after one plan ; so that if you see the interior of one you can find your way into that of another the first time of admittance. The object in building them in this way is, as I learn, that each person may know how his neighbor lives ; for the dimensions of a house being well known, no one person can receive more company than another ; and thus the system of equality so much dwelt upon and enforced by the laws of the country, is rigidly maintained. One other reason for this uniformity of size is, that the furniture of one house may fit the apartments of another. People occupy a house exactly one year, at the end of which there is a general move. On a given day a family slips out of its abode as quickly as possible and jumps into the premises of a neighbor, who in turn is careful to vacate early that in like manner he may rout out a friend in the next street. In this way families are seen crossing each other in the open air with all their furniture, children, cats, dogs and every thing belonging to them, right hand and left, the first warm day of spring, from morning till night, till they settle down. You may easily imagine therefore, that if the apartments were not of the same dimensions the furniture could not find place in the new abode, and families would be subjected to the expense of alteration and great loss of time before they could feel at home. Whereas, under the prevailing system of building, a change takes place without producing a difference; the sofa finds the same spot, the chairs the same corners; there is a nail for the husband's bootjack, and the cradle finds its accustomed station.

In every house a cell, or as it is called, an apartment, is constructed under ground, in which the husband keeps his wife and children in the day-time, where he takes his meals when at home, and where he passes his evenings. It is not so spacious as our harems, neither is the air in it so pure; yet it is what is called 'comfortable.' The rest of the house, with the exception of a chamber or two for sleeping, is filled with handsome furniture, but closed up from sight. This is one way of obtaining distinction, inasmuch as a person who inhabits a large mansion, well-furnished, is at once reputed to be very rich; although if the truth were known he may be obliged to live with great frugality in the cell. The occupant, however, to keep up the impression, opens his whole house three or four times a year to let his riches be seen, and to confirm people in the opinion of his wealth.

The cell is the sanctum of connubial life, and he who is admitted within may feel as if he were a favored person; one whom the inmates delight to honor. And here it is that I am able to acquire some ideas of the domestic habits of this singular people. This quiet unpretending place of meeting is much more agreeable than the assembly of large numbers where there is a studied effort to be witty or gay. The minds of the husband and wife are *en déshabille*, and their conversation, often marked by good sense, is rendered pleasing by a free expression of their thoughts; while their manners being no longer under the tutelage of fashion, whatever they know, whatever new emotion the conversation may create, or whatever sentiment the moment may render audible, are all thrown out with careless frankness, which shows that social enjoyment is not to be sought in crowded assemblies, but is to be found in a retired spot ' where two or three are gathered together.'

It must not be concealed from you that at times the conversation will take a turn about Mr. Tibbs' party; how such and such persons looked; what they said, and how well or ill they behaved; who was *he* and what was *she* that they should hold their heads so high? etc. This, however, less from jealousy than petty rivalry, yet neither with rancor. These little deviations from a straight line find place in all circles, and the society of New-York is not exempt entirely, though it is more common in Europe than in this country, where so much equality of condition exists among the inhabitants.

Nevertheless, an evening passed in the cell is generally a pleasant one. The husband may sometimes fall into the topic of business

he feels most interest in, but he is often brought back to a more en-
livening theme by the superior power of conversation of the wife,
who can temper his gravity by imparting her stock of knowledge in
a more agreeable form.   By this friendly intercourse I am enabled
to become acquainted with the disposition of the inhabitants indi-
vidually; and by continual observation, with proper allowances
and comparisons, I have attained to a pretty thorough knowledge
of the whole.

New-York, 28th day of the Moon Regeb, Hegira, 1260.

EVENING ON THE SEA-SHORE,

BY JOSEPH W. BENNETT.

'T was a glorious vision! the long summer's day
  Like a dolphin was dying in crimson and gold;
While before me in splendor the broad ocean lay,
  And a rainbow hung over each wave as it roll'd.

There were voices like spirits that sung in the breeze,
  A loud solemn anthem arose from the shore,
And the rocks gave responses, and murmur'd the trees,
  As though Nature in vespers her GOD would adore.

Like the shield of JEHOVAH, all lambent with flame,
  From his cloud-halo'd portal the setting sun shone,
Till the earth, sky and water in glory became
  Like the steps which the angels ascend to His throne.

On the hill-tops, like altars that tower'd in the air,
  The last rosy flashes of evening delayed;
'T was a fanciful thought that the Ghebres were there,
  Relighting the fires in their temples decayed.

Now passing away like a beautiful dream,
  Tint by tint from the landscape in darkness withdrew,
And crossing the wave with a tremulous beam,
  The moon mid her maidens smiled down from the blue.

Where a sycamore's canopy reel'd to the blast,
  On a low rustic bench that look'd over the tide,
(Oh! would that such moments forever might last!)
  I sat with the gentlest of friends by my side.

'T were folly such sweetness and worth to compare
  With a fabulous VENUS just born from the sea,
Or to boast of an angel commissioned to bear
  To this Patmos a new inspiration for me.

For lovelier far is the beauty that glows
  On the brow of a being who tenderly feels,
And link'd to mortality's pleasures or woes,
  Can lament as she chides us and smile as she heals.

O'er the silver-tipt billows the white swelling sail,
  Dimly seen through the shadows that stretched from the shore,
Came silently winging along with the gale,
  Like the SPIRIT that moved on the waters of yore.

And far, far away on the verge of the deep,
  Now hidden in vapor, now gorgeously bright,
Like meteor pleasures that leave us to weep,
  ' The light-house fire' dazzled, then vanish'd in night.

Lone fugitive mentor! alas! in thy ray,
  Was a warning that told me how soon I must sever
From a scene where the blessed might ask for delay,
  And Time fold his pinions to slumber forever.

It is gone; but that hour I can never forget,
  E'en when life shall expire like that spark on the main;
But the soul, disenthralled from the pangs of regret,
  In Heaven shall seek for its transports again.

A DAY AT RHODOS.

'DEINDE Rhodum appropinquamus, ubi tanta est viriditas arborum atque amœnitas locorum, quod est mirabile ad videndum et prosertim Paradisum a Florentiois factum.
                                                    CHRIST. BUODELMONTE. FLORENT.

MANY travellers have compared the chivalresque buildings at Rhodos with the gigantic palaces of Florence or Sienna, which resemble strong castles defended by keeps, towers and battlements. This appears to me to be an erroneous comparison, and according to my opinion the Street of the Knights is more like a dark, narrow avenue in an ancient German city, such as Nurnberg or Ratisbon. The houses at Rhodos are rather small and low; they have only two stories. The by-lanes are very narrow, dark, and every where supported by vaults and arches, in order to resist the violent earthquakes from which the island of Rhodos frequently suffers. In general it appears, that the religious knights during the fourteenth and fifteenth centuries carried on a more secluded and monastic life, than their successors at a later period at Malta.

Many armorial bearings of the proudest names, that are glittering in the history of the order may still be seen on the ancient palaces. Thus we remarked on the left, at the entrance of the street, the escutcheon of Fabrizio di Caretti, the noble Italian, who with the most brilliant courage defended the tower of St. Nicolaos during the first siege of the Osmanlis in A. D. 1480, and afterward was elected Grand Master. (1513 — 1521.)

On the right you meet the arms of Villiers de l'Isle d'Adam, d'Amboise and Mont-Begon. Then follows the great auberge of the French tongue, with the lilies and the well known device ' Montjoie Saint Denys,' the battle-cry of the French warriors in the combat. Above the arms stands the date, 1495. Farther up the street appears the escutcheon of the excellent Pierre d'Aubusson, quartered with the cardinal's hat. Now follow the mansions of other French and English knights, such as Clermont de Nesle, de Touars, de Cheron, de Lastic, de Bourbon,* and the Spanish, Portuguese and English hotels, the latter representing the three lions and lilies. The knights from Auvergne and Provence had their quarters at the upper end of the street, and we recognized here the arms of de Castro, de Montpensier et Roger de Pins. Through a Gothic arch crossing the road we went to the palace of the Grand Masters, which like an extensive and strong castle is surrounded by massive towers, and rests on the outer wall of the city. It is now a mere ruin, but earlier travellers describe it, as a magnificent building in the stern and austere style of the middle ages, and the interior is said to have surpassed the most renowned baronial castles in Germany or England, as to the splendor and romantic beauty of its interior courts, stair-cases, halls, armory and other apartments. The principal entrance is still embellished with the arms of the order, and many others of private knights are seen on the two turrets of the eastern wing. It now forms part of the harem of the Turkish commandant of the fortress, and we therefore could not get any permission to visit its precincts ; but an aged Turk offered to take us to the Church of St. John the Baptist, lying nearly opposite. On the surrender of the city, the Turks triumphantly plundered and destroyed all its ornaments and converted it to a Mohammedan mosque, though it appears to be quite abandoned at present. The principal aisle is formed by eight fine clusters of slender Gothic columns ; four others surround the high altar. On the pavement are seen remains of the sepulchral monument of the brave Fabrizio di Caretti, the last Grand Master who died in the island.

We now descended to the lower town and made some purchases in the Baazar, which on that day was found rather still and deserted, all the Greeks and Jews being busily employed with the Christian pilgrims in the harbor. Part of our company then returned on board the steamer, while I proposed to some friends, who took a particular interest in the history of Rhodos, to investigate more at leisure the famous field of battle of the Christian heroes during both the memorable sieges, and then to make an excursion to the Greek villages in the orange grove. But how were we to procure horses in such a hurry ? Some pale and starving Jews, who had followed us like our shadow, offered to furnish us with saddled mules, and we ordered them to wait for us at the Athanasian gate, formerly called 'Porta di Santa Maria della Vittoria,' whence the road ascends to the delightful Rhodini in the rose-gardens, while we in the mean time continued our wanderings along the glacis of the fortress. We therefore returned to the castle, and on the west side proceeded to the Ambrosian gate through a low passage, enclosed

---

* PERHAPS the author of the eloquent and spirited description of the second siege by the Turks in 1522.

by high and massive ramparts. In this place the walls of large squared free-stones, the deep moat, cut out in the solid rock, the advanced ravelins and out-works uniting with the principal city-wall by means of a draw-bridge, give the plain evidence, that these accumulated fortifications, which were still strengthened by the numerous cannon of the palace of the Grand Masters, formed the key to the whole defensive system of the city. Here at the Ambrosian gate, on the towers of the castle, the knights of the German tongue, led on by the Tyrolese Christoph Waldener, gloriously defended their station against the thousands of storming Turks during the last siege of 1522.[*] Their brave commander fell; but being supported by the French knights on their right, and by those from Auvergne on their left, they victoriously repelled all the repeated attacks of the enemy.

The gate, with its armorial bearings and crosses, is quite preserved. Every where we saw traces of the war. Marble balls of immense magnitude and burst falconets lie still dispersed here and there in the ditches, partly filled with rubbish, and by a wooden bridge we at last arrived on the sloping bank or glacis, outside the fortress. The eye now meets with numberless Mohammedan tombs, with small marble columns, surmounted by a roughly-carved turban, and sometimes having a gilt inscription. The sepulchres stand by thousands around the fortress, just as if they were to exhibit to posterity a monument of the prodigious loss of human life which this conquest had cost the Sultan. In Constantinople and Smyrna the Mohammedan burial-grounds are planted with thickets of sombre cypresses, and constitute the favorite walks of the gloomy and musing Turkish inhabitants. At Rhodos, on the sun-burnt, rocky level, are seen only a few straggling olive-trees or some shrubs of vitex agnus castus, here and there overshadowing a tomb; but at a distance the dreary landscape is relieved by the pretty villages Epanomaras and Turkambelas arising from out the luxuriant vineyards and orange-groves.

From the Ambrosian gate[†] the road runs south-west for more than four miles through gardens and olive plantations to the swamp, where according to tradition, the young Knight Deodat de Gozon from Provence, in the year 1342, in a dangerous combat killed a serpent or crocodile, which for a long time had been the terror of the inhabitants and flocks of the neighborhood. It is generally supposed that an egg of a crocodile had been transported with the ballast of a vessel from the banks of the Nile in Egypt, and had developed itself to the monster mentioned in the history of Rhodos. Already in antiquity huge serpents were frequent there, and the oldest name of the island was Ophis.

Three miles farther on arises the mountain Phileremos, where ruins still are seen of Jalysos, one of the most ancient Doric cities

---

[*] A PORTA Ambrosiana ad portam usque divo GEORGIO sacram, infractum robur Equitum Germanorum, vexillis aquilaribus splendens pugnabat. Fontanus de Bello Rhodio, An. 1527, cfr. CORONELLI, pag. 117.

[†] PORTA Ambrosiana, qua iter ad montem Phileremum est. Fontanus.

in Rhodos.   During the middle ages a Greek fortress stood on the
summit of the mountain, which after an obstinate siege was sur-
prised and taken by some adventurous Knights of St. John by
means of a stratagem,* and the celebrated Church of Our Lady of
Phileremos, to whose image many miracles were ascribed, and nu-
merous pilgrimages performed by the Latin and Greek Christians
of the Eastern world.

We would fain have visited these interesting ruins and enjoyed
the delightful panorama from Phileremos, extending far away over
land and sea, but the departure of our steamer the same evening
hindered us from making so far an excursion.   We therefore fol-
lowed the fortifications on the south all around the city, and having
passed the bastions of Auvergne and Spain, (Aragon,) we arrived
at the principal theatre of the most sanguinary assaults of the Otto-
mans during the last siege, the projecting English bastion on the
south-east of the city, where the confined breadth and the shallow-
ness of the moat and the want of out-works indicate the weakest
and less defensible part of the fortress.

The siege having continued for two months with great exertions
on both sides, the Turks here on the south-east of the English bas-
tion sprung a mine, traces of which are still apparent, with such
success, that dense columns of Janizaries on the fourth day of Sep-
tember, 1522, mounted the breach and forced their way to the
upper platform.   But here they were repelled with the loss of many
officers and three thousand men, by the Grand Master in person
with his chosen knights.   During the following days the attacks
were repeated with as little success; but on the twenty-fourth of
September the most tremendous battle was fought, when all the
Pashas, at the head of eighty thousand Turks, at the same time
stormed the battered and almost demolished bastions of the Span-
ish, Italian and English tongues on the south and south-east of the
city.   Knights and citizens, women and children, hurrying to the
rescue, fought with unparalleled bravery; and after the utmost
efforts, the old Isle d'Adam and his few surviving companions at last
succeeded in forcing back the enemy.   Fifteen thousand slaughtered
Turks filled up the breach and the surrounding moats.   Still the
fate of Rhodos was decided on that day!   The small band of de-
voted defenders, abandoned by the warring and wrangling mon-
archs of Europe, and suffering from want of ammunition and vic-
tuals, having for more than six months stopped the progress of the
victorious arms of Suleiman, were at last obliged to retire to the
interior part of the town, to yield up to the enemy the Spanish
bastion, and a few days later to surrender the fortress and depart
from the island.

We now arrived at the Athanasian gate, called ' Porta della Vit-
toria' to the memory of the brilliant victory which the Grand Mas-
ter Pierre d'Aubusson gained there at the Italian bastion against

---

* See the Chronicle of the Knight d'Engleure, in MICHAUD's Correspondence d'Orient, Vol. IV,
pag. 23

Mesih-Pasha on the twenty-eighth of July, 1480. You still see the ruins of the chapel of the Santa Maria della Vittoria, where the Grand Master Villiers de l'Isle Adam, fearing a repetition of the attacks on the less protected and more exposed Italian bastion, chose his head-quarters during the second siege.

The last eastern gate in the Jews' quarter, near the inner harbor, is now walled up. It was formerly called the Cosquinian gate, (Porta Cosquinii,) and is often mentioned in the Rhodian war.* On this gate the Grand Master hoisted the flag of truce, and through it the Janizaries, five days later, broke into the city in spite of the capitulation, and began their depredations.

Though many valuable works have been written on the memorable events at Rhodos, by eye witnesses and contemporaries, as well as by later erudite historians, nevertheless the most unaccountable uncertainty reigns in the different narratives as to the denominations of the gates, bastions and towers, the defensive stations of the eight tongues of the order, and the particular incidents during both the Turkish wars. Very contradictory views are to be found in the works of the distinguished historian Baron de Hammer, who, although having been himself on the spot, supposes the harbors to be situated on the south of the city, while in reality they lie on the north and north-east. Then he places the above-mentioned Mount Phileremos on the east, supposing it to be identical with the pretty hill of the hyacinths (*Symbylli*) and thus erroneously fixes the Ambrosian gate, from which, according to Fontanus and Coronelli, the road went in a south-west direction to Phileremos, at the Cosquinian gate in the Jews' quarter on the east side of the city.

That thus the whole plan of defence by Baron de Hammer, and others, blindly copying him, has been strangely misplaced, is evident from a highly interesting document by Coronelli : the detailed distribution of the bastions and towers among the eight divisions or tongues of the Order† stating, that the tongue of France held the right wing of the line of defence from the high tower of St. Michel at the mouth of the great harbor, along the bastion of St. Pietro and the whole western line of the walls as far as the palace of the Grand Masters. Then succeeded the Knights of Germany, Auvergne, Aragon, (Spain) England, Provence and Italy, eastward round the fortress, while the last and youngest tongue, that of Castile-Portugal, created in the year 1461, was intrusted with the defence of the gate of St. Caterina, and all the fortifications on the great port (Porto di Mandracchio.) This distribution of the bastions and consequently the movements and attacks of the Turks, coincides perfectly with all the accounts of Breydenbach, Fontanus, the Chevalier de Bourbon, and the often unjustly censured Abbé de Vertôt.

Before the gate, we, according to our agreement, met the small lively mules, and accompanied by a Greek *agojatis*, or driver, trotted briskly along the commodious road, paved with gravel, to the

---

* A VILLAGE still termed Coskinu (Κοσκινοι) lies four miles south of this gate, on the eastern coast of the island.

† RIPARTIMENTO delle poste del Zacosta dal quale si comprendono le fortificazioni di Rodi: CORONELLI, page 116.

beautiful hill on the south-east of the city, which the Turks call *Symbylli* (Hill of the Hyacinths) and the Greeks *Rhodini* (the Rose-bower.) It lies two miles from the fortress, and is surrounded by pretty gardens and vineyards, intermixed with olive groves and numerous lemon, orange and granate-trees. Beneath the deep shade of the plantains and fig-trees, on the bank of a cool purling brook, the lazy Turks, during the heat of summer, spend the day with their pipes and coffee. There in the paradise of Rhodos, nature had just invested all the brilliant colors of spring. The light green foliage of the trees did not yet afford any shade, nor were we in want of it, and the genial warm and vernal sun appeared to us very pleasant in comparison with the unsettled and rainy winter at Smyrna.

The straggling village, Epanomaras, inhabited by Greek Christians, runs along on both sides of the road. The houses lie embosomed in the gardens and enclosures, and every where are the vines on ledges drawn across the entrance, and thus form natural avenues and vaulted alleys. The buildings are solidly set up with squared lime stones from the adjacent quarries ; they have vaulted windows and projecting battlements, ornamented with small angular towers from the times of the Knights of St. John, and look very picturesque. No where in the Levant have I seen such prosperity, cleanliness and comfortable order among the Greeks as here in Rhodos, and on all hands the kind people called out to us in their well-known hospitable address : Καλῶς ορίζατε, ἀφεντάδες ! Welcome to you, gentlemen!

On the hill, above the village, we dismounted at the delightful source, which is led from an ancient aqueduct to a Turkish fountain and then gushing into a large, glassy reservoir, refreshes the cool and pleasing spot. High waving plantains spread their boughs over the elegant mosaïc pavement laid out with white and black stones, which border the tank, and gaily painted kiosks on slender Saracenic arches, invite to enjoyment and repose.

It happened to be the festival of St. Gregory, and as the Greeks, though generally very temperate and abstemious in their habits, never celebrate any feast of their saints without a banquet, we met with a merry party from the neighboring village, who with song and music were engaged at their dinner. We were in a great hurry to return to town, but still accepted of the kind invitation in the usual Greek style, to take coffee and a pipe, à la Turque, with them.

Our conversation turned upon the antiquities found in the gardens around. Traces of the ancient Doric city of Rhodos, marble altars with inscriptions and fragments of columns or architectural ornaments, are walled up in the buildings and enclosures. In the adjacent mountains are seen ancient quarries and artificial grottos. On the west of the present city are considerable ruins of an aqueduct from the middle ages, and at different places south of the gardens you may trace the substructions of those famous city walls which successfully withstood the battering engines of Demetrius Poliorketes. The Swedish naturalist, Professor Hedenborg, who for several years has been established in the village Neómaras, and is an admirer of antiquity, has opened several ancient sepulchres, and formed a little collection of vases, sepulchral oil-lamps of terra-cotta and the like. The villages, Epanómares, Turkámbela and Neómaras, extend in a semicircle around the fortress, and are inhabited by twenty thousand Christians. The Latins have a church and a convent of Franciscans. In the fortress live seven or eight thousand Turks and three thousand Jews, and in the rather thinly populated villages of the interior only three or four thousand Greeks and Turks.

With some reluctance we took leave of the good people on the pretty hyacinth-hill, and through the luxuriant maze of the gardens, rode on to the village Turkámbula, and the Greek church of the Panagia Elemonitra, from the height of which a most beautiful landscape opened to our view. Northward, beneath the hill, lay the green enclosures of the vineyards, from out of which many a slender palm-tree reared its lofty crown. Yonder the numberless turbaned sepulchres stretched along toward the walls of the city. Further on the castle of the Grand Masters, the cupolas and minarets of the mosques, and the gigantic towers of the harbors presented a beautiful relief against the green mirror of the sea and the distant blue mountains of Caramania.

We then returned to the castle, dismissed our muleteer, and walked down to the harbor. The only remarkable ruin of the ancient Doric Rhodos we saw was the mole or dyke so well described by Diodorus Siculus, which forms the northern galley-harbor already mentioned. Through a vaulted gate beneath the bastion of St. Pietro we went northward to the navy-yard, where at our left, on a round turret, is seen a well preserved bas-relief, representing a knight in complete armor, and behind a latticed wall a number of fine old cannon, from the fifteenth and sixteenth centuries.

Not far off stands a large Turkish tshesmé, or fountain, whose light Saracenic arches rest on foundations of ancient marble altars. The north-western city walls are high, and as well kept up as the fortifications on the interior harbor. They are without moat and out-works; but being sheltered by the batteries of the towers of St. Nicolaos and St. Michel, and bravely defended by the French cavaliers, they repelled victoriously all the attacks of the Turks.

On a wooden bridge we passed a canal, which, by means of a subterranean vault from the interior part of the city, opened a communication with the galley-port. Fontanus relates that during the siege traitors in the city, through this conduit, sent the enemy intelligence about the losses and disabled situation of the garrison. On this canal formerly stood a chapel, called *Fanum Johannis* Colossensis, and this suggested the idea, that the famous Colossus of the Lindian artist Chares, which was destroyed by an earthquake in the year 222 B. C., was placed across the canal; although there hardly can be a doubt that it stood on the great mole at the entrance of the galley-harbor.[*]

Opposite to the palace of Hassan Pasha, the governor of the island, are situated the ancient dock-yards, (Τυρσυνᾶς,) which now

---

[*] Turris Nicolea, super molem dextro cornu ante portum admirabili antiquitatis arte et sumptu in mare projectam, qua stetisse ferunt *Colossum illum Solis*, etc. Font., Lib. II.

appear to be in the same state of neglect and abandonment as all such public establishments of the Turks. During the late war of independence frigates were still built here; but now-a-days the wharfs seem to be abandoned, and only some small xebecks and barks lay in the yards for repairs and caulking.

We then went out upon the large mole, so famous in antiquity for its solidity and beauty. Immense blocks form the base. In different places columns and other fragments of marble from the ancient foundations appear on the sands, which by the negligence of the Turks now cover the fine and solid pavement and firm parapets still existing in the year 1483, according to the interesting drawing published in the travels of Breydenbach. We passed five or six windmills now standing on the higher and less exposed parts of it, and approached the strongest and most renowned bulwark of Rhodos, whose gallantly-defended walls resisted all the attacks of the Ottomans.

This powerful fortress stands three hundred paces distant from the walls of the city at the mouth of the galley-port, on the northern point of the mole, on an elevated platform. The double lines of its batteries are still mounted with numerous cannon. On the walls of the circular tower are seen inscriptions and the coat-of-arms of John, Duke of Burgundy, who in the year 1461 furnished the Grand Master Zacosta with ten thousand ducats in order to finish these extensive fortifications of the most important barrier of the city. I wished to ascend the tower, but the Turkish sentinel at the lower battery ordered us to stand back, with the impolite address, 'Jasak Diawri!' (Stand off, you infidels!) This rudeness the traveller meets with every where at Rhodos, where he cannot obtain permission to visit the walls or other interesting historical buildings. At sunset the city is shut. No Christian dares to pass the night within the gates, on penalty of the bastinado; and even on Friday, during the Mohammedan worship, no Greek is suffered to appear in the streets.

When Sultan Mohammed el Fatich, (the conqueror,) in the year 1480, ordered Misih-Pasha, with a hundred thousand Turks, to Rhodos, this general directed the whole force of his arms against the castle of St. Nicolaos, hoping by its reduction to be able to attack the city from the sea-side. But the Grand Master Pierre d'Aubusson instantly caused the mole to be fortified with breast-works and barricadoes, confided its defence to the brave Italian knight Fabrizio di Caretti, with a chosen band, and placed an ambuscade of mounted knights and bow-men in the inner harbor, who through the gate of St. Pietro might rush forward on the mole and attack the enemy in the rear, if he should attempt a descent upon the quay.

The first assault against the tower, which the Turks undertook from the sea in landing-boats and rafts tied together, miscarried altogether, as a similar enterprise in antiquity by Demetrius Pollorketes on the same spot.* The Turks fled in disorder, with a

* VIDE Diod. Sic. 20, 87-90.

loss of seven hundred slain. The furious Pasha then, on the nineteenth of June, made another attempt from the shore against the mouth of the galley-port by means of an immense floating bridge or ponton, artificially constructed, from which his columns of janizaries mounted to the assault of the outward walls of the tower. But here they were encountered by the Grand Master, who, sheathed in steel, himself led on his bravest warriors. The Osmanlis again suffered a most signal defeat; two thousand five hundred corpses floated for many days along the coast, and covered all the avenues; and the Pasha, after the above-mentioned repulse at the Gate of Victory on the east side of the city, was obliged to raise the siege and depart from the island.

There on the spot I at last obtained a clear and complete view of those interesting events, which are represented very indistinctly and confusedly by the modern historians. Both Abbé de Vertôt and Baron de Hammer confound the tower of St. Nicolaos on the northern extremity of the mole with the ancient tower of the Saracens, or of St. Michel, on the right-hand of the inlet to the great harbor, and thus appear to have inferred the occupation of the galley-port and out-works by the Turks, and their victorious advance to the inner harbor; a circumstance which in itself would have been of the highest importance, but is contradicted by all the most distinct and detailed accounts of the contemporaneous historians, the eye-witnesses of the siege.

The same fault has been committed by the greater part of modern travellers,* who already at a distance, on the approach to Rhodos from the sea, with admiration behold the high picturesque Saracenic tower, beneath the batteries of which they are going to anchor, and pay no attention at all to the more distant and now less imposing tower of St. Nicolaos, which though of a far greater importance in a historical point of view, has now been almost destroyed by the fury of the wars and the still more destructive earthquakes of latter years.

The first mentioned tower is still termed Arab-Kylesí (Stronghold of the Arabs) by the Turks, who interposed no obstacle, when, on our return to the great harbor, we desired to ascend it. At present it serves as a light-house. Having been built during the middle ages by the Saracen corsairs, it was repaired and fortified by the Knights of St. John, after the conquest of the island in 1310, and according to the warfare of the times, furnished with battering engines, (*trabocchi* and *mangani*, or *manganelle*,) and considered as the principal defence of the great harbor, (Porto di Mandracchio,) the huge chain being drawn across the inlet from its lower batteries to the opposite eastern turret of St. John.†

This magnificent quadrangular structure, solidly built with large free-stones, has four round turrets on the battlements and an octagonal beacon on the upper platform. On the south front is seen

---

* VIDE Choiseul-Gouffier's ‘Voyage Pittoresque en Grèce,’ Vol. 1, page 61. The engraving gives a faithful representation of the Saracenic tower, but the subscription refers to the ‘Tour S. Nicolas.’
† THEREFORE it is called by CORONELLI, DAPPER, and the more ancient authors, ‘Torre del Trabocco.’ VERTOT has ‘Tour S. Michel.’

the escutcheon of the Grand Master Guy de Blanchefort, representing two rampant lions in gules. We ascended to the platform on a fine stair-case of one hundred and sixty-eight steps, and enjoyed a most delightful view of both the subjacent harbors, the city, with its numerous walls and towers, and all the charming environs. The site of the ancient Rhodos, in a circumference of ten miles, enclosing all the modern Greek suburbs, the gardens and vineyards, is distinctly traced from this place.

The sun in the mean time set behind the Cum-Burnú; from the minarets reëchoed the wailing evening-prayers of the Imaums; the Christians left the fortress, and the volume of dark smoke arising from our steamer announced the moment of our departure. We descended, highly gratified with the happy hours spent in this interesting city. On our arrival on board, the anchors were heaved, we left the harbor, and standing away to the south-east during the twilight of the mild vernal night, passed along the snow-topped mountains of Caramania toward Cyprus.

THE WIFE'S APPEAL.

WHAT though, my love! thy lip has lost
　The early smile of youth,
When every word it breathes for me
　Is tenderness and truth?
And if none else a charm can see
　Upon thy care-worn brow,
I loved thee in the flush of youth,
　But oh! far better now!

And if at times a tear will fall,
　Thy pallid cheek to see,
Oh deem not that thine altered look
　Has grown less dear to me;
But that to me it tells a tale
　Of days of anxious care,
And grief and toil thou bear'st so well,
　Which I so fain would share.

What if the ones who at my side
　Launched on life's fickle sea,
Have gained a higher lot on earth
　Than I have shared with thee?
Nor stately homes nor silken sheen
　Can win from me a sigh;
Thine *heart*, beloved! is wealth enough
　Far more than earth can buy!

Perchance had fickle Fortune smiled,
　Our hearts had learned to roam,
And found a charm in wealth and power,
　To win from Heaven and Home.
But now, when all around is dark,
　Our souls at least are free,
And trust me, love! that mine is strong
　To suffer all with thee!

STANZAS: THE SUN.

BY JOHN H. KURTZ.

Dark is the moonless earth at dead of night ;
　　And o'er its vast expanse
　　Rise ragged cliff and mountain height,
At whose feet yawn huge chasms, whose depths profound
　　Defy the keenest glance ;
And forests hang their gloom o'er treacherous ground,
Where dragons lurk or prowling beasts of prey,
　　Or, bred by marshes' stagnant air,
　　The dancing wild-fires play,
And lure the traveller's feet to ruin unaware.
　　Nor paths are seen,
While every groping step may plunge him down
　　Some dark ravine ;
　　And o'er his unprotected head,
　　With fury dread,
　Storms burst, winds howl, and thunders roll ;
　　Whose mighty voices drown
All other sounds, shaking the earth and sky.
　　Dark horrors thrill his soul ;
　　Quick pants his trembling breath ;
　His lightless pathway seems to lie
Under the quivering wings of sudden Death.

　　Behold the rising Sun !
The gloomy mountains melt in tender blue :
　　Scarce is the dawn begun,
　　When in the forest, rings its matin song ;
The leaves are glancing in the light, and through
　　The vistas opening all along,
Dim distant lakes and islands meet the view.
　　The mighty monarch's rays
Pierce through the lowering fragments of the storm ;
When kindling with a bright reflected blaze,
　　Away on breezy wings
　　They fly, in quaint fantastic form,
　　Like living things
Of golden plumage, or of rosy hue,
　　Or snowy white ; and side by side,
　　Like peaceful doves, they glide
　　Along the welkin blue.
　　Or, when the sullen storm-clouds hold
In purple phalanx their retreating march,
His brilliant beams build on their latest fold
　　The love-born arch.
　　He filleth Nature's lap with light ;
　　He brings the tender flowers to birth,
And herbs, and shrubs, and trees of portly girth ;
Upward, with wondrous skill and subtle might,
　　He draws their living sap.

Through stem and twig and leaf and opening bloom,
Stores their deep cups with sweetness and perfume ;

Covers the blushing fruit with downy nap,
  And with his warmth he feeds
To full and pregnant strength their life-inclosing seeds.
  In times of dearth,
When field and forest droop, all parched and brown,
  He from the thirsty earth
  In sultry hours
Draws the thin vapours, and then drops them down
  In dewy showers.
He lights thy path, lone traveller, he cheers
  Thy steps, and banisheth thy fears.
These are his works, and countless beyond these ;
  And while they all reveal
The deepest uses Nature can require,
   The grateful mind,
  With daily growing zeal,
Throughout the boundless range forever sees
Unending forms of beauty to admire,
And may for evermore new raptures feel,
   New blessings find.
  But if, with naked eye, thou raise
Up to his burning orb thy daring gaze,
   He strikes thee blind !

   Dark is the Godless Earth
To him who wanders in its mazy wild
With eye unlightened by the second birth ;
High thrones and powers he sees, with crime defiled,
   And at their feet
Abysses bottomless of guilt and wo
  Yawn wide. Near by, his footsteps meet
Forests of old corruptions, wherein lurk
Fierce beasts of prey, that, prowling to and fro,
  Do in the dark their deadly work :
  Fanatic wild-fires, glowing bright
Where living waters have no strength to flow,
  And, dancing o'er the miry slough,
With baleful influence, like comets hairy,
  They lure to deeper, darker night
  The poor unwary.
  Nor rightful paths are seen ;
But ever close on either hand are found
  Pitfalls, and snares, and dens obscene,
   Where, underground,
Whole broods of vices hide their filth away,
  To shun the eye of day.
  And wars burst forth, with cannon roar
  And falchion-stroke ;
Battalions charge, and fall to rise no more ;
  Shouts, shrieks and groans, and curses high
Mix with the thundering hoofs of cavalry ;
While all unheeded, through the battle-smoke,
   Rise up, in naked hosts,
   The silent ghosts !
Read on their ghastly corpses, pale and gory,
   The price of glory !
  Oh, Earth ! Earth ! Earth ! hast thou no Friend ?
Will this thy night of horrors *never* end ?

   Behold the Rising Sun !
The SUN OF RIGHTEOUSNESS, who brings

The morning dawn
With light and life and healing in his wings!
As in his conquering might he marches on,
Adown the mountain's stream his glorious rays,
    Piercing the clouds of war,
That roll their curtains up as he appears,
    And shrink before his blaze ;
While thunders, storms and night are scattered far,
And hopes, like rainbows, beam 'mid falling tears.
    He filleth Earth with light ;
And, from its earliest birth, the tender soul
    Drinks in his outpoured love,
With ever-growing strength and new delight.
    Throughout the whole
    Of life's appointed term,
His spiritual warmth, with wondrous power,
    Soft beaming from above,
Sustains from bud to leaf the tender germ,
    From leaf to flower,
From flower to perfect fruit he makes it grow ;
    Nor only so,
But still, with holy seed, from sire to son,
    The stream of heavenly love flows on.

When, in this weary world of sin and wo,
The soldier quails before his ghostly foe,
Faints in the fight for his eternal crown,
And Faith can see no more Heaven's shining towers ;
Prayer, like an unseen vapor, flies aloft,
    And soon the answering times of soft
And sweet refreshing from the LORD drop down
Upon the panting soul in dewy showers.
He is about thy path, about thy bed,
    And though thy journey lie
    Through dangers dread,
Through rivers of deep waters rolling high,
    Through pestilential breaths,
Through snares, fires, sorrows, and ten thousand deaths,
They shall not hurt thee nor come nigh thy head ;
    For HE hath said :
' Lo! I am with thee ; be not thou afraid.'
These are HIS works ; and countless worlds beside
Combine to swell the immeasurable tide.
    Here mayest thou see
The deepest love, truth, grace and mercy free,
    For man unite,
And all with pure and heavenly beauty bright.
    Here mayest thou study evermore
    With heart and soul and mind,
    Be filled with raptures never felt before,
And ever find new cause to worship and adore.
    Thus shalt thou find
Life in the Light of Heaven, not death and pain ;
    But if, with naked eye profane,
    Thou proudly raise
Up to the ETERNAL LIGHT thy daring gaze,
    HE strikes thee blind!

Canst thou by searching find out DEITY?
The fringes of HIS robe suffice for thee!
    HE is THE LORD ;
    And through HIS Holy Word,

As through a glass, hath bid thee look on HIM :
A glass with solemn shadows dark and dim,
With wondrous type and mystery profound,
Beyond poor human reason's utmost bound,
With symbols, signs and prophets' song sublime,
That chaunts the ending from the birth of time :
Through *this* behold thy SAVIOUR; this supplies
A mystic twilight, meet for feeble eyes.
See how his tender love obscures the blaze
    That else would blast thy mortal gaze !
Yet not forever darkling shall thy sight
Gaze on His glory who is Light of Light :
Soon over thee the wings of Death shall pass,
And brush these earth-born shadows from the glass;
    Then face to face, and eye to eye,
In Heaven thou shalt behold the LORD of Earth and Sky.

Burlington, Vt., Sept. 1846.

THE ACQUAINTANCE OF A NIGHT.

BY HANS VON SPEIGAL.

SOME three or four summers since, while pursuing a journey on horse-back through the northern part of Indiana, night closed upon me unawares, and I found myself in the midst of the forest, occasionally stopping to listen to the peals of heavy thunder that grew more near and frequent as I advanced. To retrace my course I knew was vain, as the last log-house I had left full a dozen miles behind; so all that I could do was to press on, with a creeping conviction that I should be compelled to ' camp out' after all.

The lightning now began fitfully to reveal the straight trunks of the trees as they stretched up, without a branch, like columns, supporting the high roof of dense foliage above, which in the brightest sunshine scarcely admitted a single beam of day. Once in a while I could distinguish the long howl of a wolf, seemingly in answer to the continued hooting of an owl that kept in my vicinity, whether I rode fast or slowly; and the contingency of a solitary bivouac in the wilderness, which a few hours before seemed something agreeable for one to experience and tell of, was but little to my liking. Urging my tired horse into a gallop, I hastened forward; straining my eyes, as the lightning streamed across my path and flashed in among the gloomy recesses that yawned upon the bridle-path, to catch a glimpse of some ' clearing' ahead, and fully determined to proceed until the storm should in reality commence.

At last the wind began to sigh heavily among the trees, and to reach my forehead with a startling coolness. The tree-tops creaked against each other, as if in fear: and the owl, heretofore my annoying attendant, ceased his too-whoo, apparently awaiting the approaching storm.

As I gallopped on, half hoping, half despairing, the short bark of a dog caught my ear; and in a few moments I was off my horse, and tying him under a rude shed beside a log-cabin. Those only who have been belated as I was can appreciate my feelings when I found myself under the cover of that simple shed, which alone would have been welcome. The log-cabin, however, added something to be sure, as it gave me hope of seeing human faces, and probability of supper.

The sound of the rain rushing down on the foliage, which in a western forest can be heard for miles, became more and more distinct, till at last, as the storm marched on, it drowned even the thunder and the wind, and roared with the deafening loudness of the ocean. No sound can be more terrific to one unaccustomed to it, and although I had repeatedly listened to it before, I could hardly divest myself of the dread of danger.

After securing my horse, I knocked at the cabin, and was answered by a feeble voice bidding me ' come in.' The dog whose bark had apprized me of shelter, rushed in, as I opened the door, and fawned on the emaciated form of a man, apparently sixty years old, who lay in the centre of the floor, on a bed of deer-skins. A tin-cup, half filled with deer-fat, from the top of which protruded a string of tow which burned dimly, served as a lamp; and as it sat upon a rough bench beside him, showed the occupant of the cabin in that light which gives such effect to the wild canvass of Salvator Rosa. The old man was evidently in the last stages of a fever, and as he rested his elbow on the skins, and gazed in the blaze of his singular lamp, there was something truly noble in the features and expression of his countenance. The grey hair was straggling over his forehead, and his white beard told of long neglect; but the brightness of his heavily-shaded eye, and the determined expression of his lips, interested me at once. He pointed to a shelf, and bade me share his scanty larder; but hunger had left me, for I felt that I was with a dying man.

He told me that he had been ill more than a week, but until the night before had not considered himself dangerouslyso; yet now he had given up all hope of life. In answer to my inquiry whether he wished any last word to be sent his friends, for I did not conceal from him that I also thought his days were numbered, he told me that he had no friends to be interested in his fate, and that there was no living being whom he loved, except the poor dog that lay at his side watching every change of his features. The tears came into his eyes as he spoke, and I ventured to ask his history. It was no idle curiosity that prompted me. The very appearance of the man assured me that his was a life of more than ordinary suffering. ' Young stranger,' he answered, ' the story of my life will not be interesting to you : it is perhaps, a common one in these western wilds, where youth comes with blighted hopes and a broken heart, to seek forgetfulness and to die, away from all who might sympathize with the dreary close of an unprofitable life.' I urged him to proceed. ' Well,' said he, ' I have but little time left, and 1 may as well

give you my history, for you are the first human being whom for
many a year I have not shunned to converse with. My peace, I trust,
is made with GOD, and I have now no more to care for.   Forty
years ago,' he proceeded, ' my father died and left me, an only child,
at the age of fourteen, the only stay of my mother.   She was in ill
health, and we were very poor.   For some time I gained a scanty
livelihood in the little New-England village where we lived by cul-
tivating our small garden, and selling the produce to the neighbors,
who were ready to buy of me, and by doing little labors for them as
occasion offered.   At length, when I was about seventeen, the prin-
cipal merchant of the village took me into his store, giving me a
small compensation for my services ; and as I could thus support my
mother, and learn something at the same time, I willingly performed
the duties of my new station.

'Nearly two years passed away, and I was receiving an increased
amount of wages as I became more useful, when suddenly my mo-
ther grew very ill.   The daughter of my employer, a year younger
than myself, extremely beautiful and lovely, was the almost constant
attendant on her sick bed ; soothing her by little kindnesses, and
lighting up her short pathway to the grave.   Mary had a sweet
voice, and often did I stop of an evening before the door and listen
to her melody, which always ceased as I pressed the latch.   My
mother was always fond of music, and the soft sweet tones of Mary's
voice appeared to lull her pain ; and although she would often ask
Mary to sing when I was present, yet she never would.   When the
gate swung to, however, and she thought I was beyond the sound of
her carolling, she would again resume her singing ; and as the vibra-
tions of her delicate voice stole softly through the half-open window,
I felt them also steal into my heart.   I had seen her at church from
childhood, and had perhaps, admired her, but not till I had seen her
at the bedside of poverty did I dream of loving her.

'At last my mother died, and I followed her to the church-yard,
where she was buried beside my father, and although I ' sorrowed
as one having no hope,' yet my grief had some alleviation ; when at
the grave I saw Mary steal a glance at me, while her eyes were
dimmed with tears.   It was not wonderful that the glance came
like angel-consolation, for it told me that I had yet one in the wide
world who at least pitied me.   But oh! who can tell the grief of
an orphan, even though Pity offers the balm of sympathetic tears!
Who can lift the veil from the orphan's breast, and read the agony
of his heart?   Surely not those who neglect the poor.   Time, the
great consoler, will blunt the poignancy of grief, and heal the wounds
of sorrow.   A few weeks only had elapsed before the duties of my
employment and my growing love for Mary, blended as it was with
the remembrance of my mother's dying bed, had soothed my heart;
and I again began to regard life with joy and hopefulness.

'I had never breathed my love to Mary, yet every Sabbath afternoon
found us together in the church-yard, whither she too brought flowers
to strew upon my parents' graves ; and then, all through the lagging
week, would I think of her, and wait impatiently the Sabbath after-
noon.

'Summer passed away, and the autumn came, and yet we failed not, as the sun sank low in·the west, to be in the church-yard on the Sabbath.   I at length made known my love, and even now can well remember the afternoon.   It was communion Sabbath; and not belonging to the church, we had left the meeting-house together, for our accustomed walk to the burying-ground, which was situated on a hill-side some half a mile from the village.   The October sun shone warmly on the hills; a robin was singing on the great elm at the gate of the burying-ground, among the yellow leaves; and far off, in the grove of maples and beeches on the hill beyond, the blue-jays were screaming and chattering over their feast of mast, and occasionally a squirrel would perch himself upon the wall and sputter out his portion of the general gladness.

Mary loved me as deeply and truly as I could desire, but expressed a fear that her parents would not consent to our union.   Lovers little think of the thousand vexations and difficulties that immediately throng upon them, especially when they happen to be poor.   In the space of three short days, I had asked the consent of Mary's father; been scornfully spurned; and was again, with what little money I had saved, returning to the old house where I was born, which I had rented for a trifle to a family almost as poor as my own.   Then it was that my heart for the first time sank within me.   I could bear the cutting sneer with which the father greeted my request for the hand of his daughter, as he thought of the wan and wretched boy whom a few months before he had in compassion rescued as it were from the work-house.   I could bear the crushing and smothering sense of poverty; all, all, until I entered the door, where a kind mother used to sit and welcome me home, and saw there the faces of strangers to my childhood.   Do not wonder that I wept, young stranger; do not wonder that I weep now; for the human heart knows nothing bitterer, than to hear in the hour of anguish strange footsteps sounding upon the hearth of its early home!

'A dreary winter was that of my majority, although I obtained employment in a neighboring village, with a better compensation than before.   Spring again returned; and once or twice, on a Sabbath, I went back to my native village to strew fresh flowers on the grave in the burying-ground; but Mary was not there, and I went no more.

'The summer again began to throw its glories on the earth, when news came to me that Mary's father had failed, and was already on his way to the far West.   This came upon me like a thunder-clap. I had heard of the privations of the West, and I feared for the welfare of Mary, now that poverty had numbered her also among its children; for in those days rich men did not fail that they might grow richer.   Mr. G—— was a proud man, and cared not that those who had shared his affluence should commiserate his reverse of fortune, and so chose to bury himself in the distant West.   I found on again visiting the village, in the safe-keeping of a maiden aunt of Mary's, a letter from her, full of assurances of continued love, but expressing fears that I had forgotten her; yet concluding with the address of the new home which her father had chosen in Ohio. My decision was in a moment made to follow her and make her mine in the rough land of the West; and selling the old house for more than it was worth, thanks to the generous heart that bought it, after erecting a plain stone to the memory of my parents, and strewing for the last time fresh flowers upon their graves, I started for the West on horseback.

' It was a beautiful Sabbath afternoon in the first week of autumn that I reached the settlement where Mary lived. The half-ripe corn was high above the blackened stumps and new fences in the large clearing, whose new log-houses, roofed with bark, by courtesy were termed a village; but as yet the forest beyond was pathless, save to the hunter and the Indian, who still remained upon the borders of civilization, a daring and wily enemy.

' The log-house pointed out to me as Mr. G.'s was just on the edge of the forest, a little apart from the rest, and to approach it I passed near the burying-ground, which even then was peopled with a score of graves, although the settlement had been made but a couple of years before. A female was there alone, with a bunch of wild-flowers in her hand. She turned as the noise of my horse's tread attracted her attention, and turning pale as a winding-sheet, fell to the earth. I was instantly at her side; and then we met, by a singular coincidence, in the place allotted to the dead, nearly a thousand miles from where we first told our loves, and parted, a year before.

' I attended her home, and her father shook my hand in silence, while a tear stood in his already sunken eye. Mrs. G. appeared glad to see me, but the hectic flush was on her cheek, and told too plainly that care had done its work. The next Sabbath was fixed upon for our wedding; and when, as the sun sank into the forest, we kissed each other good evening, and I sought the dwelling of a neighbor who could provide both for myself and jaded horse, I thought that poverty and former disappointment were nothing.

' Hitherto the colonists had been unmolested by the Indians, though from time to time they had been alarmed by the reports which the hunters gave, that their deadly foe was prowling about in the vicinity, ready to attack them at the first unguarded moment; but as yet nothing certain was known, and the repeated warnings passed by with but momentary heed. Tired as I was by my journey, that night I could hardly close my eyes; and when I did, strange images danced before them, giving me, although not superstitious, an undefined yet dread presentiment of evil. At last I fell asleep, and toward morning was awakened by the blowing of horns and the cry of ' The Indians !' I feel even now the shudder which seized me when I arose, and hastily throwing on my clothes, looked out of the window of the loft in which I slept, and saw a bright blaze in the direction of Mary's house. Jumping down the ladder which led to my apartment, and disregarding the cries of the half-crazed females and children, who begged me to remain and protect them, I flew in the direction of the light. I heard rifle shots as I approached, and you can imagine my horror when I found the dwelling which I had left a few hours before, half burned down, and heard hoarse whispers among the colonists that its inmates had all been murdered! I knew nothing of what transpired afterward, until by the too certain light of the morning sun I saw three skeletons, all whitened by the fire, lying in the ashes. That of the father lay in the door-way, with the blade of a tomahawk still remaining in the skull. The others I had not the courage to approach. Many were the sobs, some of grief but most of fear, when their bones were consigned to the earth on the following afternoon, in the little grave-yard. From that day I, who had always till then been mild and forgiving, was changed. Deep hate and desire of revenge took possession of my heart. Day after day and week after week I practised with the rifle, until I was as sure of my aim as the veteran hunters themselves; and although that was the last hostile visit the Indians ever made to the settlement, yet for years I hung upon their hunting-trails, sometimes hundreds of miles from the most western settlement, picking off one by one those who ventured at a distance from the larger war or hunting parties. Eight years ago I built this log-hut, and have remained here ever since, with no companion but this dog. The horrible sin of which I have been guilty is, I trust, pardoned by that ONE who knows the motives of the heart. My story has been long, but I have done. GOD bless you, stranger, and make your life less miserable than mine!'

Here the old man sank back exhausted upon his couch of skins, and for a while seemed to slumber. My own eyes were heavy, and I half dreamed, thinking over his story; when he suddenly roused up, stared at me fixedly, a shudder seized him, 'Mary!' was breathed hurriedly from his rigid lips; he again fell back, *and I was alone with the dead!*

Those who cannot feel may talk of the passage of the soul from earth as a light matter, and may sneer at the dread we have in beholding the lifeless body and the glazed eye; but I do not blush to own that I am always struck with fear. The raven will always flap his gloomy wings over the bier, although the butterfly rests, poised in the sunshine, upon the funereal urn.

While I knelt beside the corpse the storm had gradually died away, and the lessening peals of the now distant thunder, or the occasional falling of some heavy limb in the forest, only made the loneliness of that night the more dreary. At length the morning came, and leaving the faithful dog beside the body of his master, I mounted my horse and retraced my ride of the night before. At noon I had returned with three or four kind-hearted settlers, and when the sun had slowly marched half way from his meridian toward the green line of the west, he looked down upon the grave of the subject of my narrative.

The few articles which furnished the cabin I distributed among those who had assisted in the last offices of the dead, allotting the heavy rifle and belt to the youngest of the party. The only thing which I cared to possess was a small clasp Bible, very old and worn.

On the fly-leaf was written, in a round handsome hand, '*Lizzy,
from her husband, June 15th*, 1782;' and a little lower on the page,
in trembling characters, '*Philip Morton, from his affectionate mother;*'
and again under this, in the same trembling writing, 'GOD *of the
widow, be thou with her child !*'

That mother and son are now together, in the far-off land of
spirits, where the GOD to whom she addressed her trustful prayer
smiles more nearly and perchance more tenderly than here, in this
' vale of tears.'

DARK AND LIGHT.

BY C. D. FERRIS.

I.

' HUSH, my child ;
The sound you hear is the night-wind wild !
    Nothing of fear
    Can visit you here ;
Here, in a mother's protecting arms,
Heed not and fear not the night's alarms.'

II.

' Hark, it sings !
Mother, I see the spirit's wings ;
    Its plumage bright
    Dazzles my sight,
And I hear its chanting, soft and low ;
Mother, it calls me, and I must go !'

III.

' Hush, my child ;
The sound you hear is the night-wind wild ;
    The storm is high
    And the flashing sky
Lightens the room with a fearful glare ;
But no spirit-wing can impress the air.'

IV.

' Hark, again ;
The spirit's sweet music I hear as plain
    As the thunder-peal ;
    And I 'm sure I feel
Its pinions pass o'er my aching brow ;
Mother, I must not linger now.'

V.

' Hush, my child ;
The sound you hear is the night-wind wild !
    The awful form
    Of the raging storm
Is the only vision I see to dread,
And it cannot come to thy sheltered head.'

VI.

'Hark, once more,
It sings again as it sung before;
    It bids me away
    And I must not stay;
Mother, farewell! I fly, I fly,
On its beautiful wings to the far-off sky.'

VII.

'Hush, my child:
The sound you hear is the night-wind wild!
    'T is almost done——
    Oh, my son! my son!'
And the mother wept, for she could not see
The angel form that set him free.

Buffalo, N. Y.

STRAY THOUGHTS ON ORATORY.

BY A NEW CONTRIBUTOR.

AT that early period in human affairs when the social relation began to merge in the political, when families expanded into tribes, as the young shoot branches into the stately tree, the vast field of embryo literature was as yet unbroken by a single furrow. Then, however, and before the art of writing was widely diffused, and its benefits properly understood, that branch of literature since filled by history began to be supplied in a very rude and imperfect manner by oral poetry, which is naturally the first direction of literary effort. We say *naturally;* for that men should place upon record the memory of their predecessors, was a natural impulse, and one likely to be felt before political cares had arisen to engross the mind. In the absence of writing, or while that art was in its infancy, the permanency it afforded had to be sought elsewhere, and the adaptedness of poetry to please and interest; the facility of retaining it in the memory, added to the poetic temperament which, in its purity, lies inherent in uncivilized nature; all coincided to induce the choice of the rude ballad as the substitute for an art, the capabilities of which were for the future to develope. Music also, whose strains are so fraught with rapture to the savage heart, must always, in a barbarous age, call in the aid of poetry to give it utterance. The war song, the hymn to the gods, and the traditional ballad, were thus the germs of a vegetation whose luxuriance has since overspread the wide field of literary culture.

But it was only a small portion of that field that the capacities of poetry were calculated to embrace. The memories of the past must give way to the emergencies of the present. The pæan of victory could not be sung till the war council had planned the battle : and here we find the earliest traces of that Oratory which was destined to hold unbounded sway over the popular heart. As the rude principles of public declamation by slow and natural degrees developed themselves into an art, an instrument was discovered by which mind could be brought extensively into contact with mind ; by which intelligence could be widely communicated ; by which the will, the feelings, the fortunes, the very destiny of the mass could be subjected to a single intellect. This was the first great step toward the enlightenment of the race.

From the fact just stated, that this was the only vehicle of an extensive interchange of thought, we derive the true estimate of its importance to the ancients, and the true secret of its power. Yet, however powerful an agent it may at any time have been in directing and enlightening the public mind, if we wish correctly to guage its capacity for influence, we must remember that it is *only* an agent — a means for accomplishing a certain end ; and that when other means are discovered, better adapted for the same purpose, its potency must end, and the halo with which success has surrounded it, fade away. It is only by keeping in view this fact that we can solve the problem, ' Why has oratory lost its influence ?' a problem which seems to have puzzled the minds of our greatest modern orators, while the fact involved in it has utterly blasted their ambitious hopes.

All who know any thing of ancient and of modern history, and who have labored to be benefitted by that knowledge, must have often been impressed with the change that has been effected in the sphere, the power, and the results of this art. When we look back through the misty shades of twenty centuries to the time when the Roman Forum resounded with the accents of eloquence, and the Republic was governed by its voice ; to the time when the thunders of Demosthenes shook the city of the Violet Crown, and caused even a Philip to pause and tremble, then we see what has been its power. When we view the philosophers and sages of old, surrounded by groups of disciples, discoursing in the shady grove of the academy, conversing in the gardens of Epicurus, disputing in the marketplace with Socrates ; when we find that philosophy, economy, morality, politics, were not learned out of books, but taught by the persuasive strains of oratory, then we learn how wide has been its sphere. And when we barely consider what advances in knowledge of all kinds were effected in the ancient commonwealths, remembering at the same time that they were so effected without the material aid of written literature, then we first obtain a just idea of the vastness of its results. But when we come back to our own day and see the oratorial art almost wholly superseded as a means of instruction ; when in the pulpit we see its most earnest and touching voice unsuccessful in producing emotion ; when in the senate we listen to arguments of power clothed in words of eloquence worthy of ancient days, and yet unrewarded by the change of a single vote ; then we cannot fail to acknowledge that the art has had its day. Rome is not the less fallen that its rulers still hold sway over a few square miles and some thousands of inhabitants. The night is night no less that a host of stars are striving to mitigate its darkness. So oratory is not less the shadow of a departed substance, that some traces of its past greatness still remain. Its sun has set. Its warming and vivifying power has departed, and a radiance remains whose only effect is to illumine what it cannot enliven; to shine with a cold and unimpassioned light which has no power to fructify or create.

And now to explain this change, keeping in view the fact that oratory can be only valuable and only powerful as a means of imparting thought, we inquire, has there come into use no other means of superior fitness for this purpose, whose introduction has superseded the Mercurian gift? The answer at once presents itself. Printing has wrought the revolution. In it we find the secret of the important change. In order to see this the more clearly, let us approach it gradually.

Public speaking and public writing are sister arts. Each has the human mind for its subject, and each for its object the communication of thought. The point in which of old they widely differed, was, that while the benefits of writing could be enjoyed but by a few, those of oratory were adapted to the mass, and no preparatory culture was required for their reception. The man of earnest but silent thought then as now gave utterance to his conceptions in a book; but none profited by them but such as were at once wealthy and learned. The multitude were precluded from their benefits, for they could no more procure books than use them when obtained.

This situation of things gave oratory an immeasurable advantage. Through books but few minds could hold communion, while the voice of the public speaker was a book to every member of the commonwealth. Down to the invention of printing, the scarcity of books laid the world under contribution to his art. Not only was this the case in all the departments wherein oratory now works its vain though earnest work, but the entire course of education during the middle ages consisted essentially of a vast system of collegiate lectures; a system which the practice of centuries so deeply rooted that it flourished in full vigor after the necessity which gave it birth had passed away, and the mere force of usage has transplanted it on the western side of the Atlantic. But the invention of printing gave matters an aspect entirely new. By its aid the writer was enabled to spread his thoughts as widely as his rival. Books soon forced their way into every village and hamlet, and were found at every fire-side. The vast stores of wisdom that had lain buried in monastic cells or treasured in stately castles were exhumed and scattered like autumn leaves before the wind to every corner of the land. Thenceforth books were the vehicle of knowledge, and the power of the orator was on its wane.

It was the destiny of printing not merely to rival but to eclipse. Oratory had long reigned supreme and absolute, and now a rule no less supreme, no less unlimited, was to be exercised by the renovated art. The superior advantages of books were not slow in developing themselves. The man who sought for instruction was no longer driven to seek it in the dense and tumultuous crowd, where abstracted attention was impossible, and even thought proved a weary labor. Nor was he longer obliged to rely on that imperfect memory whose confused and halting action had so often betrayed him. At his own fireside and in his own silent chamber he now listened to a voice which, at each renewed invocation, repeated to him the same truths, till they became part and parcel of his being. In perfect quietness he could ponder on them at his will. No longer hurried from one hasty glimpse to another of ideas which he had not time to dwell upon long enough to examine, he could now leisurely give each its proper weight, and contemplate it in all its bearings. And here was wrought another revolution in literature, which merits a distinct consideration.

The oral method of exchanging ideas is unsuited to the development of abstract truth. If it be not impossible, at least it is certainly not the gift of one man in a thousand, to be able to reason orally with the same order, perspicuity and absolute correctness that he would employ in arguing on paper. Much less can he who replies to an argument whose course he is obliged to follow by the ear, do so with the same satisfactory conclusiveness as if he had the argument before his eyes. It is evident therefore that where controverted points are sought to be settled by the force of reason, oratory is not the best instrument for that purpose. The constant appeals to the feelings, prejudices and sympathies, the perverted eloquence, all the sinister appliances of the oratorical art, unfit it for the grave solution of the question, ' What is Truth ?'

The fact we are about to call to mind we allude to for two purposes : first, to establish the correctness of what has just been said, and also to show how greatly, in ancient times, even the defects of oratory influenced the corresponding art. No person can have paid much attention to the classics without having noticed the miserable character of Greek and Roman logic ; the former in particular. The writings of their philosophers and the reported speeches of their orators abound with palpable sophisms, inconsequential reasoning, *argumenta ad hominem*, and the like. And this was the precise trait certain to attach itself to a literature in which oratory took the lead. What else could be expected where the public speaker taught men to cover a weak argument with a well-rounded sentence, and get rid of a troublesome objection by a brilliant sarcasm ?

As it has already been hinted, the multiplication of books subjected logic to a more rigid scrutiny, and established for it a higher standard. Fallacies that escaped detection in the hurry and glitter of a speech, could not lie unexposed under the calm observation of a thoughtful reader. Errors that had misled the world for ages, now brought to the touchstone of cautious reflection, were exploded at once and forever. The purposes of truth were subserved by the necessity which was imposed upon authors to avoid error ; and of course the consequence was that the great mass was furnished with a purer mental aliment.

One revolution is the precursor of another. Books alone would never have brought about the entire change we have been examining; but books are not the only result of printing. There was wanted a medium to spread current intelligence; to explain the movements and to discuss the questions of the day; to lead the public mind to just conclusions on every passing topic that involved the physical, intellectual, moral or political welfare of mankind. And in our newspapers and other periodicals this medium has been found. To this more than to any other single cause is owing the decline of oratory. From these sources men of all classes and conditions form their opinions; and when formed, no tongue of man has art to change them. Thus it is that we continually see political oratory employed in vain, whether addressed to legislators or their constituents; the rare exceptions only illustrating the rule. It is employed in vain, because conviction has followed quiet thought upon information derived from other quarters.

There is one exception to the general principle that oratory has been wholly superseded. It is found in the oratory of the bar. But while it is such an exception, it is likewise a strong confirmation of the truth of the causes we have assigned in explanation of the principle itself. This branch of the art still maintains its position, because literary changes have been extrinsic to its field of operation. The facts and circumstances which go to make up each particular controversy between man and man are not such as can be the subject of previous knowledge, and the ground of conviction in the minds of those to whom this sort of oratory is addressed. Moreover, the law applicable to such facts and circumstances is in a great measure unknown to the auditory who are to apply it, until laid before them by the speaker himself. In all respects therefore a different rule governs this branch of the art from that applicable to it as a whole. The very nature of things in this case prevents the utility of declamation from ceasing to exist, and it will remain a surviving branch, and as far as we can see, the only one, of an immense system, which in past days wielded the whole power, and covered the whole field of literary effort.

EPITAPH ON A MODERN 'CRITIC.'

'*FOR* PUDOR''

'Here Aristarchus lies!' (a pregnant phrase,
And greatly hackneyed, in his earthly days,
By those who saw him in his maudlin scenes,
And those who read him in the magazines.)
Here Aristarchus lies, (nay, never smile,)
Cold as his muse, and stiffer than his style;
But whether Bacchus or Minerva claims
The crusty critic, all conjecture shames;
Nor shall the world know which the mortal sin,
Excessive genius or excessive gin!

A FANTASY

FROM THE NORWEGIAN; DONE INTO RUDE ENGLISH WITH ILLUSTRATIVE MARGINAL NOTES; WHICH ACCORDING TO THE MOST APPROVED MODERN FASHION, MAY WITH EQUAL ADVANTAGE BE EITHER READ OR OMITTED.

An old Norwegian Student, in the dead of night, seated at a table covered with illuminated books and manuscripts, finds his Imagination suddenly occupied and overpowered by the Vision of his beautiful young Mistress; and after several attempts to dispel the supposed hallucination, thus remonstrates with her.

WHY dost thou come and plant thy face
　　Betwixt my page and me ?
When I would fain the legend trace,
　　The Book holds nought but Thee !

He continues his remonstrance in such terms as to make it inferable that the pestilent young enchantress had been in the habit of afflicting this worthy gentleman at night, both when he walked abroad, and as he lay upon his couch with a moon-beam in the apartment; a ray which she appears to have occupied with a Wilderness of Beauty.

Why, in the stillness of the night,
　　When even Echo sleeps
Along the silvery mountain-height,
　　And Earth its dewdrops weeps

In secret — say, why dost thou seem,
　　Noiseless and shadowless,
To glide within the moon's gay beam
　　And on my fancy press ?

This stanza contains an Ellipsis, which, however barbarous it may to some ears appear in English, is quite permissible in the Norwegian.

Peopling the magick of her light
　　With all thy beauties rare ?
And making Night, than day more bright,
　　As thou, than day, art fair ?

He ventures to ask her: if She knows she 's out ? — and, if so, whether she is sensible of the Rapture that her presence transfuses throughout every pulsation of his being.

Know'st thou these wanderings of thine ?
　　Know'st thou the Extacy
Of Joy, the Ravishment divine,
　　That, trembling, watches Thee ?

He realises her close approach; and is now satisfied, as he fondly imagines, that it is indeed and in truth, his own blessed living beautiful young Mistress that listens to his words.

Know'st thou thy lov'd, thy bright approach ?
　　And that those lips; that beam
Of Joy; now, on my sight, encroach ? —
　　Oh thou dost *live*, not ' *seem !*'

*　*　*　*　*　*
*　*　*　*　*　*

Here a pause ensues, and no reply coming from the young Lady, the old student begins to reason; and then heroically scolds himself for having been led astray by the Vision that walks in silver light.

Fool ! 't is the Vision in thine heart
　　That plays upon thy sight !
That to the Book doth life impart !
　　That walks in Silver light !

He counsels himself, by a figure taken from the Fall of the Moon-beam, to greater consistency of action and of thought, lest his mind should be altogether lost.

The beam that clothes the ivied Tower
　　Falls shattered on the Wave !
Oh let thy Mind resume its power
　　Whilst thou hast aught to save !

The last stanza exhibits the sad conviction, that he has been misled; arrives at the unpalatable confession of his age; and expresses an apprehension, since the brightness of the moon contains no more life than that of armour, that he may already have become damaged in the upper story.

There 's nought betwixt the page and thee !
　　The moon hangs sheen and cold;
The maiden sleeps, all Fancy-free;
　　Whiles thou — art craz'd and old !

JOHN WATERS.

MARY: A VILLAGE SKETCH.

IN AN EPISTLE TO THE EDITOR.

PRESCRIPTION has granted to old men the privilege of talking, and enjoined on their juniors the duty of listening to them respectfully. As I claim to be one of the former class, and have listened for many years, Mr. KNICKERBOCKER, to your agreeable discourse with feelings of great pleasure, I consider myself in some measure entitled to ask you to attend to mine at any odd moment when you may chance to have no better employment upon your hands.

I live in a smart, bustling little village, which is nothing like the Idlebergs and such-like places that have been immortalized in your Magazine. It is not far from New-York, and has an easy summer communication with your city; a circumstance which, though it does not occasion its active, business character, yet much increases it. The new cut of dress-coats is hardly a week earlier with you than with us, and of course the latest style of a lady's habit here is scarce half that time behind you. We consider ourselves not a moment 'behind the age.' The news you read at breakfast we digest at dinner. We have our baths, lectures, and libraries; our societies—

Ah! I do n't know how far I should have run on in general terms if I had not met with that word ' *societies.*' My object at this time is to make you my confidant in a little matter that occurred many years since, which arose out of a society, and which, after being long buried in a mass of varied recollections, has lately been by similar means drawn from its hiding-place, as fresh and lively as it first fell upon my heart.

This fall we had an annual exhibition of fruits and flowers; a festival season which our ' Horticultural Society' has for half a century, with much zeal and pride, commemorated. I had not attended the exhibition for several years; but this time, my grand-daughters—I wish you could see them, Sir; one is an angel and the other a fairy—in a manner compelled me to go with them. As they led me round among the tables, calling my attention at one moment to a luscious basket of nectarines, at another to a beautiful bouquet of dahlias; now pointing me to a cluster of grapes, and again to a bunch of verbenas, my thoughts went back to the time when this very society had its first exhibition; when I was a youth as full of joy and hope as these fair girls beside me; and then, dear Mary! I thought of thee.

Mary and I were in a manner brought up together. Her father was near neighbor to mine, and we were school-mates and play-fellows. I need not try to describe her to you. I am no hand at description, and I have no desire to spoil her portrait; but she was very beautiful, Sir. I do assure you, on my veracity, there are no such women now.

Perhaps you have observed that where a young man and woman
are brought up together as we were, when they cease to be children
and begin to feel the deep love that has all along been growing up
in their hearts, they are more constrained and timid toward each
other than if they had met in society as strangers, and thus become
acquainted. I think it is true as a general rule; it was certainly
true in our case.

At the time I am speaking of, I was about to leave home for col-
lege. I could not bear to think of going away to be gone so long,
(for there were not then such facilities for travelling as now,) with-
out telling her how much I loved her, and receiving a similar con-
fession from her lips; for I knew our regard was mutual. And
yet, although we met frequently, we could not converse as freely
as we had used to do; for I observed that topics of discourse very
often failed us, and then our embarrassment was sometimes very
painful. It was about this time that our 'Horticultural Society'
was formed, and an exhibition was projected, to serve as a sort of
nucleus about which to collect materials for future progress. I
had always a great taste in these matters, and being intimate with
the chief manager, I spent the day preceding the evening of the
exhibition in assisting him to receive and arrange the productions
which were brought. You may be sure, Sir, that very few of my
arrangements were made without recalling her preferences to mind,
and reflecting how I might make things most agreeable to her.

After tea that evening I called for her. Though we had made
no previous engagement, she expected, as a matter of course, to go
with me, and was waiting for me. I had not in a long time felt so
full of matériel for conversation, and I was sure from the first that
we should pass a delightful evening. From being present during
the day, and keeping a memorandum of the articles and their donors,
I was familiar with every thing. There was not a big cabbage, nor
a tall corn-stalk, nor a mammoth beet, with the whole history of
which I was not conversant. All the varieties of grapes and peaches
and apples were at my tongue's end. My memory was in full pos-
session of Mr. A.'s joke when his man brought in the queer water-
melon, and of Mr. B.'s laughable accident when he was hanging
up the bunch of turnips, and of Mrs. C.'s witty reply to the mana-
ger when he praised her flowers; and so on down the alphabet.
There was not so happy a couple in the crowd that night, as we
walked arm-in-arm through the rooms, every moment stopping to
admire something new and beautiful.

At last it was time to go home, and we left the scene of enchant-
ment. I now felt the boldness of a man in a state of intoxication;
indeed I *was* intoxicated with pleasure, and I felt that now was my
time, if ever. And Fortune was propitious to me, for Mary intro-
duced the subject that lay nearest to my heart by asking, not with-
out emotion, 'Hugh, how soon do you leave us?'

I don't know, Sir, how you like the name of Hugh, but she used
to say it was the prettiest man's name there was; and I have always

thought that Mary is a name of which an angel in Heaven might be proud. 'It is but a short time now, Mary,' I answered; 'and I could not go away without saying something to you which I have longed to say often before now.' I felt her arm tremble in mine as I said this, and then I added, before my heart should fail me, for I felt it beginning to beat thick : ' We love each other, Mary ; is it not so ?' She did not make me any answer, but her arm trembled more violently, and her steps faltered. I was not prepared for so much emotion in her, for she was of a sprightly turn, and I began to tremble myself, for fear my declaration was not acceptable. ' I hope I have not pained you, my dear girl,' I continued, as I bent forward to look in her face. 'Oh no, dear Hugh!' she replied, ' you have not pained me at all;' and then I kissed from her cheeks the tears which were glistening in the moon-beams ; and if we had been happy during the evening, how can I express the happiness we felt as we walked the rest of the way home together ?

In a few days I had left home to pursue my studies, and did not return for a whole year. I heard very little of her during my absence, for I had not told our people of our engagement, and it was not considered decorous then for young people in our situation to correspond. On my return, what sad tidings was it for me to hear that her father had become embarrassed in his circumstances, his property had been sold, and he had removed to New-York ! My first step was to lay before my parents the story of my deep and abiding love for Mary, and of my engagement to marry her. My father was a little taken by surprise, but I think my mother was not. I have a theory that women become acquainted with these matters by instinct. I went on to say that I could never forget or cease to love her ; and that now, when she was in poverty, and perhaps in want, certainly in want of many of the comforts she had enjoyed, I could never cease to reproach myself if any evil befel her. My father was a kind-hearted man, and always very kind to me. He told me that when he first was informed of her father's reverse of fortune, he had offered to place him in a situation where he could retrieve his losses ; which, from his wealth and extensive business connexions, he was easily able to do ; but her father was a very sensitive man, and declined his assistance, although expressing himself very grateful for his kindness. I said that I would go to New-York and see them ; that I would make known to him the relation his daughter and myself bore to each other ; and that under the circumstances I thought I could make him understand that we would be the parties laid under obligation by his consent to receive our assistance. My father and mother joined in recommending my intention, and wished me every success.

When I went to New-York, and after some inquiry succeeded in finding where they lived, the first words she said on seeing me (she was alone when I entered) showed her amiable, self-sacrificing disposition : ' This is very kind of you, Hugh.' Kind of me, truly, when to stay away would have been my death ! Their furniture was scanty. Every thing about them showed that they were compelled to practice strict economy. But every thing was very neat and tidy. Her father kept a small retail grocery, which occupied all his time from early in the morning till late at night; and here she sat alone, employing herself in needle-work and painting for sale. Her poor mother had been removed from the troubles of this world, and for an only child, reared in every indulgence, this was a sad change, occurring at the very time too when, from her age, the pleasures of life would have been enjoyed with the keenest relish.

But, Sir, my story has turned out longer than I intended. Old men are said to be prolix and tedious, and I suppose I am not an exception. Well, I will cut it short. After telling my story to her father, I did not have much difficulty in persuading him to listen to my proposition for their more comfortable subsistence. My father sold out to him a lucrative partnership in a mercantile house, the terms being that he should pay the interest yearly, and as much of the principal as he found it convenient. Before I left the city, I saw them established in a more comfortable dwelling, and gave Mary to understand that she must not sell her paintings and embroidery to any one but me. I then returned to college, and when I married dear Mary three years after, her father had paid off his debts, and was in a fair way of recovering the competence he had lost.

I do n't know, Sir, how you will like my story. In these days of excitement, I am afraid it will be considered tame. But it is a very interesting one to me, and would be so to all who could have known Mary. I have seen the day, too, when the circumstance that it is a *true* story would have added much to its interest; but I fear those days are gone now, and that its truth would be but a poor recommention. Yet there are so many dear remembrances connected with it that it always does me good to have some one to tell it to, and perhaps this is as good an excuse as I can offer.

SONNET: TO MY WIFE.

—

WRITTEN ON THE HUDSON.

—

IN the holy hour of moonrise, evermore,
   When o'er my heart of sin, whose light grows dimmer,
   The stars like eyes of blessed angels glimmer;
Ever-blessed angels on Heaven's happy shore!
There cometh, (oh! how oft the spell hath bound me!)
   Gliding in the starlight, from th' autumnal skies,
   A blessed form, like saint from Paradise,
Who with a kiss doth clasp her arms around me!
To-night, upon the thought-provoking river,
   While the moon struggles through the clouds above,
   That fair form cometh back with looks of love,
And holy constancy as pure as ever;
How then can I, though absent, feel alone,
When thou, though far away, art near me still, mine own!

Utica, N. Y.   H. W. R.

THE DOCTOR: A LEGEND OF NONOTUCK.

BY A LIVE YANKEE.

PART FIRST.

IN a certain fair village
Renowned for its tillage,
In the 'Old Bay State,' on a clear winding stream,
That swept lazily by like a musical dream,
And innocent yet of all knowledge of steam,
There lived a young sprig
Of a medical prig,
Who gloried in physic,
And curéd the good folks
Of all their complaints, from swamp-fever to phthisic ;
Who was great at a story, cracked wonderful jokes,
Who sung a good song, and was ripe for a hoax —
Oh ! a capital fellow was young Dr. OAKES!

The Doctor's *sanctum* was provided, you see,
With all the queer things that a sanctum should be ;
It had all sorts of oddities,
The strangest commodities,
From seven-pronged teeth to a child in a bottle ;
And nostrums enough very nearly to throttle
The whole tribe of CLARKS, from MOSES to AMOS,
For which race this redoubtable hamlet was famous,
But he became restless,
His jokes dull and zestless,
He was ' down in the mouth' and wofully ' blue,'
And what had come over him nobody knew,
Until, quite unawares, he gave us a clue,
And the secret came out,
And soon got about,
That the fog in the doctor's brain-socket was caused
By the want of a — (here the narrator paused,)
The want of a skeleton ! *There* was a want !
Think of a skeleton, grinning and gaunt !
The doctor *did* think ; and now in a flood he
Poured out his distress for the want of a body
Deprived of its flesh, to hang up in his study.

Anatomical man !
'T was a capital plan
That his friends hit upon to supply him with one,
Combined with the thought of having some fun
At the doctor's expense. So at it they went,
And told him that since they found he was bent
Upon having a skeleton, why, they would give him
A lift, in their way,
The very next day —
I mean the next night — and thus try to relieve him,
And satisfy wants that seemed so to grieve him.

The project matured, they called on the doctor,
But first got a musket, primed, loaded and cocked her,

As well as a shovel, a bar, and a barrow,
And implements such as to look at would harrow
The souls of some mortals, and dry up their marrow.
The OLD ONE himself, had he been on the spot,
'T was lucky for them that they thought he was not!
Would have flourished his tail with peculiar delight,
To see the strange tools brought together that night.

Alas! for those friends, who in hope and in trust,
  Had said ' dust to dust,'
And who, leaving the ground, had but recently started
From the mouldering home of the dear one departed,
  With a sad conviction,
  The last resurrection
Alone would disclose what they had concealed,
To sleep, as they hoped, till all thoughts are revealed,
When the dread book of Fate is brought forth and unsealed
And the saint and the sinner alike shall arise,
The one for the place where ' the worm never dies,'
The other to glory and life in the skies.

  Still, still! solemnly still!
On a night like this how the nerves will thrill,
And the limbs refuse to obey the will ;
When never a sound from valley nor hill,
Not even the note of the whip-poor-will,
Nor the shriek of the night-hawk, sharp and shrill,
Pierces the dull, oppressive air,
That spell-like hangs o'er the listener there.
How aches the sense at want of sound
To stir the breath of the dark profound!
With what intense and eager ear
We listen, as men list in fear.
Whenever the faintest leaf-fall brings
Relief to the soul's encumbered wings ;
When in the dim mysterious light
Float shadowy forms of dread and fright
Over the church-yard's tainted air,
Enough from its loosening hold to scare
The life and the shortening breath of him
Whose heart will sink and eye wax dim,
As he seems to gaze on the features grim
Of the ' terrible king,' and feels the grasp
Of an icy hand within his clasp.

But enough of this. The doctor delved
Away with the rest, for him who was shelved
  A fathom below
The spot where the lantern's fitful glow
  Began to show
That they had nearly finished their job,
The grave of its lifeless tenant to rob.

  Whiz! whiz! what was that ?
Oh, it was only the wing of a bat ;
  Whiz! whiz! there again!
But that was the sound of the dropping rain.
  Clang, clang! over his head ;
The doctor's soul was filled with dread
For he thought it to be the voice of the dead!

Clang, clang!—yet once more,
It is close to his ear, behind and before.
He dropped his spade in a terrible fright,
When before him appeared a ghastly sight,
    Which the bravest loathes :
To his agonized sense straightway there rose,
    In white grave-clothes,
    (They always come so,
They would n't be ghosts if they did n't, you know,)
    A figure that froze
    His blood, from his toes
'To the very tip-end of his rubicund nose !
In great trepidation he jumped from the grave
And ran as if running his life would save ;
Till, weak and exhausted, he sank to the ground,
On quite a peculiar-shaped sort of a mound,
Beneath which one of his patients lay taking
The last long sleep that knows no waking.

    Much perplexed,
    And thoroughly vexed,
At such a tragical turn to their joke,
    (For they thought him dead
    As herring red,)
His friends in low whispers hurriedly spoke
Of what they considered a terrible stroke ;
But a closer look convinced them soon
That the man had only gone off in a swoon ;
And heaving a long-drawn sigh, his breath
Relieved their fears of his sudden death.
    And then rang out
    A joyous shout
From the brazen throats of those godless men,
Who had been, ever since the clock struck ten,
Contriving to bring their scheme to a point,
And put the poor doctor's ' nose out of joint !'

PART SECOND.

THE doctor sat in his great arm-chair,
With a troubled face and a brow of care ;
His recent exploit had worried him much,
And he was plagued with a pretty smart touch
Of what the unfortunates term ' the blues ;'
    A horde of young devils
    Who, when in their revels,
Have a right rough way of ' putting the screws'
    To the mind of their victim,
And who to a dish of the horrors restrict him,
Until they have ' floored' and cruelly ' licked' him.

    As when from out the sparkling foam
    Gay VENUS sprang to love and light,
    And o'er the sea-god's glittering home
    Dazzled his yet bewildered sight ;
    So swept across our hero's heart
    A vision, born within the hour,
    In which revenge bore active part
    And placed his foes within his power.

'T was on a cloudless winter's night,
The earth in mantle robed snow-white,
While all around translucent flowed
Refulgence from the queen that rode
     Pavilioned high
     In the far blue sky ;
That round a brisk and crackling fire,
Which in itself would mirth inspire,
The doctor's friends, jocose and merry,
Enjoyed their steaming punch and sherry,
He having invited them all to come
And taste the fare of his bachelor home.

Oh ! were they not a jovial body,
While sipping the punch and praising the toddy ?
And as the hours waxed deep into night,
Enjoyment climbed to its utmost height.
Less and less grave the stories grew,
Till joke and wit like magic flew,
While quip and jest and repartee
With every glass jumped fresh and free.
The mirth and fun ' grew fast and furious,'
And many a story, odd and curious,
Brought forth such peals of joyous laughter
As shook the house from floor to rafter.

When merriment now to its climax had leapt,
     To the window he stepped,
And without a sound softly raised the sash.
Then from the door went out like a flash ;
As quickly returned, and held in his hand
What he who saw might well understand
     Was a dangerous thing
     For a man to bring
So near to the fire, on the hearth that was roaring ;
And still as his gimlet kept quietly boring
     A hole in the keg,
     They began to beg
To know what the desperate doctor was doing :
Their murmurs now waxed louder and louder,
When they saw he had gotten a keg of gunpowder !
But he leisurely told them that mischief was brewing,
' Remember,' said he, ' my life is embittered,
And the flattering hopes that before me once glittered
     Are dead — and I 'm done !
     So now for *my* fun !
Look your last at the moon, think your last of the sun :
Straightway to the fire this powder-keg goes,
And so to the devil it all of us blows !'
And suiting the deed to the word, in his ire
He tumbled the powder-keg into the fire.

     Like lightning sprang
     The frightened gang ;
     They were crazed and frantic,
     And many an antic
They cut in their pell-mell rush to escape
From the threatened explosion, in life-like shape ;
In eager haste from the window they jumped,
And into the snow were suddenly plumped :

Not a man of them all was left in the lurch,
And the room was soon still as the walls of a church ;
Nobody there but the Doctor alone,
Triumphantly perched on his medical throne.

I 've heard him tell what a sight was there,
In the frosty and sparkling moonlight air ;
How one poor wight lay trembling apart,
Sheltered beneath an upturned cart ;
And another, ensconced behind a tree,
Had sought him a refuge ; the while, ah, me !
One terrified mortal who in the flurry
Had tried to escape in the most of a hurry,
  Through the window had burst,
  And plunging head-first,
Down into the snow his shoulders had thrust,
So that while his head was buried below,
Deep sunk in the drift of the yielding snow,
  High sawing the air,
  Like a very large pair
Of compasses, flourished the legs of a man,
Describing an arc on a bran-new plan !
Another had made a few bounds and then fainted,
(The scene should be painted,)
And one, with his coat-tails straight on the air,
  And his head all bare,
  Let his frightened hair
Like a meteor stream in the moonlight there.

  . . . .

Now, when sojourning in that place,
A stranger sees a youthful face,
O'ershadowing which, the bleaching hair
Betokens years, and toil, and care ;
  And asks the cause
  Why nature's laws
In those poor men were so reversed,
As if to make them seem accursed ;
The boys with quizzical looks will tell
Of what to them lang syne befel ;
Tell, in their language bluff and bold,
The self-same tale your bard has told ;
And if your looks a doubt imply,
  They 'll swear 't is true ;
  And *prove* it too,
Or else the men themselves must lie.

CONSTANCY: BY MELEAGER.

STILL, like dew in silence falling,
 Drops for thee the nightly tear ;
Still that voice the past recalling,
 Dwells, like echo, on my ear,
  Still, still !

Day and night the spell hangs o'er me,
 Here forever fix'd thou art ;
As thy form first shone before me,
 So 't is graven on this heart,
  Deep, deep !

TRUSTING IN THE DEVIL.

AN EPISTLE TO THE EDITOR.

BUILDING castles in Spain is a pleasant pastime, no doubt; but when the rude breath of reality touches them, and they begin to tumble down about the dreamer's ears one after another as fast as they can come, he feels chap-fallen enough; yet after a while he will pluck up fresh courage and begin building perhaps yet more splendid aërial palaces in his aspiring imagination. This has been the case with my friend N—— C——, who is ever expecting that some lucky chance will occur to ' set him on his legs again,' as he calls it, and make a *man* of him; that is, a man of cash, who has plenty of money in his pocket and owes no man a farthing. My friend is of wealthy and respectable parentage, and in his younger years never knew the want of money, being freely supplied by an over-indulgent father, which probably laid the foundation of his subsequent improvident habits, and served to nurture his natural taste for self-indulgence and romantic and erratic notions. · He is a man now beyond the meridian of life; has a family, whom he truly loves and ardently desires to make happy and comfortable; but having by reverses, without any fault of his own, lost the greater part of his patrimony, even before he became of age, he now finds himself in the decline of life, poor and *discontented.* A severe and protracted disease has moreover contributed much to aggravate his position, having for several years cut him off from the opportunity of gaining a subsistence in some permanent employment. He is of an honest and frank disposition, industrious and temperate, and would owe no man any thing but love, if otherwise circumstanced. But to show the inveteracy of habit, although long dormant, and the singularity, nay the madness of trusting the devil to help an honest man in his straits, for any *good* purpose, I, with my friend's permission, and as a warning to others — which, alas! I fear will find but small attention in the right quarter — make known the following little anecdote, which carries with it its own moral.

Some few days ago his wife wanted some flour and other necessaries for her household, when he, as a good and loyal husband ought to do, offered to go to New-York to procure the desired articles, saying that he had some business of his own also, about printing a book, etc., and would return the same week. For this accommodation the trusting wife was duly grateful, and wished her husband GOD-speed, and a safe return home.

But for the sake of more perspicuity and directness, I must beg leave to let my friend tell his own tale as he poured it into my astonished ears. With a rueful face and in a husky voice he thus proceeded:

'The fact is, I left home with a half-formed determination to try my luck at gambling. Our necessities for money were so great and urgent, and the sources from whence the golden grains were trickling so slow and parsimonious in their supplies, that I felt a most tantalizing desire to step into the shoes of Midas, the king of Phrygia, or to be the possessor of Aladdin's lamp or the cap of Fortunatus, if it were only for five minutes. My good wife prosed considerably on pinching occasions, (and with reason, I allow,) about the extraordinary toil she had been doomed to undergo for years; and her nearest of kin looked but coldly on me for suffering her to struggle on alone as it were, hinting that now that my health was in a great measure reëstablished, it was *my* turn to labor for the support of the family. To this I did not at all demur; and Heaven knows I felt all this most keenly in my inmost soul, and determined with myself that something decided *must* be done this autumn to effect a favorable change in the posture of my domestic affairs. I had been enabled to do something, it is true, even during the period of my illness, and defrayed many lesser expenses, which do not appear on the surface, and are generally forgotten, but which in the aggregate amount to a good deal; perhaps to a couple of hundred dollars in the course of a year; but still the main burthen had been borne by my devoted companion; and it galled my proud sensibilities to the quick, and almost drove me to distraction, when I contemplated our prospects, and saw no way of relief. We have always maintained an excellent character and credit in the place of our residence, and paid our bills regularly at the end of every quarter, as far as our limited means would reach; but now some of these bills had somehow or other grown to an unwonted size, and although not of long standing, we felt ambitious to pay them off; provision was to be made for the approaching fall and a long winter; fuel and winter garments were wanted, with hundreds of little items, which a liberal fancy will quickly run up to a formidable score. Rob, steal or swindle I never contemplated, and I shrank from the bare idea of any dishonesty; but although an old man, not devoid of good common sense in other matters, the vagaries of an Utopian imagination kept suggesting to me that 'there is a tide in the affairs of men, which taken at the flood leads on to fortune,' and thus got the better of my sober judgment and past experience.

'It is now thirty years since I engaged in games of hazard, and came away a loser; but, trusting in the devil rather than in GOD, (for I consider that trusting in a fallacy or uncertainty, as are all games of chance, is on a par with trusting in the devil, the father of all lies, frauds and deception,) I thought that perhaps the fickle goddess might have changed her humor toward me by this time, and stood ready to atone for former discourtesies, by bestowing a few radiant smiles upon her humble votary on his return to his allegiance. I came away from home with a few dollars of my own money in my pocket, enough to purchase the flour at any rate, and something more; and after a little preliminary instruction from an obliging accidental acquaintance in the city, who keeps an exchange-office in one of our principal streets, provided with a protective and tasteful arras, I commenced operations with a palpitating heart, I assure you, about the first of the present month; and though I had lost two dollars previously at a private sitting with the above-mentioned obliging individual, I was now in two nights the gainer of some twelve or fifteen dollars; for I had determined to play low and prudently; at the same time I discovered that with a little more courage and resolution, and a greater degree of faith in the capricious and seductive dame, her favors might have been multiplied a hundred fold on these two occasions; for the identical painted pieces of paste-board on which I ventured my humble stakes, and having won, withdrew them to some other equally amiable member of the renowned tri-decimal family, afterward came up, again and again, and often in rapid succession, on the winning side. This was a whetter to my appetite, and was regarded as an endorsement by dame Fortune herself of her good intentions.

While pocketing the money from the '*gentlemen*' acting so disinterestedly as agents in this Court of Chance, I was inspired with no particular feelings of gratitude or regard for *them*, well-knowing how little their affections were enlisted in behalf of my welfare, but rather plumed myself on my *own* sagacity and moderation, and looked upon my 'small potatoes' as only the precursors of a richer harvest. The dispensers of ivory and paste-board were scrupulously polite, and every thing went on in the most approved business-like style; and at a certain hour a recess was announced, in order to partake of a sumptuous repast, spread on an elegant table in a splendidly-illumined apartment. Being temperate from principle and habit, and accustomed to go to bed at an early hour, I retired to my lodgings in B—— street, reserving the consummation of my destined good fortune to some other propitious hour. But, alas! my friend, that propitious hour has never come. Fortune has deserted me, like a fickle mistress as she is, and left me in the lurch; and braving her to her face, she has stripped me of nearly all my cash; the flour is yet unbought; my wife wonders what keeps me away so long, and I am at my wit's-end to know how to extricate myself out of this disagreeable dilemma. I have not the face to apply to any of my friends, for I could not do so without stating the exact truth, and that would most probably change their good-will into frigid suspicion. On the whole, I am thankful for what is. A run of good luck might have made me a confirmed gambler, and proved my total ruin. I have received a lesson, not easily forgotten, never again to trust in the devil or any of his machinery or agents. Never again will I suffer myself to be caught with chaff. Honest labor and prudence will help me through. *Ne cede malis, sed contra audentior ito: spes tutissima cœlis.* As it is no better, thank GOD it is no worse!

Here my friend ceased his lamentation. Whether he thought my opinion of small moment, or that it could not be materially affected by this gratuitous piece of intelligence, having known him intimately for quite a number of years, I will not now attempt to decide. But he imparted to me, in his own prosy way, a good deal of the mysteries and management of the profession into which he voluntarily sought to be initiated. If there exists any excuse for him, it must be his peculiar temperament and early habits. ' He does not blame any one but himself for what has happened; but while he despises his own folly, and knows that others laugh at him, he says that he wishes he had the power to destroy every *species* of gambling on the face of the earth. Surely, Mr. KNICKERBOCKER, something ought to be done to check this crying evil in our city. It could not exist were it not connived at by men of wealth and authority. It seems to me that were our public authorities in *real* earnest, faro-tables, policy-offices and ostensible exchange-brokers would at once all be swept by the board.

Your's respectfully,

New-York, September, 1846.   MEUM AND TUUM.

THE DEATH OF LANNES.

It is pleasant to turn from the selfishness of NAPOLEON's character to those touching traits of generous affection and sympathy which were exhibited toward his brave companions in arms. It was after the disastrous battle of Aspern, when the French army was painfully retreating over the broken bridge of boats to the island of Lobau, and while BONAPARTE, although smarting under this his first defeat, was still devoting the energies of his great mind to the protection of his threatened host, that a litter was brought to him, containing the shattered body of his brave marshal, LANNES. It was then that the EMPEROR forgot his defeat, his army, his own peril; and flinging himself on his knees, beside his dying friend, he wept bitterly.

It was by the Danube's tide,
   On the marchfield's bloody plain,
That brave France beheld her pride
   Humbled to the Austrian train;
There the bold imperial band
   Struck with fierce and fatal blow,
To redeem their father land
   From the stern invading foe!

Amid Aspern's straggling streets,
   By its church-yard's lofty wall,
Now the Austrian rank retreats,
   France now sees her heroes fall;
O'er the blood-bespatter'd tombs
   Lie in heaps the mangled slain,
Banners torn, and shatter'd plumes,
   Hurled down by the leaden rain!

Vain thy prowess on that day,
   Fortune's long-protected son,
CHARLES hath matched thee in the fray,
   And the laurels from thee won;
Lost to thee the magic name
   Which had never known defeat,
And consigned thee to the shame
   From thy foeman to retreat.

Fierce the pang that rent thee then,
   When above the river's tide
Came a band of weeping men,
   Struggling still to reach thy side;
Lo! they bore a hero's form,
   Victor oft in many a field,
Struck down now by battle-storm;
   Doomed no more his sword to wield.

'"T is thy LANNES, Sire; farewell!
   For the world thou still must live,
But when Death hath toll'd my knell,
   To thy friend some kind thoughts give;
I have fought for thee and thine,
   But the strife for me is o'er;
Foremost in each battle line
   Thou shalt hear my shout no more!'

Sadly knelt Earth's victor then
   By the dying hero's bed,
And the conqueror of men
   Many bitter tear-drops shed;
' LANNES, knowest thou me?' he cried,
   '"T is thy EMPEROR — thy friend!'
We will staunch this bloody tide,
   Thou shalt yet my cause defend!'

Vain thy promise, haughty chief!
   Kingdoms thou may'st give away,
But thou can'st not grant relief
   To the victims of Death's sway;
Soon the funeral-gun shall sound,
   Soon the muffled drum shall beat,
While beneath the earthen mound
   Sleeps thy friend in martial sheet!

Glory still shall deck thy path,
   Victory oft thy fame renew,
Fate shall long defeat the wrath
   Of the foes that thee pursue;
But thy thoughts shall often stray
   To the Danube's swollen tide,
To the heart that on that day,
   To protect thy banners, died!

September 25, 1846.   ROBERT M. CHARLTON.

THE SCHOLAR, THE JURIST, THE ARTIST, THE PHILANTHROPIST. An Address before the Phi Beta Kappa Society of Harvard University, at their last Anniversary. By CHARLES SUMNER. Boston: WILLIAM D. TICKNOR AND COMPANY.

MR. SUMNER's Address is a sincere and touching tribute of regard to the memory of four of the most eminent sons of Harvard University. Never, since the foundation of that venerable college, have four so distinguished of her children, passing in so brief a succession to their brighter immortality above, given such meet occasion to the scholar, the orator, and the friend, for his reminiscence, his eulogy or his tears. Nor is it flattery to say, that seldom has a theme of such solemnity and almost universal interest found a more fitting illustrator, alike of individual grief and the public loss. CHANNING, STORY, PICKERING, ALLSTON — illustrious names! Recent as the sod appears upon their graves, they have already attained in our remembrance the high seats of established renown. It is a pride as well as a pleasure to recall them; it is a kind of glory to be associated with them, even in the mere character of an 'honest chronicler.' To praise them with discrimination is better than to be one's self the subject of ordinary applause. Mr. SUMNER, in performing his sacred duty, has shown himself in some degree their disciple as well as panegyrist. He has returned us their memories perfumed with such praise as only a mind akin to theirs could have bestowed. Adorned with the flowers of unfading thought and the gems of felicitous language, the precious recollections come back to us, more brilliant, more sweet, more lasting; 'apples of gold in pictures of silver.' Mr. SUMNER, reversing the natural order of his brothers' departure, commences his eulogy with a review of the life and services of JOHN PICKERING, the scholar. In this division of his theme he displays an ability of criticism and an erudition that greatly enhance the value of his praise. Thoroughly conversant with the subject of classical learning, and imbued with the graces of the ancients, he expounds their value with a sapient judgment, but is not misled into a blind veneration of the very blots upon their pages. Here is a passage that might well be printed on the cover of almost every volume that has come down to us from the ruins of the past:

'THE classics possess a peculiar charm, from the circumstance that they have been the models, I might almost say the masters, of composition and thought in all ages. In the contemplation of these august teachers of mankind we are filled with conflicting emotions. They are the early voice of the world, better remembered and more cherished still than all the intermediate words that have been uttered; as the lessons of childhood still haunt us, when the impressions of later years have been effaced from the mind. But they show with most unwelcome frequency the tokens of the world's childhood, before passion had yielded to the sway of reason and the affections. They want the highest charm of purity, of righteousness, of elevated sentiments, of love to GOD and man. It is not in the frigid philosophy of the Porch and the Academy that we are to seek these; not in the marvellous teachings of SOCRATES, as they come mended by the mellifluous words of PLATO; not in the resounding line of HOMER, on whose inspiring tale of blond ALEXANDER pillowed his head; not in the animated strain of PINDAR, where virtue is pictured in the successful strife of an athlete at the Isthmian games; not in the torrent of DEMOSTHENES, dark with self-love and the spirit of vengeance; not in the fitful philosophy and intemperate eloquence of TULLY; not in the genial libertinism of HORACE, nor the stately atheism of LUCRETIUS. No; these must not be our masters; in none of these are we to seek the way of life. For eighteen hundred years, the spirit of these writers has been engaged in a weaponless contest with the Sermon on the Mount, and those two sublime commandments on which hang all the law and the prophets.' . . . 'Our own productions, though they may yield to those of the ancients in the arrangement of ideas, in method, in beauty of form, and in freshness of illustration, are immeasurably superior in the truth, delicacy, and elevation of their sentiments; above all, in the benign recognition of that great Christian revelation, the brotherhood of man. How vain are eloquence and poetry, compared with this heaven-descended truth! Put 'in one scale that simple utterance, and in the other the lore of Antiquity, with its accumulating glosses and commentaries, and the last will be light and trivial in the balance.'

THE orator next enters into a rapid but vigorous disquisition upon the great lawyer whom the world has so lately lost. Mr. SUMNER was his pupil; from the affectionate manner of his address, and the pathetic sincerity of his admiration, one might almost have said, his son. 'Farewell to thee!' he exclaims, Jurist, Master, Benefactor, Friend! May thy spirit continue to inspire a love for the science of the law! May thy example be ever fresh in the minds of the young, beaming as in life with encouragement, kindness and hope! From the grave of the Jurist, at Mount Auburn,' continues Mr. SUMNER, 'let us walk to that of the Artist:'

'WASHINGTON ALLSTON died in the month of July, 1843, aged sixty-three, having reached the grand climacteric, that special mile-stone on the road of life. It was Saturday night; the cares of the week were over; the pencil and brush were laid in repose; the great canvass on which for many years he had sought to perpetuate the image of DANIEL confronting the idolatrous soothsayers of BELSHAZZAR, was left, with the chalk lines designating the labors to be resumed after the rest of the Sabbath; the evening was passed in the pleasant converse of family and friends; words of benediction had fallen from his lips upon a beloved relative; all had retired for the night, leaving him alone, in health, to receive serenely the visitation of Death, sudden but not unprepared for. Happy lot! thus to be borne away, with blessings on the lips, not through the long valley of disease, amidst the sharpness of pain, and the darkness that beclouds the slowly departing spirit, but straight upward through realms of light, swiftly, yet gently, as on the wings of a dove!
'The early shades of evening had begun to prevail, before the body of the Artist reached its last resting-place; and the solemn service of the church was read in the open air, by the flickering flame of a torch, fit image of life. In the group of mourners, who bore by their presence a last tribute to what was mortal in him of whom so much was immortal, stood the great Jurist. His soul, overflowing with tenderness and appreciation of merit of all kinds, was touched by the scene. In vivid words, as he slowly left the church-yard, he poured forth his admiration and his grief. Never was such an Artist mourned by such a Jurist.'

In his masterly sketch of the character of Doctor CHANNING, our orator dwells with peculiar impressiveness upon the peaceful spirit of his ethics; upon his gentleness, and the love to man inculcated by every line of his writings. Mr. SUMNER, as is well-known, is himself a hardy denouncer of the doctrine of violence, and opposed in every form and under every disguise, to the barbarity of war; believing with the sage Lord BURLEIGH, that a soldier can never be a good Christian; that war is a trade no longer in request, and its use as little needed in an age like this as chimneys in summer. Without subscribing entirely to the great Chancellor's doctrine, we cannot but rejoice that similar principles are beginning to prevail among all sects of Christians; that war is looked upon as at least a most melancholy and degrading necessity; that the laurels of the blood-stained hero are withering before the white ensign of the PRINCE of Peace. Mr. SUMNER's Fourth-of-July oration, unsound and visionary as it may have have seemed to many, deserved the welcome it received as a herald of the glad tidings of peace. The present pamphlet is a fit successor to the more zealous character of the former. It will please more, and serve the cause of truth and justice as much. But we would look upon both as the promise of still nobler things. May they serve as the beginning of a more permanent embodiment of opinion:

'Fausto ingressui ad ampliora processuro!'

'Lo HERE AND LO THERE!' OR THE GRAVE OF THE HEART. pp. 22. New-York: Printed for the Author: BURGESS, STRINGER AND COMPANY.

UNDER this strange but appropriate title there has recently been ushered into the world a work which contains not only a guide to the detection of all religious fanaticism, but also many very bold charges and many startling revelations. In a word, the book is a very curious and remarkable one. We shall endeavor to convey some idea of its scope and design. It is a fact of no little import to the people of this country, that in various parts of the land there are little societies where superstitions are inculcated by system and by rule, which probably exceed in vulgarity and in darkness almost any thing that is revealed to us in the scrolls of heathenism; and yet these societies are controlled and inspired by such infinite financial cunning and management; their agriculture is so perfect; the articles of their domestic manufacture are so neat, useful and varied; their garden-seeds are put up in such nice little papers, and they are so sure to grow; their brethren and sisters look so sleek, and they glide so silently around such clean apartments, and there is an air of such uncommon physical attractiveness about their dwellings; there is in all their intercourse so much of the ' yea, yea' and the ' nay, nay;' in a word, these societies seem to be such perfect models of social and domestic order and fraternity, that the world we doubt not will be inclined to receive with some incredulity many of the statements in the pamphlet before us. And we confess that but for the novelty of the subject and the ability of the author in treating it, we should have laid the book aside with as much incredulity as any body. But under the specious veil which worldly cunning has drawn over this society, there seems to lurk the very genius of evil. If one in ten of the charges brought or the statements made in this book can be relied on, the world has been most wretchedly hoodwinked by a band of bold, shrewd, designing men. The writer would make us believe, (and his apparent candor and intelligence certainly entitle him to an attentive hearing,) that the institution of the society of Shakers is an ingenious decoction of superstition and civil and religious tyranny; that it is supported by gaining proselytes who have been crazed by other pseudo-religious sects, and by children taken from poor-houses and destitute families. Their tenets forbidding them to marry, they must fill up their ranks, thinned by death and desertion, in these two ways; that the unavoidable tendency of their religious system and their domestic discipline is to crush every natural and generous emotion; to blot out all intelligence and annihilate the love of it; to suppress all rational or independent thinking; to inspire contempt for the laws and institutions of civil society, and for that institution which we have been taught to believe came from Heaven, the blessed institution of marriage, which has from primitive ages proved the only bond that could unite society, give consequence or sacredness to human sympathies, or offer an attraction strong enough for the charities of home. Such in substance would seem to be the essence of this society; and after scanning with some care the proofs which our author adduces, we are constrained to admit that there is much appropriateness in the latter part of the title of the book, the ' Grave of the Heart.' This Magazine has always made war upon all new systems which have proposed 'improvements' upon the religion of the ' Son of Man.' We believe that it came perfect from its divine Founder, and that neither human wit nor human passion can better it. All such attempts have only afforded the world lamentable commentaries upon man's frailty, and have always ended in human misery.

The Shaker Society owes its foundation to an English woman who emigrated to this country toward the close of the last century. Ambitions of distinction, she hit upon a pretty bold style of action, that has ended in a drama which may be called both a farce and a tragedy, since it has been characterized by all the vulgarity of the one and the misery of the other. She personated no less a being than the HOLY SPIRIT! Of course she found followers, as every person has found and will find for false opinions till the last trump sounds. The creed and the discipline of this society are given in this book; the reader must consult it for himself. Our own opinion is, that any organization of men and women founded in this world on such a creed, and inspired by the spirit it must beget, will be the 'Grave of the Heart.' If a concoction could be made of 'Millerism,' 'Mormonism,' 'Come-Outers' and 'Get-Outers,' and the whole could be held in solution long enough to make an analysis, the precipitate would be Shakerism. It blots out the blessed name of home, feeds upon fanaticism, and tortures the word of GOD to its own liking. Like Mormonism, too, it has its new prophet, and its revelations never cease.

LIFE, TIMES AND CHARACTERISTICS OF JOHN BUNYAN, author of ' The Pilgrim's Progress.' By ROBERT PHILIP, author of ' Life and Times of WHITFIELD.' D. APPLETON AND COMPANY.

THIS is perhaps the best book which its author has presented to the world; and we cannot but rejoice that he has here assumed a task which of all others seems best fitted to his talents. If he will leave divinity to CHALMERS and DICK, with his abilities as a chronicler he might present something to his countrymen which they would not ' willingly let die.' His style in the present work, although it can lay no claim to the stateliness of GIBBON, is not ill adapted to its purpose. It is characterized by vivacity rather than energy, although we have noticed a few passages which would not disgrace noble models in the language. In condensation of thought we find a marked change for the better since the publication of the ' Experimental Guides.' One word concerning the portrait. It almost answers our conception of that venerable countenance. All the editions of the ' Pilgrim' which we have seen are disfigured by what one is well assured must be mere caricature, having, it may be, like the Athenian masks of the old comedy, just enough resemblance to hint at the victim. SOCRATES, it is related, was in the habit of confidently ascribing a noble intellect to a stranger with a comely person. We love to reverse the process; and the reader, with the noble creations of BUNYAN's mind before him, will readily infer our idea of his countenance. He has certainly succeeded in an important qualification of an allegorist, the abstraction of the reader's attention from the author, and the fixing it upon the characters represented. But not even the intense interest that attends every step of the ' Pilgrim' can altogether hide from the mental view the mild gaze of that benevolent eye, or the chastened meekness of those heavenly features.

Much praise is due to Mr. PHILIP for the manner in which he has treated one prominent feature of BUNYAN's life; we mean those terrible conflicts which raged in his soul during his earlier years. We have often been struck with the attempts of professedly religious writers to account for the unearthly struggle which agitated that powerful spirit by the cold speculations of a barren philosophy. Either there is a common FATHER of us all, or there is none. The Atheist has at least the merit of consistency. But those dreamy speculators who have established a sort of half-way house on the road to truth ; who will have a DEITY, and yet in effect have him not ; who acknowledge his attributes and yet make no account of his omniscience, appear to us to consult their reason as little as their piety. XENOPHON represents the little ARISTODEMUS, when SOCRATES confutes him in his atheism, as falling back upon cavils about a particular Providence. He seemed to suppose, and we think rightly, that there is no difference whether we deny the existence or the omnipresent agency of the DEITY. The intense mental agony of BUNYAN is indeed to be partially ascribed to the vigor of his imagination ; but the tenderness of his conscience would furnish us with a reason as philosophical, one would think, as it is obvious. Nor is the suggestion of Mr. PHILIP, although it may excite a smile with his readers, unworthy of notice. The arch-adversary, he tells us, could not fail of foreseeing how formidable an opponent was arising in the tinker, and consequently would ply him fiercely in the outset with his toils. But after all, much is to be left to the inscrutable providence of GOD; nor is there more of wisdom than modesty in presumptuously ascribing to second causes that mysterious and fiery discipline through which it has pleased the ALL-KNOWING to conduct not a few of the noblest champions of religion.

BUNYAN lived-at a most momentous crisis in the history of England. At the commencement of his life as an author the nation was but just recovering from a convulsion by which the body-politic had been well-nigh riven asunder. The English people had, under the first CHARLES, endured all the intolerable evils of a systematic tyranny. They were now, under the second, revelling with frantic excess in the license of a court which demanded no imposts nor ship-money, but drew its funds from the sale of the national honor, and, not less from policy than inclination, imposed no fasts nor thanksgivings. That noble race of stern inflexible enthusiasts who had made the name of ' Roundhead' a terror to every fawning courtier, and the name of England a terror to all Christendom, had mostly descended to their graves. A few remained to waste their scorn and pity on the reign of the strumpets, and to afford, like CHRISTIAN and FAITHFUL at Vanity Fair, a butt for the hooting and jesting of worthless buffoons, not one of whom durst wag his finger at a saint in the days of the mighty Protector. Upon a few leading minds at the restoration devolved the task of furnishing England with a moral and religious code. Venerable forms and conventional usages had been swept away together in the storm of the great rebellion. Under the former STUARTS the formal restraints of the national religious establishment had served to preserve a decent respect for the demands of modesty. The Puritans had abolished these restraints. They established in their place the mere hollow obedience of an eye-servant. Hardly were the bodies of their great old captains cold in death before one universal burst of ribaldry and obscenity announced the commencement of a general saturnalia. In the midst of this national revel, a few noble spirits remained true to their country and their faith. MILTON was indeed just sinking to his grave, and HAMPDEN had fallen in the good cause. But their mantles fell on worthy successors. The piety, vigor and learning of BAXTER, OWEN and JEREMY TAYLOR, with others, stemmed the stream of corruption among the noble and polite, while the untutored genius of BUNYAN, backed by his less gifted brethren, cast a bright light on the dark sensuality of the populace.

All of BUNYAN that was not infinitely beyond the reach of any of his friends was moulded by the Baptists. They could tell him of their spiritual conflicts, though they could not teach him how to draw the fearful scenes of the ' Grace Abounding.'

They first taught him the value of his Bible, and their example undoubtedly first led him to peruse and reflect upon its sacred pages. But it was from a far different source that he drew, to amuse his leisure hours, the vivid though grotesque imaginings of the ' Temple Spiritualized.' These remind us of the prodigious feats of a certain evil spirit, to which we are told the old wizard MICHAEL SCOT set strange tasks to keep him out of mischief. His brethren could tell the tinker of the fiery trials of the way which lay before him ; but when, having partly passed that way, he came to write about the ' Pilgrim,' he was perfectly aware that they could not have aided him, and so he kept the whole matter to himself. They could edify him by their exhortations, and induce him to display his own ' gifts ;' but when they heard his words, that acted like a spell, they were almost ready to cry out, like the astonished neighbors of a greater than he, ' Is not this the tinker's son ? — and his brethren and his sisters, are they not all with us ? Whence then hath this man all these things ?' The character of the English Baptists of that time was of just the sort to start such a genius as that of BUNYAN upon its career ; but they wanted such a spirit as could sympathize with his unbounded charity. Their virtues were many and exalted, their faults few and venial. Their souls were continually exposed to the expansive influence of the Christian faith. They differed only on a single point from many of their brethren, to whom they were bound by common sufferings, the strongest of all ties. But notwithstanding their soul-enlarging creed, BUNYAN was often obliged to rebuke the uncharitableness of his brethren of the close-communion or ' water-baptism way.' It is no small praise to an illiterate tinker of the seventeenth century that he should have cherished a Christian love more comprehensive than can be found even in the most enlightened circles of the nineteenth, except in a very few of the sects which divide the church.

Mr. PHILIP claims for the Baptists the credit of having introduced his hero to the world. However they may have encouraged him in ' exposing his gifts' in exhortation, neither they nor any other class of men can claim the honor of having ' handed the rustic stranger up to fame.' He owed it to nothing but the intense and irrepressible fire of his genius that, as he was returning home from the ' touching and comforting sermon,' he ' wished for a pen and ink that he might write.' The wish was a natural one ; and it is not improbable that there met him, though dimly, the vision of his future usefulness and deathless fame. He had been encouraged to rise while yet a youth, with fear and trembling, in the midst of the venerable GOD-fearing men and women of the church in Bedford. He had seen the big tears falling as he spoke from eyes that never wept for trifles. He had seen the rigid hands of many a stern old saint clasped in a rapture of gratitude that GOD had blessed his young servant. He had heard the groan of remorse from lips that had seldom spoken but with oaths. There arose before his imagination the prospect of addressing the same burning words to hearts which his feeble voice could never reach. He would make a book ! He would publish abroad the intense longings of his soul, that light from the other world might meet, as it had himself, the roysterers whom the holy day now found bell-ringing, or playing at hockey on the village-green. He would thunder against vice in a voice that should start the drunkard from his cups and the lecher from his night's debauch. Perhaps his little tract would reach the ear of the thoughtless King. If so, the tinker might flatter himself that his pleasure-loving Majesty, whether he would hear or forbear, should at least hear plainer names for his sins and plainer warnings to forsake them, than were wont to be uttered by time-serving bishops and velvet-fingered deans.

As BUNYAN'S character was partly moulded by the Baptists, so his exertions in the sacred desk were mainly confined to them. By his long and cruel imprisonment on Bedford bridge his own generation was robbed of twelve of the most valuable years of his life, which might have been spent in labors as extended as his benevolence. We have however no reason to complain. But for the 'certain place where was a den,' the dreamer would never have 'laid down to sleep.' The spiritual discipline of the Baptists was needful for the education of his heart. They lived in constant view of the life to come, and had trained their souls to a proud contempt for the things of time. Their only schools of learning were human nature at large; their only library was the Bible; the only end of their ambition was a golden harp and crown; the only object of their terror an angry glance from the great eye, which they felt sure was beaming in kindness above them. They had learned to despise the splendid rites of the established hierarchy. They loooked with supreme contempt on the lofty cathedrals where hireling pastors led the pompous homage of unhumbled wor- shippers. They remembered those of old, who wandered in deserts and in moun- tains, in dens and caves of the earth, of whom the world was not worthy. Conscious that the world was as little worthy of themselves, they turned without reluctance from their oppressors to the solemn shades of a temple not made with hands. They knew that a contrite heart is a worthier abode for the indwelling of the Holy Spirit than earth's most gorgeous dome. Their's was the worship of the heart.

From such a nursery did BUNYAN emerge to his work. We have said that the school of the Baptists was insufficient for the complete training of his spirit. It was so, because they knew nothing of, and of course made no allowance for, the wild vagaries of an almost omnipotent imagination. It never entered their minds that under the rough exterior of their brother there lay a faculty which was ever extend- ing before him a gorgeous panorama, crowded with all forms of life and beauty, of death and deformity. They saw in the Christian dispensation merely what any humble believer sees in it; a gracious scheme for the salvation of a ruined race. But to BUNYAN the whole scene was set in a new light. The change was like that wrought in PYGMALION's lovely statue by the transformation. If they took delight in contemplation, he was in rapture. If they were in raptures, he was already in the 'Beautiful City,' among the 'Shining Ones.' His sorrow was their agony; his agony they might thank Heaven they never felt. If they felt an inclination to do evil, he could distinctly see the malignant glance of his arch-enemy gleaming through his beautiful mask; he could feel his iron grasp dragging him down to per- dition. If they sometimes caught faint glimpses of bliss beyond the grave, he was in the very midst of the land of Beulah. The dark river shrank to a rill. He heard the voices of the inhabitants of the city; he even walked with them; 'for in this land the Shining Ones commonly walked, because it was upon the borders of Heaven.' To the vigor of his imagination was doubtless owing his fondness for the Apocalypse. By most Christians, that splendid vision, with the exception of a few brief portions, is read only as a study, with commentaries and Biblical lexicons. BUNYAN wanted no help but the magic wand of his imagination. While his brethren were quietly reading of the 'many mansions' described with such beautiful simplicity by the GREAT TEACHER, he was almost 'carried away in the spirit' and shown 'that great city the holy Jerusalem, descending out of Heaven from GOD.' Death was to them the 'thief in the night;' to him the grim monster who sat on the pale horse. They thought of the judgment as the division of the sheep and the goats; he as the giving up by death and hell of the dead that were in them, and the judging of the dead before the great white throne out of the things written in the books. Let us remark, in passing, that there is a benevolent wisdom exhibited in these various descriptions of the same scene. Archbishop WHATELY conjectures, ingeniously enough, that the framers of the liturgy paired together words of Latin and Saxon derivation, expressing the same idea, that they might meet the tastes of all worshippers. On somewhat the same principle are those wonderfully varied descriptions occurring in the Scriptures. A few instances have been given; they might be multiplied indefinitely.

Some of BUNYAN's brethren were learned. Mr. PHILIP has an anecdote of one who, when put on trial for dissenting, saved himself by pleading in Greek and again in Hebrew. His arguments were unanswerable; at least none of the lawyers could answer them. Some among the brethren were good preachers; some doubtless were good in many things in which BUNYAN was wanting; but there was no imagination that could sympathize or cope with his. They marvelled at him as boys marvel at the feats of an adventurous comrade. To the intense vividness of that imagination must be attributed the lively interest excited by 'The Pilgrim's Progress.' That was a vision rather than a dream. The relator casts a strange spell about us when we enter his magic circle. We forget all passing events while the wonderful revelation is made to pass before us. In almost every other branch of his art BUNYAN has had his superiors. But we must claim for him, in this respect, an absolute supremacy. We are pleased as we read THOMPSON's 'Castle of Indolence;' but we feel no trembling solicitude for the success of the Knight of Arms and Industry. We marvel as we read that strange episode about Death, and Sin, the portress of Hell, with her brood of hell-hounds; but we feel no earnest anxiety for the prevention of the contest between Death and Satan; nor very much about which conquers in the event of their meeting. Far otherwise with the 'Pilgrim.' Every little girl fears for his safety, when APOLLYON gets him down, as intensely as if she were herself in that terrible grasp. She is as delighted when CHRISTIAN produces the key which will open any lock in 'Doubting Castle' as if she had herself lain in the dungeon.

Another peculiar merit of 'The Pilgrim's Progress' is the skill with which a certain dignity and sacredness is cast about things ordinary and even farcical. ADDISON, in one of his ingenious criticisms on MILTON, finds fault with his favorite, for BELIAL's undignified triumph at the rout of the angels. If such mirthful sallies are improper in a heroic poem, the fault must be laid exclusively to the charge of the author. The characters and scenes of such a poem are the most exalted that can be selected. For this reason HOMER, VIRGIL, DANTE and MILTON, have all introduced superior intelligences into their plots, although no one of them has gone *below* our species, or even made prominent an unworthy specimen of mankind. Hence no possible constraint can force the writers of heroic poetry to the introduction of ludicrous scenes. It is not so with an allegory, at least with such an one as that of BUNYAN. He professes in the outset to give us the history of a Christian's journey through the world. The nature of the subject, is such that, even though treated allegorically, many familiar scenes must be introduced, especially by a writer whose first great object is the good of the people. A most incontestable proof of genius is boldly to introduce such scenes and still to maintain throughout an unbending dignity. This praise we claim for the Tinker. The only other 'first-rate' allegory in our language of much length is the 'Faërie Queen.' The best of the Edinburgh Reviewers, in comparing this great poem with the very work which we have under notice, complains of the ' tediousness' of the former. Without pretending to any remarkable critical acumen, we conceive that a single sentence which that writer has introduced, rather incidentally, contains the gist of the whole matter: ' We become sick of Cardinal Virtues and Deadly Sins, and long for the society of plain men and women?' Both SPENSER and BUNYAN had two different courses set before them. They might confine their scenes to a purely ideal world, and by avoiding all intercourse with the common affairs of life, avoid all hazard of vulgar incidents; or they might descend to the common walks of life, and take the attending hazards. SPENSER chose the former course; and owing to his continually straining after remoteness from common associations, which Mr. LEIGH HUNT affirms is one chief attraction of his work, he has lost that lively interest which is perhaps inseparable from such associations, unless we are compensated by the magnificent imagery and sonorous epithets of heroic poetry. BUNYAN chose the latter course, and his success has been complete. He has not only risked the occurrence of scenes in themselves devoid of dignity; he has even deliberately introduced such scenes; and yet under his hand they appear completely stripped of all unworthy associations. Certainly there is something very far from romantic or heroic about struggling and tumbling in the mud; yet not one reader in a thousand ever finds his mirth excited by the adventure of Christian in the Slough of Despond. Most writers would have put CHRISTIAN and FAITHFUL somewhere else at Vanity Fair than in a cage. This is perhaps a more ludicrous infliction than was ever practised in real life; yet no unworthy associations are called up to the mind by BUNYAN's narration. Instead of smiling in the recollection of the animals cooped up at the last show, the reader is filled with commiseration for the guiltless sufferers, and indignation at their persecutors. It is no small praise to say that whatever is gained for the humbler classes of the people by this homeliness of incident is *pure* gain, and by no means obtained by the sacrifice of dignity or good taste.

A great obstacle to the success of allegory has been noticed by Mr. JAMES MONTGOMERY; the anticipation of the reader's judgment by the names of personified abstract qualities. The most exquisite pleasure of which the mind is susceptible is found in discovery, as well of error as of truth. Of this pleasure we are robbed by these unwelcome titles. Every reader knows very nearly what ' Mr. BY-ENDS,' and ' Mr. HOLD-THE-WORLD,' and ' Mr. FACING-BOTH-WAYS' will say. Their names affect us like the officious kindness of a friend who takes pains to inform us when in the midst of an interesting tale how it will terminate. This nomenclature must necessarily perhaps be introduced to some extent in all allegory. Even here, however, BUNYAN has displayed his skill. To all his prominent characters he has given general and comprehensive appellations. CHRISTIAN, EVANGELIST, GOODWILL, FAITHFUL, HOPEFUL, and TALKATIVE allow, without departure from dramatic propriety, much more abundant scope for the invention than FORMALIST, HYPOCRISY, SAVEALL and MONEY-LOVE. These last therefore are soon removed from the stage. BUNYAN might have found the namesakes of nearly all his heroes among the troops of Captain FIGHT-THE-GOOD-FIGHT-OF-FAITH, and Sergeant SMITE-THEM-HIP-AND-THIGH; and all the good ladies of the ' House Beautiful' he might doubtless have seen in his own congregation. It was our purpose to have continued these desultory remarks, and to have offered some observations upon the less famous works of BUNYAN; but we have already exceeded our limits and must forbear. It only remains that we bespeak for Mr. PHILIP's book a general and thoughtful perusal; presenting as it does a most interesting account of the great master of allegory.

ETCHINGS OF A WHALING CRUISE, WITH NOTES OF A SOJOURN ON THE ISLAND OF ZANZIBAR. To which is appended a History of the Whale-Fishery, etc. By J. ROSS BROWNE. In one volume, illustrated. pp. 580. New-York : HARPER AND BROTHERS.

WE scarcely remember when we have 'run through' a new book with more pleasure than this. There is so much spirit in its pages ; such felicity in its colloquial revelations of character, events and scenes ; and throughout, such a naturalness of style, that we 'cottoned' at once to the author, and took him to our confidence with as much cordiality as we would welcome a congenial spirit to our sanctum-sanctorum. We were continually reminded, while engaged in the pleasant occupation of perusing this work ; its graphic pictures of ocean and continent ; its scenes of ship-board and shore ; its sketches of the 'small and great beasts' that inhabit the great deep, and especially of ' that leviathan that takes his pastime therein,' (which 'leviathan' we infer to be 'very like a whale,') whose capture, arraignment and *trial* are not less forcibly described and illustrated ; we were continually reminded, we say, of DANA's admirable work, 'Two Years before the Mast,' which has established so permanent a reputation at home and abroad. There is the same clearness of limning in the transfer of an ocean scene or a landscape to paper ; a greater perception of the humorous and the burlesque ; and what is of more importance, the writer has a kindred detestation of inhumanity in the petty tyrants of the deck, and equal fearlessness in exposing and animadverting upon it. The author was mainly actuated, he tells us, in publishing his work, by a desire to make his own experience as useful to others as it had been to himself ; and by a faithful delineation of the service in which he was engaged, to show in what manner the degraded condition of the sailors employed in the whaling trade may be ameliorated. He earnestly invokes the protecting arm of American law in punishing masters of whaling vessels, not only for positive acts of cruelty, but for morally degrading those under their command. We trust his voice will be heard and heeded in the appropriate quarter. The volume is a model as to type and paper, and is illustrated by several spirited engravings on steel and wood. Its extensive dissemination is already a ' fixed fact' on the publishers' day-book and ledger.

A TREATISE ON ALGEBRA. By CHARLES W. HACKLEY, D. D., Professor of Mathematics and Astronomy in Columbia College. New-York : HARPER AND BROTHERS.

THIS is a volume of over five hundred large octavo pages ; beautifully printed, and obtainable at the low price of one dollar and fifty cents. That the matter of the book is quite equal to the manner in which it is presented to the public, we should feel warranted in concluding from the general reputation of the author as a man of science, and from his great experience as a teacher ; but if farther confirmation is required, it can be found in even a cursory examination of the work itself. The abundance and variety of example and illustration will strike any teacher who has felt the poverty of most of our school-algebras in this particular. The many improvements and additions introduced, from the writings of modern German and French mathematicians, together with some things that are entirely new, and of American origin, will recommend it to the student who wishes to become thoroughly acquainted with the present condition of algebraic analysis. For beginners, an elementary or minor course is pointed out, by reference to the numbers of sections.

EDITOR'S TABLE.

THE NORTH-AMERICAN REVIEW FOR THE OCTOBER QUARTER. — No better number of this ancient and standard Quarterly than the one before us has been issued for several years. The themes of the reviews are various, and as far as we have found leisure attentively to peruse them, the merits and demerits of the works discussed are clearly and forcibly discriminated. There are in all nine articles; upon 'ALEXANDER's History of Colonization in Africa,' 'Sermons of Dr. SOUTH;' 'ELLIOTT's Carolina Sports;' 'The Progress of Society,' a review of Dr. ARNOLD's 'Introductory Lectures on Modern History;' 'SIMMS's Stories and Reviews;' GREENLEAF and STRAUSS; the Truths of Christianity;' 'MICHELET's Life of LUTHER;' 'WYMAN on Ventilation;' M'KENNEY on the Indians; and 'Was MOHAMMED an Imposter or an Enthusiast?' a review of the Koran. The article upon SOUTH's sermons is one which should be read by all clergymen, for the simplicity of pulpit style which it sets forth and illustrates by extracts and well-considered reflections upon them; a style which, without ambition or effort, has yet intensity, vitality and richness; elements in which so many modern sermons are sadly deficient. The paper upon ELLIOTT's 'Carolina Sports' embodies a warm tribute to a work which, judging alone from the liberal extracts given in the review, must possess the deepest interest. The high and cordial commendation bestowed upon this volume from the pen of an unpretending Southern writer, is evidently well deserved. The next paper, which traces the successive stages of 'Social Progress,' we have not yet read with that care which its theme demands. It is succeeded by an elaborate article on 'SIMMS's Stories and Reviews,' from the opening pages of which we take a few passages. They will confirm our readers in the estimate which we have established of the writings of this author, and another in the descending scale, in some of the later issues of this Magazine:

'THE author of 'The Yemassee,' 'Guy Rivers,' 'Life of MARION,' and a good many other things of that sort, is a writer of great pretensions and some local reputation. We remember to have read in some one of the numerous journals which have been illustrated by his genius, an amusing explanation from his pen, addressed to persons who had applied to him for information, of the difference between author and publisher; the object of it being evidently to tell the public that he was often written to by persons who, being anxious to get his works, very naturally fancied that he was the proper person to obtain them from, and to let the applicants know that the trade part of the book business was in quite different hands. We were struck by the ingenuity of the announcement, and grateful for the information thus condescendingly imparted. We availed ourselves of it to procure some of the volumes, which we proceeded forthwith to read and inwardly digest. Both of these processes were attended with no ordinary difficulties: but we believe we were uncommonly successful at last.

'The author of these novels means to be understood as setting up for an original, patriotic, native American writer; but we are convinced that every judicious reader will set him down as uncommonly deficient in the first elements of originality. He has put on the cast-off garments of the British novelist, merely endeavoring to give them an American fit; and, like those fine gentlemen who make up their wardrobes from the second-hand clothing shops, or from the 'unparalleled' establishment of Oak Hall, there is in his literary outfits a decided touch of the shabby genteel. The outward form of his novels is that of their English models; the current phrases of sentiment and description, worn threadbare in the circulating libraries, and out at the elbows, are the robes wherewith he covers imperfectly the nakedness of his invention. The *obligato* tone of sentimentality wearisomely drones through the soft passages of the thousand times repeated plot of love. To borrow a metaphor from one of the unhappy experiences of domestic life, the *tender lines* are so old that they are spoiled; they have been kept too long, and the hungriest guest at the 'intellectual banquet' finds it nauseating to swallow them.

'The style of Mr. SIMMS — we mean (for, like other great writers, he designates himself by the titles of his chief productions, rarely condescending to the comparative vulgarity of using a proper name,) we mean the style of the author of 'The Yemassee' and 'Guy Rivers' — is deficient in grace, picturesqueness, and point. It shows a mind seldom able to seize the characteristic features of the object he undertakes to describe, and of course his descriptions generally fail of arresting the reader's attention by any beauty or felicity of touch. His characters are vaguely conceived, and either faintly or coarsely drawn. The dramatic parts are but bungling imitations of nature, with little sprightliness or wit, and laboring under a heavy load of words.

'This author, as if to carry out more completely the contradiction between his statements of principle and his practice in the matter of originality, published a poem, a few years ago, in palpable imitation of Don Juan — a dull travesty of a most reprehensible model. To read canto after canto of BYRON's original, in which vulgar sarcasm and licentiousness were redeemed only here and there by a passage of poetic beauty, was a depressing task in the days of its novelty and freshness; but a pointless revival of its forced wit, its painful grimaces, its affected versification, its stingless satire, without one touch of its poetic beauty or one drop of its poignant wickedness in the stale mixture; the *heolocresia* of yesterday's debauch; was an experiment upon the patience of the much-reading and long-enduring public which could not possibly be successful. The author of 'The Yemassee' has however written some well versified short pieces, though we cannot recall a single poem which is likely long to survive the occasion which brought it forth.'

Mr. SIMMS *has* written some pleasing verse, and one or two poems that bespeak deep emotion. Examples in the former class have appeared originally in these pages, while the latter have been quoted to his honor, and widely circulated through the same medium; but we are constrained to admit that in general his verse is of that *unimpressible* description which neither pleases nor offends; which as CHARLES LAMB says, we 'at the same time detest and praise.' As to his poetical attempt in the style of 'Don JUAN,' we put it to any admirer of his, if disinterested admirers he has, to say whether his efforts in this kind do not exhibit a sort of 'heavy friskiness, most unexpected, as if the hippopotamus should show a tendency to dance?' In a notice of Mr. SIMMS's writings, in the KNICKERBOCKER for April last, we remarked that the sketches entitled 'The Wigwam and the Cabin' were 'the best things which he had written, and gave the most favorable impression of his abilities.' The 'North-American' coincides with us in opinion. Of this collection the reviewer remarks:

'IT forms part of WILEY AND PUTNAM's 'Library of American Books;' a series, by the by, which with the exception of a few of the volumes, is not likely to do much honor to American literature. It is difficult to imagine what can have seduced those respectable publishers into printing, as one of the series, that indescribably stupid imitation of DICKENS, entitled and called 'Big Abel and Little Manhattan;' * a contribution to the patriotic native American literature a good deal worse than the very worst things of 'The Yemassee' and 'Guy Rivers.' Surely, surely this dismal trash cannot have been seriously chosen as a fit representative of American originality, in a 'Library of American Books;' though it does very well to follow the silly and affected motto which some evil-disposed person has persuaded them to adopt from the Address of the American Copy-right Club.'

---

* IN justice to the enterprising publishers, it is proper to explain, that 'Big Abel and Little Manhattan' was announced, through a misunderstanding, or without their knowledge, upon the cover of a previous issue, as one of their forthcoming 'American Books.' The author was offered a cheque for a hundred dollars if he would withdraw it from the series; but as it had been printed at his risk, he would not consent to surrender an opportunity of adding to his literary laurels. It is worthy of remark also, 'in this connection,' that the 'silly and affected motto,' to which reference is had by the reviewer, is from the same luminous pen that traced of 'Big Abel and Little Manhattan' the wondrous history. A library however which includes among its volumes such excellent and attractive works as CHEEVER's 'Wanderings of a Pilgrim under the Shadow of Mont-Blanc and the Jungfrau,' 'Western Clearings,' by Mrs. KIRKLAND,' 'Mosses from an Old Manse,' by HAWTHORNE, 'The Wilderness and the War-path,' by Judge HALL, 'Typee,' by MELVILLE, and the like, should not be tabooed on account of two or three worthless or uninteresting publications, from which, at the buyer's option, they can be made to 'part company,' without derangement of the series.

These works, with the ' Tales by EDGAR A. POE,' who is described as ' belonging to the forcible-feeble and shallow-profound school,' are pronounced ' poor materials for an American Library.' In comparison with the ' infinitesimal smallness of either of these selected representatives of ' American Literature,' the ' North American' considers the tales of the ' Wigwam and the Cabin' as even ' masterly efforts,' and as well ' entitled to a place in the not very high department of literature to which they belong.' Several of them are commended for various merits, extracts illustrating which are freely given; although the ' heavy dissertations' which preface some of them, ' as if they were set up at the opening pages for the sake of warning off the trespassing reader,' the reviewer expresses small admiration. ' The stories,' observes the Quarterly, ' are not gracefully written; but being in a less ambitious style than the author's larger works, the literary faults and deficiencies are less observable, and tempered down to a less prominent and offensive point. Either from a want of original power to sustain with equable wing a long flight in the region of romance, or from a lack of sufficient culture to train his energies up to such high aims, the author of ' Guy Rivers' seems only equal to the short and easy career of the magazine tale or story.' The reviewer adds, that even in these stories coarse passages, offensive to good taste, indicate the writer's inability to discriminate, in the employ-ment of his materials, between what should have been cast aside as refuse and what was fit to be used for the purposes of art. Concerning ' CALOYA, or the Loves of the Driver,' the reviewer confirms our impression that it is ' deformed by coarseness,' that ' the plot is feeble and foolish,' and that ' the negro-driver is simply disgusting.' ' Can any thing be more absurd,' it is asked, ' than to call the resistance offered by CALOYA, the Indian wife, to the sickening advances of a greasy, woolly-headed, blubber-lipped negro, a ' triumph of virtue?' Her refusal to yield to his blandish-ments would be not so much the triumph of virtue as the triumph of nausea.' We quote the natural and just remarks of the ' North-American' upon this tale, because we once had the unhappiness to offend its author, previous to returning him the manuscript of it, by announcing it as ' under consideration' for admission into these pages; as if any thing from *his* pen required ' consideration' previous to insertion! The story was subsequently published in a Southern periodical, and was severely reprehended, we remember, in that region.

Mr. SIMMS' ' Views and Reviews of American Literature' [*] (a name ' which seems to have been adopted for no other reason than the unmeaning jingle of the words,') are held by the ' North American' to ' contain but little valuable criticism; they un-fold no principle of beauty, and illustrate no point in the philosophy of literature and art.' They are described as abounding in sounding yet baseless assumptions, of a character with the following: ' The chief value of history consists in its proper em-ployment for the purposes of art.' ' The engineer,' says the reviewer, ' who declared the final cause of the creation of rivers to be the feeding of canals, was moderate in comparison with this extravagant asserter of the preëminence of art over history, of fiction over fact, of invention over truth.' Now the preceding forcible and candid comments upon the productions of Mr. SIMMS, and those of a writer or two of his. dred pretensions, though undeniably beneath a kindred stamp, are quite coincident with our own expressed opinions in these pages; and although the ' North-American Review' is a dignified impersonality, and the reviewer in the present case obviously

---

[*] MR. SIMMS, we should here state, errs in the impression, conveyed in his prefaces, that any of these ' views' or ' reviews' ever appeared in the KNICKERBOCKER.

unacquainted with the author of 'The Yemassee,' save through his works, yet our own experience impels us to advise our old and influential quarterly contemporary that it must look to be denounced by sensitive sufferers, in terms of severe debility, as a journal influenced in its criticisms by personal prejudice; by local feeling; by 'Northern partialities,' and by 'an anti-national spirit;' all which of course will 'make it bad' for the 'North-American!' Meanwhile, we ask the especial attention of our readers to the following observations, which may be found toward the end of the review we have been considering:

'THERE has been a good deal of rather unmeaning talk about American literature. There has been in this matter, also, an operation of the principle of the division of labor. Those who have talked most about it have done the least. The men to whom American literature is really indebted have quietly planned and executed works on which their own fame and their country's literary honor rest. But certain coteries of would-be men of letters, noisy authorlings, and noisy in proportion to their diminutive size, waste their time and vex the patient spirits of long-suffering readers, by prating about our want of an independent national American literature. Of course all this prating is without the faintest shadow of sense. From the vehement style in which these literary patriots discourse, it would seem that they lamented the heritage of the English language and its glorious treasures, which are our birth-right, as a national calamity. They say, in effect, 'Go to; let us make a national literature;' and forthwith a five-act comedy of most lamentable mirth; a two or three-volumed novel of tawdry commonplaces; a witless caricature, with illustrations, like 'Puffer Hopkins;' a coarse accumulation of unimaginative vulgarities, pretending to delineate American life; spring into being, and are clamorously pushed into public notice as specimens of the genuine native-original American literature. These gentlemen forget that national literature cannot be forced like a hot-house plant. Talking about it has no tendency to produce it. They seem to think that American authors ought to limit themselves to American subjects, and hear none but American criticism; as if, forsooth, the genius of America must never wander beyond the mountains, forests and waterfalls of the western continent; as if the refinements of European culture should have no charms for the American taste. How many of SHAKSPEARE's noblest plays are laid in scenes beyond the narrow precincts of English life! How many of the greatest works of her historians trace the fortunes of countries and people having no other connection with England than the tie of a common humanity! In what portion of the British isles did JOHN MILTON place the beings that move and act in his immortal work?' · · · 'The complaint of a want of nationality in American literature is borrowed from the ill-founded judgments of English criticism. Even in this, our professed abettors of aboriginality are not original. English critics seem to expect a dash of savageness, a sound of the war-hoop, a stroke of the tomahawk or the bowie-knife; they expect to hear the roar of Niagara and the crash of the trees in the primeval forests, in the literature of America. Very prettily sounding phrases these; but neither the English originals nor the American copyists can force much meaning into them.

'American literature will do very well, in spite of these birds of boding cry. With extending literary and scientific culture, and increased familiarity with the genius of the past; with constantly enlarging intercourse among the most civilized nations, and the rapid intercommunication of thoughts, creations and inventions; the intellect of America cannot fail to go forward in the career so auspiciously begun. The work so well done already by our great orators, historians, poets and artists will not rest under the stimulating influences pouring in from every quarter upon the agitated intellect of the country. *Fervet opus;* and all the exaggerated complaints of coteries of small authors cannot make its glowing progress slower.'

A small set of self-styled author-conservators of home literature in our midst, with little brains and much tongue, are justly and forcibly rebuked in the above pregnant sentences. 'No combination of writers,' says the able critic of the *Courier and Enquirer* daily journal, 'to urge their own claims, to insist upon their own actual or imagined rights, to oppose the introduction of foreign writings, or in any way to induce literary growth by any hot-house cultivation, can ever attain any desirable result. Good books will live and bad ones will die. This is a rule as true in fact as in theory, and as just as it is true. It cannot be changed, and it ought not to be changed if it could. There is no good reason why a man should buy or read a worthless book, nor any reason why a good book, no matter whence it comes, should not be read. A stupid book is no better for being American in its origin, and a good one is no worse for coming from abroad. Books of equal merit should stand upon equal ground, without reference to their origin.' Our sentiments exactly; and we beg leave to commend them to the members of that sparse corps of reciprocal nurses to their *own* small 'literature,' who, dandle in turn as they may some diminutive authorling on their feeble knees; feed him never so near to bursting with their curds and whey, can never ' raise him ;' never impart a reputation for gifts which he has not ; least of all, for the possession of *genius*, that glorious and subtle fire, which it has been well said is in one respect like gold, since numbers of noisy persons are constantly writing about both who have neither. But hold! — we are at the end of our available space ; and although we intended to speak of the interesting and most useful article on ' Ventilation,' and that upon Col. M'KENNEY's recent work on the Indians, we must content ourselves by commending our readers to secure a perusal of them in the fair white pages of the ' North-American' itself.

' PARA, OR EIGHT MONTHS ON THE BANKS OF THE AMAZON,' is the title of a voluminous manuscript which has been left with us for ' trial and sentence.' Brazil, as our readers are aware, is ' by nature' one of the most magnificent countries in the world ; and of all its provinces, *Para*, the name alike of the province and its principal city, is the most beautiful : the luxuriant ' Amazonia' is all included in its boundaries ; and it is indeed what it is termed, the ' Paradise of Brazil.' It has been little explored, and but little is even now known of the numerous Indian tribes dwelling in the interior. The scenery of the Para river, on which the town is situated, is unsurpassed for richness and variety ; its climate is delightful ; its birds are numerous, and of the most gorgeous plumage ; it has an extensive variety of quadrupeds, from the spotted jaguar to the little Marmazete monkey ; and its insects glitter continually in the pure atmosphere, dazzling the eye as with the light of gems. Every division of natural history, in fine, teems with splendid ' specimens.' The manuscript before us is a series of fresh personal adventures and reminiscences, to which we proceed to invite the attention of our readers. The writer, it may be proper to add, while in Brazil, prosecuted vigorously his favorite study of ornithology, with actual ' illustrations ;' insomuch that he has now in his possession one of the most extensive and beautiful private ornithological collections in the United States ; all the specimens in which were killed in their native haunts by the writer and his companion, who were undismayed by obstacles, not a few of which were sufficiently serious to have intimidated older adventurers. But let us not keep the reader from the manuscript itself ; but permit him to turn over the leaves with us, taking here and there such passages as may strike our fancy or enlist our attention. Here is an interesting account of the *Toucan*, a species of bird quite abundant in Juncal, of which the ' white-throated' and the 'yellow-throated' are the finest specimens ; the first being black, with a beautifully-blended red-and-yellow bill, the second somewhat smaller, with green reflections and a less formidable beak. ' These birds,' says the writer, ' live principally on fruits, but when in a state of captivity learn to eat almost every thing. Their favorite food is the Assuby berry, and their method of eating it is very remarkable. They first seize the fruit in the extremity of their bill, and by a sudden twitch throw it several feet into the air ; as it drops, they catch it and swallow it entire, without the slightest effort at mastication. They confine themselves mostly to lofty trees, where they sit with their beaks pointed directly toward the wind, thus overcoming a power which if exerted on the broadside might considerably disturb their comfort and equanimity. Their flight is straight forward from one place to another, and it is seldom that they make a curve while on the wing. Their eyes are so constructed that they cannot see distinctly ahead, but their vision on the side is wonderfully acute. The hunter must be acquainted with this circumstance, or he will find it almost impossible to get a shot at them. They build their nests in the hollow of old trees and make a small circular aperture directly in front. The female lays but two eggs, on which she sits, and with her formidable beak protruding from the port-hole of her fortress, she is able effectually to protect herself, and repel all monkeys, serpents, or other animals or reptiles, who may be disposed to invade her sacred premises.'

The writer's companion, on his way back to Juncal, was something more than annoyed by the ' monkey-shines' of certain mischievous little rascals, the only specimens of which that one encounters in this country are ' held in slavery' by vagrant Italians, whose hurdy-gurdys occasionally resound in our public thoroughfares: ' We met,' says the manuscript, ' with but one adventure by the way which deserves mention. Passing through a part of the stream that was darkly shaded by a thick forest on one side, we heard distinctly the chattering of monkeys among the trees. ' Well,' said Mr. H——, ' I believe I 'll go ashore and give those fellows a shot. You had better remain in the boat until I return.'   I therefore landed him, and he walked noiselessly into the woods.   In a few minutes the sharp report of his gun rang through the glades, immediately succeeded by another as loud and shrill.   In a moment the woods reverberated with the horrible cries of the monkeys, who had evidently lost some of their number.   Never did I listen to such an unearthly noise ; but amid the uproar I heard Mr. H—— calling me at the top of his voice to come to his rescue. I hastily left the boat, and rushed instantaneously to the assistance of my companion. He was entirely surrounded by monkeys, and hundreds of others were coming down from the trees, while he was knocking those about him aside with the butt-end of his gun.   I fired both my barrels into the thickest of them, and probably wounded so many that they concluded it was not best farther to prosecute their attack ; for they quickly dispersed and fled in every direction.   We picked up three or four of the dead and carried them along with us.   Mr. H—— assured me that if he had been alone he would have been most seriously bitten, if not killed.'   Our narrator mentions another friend who, while in his canoe on the stream, shot a bird which fell into the water.   His dog, who was with him in the boat, jumped out to get it.   In a moment the wide jaws of an alligator twenty feet long appeared above the surface, which seized both dog and bird, and they sunk to rise no more.'

As the writer was about leaving Juncal, he beheld an example of what Scott terms ' lugging in by ear and horn :' ' We passed the day on board the schooner, to see them take in cattle. I had came down thus early in order to witness this operation.   A pen is made on the margin of a precipitous bank, into which the cattle are driven.   A lasso is first thrown around the head of one of the oxen, who is forced over the bank into the water.   A strong noose is then cast from the boat round his horns, and he is raised up by means of a pully, and put in the hold, where he is fastened. All are individually taken on board in this manner.   They look exceedingly comical while suspended by their horns, their eyes dilated, and every muscle stretched to its utmost capacity.   Although I pitied the poor animals, I could not refrain from laughter at the ridiculous appearance they made while thus hanging in the air like a bale of goods.'   While at Caripe, the name of an estate belonging to ALEXANDER CAMPBELL, Esq., a gentleman greatly esteemed for his kindness and liberality to Americans, our traveller records the following occurrence: ' We became acquainted while in the city with an Englishman by the name of GRAHAM, who had left his native country in quest of health, with his wife and only child.   He had devoted most of his time to the study of natural history, and had succeeded in acquiring by industry and perseverance a very valuable collection of specimens. His younger brother had just arrived from Europe to accompany him home. Desirous of showing him the beauties of the country, he suggested a trip to Caripe, whither, in company with a faithful black, who had been his constant companion, they all went. Wishing one day to cross over to the island of Marajo, distant about ten or twelve miles, he went out in a little montaria, with his wife and child, to gain a larger one which was waiting at anchor for him in the river, about half a mile from the shore. Through some carelessness or mismanagement, the frail boat was upset and all plunged into the water. Every exertion was made by those in the larger vessel to save them, but without avail ; husband, wife and child were drowned. This most tragic scene was witnessed by young Graham from the beach ; but alas ! he could render no assistance. What tumultuous throes of anguish must have wrung that orphan brother's heart, on beholding those most dear to him on earth swallowed up in a moment by the relentless wave ; leaving him alone, in a land of strangers ! Mr. Graham himself was an active swimmer, but he lost his life in endeavoring to save that of his wife. Their bodies, tightly locked together in the cold embrace of death, floated ashore. ' They loved in life, and in death they were not divided.' A rude grave was digged in the sand, and the sad remains of worth and beauty consigned to its bosom. Here, amid the solitude of beautiful nature, and on the banks of the king of rivers, they sweetly repose. No tear of friendship bedews the spot, but the rising tide of the mighty Amazon daily weeps over it. Martyrs to the science they so successfully prosecuted, they are calmly sleeping at Caripe :

> ' There breathes the odor of summer flowers,
> And the music of birds is there.' '

The reader having now been favorably introduced to our correspondent, we shall permit him to gossip with them ' à discretion.' He mentions this amusing occurrence at Para : ' At all the important parts of the city, such as the palace, custom-house, etc., guards are stationed, whose business it is to be vigilant during the day, and to hail all persons who pass by after eight o'clock at night. One evening a drunken English sailor was staggering past the custom-house, when he was hailed by the guard, ' *Quem var la ?*' (' Who goes there ?') The customary reply to this interrogatory is, ' *Amigo ;*' (' A friend.') Our hero, not understanding the language, nor what business any one had to address him in such an authoritive manner, in a Stentorian voice cried out, ' You d —— d screaming Portuguese son-of-a-gun, stop your noise, or I 'll send you to h — ll !' The guard, thinking of course that he could not speak the language, and that he was merely telling him so in English, let him pass in.' ' One cannot forbear noticing the extreme politeness of the Portuguese in the streets. It is the custom universally for a Brazilian gentleman on meeting a stranger, to take off his hat, and bowing, to salute him with the popular expression, ' *Viva Senhor ;*' (' Long life, Sir.') We were astonished at observing the respect that was paid us on our first arrival ; by the men who spoke and the maidens who sweetly smiled.' . . . Some idea of the success with which our adventurers prosecuted their researches, may be gathered from the subjoined catalogue of a portion of their collection : ' Our live stock was quite numerous ; consisting of monkeys, an ant-bear, an armadillo, two roseate spoonbills, and as many egrets, together with several loquacious parrots. These animals afforded us an infinite deal of amusement. The birds became so attached to us that they would come at our call, and take their food from our hands. The parrots shortly learned to repeat two of three English phrases, which they seemed to delight in pronouncing continually, even to the exclusion of their mother tongue. We had also among our feathered collection a single macaw : this bird was about two feet in length, and beautifully marked with blue and red. He was very affectionate in his disposition, and appeared to understand all we said to him. Whenever dinner or any other meal was ready, he always, at the ringing of the bell, perched himself upon the back of the chair at the head of the table, and waited patiently for us to serve him.' . . . 'An Indian brought us a live coral-snake one day, which he had recently caught in the forest. It was more than three feet in length, and regularly banded with alternate rings of black, scarlet and yellow. Although naturally very poisonous, yet the one in question had been deprived of its fangs, and consequently rendered harmless. For the sake of security we put him in a small wooden box, little thinking that it would be possible for him to get out, and then placed the box in our own apartment. In the night the reptile forced out the bottom of his cage and in the course of his perambulations found his way into the cook's room. Being awake, she aroused us by her screams. We rushed to her aid, and on discovering the cause of her fear, attempted to catch the wily serpent, but our efforts were in vain. The reptile escaped through a crevice in the floor, and we never saw our favorite ('*favorite !*') again.'

As this is the season when India-rubbers are called into requisition, the reader may like to know something of the modus-operandi of their manufacture : 'The stranger in Para cannot fail to notice the singular manner in which India-rubber shoes are transported from place to place. He will see slaves bearing long poles thickly strung with them, marching along and keeping time to a slow discordant chant. These shoes are mostly manufactured in the interior and brought down the river by the Indians. The tree (*Siphilla Elastica*) is exceedingly peculiar in appearance. It has large thick leaves, and reaches the height of eighty and sometimes an hundred feet. The trees are tapped in the same manner as the New-Englanders tap maple trees, from which a thick liquid resembling cream flows out. This is collected in earthen jars, where it is kept until desired for use. The operation of making the shoes consists in first igniting the fruit of a species of palm, which yields a thick dark smoke. They then take a wooden last, with a handle, and having poured the liquid over it, a coating of which remains, they hold it over the ignited fruit ; the action of the smoke upon the gum causes it in time to assume a black color. After the requisite number of coats have been given in this manner, the shoes are exposed to the sun to harden. India-rubber constitutes one of the principal exports of Para. More than two hundred and fifty thousand shoes are annually exported from this province ; in fact, almost all the India-rubber consumed in the United States comes from this source.' . . . Our correspondent gives an amusing description of the freaks of the electrical eel. He is writing from ship-board : 'One day, wishing to change the water in which our eels were kept, we upset the tub on the deck, and thus threw them out. Having replenished the vessel with fresh water, we requested one of the sailors to put them in. He proceeded to do so ; but no sooner had he touched it with his hand, than he received a shock which caused him to drop it in a moment. He attempted it again, but with no better success than before. Great was the amazement of his fellows, who all tried in turn to put the mysterious fish into the tub ; but none succeeded. It was amusing to see their looks of wonder at the strange sensations which they had severally experienced. The mate looked on in silence and surprise ; and being himself wholly unacquainted with the properties of the reptiles, he supposed the sailors dropped them more on account of their slipperiness than any other cause. On the strength of this opinion, he walked up boldly to the largest one, and in order to retain his grasp, seized him with great force; but the eel, little relishing such an assault, gave him so severe a shock that he ' dropped him like a hot potato,' nor could he be prevailed on to make a second trial. At length the captain procured a shovel and put them both in without any farther difficulty. The next day I observed one of the monkeys drinking from the tub; but having accidentally put his head down too far, his nose came in contact with one of the eels, by which he received a shock that made him beat a precipitous retreat. As soon however as he had somewhat recovered from its effects, he returned with vehement wrath depicted in his interesting countenance. Having mounted himself upon the side of the tub, he brought the eel a severe thwack on the head with his paw. He immediately received another shock, but being no philosopher, he struck the animal again and again, until finally he came to the conclusion that it was altogether too shocking an affair to prosecute farther; whereupon he retired, garrulously giving vent to his intense disgust.' We take reluctant leave of our young and talented correspondent's narrative; only until our next number however, unless some enterprising publisher shall in the mean time solicit the work at our hands for present publication. It well deserves that honor, as we shall still farther establish hereafter.

GOSSIP WITH READERS AND CORRESPONDENTS. — There was a friend sitting a month ago in the old cushioned *fauteuil* which spreads its inviting arms in an opposite corner of our sanctum, whose heart, then so warm and sympathetic, is now cold in the grave. And yet it scarcely seems true that HENRY LOGAN CHIPMAN is dead; ' CHIP.,' as his friends delighted to term him, in diminutive, whose love of the humorous beamed in his eyes, and played, like flitting summer sunlight and shadow upon a meadow, over his tell-tale features. But he is gone, and we shall see his face no more. A thousand reminiscences of scenes and events he had treasured up, in the numerous voyages which he had made in his country's service, are buried with him; and our readers have to lament with us the dimming of a light that shone so brightly; the untimely removal of a writer from whose natural and most facile pen they had good reason to hope so much. There was something more than usually impressive in the circumstances of his death. After several years' absence in the naval service, he found himself, on his return to his native country, in the neighborhood of a lovely and gifted young lady, to whom he had long been devotedly attached, and to whom he would doubtless before have been united, but for the objections of her relatives and friends, and her own reluctant disinclination, on the score of the long separations from each other which active service afloat would necessarily occasion. He deemed his fate a hard one at the time, but submitted to it with becoming fortitude; and not until he again encountered accidentally in town the object of his old affection was the hope of a future union reäwakened in his bosom. But the mutual flame was again rekindled between the lovers; and at the residence of her family near the city, where he was a frequent visitor, their vows were once more plighted. We have seen many happy persons in the course of our life, but we never have seen a man so *entirely* happy as our friend at this period. The last time but one that we saw him, he told us he ' would not exchange places with any king in Europe;' and he read to us a letter which ho had just penned to his aged mother, describing, in terms of the warmest affection, his happiness at the reünion with one whom he had loved so long and so fervently. On that evening, as we afterward learned, overcome with joy at his benignant and happy fortune, he invited three or four fellow-officers to a small supper-party. Here, owing to an 'intoxication of delight' and its natural enhancement by a liberal circulation of champaigne, he became somewhat elated; insomuch that when he reached his vessel the circumstance was noted by the officer on duty and officially reported at the appropriate quarter. Being one of the best officers in the service, he was overwhelmed with mortification at his error; and the next morning, in a moment of deeply-sensitive reflection upon his case, he sent in his resignation. He was solicited, almost implored, by his friends to recall it; but he for some time declined to do so, and in due course was officially apprized of its acceptance at the department. The 'iron entered into his soul' when he learned, by an affectionate but reproving letter, from one whose good opinion he would not have forfeited for the whole world, that some 'good-natured friend' had communicated his misfortune to her family, and that the intelligence had had an adverse effect upon his dearest interests. We saw poor CHIPMAN but once after this. His usually cheerful and happy face was 'sicklied o'er with the pale cast of thought' too deep for words or tears; and he was about departing for Washington to make personal interest for his restoration to the service to which he had always been an honor. A short time after his arrival at the capital he was seized with a violent brain-fever, which terminated his existence in a few hours. We shall not soon look upon his like again. He was a most kind-hearted, ingenuous, generous man; an excellent officer; a true friend, a pleasant companion, an agreeable and witty writer, in verse and prose, and an admirable *racconteur* of the various entertaining adventures which he had witnessed or experienced at different periods of his eventful life. We are not without the hope of obtaining access to our friend's miscellaneous papers, which we have had the pleasure of looking over with him; and which, independent of an uncollated subsection of the amusing sketches under the title of 'Lobscouse,' contain many things which would add to the literary reputation of the writer, as they certainly would to the enjoyment of our readers. · · · HERE is a very graceful little poem, from the pen of THOMAS MACKELLAR. It is called 'The Beautiful Land:'

'THERE is a land immortal,
    The beautiful of lands;
Beside the ancient portal
    A sentry grimly stands:
He only can undo it,
    And open wide the door,
And mortals who pass through it
    Are mortals never more!

'That glorious land is Heaven,
    And DEATH the sentry grim;
The LORD therefore has given
    The opening keys to him.
And ransomed spirits, sighing
    And sorrowful for sin,
Pass through that gate in dying,
    And freely enter in.

'Though dark and drear the passage
    That leadeth to the gate,
Yet grace comes with the message
    To souls that watch and wait;
And, at the time appointed,
    A messenger comes down,
And leads the LORD's anointed
    From th' cross to glory's crown.

'Their sighs are lost in singing,
    They 're blessed in their tears;
Their journey heavenward winging,
    They leave to earth their fears.
Death like an angel seemeth:
    'We welcome thee!' they cry;
Their face with glory beameth,
    'T is life for them to die!'

We should be glad to hear often from the author of these lines. · · · AMONG the remarkable specimens of aboriginal eloquence recorded by Colonel M'KENNEY, in his interesting work on the Indians, is the following by SKENANDOAH, the 'good Oneida,' who lived upward of a century. A while previous to his death a friend called to see him, and inquired after his health. 'I am an aged hemlock,' was the reply of the old chief; 'the winds of an hundred winters have whistled through my branches, and I am dead at the top. Why I yet live, the great GOOD SPIRIT only knows. When I am dead, bury me by the side of my minister and friend, that I may go up with him at the great resurrection.' KUSICK was a chief of the Tuscaroras. He was in the old war, and bore a lieutenant's commission from the hand of WASHINGTON. He was placed on the pension-list at the instance of the agent and the Register of the Treasury. Some years after, Colonel M'KENNEY, when passing through the Tuscarora reserve, on his way to the wilderness, stopped opposite to KUSICK's cabin, and walked up to see the old chief. He found him engaged in drying fish. After the usual greeting, the agent asked him if he continued to receive his pension. 'No,' answered KUSICK, 'no; Congress passed a law making it necessary for me to swear that I could n't live without it. Now here is my little log-cabin, and it is my own; here 's my patch, where I can raise corn and beans and pumpkins; and there 's Lake Oneida, where I can catch fish. I can make out to live with these, without the pension; and to say I could not, would be to *lie to the Great Spirit.*' What a lesson to many a 'lordly white!' · · · THE sun to-night has gone down behind the fading yellow woods that look from the heights above the Hudson upon its turbid waves; the hollow winds, freshened from the far hills that rise cold and pale, the oceanward barriers to 'the vast inland stretched beyond the sight,' are sighing, 'mournfully, O! mournfully,' about our silent sanctum, and whirling the dead leaves around the creaking shutters. How can we choose but think, that so descended the red sun, so looked the faded woods, so rolled the river its angry waters to the main, so swelled the anthem of the hollow winds, but a brief twelvemonth ago? Some such thoughts too were in the mind of our friend and correspondent, 'J. HONEYWELL,' when he penned and despatched to us these admirable lines:

'AGAIN, oh! month of melancholy,
 Full of pale thought and sad presage,
Thou callest up each youthful folly,
 To haunt me in my pilgrimage.
Why urge, with hollow voice and cold,
 Disheartened Manhood to remember?
I feel that I am growing old
 Without thy warning, bleak NOVEMBER!

'Wild and remorseless winds are singing,
 In mournful tones, the dirge of Summer,
And the hoar Frost is broadcast flinging
 The blight of an unwelcome comer;
I meet you now o'er times to sigh,
 Which I would not, but must remember,
When ye, oh! winds and frost and I
 Met in a happier past November!

'Thou dost evoke, in swift transition,
 A shadowy and tumultuous throng
Of scenes that once were all Elysian,
 When the heart beat with pulses strong;
But only with malicious smile,
 To ask if I youth's hopes remember,
Which have been tombed this weary while,
 Back in a long, long gone November!

'Thou bring'st me not my promised pleasures;
 Thy dead leaves fall with plaintive sound,
And like those leaves, life's hoarded treasures
 Fall withering on the waste around.
'T is said the woods are glorious now,
 And that thy robes are gay, November;
But tears obstruct my sight—and thou
 Dost make me sad with thy 'Remember!''

One *feels* these fine lines. · · · '*Remembrances of Boyhood*' shall appear,; we *do* 'think the article worthy.' Speaking of boyhood, we may as well add, that we have recently had quite a practical illustration of the pleasure to be derived from certain of its reminiscences. During a recent visit to an esteemed friend in the country, whose hospitable mansion rises amidst its painted autumnal trees, within sound of the cataract of Cohoes, we joined a pleasant party to visit, over the Hudson, the lofty summit of '*Mount Rafinesque*,' (named after an old contributor to this Magazine,) from which a magnificent and most varied view may be commanded. As we alighted from our barouche, at the foot of the last great acclivity, and began to ascend through the forest that skirts its base, so it was that the fresh mountain air did greatly dilate the heart and expand the spirits of ' OLD KNICK.,' who left the ' honorable member,' his guests and the charming ladies of his household behind him, while ZACCHEUS-like, he ran on in advance, and climbed some forty or fifty feet to the top of a small ' staddle,' having it in mind to perform a common feat of his boyhood ; namely, to ' sway' the same by grasping its top and dropping slowly to the ground with the yielding trunk. Now look you what befel : ' Do me the favor to observe !' exclaimed ' OLD KNICK.,' as he threw himself free from the body of the sapling. Down he went, with a sensation as of sinking slowly in a balloon, when presently, while yet about fifteen feet from the ground, he suddenly ' *heard something drop !*' The individual who emerged from under the bruised branches of that prostrate ash, (so unlike the lithe saplings familiar to his boyhood,) was rubbing several of his own limbs, for some cause or other ; and we can answer for him, that when he saw the 'honorable member' smothering a titter, and his fair household suppressing a large amount of giggle ; when he heard them say that they were ' *sorry* that the tree had broken so soon ; *very sorry* ; did n't know the time, in fact, for several years, when they had been *quite so sorry* ;' when ' OLD KNICK.' saw and heard this, he was discomforted within himself, and his countenance fell ; for then he knew that they were laughing at him. There was a lame male ' human' about the house that night, doing something with laudanum and opodeldoc ; yet he did not forget, amidst his thoughts of ' the toil to that mountain led,' the matchless view of city, village, mountain, ' field and flood,' which was commanded from its lofty summit, on that glorious October afternoon. But we ' gossip out of season.' . . . AN Easton (Pa.) correspondent (would we were there at this moment, with our friends B —— and L ——, on their way to the Delaware Water-Gap !) sends us the following. It is one of the *vérités veritables,* and is taken from ' The Yellow Dwarf,' an original extravaganza on the fairy tale of that name :

> 'THE question is, 'To be or not to be ;'
> If 't is to be, to be of course it will,
> If not to be, then something must be, still ;
> What must be, must be ; that appears to me
> To be as plain as even A. B. C.
> Take one from two, and it is very plain
> That one will very probably remain ;
> But if that two should not be two, but one,
> Deduct, and the remainder will be none ;
> So if from six you take the figure four,
> Two will be left, and not a fraction more ;
> Although by adding six to four, 't is plainer,
> The four will be of course by six the gainer.'

These ' premises' are as impregnable as the assumptions ventured by the author of a poem entitled ' Incontrovertible Facts,' which opened as follows :

> ' BOSTON is n't in Bengal,
> Flannel drawers are n't made of tripe ;
> Lobsters wear no specs at all,
> And cows do n't smoke the German pipe !'

' Clear as mud !' . . . IF we were to say on this side of the water what plain-speaking Englishmen say of themselves, it would be set down we fear to something like national ill-will. PUNCH, for example, avows that ' in his heart' he thinks an English snob, for self-sufficiency and braggartism, without a parallel in his way :

' ABOUT the British Snob there is commonly no noise, no bluster, but the calmness of profound conviction. We are better than all the world ; we do n't question the opinion at all ; it's an axiom. We are the first chop of the world : we know the fact so well in our secret hearts, that a claim set up elsewhere is simply ludicrous. My dear brother reader, say, as a man of honor, if you are not of this opinion ? Do you think any body your equal ? You do n't — you gallant British Snob — you know you do n't. And I am inclined to think it is this conviction, and the consequent bearing of the Eng-

acquainted with the properties of the reptiles, he supposed the sailors dropped them more on account of their slipperiness than any other cause. On the strength of this opinion, he walked up boldly to the largest one, and in order to retain his grasp, seized him with great force; but the eel, little relishing such an assault, gave him so severe a shock that he 'dropped him like a hot potato,' nor could he be prevailed on to make a second trial. At length the captain procured a shovel and put them both in without any farther difficulty. The next day I observed one of the monkeys drinking from the tub; but having accidentally put his head down too far, his nose came in contact with one of the eels, by which he received a shock that made him beat a precipitous retreat. As soon however as he had somewhat recovered from its effects, he returned with vehement wrath depicted in his interesting countenance. Having mounted himself upon the side of the tub, he brought the eel a severe thwack on the head with his paw. He immediately received another shock, but being no philosopher, he struck the animal again and again, until finally he came to the conclusion that it was altogether too shocking an affair to prosecute farther; whereupon he retired, garrulously giving vent to his intense disgust.' We take reluctant leave of our young and talented correspondent's narrative; only until our next number however, unless some enterprising publisher shall in the mean time solicit the work at our hands for present publication. It well deserves that honor, as we shall still farther establish hereafter.

GOSSIP WITH READERS AND CORRESPONDENTS. — There was a friend sitting a month ago in the old cushioned *fauteuil* which spreads its inviting arms in an opposite corner of our sanctum, whose heart, then so warm and sympathetic, is now cold in the grave. And yet it scarcely seems true that HENRY LOGAN CHIPMAN is dead; 'CHIP.,' as his friends delighted to term him, in diminutive, whose love of the humorous beamed in his eyes, and played, like flitting summer sunlight and shadow upon a meadow, over his tell-tale features. But he is gone, and we shall see his face no more. A thousand reminiscences of scenes and events he had treasured up, in the numerous voyages which he had made in his country's service, are buried with him; and our readers have to lament with us the dimming of a light that shone so brightly; the untimely removal of a writer from whose natural and most facile pen they had good reason to hope so much. There was something more than usually impressive in the circumstances of his death. After several years' absence in the naval service, he found himself, on his return to his native country, in the neighborhood of a lovely and gifted young lady, to whom he had long been devotedly attached, and to whom he would doubtless before have been united, but for the objections of her relatives and friends, and her own reluctant disinclination, on the score of the long separations from each other which active service afloat would necessarily occasion. He deemed his fate a hard one at the time, but submitted to it with becoming fortitude; and not until he again encountered accidentally in town the object of his old affection was the hope of a future union reäwakened in his bosom. But the mutual flame was again rekindled between the lovers; and at the residence of her family near the city, where he was a frequent visitor, their vows were once more plighted. We have seen many happy persons in the course of our life, but we never have seen a man so *entirely* happy as our friend at this period. The last time but one that we saw him, he told us he 'would not exchange places with any king in Europe;' and he read to against the 'North-American Review.' This was in bad taste, surely, and as certainly so deemed; but something was to be pardoned in consideration of the lacerating thorn that rankled in his side. Yet we think the true policy for him would have been to smother his rage, and leave the hard words unsaid; for there were those present who had taken the 'North-American Review' for upward of thirty years, and half-a-dozen travelled gentlemen who had been made aware of the distinguished honor which this able Quarterly had reflected and still reflects abroad, upon the literary progress of the United States. . . . Mr. H. W. HEWET, the original publisher and engraver of the 'Illustrated SHAKSPEARE,' now issuing in numbers by the BROTHERS HARPER, has discovered or invented a method of printing engravings in colors, by one impression, which will form one of the most important pictorial improvements of the day. Nothing can be more beautiful than the specimens we have examined. They are equal to, and very much resemble, fine water-color drawings. Mr. HEWET has in preparation, for some enterprising publisher, the '*Arabian Nights' Entertainments*,' a new translation from the Arabic, with copious notes by LANE, author of 'The Modern Egyptians;' illustrated by many hundred superb engravings on wood, from original designs by WILLIAM HARVEY. The American edition will be *complete*, with all the engravings, notes, etc. It will appear in thirty-two copious numbers, in the first style of pictorial and typographical art. Won't *there* be a book for all lovers of Arabian romance? Rejoice, ye youths of both sexes, around the winter fireside! · · · OUR thanks are due to 'E. K.,' of Brooklyn, for the '*Autumn Thoughts*.' He is right in his impression that the lines were written by the late WILLIS GAYLORD CLARK. The poem is one of that lamented writer's less carefully-finished effusions; yet the last two stanzas will strike the reader, we think, as being felicitous:

'I MAY not ask, as thronging back
   To my lone soul, these memories come,
Why the dim cloud o'er Pleasure's track
   Came with its shadowy fold of gloom:
I may not ask why LOVE again
   May never bless my lonely hours,
Or o'er life's dull and weary plain
   Scatter its sunlight and its flowers.

'I may not *ask*, but this I *feel*,
   That clouds have dim'd my brightest sky;
That cankering cares have come to steal
   The light from manhood's thoughtful eye;
Yet still I gaze, and feel as one
   Who, travelling, marks a landscape passed
Where streams the influence of the sun,
   While cloud and storm are round him cast!'

AN esteemed Southern friend and correspondent, writing us from 'Rowland Springs, Cass county, Georgia,' and enclosing us one of his always welcome communications, observes: 'I had thought that I was done with verse for the rest of my life, but the holiday of a few weeks in this mountain region, where the wild Indian so lately roamed, has brought back some faint memories of my romantic days, and I have endeavored to woo the coy muse. She has become so cold, however, from my long neglect of her, that I could coax but little out of her. You gentleman of the north can scarcely believe that we have in Georgia so many fine things as are grouped in this region; but it is *true* that we have here, within the compass of a few miles, mines of gold, iron, lead and coal, to say nothing of the diamonds that lie scattered about, and the beautiful scenery spread broadcast over the land. But I have lingered out my few days of holiday,

'And have looked on hill and plain
   That I ne'er shall see again;'

for I am on my way back to the dust and toil of week-day, work-day life, and to my allotted task of helping to drag the so-called car of Justice. And so, farewell poetry, mountain stream, and woodland nymph! — and come on, ye ill-shapen, strife-begetting demons of the law! But while *you* roam through the garden-walks of literature, cast some passing thoughts on the poor pilgrim who is struggling with weary steps over the desert ways of strife.' While our friend was hastening back to his official 'bench' at the capital, we were with kindred reluctance hurrying back (from our only summer jaunt) to our professional chair. Yet the scenes we then saw are sometimes before us in our silent sanctum. They even come in the night-watches; and often,

> 'WHEN sleep the eye-lids fills.
> Our spirit seems to walk abroad
> Among the mighty hills!'

And so has it been, we doubt not, with our friend. . . . A NORTHERN correspondent sends us the following, which was suggested by the 'Number twelve, pegged heel' anecdote in our last gossipry: ' An amazing pair of feet appeared in the bar-room of an ambitious village-inn, late one evening, the owner of which inquired anxiously for the boot-black. The bell rang nervously, and in a moment a keen Yankee illustrator of 'DAY AND MARTIN's best' popped into the room.' ' Bring me a jack!' exclaimed the man of great 'under-standing.' The waiter involuntarily started forward, but chancing to catch a glimpse of the boots, he stopped short, and after another and closer examination said, with equal twang and emphasis: 'I say yeŏu, you aint a-goin' to leave this world in a hurry; you've got too good a hold onto the ground. Want a boot-jack, eh? Why, bless your soul, there aint a boot-jack on airth big enuff for *them* boots! I don't b'lieve that a jack-*ass* could get 'em off.' My stars! man!' cried our friend of the big feet, ' what 'll I do? I can't get my boots *off* without a jack?' ' I tell you what *I* should do,' replied ' BOOTS,' ' if they was mine; I should walk back to the *fork of the road*, and pull 'em off there! *That* would fetch 'em, I guess!' . . . IT was an exceedingly pleasant surprise to us the other evening, after dining with an old and long-esteemed friend, to walk into the drawing-room to witness the opening of a fine marble statue, from the chisel (and head) of Mr. H. K. BROWN, a young but already very distinguished American sculptor, recently returned to this country from a long residence in Rome. The figures are of a boy and dog; the former holding the latter back by his chain and collar from lapping a bowl of milk which stands upon the floor. The boy. in position, drawing and expression, is a very charming conception. The surface of the body and limbs is flesh-like, and the head and face are full of grace and beauty. The eagerness of the animal is forcibly depicted in every feature of the head, including the ears and fore-shoulder. There are other works of the same sculptor recently arrived, but not unboxed as we write, to which we shall pay our respects hereafter. Mr. BROWN is a young artist of the first order of genius, and what is not always the case, as modest as he is gifted. . . . WE have received from Pittsburgh, (Penn.,) a poem addressed to the *Steamer New. Hampshire,* a very popular boat, which under the capable supervision of the Messrs. ALLENS has acquired a wide repute on the western waters. If the poem were not much too long, we would insert it with pleasure; for we hear on all sides that the boat whose long and varied voyage it describes is worthy of all the praise which she has elicited at the hands of our correspondent. . . . WE do not often envy any human being; but we confess to having entertained something of this feeling toward the possessor of a beautiful house and charming grounds, which we passed daily, in a fashionable quarter of the town, during the pleasant October days. But one morning we saw the owner among his grapes and flowers and fountains; a tall, care-worn, thin-visaged man, who stood tremblingly on ' his pins' and surveyed his beautiful possessions. Ah! thought we, there is a ' compensation' in every thing. ' What pleasure can it be to thee,' says an eloquent divine, ' to wrap the living skeleton in purple, and wither alive in cloth-of-gold, when the clothes serve only to upbraid the uselessness of thy limbs, and the rich fare only reproaches thee, and tantalizes the weakness of thy stomach.' So ' let us to our mutton,' with that good digestion which waits on an appetite that is most like a hungry anaconda's. · · · WE are well pleased to learn that the extensive piano-forte establishment of Messrs. STOD-ART AND DUNHAM, which was some time since destroyed by fire, has been again re-built, and is now in successful operation, with its full complement of workmen. As the pianos from this old established house are held second to no instruments in the world, we are performing a public service in mentioning that all orders can now be supplied by the proprietors with ' promptness and despatch.' · · · OUR readers will have been made aware, before these pages are before them, of the sad death of Mr. WILLIAM KIRKLAND, of this city. He was about to return from Newburgh, in the neighborhood of which place he had gone to see his little son who was at school. ' The wind was high, the night was dark,' when he left the hotel at Newburgh to take the night-boat to town ; and being somewhat near-sighted, with impaired sense of sound, he must have walked off unperceived from the very indifferently-lighted dock. ' Mr. KIRKLAND,' justly remarks a contemporary, ' was a man of ripe scholar-ship, of amiable and upright character, and singular disinterestedness. He had just begun, in connection with his wife, well known as one of our most lively and popular writers, a new weekly religious paper, which promised the most abundant success. He has departed in the prime of his years, and when the studies and experiences of a laborious life were about to be turned to the greatest avail for the good of mankind.' With his deeply-afflicted wife and family a warm sympathy is universal ; for of few among us could it so truly be said, ' He lived beloved and died lamented.' He was only forty-five. · · · THE moon *is* poetical, dear ' Babylonian,' but *you* are not, exactly. We never look at our ' pale mistress' without thinking how the dead have gazed upon her as *we* are gazing, noting the marks upon her face ; how ' they who go down to the sea in ships' have dwelt upon her, a track of calm effulgence streaming the while to the vessel's side ; and they too who in sweet country haunts sit under tall trees and drink in the quiet loveliness of the landscape, ' silvery in her chaste light.' Yes, there *is* poetry in this ; it is not ' all moonshine,' as some may perhaps sup-pose. · · · WE do not know when we have encountered a more explicit ' declaration of principles' than will be found in the following anecdote, which reaches us in a note from an Albany correspondent : ' A fashionable JEREMY DIDDLER not long since ordered a suit of clothes of a ' crack' merchant-tailor in town. At the proper time he called and asked if they were done. ' Done ? No, Sir !' replied the tailor ; ' how could you expect them to be made up unless you first secured me ? You do n't pay your debts, and I cannot afford to *give* you a suit of clothes.' Our DIDDLER stared with comi-tragic earnestness at the ' SNIP,' then stepped back, and with a look and manner that are utterly indescribable, replied : ' Well, that's d — d bad ; for some-body's got to do it !' · · · THE '*Scratches on the Road with a Pewter-Headed Cane*' record a remarkable instance of a noble dog standing up in defence of a wounded pig against the attack of a cross-grained cur ; the pig mean while mani-festing his knowledge of the kindly intentions of his defender, by standing perfectly still and permitting him to lick his wounds. It 's curious, certainly, but ' no *great* scratch,' Mr. HOOD ; you can ' come up' to a better, certainly. Indeed, we have evidence in our portfolio that you *have* done so. · · · ' THE whirligig of Fate brought about the revenges' of *one* man of our acquaintance, when he was a boy. He had been watched by a 'tiding-man' at church, on a sultry Sunday, when he was relieving the tedium of listening to a long doctrinal sermon by cutting oblong holes and deep initials in the side of the pine pew in which he sat in the gallery; and was led by the ear, in presence of the whole congregation, to the 'condemned pew,' where all bad boys were placed as in a criminal dock. While he was in this conspicuous duress, his cheeks burning-red with shame, the holy tiding-man had seated himself at the foot of the gallery-stairs, by the open porch-door, where, owing to the sultry day and the somnolency of the discourse, he presently began to nod. Now there was a huge goat belonging to a deacon, who lived near the church, and this goat had been taught, by playing frequently at 'bunt' with a negro-boy of the family, to 'run into' every body who appeared to 'address themselves to action' in his line of warfare. 'Nothing could be more ludicrous,' says our friend, 'than to see this goat, who had been nipping the short grass in front of the church, clatter up opposite the nodding 'tiding-man,' and stamp two or three times with both feet at once, and turning his head under, as if 'ready for the fray.' Presently he retreated two or three steps, and with one rush knocked the sleeping sacristan clear into the side-aisle, and administered an additional 'dig' or two after he lay there. The man bled profusely, and his face was much swollen. He was removed to the deacon's house, and did not leave it until after the lapse of three weeks. Our friend observed, that he was 'very sorry' that such an accident should have happened! . . . WHAT a blessed and blessing thing is the wide social bond of friendly sympathy! We were ruminating this moment, while gazing into the fire that flashes fitfully in the grate, how many and how widely separated are they, who in our pleasant home-sanctum have communed with us in cordial fellowship within the last twelvemonth. Some, alas! have fallen gloriously in their country's service; others are now sailing on the 'great and wide sea' in another hemisphere; some are in far cities of the Orient, others in towns of the distant Occident; and many are they, in almost every division of our own land, whom we can recall mnemonically by a single glance around our apartment. Friends! on land or sea, at home or abroad; on the mountains of the North or the plains of the South; in the far, far West, or extremely down East — Friends! 'have with you' all to-night! . . . IN these humbugeous days of false pretence in literary matters, one hardly receives credit for a plain statement of fact; but we must beg our readers to believe that '*The Saint Leger Papers*' have been delayed through failure in the receipt, by late arrivals, of the continuous manuscripts. It was fortunate that this hiatus occurred just at the conclusion of 'Part First,' for it would otherwise have been very provoking for our readers to be compelled to wait until our next number. . . . Mr. T. ROMEYN BRODHEAD has sailed for England, to enter upon his official duties as Secretary of Legation at the American Embassy. Mr. BRODHEAD is an accomplished scholar, an excellent writer, a gentleman of polished address and a good heart. The embassy will be honored by his appointment. · · · WE have had little opportunity to examine the merits of the new 'science' of '*Phonography*.' We are quite willing to admit, however, that there is wide room for improvement in much of the spelling of the day. We have a case in point. A friend informs us, that being in a shop the other day, he remarked a dashing-looking person writing a letter at the tradesman's desk. When he had sealed and directed it, he examined the superscription with some scrutiny, and finally asked the shop-keeper, 'How do you spell Philadelphia?' '*Fel-a-del-fy*,' replied the shop-keeper. 'Then I've got it right!' said the 'New-York correspondent;' I was thinking praps I 'd made a mistake !' . . . YES, we *are* 'in for it now,' friend ' P.,' past peradventure :

> 'THE clover-fields have lost their tints of green,
> The beans are full, and leaves are blanched and lean,
> And winter's piercing breath prepares to drain
> The thin green blood from every willow's vein.'

' Well, who cares ?' Now for theatres, concerts and town-parties ; those sadly ' genteel' gatherings, where one meets with ' wonderful foreign counts with bushy whiskers and yellow faces, and a great deal of dubious jewellery; young dandies with slim waists, self-satisfied simpers, and flowers in their button-holes; and old stiff, stout bald-headed conversazione-roués, whom one meets every where,' together with the very last-caught lion of the season. . . . WILL the kind friend, whose munificent present is enhanced by the delicate manner of the donor's concealment, permit us to tender him here the gratitude of a warm heart? The golden token of his noble generosity, whenever we ' take note of time,' passing in golden hours, will remind us of one of those true spirits who enact generous deeds by stealth, and seek no reward but the pleasure which springs from doing good. Kind UNKNOWN ! may your heart know no change, your sky no cloud ! . . . ' THERE goes the old Dutchman who had the dangerous geese !' exclaimed a friend in the country the other day, calling our attention to a Dutchman of the oldest ' school,' who was walking slowly along the road.' We asked an explanation. Why, when the Yankees first began to settle in here, he was joined one morning by a slab-sided specimen of 'em, as he was picking up the quills that his geese had dropped, in their chattering morning waddles, by the edges of an oblong pond at the roadside. Presently one of the geese stretched out his long neck at the Yankee, who started and ran as if a mad dog were at his heels. ' I dold him,' said the old Dutchman, ' not to be avraid ; dat de geese would n't hurt um any ; but de geese *did* run after him dough, clear over de hill a ways; and none of 'em would n't give um no rest any more, whenever he come along the sdreet. I p'lieve dey had a shbite ag'in de Yankees. Mein GOTT ! it 's curious, dough, but de geese always went away, and did n't come back any more !' The secret of that was, that the Yankee, who was so afraid of the Dutchman's geese, had thrown out kernels of corn, among which was one with a fish-hook attached. Once swallowed, the angry goose was soon in tow after the flying fugitive. · · · '*A country ' Old Mortality,'* ' impressed with the two or three epitaphs given in our last number, has despatched us another one, which he assures us is indisputably genuine. It was copied from a tomb-stone in the ' old country :'

> 'HERE lies old VANDERHILDEBROD !
> Have mercy on his soul, oh GOD ;
> As he would have, if he were GOD,
> And you were VANDERHILDEBROD.'

THE ' *Scene at an Auction-Room,*' in which our eloquent friend THOMAS BELL bears a conspicuous and honorable part, will appear in our next.— WHAT has become of FLANEUR ? Some scribbler is usurping his style and cognomen in a London magazine. — THE lines of our clever correspondent, E. CURTIS HINE, (*of* whom and *from* whom more hereafter,) will appear in our next. Mr. J. BAYARD TAYLOR will please accept our thanks for his '*Lines to an American Child in Italy.*' They are filed for immediate insertion. ' J. L. C.' of Vermont is under consideration.— NOTICES of several new publications are unavoidably crowded out, together with criticisms upon the performances at the Park and Bowery Theatres.

LITERARY RECORD. — No metropolitan publishers 'open' upon the public so richly the present month as Messrs. D. APPLETON AND COMPANY. First we have, in a second edition, enlarged, the poems of the charming Kentucky poetess, 'AMELIA,' now generally known as Mrs. WELBY; a volume replete with imagination, informed by a spirit of deep feeling and affection, and remarkable in many instances for the exquisite melody of its versification, and a wide range of felicitous similitude. Next we have, gorgeously illustrated and bound, the '*Poetical Works of Thomas Moore*,' complete in one volume, prepared and revised by the author. The book is admirably executed, and the steel engravings, (which include a noble portrait of the poet, and a view of his country residence,) are of the first order of beauty and excellence. This is followed by another attractive book, '*Childe Harold's Pilgrimage*,' quite as elegant in its externals, and considering the size of the work, even more profusely illustrated. Then come the '*Poetical Works of Robert Southey, collected by Himself*;' a new edition, including 'OLIVER NEWMAN and other Poems,' now first published; illustrated with eight fine steel engravings, from drawings by the best artists in England. Preliminary notices are affixed to the long poems, the whole of the notes retained, and such additional ones incorporated as the author, since the first publication, has seen occasion to insert. This beautiful edition will find a place in the library of every man who is fond of elegant literature. From the same publishers we derive two other valuable books by American authors: '*A Course of Reading for Common Schools*,' by Professor MANDEVILLE, of Hamilton College, on the plan of the 'Elements of Reading and Oratory,' (a volume by the same author, which has been properly commended in the KNICKERBOCKER,) and '*Warner's Rudimental Lessons in Music*,' a small volume, yet containing the primary instruction requisite for all beginners in the art, whether vocal or instrumental. Of the first of these two last-named works we may have more to say hereafter. · · · FROM the enterprising house of Messrs. WILEY AND PUTNAM we have, in a portly volume, '*The Water-Cure in Chronic Disease*;' an exposition of the causes, progress and terminations of various chronic diseases of the digestive organs, lungs, nerves, limbs and skin, and of their treatment by water and other hygienic means; unquestionably the most complete work upon its theme extant. The author is the eminent Dr. GULLY, who appears to be a licentiate and fellow of all the royal and medical colleges in Great Britain. Also a very interesting volume, entitled '*Notes on the North-west, or Valley of the Upper Mississippi*,' which covers new ground geographically, and differs in design, plan and mode of treatment from other works descriptive of the vast region of which it treats; a region almost wholly unknown to American geographers twenty years since. It is strictly authentic, and would seem to be indispensable to persons seeking information in relation to that portion of the United States. In the popular '*Library of Choice Reading*' of the same publishers, we are glad to find CARLYLE's 'Heroes and Hero-Worshippers,' HAZLITT's 'Spirit of the Age,' (both heretofore noticed in these pages,) and the Poems of CAROLINE BOWLES, or Mrs. SOUTHEY, a collection which we trust may find a wide circulation in this country, for the purity, the simple domestic and devotional feeling, and the love of nature and of man, which are its characteristics. Of the '*Library of American Books*,' Miss S. MARGARET FULLER's 'Papers on Literature and Art,' and 'The Early Jesuit Missions in North America,' translated by Rev. WILLIAM INGRAHAM KIP, are the latest issues. Their tardy receipt must constitute our apology for not noticing them more particularly in the present number. The same publishers have given us, in a handsome single volume, '*The Christmas Carol*,' '*The Chimes*,' and '*The Cricket on the Hearth*,' by CHARLES DICKENS; (what a delightful feast for autumnal and winter evenings!) and they will also publish, in the course of the present month, in connection with Messrs. JAMES MUNROE AND COMPANY, Boston, '*Poems by William Thompson Bacon*,' a gentleman with whose poetical productions our readers are familiar, and being so, will be glad to secure a copy from the forthcoming edition, which is to be very beautiful in its externals. . . . Messrs. BAKER AND SCRIBNER have among the recent issues of their press a little volume entitled '*The Convict's Child*,' by CHARLES BURDETT. The tears of the 'little people' to whom it was read in the sanctum hereabout attested the power and simplicity which mark its contents. The author is certainly a pleasing and forcible writer, and we are not surprised at his growing reputation. '*Clement of Rome, or Scenes from the Christianity of the First Century*,' by Mrs. JOSLYN, is the title of a new volume, as yet unperused, from the same press. . . . WE receive (at a late hour) from the New-Jersey Historical Society, a work which promises much interest; namely, '*East-Jersey under the Proprietary Governments*.' It is a well-written and perspicuous narrative of events connected with the settlement and progress of the province until the surrender of the government to the crown in 1702, drawn mainly from original sources. The author, WILLIAM A. WHITEHEAD, Esq., closes his volume with an appendix, containing 'The Model of the Government of East New-Jersey in America,' by GEORGE SCOTT of Pitlochie, here first reprinted from the original edition of 1685. Mr. WHITEHEAD'S extensive and authentic researches seem to have exhausted all the demands of his subject. There are many instances of the teachings of History by example, and not a little 'comparative' amusement, in the civilized sense, in this volume; and of these it is our purpose to avail ourselves hereafter. · · · THE writer, whoever she may be, of '*The Wild Rose,*' a pretty little 'booklet' published recently by Messrs. HENRY M. ONDERDONK AND COMPANY, has little need to send her verse forth to the public under a *nom de plume.* 'GENEVIEVE' may rest assured that she has a warm fancy and a facility of graceful versification. Take this example, selected quite at random, of her poetical powers :

'I SAW the fair and smiling moon
   Rise in the eastern sky,
And as her beams played round me,
   There seemed an angel nigh,
But a cloud of fleecy whiteness
   Passed o er her face so pale,
Which, though it dimmed her brightness,
   Was still a lovely veil

'I saw a pure and silver lake,
   Placid and clear and still,
Sleeping beneath the moon-beams,
   While rose a purple hill
Which o er the lake's calm bosom
   Its lengthened shadow threw,
And the mingled light and darkness
   Were beautiful to view

'I saw a rose whose beauteous form
   And fragrance seemed to speak
Of maiden grace and purity,
   But a tear was on its cheek
It seemed to breathe of sadness,
   That flow'ret bright and fair,
And yet 't was all the lovelier
   For that pure tear-drop there.

'So like the mountain shadow,
   And like the cloud so pale,
And like the tears upon the rose,
   As a pure filmy veil;
Like beauty in which sadness
   Doth gently bear a part,
Like all that a sweet yet mournful,
   Young LOVE comes o'er the heart.'

As we are closing our number for the month, we receive from the press of Mr. BENJAMIN B. MUSSEY, Boston, an exceedingly handsome volume, containing the '*Sacred and Miscellaneous Poems of William B. Tappan.*' If our readers had not already been made favorably acquainted with Mr. TAPPAN's poetical talents, as developed in his communications to the KNICKERBOCKER, we should regret the necessity which compels us thus briefly to announce the present collection. As it is, however, the mere announcement will be all that his admirers will be likely to require. · · · AMONG the recent publications of W. H. GRAHAM, Tribune-Buildings, are FARNHAM's '*Life, Travels and Adventures in California, and Scenes in the Pacific Ocean,*' a very interesting work, and Hon. JOHN QUINCY ADAMS' '*Lives of Celebrated Statesmen,*' with a sketch of the author by CHARLES W. UPHAM. · · · JUDGE HALL's matter-full '*Address before the Young Men's Mercantile Library Association of Cincinnati,*' recently published, arrived too late for farther notice than the mere announcement of its publication in the present number. · · · WE have seldom encountered a more chaste and beautiful publication than '*Greenwood Illustrated,*' in a series of picturesque and monumental views, in highly-finished line-engraving ; from drawings taken on the spot, by JAMES SMILLIE. The engravings are on steel, and are of the first order of execution. The artist who drew them has a fine eye for the picturesque and the beautiful. The literary department is in the hands of Mr. N. CLEAVELAND. We are sorry that while copying the poetical inscription from the monument to the young Indian wife, DO-HUM-ME, the editor should not have rendered that justice to BRYANT which the sculptor has denied him. The verse should be:

'Thou 'rt happy now, for thou hast past
The long, dark journey of the grave,
And in the land of light at last
Hast joined the good and brave '

The last line, on the monument, has two words added to it, which spoils the measure without adding to the sentiment, and there is also an error from the original in the second line, although less material. Poor beautiful DO-HUM-ME! how well we remember her as she sat, a few days before her death, in one of the apartments of the American Museum, gazing up into her young husband's face, her hand clasped the while in his. But ' speaking of inscriptions,' that is an admirable one recorded upon the tablet of a young mother, laid to rest in Greenwood with an only and infant child, whose death occurred a little while before her own : ''Is it well with thee ? Is it well with the child ?' And she answered, ' It is well.'' How simple, yet how touching, is this passage of Holy Writ in this connection ! · · · WE wish we had received a little earlier from the publishers, Messrs. CAREY AND HART, Philadelphia, our friend T. B. THORPE's late work, '*Our Army on the Rio-Grande,*' comprising ' a short account of the important events transpiring (occurring, the author means,) from the time of the removal of the 'Army of Occupation' from Corpus Christi to the surrender of Matamoras ; with a description of the battles of Palo Alto and Resaca de la Palma, the bombardment of Fort Brown, and the ceremonies of the surrender of Matamoras ; with descriptions of the city,' etc., etc. ' TOM OWEN, the Bee-Hunter,' has done his best in this work, and *his* best is good-enough reading

LITERARY RECORD.—No metropolitan publishers 'open' upon the public so richly the present month as Messrs. D. APPLETON AND COMPANY. First we have, in a second edition, enlarged, the poems of the charming Kentucky poetess, 'AMELIA,' now generally known as Mrs. WELBY; a volume replete with imagination, informed by a spirit of deep feeling and affection, and remarkable in many instances for the exquisite melody of its versification, and a wide range of felicitous similitude. Next we have, gorgeously illustrated and bound, the 'Poetical Works of Thomas Moore,' complete in one volume, prepared and revised by the author. The book is admirably executed, and the steel engravings, (which include a noble portrait of the poet, and a view of his country residence,) are of the first order of beauty and excellence. This is followed by another attractive book, 'Childe Harold's Pilgrimage,' quite as elegant in its externals, and considering the size of the work, even more profusely illustrated. Then come the 'Poetical Works of Robert Southey, collected by Himself;' a new edition, including ' OLIVER NEWMAN and other Poems,' now first published; illustrated with eight fine steel engravings, from drawings by the best artists in England. Preliminary notices are affixed to the long poems, the whole of the notes retained, and such additional ones incorporated as the author, since the first publication, has seen occasion to insert. This beautiful edition will find a place in the library of every man who is fond of elegant literature. From the same publishers we derive two other valuable books by American authors: 'A Course of Reading for Common Schools,' by Professor MANDEVILLE, of Hamilton College, on the plan of the 'Elements of Reading and Oratory,' (a volume by the same author, which has been properly commended in the KNICKERBOCKER,) and 'Warner's Rudimental Lessons in Music,' a small volume, yet containing the primary instruction requisite for all beginners in the art, whether vocal or instrumental. Of the first of these two last-named works we may have more to say hereafter. • • • FROM the enterprising house of Messrs. WILEY AND PUTNAM we have, in a portly volume, 'The Water-Cure in Chronic Disease;' an exposition of the causes, progress and terminations of various chronic diseases of the digestive organs, lungs, nerves, limbs and skin, and of their treatment by water and other hygienic means; unquestionably the most complete work upon its theme extant. The author is the eminent Dr. GULLY, who appears to be a licentiate and fellow of all the royal and medical colleges in Great Britain. Also a very interesting volume, entitled 'Notes on the North-west, or Valley of the Upper Mississippi,' which covers new ground geographically, and differs in design, plan and mode of treatment from other works descriptive of the vast region of which it treats; a region almost wholly unknown to American geographers twenty years since. It is strictly authentic, and would seem to be indispensable to persons seeking information in relation to that portion of the United States. In the popular 'Library of Choice Reading' of the same publishers, we are glad to find CARLYLE'S 'Heroes and Hero-Worshippers,' HAZLITT's 'Spirit of the Age,' (both heretofore noticed in these pages,) and the Poems of CAROLINE BOWLES, or Mrs. SOUTHEY, a collection which we trust may find a wide circulation in this country, for the purity, the simple domestic and devotional feeling, and the love of nature and of man, which are its characteristics. Of the 'Library of American Books,' Miss S. MARGARET FULLER's 'Papers on Literature and Art,' and 'The Early Jesuit Missions in North America,' translated by Rev. WILLIAM INGRAHAM KIP, are the latest issues. Their tardy receipt must constitute our apology for not noticing them more particularly in the present number. The same publishers have given us, in a handsome single volume, 'The Christmas Carol,' 'The Chimes,' and 'The Cricket on the Hearth,' by CHARLES DICKENS; (what a delightful feast for autumnal and winter evenings !) and they will also publish, in the course of the present month, in connection with Messrs. JAMES MUNROE AND COMPANY, Boston, 'Poems by William Thompson Bacon,' a gentleman with whose poetical productions our readers are familiar, and being so, will be glad to secure a copy from the forthcoming edition, which is to be very beautiful in its externals. . . . Messrs. BAKER AND SCRIBNER have among the recent issues of their press a little volume entitled 'The Convict's Child,' by CHARLES BURDETT. The tears of the 'little people' to whom it was read in the sanctum hereabout attested the power and simplicity which mark its contents. The author is certainly a pleasing and forcible writer, and we are not surprised at his growing reputation. 'Clement of Rome, or Scenes from the Christianity of the First Century,' by Mrs. JOSLYN, is the title of a new volume, as yet unperused, from the same press. . . . WE receive (at a late hour) from the New-Jersey Historical Society, a work which promises much interest; namely, 'East-Jersey under the Proprietary Governments.' It is a well-written and perspicuous narrative of events connected with the settlement and progress of the province until the surrender of the government to the crown in 1702, drawn mainly from original sources. The author, WILLIAM A. WHITEHEAD, Esq., closes his volume with an appendix, containing 'The Model of the Government of East New-Jersey in Ame-

ORIGINAL PAPERS.

NOTICE.

COUNTRY SUBSCRIBERS who are in arrears should recollect to make returns for what we send them. Remittances to be made to   JOHN ALLEN,

139 Nassau-street,

New-York.

MR. T. P. WILLIAMS is our Agent to receive the names of Subscribers in the West and South. Editors and others kindly interested in the circulation of this Magazine, will oblige us by facilitating his designs.

O. D. DAVIS and JOHN STOUGHTON, Jr., are canvassing for subscribers to this work in the state of New-York.

THE KNICKERBOCKER.

Vol. XXVIII.   DECEMBER, 1846.   No. 6.

THE SAINT LEGER PAPERS.

PART THE SECOND

'Quidquid agunt homines, votum, timor, ira, voluptas,
Gaudia, discursus, nostri farrago libelli.'

Two years!
                                    Time, that mighty leaven, which
leaveneth the great current of events, maturing and evolving each
in its appointed order, had worked restlessly through two more
years, and these were added to the eternity of the past.

And what were those two years to me? Much, every way, save
in actual results. In these, nothing.

The result is slow and sudden. Slow, to the anxious one, who
labors wearisomely, and with an almost omnipresent energy, to bring
somewhat to pass. To such, how slow and painful are the steps
toward the summit, though from the plain its towering height de-
light the eye!

Sudden, to the wondering many who behold what *has* come to
pass, but who know not, nor think, nor imagine any thing of the
preparation-work. To such, how suddenly doth the patient laborer
emerge from obscurity, and take his stand upon the pinnacle of fame!

This is also true of that which tends downward unto perdition.
For men look at the *results* of evil, not at the *causes* of it. The
result is nothing without *exclusion*. For to attain it, one must
exclude all that is foreign to the pursuit. If a man serve his pas-
sions, he must exclude the higher enjoyments of the moral and in-
tellectual. Or if he seeks the intellectual, he must exclude those
baser things which enervate and enslave the mind. If he deter-
mine upon moral and religious culture, he must exclude the influ-
ences of 'time and sense.'

Self-denial, which is another word for exclusion, is a necessary
exercise. No matter what the object sought; without it, all labor
is empty effort. For no person can at the same time walk in a given

about the revenges' of *one* man of our acquaintance, when he was a boy. He had
been watched by a 'tiding-man' at church, on a sultry Sunday, when he was relieving
the tedium of listening to a long doctrinal sermon by cutting oblong holes and deep
initials in the side of the pine pew in which he sat in the gallery; and was led by the
ear, in presence of the whole congregation, to the 'condemned pew,' where all bad
boys were placed as in a criminal dock. While he was in this conspicuous duress, his
cheeks burning-red with shame, the holy tiding-man had seated himself at the foot
of the gallery-stairs, by the open porch-door, where, owing to the sultry day and the
somnolency of the discourse, he presently began to nod. Now there was a huge goat
belonging to a deacon, who lived near the church, and this goat had been taught, by
playing frequently at 'bunt' with a negro-boy of the family, to 'run into' every body
who appeared to 'address themselves to action' in his line of warfare. 'Nothing could
be more ludicrous,' says our friend, 'than to see this goat, who had been nipping the
short grass in front of the church, clatter up opposite the nodding 'tiding-man,' and
stamp two or three times with both feet at once, and turning his head under, as if
'ready for the fray.' Presently he retreated two or three steps, and with one rush
knocked the sleeping sacristan clear into the side-aisle, and administered an additional
'dig' or two after he lay there. The man bled profusely, and his face was much
swollen. He was removed to the deacon's house, and did not leave it until after the
lapse of three weeks. Our friend observed, that he was 'very sorry' that such an ac-
cident should have happened! · · · WHAT a blessed and blessing thing is the wide
social bond of friendly sympathy! We were ruminating this moment, while gazing into
the fire that flashes fitfully in the grate, how many and how widely separated are they,
who in our pleasant home-sanctum have communed with us in cordial fellowship
within the last twelvemonth. Some, alas! have fallen gloriously in their country's
service; others are now sailing on the 'great and wide sea' in another hemisphere; some
are in far cities of the Orient, others in towns of the distant Occident; and many are
they, in almost every division of our own land, whom we can recall mnemonically by
a single glance around our apartment. Friends! on land or sea, at home or abroad;
on the mountains of the North or the plains of the South; in the far, far West, or
extremely down East — Friends! 'have with you' all to-night! · · · IN these
humbugeous days of false pretence in literary matters, one hardly receives credit for
a plain statement of fact; but we must beg our readers to believe that '*The Saint
Leger Papers*' have been delayed through failure in the receipt, by late arrivals, of
the continuous manuscripts. It was fortunate that this hiatus occurred just at the
conclusion of 'Part First,' for it would otherwise have been very provoking for our
readers to be compelled to wait until our next number. . . . Mr. T. ROMEYN BROD-
HEAD has sailed for England, to enter upon his official duties as Secretary of Legation
at the American Embassy. Mr. BRODHEAD is an accomplished scholar, an excellent
writer, a gentleman of polished address and a good heart. The embassy will be hon-
ored by his appointment. · · · WE have had little opportunity to examine the merits
of the new 'science' of '*Phonography.*' We are quite willing to admit, however, that
there is wide room for improvement in much of the spelling of the day. We have a
case in point. A friend informs us, that being in a shop the other day, he remarked
a dashing-looking person writing a letter at the tradesman's desk. When he had
sealed and directed it, he examined the superscription with some scrutiny, and finally
asked the shop-keeper, 'How do you spell Philadelphia?' '*Fel-a-del-fy,*' replied the
shop-keeper. 'Then I've got it right!' said the 'New-York correspondent;' I was

saw it years, years before. The landscape, the mansion, a particular apartment, the books, the furniture, and the little articles of use or fancy which lie scattered around. Other things have been changing—changing; these have remained the same; and they speak to him as if they knew not that *he* had changed. They speak the language of by-gone days; they know no other, and *therefore* lingers the wanderer, ere he resumes his pilgrimage.

But I will proceed. I had returned from Glencoe an altered being. I felt that an epocha had taken place in my existence. Before, I sought eagerly after some explanation of the outward form and manner of this world. I expected to get at the centre from the surface. The consequence was, that whatever I learned sufficed only for the occasion; it furnished me with nothing inductive. I was still under a cloud, and saw every thing 'as through a glass, darkly.' As the tendencies of manhood began more strongly to be developed, which by-the-way received a tremendous impetus from the strange adventures of the previous summer, I felt that there must be some way to break the charm of mystery that enveloped all around me. So far, nothing had indelibly impressed me. Perhaps I may except the meeting with the Wœdallah and my acquaintance with Leila, which beyond question were the strongest incidents that had come to affect me.

From Leila I had heard nothing since leaving St. Kilda, though months had elapsed; so that even the singular occurrences at that remote island began by degrees to lose their hold upon me. Perhaps I was a little piqued at the silence of my fair relative, after her promise that she would acquaint me with her movements; beside, I was in no state to cherish recollections of any kind. I desired to get upon some system of living which would give me peace of mind. At the same time I felt dissatisfied with every thing I had ever tried. I longed for something new. Restraint of every kind had become irksome, oppressive, unendurable. I resolved to throw off the fetters of former influences, and learn afresh. This was a hardy resolution for a youth, but it was taken.

Fearful indeed it is thus to unsettle every thing which previous education has tended to make firm. But it is still more fearful to find, too late in life, that one is *adrift*. When I came home, I began to commune with myself. The return to familiar scenes had nothing of their usual enlivening welcome effect upon my spirits. By and by I went to the old library. It was dustier and more gloomy and more neglected than ever; but I loved it. I resolved there, in that ancient and deserted chamber, to put my resolution in practice. I declared to myself that I would think with freedom; that what seemed to me to be inconsistent I would call inconsistent, and that whatever did not commend itself to my reason I would reject. Full of these notions of a new-fledged independence, I began to study.

It happened about this time that my father employed as a tutor for me a man highly recommended to him by a particular friend, as thoroughly learned and accomplished; and in consequence, FREDERICK DE LISLE was domesticated at Bertold Castle. He was an Englishman by birth, a Frenchman by descent, and a German by education. How my father was induced to break over his prejudices and receive into his house any one with Gallic blood in his veins, I cannot tell, except that he was carried away by the persuasions and recommendations of his friend, upon whose opinion he placed great reliance. De Lisle was about five-and-thirty; old enough to have formed settled opinions, and maintain them with powerful arguments; young enough to commend himself to my companionship by a tolerably youthful air and demeanor.

I have said that he was of French descent, but he had nothing of the easy volatility of the Frenchman in his manner or in his character. His parents were Huguenots, who escaped into England to save their lives and enjoy religious freedom. England, to be sure, could not at that time boast of universal tolerance, but the elder De Lisle had some friends in the country, and to England he came. His son was born some time after the settlement of the parents in their adopted land. His early training had been carefully looked after, and by the assistance of the friend who had recommended the young man to us, he was sent to Germany to be educated. Naturally contemplative and thoughtful, without possessing a deep-reasoning, cause-discovering mind, the young De Lisle found, in the mazy philosophy of a certain class of German writers, a ready-made system, just fitted to his powers of contemplation, and apparently explanatory of the theory of life which he had been accustomed to consider as entirely beyond his grasp. He yielded therefore a blind assent to the new philosophy, and became, really without being aware of it, a very religious Pantheist.

I must not do him injustice. He had far more than ordinary powers of mind. He was a finished scholar, a proficient in the ancient and modern languages, and possessed of a fine critical taste. He had nothing of that malignant sarcasm which the doubter is apt to use with so unsparing a hand, with those who do not give a ready assent to his doctrines. De Lisle, on the contrary, was satisfied with having found a theory in which he could himself rest, and which he was happy to commend to others, without assailing their own. In conclusion, I must add, that he was naturally amiable, and his habits of life unexceptionable in every respect.

Such was the person, (nearly twenty years my senior,) who at this stage of my mental and moral progress was introduced as my preceptor and guide.

Was I not in danger?

I continued some time pursuing different studies under the direction of De Lisle, without making him acquainted with the state of my mind, although I was won by his pleasing, I may almost say fascinating deportment. Perceiving how much time I spent by myself, he at last asked me, in a delicate manner, what it was that so constantly occupied my leisure? I was not disposed at first to be communicative, but I finally determined to give him a full account of myself. I proceeded with considerable trepidation to recount all that I had experienced, showing evidently by my manner that I considered the history of my mental trials as something very extraordinary. When I had concluded, De Lisle, much to my surprise, smiled complacently upon me, and with an air half of commiseration and half of superiority, exclaimed :

'My young friend, you are but going through with the experience of every one who escapes from the thraldrom of superstition and bigotry into the clear atmosphere of intellectual freedom. You tell me of fears. Man in his proper element can have no fears. Why should he have them ? *What* has he to fear ? — WHOM has he to fear ? Is he not a part and portion of the Almighty Essence ? Can you resolve his spirit into aught else ? Can Self war with Self? Nay, resolve man into what you will, why should he play the trembler ? St. Leger,' continued De Lisle, kindly, 'I appreciate your distress; I feel with you. Trust therefore to my experience. The ground over which *you* are passing *I* have passed. I too have been in darkness ; have had my apprehensions and my fears; my forebodings, my trials and my doubts. I have escaped from them all, into glorious liberty, and in the path which led to my emancipation I would conduct you.'

I was completely astounded by these remarks. I supposed that all my experience was peculiar to myself; and I felt no small degree of mortification to learn that I had been travelling a beaten track, and that an ordinary acquaintance could readily describe the journey. I believe I may say with truth that I had a stronger intellect than De Lisle. But so completely was I taken by surprise at this unlooked for denouément, and so entirely did my friend seem to understand my position, that almost without knowing it, I yielded to his guidance. This certainly was not extraordinary. It probably would have occurred in ninety-nine cases out of a hundred. At all events, it occurred in mine.

In this way did Frederick De Lisle come to exercise a great influence over my mind. Still, I made very slow progress in my new course. Although I had thrown all former opinions to the winds, they would steal back upon me unperceived, knock softly at the door, and Conscience (for the first time an unfaithful janitor) would let them in without my consent; true, they were instantly turned out of doors again; but they gave me much trouble, nevertheless.

I was not without my misgivings. After all, I disliked to be, convinced that my life had been one grand error, and that I had just discovered it. Was I then so enslaved ? Was not my reason free ? Had my education been so entirely perverted and misdirected? These were questions that I asked myself daily, and daily I tried to answer them.

Just at this time I came across, in the old library, the '*Tractatus Theologico Politicus*' of BENEDICT SPINOZA. I perused this work with avidity. De Lisle, who seemed to understand my disposition, took care not to alarm my pride by too much dictation. He would assist me in a difficult passage, or throw in a remark to corroborate my author, and afterward leave me to myself. Although the doctrine of Spinoza appeared to be a sort of revival of the docman by birth, a Frenchman by descent, and a German by education. How my father was induced to break over his prejudices and receive into his house any one with Gallic blood in his veins, I cannot tell, except that he was carried away by the persuasions and recommendations of his friend, upon whose opinion he placed great reliance. De Lisle was about five-and-thirty; old enough to have formed settled opinions, and maintain them with powerful arguments; young enough to commend himself to my companionship by a tolerably youthful air and demeanor.

I have said that he was of French descent, but he had nothing of the easy volatility of the Frenchman in his manner or in his character. His parents were Huguenots, who escaped into England to save their lives and enjoy religious freedom. England, to be sure, could not at that time boast of universal tolerance, but the elder De Lisle had some friends in the country, and to England he came. His son was born some time after the settlement of the parents in their adopted land. His early training had been carefully looked after, and by the assistance of the friend who had recommended the young man to us, he was sent to Germany to be educated. Naturally contemplative and thoughtful, without possessing a deep-reasoning, cause-discovering mind, the young De Lisle found, in the mazy philosophy of a certain class of German writers, a ready-made system, just fitted to his powers of contemplation, and apparently explanatory of the theory of life which he had been accustomed to consider as entirely beyond his grasp. He yielded therefore a blind assent to the new philosophy, and became, really without being aware of it, a very religious Pantheist.

I must not do him injustice. He had far more than ordinary powers of mind. He was a finished scholar, a proficient in the ancient and modern languages, and possessed of a fine critical taste. He had nothing of that malignant sarcasm which the doubter is apt to use with so unsparing a hand, with those who do not give a ready assent to his doctrines. De Lisle, on the contrary, was satisfied with having found a theory in which he could himself rest, and which he was happy to commend to others, without assailing their own. In conclusion, I must add, that he was naturally amiable, and his habits of life unexceptionable in every respect.

Such was the person, (nearly twenty years my senior,) who at this stage of my mental and moral progress was introduced as my preceptor and guide.

Was I not in danger?

I continued some time pursuing different studies under the direction of De Lisle, without making him acquainted with the state of my mind, although I was won by his pleasing, I may almost say fascinating deportment. Perceiving how much time I spent by myself, he at last asked me, in a delicate manner, what it was that so constantly occupied my leisure? I was not disposed at first to be communicative, but I finally determined to give him a full account of myself. I proceeded with considerable trepidation to recount all that I had experienced, showing evidently by my manner that I con-

this, he was careful not to alarm me by his suspicions, but maintained his usual calm and complacent manner.

I was truly in a pitiable state, but I did not relax my efforts to get free. I studied and read and thought more assiduously than ever. My soul was burning up within me.

One morning, after the arrival of the post, a letter was placed in my hands, bearing my address. The superscription was in a small, delicate hand, but every character was traced with singular distinctness. I opened the letter, and read as follows :

'I have not forgotten you; I never shall forget you; never! never!

'At present, I write few words. My father has conversed with me as a parent with a child. He has given me his confidence, and I love him. I owe this to your visit. I love my parent; but I do not release you from your promised friendship. Let it be abiding; GOD only knows how soon I may require it. We shall meet by-and-by, but not yet; for as yet I know not where my destiny will lead me. Wherever I am, my consolation shall be, that in the hour of need I have one real heart-friend. Your promise is pledged — *forget it not !*   'LEILA ST. LEGER.'

'This is *from* a St. Leger *to* a St. Leger—from kin to kin. You cannot misconstrue it.   'L. ST. L.'

How opportune was the arrival of this short epistle! I read it over and over again. I examined it word by word and syllable by syllable, and then letter by letter. The postscript, although written for explanation, pleased me less than any part. I felt a thrill of joy dart through me, as the recollection of our last interview came back fresh to mind.

And this simple bit of paper, with these small characters traced upon it, had the effect to relieve my spirit, which was nigh on the verge of madness. Here was humanity interposed between me and the fiend. A young, beautiful, and almost unprotected girl claimed something at my hands — at least friendship; and whatever *was* or *was not*, either in heaven above or in hell below, if hell or heaven there were, yet here, upon the round earth, something real, something delectable, something (as I thought) *holy* presented itself, not for my contemplation — I had had enough of that — but for positive thought and action and feeling. Something objective, something real, something true.

[Bear in mind, thus I reasoned *then.*]

Of course I knew not when I should hear from Leila again. It did not matter much, so long as I was assured of the tie between us. I could now resume my studies; I could look more minutely into De Lisle's theory of life. Strange to say, I felt less repugnance to it than before. I began to take a deeper interest in things about me. Nature seemed more joyous; and when De Lisle exclaimed, in his tranquil, quiet tone, 'See you not GOD stirring through all this ? — here and there? above, around, every where? All is GOD, and GOD all!' I murmured an almost satisfied assent.

Yet I was *not* happy.

SEEDS.

A POETICAL ESSAY BY JOHN M. RHEIN.

WHEN the third morning of Creation shone,
    And from the naked earth
Rose the green herb, and grass, and branching tree full-grown,
      'T was thus decree'd
    By the Eternal MIND
And Voice of GOD that called them into birth,
    That they should grow:
    ' The green herb yielding seed,
The fruit-tree yielding fruit after his kind,
Whose seed is in itself, upon the earth:
      And it was so.'

Thus sprang that living verdure into being,
    Whose annual generations reach
Beyond the birth of ADAM. All agreeing,
A lesson of obedience do they teach;
Obedience to the voice that brought them forth:
    For, whether all alone they grow,
    Scattered by breezes to and fro,
      Or, side by side,
They cover fields or spread in forests wide,
Or struggle heavenward in the frozen North,
Or clothe in endless green the burning Line;
From age to age, with faith that never sleeps,
The vegetable world unbroken keeps
      That Law Divine.

    But never to the curious eye
Do they unfold their hidden mystery;
      Nor any seed e'er tells
How, in itself, its life mysterious dwells.
While in thy hand, or in the light of day,
    It seems an inert thing,
All dry and dead; nor life nor motion shows
      Within its rounded ring;
      But bury it away
Down in the dark damp earth, it dies and grows.
    The blade comes first,
      Soon the green leaves are shown;
Then buds appear, that shortly burst,
And opening show the tinted flowers full-blown,
Of purple, white, yellow or orange hue,
    Of pink or bright carnation,
Or velvet brown, deep-red, or purer blue.
All this is beauteous preparation;
      But now, at length,
      And all unseen,
The plant mature puts forth its chiefest strength.
    Within the pod of tender green,
Or stronger sphere o'ertopped with crown imperial,
    Under the shag-bark's russet suit,

Or veiled 'neath gauzy wings for flight aërial,
Deep in the swelling womb of pulpy fruit,
  Or housed within the rugged cone,
Or tough-ribbed shell, or hollow-chambered stone ;
    The plant, with patient care
    And instinct rare,
Gathers from every fibre of its frame
  The express idea of the same ;
(Ideas which, like those within the brain,
    Seem to maintain
    A certain place,
  Yet occupy no space ;)
Slowly with sap the ripening globes it feeds,
And in the germ of all the thousand seeds
    Within its teeming cup,
    Stores its own image up,
Even to the seed wherein that image lies ;
    And in their memories,
  With wondrous power, stamps both
The time and order of their birth and growth.

    And all the while the secret cell,
Where this mysterious labor is perfecting,
    Is guarded well,
By prickly beard its pointed spears erecting,
    Or shielded by tough rind
      Or tangled furze,
    Or else entrenched behind
A rampart bristling thick with barbed burrs ;
  Or stinging thorns do guard the approach,
Or 't is perchance by waxy husk defended,
    Lest insect foes encroach
Ere Nature's last and greatest work is ended.

    Life, wondrous Life, hath here
Begotten wondrous Life ; yea manifold,
    In silence dark, and secrecy ;
And these heirs, in thèir tiny bosoms, hold
The hoarded life-spring of another year.
    And yet no mortal eye
    Hath seen the mode, nor listening ear
    Hath heard the story told ;
  While boastful Science, like the mole,
    With microscopic eyes
But burrows in the dark and cannot rise
To see the ethereal spirit that informs the whole.

    Here is the grand climacteric
Of this their annual life. And now for them
No more is left but gradual decay.
    The shrunken stem,
  Erewhile so vigorous and thick,
Like cord umbilical, in time gives way,
    And drops the fruit to earth,
Again to die ; and dying, to bring forth
Another generation to the birth.
Soon fade the leaves to shades of lifeless brown ;
Awhile they shiver in the frosty air,

SEEDS.

A POETICAL ESSAY BY JOHN M RHEIN.

When the third morning of Creation shone,
    And from the naked earth
Rose the green herb, and grass, and branching tree full-grown,
    'T was thus decree'd
    By the Eternal Mind
And Voice of God that called them into birth,
    That they should grow :
    ' The green herb yielding seed,
The fruit-tree yielding fruit after his kind,
Whose seed is in itself, upon the earth :
    And it was so.'

Thus sprang that living verdure into being,
    Whose annual generations reach
Beyond the birth of Adam. All agreeing,
A lesson of obedience do they teach ;
Obedience to the voice that brought them forth :
    For, whether all alone they grow,
    Scattered by breezes to and fro,
    Or, side by side,
They cover fields or spread in forests wide,
Or struggle heavenward in the frozen North,
Or clothe in endless green the burning Line ;
From age to age, with faith that never sleeps,
The vegetable world unbroken keeps
    That Law Divine.

But never to the curious eye
Do they unfold their hidden mystery ;
    Nor any seed e'er tells
How, in itself, its life mysterious dwells.
While in thy hand, or in the light of day,
    It seems an inert thing,
All dry and dead ; nor life nor motion shows
    Within its rounded ring ;
    But bury it away
Down in the dark damp earth, it dies and grows.
    The blade comes first,
    Soon the green leaves are shown ;
Then buds appear, that shortly burst,
And opening show the tinted flowers full-blown,
Of purple, white, yellow or orange hue,
    Of pink or bright carnation,
Or velvet brown, deep-red, or purer blue.
    All this is beauteous preparation ;
    But now, at length,
    And all unseen,
The plant mature puts forth its chiefest strength.
    Within the pod of tender green,
Or stronger sphere o'ertopped with crown imperial,
    Under the shag-bark's russet suit,

Till, one by one, are all
The loved ones carried forth to meet the call.
        Nor are we ever left
Alone with happiness, while here below ;
        Nor are our feeble souls bereft
Of all the aids of pain and grief and wo,
        That wean our lingering hearts away
From glittering dust and bubbles of a day.
        We need this rough and thorny hedge
To keep the base defiling world aloof,
Lest our bright Spirit-sword, of heavenly proof,
Should cloud its beaming blade, or blunt its edge.

        Nor all alike can sow
The holy seed : some, like a fruitful tree,
        May live to see
        The germs they scatter bud and grow,
        Till far and wide, all round,
The rising forests shade the fertile ground.
        Others, like annuals frail,
        At earlier ages fail,
Die ere they conquer in the fruitless strife,
And dying, quicken some loved soul to life.

        Thus from the time
        When first that Sower went forth to sow,
        In every age, in every clime,
The Holy Seed hath grown, and still doth grow.
Each generation as it rose, receiving
The precious germs from those that went before,
        Planted them deep in hearts believing ;
        While these the burthen bore
To sons and daughters, who again brought forth
Another generation to the birth.
And yet no eye hath seen, nor listening ear
        Hath heard, nor mortal mind
Can comprehend that life-birth here.
        'T is like the wind,
        That where it listeth, bloweth ;
We hear the sound thereof, yet no man knoweth
Whence it hath come, or whitherward it goeth.
        Thus it hath been, and still shall be,
Till He that sowed the seed again shall come,
And angel-reapers, both from land and sea,
        Gather the harvest home !

        Another Sower, at the time
When righteous Abel fell, went forth to sow.
        And, from the world's young prime
        Even until now,
        His never-resting hand hath sown
        Seed for an harvest not his own.
Charnels and catacombs, church-yards and graves
        He fills ; nor only these,
But on all hills, vales, plains and mountains high,
Or inland far or washed by ocean-waves,
        He strews the ripened grain ;
While, buried in the furrows of the sea,
Deep down the bosom of the sounding main,
        His countless myriads lie.

Then flutter down
To rise no more,
Leaving the face of Nature drear and bare ;
And all is o'er !

A Sower went forth to sow :
The field wherein he sowed,
The wayward heart of man while here below ;
The Seed, the Word of God.
That living Word, which, to the worldly eye,
Or on the cold unfeeling tongue,
Long powerless and dead
Appears to lie,
Like bread
For naught upon the waters flung,
Will, when the heart is soft and young,
Or its tough soil is broken up by wo,
Or by sharp anguish wrung,
Take root ; and soon the tender fibres grow,
Spreading like silvery threads in every part,
Until their heavenly net-work fills the wounded heart.

Repentance first appears,
Scarce rising from the ground through humble fear ;
Drying her bitter tears,
Soon child-like Faith, with vision clear,
Beholds things yet unseen by mortal eye ;
Hope like the bud of promise swells ;
And crowning Charity
Openeth like the flower in perfect bloom,
Within whose bosom are deep wells
Of sweets, where not in vain the hungry calls,
Wherein the thirsty findeth drink,
And round the brink
The dew of gentle pity softly falls ;
While universal love, like rich perfume,
For ever breathing forth,
Rises to heaven, and floats along the earth.

But yet a higher effort of the soul
Is needed to impart
The good seed to another heart.
For this great end, the whole
Of grace and nourishment and power divine
Is drawn to secret action ; while without —
A faithful sign
Of love — the heart is warded all about
With trials and afflictions sore ;
Heart-weariness we feel, and pain ;
Gaunt Poverty, with all his hungry train ;
And o'er and o'er
Our hopes are crushed, our longings blighted ;
Friends that once loved, now love no more ;
Envy and malice, in close league united,
Sting with envenomed tongues our name,
And feel no shame ;
Diseases, slow or sudden, waste the frame,
And where they go before,
Death follows after, knocking at the door,

Till, one by one, are all
The loved ones carried forth to meet the call.
Nor are we ever left
Alone with happiness, while here below;
Nor are our feeble souls bereft
Of all the aids of pain and grief and wo,
That wean our lingering hearts away
From glittering dust and bubbles of a day.
We need this rough and thorny hedge
To keep the base defiling world aloof,
Lest our bright Spirit-sword, of heavenly proof,
Should cloud its beaming blade, or blunt its edge.

Nor all alike can sow
The holy seed: some, like a fruitful tree,
May live to see
The germs they scatter bud and grow,
Till far and wide, all round,
The rising forests shade the fertile ground.
Others, like annuals frail,
At earlier ages fail,
Die ere they conquer in the fruitless strife,
And dying, quicken some loved soul to life.

Thus from the time
When first that SOWER went forth to sow,
In every age, in every clime,
The Holy Seed hath grown, and still doth grow.
Each generation as it rose, receiving
The precious germs from those that went before,
Planted them deep in hearts believing;
While these the burthen bore
To sons and daughters, who again brought forth
Another generation to the birth.
And yet no eye hath seen, nor listening ear
Hath heard, nor mortal mind
Can comprehend that life-birth here.
'T is like the wind,
That where it listeth, bloweth;
We hear the sound thereof, yet no man knoweth
Whence it hath come, or whitherward it goeth.
Thus it hath been, and still shall be,
Till HE that sowed the seed again shall come,
And angel-reapers, both from land and sea,
Gather the harvest home!

Another SOWER, at the time
When righteous ABEL fell, went forth to sow.
And, from the world's young prime
Even until now,
His never-resting hand hath sown
Seed for an harvest not his own.
Charnels and catacombs, church-yards and graves
He fills; nor only these,
But on all hills, vales, plains and mountains high,
Or inland far or washed by ocean-waves,
He strews the ripened grain;
While, buried in the furrows of the sea,
Deep down the bosom of the sounding main,
His countless myriads lie.

But are not these all *dead ?*
How can they then
Be made to rise again ?
Long before Egypt's days of glory fled,
And when her swarthy sons
Embalmed for burial, in the fond conceit
. That so their loved ones
All incorrupt might slumber,
Till they should rise to meet .
Their final judgment, when the mystic number
Of this world's age should be complete ;
A single corn of wheat,
Grown in her Nile-enrichéd glebes,
Was in a dead man's spicy shroud enclosed,
And buried in the catacombs of Thebes ;
There undisturbed reposed,
Till after thrice a thousand years had flown,
As if arisen from the dead, behold
That seed was disentombed and sown,
And grew, and brought forth fruit an hundred fold.

Now shall our FATHER, who, in love for all
His wondrous works, doth mark the sparrow's fall,
Shall HE remember this one little seed,
That its frail life shall be for ages kept,
And perish never ;
And yet hath HE decreed
That the *man's* body, by whose side it slept,
Shall lie forgotten in the bonds of Death forever?
Nay, shall his hand thus clothe the grass,
Whose fading glories quickly pass,
And not much more clothe us, when we
Though mortal, put on immortality ?
Soon shall the trumpet sound,
Whose piercing note proclaims to earth and ocean
The Spring-time of the Dead.

Then shall we see
These mortal seeds of immortality,
No longer winter-bound
By that corruption wherein they were sown,
But raiséd incorrupt to life and motion
Forth from their earthy bed,
Swift as the light, behold them high upgrown ;
They lift their heads to heaven ; their leaves
Glance in the beams from Zion's TEMPLE shed ;
And as the quickening SPIRIT gently breathes,
The waving harvest bows the adoring head.
In this their perfect glory clad,
The whole round world and all that it contains
Burst forth in triumph glad.
Hills nod to hills, and plains to plains
Their answering salutation fling ;
For now the praises of the LAMB employ
New-tunéd voices ;
The swelling chorus bounds from lands to lands ;
The valleys laugh and sing,
The sea makes merry with her liquid noises,
Floods clap their hands,
And hoary mountains leap and shout aloud for joy !

Burlington, Vt., Oct., 1846.

HOPEFUL VIEWS.

Και ετυγχανον λεγων, πολλαι και καλαι ελπιδες ημιν ειεν ευδαιμονες.

I OPENED a Greek book in the room of a college student to-day, and I chanced upon the words of my motto : ' And I happened to say, many and beautiful hopes ought to make us happy.'·· Yes, indeed ! happy and brave to bear our trials, to rejoice in the contest óf life.   In all my practice I am convinced that men need medicine for the mind more than for the body.   How often does the timely visit or letter of a friend drive away nervous pains ! · What refreshment to the spirit is there in a hearty grasping of the hand !

There are men who walk our streets, bestowing happiness all along their path, by the benevolent approval they smile upon the high and the lowly.   They feel human brotherhood.   It is no affectation of sympathy, no patronizing air, but a real feeling from the heart, beaming out from the countenance, and doing good ' like a medicine.' They are full of hope for human nature.   They believe that GOD made man and still regards the work of HIS hands ; that our world is under the direction of a FATHER and not of the Devil.

Let me not be rough in what I have to say in this paper ; but I cannot help remarking, that from the way many stagger through life, afraid and doubting, dodging and cowering, it would seem that the universal belief is, that some malicious and powerful demon sits at the helm of affairs and directs events.   Distrust of themselves, anxiety and fear take hold of men, and they stumble from their want of confidence. ' *But many and beautiful hopes ought to make us happy.*'   This want of confidence in GOD, in the course of events that happen to us, as the best for us possible, upon the whole ; this want of a faithful acquiescence in the will of GOD, is the cause of almost all unhappiness and discontent.

See how necessary, my dear reader, confidence is to you as you walk the pavement.   Could you take the same steps you now do as you go to your place of business, if your path was over a deep black gulf, with no more space to walk in than that which you occupy in your path in the way ?   Why cannot you take the same steps ? You fear to fall ; and your fear makes you weak and giddy.   The boy walks on the top of the fence ; but if it were ten feet higher he could not do it.   So men blunder along through life, distracted and enervated by unmanly fears and want of confidence.   Do we not know Trumperly, a very regular man and a most respectable shop-keeper ! He taketh his Sabbath walk.   He looketh round upon a wide expanse.   The heath is illuminated with flowering furze.   He stands upon a veritable field of cloth-of-gold.   He is about to smile upon the natural splendor, when again he recollects the bad half-dollar taken ten days ago, and at the extremest corners of his mouth the smile dies a death of suddenness. And Grizzleton? Did he not travel for enjoyment, and did not some past particular wrong always blot out and destroy the present beauty? He made a pilgrimage to Niagara. He was about to be very much rapt, astounded by its terrible grandeur, when the spray fell upon his new hat, and he could not but groan for the cotton umbrella, price one dollar, that he had lost at New-York. And in this way do we often shadow present pleasures with the thought of some sort of counterfeit money, some sort of departed umbrella.

It would seem, I say, that men believe in a demon rather than a God. From youth it is taught that sorrow is our lot, and every smile of joy is seized as a happy exemption from the common fate. What a miserable appearance does the world present as we look at it struggling for the very means of livelihood; friend overreaching friend in a sharp bargain; each intent upon warding off want and penury; as if to live were to eat and drink and wear fine clothes and seem to others to be happy! What a miserable state is that when every thing is done for appearance! — and people cheat themselves into the belief that they are happy, when they can impose upon the world with an appearance of happiness! Here is mean fare, stingy fare, sordid clothing, and no books at home, that the daughters, to be married, may appear at church in fifty-dollar shawls and feathers in their hats. They believe, such people, that the devil is king, and virtue a physical state of the person. Their hopes are not many nor beautiful. They bound their life by a narrow object, and are willing to be miserable themselves, so they appear to be happy in the eyes of others.

Let the father and mother answer: What are your hopes for your children? Do you look forward to the time when they shall fulfil beautiful hopes?—become cultivated, religious and elevated beings? No; you are rather anxious that your daughters should marry rich men; that your sons should amass money and become independent. You look not beyond the present life; you bound your view by a narrow span of years. You are not happy, for you do not make the most of life; you indulge not in those many and beautiful hopes that might make you happy.

It is a fair presumption that God made man to be happy. Every thing in the outward universe seems made to minister to his felicity. The firmament alone ought to dispel all doubts of an unhappy fate to him who strives to obey the laws of his being. Here seems to be a theme for many and beautiful hopes. Who made those shining stars, distant worlds, now moving in their appointed orbits, while they seem all motionless to us? There will be a time to you, mortal, when all the mysteries of your own being and the laws of those silent planets shall be unfolded! How can any one be unhappy and distrustful for whom such a fate is in store? What matters it to you whether you live in splendor or poverty for a few years! Your condition now, your outward condition, cannot affect your claims to a place in the world of God. All these invidious distinctions will vanish in a few years, and you will only be known for what you were morally. Who will take this view? How many are able to rise to a sense of the beautiful hopes that belong to us as immortal beings?

As a country practitioner, my words may not have the weight they would if I drove a curricle and livery; but it verily seems to me that the world needs now the simplest common-places of wisdom. It has groped after wisdom and power, and thought them great and distant objects, when they were to be sought in the heart, and were nigh to us, even in our very homes, while we have been looking out of the window. It has thought that influence and wealth were only to be attained by unusual means; as if GOD had made success the exception in human affairs, while the majority of the race were made to pine in hopeless despondency. It is appalling and distressing to me in the last degree to see the laborer going to his work like a whipped dog; to see widows and orphans bowing to their fate as if it were an awful dispensation of Providence; to see nine-tenths of my fellow mortals broken-hearted and weary, and only living because they are afraid to die. It breaks my heart to see a man of vigorous frame and honest, simple mind, drop his eye before some apology for manhood, dressed in showy attire. Poverty and want and habitual degradation have killed out the finer emotions in many a human being, and the luxurious and idle live upon the blood of their fellows.

Every man lives by somebody's labor; if not his own, then another's. Yonder vagabond, a cumberer of the ground, is living upon the sweat and toil of a man who died a thousand years ago. He thinks it is his fate to live a life of ease. There is no such permission. The idler thrives upon human sweat; he lives upon somebody. No wonder he is enervated and desponding; living a false life, he has no beautiful hopes to make him happy.

The absence of hope, the belief that any one entertains that he is fated to lead a dark, obscure and gloomy life, I say, is the cause of much of the disease and ill-health in the world. Sorrowful and despondent views derange the digestive organs, and soon the springs of life are undermined. Men need hope as much as they need bread; man lives not by bread alone. He needs heart, hope in his work; and an approving, encouraging word nourishes him more than a biscuit.

The same ought to be done in morals as we are doing in physics. We are coming back to the simplest elements; cold water externally and internally, sleep and quiet, pure air and no medicine. We reach the seat of the disease through the mind. We exorcise the devil. We do not drive him out with calomel and other purges, but with that power of resistance which exists in every frame to expel foreign matter, things prejudicial to its being. The faculty now but clear away the rubbish and give nature a chance to act, as the gardener rakes the leaves from the flower-beds, and the sun and the internal fires of the earth throw out the violets and daisies.

Let every man then rest in his reserved rights, and be happy in the beautiful hopes that belong to him as an immortal being; and the first thought, it seems to me, which ought to be in every body's mind, as a constant presence, is this : *What you do, you do forever.* Be it sin or be it sacrifice, what you do, you do for a long pull. The thought, the act of to-day will never cease in their influence over your being. Now if this was understood and believed, as it ought to be, it would do away with severe laws and penalties, and be like the return to cold water in the healing art. Hanging, like calomel, would soon be out of fashion. Imprisonment for life would be thought as unnecessary as sleeping in a feather-bed to cure a fever. Fines would disappear with fees, and beautiful hopes would sway mankind and produce peace and an elevated state of society.

Almost all intemperance is an attempt to get up by steam hopeful views. As things are going on, men must intoxicate their brains before they can entertain hope. This is not true ; but they think so. For no poverty, no sickness, no deformity, no misfortune, can shut a man out from having then 'many and beautiful hopes which ought to make us happy.'

DIRGE.

'REQUIESCAT IN PACE.'

A DIRGE for the flower that 's lying there,
  Down in the low moss laid !
Its leaves are crumpled and growing sere ;
  O ! dim is their lesson made !
Gild its grave with a prayer, as scholars their books
  Edge with gold when the letters fade.

Fall back and pray, for it's spirit's gone !
  O'er the dust of its once sweet fame,
Ranged thickly, are crossed its spears of thorn,
  To shield its grave from shame ;
Hung up like the lances and sacks that deck
  Each tomb of old knightly name.

With thee, poor rose ! I lay down this sad heart,
  Its beauty crushed by harder fate than thine ;
Thy time was come, and thou had'st played thy part ;
  Hadst won fair ladies' praise ere thou didst pine.
E'en thus would I. But when my Spring did shine
  Rich in its flushing pride, a cruel maid
Envied my grace, and struck me with her eyne ;
Down at *her* bidding sinks this broken heart of mine !

Round my fresh mound, sweet lady ! twine one wreath.
  Over the glory thou hast ruined so
Shed but one tear, or murmur but one breath
  Ending in prayer ! It will not bring thee wo,
May bring thee mercy. Lest from my dwelling low
  Alas ! some thorn should spring to make thee know
Requiting angels watch the heart's hard death ;
  Yes, and beyond its grave their influence will go !

Ave MARIA !
Requiescat in Pace !   O B. F.

The Egyptian Letters.

NUMBER TWO

Letter the Fifth.

FROM ABD' ALLAH OMAR, TO SEYD AHHMAD EL HAJI, CHIEF SECRETARY OF THE CÁDÁS AT CAIRÓ.

A MARKED difference is observable, dear Ahhmad, between the way youth are brought up in this country and in Egypt. I refer chiefly to domestic education, or rather manners. With us, you know, the first precept given to children is obedience. We are taught to look upon our parents not only with respect but with awe; to consider their command as law and their advice as the oracles of wisdom. We speak only when we are spoken to, and then in few and respectful terms. As a mark of reverence, we receive instruction in a kneeling posture, and never presume to address a superior unless the head be covered. You would be astonished to observe in this country how differently youth (I speak now of the male sex,) are allowed to behave themselves. They treat their parents with the same familiarity they would strangers, their equals; reply to them in the same language; sit down in their presence, and appear before them without their turbans. They are permitted to range at large and eat with them at the same table; and here in an especial manner is exhibited the unbounded liberty in which children are indulged. Not unfrequently they are seen serving themselves to such of the meats as are near, or if at a distance, reaching unceremoniously to those dishes for which they have most relish. It is the custom for each person to have before him a flattened piece of baked clay, on which his meal is put; and such an assemblage as may there be seen is quite disgusting to all those who conform to the precepts of our holy prophet.

Fish, flesh, vegetables of two or three different kinds, apples or other fruit made into a pulpy substance, the whole floating in the juice of the meat, made rich by the addition of various condiments to render the whole exciting to the palate; and as if this were not sufficiently gross, many persons spread layers of butter on pieces of bread, which they eat at the same time. This heterogenous mass is swallowed with little labor of mastication, varied by an occasional pause to drink, when the mouth is seldom wiped, and frequently a portion of the meat rests on the edge of the drinking cup, for the purpose probably of marking where they may drink again. The boys can hardly be blamed for these practices, for they have before them the example of their fathers; and indeed some of the mothers are not more delicate. There are exceptions to this assertion, but they are not numerous.

You will admit with me that our own method is much better, by being more cleanly. When we take our food with the fingers they have always been previously washed, and at our repasts the hands are dipped into water-cups several times; so that none of the eatables remain upon them. Our holy religion, as well as our native purity, enjoins a rigorous attention to personal cleanliness. But, alas! this benighted people are for wise purposes left to their own ways, and we must bow to the decrees of Providence.

It is not at meals alone that the rude habits of children are most visible : in the streets they brush by without reverence for age or sex, and in their homes they are often supremely annoying. Parents expect all visitors to take notice of their children; indeed it is regarded as an affront or want of good breeding if they do not. This might be passed over ; but if, to ingratiate himself with the parents, a stranger to their youthful ways should attempt to be particularly attentive, he becomes at once a victim to their boisterous mirth. They almost pull his clothes from his back; overwhelm him with questions, which they do not give him time to answer; interrupt him in conversation, or when he can speak, drown the sound of his voice by the noise of their own. All this time the delighted parents, unknowing or unwilling to know the pain that is inflicted, look on without chiding this impertinence, while the poor visitor, instead of the agreeable converse which he came to enjoy, is made a victim to relieve the mother from the burden of maternal care. Children are always interesting objects; no one can help being delighted with their artless ways; and in America, where they are very beautiful, one is irresistibly attracted toward them ; but a close contact, by showing the unrestrained freedom in which they are indulged, weakens the impression of their loveliness.

With this negligence of the cultivation of manners in early life, comes a roughness of deportment, which, as boys advance to manhood, they seldom leave off. A few, by an effort of good feeling, or by better knowledge derived from travel abroad, where good manners form a part of education, converse and act as men of good breeding do in all countries; while those who remain at home without good models for imitation, or natural disposition to be gentle, preserve a coarseness of manners which to strangers is very repulsive.

When a young man of the present day begins to mingle in society, which he does very early, the first object of his regard is his hair, especially that which grows on the face. The beard is not here, as with us, an invariable portion of costume, if I may so speak, for none of the elder part of the community wear it; but it is a fancy addition, got up by the young. I must say it is very unbecoming when seen with the ill-made tight garments worn in this country. It is only with the graceful turban and the full flowing robes of our Mussulmen that the beard adds manliness and dignity to the figure. The beards of our Sheyks and our Imaams command respect, while those of the *élégants* of our city of Cairo give a charm to the person of youth which no one can behold without pleasure.

Here, it is the mere quantity of hair that excites admiration; and he who can exhibit most, rises highest in the favor of the sex which is born without this appendage to the face.

How long this fancy will last no one can tell; but according to the present fashion, it seems to be a passport to a lady's regard. It is believed that he whose face is covered with the greatest quantity of hair has his head the best stored with brains; and a lady will receive with great complacency the attention of a gentleman transformed to an animal, in preference to the addresses of a sensible youth who can only present a smooth chin. A beard disproportionate to the size of the person is ridiculous, even in Cairo:

'WHEN I behold thy little feet
  After thy beard obsequious run,
I alway faucy that I meet
  Some father followed by his son.

'A man like thee scarce e'er appeared;
  A beard like thine, where shall we find it?
Surely thou cherishest thy beard
  In hopes to hide thyself behind it!'

New-York, fifth day of the Moon Shaaban,
  Year of the Hegira, 1260.

Letter Sixth.

FROM THE SAME TO THE SAME.

IT gratifies me, dear Ahhmad, to bear testimony to the kindness of the people with whom I now live. They not only treat me with civility, but are friendly, and the hospitality they show in their dwellings, while it is very pleasing, affords me an exceedingly good opportunity to become acquainted with the character of individuals. It is only by long residence, mingling freely with people, and being observant, that one is put in a position to obtain this knowledge; and it is seldom that these advantages are thrown in a stranger's way at once. Many people are very reserved, and treat you merely with cold civility, so that from them you learn nothing; others, who are disposed to be more familiar, are yet slow in bringing you into their families; but here in this hospitable city these barriers are not raised against me, and I have free admission into every place I wish to enter. As soon as I make my appearance, the 'Stranger from Egypt' is announced, and I am admitted at once into the immediate presence of the owner, even when he is surrounded by his wife and children. This facility of intercourse not only shows an unreserved confidence which flatters me, but serves to hasten the acquirement of the knowledge which is the principal object of my voyage to this distant land; and I am already so far identified with the inhabitants, that I have as intimate an acquaintance with their habits and manners as if I had been a resident among them several years.

You are not aware that females are not secluded here as in the Hhareems of Egypt, but have equal personal freedom with the men, to go into the open streets at all times of the day, receive and make visits, with full liberty to converse with any person whom the husband admits into his house. Knowing this, and profiting by the invitations often given me, I pass many hours in the company of women; and I must confess that their society is at all times much more agreeable than that of the men. They are more affable and frank; more willing to take the trouble of instructing me in ways of the New-York world; more indulgent to my ignorance, and more ready to point out the objects that are most worthy of my attention as a stranger.

From what I can perceive, dazzling beauty is not common. A woman of commanding figure, accompanied by great personal charms, is rarely to be seen; but pretty women are very numerous. The females are generally low of stature, which, though a physical property favorable to comeliness, does not produce the effect to enforce respect, while it subdues the heart. Their moral education is strict, which makes their minds pure; yet a too rigid interpretation of the moral code gives to their manners a tinge of stiffness which at first is a little repulsive. Their natural temperament is cold; but this produces a habit of reflection from which springs much good sense. When they show ardor, it is in a measured tone, showing it to be more of manner than of deep feeling. They are sprightly in conversation, without however the warmth of the French or the self-possession of the English. They are quick enough in their perception, but deficient in the experience of managing their own feelings, and want tact in discovering and obtaining an influence over those of others. They are possessed of excellent natural capacity, but unfortunately this is not well developed; their education well begun, is left half finished; while they are brought so early from school and marry so young that they have not sufficient time to improve all the inherent qualities they actually possess. When once married, the cares of maternity soon absorb all their attention, and study, when no longer habitual, ceases to be a pleasure. If they are passionately fond of dress, it is a fault for which the men are chiefly to blame. Women, like all the rest of mankind, are fond of power, and if men refuse it to them in one way they will try to obtain it in another. If to beauty be added array of dress, man with all his pride and pretended love of simplicity is often subdued. A 'floating robe' has softened many an obdurate heart, and has on many occasions proved an 'appeaser of husbands.' While they are left to consult their own fancy in the choice of their apparel, the husbands leave to them the selection of furniture for their houses; and in this last is displayed more of wealth than of pure taste. Their persons and dwellings are apt to be overloaded with ornaments, and these not always of a kind befitting their station or fortune. All this has an unfavorable effect upon the character. It leads the mind to dwell on frivolous objects, by which the conversation is rendered light and unsubstantial. It precludes it from vigor, and makes the virtues all negative. Hundreds may be found who by patient endurance show a passive heroism that few men can imitate; but none are seen of those exalted beings that lead and control by intellect alone.

If however few possess those commanding talents which enforce the respect due to intellect, or those high personal endowments which exact homage, many, very many exhibit those milder attributes which excite admiration and win affection. As matrons their

domestic virtues are all their own ; and in no country are they sur-
passed in the gentle offices of regard, or in the warmth of sympathy
for others' pains ; while they are steadfast in their friendship and
active in their benevolence.   The sphere of the American women
is especially domestic ; and to confine them more closely within these
bounds, they are denied many privileges held by females in other
countries.   They cannot hold property in their own name while in
the marriage state ; if they possess any before marriage, it falls to
the husband of right, unless some previous legal provision be made
to secure it to her ; and the custom of society does not permit a wife
to engage in any pursuit independent of her husband, or to become
associated with him as a partner in his calling or profession.   Thus
they have no scope for practical energy, and their capacity is not
allowed to develope itself in the active and rougher pursuits of life
wherein their power of usefulness might be brought into practice.
The most they can do is to exert their abilities as writers ; and even
this can rarely be done by those who have families dependant upon
their maternal care.   These customs and laws are of very ancient
date, and were most probably made not only to secure the supremacy
of the men, but to prevent females from neglecting duties which
nature prescribes, and which are essential to the formation and well
being of all human society.

Beside these legal and social restraints, the women of America
are much curbed by many minor checks, which, taking their origin
in mere custom, or in some over-scrupulous notions of propriety, are
not less burdensome for being, many of them, puerile.   These have
obtained the sanction of public opinion, a despotic power created in
this country, to which the people bow with abject submission, while
they are loud in their boast of uncontrolled freedom of thought and
action.   As if to lighten their burthens, and render women forget-
ful of their subjection, they are treated with a degree of respectful
attention not observable in other countries ; as beings set apart for
reverence, and regarded as goddesses while they are denied the at-
tributes of divinity.   These various restrictions set round the facul-
ties, mental and physical, of women, have an effect to deprive the
character of strength.   Never being permitted to start forth from a
secluded sphere, they are not conscious of their latent powers ; and
when assailed by misfortune, they exhibit only calm resignation in-
stead of the vigorous effort which might throw the burden from their
minds or create resources which would deprive calamity of its terrors
by a bold resistance.

Notwithstanding these numerous impediments thrown in their way,
women are able by their intrinsic qualities to acquire a marked in-
fluence over men.   The foundation of this influence, is in this coun-
try above all others, laid in the position they hold as mothers, on
whom devolves the duty of giving the first impressions to children.
It is they who guide the early affections, control youthful propensi-
ties, and give to the character all those softer impulses that render
the future man tractable and prepare him for the enjoyments of
social life.   They may make mistakes in the estimate of their chil-

dren's capacities, but rarely do they fail to detect the hidden motions that lurk about the heart, and *never* do they fail to instil into their minds sound moral principles and religious truths. The hold thus acquired over the children, by an easy transition, extends itself in silence over the mind and conduct of the husbands. No being can be so hardened as to withstand the calm persuasion, the disinterested council, that comes from the mother of his children; the woman whom of all others he most loves. And the clinging affection which binds together husband and wife under the most endearing forms, deprives man of all his sternness, and gives to the weak an irresistible power over the strong.

The quiet influence exercised by women in enlightened countries, of which this is one, is mighty, and not the less powerful for being visible only by its effect. By the laws of nature and moral culture they are removed from many of the temptations which beset men. They are not sordid, nor rapacious; and being separated from the immediate action of the selfish passions, which are too apparent here as elsewhere, they are well qualified to give wholesome council on subjects within their comprehension. However much the state of society may give power to the men, and retain women within limits in some respects too strict, the marriage state seems to be one of contentment, to which I have reason to believe female virtue greatly contributes.

New-York, twelfth day of the Moon Shaaban,
Year of the Hegira, 1260. } —

Letter Seventh.

FROM THE SAME TO THE SAME.

In the course of my historical studies it came naturally in my way to read of the customs of different people of ancient times; and however singular many of these customs were, their origin could be traced, and the reason for establishing them could generally be explained. They have however in this country a custom, the origin of which is lost in the mist of antiquity, notwithstanding the people as a nation are of very recent date. The custom is this: At the end of every fourth year, by a process that I cannot explain, the nation is utterly ruined. You may think this is accidental, or brought about by some of the ordinary vicissitudes that attend human affairs; not so; for the catastrophe is expected, and the coming event is always recorded in their calendar with the same accuracy of calculation as if it related to the changes of the moon or the return of an eclipse.

What is truly remarkable, this melancholy occurrence appears never to produce the least change in the manners or habits of the sufferers; indeed it does not depress their spirits. They eat, drink and sleep quite as well as when in a prosperous state, and laugh, dance, go to the places of public amusement, and keep up the usual gayeties with quite as much joy as if the country had overcome an enemy, gained an accession of territory, or the Pasha's family was increased by the birth of a son. In imitation of this periodical misery, cities, towns and even villages, have private destruction on a smaller scale, which comes upon them at shorter intervals.

You must know that this government is elective, and that every four years the head man is turned out of office and another person is put into his place. Wherefore, when Sultan Selim is turned out, the country is ruined; in like manner when Sultan Osman is put in, the country is ruined again. So it is with the officers of cities and towns; when the Sheykh who is in power is told he must go home, attend to his personal affairs, get wealth and relief from cares, the city or town over which he presided is ruined in like manner as is the country at large, and the inhabitants express their wretchedness in the same way. How universal ruin should follow all this, none but the people themselves can give a reason, and even from them I never could obtain one that was at all satisfactory. Would you believe also, they go about telling each other that the eyes of the whole world are upon them while these things are in progress? They have an idea that our Pasha Mohhammed Ali (may he always prosper!) is on the watch to see their actions, and is pleased or angry whenever they do well or ill. It is in vain that I endeavor to undeceive them. I daily tell them that our merciful ruler, if he ever heard of them at all, looks upon them with as little concern as he would at seeing a Fellah impaled for secreting his only son from the conscription.

Singular as this people are in many of their ways of acting, I am at a loss to imagine how they get possessed with this periodical fit; for wherever I go the signs of prosperity are visible. New houses are constantly in progress, which when completed are soon filled with expensive furniture, and inhabited by persons who are far above want. Ships too are constructed while this misery abounds, to carry away the raw materials of the country and bring back luxuries from other climes; while on the quays and in the streets the same activity is apparent, and every person follows his accustomed occupation, as if the world was to last forever. We have abundant misery in Egypt, but it arises from known causes; is not derived from custom, but rather from some well-understood calamity. For instance, a sudden call of men to fill up the ranks of the army or to man the fleet; a failure in the inundation of the Nile; or when a person has lost his *Hhegab*, (charm against the 'evil-eye;') these are real miseries which come home to all classes. Men are forced from their abodes into a service they dislike; agriculture suffers, and people are pinched for food; while the last-mentioned persons are exposed, without shield, to all the horrid treatment Satan knows so well how to inflict.

Here however no such evils are to be dreaded, or need to be guarded against. The country possesses very few armed ships, and the number of men required to man them is very small; hardly troops enough to be called an army, which is recruited without burden to the laboring classes; and the agriculture of the country is not dependent upon inundations, though rivers abound; for seldom a month passes without copious showers which refresh the soil. As to the evil-eye, they learn to bear this of necessity; for how can a people who know not the Kooran hold any charm that can ward off its malice ?

You know I am much given to meditation ; of course this subject has occupied my mind; at times I have thought upon it intensely ; still I am not able to arrive at the source of this mysterious influence. I often hear a people spoken of, who lived at a very remote period of the history of this country, who are called by the name of ' venerable and pious ancestors,' and who, it is said, possessed many odd notions. It is probable therefore this custom was prevalent among them, for some good cause which does not now exist ; this people continue it for the purpose of keeping these patriarchs in remembrance ; add to which, climate, education and habit, no doubt tend to confirm the observance.

Peace be upon you, my friend ! you who neither sleep on the bed of indolence nor on the pillow of stubbornness ! May the favor of the prophet be shed upon you, and your labors be lightened !

New-York, nineteenth day of the Moon Shaaban,
Year of the Hegira, 1260.

Letter Eighty.

FROM THE SAME TO THE SAME.

As I was leaving my apartment a few days ago, the following letter was put into my hands :

' STRANGER : I am told you have come from the country where Pharaoh once lived and where Moses was raised, to see what you can pick up at the West ; but I make bold to tell you that so long as you remain cooped up in these diggin's you will have no notion at all of the real West. I now write to offer you a chance to see the world. I live on the Platte River, about two hundred miles west of St. Louis, and a few of us want to make up a party to *go West;* so if you would like to make one of us, just say the word. It 's the greatest place in all creation, and you 'll think so too when you get there. It 's only about two thousand miles from where I live, and it won't take you more than six months to go ; and when you get there, you may do what you like. We 'll make you a justice of peace at the start ; you can study law enough as you go along; and as soon as we get settled, you shall be made head judge. You need not take much baggage. As you never shave, you won't want razors ; the fact is, you won't want hardly any thing except a good rifle to kill game as we travel.

' We should be glad to have you go ; so say the word, quick.

' Yours,   DAN. TUCKER.'

This epistle caused me much surprise, the more so as I never before heard of the writer; and the ' West' he speaks of is a region utterly unknown to me. I have certainly come already an immense distance toward the west ; indeed, I supposed I had reached the extreme point, and could go no farther. But here is a man who lives fifteen hundred miles west of this city, who yet talks of going two thousand miles farther on a party of pleasure! I was so much astonished at this proposal, that before answering the letter I determined to ask my friends where this never-ending West was situated, and whether it would be advisable to go so far from home among strangers. The honors proposed to be conferred upon me were sufficient to tempt many persons, yet they had no charms for a quiet man like myself; wherefore, after reflection, I respectfully declined Mr. Tucker's offer.

I have reflected much on this subject, and am at a loss to imagine what induces people, comfortably provided for, all at once to break up fixed habits, pleasant associations, and the like, to travel thousands of miles into an undefined region they know nothing about. As far as I can perceive, it arises from a restless spirit that is not easy to check; it seems to be a longing desire to remove somewhere; and no other place than the West presents itself to their minds. And after deep consideration, I am persuaded that with this people it is an impulsion to which they are forced to submit. In yielding, however, they have ever ready some plausible excuse, which, if it does not satisfy people's minds, silences inquiries. The land is better than where they are, say they; yet this is not the case with all, for many go whose land on which they reside is good enough. Rather go to places where they *hope* to do better, than try to improve their condition, resting where they are—thinking removal brings less of labor. They do not bring sickness and privations into the account.

The inhabitants of the northern parts of Europe migrated because their climate was unfavorable and Nature was slow in producing. The climate of Southern Europe was genial; the soil more fertile, the warm season longer. When the northerners got sight of the land they would not go back; they were not a little stimulated too by the thirst of plunder. The American wanderers have none of these inducements. The people of Asia came westward because their country was over-populated; they were pinched for room and pressed hard upon subsistence. According to old records, they left their homes and came to Egypt; which country becoming in its turn over-peopled, as we may readily suppose, a large number emigrated to Canaan and Phœnicia, while at the same time other colonies went into Greece. The same cause operating on these last countries, drove the inhabitants forth into the southern parts of Europe. Here seems to be abundant cause; to which may be added what is possible, a few might be prompted by a voluntary desire to better their condition. The people of America are not moved by the first cause, because they have room enough; even more than is quite good for them; they seem therefore to be actuated by mere love of change. They place their happiness in being in some one spot where they do not happen to be. The fixed home is dull; they pant for excitement, sigh for the unseen and unknown, and want to be founders of cities which they soon get tired of, leaving the enjoyment of them to those who follow in their track.

That the people of Asia became numerous and pressed hard on the means of subsistence, is sufficiently clear, from the fact of their frequent expeditions into Egypt in search of corn. This produced then the same effect it did in later times, and many had to seek a livelihood elsewhere. Here was a *necessity* for emigrating.

The south of Europe became populous, and frequent wars raised up a body of men who were no longer fit to cultivate the soil; they became restless and adventurous, and rather an incumbrance to society, which was willing to reject them. This, with disorderly habits, such as soldiers acquire, made them resist the restraints social life imposes, and led them to seek a place where they could enjoy a wider range, and where they could live uncontrolled; they could not remain at home, so they came to America; more especially to the southern portion of the continent. Here was a tolerably fair cause for emigrating.

The Americans of the present day have none of these reasons for their movements. These hordes came from the East to the West from a sort of necessity, more or less strong, while the Americans go apparently for the pleasure of going. They never think of trying any other place than the *West*, the *West*. The propensity to roam may, nay, I might say *will*, never subside. The Anglo-Saxon race is destined to overrun the western hemisphere, and Mexico and all the southern regions, almost boundless, must yield to what appears to be destiny. There must be some hidden cause that drives mankind onward in this direction, or it would not be going on as it has done for five thousand years. Do the inhabitants of the world go with the sun, and *because* the sun comes this way! Are they drawn to the point by electricity, animal magnetism, or chemical affinity?

Another view of the subject may be taken. When mankind congregate and form societies, they necessarily, for the purpose of promoting harmony with each other, impose certain restraints upon their own actions, and mutually agree to make sacrifices of personal liberty so far as is requisite to maintain order and prevent the strong from oppressing the weak. In short, they of themselves make laws to bind themselves. Now your seekers after the Eldorado of the far West do not incline to this, for they hate restraint of all and every kind; and no sooner do they perceive settlements thicken, and that laws of control begin to be talked of, than they fly to some other place where no such things are needed. They wish to range over boundless space, to know no law but their own will, to live after their own fashion, where no one shall be near to make them afraid. This is one of the inducements, and an all powerful one, to go to the West.

This is the only nation that does or ever did exist, with a people who move in large masses, chiefly for mere love of change. Most people prefer staying at home; leave it with reluctance, and not till they are oppressed by bad laws, burdened by heavy taxes, or straightened for the means of support. Settled habits, uncertain fortune and change of climate, are with the generality of mankind obstacles to a desire to remove ; but there are no impediments to these restless far-west-seeking folks, who go onward fearing nothing and hoping every thing.

If there has been a tide of population always setting to the West from all countries in the East, then Japan, China and Thibet must have come from America, and they have transmitted their knowledge, civilization and arts through Chaldee to Persia; thence to Egypt, and thence to Europe, till it has reached its original source. If this circular movement be the natural course of things, is it then wonderful that mankind should crowd onward to the West, when it seems to be their destiny ? It appears to be so uniform that it can hardly be blind chance or wayward propensity, but must, one would think, be designed in order that the world as it turns round shall receive on each part its due proportion of the rays of knowledge, the light of science, the benefit of husbandry and advantages of civilization, or other things, we know not what.

The Millenarians say the world is to be full to overflowing of people. It may be so, but I rather think in a different sense. The world shall be fully peopled, but not all parts of it at the same time. If what they say should come to pass, how will restless spirits find a vacant place in the West, when the West as at other points of the compass will be full ? A spare spot must be left where rovers may bestow themselves. Fill up all parts, and the inhabitants of the world would crowd together and become stagnant; or what is more probable, would quarrel for elbow-room. The lion and the lamb could not lie down together, for there would not be space enough for both, and the strong would be apt to kick the weak out of bed. Let there be then a safety-valve ; an open space where people may breathe freely without risk of suffocation.

We cannot say that civilization is a direct cause of emigration, yet there is a connection between the two which shows that they both work to produce the same ends. Civilization is not man's precursor in his progress onward, but rather a companion who overtakes him on the way and who renders the travelling agreeable. In the present case, civilization is not an active principle to stimulate man to exertion, but rather a passive agent, which is ready at his call to show how his labors may be lightened. As man advances, civilization is not far in the rear ; for however he may be uncivilized, he yet carries with him the seeds of moral and physical improvement ; and those who go to the West are instruments to produce an ultimate good they do not dream of at the outset. It cannot therefore be denied that emigration extends the boundaries of civilization, even although after reaching a certain point it has its decline, as history teaches ; and it is well that a race of men exists who preserve and keep alive this blessing, that it may be transmitted to future generations, who like their predecessors shall emigrate to the West, and diffuse it over every part of the globe. On the whole, although the people have no valid reason for leaving their homes, if they are impelled by their destiny, *Inshallah!* (in the name of God,) let them go.

I present this matter to you in all its bearings, without feeling sure you will take much interest in it, or that my stray thoughts are expressed in a way to give you pleasure. The subject must to you be novel, and we all like to learn something out of the beaten track, beside being amused with every new feature of character. For myself, I am not linked to the destiny of the Americans, and am determined not to follow in their path to the other end of the world. I persist in this seemingly refractory spirit, although by so doing I forego the honor of being appointed to a high office, believing it will be time enough to administer justice when I learn that justice is established in the land.

New-York, twenty-sixth day of the Moon
Shaaban, Year of the Hegira, 1260.

THE BATTLE OF BUNKER-HILL.

A REMEMBRANCER OF THE PAST.

THE moon behind the hills had sank,
When through the tall grass waving rank,
  A long procession led;
There, side by side, the aged sire
The stripling in his youthful fire,
Each burning with a fierce desire,
  The dreary pathway tread.

And peaceful gleamed the stars of night,
As silent they ascend yon height,
  Unseen by foeman's eye;
No sounds upon the breezes float,
Save now and then a martial note
Came mellow from the trumpet's throat,
  Like spirit passing by.

But morn their giant toil reveals;
A gun along the water peals,
  To break the soldiers' sleep;
Lo! Freedom's hills have found a tongue,
And the defiance back is flung,
And Freedom's rally-shout hath rung
  In echoes long and deep.

'T is noon! the sun in torrid heat
On moving columns fiercely beat,
  Or sparkled on the wave;
Where England's thousands, ferried o'er,
The rolling tide should cross no more,
But on the field their life-blood pour,
  As tribute to the brave.

Hark to the shout! the trumpet-blast
' For England !' is the war-cry passed,
  ' New fame to-day she reaps :'

Lo! volleyed round on round has pealed,
But from the hill no sign revealed
That in its crater-top concealed
    Volcanic fury sleeps.

But look! behold yon bursting flame!
They shrink before that deadly aim —
    Their columns are o'erthrown;
Fancy is truth, if it but deemed
That where that fire so brightly streamed
Death's scythe in the bright sunshine gleamed,
    And through their ranks had mown.

The eye that with defiance blazed
In cold unconsciousness is glazed —
    Its lightning glance is gone;
As if the soul for freedom yearned,
And through the eye its passage burned,
And left upon the clay it spurned
    The lip-curled mark of scorn.

The voice that rang in trumpet-tone
Hath melted to a dying moan,
    As if it prayed to Death;
While on the brow in clammy sweat
His dark baptismal seal is set;
Mortality hath paid its debt,
    And yields its struggling breath.

Now darker, fiercer grows the fight,
And bursting on the 'wildered sight
    See clouds on clouds ascend;
The burning town, the rising flames,
Britannia's hard-earned glory shames;
Oppression's funeral-pile proclaims
    Her boasted triumphs end!

Oh! Freedom's altar is a land
Not by the low horizon spanned,
    But stretching far and wide;
Yon rising flames that scorch the skies
Consume the votive sacrifice;
Yon rolling clouds like incense rise
    To GOD, the freeman's guide!

Now England triumphs o'er her foes,
But heaps on heaps of dead repose
    On war's red mantle spread;
GOD hath rebuked the insatiate,
And granted on this day of fate
Their triumph to commemorate,
    A monument of Dead!

'T is night; the holy stars look down
On battle-field and ruined town,
    Desolate, sad and drear;
But where the cotter's windows glare
The wail of comfortless despair,
Or the half-uttered voice of prayer,
    Proclaim the Dead are here!

THE REIGN OF THE PEOPLE.

A SCENE IN THE FRENCH REVOLUTION

ALL Lyons was astir. The public halls and the places of amusement were thrown open, and the happy multitudes turned their steps alternately to the scenes of rejoicing for the success of the people in the past, or to the tribunes where revolutionary orators communicated their own wild ardor to their hearers, in the contemplation of the future. And how could Lyons avoid sharing in the general intoxication of France, induced by one word, so universally misunderstood — A REPUBLIC!

It was September, 1791, and the choice of primary electors had just been followed by the election of national representatives to succeed the constituent assembly. There were not a few however who could not sympathize in the general joy, for their sagacity caught a glimpse of an unhappy future. But among the successful candidates for the assembly, was PIERRE AUGUSTE DE CHABOTTE, who was descended from a noble family, and was the presumptive heir to their possessions. Legitimately therefore he seemed to belong to the part of the royalists. But he had enjoyed a liberal education, and the lives of the classic heroes had inordinately excited his imagination, while the vicious philosophy of the day had biassed his judgment. Early sent to Paris, he had listened with enthusiasm to the harangues of MIRABEAU, and the conversation of LA FAYETTE had confirmed his adhesion to the popular party. The city of Lyons, never jacobinical, although republican, had welcomed his accession to them, and he on his part rejoiced in a victory which seemed to him the presage of a renewal of the interrupted national prosperity.

But while these feelings were active in his mind, others of a less agreeable character forced themselves upon him; and as he rode slowly away, amid the cheers of the populace, toward his chateau, a league from the city, the apprehension of a father's anger made him almost regret a course which nothing but the conviction of a high-toned mind could have induced him to adopt. It was not therefore without painful forebodings that he entered one of the old mansions which adorned the environs of the city. Built a century before, the loyalty of the owner had made the internal arrangements accord with the style of the architecture, and both carried the mind back from the scenes of revolutionary excess to the serene splendor of the monarchy, in the days of LOUIS LE GRAND. The young heir sighed as he thought of the necessity of change, and for some time he wandered through the long corridors alone; until opening a side-door, he found himself in a little oriel, by whose curiously-carved window sat a lady. She raised her head, and the traces of grief were clearly manifest. 'Sister,' he said, sympathizingly; but as he approached her, she rose.   The pride of the daughter of nobles was in her mien, and as she vanished she said :

'Dishonorer of your house, soon to be the betrayer of your king, go !   I love you, but I leave you ; thus will all forsake you.'

He did not answer; for a moment he staggered, and the floor seemed to glide away from under him.   Then his own pride came to his aid.   It nerved as well as conquered him ; and his first impulse was to seek his father and upbraid him for thus casting him off. Thus impelled, he strode hastily to the more retired suite of apartments occupied by him.   He paused in the ante-chamber to collect himself, and better thoughts came over him.   Filial love, and the habitual deference of education, softened his injured pride a little, and he resolved to part in peace if not in love.

It was a scene for the pencil of genius.   The mellow light was streaming in through the gilded and partially-darkened windows, lending a soft hue to the antique tapestry which covered the walls. The setting beams rested mildly on the venerable forehead of the old baron.   He leaned upon his sword.   He did not speak, but his whole bearing told of the haughty, high-bred noble, who, trained in the palaces and battles of France, had been accustomed to sustain her honor and his own in both.   Age, while it had diminished his physical vigor, had not dimmed his eye, and had increased the dignity of his aspect.   That eye now rested full and clear upon the intruder, and the severe but dignified displeasure visible upon his features gave them an expression much more stern and commanding than they were wont to exhibit.   Unaccustomed to govern his feelings or restrain their expression, his son stood before him destitute indeed of his calm self-command, but sustained by his own convictions of rectitude and his own pride.   In the younger as in the elder descendants of the family could be easily discovered the indescribable manner, of which no situation can deprive its possessor, and which a mere familiarity with refined society cannot of itself produce.

Thus they confronted each other in silence.   At length the armed heel of the young Count rung on the oaken floor as he advanced a step.   Kneeling on one knee, he commenced, ' My father.'

'Call me not ' father,' boy !' interrupted the Baron.   'When your assembly abolished the old realm upon inheritance, they cut you off from property, as the previous acts robbed me of title.   This very morning, as I heard the shouts of the rabble heralding your victory, I swore to Heaven that you should cease to be my son !'

While the old man spoke, the youth had risen, but his emotion had vanished.   Strong minds, often weak before, acquire unwonted fortitude in the moment of crisis, and his eye now flashed as he replied :

'I seek not your title, Sir ; I do not want your possessions ; let them solace your old age, and then go where they belong, to the people. I sought you only that we might part at least in amity. The Heaven to which you swore is witness of the purity of my motives.   I have indeed adopted a course which I feared would deprive me of your favor, though I could not anticipate the extinction of your love. The honors of high lineage too I knew must perish in the march of the revolution. But I saw France burthened by oppression. A privileged order monopolized her honors and emoluments. Under the insolence of aristocratic pride and unscrupulous exaction, the interests of the multitude were neglected and their energies' crushed. Industry was paralyzed and commerce languished, while even philosophy and letters struggled to rise, and gained but a precarious eminence by a purchased title. Then I looked to other lands and other times, and in the glories of ancient Athens I read a testimony to the power of the people's energy released from restraint. Thus I saw that France would be happy only when in giving freedom to all orders of the state she should imitate the republic for whose liberty she so lately fought; and then from universal activity she might derive unlimited prosperity.'

The Baron's face flushed as he spoke, and pointing to his armorial bearings suspended above.them, he rejoined :

' On the field of Ivry my ancestor won his spurs, and as King HENRY dubbed him knight, he bade him strike boldly for king as well as kingdom. This sword in my hand the Regent Orleans gave your grandfather as a tribute to his loyalty. But before he died he warned him that the youthful monarch would soon need all his true friends. The catastrophe he feared has been averted until now; and now his son, like his fathers before him, will live or perish with his sovereign, and with him the name of a loyal and ancient house shall be extinct.'

' Let it become extinct !' warmly replied Auguste ; ' I too will peril all ; but it will not be in the cause of a false man, but of an injured people. I may strive to emulate the deeds and the virtues of a Harmodias and a Brutus ; and when in the support of a falling dynasty your fortunes too have fallen, I will win a historic name from nobler sources — from a grateful *Nation !*'

' Say rather, vain and thoughtless boy!' replied his father, ' that when your freed rabble have overturned the throne and trampled on the altar, they will signalize your name as one of the first victims of your boasted energy of the people. So, traitor to the memory of your ancestors; so, representative of the *canille ;* the success of your party will be the seal of your doom.'

Deeply wounded by the contemptuous tone of his father, although sensible how keenly the old royalist felt the destruction of the hopes he had reposed in him, he only answered, ' May GOD pardon you, my father, as I do !' And thus they parted.

As he passed the little oriel to which we have referred, he heard his sister's voice, and he lingered long enough to catch her broken tones supplicating the blessed VIRGIN to pardon and preserve him. Then he turned away; he was firm, though his heart was beating and his pulse throbbing with deep emotion. Possessed of all his father's character, although without a particle of his loyalty, he looked back on the turrets of his house, and felt conscious of a resolute determination, not unlike that which animates the leader of a forlorn hope.

It was the last time he was destined to see those towers, for ere long the silver hammer of Collot d'Herbois levelled the ancient mansion to the ground.

CHAPTER SECOND.

AT the corner of the Rue Richelieu and the Rue St. Honore in Paris there stands a small three-story house. It appears to be built upon the dilapidated walls of its predecessor, and show-mongers point with avidity to balls imbedded in its more ancient parts, which have been there, they affirm, since the tenth of August, '92. The present building however is nothing to us ; but the evening before the tenth a man was in the naked atelier of the house which stood there then, alone. The faint light which struggled in through the broken and slanting window showed him to be young ; and as he walked impetuously up and down the creaking floor, the full development of his ample chest and swelling muscle contrasted happily with his otherwise light and graceful form. His features were regular, but they seemed rather too bold and prominent for his native district, the Lyonnois. The approach of darkness did not cause him to intermit his walk or cease his irregular gestures. Now and then his breast heaved, and muttered words escaped him unwillingly : 'Aristocrat!' 'Sans-Culotte! Die, fool!' and the like. Anon, other considerations seemed to present themselves, and in a moment of tranquillity he murmured a woman's name : 'Emilie! Emilie! for her sake, for *her* sake, live!' Thus the contest of love and hate continued until the bells of the neighboring St. Roche struck. He listened. The eleventh stroke warned him of the approach of midnight and aroused him to other things. He went to the window, and leaning his body out, looked over the eaves far down into the street. It was filled and noisy as at noon-day. Alas! it was not the activity of peaceful toil. 'One hour more,' he said, gloomily ; then taking a mouldy bit of candle from a decayed shelf which seemed scarce able to sustain it, he struck a light, and sitting down on his little cot, placed before the fire-place, he thrust his hand up the chimney and drew out some papers, a book and a portrait. One by one he burned the papers : 'Thus let all property perish!' he exclaimed, 'but that of the people.' He opened the book. It was one of the inflammatory productions of the day, a parallel between Brutus and Cromwell. For some time he continued absorbed in its perusal ; at length his eye glanced to the portrait which he had kept in his hand. With a shout, he started up! 'Jacque Clement, king-killer ; immortal!' No name, ha! ha! Cromwell, I follow thee!' And so saying, he sprung out of the room.

He had hardly gained the street when the clock struck twelve : midnight ; there was stillness for an instant. The pause presaged the earthquake ; the next moment the thundering report of a cannon shook the air. The clang of the tocsin followed quick and sharp. Drums beat in all quarters of the city, and the men of the sections hastened to the various rendezvous of the faubourgs.

Amid the general confusion, ferocious bands of swarthy and half-naked men rushed through the streets, trampling down whatever opposed, and drowning by their clamors the rattling of the heavy artillery wagons, whirled along with them.

A vast crowd soon choked up the Rue St. Honore, while a tumultuous mob forced their way slowly to the house of the Jacobins, whither Henri Graubnèr directed himself. It was not far from the Rue Richelieu, but it took him more than an hour to get there. The spectacle there presented to the eye was a remarkable one. The building was vast; it had been originally a church. All vestiges however of its consecrated character had disappeared except the broad and sweeping galleries, extending the whole length of the edifice. The few lights which glimmered here and there in the expanse could not dispel the thick darkness above, or even render the dome visible ; and the gloomy feelings naturally excited by this funereal pall were not diminished by the inharmonious voices proceeding from it ; for the bats, scared by the tumult from the vaults, had taken refuge in the decaying cornices, and flitting about in terror, mingled their screams with the din below. The massy pillars were adorned with bruised and scorched busts of revolutionary heroes, and the faded flowers encircling their brows evinced their respective popularity. Behind the fragment of black marble on which the president sat, two large pictures of Clement and Ravaillac could be indistinctly seen, though the names of the victims and their eulogies, contained in the inscription below, were hardly discernible. The frames of these paintings had been appropriately fabricated by some ardent Jacobin from the instruments of torture which hung neglected on the wall. Two thousand members were now assembled on the floor, and their numbers were momentarily augmented by the more audacious of *the people*, who refusing to be restrained to the galleries either burst in at the gates or clambered down the great pillars at the hazard of their lives.

For a long time the cries of the mob in the galleries, composed of the lowest of the populace, prevented all action, and the outrageous bellowing of the chorus of the ' Ca Ira' stunned and terrified the deputies themselves. The president and deputies strove in vain to still the clamor, and the last resort, the discharge of muskets into the vaulted dome, procured no cessation of the tumult. At length the great gates were thrown open. The already dense multitude crowded still closer, and an alley was thus formed through which a hundred of the revolutionary Marseillois troops marched in. They came from the club of the Cordeliers, and they bore with them one whose voice had never yet failed to be heard. Ranging themselves behind the rough scaffold which served for a tribune, their torches illumined the surrounding space and brought clearly into view the atra-bilious countenance of the sanguinary Jacobin chief, the president Robespierre. He did not need to command silence again, for Danton had mounted the tribune, and his stentorian voice was echoing in every part of the house : ' Men of France !' he said, ' we are betrayed ! the traitor LA FAYETTE goes free. Already the Austrian armies are on our frontiers, and this night the perjured Louis gives your capital to carnage and conflagration, while you and I perish as he embraces his allies.   To arms! to arms! — no other chance is left us!'

'This night Louis dies!' shouted a voice in the galleries; 'Jacques Clement!'

Henri's voice was lost in the answering cries of thousands: 'To arms!   Let us march!'

The drum of the Marseillois beat the 'Generàle,' the mob struck up the Marseilles Hymn, and the cannon led the way to the Tuilleries.

THE   FAIR   INCONSTANT.

BY E. CURTISS HINE.

'T was in a crowd where last I met her;
   A frown was on her snowy brow,
For I, who long had worn her fetter,
   And uttered many an earnest vow
Of love, had burst the chain that bound me,
   And learned to smile as cold as she;
Look'd through the mists she 'd thrown around me,
   And set my heart from thraldom free!

Though long her fairy form was painted
   In glowing colors on my soul;
Though long I deemed her angel sainted,
   Who o'er my senses held control;
The rainbow's hues at last had faded,
   And left the heavens black with night;
Reflection's cloud my star had shaded,
   That star could never more be bright.

She knew the power was gone forever
   That held me captive in her train,
And that her syren voice could never
   Like music thrill my heart again;
She felt the spell that once enchanted
   Was swept away, and passion's thorn,
Which in my boyish breast she 'd planted,
   Was dead, and flowerets there were born.

'T was in a crowd where last we parted,
   Coldly as in that crowd we met;
I saw, while tears of anguish started,
   That tears were in *her* eyes of jet:
But mine were shed, that one so gifted
   No more could reign my bosom's queen;
And her's, because the veil was lifted,
   And that her inmost heart was seen!

THE MAGNETIC AGE.

BY S. M. PARTRIDGE.

IN the enlightened nineteenth century, when knowledge has become intuitive, and even the children are born, Minerva-like, with a matured judgment, it would be alike irrelevant and impertinent to bring proofs of the truth of animal magnetism to a people who, through the gifts of nature alone, possess such an uncommon capacity that they can march directly up, and at a glance pronounce instanter an infallible decision on the most complicated questions in science, morals and politics; in fact, on all those momentous subjects which in less favored ages required years of study for their comprehension. We are dumb from amazement at the natural proficiency and attainments of the present generation. Men who all their lives have sat with their legs under a table know Bonaparte to have been a coward, and women who have only been taught to torture music into innumerable discords, and distress worsted into grotesque libels on nature, lisp oracular decisions upon all things. In the blaze of this universal illumination, antiquity, experience and evidence are but a breath blown upon glass; and we doubt whether it were an amusement worthy of even the children of the present to draw their own figures over these, and then rub all out together. So without stirring dusty proofs or old worm-eaten recollections, we will at once ride triumphantly into the science of Animal Magnetism. Who would not rather soar with a new-born phœnix than grub among its ashes? The entire perfection of modern popular judgment has buried old Empiricism; therefore whatever the aforesaid judgment pronounces to be true must henceforth be considered and recognized as established science. This being the case, we will say nothing about the sorcerers of India or Egypt, nor of the convent that was suppressed on Mount Athos in the fourteenth century for practising clairvoyance.

But one request we cannot refrain from making, the justice of which is self-evident on the surface; and this demand, for it is a demand in equity, imperatively calls for a reversal of that decision which the present century has so unjustly recorded against their fathers for the punishment of witchcraft. Witchcraft and animal magnetism are one and the same power in essence, although practically the effects may differ according to the will of the magnetizer; and it is certainly not to be wondered at, if in a comparatively ignorant age, wielded by illiterate old women, it should have presented itself under a different aspect from the present, when practised by skilful doctors and learned professors. Perhaps nothing has occurred in the whole march of civilization so strongly illustrative of moral progress as the immense improvement in the employ ment of this mighty social and intellectual fulcrum, which is destined ultimately to upheave and remodel society on an entirely different basis; so that when perfected, mankind will be able to dispense with the greater part of labor, study, and all that train of mean and vulgar virtues which have hitherto restrained free and generous impulse, and made them slaves to circumstances. How truly providential, and likewise what a testimony of its truth, that this immense power was not entirely trusted to and understood by man, until he had become so wise and pure that his native goodness constrained him to use it for general benefit!

Hurry! hurry! Assemble quickly a World's Convention, and re-baptize this mundane sphere; it is gross sacrilege to call it earth, and the illuminated specks that corruscate on its surface, men and women: unawed, we must be in heaven, walking among favored angels, for surely to no lower beings would the great CREATOR abdicate the moral government of immortal souls. We trust that prejudice and ignorance have entirely vanished; but if a vestige of those old dark feelings should unhappily linger in the bosom of any human being, behind his or her age, let them not, blinded by their benighted judgment, exclaim, ' Why, angels would never have ran away with the wives and silver-spoons which these Animal Magnats have now and then attracted from out of their legitimate orbits!' Such persons, if any there be, must remember that they know little about angels, and like the lawyers, put in a demurrer that at that time the world was not perhaps as perfect as at present; and these scientific professors who read futurity might from the fulness of their generosity have troubled themselves with the care of these chattels to prevent future strife, which might have led to bloody murders too horrible to contemplate, and to the pawning of silver-spoons for glasses of those liquid poisons which were formerly used for the purposes of intoxication. We are told that charity requires us to put the best construction on all things; therefore the better we can make a bad act look, the greater our charity! But on this account let us not indulge in self-complacency; for if we could hear the ' OLD SCRATCH' plead his own cause, it is likely that he would put a better construction upon his evil deeds than any of us would be able to do : hence, according to the aforesaid definition, the devil has more charity than man.

By-the-by, this old gentleman—for every one who holds office, let him behave or misbehave as he may, is now considered a gentleman—is one of the most reliable proofs of the antiquity of animal magnetism. For in earlier ages, when, as geologists tell us, the surface of the earth was much warmer than at present, and there was not that danger of catching cold from too sudden a change of climate, His Satanic Majesty sometimes vouchsafed a personal inspection of his subjects; but his courtiers, unlike all others, though they did the bidding of their monarch, endeavored to keep a respectable distance; for in his manipulations to subject their wills, which were exactly like those of animal magnetism, his sharp claws would approximate rather nearer than was quite comfortable to their skins; and from this circumstance arose the otherwise inexplicable name of 'Old Scratch.' Wonderful as the power and effects of animal magnetism have shown themselves to be, yet these are but as the dawn compared with noon-day in relation to its future efficacy; which in a short time is no doubt destined to renovate and regenerate the whole moral state; as it must infallibly interfere and subvert all the laws which have hitherto been called those of nature, overturn every recognized system, and assume an uncontrollable and irresponsible agency over all human affairs, from the highest offices of state down to the minutest ramifications of social life.

We confidently anticipate the time—although, like all good, it may be achieved through conflict, bloodless we trust, as *wills*, not *bodies*, are to be engaged in the contest—when freemen will not be under the disagreeable necessity of subscribing their money to bribe voters to elect members of legislature, and senates to oppose corrupt government; and then what really must be done, when these governments have any private profitable speculation in view, for which blood and treasure must pay, supply funds a second time to re-purchase from themselves those members whose election they had previously bought; so that they may aid in levying a third contribution to carry into effect the very object that they were originally purchased to oppose. We do not say that this could be the case at present; but from mere curiosity we should like to see a list (and by-the-by, it could be quite as regularly kept as the 'Red-Book,') of all the members of the different legislative bodies, from Walpole's parliament up to the present time, with adjoining columns of the prices paid for each, under separate headings of 'Elections,' 'Government Bribes,' and 'Votes for Useless and Injurious Expenditure.' It would be a valuable historical document, and would specify the price that the people have been willing to pay for freedom; thus exalting them exceedingly in the eyes of posterity.

The magnetic telegraph wires, about which the world has made such a fuss, are but strings on the fiddle of Animal Magnetism; and not till they are stretched from pole to pole can a perfect tune be expected; then will it raise its immense fiddle-bow wide as the heavens, and strike a harmonious movement that shall rock all earth into a slumber. This they have imparted to us as their future plan of operation. But the communication with which we were honored does not (and it is a matter of especial regret,) disclose whether the power is to be directed under the republican form of an orchestra, or by the regal hand of a monarch; and we hope when more definite proceedings are rendered necessary, that there may be neither delay nor disagreement on this head, but that they may keep in mind the old adage, 'Between two stools,' etc.; for the height would be bone-smashing to fall from; far worse than a fat boy plunging from between high stilts; it would be a real avalanche of lead into a dark measureless profound. But in our over-anxiety, for sensitive people always tremble most when their hopes are strongest, we have for a moment let slip the thread of communication.   Hitherto the efforts of the Animal Magnats have been rather to display the wonders of the science than to reap from it pecuniary benefits ; but now a magnetic alliance has been effected, which embraces all civilized countries ; and such a perfect system has been adopted by the members that they can all at the same moment of time feel the pulse of the moral world, and instantly communicate with each other the most effectual remedies for its various diseases ; and this union and understanding is no doubt the sole though concealed cause of our late improvement.   They calculate also to discover and explore all the valuable mineral treasure that lies concealed in the earth ; designate its various situations, and draw correct maps of all lodes and veins, so as to save the Future that enormous expenditure of toil and money which has been lavished from time immemorial on ever-flitting El Doradoo.

This moral transit will no doubt overwhelm, and perhaps entirely abolish, many professions that have been considered of vital importance to the social state ; such as law, physic and divinity.   For what a complex, clumsy contrivance courts, witnesses, lawyers, judges must seem, in comparison with the employing of one single simple clairvoyant, who is capable of entering all places and every mind, and instantly seeing all that has ever been done in the one, or thought of and executed by the other ; and who can reveal this with a clearness and certainty far transcending all legal comprehension ?   They will also possess the same advantage in medicine, as they can detect and apply remedies for every disease, and may possibly make known new ones that physicians have never thought of.   If ever man can conquer old Death, rely upon it that it will be through their means.

They will also be able, it is confidently thought, to resolve historical questions and dates which have provoked so many learned quarrels ; and our informant assured us that he had actually seen several pieces of Greek music, pricked off as sung from the lips of a clairvoyant; and that he confidently anticipated the entire recovery of that wonderful harmony, the loss of which the world had so long deplored. Our informant stated that they had invented a social guage, or as they called it, ' *Moralometer*,' by which they were able to measure and ascertain the exact state of morals among any people; and they propose that each nation shall select a ponderous and profound Animal Magnat, whose especial business it shall be to consult this ' moralometer' once in every twenty-four hours ; and when any moral deficiency is observable, magnetize that national bump until it rises to the required height.

And here it is that the science will interfere with the profession of the clergy.   The Magnetic Alliance say, in proportion as they gain influence and power in human affairs it must become obvious to every intelligent mind that the same amount of physical force will not be necessary that is requisite at present; and as nothing has been created in vain, but every thing with reference to some especial purpose of usefulness, they suppose that the material part of man will decrease in the same ratio as mind increases ; for as a philosophical Animal Magnat pertinently observed, 'Why send bodies into the world, when Will alone can do its work ?' At Munich, in Bavaria, they have discovered a most ingenious mode, by means of which the future can be actually read, and with unerring certainty. Every one in this country is aware that in Germany there exists able Animal Magnats who are capable of suspending animation for days, weeks, months, years or centuries; so that the magnetees lie in a state exactly resembling that of death; but with this difference, that at the termination of the time specified they will awake alive and in full vigor, just as the seven sleepers did many long years ago, or the 'Sleeping Beauty' in more modern times.

Last year there resided in Munich a lady, young, beautiful, graceful, wealthy and noble, whose desire to see the future so strongly overcame her love of the present that she turned from all the most valued enjoyments of life and sought in the magnetic trance a suspension of sense and soul for five hundred years. She may there be seen lying in an alabaster sarcophagus, her beautiful hands folded across her breast; on the third finger of the left hand sparkles a most singular magical ring, which it is said was given to an ancestress of the tranced lady by PARACELSUS himself. It looks like a small eye of red and green flame, and possesses a wonderful and unaccountable power over all who gaze upon it. They feel as if held by the hand of fate under the spell of a demoniac fascination; a cold chill, like that of death, passes between the bones and flesh, and the trembling nerves relax with the languor and faintness of expiring life.

Persons before entering are warned not to fix their eyes too daringly on this magnetic gem. The perfect beauty of her features, and their seraphic expression of peace and purity, have given her the name in Munich of 'The Sleeping Angel,' and she is known by no other designation. But while the mass, struck dumb by romantic admiration, were merely worshipping her beauty, the searching minds of the Animal Magnats have, through her means, opened out a wide field of discoveries, through which Science can lift the veil from off the hitherto shrouded future. Their mode of effecting this, and the vast stores of curious, unexpected and startling knowledge which they have gained, are under compilation, and will, with the sanction of the most renowned Magnats, soon be presented to the inspection of the public.

CHRISTMAS.

SEE, the dawn from Heaven is breaking,
    On our sight,
And Earth, from sin awaking,
    Hails the light !
See those groups of angels, winging
    From the realms above,
On their brows from Eden bringing
    Wreaths of Hope and Love.

Hark, their hymns of glory pealing,
    Through the air,
To mortal ears revealing
    Who lies there !
In that dwelling, dark and lowly,
    Sleeps the Heavenly Son,
HE whose home 's above — the Holy,
    Ever HOLY ONE.

THE SONG OF NIGHT.

BY A NEW CONTRIBUTOR.

I.

I come, I come from the land of dreams,
And shadows I throw on the day's last beams;
I come at the gentle twilight hour,
And softly close the bright-leaf'd flower.

II.

I steal from the lake and winding stream
The silvery glow of the sun's last gleam;
I breathe on the crest of the gorgeous cloud,
And its gilded head is in dimness bowed.

III.

The fleecy foam of the ocean wave,
As the sandy shore its waters lave,
But sparkles dim, as sea and land
Are curtain'd by my sable hand.

IV.

On the violet's breast, on the beechen tree,
I fold the wing of the murmuring bee;
I check the bound of the graceful fawn,
And his bright eye close till the opening dawn.

V.

The liquid notes of the woodland bird
At my approach are faintly heard;
As sinking 'neath the dark green leaves,
Her parting song she sweetly breathes:

VI.

My finger still on the infant I lay,
And close his lids in the midst of play;
And I gently steal on the maiden fair,
As she softly murmurs her evening prayer.

VII.

At my coming the peasant seeks his cot,
And in peaceful dreams are his cares forgot;
While the sons of toil their labors close,
And a refuge find in deep repose.

VIII.

My shadowy mantle around me I fold,
As the mountain mists are backward rolled;
When morning's light o'er my pathway is cast,
I vanish from earth—a dream of the past.

Boston, October, 1846.

G. A. A.

SOME THOUGHTS ON CRIPPLES.

BY A NEW CONTRIBUTOR.

CRIPPLES always interest me strangely, whenever and wherever I see them. I have been most impressed with their appearance when I have met them, as one often does, in the business streets of our populous cities. In such places the contrast is more striking between the activity of whole-limbed, sound-bodied business men, and the painful, snail-like halt of cripples, than in villages, where business moves slowly, and every one's pace corresponds with it. How often have I stood in my old observatory, the door-way of my New-York life, and watched the two opposing currents of people rushing up and down Broadway, each struggling for precedence; and in the midst of the whirling stream would be seen a shapeless body, heaving slowly along, now half-hidden by the waves, and then rising to the surface, till coming nearer, the body takes enough of human form to show that the nobler part of humanity still remains. You look upon his shattered frame with that kind of respect which one feels for the tottering ruins of some ancient castle. You cannot believe that the cripple has lived only the ordinary length of time allotted to mortals. His disfigured members show like old mutilated statuary. He has lived in another world, or in a state of the world differing from that in which other men spend their days. His experiences have been more various and of longer duration. His scars are venerable. They must have been caused by some convulsion of nature in times long gone by. His limbs are rent asunder as a tornado will sometimes rend the limbs of a mighty oak that has long been old. His dress is near enough the present fashion, but it has an antique look. You cannot believe it to be a modern dress. In the constant changes of fashion, one may fancy that the present style has before prevailed; and that with an admirable foresight, this dress had been carefully boxed up by some provident great-grandfather, for the use of one of his descendants who might live when the revolving wheel of fashion had carried the same style into modern times. And the old clothes have fallen into good hands. While he occupies them they will never look older than they now do. You may meet him a hundred times; still the same dress, unchanged. It is as durable as his weather-beaten frame. His clothes cling about him like moss about a rough old tree-trunk. Why should they wear out? He is not a business man.

I am speaking now of those who are cripples in the strictest sense of the term; those beings who move about the world on two stumps instead of legs, and pick up with one hand whatever good things Fortune or their more fortunate neighbors are pleased to favor them with; or those, still more unfortunate, whose withered bodies are chained to a pair of trundle-wheels by the strong arm of Adversity, as the Roman emperors used to chain captives to their triumphal cars, and drag them through the streets of the imperial city. There is another class who walk on crutches; and still another, more common, who use canes, not for fashion's sake, but compelled by their lameness. I hardly know whether it is strictly proper to include under the general denomination of cripples those who have sought out many inventions to remedy their defects; such as cork legs, wooden legs, etc.; for they, by bringing Art to the help of Nature, have almost placed themselves beyond the pale of crippleism.

There are two grand divisions of cripples; those who are lame from their birth, and those who become lame by accident. The former may be styled the ' ancient and honorable' order of cripples; who are accustomed to regard the latter in the light of interlopers. We cannot withhold our respect from either class; but we confess there is some show of reason in the slighting manner which natural cripples adopt toward accidental ones. The pedigree of the former seems to be better established than that of the latter. We feel the same instinctive reverence for them that we do for an ancient barony, which has kept its titles unchanged and its honor untarnished through a long succession of generations.

In this age of hurry and excitement, cripples attract unusual attention, from their antagonism to the prevailing characteristics of the times. This also wins for them an increased respect from all who look below the surface of things. They form a conservative principle in society. Calmly but steadily do they oppose their slow motion to the hurry of business. They are ripples in life's swift-rushing stream, checking its impetuosity. Their maimed limbs are *realities ;* and as such serve to offset the falsities of a life where little else is real. They have their mission, and it is one not to be despised; that of keeping us constantly reminded that adversity may one day take any of us by the hand, lead us for a season into his dark domain, and then send us back into the world to tell our experience and show our scars to old associates.

A little incident occurred the other day, which, as having some connection with this subject, it may not be amiss to relate here. I was riding over one of our rail-roads toward Boston; and as we passed through the outskirts of a small village, I noticed an aged cripple seated on a sloping bank near the rail-road track, watching, with great apparent interest, the swift motion of the cars as they passed, headed by their panting iron horse, which seemed tired of the stillness of green fields, and eager to join its more noisy city mates. The cripple had laid his crutches down by his side; and although he was a poorly-dressed man, and not of that station in life from which we are apt to expect more than common-place thought, still it was evident to me that both memory and fancy were busily at work in that old man's brain. What would I not give to know his thoughts, as that mighty contrast to all his past and present life swept by him on the lightning wings of modern invention ! His lameness was evidently caused by accident; and years ago, when a boy, he was doubtless as active as any of his playmates. But there were no rail-roads then. Men had not then dreamed of the wonder-working power of steam; how that in a few years that great agency was to wake up the drowsy world, and give a new impetus to all civilized life. As he grew older, and the march of improvement began to tramp along with hastier steps, a strong grasp was laid upon him, and an unwelcome voice called to him to stand aside and let the procession pass. He might gaze at them as they went by, but his step had become too slow and feeble to keep pace with them. And thus this great drama of life was being enacted before his eyes, while he sat a passive spectator, gazing in deep meditation upon the shifting scenes. At times he had vainly essayed to join the crowd, and bury the remembrance of his cares beneath the troubled waters that heaved around him. He had clutched at the skirts of the passing world, but had been rudely shaken off; for his part was not to *do*, but to 'suffer and be strong.' Slowly and painfully had he learned this lesson, and the study had not been lost. It had nerved him to bear up, with cheerful heart, whatever burthen might fall to his share, and the world, when it ceased to sneer, had learned to respect him.

What that man has suffered can only be known by those who have shared with him this imprisonment of the bodily powers, this blighting of life's first-fruits. O, ye of the sound limb and robust frame! little can you appreciate, even in fancy, the feelings which such terrible desertion of manly energy must cause in a hopeful, vigorous mind! With the rough pathway of life stretching far before him; deprived at one blow of the strength which might have aided him to bear up firmly against misfortune and danger; old friends fleeing at the first sign of trouble; if he yet can finish his earthly career triumphantly, he must be formed of no ordinary mould. To place every vain regret for the faded hopes of youth, the first heartless indifference or thoughtless sneer of a gaping world, the grim phantom or more dreadful reality of want, which always haunts the unfortunate, in the scale of human destiny, and have a noble nature outweigh them all, this demands the truest heroism. It is the fiery ordeal through which he must pass who stumbles in the march of life. Nothing but a real unflinching soul can bear him bravely through it; and if he conquers, it is a victory worthy to be inscribed in letters of gold on his after life, and he may well be ranked among the nobility of the human race.

Thinking of this class of our fellow-beings, brings thoughts of that terrible scourge which so much increases their number; and with it comes an involuntary shudder at the recollection of how much misery war has caused. Almost every year this terrible destroyer sweeps over some fair land, blighting all that is lovely, and leaving only blackened ruins as traces of its mad career. Would that the sight of those shattered remnants of humanity who have shared so largely in the *spoils* of war might infuse a more peaceable spirit among our belligerent statesmen and politicians! Until that desirable time shall come, let us gather from this mass of evil what grains of good we may. Let us profit by the teaching of these eloquent ambassadors whom war sends out into the world, halt and maimed, but bearing always a gospel of patience and endurance to men.

What a perpetual reminder the lame man carries about him! He needs no lectures on humility. That lame leg is worth to him more than a whole barrel of sermons. His crutch is a monitor whose teachings, although inaudible to others, sound loudly in his ears; a constant warning to him to beware of pride. It teaches him also a just regard for others' feelings, for it shows him that he too is mortal. Our pity is awakened at the first sight of a cripple, but on farther reflection we are half inclined to envy him. How easily and naturally his hobble-foot pushes its way through the flimsy web of custom! To him fashions and customs are mere toys; play-things with which the children of men amuse themselves upon the green earth. He can afford to dispense with them all. He has no personal charms to display. Fashion and he have long since ceased to exchange goods. She cannot add a new grace to him, and he would only mar the splendor of her train. He is a lone man; independent, original. His actions spring from himself, and are governed by a law of his own being. He pleases himself; and no one whose good opinion is worth having can fail to be pleased with him. He is respected by all; his lameness is a badge of authority. The beauty and strength that once resided in his withered limbs have retired into his mind, as fallen autumn leaves impart their richness to the soil from which they sprung. Hence his superiority is not merely admissive; it is real. His great soul sits in the ruined temple of his body, as you may imagine Marius seated amidst the ruins of Carthage.

FADING AUTUMN: A SONNET.

BY MRS. E. C. KINNEY.

Th' autumnal glories all have passed away !
  The forest-leaves no more in hectic red
Give glowing tokens of their brief decay,
  But scattered lie, or rustle 'neath the tread,
  Like whispered warnings from the mouldering dead ;
The naked trees stretch out their arms all day,
  And each bald hill-top lifts its reverend head
As if for some new covering to pray.
  Come, WINTER, then, and spread thy robe of white
Above the desolation of this scene ;
  And when the sun with gems shall make it bright,
Or, when its snowy folds by midnight's queen
  Are silvered o'er with a serener light,
We 'll cease to sigh for summer's living green.

Newark, Nov., 1846.

BALLAD OF JACK RINGBOLT.

BY JAMES KENNARD, JR.

JACK RINGBOLT lay at the 'Seaman's Home,
  And sorely grieved was he,
Lest he should end upon the land
  A life spent on the sea.

He was born upon the ocean,
  And with her dying groan
His mother gave him being,
  Then left him all alone.

Alone upon the desert sea!
  With not a female hand
To nourish him and cherish him,
  Like infants on the land!

The storm-king held a festival
  Upon the deep that night;
His voice was thundering overhead,
  His eye was flashing bright:

The billows tossed their caps aloft,
  And shouted in their glee;
But oh! it was for mortal men
  An awful night to see!

Among the shrouds and spars aloft
  A host of fiends were shrieking;
And the pump-brake's dismal clank on deck
  Told that the ship was leaking.

The ship was lying to the wind,
  Her helm was lashed a-lee;
And at every mighty roller
  She was boarded by a sea.

The doom-struck vessel trembled,
  As the waves swept o'er her deck;
She rolled among the billows,
  An unmanageable wreck.

To their boats they took for safety,
  The captain and his men;
And the helpless new-born infant
  Was not forgotten then.

A rough, hard-featured countenance
  The storm-tossed captain wore;
But his heart, for tender innocence,
  With love was flowing o'er.

'He shall not perish here alone,
  Upon the ocean wild!
But only GOD can nourish him,
  The motherless young child!'

But all in vain his kindness,
  Had they not, at break of day,
Glad sight! beheld before them
  A vessel on her way.

They were rescued, and on board her,
  As the passengers drew round,
In woman's arms the orphan boy
  The needed succor found.

He lived; but to his inmost soul
  His birth-night gave its tone;
The spirits of the stormy deep
  Had marked him for their own.

He lived, and grew to manhood
  Amid the ocean's roar;
His heaven was on the surging sea,
  His hell was on the shore!

He joyed amid the tempest,
  When spars and sails were riven;
And when the din of battle drowned
  The artillery of heaven.

He often breathed a homely prayer,
  That when life's cruise was o'er,
His battered hulk might sink at sea,
  A thousand miles from shore.

And now, to lie up high and dry,
  A wreck upon the sand!
To leave his weary bones at last
  Upon the hated land!

The thought was worse than death to him,
  It shook his noble soul;
Strange sight! adown his hollow cheek
  A tear was seen to roll.

Could I but float my bark once more,
  T' would be a joy to me,
Amid the howling tempest
  To sink into the sea!

Then turning to the window,
  He gazed into the sky ;
The scud was flying overhead,
  The gale was piping high :

And in the fitful pauses
  Was heard old Ocean's roar,
As in vain his marshalled forces
  Rushed foaming on the shore.

Look now ! his cheek is flushing,
  And a light is in his eye ;
' Throw up the window ! let me hear
  That voice before I die !

' They 're hailing me, the crested waves,
  A brave and countless band,
As rank on rank, to rescue me,
  They leap upon the land !

' T is all in vain, bold comrades !
  And yet, and yet so near !
Ye are but one short league away —
  Good God ! must I die here !

'No ! the ship that brought me hither
  Is at the pier-head lying,
And ere to-morrow night she 'll be
  Before a norther flying.

' Now bless ye, brother sailors !
  If ye grant my wish,' he cried ;
'But curse ye ! if ——' He spake no more,
  Fell back, and gasping, died.

—

PART SECOND.

They sewed him in his hammock
  With a forty-two pound shot
Beneath his feet, to sink him
  Into some ocean grot.

Adown the swift Piscataqua
  They rowed with muffled oar,
And out upon the ocean,
  A league away from shore.

'T was at the hour of twilight,
  On a chill November day,
When on their gloomy errand
  They held their dreary way.

The burial service over,
  He was launched into the wave ;
Now rest in peace, JACK RINGBOLT !
  Thou hast found an ocean-grave.

Down went the corpse into the sea,
  As though it were of lead ;
But it sank not twenty fathoms,
  Ere it touched the ocean's bed.

Then up it shot, and floated
  Half-length above the tide ;
A lurid flame played round the head,
  The canvass opened wide.

No motion of the livid lips
  Or ghastly face was seen ;
But a hollow voice thrilled thro' their ears,
  ' Quarter less nineteen !'

Then eastward sped the awful dead,
  While o'er the darkened sea
Upon the billows rose and fell ·
  The corpse-light fitfully.

They gazed in fearful wonderment,
  Their hearts with horror rife ;
Then, panic-stricken, seized their oars,
  And rowed as if for life.

Their eyes were fixed with stony stare
  Upon the spectral light ;
They rowed like corpses galvanized —
  So silent and so white.

They darted by ' The Sisters ;'
  They went rushing past 'Whale's Back ;'
With tireless arms they forced the boat
  Along her foamy track :

But not a single face was flushed,
  Not one long breath they drew,
Until Fort Constitution
  Hid the ocean from their view.

—

PART THIRD.

'T was midnight on mid-ocean,
  The winds forgot to blow ;
The clouds hung pitchy black above,
  The sea rolled black below ;
On the quarter-deck of the ' Glendoveer'
  The mate paced to and fro.

There was no sound upon the deep
  To wake the slumbering gales,
But the creaking of the swaying masts,
  The flapping of the sails,
As the vessel climbed the ocean's hills
  Or sank into its vales.

The mate looked over the starboard rail,
  And saw a light abeam ;
The lantern of a ship, mayhap,
  A faint and flickering gleam :
Was it beaming down on the Glendoveer,
  Or did the mate but dream ?

A phantom-ship on a breezeless night
  To sail ten knots an hour !
Now on the beam, now quartering,
  Now close astern it bore :
All silent as the dead it moved,
  A light — and nothing more !

It broke upon the still night-air,
  A hoarse sepulchral sound :
'What ship is that ?' A moment,
  And the mate his breath has found :
' The Glendoveer, of Portsmouth,
  From Cadiz, homeward bound !'

No creaking block, no rumbling rope
  Was heard, nor shivering sail ;
But luffing on the larboard beam,
  A voice was heard to hail,
That made the hearts of the Glendoveer
  Within their bosoms quail.

A livid glare, a ghastly face,
  A voice — and all was o'er ;
' Report JACK RINGBOLT, sunk at sea,
  A thousand miles from shore !'
Silence and Darkness on the deep
  Resumed their sway once more.

Portsmouth, N. H.

A BULL-FIGHT IN PERU.

BY JOHN A. BRYAN.

DURING my residence in Lima, in Peru, I once became a witness of one of those sporting and novel exhibitions, so common in all Spanish countries, called a BULL-FIGHT. This was in the summer of 1845 ; and such a spectacle, to those unaccustomed to such scenes, was peculiarly appalling. The deeply-agitating sight had certainly enough of the horrid in it to satisfy the sensitive mind for a life-time. For one, I can never have sufficient curiosity for its repetition. The performance, it is true, was full of excitement. This very naturally arose from the great national importance that seemed to be attached to it on this occasion, and from the uncommon display with which it was attended. It was made doubly interesting from the fact that it was given in honor of the recent elevation of General CASTILLA to the presidency of that republic. This of itself threw around the grand occasion an additional interest. All seemed to anticipate its coming with deep emotion. Every countenance lightened up at its approach. The public offices were early put in order for the great festival ; mass was said in all the churches ; and the bells chimed a rapturous welcome. At sun-rise the broad banner of Peru was streaming from the palace balcony, and the flags of every nation holding any commercial relations with the republic floated over the official departments of all the foreign diplomatists throughout the city.

Three o'clock P. M. was the hour of exhibition. All the stores and shops were closed. The day opened brightly and finely, and the dank morning dews had scarcely been borne away by a brilliant and scorching sun, before the streets were thronged with a bustling populace, impatient for the opening scene. A few hours in advance of the time a thronging procession paraded the streets, composed of all sorts of people, of all conditions and hues, grades and colors, from the lusty donkey-driver of the mountains up to the rich and polished Castilian blood, in his epaulettes and buttons, robes and lace. These, under full escort, were perambulating the city at an early hour. Thrilling music, the proud boast of Peru, gave a spirit-stirring movement to the national guards, on prancing steeds, and the drums and equipments of the day were all splendid and gorgeous. Here the embroidered body-dress of the victim of the slaughter was paraded, and here too, amid sparkling brocades and glittering pearls, the keen-edged instruments of death were displayed with which the chivalrous knights of the ring were to show off their adroitness and skill in the impending fight.

Accepting of the polite invitation of that accomplished Spanish statesman, General ROCAFUERTE, then sojourning in Lima, to take a seat in his *calisa*, we arrived before the opening of the main scene of the day. To the gentleman thus accompanying me I had been under many obligations while in Peru. He was one of the great men of South America; was the early friend and companion of SIMON BOLIVAR in his noble struggle for the freedom of Columbia; was subsequently minister from Mexico to England, and for many years president of the republic of Equator. In his society I had many advantages, in obtaining a knowledge of the country, its resources, customs, manners and habits; and I tried to profit by his learning and intelligence. As we approached the Plaza del Acho a cloud of people thronged the way. Each side of the street was literally lined with small dealers in drinks and sweet-meats, and most bountifully supplied with huge goblets of *Chincha* and the famous 'Nectar of Peru.' Hilarity and joy were the watch-words of the hour. All was life and gayety. Dashing bloods flew by us like the wind, and Peruvian belles, beautifully attired, and languishish beneath glittering diamonds and costly decorations, were all rushing forward with impetuosity to the grand amphitheatre. What a holiday for the South American Spaniard! But I felt little of its inspiration, and had no foretaste of the approaching festivity.

Crossing the main bridge leading over the river Rimac, and arriving early at the Plaza, nearly a mile distant, we were allowed leisure for a hasty glance at the different apartments and decorations. Ascending a narrow stair-way to the principal tier of boxes, we halted for a moment to take a look at the animals. They were in an adjoining pen, just back of the prefect's station. Here sixteen beautiful specimens of South American growth were huddled together. They appeared to be almost another race from our English and North-American breeds. They were tall and slender, with long projecting horns, but of fine shape and color, and of remarkable agility and sprightliness. One at a time they were to be pushed into the conflict awaiting them.

Passing rapidly around, I readily saw that the principal structure composing this vast amphitheatre was a shammy-built concern, rude and rough, except perhaps the gallery of the president, which seemed to be hung with ribbands and roses, flowers and festoons. The great circle is about four hundred feet in diameter, and is said to be of sufficient capacity to contain twenty thousand people. The outer barrier is about seven feet high. Eight inner rows of benches, one above another, stretch around the arena. From the immense size of this edifice, and the ground it encloses, particularly if there be any correctness in the estimate of its capacity for the public accommodation, there must have been at least eighteen thousand people present. Every avenue was filled; not a vacant space was to be seen.

Quietly dropping into our seats, I supposed the first fight was about to come off; but a queer caper, called 'the Dance of the Handkerchief,' was then performing. This was a real 'darkey' affair, black as South-Africa, and similarly performed. Such a kick-up, I am sure, has seldom been seen this side of Congo. All sorts of pranks, with horrid masks and contortions, were cut up in this rough-and-tumble mountaineer fandango. But this shining prelude soon passed off. An evolution or two from a platoon of the military followed, which was more in keeping with the occasion. It was a tasteful performance in honor of the president. The sound of the bugles gave out the orders; time was marked with great precision. Every movement was skilfully executed, and with such fidelity and faithfulness as would have done credit to any military school in Christendom. On marching from the ground, President CASTILLA found himself most tastefully complimented by seeing his name in large capital letters before him, left by the military in their last evolution; an evidence of itself of the consummate perfection and skill of the Peruvian soldiery, and of the national attention paid to a military education in that republic.

The grand drama of the day was now about to open. The trumpet sounded, the band struck up a national air, the signal flag was hoisted, and the excited throng were all in a blaze. Near the centre stood a kind of safety-post, to become the resort of the flying victim when hotly pursued. It was of simple construction, composed of some dozen or more posts driven into the ground just wide enough apart to admit the body of a man, and to give him an advantage over his antagonist. The insurgents of the ring were often sheltered here. Contiguous to this and but a few feet from it was planted the kicking, snapping fire-image, to startle and annoy the bull in his furious rounds. When all was in readiness, the signal-rocket whirled through the air. Bustle and confusion reigned for the moment. The guards were all stationed; ladies flirted their fans; children giggled and chattered; plumes waved; diamonds glittered, and tens of thousands of bright eyes glistened with an intensity that nothing but a scene of the deepest interest could have enkindled.

Soon a troop of six horsemen and as many footmen, bearing swords, lances, spears and flags in their hands, swept into the ring, amid the cheers of the multitude. Bright and shining armor enshrouded them. In a moment the entrance-gate flew back, and through it rushed the enraged animal, as if a thousand furies had sent him ahead. At first I could not account for the crazy ferocity of his rapid plunge upon his foes. My sympathies in advance had been all on his side, but were now as suddenly reversed, with the natural reflection, that if this was the way he was disposed to poke his curly bull-head after human flesh, it mattered little what amount of tribulation and suffering he might be doomed to endure; but a revulsion just as speedily came over me, when told that in the dark and narrow den from which he issued he had been purposely cut and gashed, pricked and tortured, to enrage him for the battle, and that the enamelled body-blanket he wore upon his back was actually fastened there by being sewed through his hide!

A chivalrous horseman received the first attack. They flew around the arena, the bull hanging close upon the horse's flank, with tremendous spirit. Others came soon to his relief. Crimson flags were now flying in all directions; when, dashing suddenly at one of these provoking symbols, a poor footman was put to a terrible chase, and came near paying the forfeit of his prowess upon the point of the animal's horns. A fatal lance had already struck the bull in the back, and he writhed with agony as he bounded after his prey. Here the red flag of a horseman again attracted his fury, and they had an exciting round for a few minutes, the horse being finally severely gored in the struggle, and the scarlet banner borne triumphantly away upon the head and shoulders of the bull, amid the thundering applause of the giddy assembly. Here, too, receiving a dreadful plunge from a short sword, he soon began to evince its effect. Still trotting on, however, with a spirit unquailing, he encountered his eager pursuers until the third lance brought him to his knees, when he was soon despatched.

Four beautiful horses, attached to a pair of low truck-wheels, now pranced into the arena, to which the head of the fallen victim being made fast, the body flew from the arena through the great gate like a whirlwind. None but the animal fell in this conflict, though several had pretty narrow escapes. The music again struck up. Hand-waiters and goblets, loaded with a profusion of sweetmeats and drinks, were now flying all around us. They seemed to fill up the rhapsody of the interlude, which was but short. The drums now again began to roll, and that bright ensign of the occasion, the blazing sky-rocket, foretold that the *second* scene in the grand drama of the day was about to open. Impatience had already began to show itself. The motions of the turnkey were eagerly watched. Refreshments were huddled aside, and the mock-warriors were all at their stations, when the ferocious animal, rushing wildly into the ring, soon put the bravest of his foes to flight. A bold horseman ventured at length to give him battle, but he soon seemed to conclude that ' discretion was the better part of valor.' Pitching first at one and then at another, all were soon in active motion around the bull ; but, while pressing upon his victim at a full jump, an aged veteran in the arena plunged his lance full half its length into his body, where it was left dangling. For this intrepid feat handfuls of money were showered down from the prefect's gallery. Bowing in acknowledgment, he returned to the attack for another triumph, but was soon foiled. The hand of one more fresh and vigorous bore off the palm. Hitting the bull just back of the horns, he crippled and fell. The next moment he was to be seen at the heels of the prancing steeds, flying rapidly through the great gate. Again the bugle sounded, the band played, and a similar round of hilarity mingled among the throng.

The flaming signal, now bursting and cracking high in the air, announced that the third combat was then to commence; and this proved more exciting than any that had preceded it. It was most skilfully contested on both sides. The bull, though less furious at the outset, was more desperate in the final encounter. On entering he stood for a moment, as if to survey the armor of his enemy. He was a noble-looking fellow, of a dark chesnut color, with lofty horns and fine symmetry. In waiting to receive him stood a sturdy ' darkey,' in yellow satin pantaloons and blue undress, who had previously cut some pretty successful pranks with the short sword. This precious representative of the Banjo race was so complete a specimen of the real African that I imagine it might have puzzled the most acute anatomist in Christendom to have told which end of his foot held the balance of power, or whether he did not first put his shoe on the heel and draw it over his toes; but he was brave as Julius Cæsar. He fairly grinned defiance to his foe. His ivories glistened, and he turned up the white of his eye most furiously. He seemed to stand so much upon a par with the bull in every intellectual quality, that like the loving wife when her husband was in close hug with a bear, no one seemed to ' care which whipped.' He flourished the red flag so provokingly around and over his head that the enraged animal could stand it no longer. Plunging suddenly and furiously upon him, for a few moments the victory seemed uncertain, and the excitement was intense; but Cuffee repulsed every plunge with great dexterity and success; when, watching his opportunity and making a sudden and rapid dash at the bull, he planted his weapon to the very hilt into his vitals. The plaudits now fell thick and heavy around him; but the bull became still more restive and enraged. The demonstrations of his fury were now rapid and terrible. Flying at one of the horsemen, he ran him full half around the arena, to the very top of his speed, finally tossing the horse upon his horns, and prostrating the rider. Still hot in the pursuit of the retreating foe, though bleeding and panting and jumping and flouncing on his crazy course, he made sad havoc of every thing that came in his way.

In this terrible paroxysm of rage and agony, and when bounding and bellowing around the arena, he pitched wildly and madly at one of the flag-men on foot, who at first repulsed his attack with sword and scarlet. Soon finding however from the desperation of the onset that he must fall or fly, he turned heel to run; but so close was the pursuit of the bull that all saw the fate of the poor fellow to be inevitable. There seemed no possible chance of escape. At every jump the bull was gaining. Loud huzzas for the bull in the Spanish tongue now resounded from every quarter. Close upon his victim, screams and screeches reëchoed from every side. ' There, he gains!' 'See! he's upon him!' 'He's killed!' 'He's gone!' At this thrilling moment, amid smoke and dust and blood and carnage, the heels of the fated man were seen flying high in the air. He fell, and in his fall the rapid grapple of the animal, jumping with wild fury upon his prostrate antagonist, was most fearful and horrid. The audience in an instant were mostly upon their feet. The vast amphitheatre was now one promiscuous scene of noise and confusion; some shouting and rejoicing, some sighing and groaning, and every eye sparkling with deep animation. All thought the fallen matador was torn to atoms; but it proved otherwise. He escaped with his life. The red flag was so skilfully hurled in the face of the crazy creature at this fatal moment, that in plunging upon it he floundered over his prey, who at the instant, dexterously jumping to his feet, was speedily hustled off to a port of safety. The activity and adroitness of this fellow was miraculous. When hotly pursued in the race, and perceiving that to escape would be impossible, he so expertly turned back his eye upon the bull as to slide directly between his horns; and to this sudden dexterity of his he owed his life. Though somewhat lacerated and wounded in the encounter, I believe he was soon enabled to make his reappearance in the ring.

The bull was still on his round of desolation and ruin. Mad and furious, with several bloody weapons then in his body, and swinging from his sides, he had a desperate conflict with an expert horseman on his way, from whom he barely escaped with a terrible gash in his side. Still plunging on with increased desperation, he dashed wildly at every opposing obstacle that met him in his course. Bounding rapidly at the fire-image standing in the centre of the arena, he rattled it high upon his horns, where, roaring and blazing, and cracking about his ears, he bellowed and foamed and kicked his way, through horse and foot, lances and flags, to a distant part of the circle. Here, streaming in blood, with the gay ribands hanging in tatters from his horns, and several of the fatal weapons still clinging to his body, he turned to behold the scene of havoc that had marked his progress. The noble animal seemed to look defiance in the very face of his pursuers. He raised high his head, first turning to one side and then to the other; and surely never could a victorious warrior fresh from the battle-field and flushed with the panoply of success, when the smoke of the conflict had cleared away from above the wounded and the fallen, have evinced more heart-felt exultation or composure. Such a scene would indeed have been worthy of the finest touches of the painter; but worn down with the struggle, faint and weary, the red gore rolling in torrents from his sides, he soon began to writhe and tremble with pain and weakness. Perceiving this, two valiant horsemen, fresh in the attack, now rushing rapidly upon him, suddenly brought him to the earth. The poor creature thus lacerated and torn, cut and mangled, soon rolled upon his side and was at peace.

I looked around me to see if any bosom seemed to beat responsive to my own over a scene so repulsive and horrid; but I found all was joy and gladness throughout the assembled throng. A group of Limanian ladies, sitting directly in front of me, and whose excessive transports of delight I had before witnessed, appeared now to have come to the very climax of their joy and exultation. They giggled incessantly; and while coolly and inhumanly recounting to each other, in their own favorite Spanish, the various rounds of torture and cruelty they had witnessed in the fight, seemed to evince little of that refined delicacy of feeling so becoming to their sex. But this heartless specimen of inhumanity, though more or less common to all such exibitions in South America, is by no means universal among the giddy and the gay of Peru. Honorable exceptions there are, and such as reflect the highest credit upon female society throughout that hospitable clime. Close by my side sat an elderly Spanish lady, whom I subsequently found to be the wife of a distinguished merchant of the city. She was evidently of high Castillian blood, proud of her ancestry and of herself. Disposed to see how she seemed to enjoy so bloody a tragedy, I watched her emotions with some attention; and I was pleased to discover that she often turned her eyes from the brutal conflict with disgust. She seemed to shudder at the shocking picture before her, though it might be difficult perhaps, upon any principle of enlightened humanity, to account for her ever having become the willing patron of such scenes by honoring them with her presence.

Here ended the third scene. The usual preliminaries of the interlude then followed. These over, the fourth victim of the slaughter came boldly galloping into the arena, loaded with dazzling festoons, and sparkling with gold lace and ribands. But he made a bad start of it. At the very outset he was unfortunate. Encountering a more desperate and skilful adversary than any of his predecessors, the bloody poniard was wielded with too great exactness and success. It struck him between the horns, when on his first round, and he sunk beneath the blow. Struggling still to recover, the spears and lances and short swords flew thick and heavy around him, piercing his very vitals, until the blood flowed in streams from his head and sides. The next moment his body was to be seen whirling swiftly through the broad gate; after which, with little pause, the fifth scene of the day opened before us; and this proved the most shocking of them all. It was the last I witnessed, though not the last of the exhibition. The preparations which were making gave evident signs of what was to follow. The many thousands of sparkling eyes around me sufficiently attested that some unusual specimen of torture was now about to come off. The tragic instrument for the intended execution was here brought into the arena. It was a sharp two-edged lance, of about the width of a man's hand, and some eighteen inches in length. This was firmly fixed into a substantial staff, apparently from twelve to fourteen feet in length, and about three times the size of a common hay-fork. The end of this staff was planted against a projecting timber, driven into the ground some thirty feet from the gateway. It was to be manned, as I was informed at the time, by a convict from some of the prisons, who, if he escaped with his life, was to be set at liberty.

In a moment, flag in hand, he was at his post. Crouching low upon one knee, and so resting the staff upon the other as if to catch the bull on his first plunge into the circle, he awaited his destiny. Every feeling heart must have bled over the dreadful picture. The bull was of a jet black, rather a fit emblem of the dark deed about to be committed upon his body. At the whirl of the gate, he dashed furiously at the flag of the convict. The lance struck him in the under jaw, tearing it most shockingly, and passing directly through the skinny part of the neck, projected about two feet above his head. With this dragging and dangling at his side, he still pressed rapidly upon his antagonists. The poor convict, though completely run over and prostrate, was so little injured that he was enabled to scramble to a place of safety. The noisy throng now cheered on the bull. Opening the bowels of one horse, and tossing another against the ballustrade, he was making tremendous strides around the arena, when, fatally struck by a *matador* with a spear, he writhed, quivered and fell. A severe lunge from a short sword here ended his career; and with it I returned from a performance which, in spite of myself, had worked up all my better feelings to an intensity of excitement before unknown ; perfectly willing to leave all such exhibitions, for all time to come, to those who could look upon them with a smile of pleasure.

Turning from a scene so exciting and absorbing, and yet so repulsive and revolting, we hurried away to the city. All there was serene and peaceful as the shades of night. The sun still cast its last departing rays over the distant horizon. Vesper prayers had not yet been said in the churches, nor had the solemn toll of the church bells, in chiming the symphonic Catholic *oracion*, lifted the hats of the scattered few in the streets in silent reverence to GOD and HEAVEN. Every thing above us and around us seemed to proclaim that the festive day was nearly closed, and that the awakening inspirations of the hour, though mingled with butchery and blood, were still left to warm the affections of the human heart ; to draw the curtain of forgetfulness over the past, and to shed around our path the halcyon light of encouragement and hope for the future.

A PICTURE FOR YOUNG PARENTS.

—

FROM 'A TALE OF PARAGUAY.'

—

> OH ! bliss for them when in that infant face
> They now the unfolding faculties descry,
> And fondly gazing, trace — or think they trace —
> The first faint speculation in that eye,
> Which hitherto hath rolled in vacancy !
> Oh ! bliss in that soft countenance to seek
> Some mark of recognition, and espy
> The quiet smile which in the innocent cheek
> Of kindness and of kind its consciousness doth speak !

A WELCOME TO WINTER.

BY J. HONEYWELL.

I.

BRIMMERS to WINTER! Winter wild and weird,
  Frost-crowned and peerless! To his jocund laugh,
And frolic eye, and long white flowing beard,
  Let us with right good will our bumpers quaff!
O why should poets paint the jovial sage
  So fiercely grim, and not his beauties sing?
Why call him blear-eyed, crabbed, curst with age,
  And slander thus the good old roystering king?

II.

Not so do we behold him. Glowing hearts
  Welcome with joy their ancient, loving friend,
While he ungrudgingly to them imparts
  Pleasures that multiply withouten end.
Who brings delight, to wile the evenings long?
  Who drives off cares that pained the summer time?
Who crowns long months of toil with mirth and song,
  But brave old Winter in his lusty prime!

III.

Hark to the sleigh-bells on the snow-piled plain,
  Whose witching music charms the frosty air;
While riant voices, like a gay refrain,
  Tell that red lips and sparkling eyes are there.
And mark yon skater on the ice-bound stream;
  Such magic circles spring beneath his heel,
And such his dext'rous feats, we almost deem
  Some tricksy ARIEL rides the ringing steel.

IV.

And thou, O Winter! bringest us again
  Our harvest home, Thanksgiving! When dear friends
Cluster once more, to bind anew the chain
  Of fond affection; and to make amends
For absence past. Hearts long have yearned to meet,
  That now, beneath the patriarchal roof,
Find in a blest communion, brief but sweet,
  Assurance strong that love is absence-proof.

V.

I love hoar Winter for the boisterous glee
  With which he ministers to young and old:
A bounteous gentleman indeed is he,
  Who comes with joys and blessings manifold.
He lends new beauties to the maidens fair,
  That they the more may captivate our hearts,
And he it is, not Cupid, that should bear
  The twanging bow and the resistless darts.

VI.

Where should love's home be, but around the hearth,
　　Where great fires up the ample chimney roar?
When care is banished, and light-hearted mirth
　　Flingeth broadcast his long-time hoarded store.
Grandsire and sire, all garrulous with delight,
　　Their rugged features brightening in the blaze,
Grow young again, and fill the ear of night
　　With tales and legends of the elder days.

VII.]

Though winds may rave, and the wide drifting snow
　　Give to the shrouded world an aspect drear,
'T is home's triumphal hour; and the rich glow
　　Of rosy love beams all around us here.
Hail! to brave Winter! honored be his name!
　　The bard, delighted, lingers o'er the theme,
Forgetful of Ambition, Fortune, Fame,
　　While Love, heart-throned, sits here and reigns supreme.

A CHRONICLE OF OUR NAVY.

BY NED BUNTLINE.

'BLESS your starry top-lights, youngster! how are you? Where are you from and where bound to? I have n't seen you for a year o' Sundays! You look pale, boy; are you under the weather?'

Thus was I hailed a few days since, while passing down Broadway. I looked up and my glance fell upon a countenance as familiar to me as the face of old ocean. I saw the bright eye, ruddy cheek and weather-beaten figure-head of my gallant old commander, Captain J. M. M——, and felt the hearty grasp of his warm right hand. While I responded to his congratulations and inquiries, Memory overhauled her log-book. Many and varied were the scenes she brought to view. How often with him had I stood upon 'the peopled deck,' and gazed forth upon the wild majesty of the war of elements; how often in the southern ocean, when the winds and waves seemed all asleep, and the stars above winked at the stars in the sea, have I with him paced the quiet deck and talked of home, our native land, and loved ones there; how often in those sweet climes

　　'WHERE the flowers ever blossom, the beams ever shine,
　　Where the virgins are soft as the roses they twine,
　　And all save the spirit of man is divine,'

have we wandered together, joining in the banquet or the festive dance! Times of pleasure and scenes of peril have we shared. We have faced death together. Time hath dealt gently with thee. Thou art still the same, brave and generous friend of my lonely youth; thy step is still firm; thy grasp strong, thine eye as bright now as when it first looked up in the pride of young ambition upon the stripes and stars in the robe of liberty.

From that same log of Memory, reader, accept an extract. It is a chronicle of a cruise made long years age with Captain M——.

We were lying at Norfolk in 18——, in the schooner Porpoise; Captain, then Lieutenant M——, commanding her. Orders came to us suddenly and unexpectedly from the Navy Department to fit out for sea without delay, and to make sail for the vicinity of the Cape de Verd islands, in search of a piratical schooner which had captured the American merchant brig Mexican, robbed, and then set her on fire. One of the crew of the brig had concealed himself in the hold at the moment when the pirates boarded her, and there remained undiscovered while his shipmates were all murdered. The pirates stripped the vessel of every thing valuable and then set her on fire, returning to their own vessel and making sail. The poor fellow who had been hidden in the hold soon began to feel the increasing warmth of the climate below, and cautiously crept from his hiding place. When he got above hatches, he found the forward part of the vessel entirely enveloped in flames, which were running up the spars and rigging, and rapidly extending aft. He cast one hurried glance upon the bloody figures of the crew, then shuddering as he passed them, rushed to the jolly-boat which hung at the stern davits. It was the work of only a moment for him to cast loose the davit-falls and lower her down into the water. Another instant, without food or water, and with but a single oar he was alone in her on the broad Atlantic. With his single oar he sculled his boat clear of the burning brig. Fortunately he was not discovered by the pirate, who was crowding sail in an opposite direction. As soon as he was clear of the brig, poor Jack sat down and watched mast after mast fall hissing into the water; he fancied that he saw the crisped and burning bodies of his dead comrades dance around the flaming deck; he saw the red fire eat the noble hull of his vessel down to the water's edge, until it was nothing but a black and shapeless mass, and then it vanished from his sight.

For three long days that poor fellow drifted to and fro upon the waters. Hope had nearly deserted him; he began to feel the intolerable fever of thirst, when his wandering glance fell upon a speck in the horizon. At first he thought it a cloud, but soon he knew it to be a sail. Her course happily lay athwart his track, and his shirt hoisted upon the oar attracted the observation of her crew. He was taken on board. She proved to be an American, homeward bound, where she arrived safely. Poor Jack's story was told to the proper authorities, and he was sent in person on board of our craft, to aid in recognising the pirate, should we fall in with her.

We sailed in seven hours after our orders arrived, and after a quick but very rough passage, wherein our craft proved herself as wet as the fish which she was named after, we arrived at Porto Grande in the island of St. Vincents. Here we watered ship and then stood out to sea on our cruise after the buccaneer.

On the third day out, when we were not far from Brava, we discovered a sail on our weather-bow. She was a fore-and-aft schooner, very rakish, and seemed to be running free, heading down toward us.   The vessel which took the Mexican was a fore-topsail schooner; and this a fore-and-after, but we knew how easy it was to send down square yards and change a two-masted rig, and accordingly hauled our course for the stranger, hoisting Portuguese colors at our peak, shutting in our ports and showing very few men about decks, so as to try and disguise our schooner until she was in gun-shot.

As the stranger neared us, our suspicions became more and more excited.   Our schooner was cleared for action.   Through the glass, the strange sail showed a long hull, painted black, with the muzzles of eight guns on a side, run out, her spars were taunt and very heavy, and her deck was full of men.   The survivor of the brig, as soon as he saw her figure head, (a Turk with a green turban) pronounced her the same vessel which had captured the Mexican.

She was now within a mile and-a-half of us, rapidly coming into range, and we all felt that a fierce and bloody struggle was at hand. Our arms were in hand, the decks sanded down, the port fires alight; all was ready, the crew burning with impatience, our brave skipper walking up and down the quarter-deck, calm and thoughtful, but firm as the bright sword in his hand.

Suddenly there seemed to be a strange commotion on board the stranger; she flattened in her sheets and hauled on a wind, heading in for the islands.   She had evidently discovered our character. We had been standing on under short sail, more completely to deceive her, but now we saw that it was time to crowd canvass, for the build of the stranger denoted a speed which even our fancy clipper might fail to exceed.

'Aloft, topmen!' shouted Lieut. M——, 'lay aloft and loose to'-gallant sails!   Another pull on the lee-braces; haul out the bow-lin's; keep her full and by, quarter-master!   Run out the guns! Tell Mr. Meade to try a shot with the long eighteen forward, and heave it across that rascal's fore-foot!'

The gun was fired and the shot fell but a little short.   The schooner fired a weather gun in defiance, and then out from each mast-head floated the red flag.   She had cast away deception and evidently depended upon her speed to escape us.   We soon saw men at work in her rigging, and in an inconceivably short space of time she had yards crossed and a top-sail and top-gallant-sail set.   On the first start we seemed to gain upon her, but as she made more sail, she evidently put the boot on the other leg.

' Mr. Meade, we must cripple that craft in her spars or she 'll get away,' said the lieutenant to our little first luff, than whom not a nobler fellow ever trod a plank.

' I 'll try her, Sir!' was the reply, ' but it's a long range for us, and we pitch so in this infernal head-sea that it 'll be more a matter of chance than skill!'

The young officer carefully levelled the long gun, and after a moment's steady sighting applied the match.   As the smoke cleared up, a huge rent could be seen in the main-sail of the schooner. This proved her still to be within range, and we felt sure of her. The wind was very fresh, and we were both on the same tack, heading in for some high rocky islands that lay a little to windward of Brava. Three more shots were fired unsuccessfully at the pirate.

'We 'll try a broadside,' said our commander. 'Stand by the starboard guns! Quartermaster, luff her up in the wind! Ready, fore-and-aft! With the weather-roll—fire!'

For a moment our little craft quivered under the heavy discharge, and then as the cloud of smoke lifted and left a clear view of the enemy, our crew raised a cheer, such as none but American sailors can give in the hour of victory. Both top-masts of the pirate had gone by the board; her crew were aloft trying to clear the wreck.

'No more firing!' cried Lieut. M——; 'we 've got her now! there 's no need of wasting Uncle Sam's powder.'

Scarcely were the words out of his lips before we saw the bows of the pirate fall off before the wind; then her broadside ranged full upon us, and as we saw the smoke from her guns, crash! whiz! rattling through our spars and rigging came the iron hail. For a moment we scarcely knew where we were. The pirate had fully returned our compliment. He had literally riddled our sails; our fore-yard was gone in the slings; the main-top-mast shot off close down to the fid; the jib-stay shot away, and three or four of his shot were sticking in the hull, leaving room for carpenters' plugs as big as a man's leg.

We at once set to clearing the wreck, and as fast as possible made sail. The pirate however was ahead, and before we got under headway again, rounded the high rocky point of an island about a mile and a half to windward of us. We still felt sure of overhauling him before he could get clear of the islands; but when we rounded the point he was nowhere in sight. For three days we cruised about among those rocks, keeping a bright look-out day and night, but we never caught another glimpse of the schooner. Some of our tars would shake their heads and talk of Flying Dutchmen and buccaneer compacts with his sulphuric Majesty, the Devil, when trying to account for the sudden disappearance of the pirate; but we never saw her more. For three weeks we cruised about in those waters, and then made sail for Pensacola, via the island of St. Thomas and the old Bahama Channel.

In running along the north side of Cuba, just after we got clear of the Banks, we had very heavy weather. One morning, just at dawn, when we were under close reefs, we made out a vessel at anchor close in under the land; and as the light cleared, we saw that she was one of the little English schooners that are kept cruising round the islands to intercept the slavers, who generally run this channel on their way from the African coast. As soon as she saw us she weighed anchor, made sail and stood out, hoisting her colors. Heading across our forefoot, she fired a gun, which sent a shot hissing through the foam but a few fathoms ahead of us. Our colors were hoisted at the peak, as also our man-o'war pennant at the main-truck; therefore it was not strange that our commander should be a little 'miffed' at this act of impertinence.

'Beat to quarters!' shouted he; 'I 'll heave to for no d—d Englishman, who talks in *that* way! Hold your course steady, quartermaster!'

The Englishman was heading across our bows and very rapidly nearing us; but finding that we did not regard his shot, fired again, and this time his shot flew right between our masts, but touched nothing.

'By Jupiter! I won't stand this!' shouted Lieut. M——; 'stand by with that bow-gun and heave a shot right into his hull! D—n him, I 'll sink him for daring to insult the flag of my country!'

The shot fortunately struck close under the cutwater of the Englishman, but did no injury. Our course was altered for her, and in a few minutes we were in hail of her; our commander and her's both standing on the hammock-nettings of their vessels; our captain as mad as a disappointed old maid.

'How dare you fire into a United States vessel, Sir!' shouted Lieut. M——, as the vessels came within hail.

'Because you did n't show your colors!'

'You lie, you bloody Englishman! My colors were up before your dirty dish-cloth hung at the peak!'

'I 'll make a personal matter of it, Sir!' replied the English captain, now quite as angry as our own.

'Very well, Sir! that 's just what I want. We are within ten hours' sail of Havana; I 'll run in there and wait for you. I 'll teach you to insult the flag of my country!'

The whole affair might easily have been explained. We were running down the channel before the wind, and our colors, though hoisted, were becalmed under the lee of the main-sail, and did not blow out where the Englishman could see them. He at first had mistaken us for a slaver.

On that evening we anchored in Havana, and had hardly dropped anchor, before our brave young skipper had his pistol-case out, cleaning and preparing his weapons. We waited in port a week, but the Englishman never made his appearance to get the 'personal' satisfaction he had claimed.

There were no more incidents on that cruise that will interest the reader; but there are other chronicles in connection with Captain M—— and my later cruisings which 'Old Knick.' will hereafter register. Commander M—— will, I hope, pardon these reminiscences, which I trust will not fail to remind him pleasantly of the past. May he live till every hair of his head becomes a sprig of laurel to form a wreath for his brow!

New-York, November, 1846.

THE MISANTHROPE: AN EPIGRAM.

He has a grief he cannot speak,
    He wears his hat awry;
He blacks his boots but once a week,
    And says he wants to die.

L O O K   A L O F T .

ADDRESSED TO A GIFTED FRIEND, TOO EASILY DISHEARTENED.

'Qui osetout, peut tout ce qu'il ose.' — BERNARD.

GIVE not thus to listless sadness
    Hours the partial Muse would claim;
Up! and with enthusiast madness
    Storm the rugged steeps of fame!

Not by wishing, but by willing
    O'er the clouds to lift his flag,
Genius, aim with act fulfilling,
    Proudly climbs the laureled crag.

Did the youthful Swiss,* long dreaming
    Europe's topmost round to scale,
Sit him down to idle scheming
    In Chamouni's murmuring vale?

No; but o'er the glacier pressing,
    Up the granite's icy flank,
Step by dauntless step progressing,
    Trod he first thy scalp, Mont Blanc!

Be like him a bold advancer,
    Nor the mocking laggard heed:
Upward! — from the summit answer,
    They who win may laugh indeed.

When the Scottish Jove's mad levin
    Laid the noble minstrel low,
Swifter tow'rd the Muse's heaven
    Rose he, strengthened by the blow.

He who launched at eve the thunder
    On the young aspirant's name,
Waked to see him throned in wonder
    On the Himmaleh of fame.

Though than Newstead's bard less gifted,
    Tune thy harp to higher strain,
And its voice for Truth uplifted
    Shall a nobler audience gain.

Ask not, darkly musing, whether
    Glory's dawn be far or nigh,
Clash the flint and steel together,
    And the sparks shall flash reply.

Chance speeds all, the weak assure us,
    On or from the lurking shelf;
Nay! be thy own PALINURUS,
    Be thou Fate unto thyself!

New-York, 1846.

---

* SAUSSURE.

LITERARY NOTICES.

RUDIMENTAL LESSONS IN MUSIC: containing the Primary Instruction requisite for all Beginners in the Art, whether Vocal or Instrumental. By JAMES F. WARNER, translator of WEBER'S 'Theory of Musical Composition, KUBLER's 'Anleitung zum Gesang-Unterrichte,' etc. New-York: D. APPLETON AND COMPANY.

To no individual probably is the musical public more indebted for first-class works upon the science of music than to Mr. WARNER. And although it may perhaps be regretted by some that instead of translations he had given us original works of his own, yet the merit of the works he has translated renders them most acceptable to well-instructed artists ; and we may doubt whether an author deserves more credit for writing a good book, or for selecting one equally good in a foreign language, and giving it to his readers in a correct and attractive style. We hail with delight any thing that can render the study of musical elements more attractive ; and if simplicity of plan and clearness of statement, combined with well-selected exercises, make a book valuable both to the teacher and the scholar, then we may congratulate our music-studying community on the appearance of the ' Rudimental Lessons.' The author has given us an elementary book, not exceeded, to our knowledge, in any language. His aim as a teacher and writer seems to have been to combine in the shortest compass the greatest amount of knowledge, communicated in the simplest and clearest manner. Bringing to his task a highly-cultivated intellect, he possesses advantages in the power of few who make music their profession ; for among the children of song there are not many who have enjoyed the advantages of a liberal education ; and hence in preparing musical works most musical authors among us are found unequal to the production of what will bear comparison with elementary works on other subjects. But Mr. WARNER's general scholarship is of such a rank as to afford him every prospect of success among the better intellects of the day ; and there will be but one voice among well-trained artists as to the manner in which he has acquitted himself in the work before us. The first thing in musical instruction is to afford a clear and correct idea of such sounds as enter into the formation of correct melody. Secondary to this, and of scarcely less importance, is the skill to convey clear ideas to pupils of the same sounds when represented upon the printed pages. Whatever will accomplish both these objects soonest must be the best. Expedients for this purpose are almost innumerable ; and each has its advocates, who are ready to bring certificates from the four winds, each to show that his own system is the only one, and music shall die with it. Thus we have zealous advocates of patent notes with the staff; others as zealous for the disuse of the staff; others again would reduce all things to a few mumerals with marks; others glorify the method of fixed syllables, as used by the French; while others vary the syllables with the pitch of the scale, and use only fixed letters to denote the degrees of the staff. But Mr. WARNER has aimed, and we think successfully, to strike out a middle course, by which he avoids all extreme and exclusive views, and renders musical study at once simple, clear, and consistent in its whole course. The first chapter of his work treats of musical sounds as they exist in the practice of singing. He has used the old term *tones* for the notes of the scale; while he avoids the old, and to beginners scarcely intelligible distinction, of 'Tones' and 'Semi-tones,' by treating all the proximate intervals of the scale as either *great* or *small seconds*. As the basis of representing sounds upon the staff, he has adopted the German method of marking the letters, so much commended by CALCOTT, but which has been little known in this country. The writer has long used it privately in teaching the piano-forte; and would not dispense with it upon any condition; but it has not appeared in elementary works on this side of the Atlantic, until Mr. WARNER brought out WEBER's theory; and now with all its clearness and beauty it has for the first time publicly assumed the rank due to it in an elementary treatise. The advantages of this over the method of fixed syllables cannot be estimated; as it gives to every key or stop of a musical instrument, and also to every place on the staff, a definite name that distinguishes it from all others. It also affords the best method known by which persons not used to keyed instruments may be taught to comprehend the difference of pitch among the various parts of vocal music. The next step is to treat of letters as affected by flats and sharps; after which the staff is introduced; in treating which, his method is remarkably clear; although we could have wished a shorter and simpler method of naming had been used for the added lines. The article on the clefs is all that one could wish; he gives all that can be useful on that head. We are next introduced to notes, as in practice substituted for letters upon the staff to show the relative length of sounds employed in a movement. The whole matter of notations is treated in a manner clear and satisfactory; both as to forms and the manner of their presentation. The article on Measures is peculiarly rich. We would venture however to suggest whether the subject of accent should not *precede* that of measure, as it is the basis of the latter, though it is not so treated in any work with which we are acquainted. The mode of naming the intervals seems to be all one could desire for correctness and clearness. In treating the now much-neglected minor scale, Mr. WARNER has, we perceive, allowed a superfluous second between the sixth and seventh, while most authors allow of no such interval. In this however he coincides with the practice in Germany; though it were to be wished that the minor scale might be presented as it sometimes appears in practice, without accidental sharps; but with the remark that the sixth and seventh are liable to be elevated by sharps in certain cases. The article on transposing scales will be found to afford to our elementary teachers many views of importance that they are not likely to find in any but expensive volumes, with which most musical persons are not likely to come in contact. In the chapter on harmony, as a branch of elementary study, we are presented with a concise view of the most important chords and their successions. That this most obscure and difficult branch of musical inquiry can be made plain and comprehensible to learners we can have no doubt; and we trust Mr. WARNER will attempt the task more in full hereafter. Some excellent views of the usual modulations are added in a separate chapter; and the work closes with a copious list of abbreviated forms, and some excellent remarks on style. As the volume becomes known to teachers, it will undoubtedly be adopted as a standard work ; for it contains more valuable matter, and is 'got up' in a clearer and purer style, than any other work in the same compass, with which we are acquainted.

URANIA: A RHYMED LESSON. By OLIVER WENDELL HOLMES. Pronounced before the Boston Mercantile Library Association, October 14, 1846. Boston: W. D. TICKNOR AND COMPANY.

MEMORY is an excellent critic ; trustworthy always, at least with us, in designating the natural and truthful writer, whether of poetry or prose. And this, in the example of Mr. HOLMES, is a test so complete, that we scarcely know of a production of his, long or short, in which some striking thought or rare felicity of versification has not fixed itself indelibly upon our mind ; and in several instances whole passages, almost at a single perusal, have remained fastened as with hooks of steel upon the memory. There is one remark in relation to this popular poet which we deem it proper to make here. Because he has on many occasions wielded the polished lance of ridicule and satire ; because his conception of the burlesque is vivid, and his wit and humor pre-eminent, he is by many persons, not otherwise acquainted with his writings, held to be little more than an amusing satirist or a pleasant farceur. This is a great error. Mr. HOLMES has otherwise exhibited an intensity of poetical sensibility and a depth of poetic power, as marked as those of any American poet we have ever encountered. His natural compass of thought is wide and various ; and whether he sports with language as if it were a play-thing, or uses it as a medium wherewith to wreak upon expression thoughts that breathe or burn, he leaves upon the mind an ineffaceable impression of genius united with the highest order of artistic skill. If the reader has ever heard Mr. SAMUEL LOVER repeat his intensely interesting sketch of 'SHAWMUS O'BRIEN,' he will understand our impression of the characteristics of Mr. HOLMES's poetry, in those examples where external Humor and internal Pathos jostle each other in successive stanzas, as in 'The Last Leaf,' and many other poems of a kindred character from his pen. In a late number of this Magazine, in a notice of the beautiful London edition of Mr. HOLMES's writings, we dwelt at some length upon the peculiarities of his genius : we proceed therefore, in the present instance, to segregate a few passages from the 'Rhymed Lesson' before us, leaving our readers to derive from these their impression of its character. The following fervid lines remind us of a passage in CARLYLE's 'Sartor Resartus,' commencing 'Who am I? What is this *Me?* Sure enough I am, and lately was not ; but Whence? How? Whereto?' etc. :

'BETWEEN two breaths what crowded mysteries lie —
The first short gasp, the last and long-drawn sigh !
Like phantoms painted on the magic slide,
Forth from the darkness of the past we glide,
As living shadows for a moment seen
In airy pageant on the eternal screen,
Traced by a ray from one unchanging flame,
Then seek the dust and stillness whence we came.

'But whence and why, our trembling souls inquire,
Caught these dim visions their awakening fire?
O, who forgets, when first the piercing thought
Through childhood's musings found its way unsought,
I AM ! I LIVE ! The mystery and the fear
When the dread question, 'WHAT HAS BROUGHT ME HERE?'
Burst through life's twilight, as before the sun
Roll the deep thunders of the morning gun !'

'NATURE has placed thee on a changeful tide,
To breast its waves, but not without a guide;
Yet, as the needle will forget its aim,
Jarred by the fury of the electric flame,
As the true current it will falsely feel,
Warped from its axis by a freight of steel ;
So will thy CONSCIENCE lose its balanced truth
If passion's lightning fall upon thy youth ;
So the pure impulse quit its sacred hold,
Girt round too deeply with magnetic gold.

'Go to yon tower, where busy Science plies
Her vast antennæ, feeling through the skies ;
That little vernier on whose slender lines
The midnight taper trembles as it shines,
A silent index, tracks the planets' march
In all their wanderings through the ethereal arch ;
Tells through the mist where dazzled Mercury burns,
And marks the spot where Uranus returns.
So, till by wrong or negligence effaced,
The living index which thy MAKER traced
Repeats the line each starry Virtue draws
Through the wide circuit of creation's laws ;
Still tracks unchanged the everlasting ray
Where the dark shadows of temptation stray ;
But once defaced forgets the orbs of light,
And leaves thee wandering o'er the expanse of night!'

If the reader would enjoy an example of graphic limning, let him turn to pages
twelve and thirteen of the poem before us, and introduce for himself this admirable
picture of metropolitan church-going :

'SEE through the streets that slumbered in repose
The living current of devotion flows ;
Its varied forms in one harmonious band,
Age leading Childhood by its dimpled hand,
Want, in the robe whose faded edges fall
To tell of rags beneath the tartan shawl,
And Wealth, in silks that fluttering to appear,
Lift the deep borders of the proud cashmere.

'See, but glance briefly, sorrow-worn and pale,
Those sunken cheeks beneath the widow's veil ;
Alone she wanders where with *him* she trod,
No arm to stay her, but she leans on GOD.
While other doublets deviate here and there,
What secret handcuff binds that pretty pair?
Compactest couple ! pressing side to side—
Ah, the white bonnet that reveals the bride!
By the white neck-cloth with its straitened tie,
The sober hat, the Sabbath-speaking eye,
Severe and smileless, he that runs may read
The stern disciple of Geneva's creed ;
Decent and slow, behold his solemn march,
Silent he enters through yon crowded arch.
A livelier bearing of the outward man,
The light-hued gloves, the undevout rattan,
Now smartly raised or half-profanely twirled —
A bright, fresh twinkle from the week-day world—
Tell their plain story ; yea, thine eyes behold
A cheerful Christian from the liberal fold.

' Down the chill street that curves in gloomiest shade,
What marks betray yon solitary maid ?
The cheek's red rose, that speaks of balmier air,
The Celtic blackness of her braided hair;
The gilded missal in her kerchief tied ;
Poor NORA, exile from Killarney's side !
Sister in toil, though born of colder skies,
That left their azure in her downcast eyes,
See pallid MARGARET, Labor's patient child,
Scarce weaned from home, the nursling of the wild
Where white Katahdin o'er the horizon shines,
And broad Penobscot dashes through the pines ;
Still as she hastes her careful fingers hold
The unfailing hymn-book in its cambric fold.
Six days at drudgery's heavy wheel she stands,

The seventh sweet morning folds her weary hands ;
Yes, child of suffering, thou may'st well be sure
He who ordained the Sabbath loved the poor !'

We regret that we have not space to exhibit the liberal and catholic feeling mani-
fested in the lines which follow these, inculcating love to men in all who inculcate
love to God, and the banishment of sectarian impulse from the bosoms of those who
would worship Him in spirit and in truth, by what form soever their outward service
may be distinguished. But oh ! town-reader, if you have ever been bored to extinction
in the public thoroughfares ; if any prolonged nothingarian has a peck or so of your
buttons at home ; if you have been tortured by the man who with a double-stroke
introduces the slow auger into your breast, or that other specimen of the genus bore
who twists a small gimlet into you in divers places, removing it occasionally to blow off
the chips ; if a large piece of sticking-plaster has been spread over your too suscep-
tible person in Broadway ; pray read to the culprits these lines when next they en-
counter you. We shall carry a strong-bound copy of Holmes's poem about us as a
talisman hereafter, whenever we go forth upon the street :

' I tell in verse—'t were better done in prose—
One curious trick that every body knows ;
Once form this habit, and it's very strange
How long it sticks, how hard it is to change.
Two friendly people, both disposed to smile,
Who meet, like others, every little while,
Instead of passing with a pleasant bow,
And ' How d' ye do ?' or ' How 's your uncle now ?'
Impelled by feelings in their nature kind,
But slightly weak, and somewhat undefined,
Rush at each other, make a sudden stand,
Begin to talk, expatiate and expand ;
Each looks quite radiant, seems extremely struck,
Their meeting so was such a piece of luck ;
Each thinks the other thinks he 's greatly pleased
To screw the vice in which they both are squeezed ;
So there they talk, in dust, or mud, or snow,
Both bored to death, and both afraid to go !
Your hat once lifted, do not hang your fire,
Nor like slow Ajax, fighting still, retire ;
When your old castor on your crown you clap,
Go off ; you 've mounted your percussion-cap !'

We have always contended that the mouth is the best external criterion of a man's
character. While we should always suspect the person who could not look one in the
face, we should yet scan the lines of his mouth to detect insincerity or falsehood.
Something like this we take to be the judgment of our poet in this regard :

' Our cold Northeaster's icy fetter clips
The native freedom of the Saxon lips;
See the brown peasant of the plastic South,
How all his passions play about his mouth !
With us, the feature that transmits the soul,
A frozen, passive, palsied breathing-hole.
The crampy shackles of the ploughboy's walk
Tie the small muscles when he strives to talk ;
Not all the pumice of the polished town
Can smooth this roughness of the barn-yard down;
Rich, honored, titled, he betrays his race
By this one mark—he 's awkward in the face ;
Nature's rude impress, long before he knew
The sunny street that holds the sifted few.

' It can 't be helped ; though if we 're taken young,
We gain some freedom of the lips and tongue ;
But school and college often try in vain
To break the padlock of our boyhood's chain
One stubborn word will prove this axiom true ;
No late-caught rustic can enunciate *view.*'

'Speak clearly if you speak at all;
Carve every word before you let it fall;
Do n't, like a lecturer or dramatic star,
Try over hard to roll the British r;
Do put your accents in the proper spot;
Do n't—let me beg you—do n't say ' How !' for ' What ?'
And, when you stick on conversation's burr,
Do n't strew your pathway with those dreadful urs !"

Mr. Holmes is equally authentic in his opinions upon dress; and when one finds his own propensities and practices in this respect entirely described, he has but to assure himself that good taste is of no city; although Philadelphia may turn up its solemn nose at New-York, New-York taboo Boston 'habits,' and Baltimore frown upon both. We take a reluctant leave of this ' Rhymed Lesson ;' but yet with the pleasant reflection that those readers who may act upon our advice to go at once to the nearest book-store and secure its perusal entire, will have an opportunity of enjoying what would not have been *new* to them had our space been commensurate with our desire to entertain them.

Life of Stephen Decatur : a Commodore in the Navy of the United States. By Alexander Slidell Mackenzie. Volume Eleven of Sparks' 'American Biography.' In one volume. Boston: Charles C. Little and James Brown.

Beside ample recorded facts in the public chronicles of the time, the author of this very interesting work has been indebted for his materials to various authentic private sources, embracing a wide connection of those who had the best means of being acquainted with the personal history and career of its distinguished subject. Thus the incidents connected with Decatur's early service in the navy ; details in relation to the burning of the Philadelphia, and minute information concerning its capture, with the various attacks on Tripoli; incidents occurring in the capture of the frigate President and of the Algerine frigate Mashouda; original letters, detailing circumstances connected with the closing scenes of Decatur's life, etc., are given with much fulness, from the most reliable testimony. The author has been indebted also to Mrs. Decatur for all the public papers of her husband that remained in her possession, and for freely communicating whatever information was requested. The minute details of the inception, progress and final result of the fatal duel with Commodore Barron, by which Decatur lost his life, are very interesting; and all who read attentively the correspondence in this connection will be satisfied, that in the *manner* of either antagonist, previous to their final meeting, there was much that no faithful historian could conscientiously commend. ' The painful incidents of this portion of the work,' remarks its author, ' were found not a little embarrassing in the narration.' Some allowance, he is quite right in assuming, should be made for the inherent difficulties of the task. We have full faith in the justice of his claim to be considered as having sought diligently for truth, from every source within his reach; but as he himself remarks, the search for truth, however sincere, does not always result in its being found; experience having demonstrated that contemporary history is quite as fallible as that of the past. Various errors, he adds, which he has had occasion to rectify on obtaining information, leave him without the hope that others may not yet remain. These however, whether detected by the indulgent or the censorious he says he shall be happy to have an opportunity to correct. The work is well executed, and embellished with a fine portrait of Decatur by Sully, with a fac-simile of his hand-writing.

MEMOIRS OF THE COURT OF CHARLES THE SECOND. By COUNT GRAMMONT. With numerous
Additions and Illustrations, as edited by Sir WALTER SCOTT. London: BOHN. New-York: BART-
LETT AND WELFORD.

THE enterprising New-York publishers of this very handsome and comparatively
cheap volume have laid us under obligations to them for affording us many hours of
pleasurable employment. The ' Memoirs of COUNT GRAMMONT,' ' which paint the
chief characters of the court of CHARLES the Second with an easy and exquisite
pencil,' are enough in themselves to make up a most attractive volume; but to these
are added in the present work, (which is published entire as revised by Sir WALTER
SCOTT in 1811, with all the notes, and a number of illustrative anecdotes, gleaned
from the most authentic sources,) the personal history of CHARLES the Second, com-
piled with care from all previous authorities, and presenting in a small compass the
most complete picture of the merry monarch in dishabille yet given to the public. If
we could command the space, we should be glad to quote largely from the King's ac-
count of his escape after the battle of Worcester. It was dictated by himself, and is
one of the most romantic pieces of English history we have ever read. The minute
and personal character of the narrative, its lively and careless style, and the collation
of it with other accounts, prove it to be unquestionably genuine. In addition to this, we
have the so-called ' Boscobel Tracts,' contemporary narratives, written in the quaint
language of the time, by THOMAS BLOUNT. These give curious variations and highly
interesting additions to the King's own narrative, and are, to use the words of the
' Retrospective Review,' ' now among the most scarce and highly-prized historical
pamphlets of the seventeenth century.' A beautiful engraving of the beautiful NELL
GWYNNE fronts the title-page.

A TREATISE ON THE PRACTICE OF THE SUPREME COURT OF THE STATE OF NEW-YORK, with
an Appendix of Practical Forms. By ALEXANDER M. BURRILL, Counsellor at Law. Second
edition. In three volumes, 8vo. New-York: JOHN S. VOORHIES.

THE second edition of this work, laboriously revised and greatly enlarged, has just
been completed by the publication of an Appendix, in a separate volume, containing
the Forms referred to in the first and second volumes. From the favorable reception
given to the first edition, and the care with which the task of revision appears to have
been executed, we should think the present publication would be preferred by the pro-
fession in this State to any other work on the subject of which it treats. The ele-
mentary explanations and historical illustrations of the various rules and proceedings,
of which the text and notes are full, which must render it of peculiar interest to the
law-student, are to be met with, to the same extent, in no other treatise of the kind,
American or English; while the practical directions which are interspersed through-
out, and which constitute another characteristic feature, recommend it as a valuable
daily manual for the practitioner. The author's attempt to produce an intelligible and
readable book on a subject, which, as hitherto usually handled, has been any thing
but attractive, has we think been quite successful; and to those who desire to know
whether *true* practice be, in fact, the ' mysterious jargon' which it has of late become
fashionable, in certain quarters, to designate it, we recommend an attentive perusal
of its pages. The work is clearly and correctly executed by Mr. WILLIAM OSBORN.

EDITOR'S TABLE.

'PARA, OR EIGHT MONTHS ON THE BANKS OF THE AMAZON.'—We resume our survey of the entertaining manuscript thus entitled, of the variety and pleasantness of which our readers had an agreeable foretaste in our last number. We pass at once to extracts. The subjoined is one of the writer's jottings-down at the island of Marajo: 'Beautiful birds were very plentiful, such as Toucans, Scarlet Ibis and Roseate Spoonbills. We shot them for amusement, ate them for nourishment, and preserved their skins as ornithological specimens. Beside these, there were many gigantic cranes constantly feeding on the campas, some of which were upward of ten feet in height. One day I heard the report of a gun, and soon after the voice of Mr. J——, who was calling me as lustily as he was able. I rushed out, gun in hand, to ascertain what the matter was, but was nearly convulsed with laughter when I discovered the cause. He was running with incredible velocity over the meadow, while a large crane which he had wounded was in rapid pursuit. A shot from my gun soon brought the bird to the ground, and we immediately secured him. He was a most formidable-looking fellow, and I should have been almost as willing to encounter a wild-cat in single combat as him. Their beak is sometimes more than a foot in length, and they use it with wonderful dexterity and power.' Our correspondent is a much better sportsman with his gun than with his fishing-rod. Out of his own mouth let us make our assertion good: 'On one occasion I went out with a friend, in order to procure a few delicate little fishes for supper. After walking several miles through groves and brooks, and over the campa, we at length arrived at the desired spot. Here flowed a charming rivulet; and having baited our hooks, and made all other necessary arrangements, we sat down on the bank, under the shade of some spreading trees, and commenced operations. Little did I imagine the sequel of all my extensive preparations! Just consider for a moment that I was in a delightful situation, in a southern forest; that the atmosphere was balmy and sweet, and every thing conducive to quiet and repose; and you will not be much surprised to learn that I involuntarily fell asleep! From this state of inactivity I was suddenly awakened by sliding off the bank into the water. What a *damper* upon farther operations! Being excessively afraid of alligators, I jumped out of the stream as soon as possible, and shortly went home, comforting myself with the assurance that although I had caught no fish yet I had caught a decided ducking.' This would never do on the banks of the Mongaup and the Callicoon. Here is a crowded sketch in the 'animated nature' way. The writer is rowing slowly up a stream near Juncal, in a little montaria, loaded down with various 'game' to the water's edge:

' Now and then we would shoot a brilliant bird, that lucklessly chanced to fly a perch before us, and sometimes send our shot rattling against the mailed tyrants of the stream. As we were gliding by we heard a considerable noise in the bushes, and looking in the direction from whence it proceeded, we perceived a large tapir running along the bank, as expeditiously as he was able. We both fired at him, but although we evidently gave him the entire contents of our guns, yet it was without any visible effect. He was an animal of the size of a small cow, quite corpulent in appearance, and having a long nose, somewhat resembling the trunk of an elephant. We also saw many monkeys among the branches, who yelled terribly at us, appearing to be irritated at our invasion of their premises. A flock of parrots would occasionally salute us with their discordant notes, and sometimes a diminutive and glittering humming-bird, like a sprite from fairy-land, would gleam for a moment before us, then vanish forever.' · · · ' Bright-winged birds of every hue continually flitted before us as we swept along the flowing tide ; and anon a troop of monkeys would be seen, playing among the branches of the brook-side forest. Occasionally we would level our gun at some of them, who stopping suddenly in their sports and looking directly at us, as if fully aware of our intentions, would break out into the most piteous cries. Under these circumstances we were not able to shoot, but invariably turned our gun aside and let them gambol on. He who can listen unmoved at the call of mercy, even from the mouth of a dumb animal, deserves not pity himself.' There is a very fine live specimen of the *Tapir* in Messrs. RAYMOND AND WARING's menagerie ; and it is justly deemed a great curiosity. Here is another snake-story : ' The greatest curiosity to us was a boa-constrictor, in a strong box, which Mr. C—— had presented to us. It was under the charge of the captain, who occasionally gave it a chicken or duck to masticate. On the passage back to the United States this snake forced himself out of the box in which he was confined, and went no one knew whither. Some supposed he had gone overboard ; others that he had concealed himself in the hold of the vessel. This last proved to be the case ; for while the vessel was being discharged of her cargo, the boa was found perfectly stiff among the goods, and as we supposed, dead. We put him however in a tub of warm water, and to our infinite surprise and joy, he shortly recovered his former life and activity.' What pleasant thoughts the passengers on board that vessel must have had at night, when they reflected upon the probability of a visit from his snakeship before morning ! But here is a longer story of a still longer serpent : ' Having proceeded up the stream almost as far as possible, and being about to change my course, I perceived something tumbling and rolling in the water but a short distance in front of the boat. Gazing at it intently, I soon discovered that it was a large amphibious snake, not less than twenty feet in length. I immediately levelled my gun at him and fired, when he at once floated ashore, apparently without sense or motion. Being little anxious to meddle with his snakeship until fully convinced that life was extinct, I proceeded to give him the contents of my remaining barrel. Upon the receipt of this, to my great astonishment, he suddenly recovered animation, and swam quickly to the opposite side. But he appeared to be considerably 'sick,' and opening his mouth to its fullest extent, out came a Muscovy duck, of the largest size, which evidently had but recently been swallowed ! While in the act of ejecting this bird, I stationed myself within a few feet, directly before him, prepared to fire down his throat the moment an opportunity was offered by the exit of the duck. To my exceeding chagrin, however, the cap exploded without igniting the powder. Indulgent reader, the writer possesses a vast deal of patience, but at that critical moment it was overcome, and he was wonderfully provoked, both with his gun, the snake and himself. Being now relieved, the boa plunged into the water and appeared to be entering a hole in the bed of the stream. The extremity of his tail alone remained above the surface. Fearing lest he might escape, in my desperation I seized hold of this dishonorable part of his person and gave it a powerful pull. In a moment, to my great consternation, the head of the snake emerged from the water, thus proving that he had merely been lying on the bottom in the mud. A third and last discharge from my gun broke his neck, and he floated again ashore, as I then conjectured, to die. But in this supposition I was altogether mistaken. More than an hour had elapsed, and still the snake was alive and evidently gaining strength. I had not a single serviceable cap left, and was consequently unable to molest him more. At length he slowly began to ascend the bank, and finally vanished among the bushes.'

A melancholy instance of somnambulism occurred in the house in which our correspondent was living at Para, of which he gives the following account: ' I was residing in one of the loftiest houses in Para, and tenanted, in company with a young man of about my own age, a room on the fourth floor. The apartment was small, and had but one window, which, unprotected by a balcony, looked out upon the street. My companion was a noble although mysterious young man, and singularly given to a habit of rising and walking in his sleep. Hardly a night passed that I was not awakened by his perambulations through the room. He would sometimes take down his guitar and play a plaintive air; at other times he would unbolt the door and visit different parts of the house, without meeting with any accident. I finally became so accustomed to his singular habits that I lost all apprehension of danger arising from them. Once, however, about midnight, while lying in my hammock in a state of half-unconsciousness, with but a dreamy appreciation of material objects, I perceived my friend arise, walk to the window, deliberately open it and then jump out! The horror of the scene aroused me to a perception of its reality. I looked at his hammock; it was vacant. I then tried the door; alas! it was locked. Rendered desperate by terror, I endeavored to believe that all I had seen was but a dream. I could not acknowledge its truth. In my frantic state of mind I rushed to another room, where some men of the household were sleeping, and having awaked them, asked them, hardly knowing what I said, if they had seen my companion. They conjectured immediately from my agitated appearance that all was not right, and inquired what was the matter. I told them in few words that my room-mate had probably jumped out of the window. Startled by the intelligence, they hastily arose, and having procured a lantern, we went down into the street; and there, on the pavement directly under the fatal window, lay the mangled and lifeless corpse of poor F——.' Our entertaining traveller has much to say of the Brazilian women in general; and judging from his description, we should certainly infer them to be rather a free-mannered race, with certain customs that would hardly 'do' in this region. Beautiful young ladies, in the light dress of our ' first mother,' would hardly go in bathing with single gentlemen in any of the New-England rivers; but it seems they may do so without comment in the Para and the Amazon, and other things scarcely less noteworthy. Speaking of the ladies, by-the-by, we may as well quote in this place the love-and-matrimony story of an excellent but rather romantic young American planter, from the island of Madeira, whom our correspondent encountered at Maguary: ' About a year previous he left the United States for Spain, with a single companion of his own age, who was also a planter. Having spent some nine months in rambling over the mountains and plains of that interesting country, they became satiated with its various attractions, and finally started in a heavily-laden vessel to return to their native land. On the passage, which was an unusually tempestuous one, the vessel sprung a leak, and was soon reduced to a sinking condition. A great proportion of the cargo was thrown overboard, and the vessel piloted into the nearest port, which chanced to be that of the enchanting island of Madeira. So delighted were our adventurers with the charms of this island, and so grateful for their recent escape from the perils of the sea, that they resolved to take up their residence in Madeira for a few weeks, before again trusting to the vicissitudes and dangers of the deep. In three days our hero was head-and-ears in love with one of the island beauties. She was a young girl of Portuguese extraction, not more than sixteen or seventeen years of age, and of exceedingly prepossessing appearance. Her parents were wealthy, and of the first rank and respectability. She however could not speak a word of English, and our adventurer was wholly unacquainted with her native tongue. This was at first somewhat discouraging to the latter; but he was at length entirely relieved from his doubts and apprehensions by discovering that the brother of his intended was able to converse equally well in both languages. To him he procured an introduction, and made known his tender feelings concerning his sister; desiring at the same time that he might be permitted to offer his addresses to her. This was assented to, and a courtship was commenced which was carried on by means of the brother, until in the course of three or four weeks it resulted in the complete discomfiture of the pretty Senhora, who yielded up her captive heart to her victor, and promised to marry him; upon condition, however, that he would abandon Protestantism and become a believer in the Roman Catholic faith. These were certainly hard terms; but what could he do? If he objected to them, he would lose the pretty Senhora forever; if he accepted them, he would gain a young and beautiful wife, who would be his forever, and who might probably with him, at some future period, return to his temporarily-abandoned creed. What should we have done, reader, under the circumstances? Why, I think we should have done just as our adventurer did; marry the charming Senhora and take the new religion; the former forever, the latter until we regained our native land. We could then return to our abandoned faith, to which we might endeavor to add a lovely convert. Our hero's description of the ceremony of his conversion was exceedingly amusing: 'A number of richly-dressed priests,' said he, 'asked me an innumerable number of questions, to all of which, without understanding them, I replied by an affirmative nod of the head. Then, having prayed and performed a variety of exercises, they wound up by crossing my face and breast, and in fact every part of me, with 'the sign of the cross,' and finally rolled me up in a cross. All this I bore with the resignation of a martyr; but the moment the ceremony was over, these words burst instinctively from my lips: 'My dear fellow,' said I to my companion, 'is n't this a most confounded humbug!'' Desiring to see Brazil before his return home, he took passage on board of a vessel bound for Para. His brother-in-law accompanied him, and I suppose made himself exceedingly useful as a medium of communication, or mental telegraph, between the newly-married pair during the blissful hours of their honeymoon.' But our friend has not permitted the romantic young planter to usurp all the love-adventure of his pages. He had occasional 'transactions' in that kind on his 'own account.' Let us premise that on 'a very charming day in that charming climate,' our correspondent encounters, under the shade of an ornamental verandah, four love-inspiring maidens, to each of whom he offers a cigar; and while they are smoking them, which the reader is to understand they are doing with the utmost *goût*, we will listen to his description of one of them: 'She was without exception the most beautiful girl I ever saw. Her form was fairy-like, and her stature rather small than otherwise. However, not more than fifteen years had rolled their summers over her head, and her height was therefore well-proportioned to her age. Half an inch more would certainly have detracted from the perfect symmetry of her person. She *was* a most lovely being, and was christened and known by the euphonious name of 'Louisa.' Her face was oval and full, and her countenance indicated the possession of the finest feelings and most tender sentiments of human nature. Never, *never* had I beheld such a pair of lips!—so prettily-formed, so ruby-like, so tempting! The emotions óf the poet, who though dead still lives in his works, arose in my mind:

> 'Oh! might I kiss those lips of fire!
> A thousand scarce could quench desire!'

But the passion of the moment was suppressed, and I conversed with her as I would have talked with a sister. Her head was decorated with luxuriant hair, which hung in dishevelled wavy tresses upon her white symmetrical neck and well-developed bosom. A few flowerets were entwined in her hair, which were indeed all the ornaments she wore. Her exquisite simplicity was itself a charm; a charm which jewels and precious stones would inevitably have destroyed. Beautiful girl! she did not need them! Innocent as childhood, she used only that garb which necessity and custom compelled. Her dress was so low in the neck that it distinctly disclosed those charms which it is customary for females to conceal in more civilized countries, and terminated so high above ground as to expose the smallest and most symmetrical foot and ankle ever beheld by mortal man. Such was the beautiful maid of Vigia. My conversation with the charming Senhoritas was abruptly brought to a conclusion by the announcement of the morning meal. So commending them to GOD till by-and-by, I hastened away.' But this was not the last of the beautiful maid of Vigia. Our friend sees her daily promenading in the garden, and on the balmy moonlit evenings he would often converse with her through the lattice-work of her window. And as he is about to depart from Vigia for the United States, look you what a pretty love-incident he records: 'A few hours before my departure, as I was walking in the rear court-yard, I heard the sound of a gentle voice. Looking in the direction whence it proceeded, I beheld the lovely maiden peering with her large bright raven eyes through a narrow aperture of the fence, and holding a solitary rose in her hand. 'Senhor,' said she, in a melodious, rich whisper, 'take this rose—and remember me!' I cannot say that I truly loved the girl, beautiful as she was; but being addressed at such a time in so affectionate a manner, by so charming a creature, who appeared then if possible more lovely than I had ever seen her before, had a most favorable effect upon me. Who then will blame me, when I say that I accepted her fragrant tribute, and that our lips met while I was breathing to her my last adieu? 'If any, speak; for him have I offended!'' No offence in the world, dear Sir; and we should like to hear the first man 'speak' to the effect that there was! His popularity with the ladies (GOD bless them!) would be gone forever. But now ensueth a pause. We have run cursorily through our correspondent's voluminous manuscript, taking here and there a passage, quite at random, as it arrested attention in a hasty perusal. But we have presented extracts enough to show the interesting character of the writer's observations; and we trust before long to encounter the manuscript transformed to a printed book, with illustrations, like BROWNE's ' Etchings of a Whaling Cruise.' It would well repay any publisher's ' venture.'

A YANKEE IN WESTMINSTER ABBEY.— An esteemed friend, to whose port-folio our readers have more than once been indebted, sends us the following welcome communication : ' Almost my first visit in London was to Westminster Abbey ; and although I have since gazed with admiration and astonishment, mingled with awe, upon St. Paul's, York Minster, the cathedrals of Cologne, Strasbourg, Milan, St. Peter's ; and have stood in the Pantheon, where one feels as though he were shaking hands with Antiquity itself ; yet I have experienced no emotions like those inspired by the old abbey. Larger, loftier, more magnificent, grander in a certain sense, they may be ; nay, undoubtedly are. Munificence may have invoked art, and art exhausted science, and both the world, to supply the precious stones and marble and silver and gold ; and cunning hands may have fashioned them into exquisite monuments of piety or of taste ; yet there stands the old Abbey, honorable in years but fresh in preservation, with her nave and choir and transepts and arches, and windows through which streams the soft and sombre light ; and old tombs, some crumbling to decay and others by sacrilegious hands defaced or broken ; but there she stands, alone in her glory, that neither time nor violence can obliterate or destroy !

' We enter this ' magazine of mortality,' as ADDISON appropriately calls it, by a door in the transept, and find ourselves among a crowd of visitors, drawn thither perhaps by the same feelings that influence us, and standing immediately in the ' Poet's · Corner.' This appears to be a privileged spot, where all may freely come ; but at a short distance, and between two columns, is a gate that bars our farther entrance. At this gate stands a sturdy verger, dressed in a dark cassock and grasping an official wand. Visitors are kept in waiting 'here until a goodly number are collected, when the verger proceeds to pocket the required pence,* (I could n't but think of ' St. PETER sitting at the celestial gate,') and handing you over to ' another of the same sort,' you are ' rushed' through. But being in a spot we most wished to see, and in no haste to advance under the locomotive process, we took our stand and looked around. Familiar names meet the eye at every point. What cathedral, what city, what nation can boast such great wealth, the accumulated treasures of centuries? — philosophers, historians, poets, sages, artists? —the great and distinguished men of England. And herein is the glory of the old Abbey.

' Look around. CHAUCER, SPENSER, MILTON, BUTLER, PRIOR, DRYDEN, SHAKS-PEARE, THOMPSON, ADDISON, GOLDSMITH, ' O! rare BEN. JOHNSON !' and he of like cognomen, the great Leviathan of Literature himself, are slumbering beneath my feet ; and SHERIDAN, and he who died but yesterday, CAMPBELL — they are gathered in here ; not that the mortal remains of *all* are in this spot interred, but here are their monuments, and of most of them their remains—fit place for either—to be

---

* WE are here reminded of HOOD's thoughtful man, whose solemn reflections on hearing the organ in the Abbey, at the close of the service, were abruptly interrupted by the verger with :

' Service is done, it 's tuppence now
For them as wants to stop !'

gathered as it were into one fold. I could not but reflect, that if in the general re-surrection we reässume our 'mortal coil,' what an army of illustrious spirits would rush out of the old Abbey!

'But, premising that we have paid our toll to the gate-keeper, let us advance under the charge of this intelligent old verger. But do n't ask him any questions; it takes up time, and he cannot answer them; he has his lesson by rote, and like HAMLET's grave-digger, 'We must speak by the card, or equivocation will undo us.' Sir ISAAC NEWTON, Sir GODFREY KNELLER, the great Earl of CHATHAM, and his son, England's illustrious minister, WILLIAM PITT, his rival, CHARLES JAMES FOX — General WOLFE! (how the great names crowd about us!) and presently we come to poor ANDRE; but this sounds too much like a catalogue. Kings and queens and princes and dukes are commingled with viler or more illustrious clay. Yonder stands the coronation-chair, in which how many sovereigns have been crowned! It is just as good as new, and will answer the like purpose, if *needed*, these many, many years; and the old stone under it, brought from Scotland in the thirteenth century, will last 'till the crack of doom.' But where are they who sat in that chair! What a soft mellow atmosphere pervades the Abbey! If one were dead he could not feel lonesome here, there is such goodly company, and so many inquirers searching for one, and such a constant reverberation of sound above and around.

'The old verger's monotonous voice arouses us, as in his 'accustomed walk' he is relating how in such a year JOHN JONES, the Duke of SMITH, died and was here buried; as was also the Dutchess his wife, and the little infant, their illustrious offspring; and their figures are all sculptured in high relief in marble, cumbent, with their hands folded across their breast; 'undoubted true portraits,' except that their noses had been knocked off by CROMWELL or his blood-thirsty followers. By the way, CROM-WELL, according to these veritable vergers, committed all the outrages that time, mis-chievous boys and thieves ordinarily do in other countries. There was scarcely a church in England, Scotland, or even *Ireland*, as we afterward found, where CROM-WELL had n't played the very devil; but they are giving him a *statue* in the new houses of Parliament for all that. We could not but observe, in passing along, with what sedulous care some 'Old Mortality' had dug out the brass or silver with which many of the marbles had been inlaid.

''This,' proclaimed the verger, 'is the tomb of JOHN, Lord RUSSELL, son and heir to FRANCIS, Earl of Bedford. And his son FRANCIS by ELIZABETH daughter of ANTHONY COOK, Knight, and widow of Sir THOMAS HOBY, Knight.'

''*Is that Lord John Russell?*' exclaimed a Voice.

'It was strongly nasal, and seemed familiar to my ear; yet I was doubtful of its identity. I only retreated to the periphery of the circle; the crowd were not violently agitated with the anachronism. It might have been that they did not hear it, or hearing, did not heed it. We swept on. Presently we came to the tomb of 'ELIZA-BETH, Countess of Derby, wife of WILLIAM STANLEY, Earl of Derby, eldest daughter of EDWARD DE VERE, Earl of Oxford, grand-daughter of Lord BURLEIGH, who died in 1624.

''*Is that Lord Stanley?*' inquired the same Voice.

'The corn laws and free trade were evidently running in our friend's head, and not chronology. I was certain now of being in the vicinity of a live Yankee. I knew from what direction the voice came; but bashful of a recognition, I avoided turning my eyes to that quarter. The verger resurrectionized one of the SPENCERS; then came the same interrogatory:

" *Is that Lord Spencer ?'*

Now all these old gentlemen and ladies had been very dead for several centuries, and were entirely innocent of knowing any thing at all about Sir ROBERT PEEL, or Lord JOHN RUSSELL, or the corn laws, or free trade ; but ignorance being bliss, I had no idea of disturbing the fancies of my Yankee countrymen or his erudite cicerone ; so after satisfying myself that the anxious inquirer was the identical ' Colonel,' formerly a grocer in my own city, but retired from business, I gave him, as sailors say, ' a wide berth ;' not however until I saw him standing in front of WOLFE's monument, on the façade of which is a bas-relief, representing the storming of the heights of Quebec by that gallant general. He was saying to his listeners : ' I *ben* to that place ; I *seen* that ; I was there two *year* ago ; 't 's a good ways off, that is ; much as three thousand *mild.'*

' Not being anxious to renew an acquaintance temporarily formed with the Colonel in Liverpool, on my arrival there some fortnight before, and my reflections taking a different direction from what they had been on entering, I left the Colonel in undisturbed possession of the Abbey, intending to renew my visit at some future time.'

DEATH-WARNINGS: OR VOICES FROM THE SPIRIT-WORLD. — Our readers will have seen, among the Moslem traditions recorded in these pages by our oriental correspondent, the fact mentioned that dreams are regarded by the inhabitants of the East as often true warnings or indications of future events. This belief of celestial communings with the ' under-world' is well illustrated by the subjoined anecdote, which was related to Mr. LANE, the editor of the ' Illustrated Arabian Nights' at Cairo, shortly after the terrible plague of the year 1835. His authority was a distinguished sheykh, who had taken the trouble to investigate the fact, and had ascertained its truth : ' A tradesman, living in the quarter of El-Hanafee, in Cairo, dreamed during the plague that eleven persons were carried out from his house to be buried, victims of this disease. He awoke in a state of the greatest distress and alarm, reflecting that eleven was the total number of the inhabitants of his house, including himself, and that it would be vain in him to attempt, by adding one or more members to his household, to elude the decree of GOD, and give himself a chance of escape : so, calling together his neighbors, he informed them of his dream, and was counselled to submit with resignation to a fate so plainly foreshown, and to be thankful to GOD for the timely notice with which he had been mercifully favored. On the following day, one of his children died ; a day or two after a wife ; and the pestilence continued its ravages among his family until he remained in his house alone. It was impossible for him now to entertain the slightest doubt of the entire accomplishment of the warning : immediately therefore after the last death that had taken place among his household, he repaired to a friend at a neighboring shop, and calling to him several other persons from the adjoining and opposite shops, he reminded them of his dream, acquainted them with its almost complete fulfilment, and expressed his conviction that he, the eleventh, should very soon die. ' Perhaps,' said he, ' I shall die this next night: I beg of you therefore for GOD's sake to come to my house early to-morrow morning, and the next morning, and the next if necessary, and to see if I be dead, and when dead, that I am properly buried ; for I have no one with me to wash and shroud me. Fail not to do me this service, which will procure you a recompense in heaven. I have bought my grave-linen ; you will find it in a corner of the room in which I sleep. If you find the door of the house latched, and I do not answer to your knocking, break it open.'

' Soon after sunset he laid himself in his lonely bed, though without any expectation of closing his eyes in sleep ; for his mind was absorbed in reflections upon the awful entry into another world, and a review of his past life. As the shades of night gathered around him he could almost fancy that he beheld, in one faint object or another in his gloomy chamber, the dreadful person of the Angel of Death ; and at length he actually perceived a figure gliding in at the door, and approaching his bed. Starting up in horror, he exclaimed, ' Who art thou ?' — and a stern and solemn voice answered :

" ' Be silent ? I am Azrael, the Angel of Death !'

' ' Alas !' cried the terrified man ; ' I testify that there is no deity but God, and I testify that Mohammad is God's apostle ! There is no strength nor power but in God the High the Great ! To God we belong, and to Him we must return !'

' He then covered himself over with his quilt, as if for protection, and lay with throbbing heart, expecting every moment to have his soul torn from him by the inexorable messenger. But moments passed away, and minutes and hours ; yet without his experiencing any hope of escape ; for he imagined that the Angel was waiting for him to resign himself, or had left him for a while, and was occupied in receiving first the souls of the many hundred human beings who had attained their predestined term in that same night and in the same city, and the souls of the thousands who were doomed to employ him elsewhere. Daybreak arrived before his sufferings terminated ; and his neighbours, coming according to their promise, entered his chamber, and found him still in bed ; but observing that he was covered up, and motionless as a corpse, they doubted whether he were still alive, and called to him. He answered, with a faint voice : ' I am not yet dead ; but the Angel of Death came to me in the dusk of the evening, and I expect every moment his return, to take my soul : therefore trouble me not ; but see me washed and buried.'

' ' But why,' said his friends, ' was the street-door left unlatched ?'

' ' I latched it,' he answered, ' but the Angel of Death may have opened it.'

' ' And who,' they asked, ' is the man in the court ?'

' He answered, ' I know of no man in the court : perhaps the Angel who is waiting for my soul has made himself visible to you, and been mistaken, in the twilight, for a man.'

" ' He is a thief,' they said, ' who has gathered together every thing in the house that he could carry away, and has been struck by the plague while doing so, and now lies dead in the court at the foot of the stairs, grasping in his hand a silver candlestick.'

' The master of the house, after hearing this, paused for a moment, and then throwing off his quilt, exclaimed : ' Praise be to God, the Lord of all creatures ! That is the eleventh, and I am safe ! No doubt it was that rascal who came to me and said that he was the Angel of Death. Praise be to God ! Praise be to God !'

' This man survived the plague, and took pleasure in relating the above story. The thief had overheard his conversation with his neighbors, and coming to his house in the dusk, had put his shoulder to the wooden lock, and so raised the door and displaced the latch within. There is nothing wonderful in the dream, nor in its accomplishment ; the plague of 1835 entirely desolated many houses, and was mostly fatal to the young ; and all the inhabitants of the house in question were young excepting the master.'

THE DRAMA.

KING JOHN AT THE PARK-THEATRE. — The great feature of the past month has been the production of *King John*, with such an array of scenery, costume and appointments as quite eclipses Mr. KEAN's late revival of RICHARD the Third. The great fidelity of the dresses and other paraphernalia of the characters; the immense multitude of personages represented, and the faithful views of places and scenery upon which the events of this play transpire, render it altogether a historical picture, wherein are worthily and forcibly portrayed the immortal imaginings of SHAKSPEARE. In the production of this play Mr. CHARLES KEAN has displayed a degree of historical research, a close and scrutinizing investigation of the manners and dress of the middle ages, which would do credit to a professed antiquary ; not that it is a work of great labor to find authority for the mere costumes of the kings, cardinals, and other great personages of the times ; but to dress every character in his fitting garb, from the king on his throne down to the merest lackey and camp-follower ; and this not in his simple garb alone, but with every appointment belonging to the costume ; so that each dress is a study, a perfect picture in itself; defying criticism, even upon its minutest points ; all this requires a refined taste, great study, laborious research and a true love of art for its own sake, to accomplish. There can be no doubt that a certain influence of sundry dollars and cents to accrue upon the succcess of the undertaking had its effect upon the mind of Mr. KEAN and eke upon that of the manager in the production of these expensive SHAKSPERIAN revivals ; but there is good evidence that a higher and nobler inducement had its effect also in urging their accomplishment. Every friend of the true drama, every lover of art, every reader of SHAKSPEARE, every admirer of the beautiful in any shape, must feel grateful to Mr. KEAN and the manager of the Park for the great gratification which they have thus afforded them. It is not necessary at this time to particularize the gorgeous pieces of scenery, or the rich and magnificent or the homely yet faithful dresses and appointments of this production. Every daily journal has told its readers of their wonders, and thousands have feasted their eyes and minds with a sight of them ; but it is always in season to commend good acting, whether performed under the liberal means and appliances that surround the dramatis personæ in ' King JOHN' and RICHARD the Third, or whether portrayed in a barn, with a hay-rack for the King's throne and a horse-blanket for His Majesty's most royal tent ; so we will pretermit the accessories, and speak of the personations of the players.

The great character in this play is the queenly, motherly, sorrowing CONSTANCE. There is but little in words and dialogue even for her to do ; and well it is that there is not more of this affecting, sorrowing vein ; if there was, and it was portrayed by Mrs. KEAN, she would literally drown the stage in tears. A more painfully true piece of acting was surely never witnessed than the CONSTANCE of Mrs. KEAN. It is the vivid truth of nature itself, most masterly expressed. Her whole manner is most touchingly impressive. There is a majesty in her sorrow that bends all before it. She is the very queen of sadness ; her's is a commanding grief, that will not be controlled. When she speaks of her lost ARTHUR, she does it in such sweet accents of grief and love that the most unsympathetic heart pities and grieves with her. A mighty sorrow fills her whole being ; speaks in her eyes and gives out its seeming in every attitude and gesture. Nothing could be more full of majestic sadness than her attitude and accents in the passage:

> ' To me, and to the state of my great grief,
> Let kings assemble ; for my grief 's so great
> That no supporter but the huge firm earth
> Can hold it up. *Here I and Sorrow sit ;*
> *Here is my throne ; let kings come bow to it !'*

In every character in which this great artiste has appeared we ' have been there to see ;' but by none have we been so impressed with her great power as by her personation of CONSTANCE.

KING JOHN himself we consider as a mean, cruel, crafty, and but that he is a king, a very contemptible sort of person ; and all that could be done to keep these peculiarities in all their revolting hideousness before the audience was most successfully accomplished by Mr. KEAN. The scene with HUBERT, the only really great one for the king in the play, was forcibly given, and reminded us somehow most strangely of the elder KEAN. The death in the last act was also painfully impressive ; but the character itself is a feeble one, compared either with CONSTANCE or FALCONBRIDGE, and Mr. CHARLES KEAN certainly does as well with it as its limited scope admits of. Mr. VANDENHOFF'S FALCONBRIDGE deserves the high praise which attends all the personations of this most excellent actor. The bold, careless, soldier-like bearing, the almost reckless independence of the character, was admirably given, and the merry humor of the part was portrayed with all the freedom that belongs to it. It was sparkling, gay and satirical, without descending to farce ; it was full of a quiet, gentlemanly humor, which, although it might not mount up to the broad expectations of the groundlings, could not fail to please the discriminating taste of his audience. Mr. DYOTT's *Hubert* was well sustained, and acted with the discriminating judgment which is always expected from this gentleman. Mr. BASS as *Cardinal Pandulph* delivered his text with all due emphasis and discretion, and was dignified and lofty to a degree ; but connecting Mr. BASS as we always do with something exceedingly comic, the contrast of the austere demeanor of the Pope's Holy Legate and the quips and quirks of merry *Jack Falstaff*, came very unfairly and provokingly to the mind, somewhat to the prejudice of a just appreciation of his merits as the Cardinal. Mrs. Abbot played the Queen Mother well ; but to our thinking this lady is altogether too amiable in disposition and too handsome in person to represent faithfully the character of this abominable she-wolf. Miss DENNY played the part of *Arthur* to admiration. Her naiveté and innocent manner throughout her scene with Hubert was touchingly pathetic, and evinced a wonderful degree of talent and judgment for so youthful an aspirant. Mr. STARK as *The Dauphin*, bating some starchiness of manner, got through his part with credit. In short, the play altogether is brought upon the stage, and represented there by all engaged in it, in a manner that makes it a most intellectual treat to witness, and one which will be treasured up to be enjoyed hereafter as a ' most sweet remembrance.' . . . . THAT charming danseuse, Madame AUGUSTA, contrary to expectation, has given her friends an opportunity of enjoying her exquisite performances for a few nights at the Opera House. Great as has been the admiration which has always heretofore attended AUGUSTA, it has been increased many fold during this short engagement. With all the lightness of one of the divine Peris of song, she adds a grace as bewitching and angelic as any that floated in the imagination of MOORE when he dressed his gay immortals. But in plain prose, our Queen of the Dance has improved greatly since her last appearance in this country ;

and this is saying much, where there appeared so little room for addition. As a graceful artiste in the pantomime of the ballet, Augusta has never had but one equal. She seems to speak with her eyes and fingers, and every motion of her graceful frame, as eloquently as the most famous histrion in words. But it is the graceful fairy-like lightness of her steps that charms and wins all hearts toward her. She floats along the scene as if she spurned the ground beneath her, or as if the occasional touch of her tiny foot to the grovelling earth was merely a submission to custom, and not at all necessary to sustain her airy form in its passage. There is nothing of the earth about her; all is spiritual and sylph-like, as if she had just flown down from the spirit-land to glide for a moment before the wondering eyes of mortals, a thing of airy light, and then to fade away again like the bright spirit of a happy dream. But Beranger, with his pencil of light, has drawn her portraiture, and here it is:

> 'Oui, vous naissez au sein des roses,
> Fils de l'Aurore et des zephyrs;
> Vos brillautes metamorphoses
> Sont le secret de nos plaisirs.
> D'un souffle vous séchez nos larmes;
> Vous epurez l'azur des cieux:
> J'en crois ma Sylphide et ses charmes,
> Sylphes légers, soyez mes dieux!'

Gossip with Readers and Correspondents. — 'Well, here we are *again!*' at the end of our twenty-eighth volume; and on the first of next month we 'shall have the honor of appearing before you' with the first number of our *Twenty-Ninth Volume.* If you did not *know* us, reader; if we had not been companions for so many years; and if we thought there was any *necessity* for so doing, we might entertain you with a long list of attractive promises, impossible of fulfilment; but 'being that circumstances are as they are,' we shall do no such thing. This much only we *do* say, that our port-folios are full of most acceptable matériel; that we have an unapproachable corps of contributors of whom we are not more proud than our readers themselves; and that beside matter in hand we have articles engaged from the pens of some of the first writers in the land; and with these facts our readers will soon be made acquainted, 'by the seeing of the eye and the understanding of the heart.' Grateful for long-continued and increasing patronage, we have pleasure, by way of reciprocity, in assuring our readers, that in the quality and variety of literary viands, in neatness and beauty of typographical execution, and in early and secure transmission, we anticipate remaining in no respect behind the best of our contemporaries. 'And farther this deponent sayeth not.' . . . '*Sweepings from the Study of a Septuagenary*' contain many excellent things. We subjoin the following: 'Time has no identity. It is a fiction in philosophy, which represents passing events; and the annual revolution of our earth, with the return of the seasons, are its exponents. Time is to eternity what space is to matter; hence Time, Destiny and Fate are fictions which may flourish in poetic fancy and philosophical abstractions, but have no identity in physical reality. The following poetic sonnet on Time, Fame and Oblivion is a fine imitation of the Italian by Dante, from the pen of Mr. Edward Coxe, of Hampstead Heath, Middlesex, London; and affords a rich specimen of the copious beauty and poetic power of the English tongue:

> 'I asked of Time for whom those temples rose,
> That prostrate by his hand in silence lie?
> His lips disdained the mystery to disclose,
> And borne on swifter wing, he hurried by.

> These broken columns whose? I asked of Fame;
> (Her kindling breath gives life to works sublime;)
> With downcast look of mingled grief and shame,
> She heaved th' uncertain sigh, and followed TIME.
> Wrapt in amazement, o'er the mouldering pile
> I saw OBLIVION pass, with giant stride:
> And while his visage wore Pride's scornful smile,
> 'Haply *thou* know'st; then tell me whose!' I cried;
> 'Whose these vast domes, that e'en in ruin shine?'
> 'I reck not whose,' he said, 'they now are *mine!*'

IN the following graphic delineation, Destiny and Fate are to be considered as imaginary agents, placed out of connection with realities. To draw aside the veil which covers such gloomy abstractions, representing in their place poetic flowers, might injure the nice texture of fancy, and only convey absurd contradictions instead of healthful truth. Here are fine thoughts ' On contemplating a Starlight Night:' 'Ye mystic lights! ye worlds beyond worlds! incalculable — infinite! rolling forever at immeasurable distances from our petty sea of mortality, as wave after wave we fret out our little life, then sink into the dark abyss! Can we look upon you, ye bright defiers of rest, note your appointed order and your unvarying course, and not feel that we are indeed the poorest puppets of an all-pervading and resistless Destiny? Shall we see throughout the universe each orb fulfilling its preördered course; no wandering from its orbit; no variations in its seasons; and yet imagine the great ARCH-ORDAINER will hold back the tides he has sent from their unforeseen source at our miserable bidding! Shall we think that our prayers can avert a doom interwoven in the web of events, when to change a particle of our fate might change the fate of millions? Shall the link forsake the chain, and yet the chain remain unbroken? Away then with your vague repinings and blind demands! All must on to the goal. The colors of your existence, your crimes and your sorrows, were doomed before your birth. Millions of ages back, when this hoary earth was peopled with other kinds; yea, before its atoms had formed one layer of its present surface, destiny had fixed the moment of our birth and the limits of our career!' These thoughts may be vague, yet they are forcible. · · · WE came across recently, in looking over the extensive correspondence of the late lamented ' OLLAPOD,' (of which more hereafter,) the following remarks, addressed to a hypercritical reviewer of his ' Spirit of Life,' who among other things had taken exception to the terms here italicised:

> 'WHERE the *sere blooms of man's decline* are shed,
> And sterile snows the brow of age o'erspread;'

and to the last line of the following passage, farther on in the poem:

> 'WHILE leaves and birds and streams their songs attune,
> And steep'd in music, smiles the rose of June;
> Making the freighted bliss it scatters there
> Seem like *the breathings of ambrosial air.*'

' The reviewer,' says OLLAPOD, 'asks ' What are the blooms of man's decline?' A yankee might reply by calling them withered flowers. When SHAKSPEARE made one of his heroes say that his way of life had fallen into ' the sere and yellow leaf,' he meant the sere blooms of his decline — precisely. There is no getting over the meaning, or changing the propriety of the phrase. It exceeds no poetic license, and is perfectly defensible. You seem, Sir, to have been marvellously puzzled with the lines:

> ' Making the freighted bliss it scatters there
> Seem like the breathings of ambrosial air;'

but if you had read the best English and American poets attentively, your wonderment would have ceased, and your enlarged comprehension grasped the emblem. You confess you do not know what ambrosial air is. MILTON tells you. When EVE stood in Eden by the Tree of Knowledge, she saw

> 'One shaped and winged like one of those from Heaven;
>   •   •   his dewy locks *distilled*
> *Ambrosia.*'

'Now what was this but fragrant air? Was it oil that they dropped? What did they distil? Actual fruit, think you? When the lady in SOLOMON's song got up to open to her beloved, think you that her fingers dropped *real* myrrh upon the handles of the lock? or was it the odor only which she left around them? Let me refer you to the precedent set me, though only seen of late, by an American poet, HILLHOUSE. In his noble 'Hadad' occurs the following colloquy between two cherubs:

> SECOND CHERUB.   •   •   •   'Methinks
> A sudden sweetness fills the air around me.'
> FIRST CHERUB. '*Ambrosial.* It betokens some blest presence.'

'Now what is that but air? We say the air is foul, when the pestilence is abroad. MILTON makes 'sewers *perfume* the air;' and if one cannot say *ambrosial* air with the most perfect propriety, then never was poetic simile or phrase defensible.' —— THE following amusing anecdote was jotted down on the same paper, with the evident intention of introducing it into the '*Ollapodiana.*' It was of a scene in an English court of justice, wherein three parties, a poor man, his wife, and a boy of seven years, appeared before 'His Worship,' to explain why it was that a donkey belonging to the family had been so unmercifully beaten as to bring them in jeopardy of the penalty attached to the offence of cruelty to animals. 'The man denied that the donkey had been abused; he said he had 'too much respect for the poor dumb hanimal,' and requested that the alleged sufferer might be sent for. The donkey being at the door, it was ordered by the magistrates to be brought to the bar and examined. The long-eared witness walked into the office with a look of profound gravity, and put its head meekly over the bar. Its sleek condition and freedom from bruises was soon established. The owner was overjoyed at his dismissal. 'My donkey,' said he, 'is in a slap-up condition, and I takes a pride in keeping on him so. LORD love your worship! he's never wolloped more nor vot does him good; he's just like von of my family, and as fond as a baby. I can't see no difference atwixt *him and von of my hown!*' · · · WE have been reflecting (while wafering a blank strip of paper upon the above, whereon to pursue our gossippings,) upon the power of association connected with the familiar hand-writing of a departed friend. 'The hand which traced it may lie, cold and forgotten dust, in the grave; it may have become

> 'An empty sound,
> To which no living thing lays claim;'

but its magic power remains. We feel, while we look on it, that we behold the certain and visible stamp and impress of a human existence, since passed away like a shadow from the earth.' That silent page makes oath to us that a being *was*, with health, strength and reason; who hoped like ourselves, laughed like ourselves, and breathed the air we breathe: '*C'est une étinecelle de sa vie;*' a spark which burns on after the lamp of life is extinguished; a moment of the human energy of body and soul, saved from the blank of a passed existence. · · · WE have been scrutinizing, for the last half-hour, a miniature of our friend and occasional correspondent, Professor JAMES J. MAPES, by Mr. OFFICER, an artist who has no superior among us in the line of his profession. We never saw a more perfect likeness, or a more soft and admirably-colored painting. There is not a touch of the *pencil* to be seen on the entire surface of the picture. Apropos of Prof. MAPES: our readers will be glad, and not at all surprised, to hear that this gentleman, who never yet lost an opportunity of doing a kindness to the gifted and the deserving, has been triumphantly acquitted of certain *uncertain* charges which were recently prosecuted against him by a mercantile firm in the city of Philadelphia. The abundant testimony of long-established personal character which he adduced, from the first sources in this metropolis, as well as the utter failure of the prosecuting parties to make out their case, must have had weight with the jury in inducing them, in their verdict of honorable acquittal, to throw the entire costs upon the county. · · · 'THE Night-wind in Autumn!' exclaims a new and clever correspondent, (E. C. HINE,) 'the night-wind in Autumn! it has a sweet but melancholy voice, as it comes hovering around your casement in the dark solemn midnight, and seizes with its unseen hand upon the rustling curtain of your apartment, swaying it aside, looking in upon your couch, and muttering something in an unknown tongue; and then, because you cannot understand it, it goes sighing and moaning away! It is a requiem for the dying year. 'T is the Spirit of Summer, that still lingers around the graves of the flowers, bewailing the lovely ones that have perished forever. The night-wind! It has wandered amid the silent church-yards, bearing with it their spectral meteor-lights, that it might read the inscriptions on the white stones that watch above the dead. The night-wind in Autumn! Listen to its plaintive voice, as it steals softly along to its unknown goal :

'T is the voice of a spirit that whispers at night,
Of a fond one who faded away from thy sight;
'T is a messenger sent to this cold world of pain,
To tell thee that loved one shall meet thee again!

''T is the low plaintive night-wind! O, list to its strain!
Like the music that floats, o'er the moon-lighted main,
From a bark of the dead; even thus to thine ear
It murmuring comes, from the grave of the year!

'That voice to the night-wind of Autumn is given,
To warn us of DEATH and to tell us of Heaven;
And sweet as the sound of a bright seraph's wings,
When hov'ring around us, the song that it sings!'

IT might, without any impropriety, be inscribed with '*Imperator*,' that gigantic car which towers aloft with all its golden embellishments, on the melancholy site of the late 'NIBLO's Theatre' in Broadway, reminding one, not of any lesser ovation, but of the gorgeous Roman 'triumph,' at what time the victorious generals came in from the East, to Rome, the 'mistress of the world,' with treasures and princes captives, to adorn their train. Eager hearts are beating with curiosity to behold the *opima spolia* heralded by a big-wheeled chariot such as this. Nor does the illusion vanish at the blast and flourish of many brazen instruments, which play proudly a 'grand march,' spirit-stirring, and expressive of the march of empire; while slowly, with majestic footstep, comes in the Elephant of Siam, surmounted with the tower which once bristled with the spears of warriors, but is now resplendent with the light of woman's eyes. 'Hail Columbia, happy land!' Cast your eyes around the area, not quite so large as that which used to drink the blood of gladiators, and to resound with the bellowing of beasts; yet the beasts are there, in all the sleekness and beauty of their savage natures; various, and of greater or lesser fury; yet domineered over and subjected to the nobler man; just as the brutal passions of the man himself are governed by the nobler reason. There crouches in his lair, at perfect rest, the Lion of Numidia; magnificent, with his vast head, and manner full of royalty. There moves, with distinguished gracefulness, the leopard, which cannot change its spots, (except by leaving one spot and going to another,) and would be deprived of a large share of its beauty if it did. There stands the wolf, to whose class HORACE recalls us, as the memory of his ode comes down to us from school-boy days; and especially of that loving adventurer, who was shielded from one in the Sabine wood, (as he sang his own LALACE) by the guardianship and charm of native Innocence. Very few men have been shielded from wild beasts by the power of purity, since the fall of man. A feeling of insecurity still creeps over you, as you look through the massive bars of the cages which cramp the monarchs of the forest. Will they not make one grand strike for freedom? And then what will become of the motley crowd who are looking at the monkey in the ring? No doubt they will form an example of the brittleness of human bones; cracked up in the jaws of monsters with the celerity of a big icicle hit with a broom-stick. A feeling of anxiety may have come over you as you have laid down to rest over a big boiler of four hundred horse power; and if the explosive spirit should burst the bars and nails which clamp the strong cage, what will become of the sleeper? But think of that rush of fiery spirit, elephant, tiger, lion, zebra and hyena-power, bursting forth to tear the cuticle, to roar, hiss and throw up into the air the unresisting victims! Such an event is too terrible even to think of; we will therefore set it down as impossible; at any rate 'dismiss the subject as unpleasant.' To pass over the pleasure of an intellectual and rational man in such a collection of wild beasts as we now allude to, there are one or two objects of so ludicrous a nature as to attract the attention of most spectators. What a curious bird is that stork! Can it be possible that *he* is the bird quoted in the spelling-book (with picture to match) for filial piety? Standing on one leg, and quite uncertain what to do with the other; with a flat bald head, and a blinking eye which winks upward, and a horridly clumsy bill, as long as your arm. Altogether, he is as gawky as a clown at Almack's. With a slow motion he turns around from presenting his side to face the spectator. Dear bird! that does not alter you for the better. You *are* ugly, and 'no mistake;' calling to mind that departed flamingo of the Bowling-Green, lately celebrated by poor CHIPMAN in these pages:

> 'Oh! have you ever ever seen a long-legged flamingo?
> Oh! have you ever seen in the water him go?
> Oh yes! at the Bowling-Green I've seen a long-legged flamingo!
> Oh yes! at the Bowling Green I've seen in the water him go!'

We might mention the numerous company of parrots, paroquettes, and cockatoos, quietly seated on perches, with their green and gorgeous plumage so strongly contrasting with this ungainly bird; and indeed ornithology is an agreeable study, as the great JONES said when he inspected the cabinet of minerals. But we are startled from this contemplation by a roar as terrible as ever resounded in the great woods. It may be compared, though in a peculiar sense, to that voice which VIRGIL mentions as belonging to the ghosts in Tartarus. Was n't it a *voice?* — or to translate in a new fashion, *vox et preterea nihil?* 'It warn't nothin' else,' we heard it 'correctly observed.' The cause of all this is the gentle thrusting of an iron bar into the cage of a tiger, who has taken it into his head to fall out and fight with one of his fellows. 'BILL!' quoth the keeper, 'what yer beöut?' The kind salutation of the iron bar produces its effect, and 'Bill's' growl subsides. Next to 'horsemanship' and 'still vaulting' by the monkey, perhaps the most interesting exhibition is that of the great

American Anaconda; the keeper wearing him around his neck, and introducing him in a set speech, as thus: 'Ladies *and* gentlemen: This is the great South American Anaconda; of vast size and growing into a warm climate. He feeds on rabbits as well as birds of that nature, besides whatever he can git — if they falls in his way; as is very liable — especially in those climates, which are very healthy for invalids, especially consumptives. His skin as you see is speckled on the back and on the belly; either one — it makes no matter which. He will fast three weeks, but sometimes I have known him to do it three months without eating any thing, or rather two rabbits, which takes him several days. That there is p'ison in the fork of his tongue is a vulgar error; for his muscular power is at the end of his tail, which he swings with great energy, and crushes his victim. He is of greater or less longevity, but as he never ceases to grow as long as he lives there is no criterion for his life.' But the more intense interest is reserved for the last act of an entertainment which ought to be seen by every man, woman, or child, who would be instructed by the glorious works of nature. It is the acting upon a narrow stage, where the curtain is ever down, yet of so coarse a texture that you behold the actors upon the scene. *Dramatis personæ,* lion, tiger, leopard, panther, bear, wolf, man — the characters in full dress, the leopard especially in a very rich and brilliant costume; the man also vying in the splendor of his tunic; but the lion we think more respectably dressed in the main. The exits are numerous; the single combats furious; the alarums many; passions are torn to tatters; but above all, the illusions of the ordinary theatre set at nought by the vision, fleeting yet true, of a lion harnessed to a chariot, such as you have seen graven on ancient gems. The whole piece closes happily and with affectionate embraces. *Vivat Republica!* Proceed at once to RAYMOND and WARING's menagerie, and verify the foregoing description. . . . 'Do not the undeniable revelations of Mesmerism,' asks a Boston correspondent, 'warrant the belief that no long time will elapse before 'coming events' may be predicted with almost unerring certainty?' The answer is obvious; but even if such a thing *were* possible, it could not be desirable. Well is it that, from infancy to the grave, clouds and darkness hang around the future:

'WHEN another life is added
　To the heaving turbid mass:
When another breath of being
　Stains creation's tarnished glass:
When the first cry, weak and piteous,
　Heralds long-enduring pain,
And a soul from non-existence
　Springs, that ne'er can die again;
When the mother's passionate welcome
　Sorrow-like bursts forth in tears,
And the sire's self-gratulation
　Prophecies of future years —
　　It is well we cannot see
　　What the end shall be.

'When across the infant features
　Trembles the faint dawn of mind;
When the heart looks from the windows
　Of the eyes that were so blind;
When the incoherent murmurs
　Syllable each swaddled thought,
To the fond ear of affection
　With a boundless promise fraught,
Kindling great hopes for to-morrow
　From that dull uncertain ray,
As by glimmering of the twilight
　Is foreshown the perfect day—
　　It is well we cannot see
　　What the end shall be.

'When the youth beside the maiden
　Looks into her credulous eyes;
When the heart upon the surface
　Shines too happy to be wise;
He by speeches less than gestures
　Hinteth what her hopes expound,
Laying out the waste hereafter
　Like enchanted garden-ground;
He may palter—so do many,
　She may suffer—so must all;
Both may yet, world-disappointed,
　This lost hour of love recall—
　　It is well we cannot see
　　What the end shall be.

'When the altar of religion
　Greets the expectant bridal pair;
When the vow that lasts till dying
　Vibrates on the sacred air:
When man's lavish protestations
　Doubt of after-change defy,
Comforting the frailer spirit,
　Bound his servitor for aye;
When beneath love's silver moonbeams
　Many rocks in shadow sleep,
Undiscovered till possession
　Shows the dangers of the deep—
　　It is well we cannot see
　　What the end shall be.'

OUR old friend ANDREW STEVENS, we are glad to perceive, has returned to us from Virginia, and resumed his manufacture of fine jewelry, and the supplying and re-setting of diamonds, pearls, etc., in the rear building of Number 183, Broadway, up stairs. We can state, of our own knowledge, derived from a long acquaintance with Mr. STEVENS, that for chaste and correct taste in re-setting precious stones, gems and cameos, of the antique or modern school, he cannot be surpassed; and one reason of this is, that every thing is executed by himself, or under his immediate supervision. Any of our readers, ladies or gentlemen of taste or *vertu*, who may require the facile skill of Mr. STEVENS, will have occasion to thank us for advising them of his where-about, which we may add is in a very central situation, but a door or so from MAR-QUAND'S. . . . A FRIEND of ours, walking thoughtfully along the Third Avenue recently, on a pleasant Sunday, was much struck, and not a little amused, by ' *The B'hoys*,' returning from their Sunday drives, with all sorts of steeds and vehicles, in the former of which they are especially wise. A true 'B'hoy' 'knows vat an 'oss is; he 's not a hass, *he* aint.' We heard one complaining the other day to a livery-stable keeper of the animal that had been 'let' to him: 'I told yer I wanted a twelve-mile horse; and you guv me——' 'Well, *warn't* he a twelve-mile 'orse?' 'Yes, *he* was, and nothin' else! We could n't get *another* mile out of him, nohow. W'y did n't you give me as good a animal as you did BILL SYKES — sa-ay?' 'I did.' 'You *did n't*; BILL's went over thirteen mild, 'fore he dropped.' 'Well, he had a peck more oats, than your'n. Oh! he *did*, did he? Well, you 'll get no more of my cus-tom, old mutton-head, that 's all!' . . . MRS. MOWATT has left the city on a tour to the south, to fulfil engagements in the various theatres at Charleston, Mobile, New-Orleans, etc.; thence she visits most of the western cities. She is accompanied by Mr. EDWARD L. DAVENPORT, a very promising young actor, who is winning golden opinions wherever he appears. . . . '*Parental Government*' would be an excellent paper for Mrs. ALLEN's admirable '*Mothers' Journal.*' It is conceived in the right spirit, and well written. These lines, quoted in it, are worthy to be recorded in letters of gold:

'SPEAK gently : love doth whisper low
    The vows that true hearts bind ;
And gently friendship's accents flow,
    Affection's voice is kind.

'Speak gently to the little child,
    Its love be sure to gain ;
Teach it, in accents soft and mild,
    It may not long remain.

'Speak gently to the young, for they
    Will have enough to bear ;
Pass through this life as best they may,
    'T is full of anxious care.

'Speak gently to the aged one,
    Grieve not the care-worn heart ;
Their sands of life are nearly run —
    Let such in peace depart.

'Speak gently, kindly to the poor,
    Let no harsh tone be heard ;
They have enough they must endure,
    Without an unkind word.

'Speak gently to the erring ; know
    They must have toiled in vain ;
Perchance unkindness made them so —
    Oh! win them back again !

'Speak gently ! HE who gave his life
    To bend man's stubborn will,
When elements were fierce with strife,
    Said to them, 'Peace! be still !'

'Speak gently ! 't is a little thing
    Dropped in the heart's deep well ;
The good, the joy which it may bring,
    Eternity shall tell !'

THE Anniversary Festival of our good *Saint Nicholas*, (blessings on his memory!) will take place on the seventh instant at the City-Hotel. Arrangements have been made to have it one of the very best of these annual gatherings. On the same day the Rev. Dr. DEWITT will deliver at the old Dutch church the usual anniversary address. It will be a rare treat, and should be attended by all good KNICKERBOCK-ERS. . . . How much the public are indebted to Messrs. CAREY AND HART, Philadelphia, for their beautiful illustrated editions of the writings of our best American poets! We have already had a superb edition of LONGFELLOW's poetical works, and now we have a still more elegant volume, in the '*Poems by William Cullen Bryant, with Illustrations,*' engraved by American artists. It has *twenty* most admirable engravings on steel, after pictures by that true child of genius, LEUTZE, including a most faithful likeness of BRYANT, from the pencil and burin of the Brothers CHENEY. Of these we shall speak more at large hereafter. The collection of the poems is large and complete ; the paper and printing are worthy of the most distinguished English press ; every thing in short about the book, external and internal, is *beautiful.* It must have an unwontedly large sale. What a gift-book it will be! · · · DID you ever know a case of decided *Twaddlum,* reader? We never did ; but FIELD, of the ' St. Louis Réveille,' describes one :

'DOCTOR,' said a young and enthusiastic new-school physician the other day to an elder and more experienced practitioner of the same system, (he happened to be within ear-shot at the time of a *regular,*) ' Doctor,' said he, 'you have experience, and I wish to consult you with regard to a case of *Twaddlum.*'
'Proceed, my young friend,' said the man of experience.
' Well then, Doctor, I have a female patient who has a derangement of the *twaddlum* of her stomach, occasioned, as I think, by a warring of ulcers against the veins. I give her pills and relieve the twaddlum, but this invariably increases the action of the ulcers.'
' Ah!' interjected the elder Experience.
' Well, then again, Doctor, I give her *more* pills, and subdue the action of the ulcers ; but this again produces greater derangement of the twaddlum ; and so it goes on, the twaddlum ag'in the ulcers and the ulcers ag'in the twaddlum, and the pills g'in out too, and no good done.'
' Ah! my young friend, you do n't understand these cases : I have perhaps had more cases of *twaddlum* than you have met with.'

And here he went into a minute explanation of the entire case ; but the ' notes' were lost. Physician's fees, by-the-by, are sometimes for complaints quite as ima-ginary as ' the twaddlum.' An anecdote is related of an English clothier, who, after long drinking the Bath waters, took it into his head to try the Bristol hot wells. He procured from his physician a letter to a brother GALEN, stating his case, etc. ; but after he had proceeded half way on his journey, his curiosity induced him to pry into the contents of the letter, when the following words presented themselves to his astonished vision : ' Dear Sir : The bearer is a fat Wiltshire clothier ; make the most of him !' It is needless to add that his cure was at once effected, and he immediately turned his horse toward home, ' a sadder and a wiser man.' · · · IT was most especially cool in Mr. (or Miss) E. DENTON to send us ' *Thoughts of the Season ;*' as if *we* should not at once discover that the second and third verses were bare-faced plagiarisms from these two stanzas of ' W. G. C.,' in his well-known lines to October :

' I LOOK to Nature and behold
 My life's dim emblems rustling round,
In hues of crimson and of gold,
 The year's dead honors on the ground :
And sighing with the winds, I feel,
 While their low pinions murmur by,
How much their sweeping tones reveal
 Of life and human destiny.

' When Spring's delightsome moments shone,
 They came in zephyrs from the west :
They bore the wood-lark's melting tone,
 They stirred the blue lake's glassy breast ;
Though Summer, fainting in the heat,
 They lingered in the forest shade ;
But changed and strengthened now, they beat
 In storm, o'er mountain, glen and glade.'

Perhaps our would-be correspondent never saw the foregoing stanzas before? ' Oh, no! by no means ; oh, certainly not !' · · · WE ask for Mr. LEONARD, the Irish comedian, who is now on a professional tour to the South and West, the atten-tions and good offices of our friends in those regions. Mr. LEONARD is a gentleman of education, a most worthy man, and the nearest akin to POWER of any actor who has undertaken the parts of that lamented comedian. · · · THE following parody was found inscribed on the newspaper-board of a ' lunch-house' in Saint Louis, Missouri,

The excellence of the sentiment may perhaps excuse the liberty which the writer has taken with a well-known sacred melody :

'I WOULD not drink alway; I ask not for punch,
Where crowds at eleven are gathered to lunch;
The few hasty toddies I 've had at the bar
Are enough for one morning — I 'll light my cigar!

'Who, who would drink alway, away from his wife ?
Away from his children, the solace of life ?
When his home is illumin'd and glowing with love,
And the honeymoon's lustre eternal shall prove ?

'There his pledges of love all in harmony meet,
Euraptur'd their father's lov'd presence to greet;
And the tears of rejoicing unbidden may start,
For the smile of his MARY 's the feast of the heart!'

—

A FRIEND of ours, who is trying the water-cure at New-Lebanon, writes us : ' It seems a mighty hard place for *a gentleman*, this establishment. Sometimes I feel as though I was the inmate of a lunatic asylum. At table, the food and appearance of the guests forces very strongly upon me the unpleasant supposition that I am in a penitentiary, and nothing but the rectitude of my conscience relieves the effect of such an impression. At other moments I am convinced that I am in a public hospital. But for the sake of health I am willing to endure every thing. In two or three weeks I hope I shall know my fate, so far as water is concerned. . . . WE quite agree with ' R. W. H., Jr.' that mob law, in *any* case, is to be greatly deprecated. Mobs may sometimes *reason* rightly, but they always *act* wrong. Still, as to the work to which ' R. W. H., Jr.,' refers, we hold that if what is there set down as true, *be* veritable, then are the animadversions upon them neither undeserved nor too strong. Are we not right ? . . . ON the hill which overlooks the town of Plymouth (Mass.) and the sea, is the old burying-ground, where sleep in the barren soil the ancient Pilgrim Fathers. At a mile distant, in a beautiful grove, is the modern cemetery, with its marble monuments, which gave rise to the following epigram :

'THE rude forefathers of the hamlet sleep
Where scanty grass is picked by famished sheep ;
Within yon shade, beneath those marble stones,
We, their descendants, lay our polished bones.'

—

' HALL's newly-invented ' *Hydrostatic Ink-Fountain*' seems to us one of the most perfect inventions of the kind we have ever seen. The flowing of the ink is free ; it is preserved always clear and pure, and uninfluenced by atmospheric air; the fountain, if overturned, will not spill its contents; and *altogether*, the 'Hydrostatic Fountain,' with its convenient receptacles for pens, etc., completely supplies a very important desideratum. They are manufactured by Messrs. THOMAS WILDE AND COMPANY, No. 30, Old Slip. . . . OUR friend DEMPSTER, at the last advices, was at Liverpool, where he had given two concerts, with a success not exceeded by any of his ' illustrious compeers.' His houses were truly excellent, and his songs received with great applause, and honored with *encores*. He had previously at Aberdeen, near his native place, given two entertainments, which like those at Liverpool were fully attended by enthusiastic auditors. ' The May-Queen,' with many other of his fine musical compositions, are cordially commended by the public journals of Aberdeen and Liverpool. Mr. DEMPSTER's continued success is quite certain. . . . 'A zealous person,' writes a correspondent, ' was recently arguing fiercely with a Methodist minister hereabout, concerning some knotty points of faith ; and the better to support his position, quoted Scripture. 'Well, truly,' said the disciple of WESLEY, nothing confounded, 'if JESUS said that, it must have been when he was a very young man, and did n't know much about those things !' . . . SEVERAL notices of new publications, with four pages of gossipry, including many explanatory words to correspondents, are unavoidably omitted till our next number.

LITERARY RECORD.—Our '*Literary Record*,' for causes elsewhere stated, must be brief this month. From Messrs. LEA AND BLANCHARD we have '*Legends and Stories of Ireland*,' by SAMUEL LOVER, Esq., complete from the author's last revised London edition; with illustrations by W. HARVEY and the AUTHOR. Here are some twenty-five capital sketches, many of them admirably illustrated, including among them 'The Gridiron,' 'The White Horse of the Peppers' and other equally well-established favorites, and all for *fifty cents*. The same publishers have issued the ninth volume of their '*Lives of the Queens of England from the Norman Conquest*,' an authentic and valuable work. · · · MESSRS. HARPER AND BROTHERS' latest publications are, '*Salkeld's Compendium of Roman and Grecian Antiquities*,' with a sketch of Ancient Mythology; a revised and enlarged '*History of the American Revolution*,' with several numbers of those excellent serials, the 'Pictorial SHAKSPEARE' and the 'Pictorial History of England.' · · · FROM Messrs. WILEY AND PUTNAM we have CARLYLE'S '*Sartor Resartus*,' a work too well known to require comment; '*Poetry of Wit and Humor*,' by LEIGH HUNT, a volume of which we purpose to speak hereafter; and the best American edition yet issued of DICKENS'S '*Dombey and Son*,' and the only well-printed one, we believe. · · · Messrs. D. APPLETON AND COMPANY have published several new works, for the which we must refer our readers to their catalogue, accompanying the present number. · · · H. LONG AND BROTHER give us '*Woman's Reward*,' a novel by Hon. Mrs. NORTON; a work which attracts much attention, from the fact that it is supposed to embody many scenes and events in the real life of the gifted author. . . . MESSRS. BAKER AND SCRIBNER have published a volume entitled 'The *Sacred Mountains*,' by J. T. HEADLEY. It is highly commended by the metropolitan press. · · · WE have also from Messrs. LEA AND BLANCHARD, in one volume, all of DICKENS' '*Christmas Stories*,' and his '*Pictures from Italy*;' and in numbers, his '*Dombey and Son*,' with illustrations. Of the 'Small Books on Great Subjects,' of these publishers, we have two issues, namely : '*A Brief View of Greek Philosophy*,' from SOCRATES to CHRIST, and '*Christian Sects in the Nineteenth Century*.' · · · WE have received from Mr. GEORGE VIRTUE, 26 John-street, the first two numbers of a very superbly-illustrated '*Devotional Family Bible*.' The paper and printing are of the first order of excellence, and the engravings unsurpassed. The whole is accompanied by notes from the Rev. ALEXANDER FLETCHER, A. M., author of the 'Guide to Family Devotion,' etc. · · · THE following tribute to the merits of '*Hazen's Grammatic Reader*' is from the pen of Mr. ROBERT CHAMBERS, in a letter to a friend in this city: 'The New-York school-book which was sent me by the publisher through you, astonishes me by the beauty of the typography and wood-engravings. Just to-day I found one of our people showing it to the MARQUIS OF STAFFORD, as he was going through the office as a visitor. We were all remarking that even VAN VOORST'S books of natural history, which stand so high in respect of wood-engraving, do not excel this little series of books.' · · · · 'COSMO-PHONOGRAPHY,' a voluminous work, *edited* by Prof. GOURAUD, and soon to be published, we are informed is not a system of 'Phonography,' crowded with all sorts of difficulties, like that which has of late made its reäppearance in the world under the name of *Phonotypy*, which assumes to reform, but in reality caricatures, the English language. Mr. GOURAUD 'protests formally' against any supposition that he has in view the 'reformation' of any language whatever, 'and especially of that in which ADDISON, POPE, BYRON and others have raised our Anglo-Saxon literature to a level with that of classical Greece and Rome.' This achievement 'he leaves to the JOHNSONS, WALKERS and WEBSTERS of coming ages; or rather to the old man Time, that remorseless reformer of all reformable things.' The Professor's System has a wider and much more practical aim than this. It will apply not to a single nation, but to all nations, as is implied by its comprehensive title: '*Cosmophonography*: a *system of writing with mathematical exactness the pronunciation* of any spoken language in the world.' The work will contain written specimens of its adaptation to over one hundred different languages, with their original typography; while the immediate application of this extraordinary system 'for learning languages' takes hold of no less than the English, the French, the German, the Spanish, the Italian, the Portuguese, and incidentally, of the Latin and the Greek. If the author fulfils his plan, his work must prove to be a great and most extraordinary philological production.

THE

Knickerbocker.

BOUND VOLUMES.

28

CONTAINING CONTRIBUTIONS FROM

WASHINGTON IRVING,
FITZ GREENE HALLECK,
J. K. PAULDING,
Sir E. L. BULWER,
JAMES G. PERCIVAL,
NATH. HAWTHORNE,
Dr. O. W. HOLMES,
Rev. J. PIERPONT,
RICHARD B. KIMBALL, Esq.,
Prof. CHARLES ANTHON,
W. H. C. HOSMER,
WILLIAM NORTH,
DONALD McLEOD,

WILLIAM C. BRYANT,
Prof. H. W. LONGFELLOW,
Hon. LEWIS CASS,
J. H. PRESCOTT, Esq.,
Gov. W. H. SEWARD,
Rev. Dr. BETHUNE,
THOS. W. PARSONS,
JOHN T. IRVING,
PARK BENJAMIN,
ALFRED B. STREET,
WM. H. C. PALMER,
JOHN P. BROWN,
JAMES LINEN, Etc.

WITH THE INIMITABLE TABLES OF

LOUIS GAYLORD CLARK, Editor

☞ For No. of Vol., *vide* Index. ☜

NEW-YORK:

JOHN A. GRAY, 16 & 18 JACOB STREET.

DEXTER & BROTHER,
SOLE AGENT FOR THE UNITED STATES.

LONDON: John Chapman, 142 Strand.

POPULAR LECTURES

ON

SCIENCE AND ART;

DELIVERED IN THE

CHIEF CITIES AND TOWNS IN THE UNITED STATES,

BY DIONYSIUS LARDNER,

Doctor of Civil Law, Fellow of the Royal Societies of London and Edinburgh, Member of the Universities of
Cambridge and Dublin, and formerly Professor of Natural Philosophy and Astronomy
in the University of London, &c. &c.

AFTER Dr. Lardner had brought to a close his Public Lectures in the United States, he was prevailed upon by the Publishers to prepare a complete and authentic edition for publication.—The general interest which, for a period of several years, these beautiful expositions and commentaries on the Natural Sciences had excited, and which was so universally felt and acknowledged, induced the Publishers to believe that their publication would be most acceptable, as well as permanently beneficial, to the American public. In these published Lectures it will be found that the Author has preserved the same simplicity of language, perspicuity of reasoning, and felicity of illustration, which rendered the oral discourses so universally popular. While the Work was passing through the press, and as the different Numbers or Parts were circulated, the Publishers received from all sections of the Union the most flattering encomiums of the usefulness of the work and of the manner in which it was printed and illustrated. It was gratifying to the Publishers to notice the interest taken in the work by MECHANICS. In one workshop in New-York, Thirty of the Journeymen purchased the Numbers as they were published; and, in several large establishments, the workmen formed clubs and purchased the work at the wholesale or dozen price. The number of Lithographic and Wood Engravings, large and small, in the whole series, is 380.

We do not know that we can give a better idea of the work, to those who have not seen it, than by publishing the following summary of the matters treated of in the different Lectures:

LECTURE I....THE PLURALITY OF WORLDS.

Contemplation of the Firmament—Reflections thereby suggested—Limited Powers of the Telescope—What it can do for us—Its effect on the Appearances of the Planets—Are the Planets Inhabited?—Plan of the Solar System—Uniform Supply of Light and Warmth—Expedient for Securing it—Different Distances of the Planets do not necessarily infer different Temperatures, nor different Degrees of Light—Admirable Adaptation of the Rotation of the Earth to the Organization of its Inhabitants—Minor and Major Planets—Short Days on the latter—The Seasons—Similar Arrangement on the Planets—The Atmosphere—Many Uses of the Atmosphere—Clouds—Rain, Hail, and Snow—Mountains on the Planets—Land and Water—Weights of Bodies on the Planets—Appearances of the Sun, &c. &c.

LECTURE II.....THE SUN.

The Most Interesting Object in the Firmament—Its Distance—How Measured—Its Magnitude—How Ascertained—Its Bulk and Weight—Form—Time of Rotation—Spots—Its Physical Constitution—Luminous Coating—Temperature—Luminous Matter, &c. &c.

LECTURE III.....ECLIPSES.

Lunar and Solar Eclipses—Causes—Shadow of the Earth—And Moon—Magnitude—When they can happen—Great Solar Eclipse described by Halley—Ecliptic Limits, &c. &c.

LECTURE IV.....THE AURORA BOREALIS.

Origin of the Name—Produced by Electricity—General Phenomena of Auroras—Various Examples of this Meteor—Biot's Excursion to the Shetland Isles to observe the Aurora—Lottin's Observations in 1838_9—Various Auroras seen by him—Theory of Biot—Objections to it—Hypothesis of Faraday—Auroras seen on the Polar Voyage of Captain Franklin, &c. &c.

LECTURE V.....ELECTRICITY.

Electric Phenomena observed by the Ancients—Thales—Gilbert de Magnete—Otto Guencke's Electric Machine—Hawkesbee's Experiments—Stephen Grey's Discoveries—Wheeler and Grey's—Dufaye's Discovery—Invention of the Leyden Vial—Singular Effects of the first Electric Shocks—Experiments of Watson and Bevis—Experiments on Conductors—Franklin's Experiments and Letters—His Experiments on the Leyden Vial—His Discovery of the Identity of Lightning and Electricity—Reception of his Suggestions by the Royal Society—His Kite Experiment—His Right to this Discovery denied by Arago—His Claim Vindicated—Invention of Conductors—Canton's Experiments—Discovery of Induction—Inventor of the Condenser—Works of Æpinus—Theory of Symmer—Experiments of Coulomb—Balance of Torsion—Electricity of the Atmosphere—Effects of Flame—Experiments of Volta—Lavoisier and Laplace—Analytical Work of Poisson.

LECTURE VI.....THE MINOR PLANETS.

Mercury—Transit over the Sun—Relative Position—Difficulty of Observing it—Venus—Diurnal Motion of Venus and Mercury indicated by the Shadows of Mountains—Axis of Rotation—Seasons, Climates, and Zones—Orbits and Transits of Mercury and Venus—Mountains on Mercury and Venus—Influence of the Sun at Mercury and Venus—Twilight on Mercury and Venus—Mars—Atmosphere of Mars—Physical Constitution of Mars—Has Mars a Satellite?—Appearance of the Sun at Mars, &c.

DR. LARDNER'S LECTURES.

DR. LARDNER'S LECTURES,

DR. LARDNER'S LECTURES.

ages—Working Apparatus—Mode of Operation—Defects of Savery's Engine—Newcomen and Cawley's Patent—Accidental Discovery of Condensation by Injection—Potter's Invention of the Method of Working the Valves—His Contrivance improved by the Substitution of the Plug-Frame.

LECTURE LVII.....THE STEAM-ENGINE.
(Second Lecture.)

Mechanical Force of Steam—Watt finds Condensation in the Cylinder incompatible with a due Economy of Fuel—Conceives the notion of Condensing out of the Cylinder—Invents the Air-Pump—Substitutes Steam Pressure for Atmospheric Pressure—Invents the Steam Case or Jacket—His Models—Difficulties of bringing the Improved Engine into Use—Watt employed by Roebuck—His Partnership—His first Patent—His Single-Acting Engine—Discovery of the Expansive Action of Steam—Extension of the Steam-Engine to Manufactures—Attempts of Papin, Savery, Hull, Champion, Stewart, and Wasbrough—Watt's Second Patent—Sun-and-Planet Wheels—Valves of Double-Acting Engine.

LECTURE LVIII....THE STEAM-ENGINE.
(Third Lecture.)

Methods of Connecting the Piston-Rod and Beam in the Double-Acting Engine—Rack and Sector—Parallel Motion—Connection of Piston-Rod and Beam—Connecting-Rod and Crank—Fly-Wheel—Shuttle-Valve—Governor—Construction and Operation of the Double-Acting Engine—Eccentric—Cocks and Valves—Single-Clack Valves—Double-Clack Valves—Conical Valves—Slide Valves—Murray's Slides—The D Valves—Seaward's Slides—Cocks—Pistons—Cartwright's Engine.

LECTURE LIX.....THE STEAM-ENGINE.
(Fourth Lecture.)

Analysis of Coal—Process of Combustion—Heat evolved in it—Form and Structure of Boiler—Wagon-Boiler—Furnace—Method of Feeding it—Combustion of Gas in Flues—Williams's Patent for Method of Consuming unburned Gases—Construction of Grate and Ash-Pit—Magnitude of Heating Surface of Boiler—Steam-Space and Water-Space in Boiler—Position of Flues—Method of Feeding Boiler—Method of Indicating the Level of Water in Boiler—Lever Gauges—Self-Regulating Feeders—Steam-Gauge—Barometer-Gauge—Watt's Invention of the Indicator—Counter—Safety-Valve—Fusible Plugs—Self-Regulating Damper—Brunton's Self-Regulating Furnace—Gross and Useful Effect of an Engine—Horse-Power of Steam-Engines—Table exhibiting the Mechanical Power of Water converted into Steam at various Pressures—Evaporation Proportional to Horse-Power—Sources of Loss of Power—Absence of good Practical Rules for Power—Common Rules followed by Engine-Makers—Duty distinguished from Power—Duty of Boilers—Proportion of Stroke to Diameter of Cylinder—Duty of Engines.

LECTURE LX.....THE STEAM-ENGINE.
(Fifth Lecture.)

Railways—Effects of Railway Transport—History of the Locomotive Engine—Construction of Locomotive Engine by Blinkinsop—Messrs. Chapman's Contrivance—Walking Engine—Mr. Stephenson's Engines at Killingworth—Liverpool and Manchester Railway—Experimental Trial of the "Rocket," "Sanspareil," and "Novelty"—Method of Subdividing the Flue into Tubes—Progressive Improvement of Locomotive Engines—Adoption of Brass Tubes—Detailed Description of the most Improved Locomotive Engines—Power of Locomotive Engines—Position of the Eccentrics—Pressure of Steam in the Boiler—Dr. Lardner's Experiments in 1838—Resistance to Railway Trains—Dr. Lardner's Experiments on the Great Western Railway—Experiments on Resistance—Restrictions on Gradients—Compensating Effect of Gradients—Experiment with the "Hecla"—Disposition of Gradients should be Uniform—Methods of surmounting Steep Inclinations.

☞ The above Work was originally published in Fourteen Numbers or Parts, and sold at the extremely low price of 25 cents per Number. Any of the Numbers can still be purchased. The entire Work is now completed and sold in two large octavo volumes of about 600 pages each, well bound in full cloth, illustrated by 380 Engravings, and sold at $4 50.

☞ District School Libraries can order these Lectures through any of the Booksellers or Country Merchants. Parents, Teachers, Superintendents and Trustees of Common Schools, Farmers, Mechanics, and all, indeed, who have any desire to increase their store of useful information on the subjects embraced in these volumes, are earnestly entreated to examine this Work before they throw away their money on the trash, or even worse than trash, that is now so rapidly inundating the country.

From among the numerous Recommendatory Notices which the Publishers received during the progress of the publication, we have only room to give the following:

From D. MEREDITH REESE, A. M., M. D., Superintendent of Common Schools in the City and County of New-York.

NEW-YORK, Oct. 20th, 1845.

Messrs. GREELEY & McELRATH:
Gentlemen: I have examined the Popular Lectures of Dr. LARDNER, ON SCIENCE AND ART, with much satisfaction, and take pleasure in expressing the opinion that you are doing a valuable service to the people of our common country by their publication, and especially by issuing them in numbers, and at so cheap a rate.

To popularize Science and cheapen Knowledge, must be regarded by the philanthropist as worthy of the mightiest minds of the age, and to be successful in such efforts, constitutes their authors public benefactors. These Lectures of Dr. Lardner are addressed to the common mind, and though treating upon the loftiest of the Natural Sciences, are so plain and practical, so simple and attractive, that all who can read may readily profit by their instructions. The clear and familiar illustrations and diagrams, which abound in every department, are skilfully adapted to the apprehension of youth, who should be encouraged every where to read and study them and thus promote their own happiness and usefulness.

I could wish that they were found in every School Library, to which their scientific accuracy and numerous moral reflections upon the wonderful works of God should be esteemed no small commendation. But they should be found in every work-shop in the land; for Science and Art are here exhibited in their true relations; and the working men of our country would find here both entertainment and instruction, calculated to improve alike their intellects and their morals.
D. M. REESE.

ALBANY, May 5, 1846.

GREELEY & McELRATH:
Gentlemen: I cordially and cheerfully concur with my friend, Dr. REESE, in the high appreciation which he places on your edition of Dr. Lardner's Lectures, and have no hesitation in recommending them as a most valuable acquisition to our School Libraries.
SAML. S. RANDALL,
Dep. Supt. Com. Schools.

"These publications are admirably adapted to interest and instruct the general reader."
[Norwich Gleaner.

"No man has succeeded better in giving popular interest to abstruse subjects than Dr. Lardner."
[Worcester Ægis.

DR. LARDNER'S LECTURES, &C.

"The work will be a very interesting and valuable one, and ought to be found in many places now monopolized by the worthless rubbish of the day; we mean cheap novels. We think great credit is due to Greeley & McElrath, for their effort to bring Science within the reach of so many, and make it the fireside companion of almost every home. Let them be liberally patronized." [*White Mountain Torrent.*

"The work will be a valuable one, and the sale must be immense." [*Bellows Falls Gazette.*

"We hope these enterprising publishers may be liberally encouraged in the effort to furnish reading for the people." [*Christian Freeman.*

"The citizens of small country towns which are not visited by such Lecturers as Dr. Lardner, are under weighty obligations to Messrs. Greeley & McElrath for the opportunity thus afforded, to put themselves in possession of a work of much merit." [*Whig, (Wayne Co. N. Y.)*

"A valuable accession to the Scientific Literature of the day; worth a ton of the sickening love stories that flood the country." [*Eastport Sentinel, (Me.)*

"One happy and remarkable trait of the work is, its perfect adaptation to the most common minds. We trust that such a work will receive, from the reading community that encouragement which it so justly merits; that it will be found on every farmer's table, and in every library." [*Enterprise, (Md.)*

"If our youth would once taste, and get interested in Science thus taught, they would find a method of employing their reading hours more happy and useful for themselves as well as for all whose character and happiness are affected by them, than in devouring the light and often immoral stories and romances which flood the country." [*Christian Mirror.*

"The most valuable Lectures ever published in the United States." [*Talladega Reporter, (Ala.)*

"A work of high value, and must find a wide circulation." [*Baltimore Patriot.*

"We consider these Lectures among the most valuable reading that has ever been offered to the American public." [*Cultivator.*

"We know of no publication in this department of Literature which has succeeded so well, in stripping an unwise and erudite philology from a vast mine of mental wealth, and exhibiting its attractions to the delighted gaze of the 'unlettered hind,' as well as to the student of Nature's manifold mysteries.

"We would be glad to see these interesting dissertations in every family, (and we think their cheapness renders them easily accessible to most,) because there is a solidity of matter and a vigor of style about them, which will render them as instructive and impressive to succeeding generations as to the present." [*The Virginian.*

"We wish our readers may, one and all, have the gratification and the benefit of using such mental food as these Lectures afford." [*American Freeman, Wis. T.*

"These Lectures of Doct. Lardner are of great value. They treat of interesting and important subjects and embody a vast amount of valuable information in an attractive and agreeable style. If our young men and girls would save the ninepences and quarters to buy this work which they now spend for the disgusting and sickening love stories which flood the country, and which they so eagerly seek for, they would find their heads filled up with something useful and instructive, instead of vulgar trash." [*Thomaston Recorder.*

"This work ought to be in the hands of every young mechanic in the land, as well as the astronomer and man of science, as mechanics and mechanism occupy a large place." [*People's Advocate, York, Pa.*

"We cannot forbear to recommend this work to the attention of all who wish to acquaint themselves in the easiest and cheapest way with the wonderful and mysterious agencies of physical nature. To the student and the teacher, the professional man and the day laborer, it is a work equally valuable and interesting. The whole series will comprise, at a comparatively trifling expense, one of the most valuable compendiums of Natural Philosophy and Mechanical Science to be found in the language. To young men and mechanics who want the leisure to delve through more abstruse and voluminous works, these Lectures will be found invaluable." [*Independent Democrat, Concord, N. H.*

☞ Any person wishing to procure this valuable work may apply to our Agents, or to any of the Booksellers or Country Merchants in any part of the United States. Orders are respectfully solicited. GREELEY & McELRATH, Tribune Buildings, New-York.

HUMAN RIGHTS.

ESSAYS ON HUMAN RIGHTS AND THEIR POLITICAL GUARANTIES. By ELISHA P. HURLBUT, Counsellor at Law of the City of New York. 1 vol. 12mo.

Its several chapters discuss the following topics: I. The Origin of Human Rights; II. The true Function of Government; III. The Constitution of Government; IV, V. Constitutional Limitations and Prohibitions; VI. The Elective Franchise; VII. Rights emanating from the Sentiments and Affections; VIII. The Rights of Woman; IX. The Right of Property and its Moral Relations; X. Intellectual Property ☞ The Work is printed on a fair, large type, and sold retail at 50 cents per copy.

LECTURES ON ASTRONOMY,

Delivered at the Royal Observatory of Paris. By M. Arago, Member of the Institute of France, &c. With extensive additions by Dionysius Lardner, former Professor of Astronomy and Natural Philosophy in the University of London. Illustrated with numerous cuts and diagrams.

APPENDIX.—Table of the Constellations, with the number of stars in each, as far as those of the sixth magnitude. Summary.

Price 25 cents; five copies for $1. Agents and Booksellers supplied on the usual terms.

HISTORY OF THE SILK CULTURE.

THE SILK CULTURE IN THE UNITED STATES—embracing complete accounts of the latest and most approved mode of Hatching, Rearing, and Feeding the Silk-Worm, Managing the Cocoonery, Reeling, Spinning, and Manufacturing of the Silk, &c., &c., with Historical Sketches of the Silk Business; Natural History of the Silk-Worm, the Mulberry, &c. Illustrated by numerous engravings of Machinery and Processes, and a Manual of the Silk Culture. Price 25 cents; five copies for $1.

GREAT BOOK FOR FARMERS!

LET EVERY FARMER IN THE UNITED STATES HAVE A COPY!

Let every Farmer in the United States subscribe for a Copy for his Son. It may prove of more value to him than a Horse, or even a Farm!

THE FARMERS' LIBRARY

AND

MONTHLY JOURNAL OF AGRICULTURE.

JOHN S. SKINNER, EDITOR.

EACH number consists of two distinct parts, viz:

I. THE FARMERS' LIBRARY, in which are published continuously the best *Standard Works* on Agriculture, embracing those which, by their cost or the language in which they are written, would otherwise seem beyond the reach of nearly all American Farmers. In this way we give for two or three dollars the choicest European treatises and researches in Agriculture, costing ten times as much in the original editions, not easily obtained at any price, and virtually out of the reach of men who live by following the plow. The works published in the Library will form a complete series, exploring and exhibiting the whole field of Natural Science, and developing the rich treasures which Chemistry, Geology, and Mechanics have yielded and may yield to lighten the labors and swell the harvests of the intelligent husbandman.

II. THE MONTHLY JOURNAL OF AGRICULTURE will likewise contain about 50 pages per month, and will comprise, 1. *Foreign:* Selections from the higher class of British, French and German periodicals devoted to Agriculture, with extracts from new books which may not be published in the Library, &c. &c. 2. *American:* Editorials, communicated and selected accounts of experiments, improved processes, discoveries in Agriculture, new implements, &c. &c. In this department alone will ours resemble any American work ever yet published. It can hardly be necessary to add that no Political, Economic, or other controverted doctrine, will be inculcated through this magazine.

Each number of the Library is illustrated by numerous Engravings, printed on type obtained expressly for this work, and on good paper—the whole got up as such a work should be.

This Monthly, which is by far the amplest and most comprehensive Agricultural periodical ever established in America, was commenced in the month of July, 1845, and before the close of the first year among its subscribers were embraced many of the most intelligent farmers, professional men, and retired gentlemen in every City and State in the Union. The reprint of standard works and the variety, elegance and costliness of the Engravings will always render this one of the most useful and interesting, and, in view of the amount of reading matter, the cheapest Farming periodical in this or any other country. The beautiful work of PETZHOLDT ON AGRICULTURAL CHEMISTRY was published complete in the first two numbers of the FARMERS' LIBRARY; and the great work of VON THAER on the PRINCIPLES OF AGRICULTURE, TRANSLATED BY WM. SHAW AND CUTHBERT JOHNSON, WITH A MEMOIR OF THE AUTHOR, &c. was commenced in the number of the LIBRARY for September, 1845, and will be completed entire, without abridgment, in the June number for 1846. This justly celebrated work is alone worth the full subscription price of the FARMERS' LIBRARY, and yet it is not more than one-third of what each subscriber to the Work receives for his subscription money. This work of Von Thaër was originally written and published in the German language, translated and published in the French and afterward in the English language. It is pronounced by competent judges to be the most finished Agricultural Book which has ever been written. The London edition is printed in two octavo volumes, and is sold at about $8 per copy.

Von Thaër was educated for a Physician, the practice of which he relinquished for the more quiet and philosophical pursuits of Agriculture. Soon after he commenced farming he introduced such decided improvements upon his farm that his fame was soon known from one end of Europe to the other. The most celebrated farmers of England, France, Denmark, Germany, &c. courted his friendship, and his writings were everywhere sought and studied.

The following subjects are discussed in the work of Von Thaër, and the manner of treating each subject is original, philosophical and practical.

SECTION I. THE FUNDAMENTAL PRINCIPLES:—A Sketch of Systematic Agriculture; The Bases of the Science of Agriculture; The Bases of Enterprise; Capital; The Farm, and the Manner of taking Possession of it; Leasehold Estates; Hereditary Leases.

SEC. II. THE ECONOMY, ORGANIZATION AND DIRECTION OF AN AGRICULTURAL ENTERPRISE:—Labor in General; Draught Labor; Manual Labor; The Proper Method of keeping the Journals, Registers, and other Books connected with an Agricultural Undertaking; Proportion of Manure to the Quantity of Fodder and the number of Cattle; The various Systems of Cultivation. Class 1—The Cultivation of Corn—Alternate Cultivation—Alternate Rotations with Pasturage—On the Succession of Crops—Alternate Cultivation, accompanied by a suitable Succession of Crops and Pasturage—Alternate Cultivation, with Stall-Feeding of the Cattle—Four Crop Divisions—Five Crop Divisions—Six Crop Divisions—Seven Crop Divisions—Eight Crop Divisions—Nine Crop Divisions—Ten Crop Divisions—Eleven Crop Divisions—Twelve Crop Divisions—Twelve Crop Divisions—The Transition from one Rotation to another.

SEC. III. AGRONOMY; OR A TREATISE ON THE CONSTITUENT PARTS AND PHYSICAL PROPERTIES OF THE SOIL, AND THE BEST METHOD OF ACQUIRING A KNOWLEDGE OF THE DIFFERENT EARTHS, AND ASCERTAINING THEIR VALUE:—Silica; Alumina; Clay; Lime; Gypsum, or Sulphate of Lime; Marl;

Magnesia; Iron; Humus; Peat; The Different Species of Earths, their Value, Employment, and Properties, in their Relations to the Constituent Parts of the Soil.

SEC. IV. AGRICULTURE:—Part 1—On Manuring and Ameliorating the Soil: Vegetable Manures—Mineral Manures. Part 2—On the Tillage of the Soil, or its Mechanical Amelioration; Agricultural Implements; On Plowing; On Clearing Land; Hedges, Fences and Enclosures; On the Draining of Land; On the Draining of various kinds of Marshes; Irrigation; On Earthing and Warping; On the Management of Meadow Land; The Hay Harvest; On the various kinds of Pastures.

SEC. V. ON THE REPRODUCTION OF ANIMAL AND VEGETABLE SUBSTANCES:—Vegetable Reproduction; Wheat: Spring Wheat—Spelt—One-grained Wheat (*Einkorn* of the Germans).—Smut, or Caries in Wheat (*Brand*);—Rye; Barley: Common, or Small Quadrangular Barley—Two-rowed, Long-eared, or Large Flat Barley—Siberian, or Quadrangular Naked Barley—Naked Flat Barley—Six-rowed, or Winter Barley;—Oats (*Avena Sativa*); Millet (*Panicum*); On the Cultivation of Grain in Rows, or with the Horse-hoe; Leguminous Crops; The Pea; The Lentil; Kidney-Beans, (Haricots); Beans (*Vicia Fabia*); Vetches: Common Vetch (*Vetch Sativa*); Buckwheat (*Polygonum Fagopyrum*); Meslin—Mixtures of Different Kinds of Grain; Culture of Hoed or Weeded Crops; Vegetables for the Market; Oil-Plants; Colza and Rape (Autumnal Varieties)— Spring Colza, or Spring Rape—Mustard—Oily Radish (*Raphanus Chinensis Oleiferus*)—Cultivated Gold of Pleasure (*Myagrum Sativum*)—Common Poppy (*Papaver Somniferum*);—Thread Plants: Flax— Hemp (*Cannabis Sativa*);—Other Plants, the Cul-

ture of which has been proposed for the sake of their Thread: Syrian Swallow Wort. or Virginian Silk Asclepias *Syriaca*)—Common Nettle (*Urtica Diaca*)—Fullers' Teasle (*Dipsacus Fullorum*); - Coloring-Plants: Dyers' Madder (*Rubia Tinctorum*)—Dyers' Woad (*Isatis Tinctoria*)—Dyers' Weld (*Reseda Luteola*)—Bastard Saffron (*Carthamus Tinctorius*);— The Hop; Tobacco; Chicco·y; Carraway (*Carum Carui*); Common Fennel (*Fœniculum Vulgare*); Anise (*Pimpinella Anisum*); Culture of Fodder-Plants: The Potato—The Field-Beet—The Turnip (*Brassica Rapa*)—Turnips which will not bear Transplanting—Turnips so properly called—Turnips admitting of Transplantation—The Turnip Cabbage— Common Red and White Cabbage (*Brassica Oleracea*; var. *Capitata*)—Carrots—The Parsnip—Maize, or Indian Corn (*Tea Mais*);—Herbage Plants: Common Purple Clover (*Trefolium Pratense*, var. *Sativum*)—White, or Dutch Clover (*Trifolium Repens*)— Strawberry Trefoil (*Trifolium Fragiferum*)—Lucerne (*Medicago Sativa*)—Sainfoin (*Hedisarum Onebrychis*)—Yellow Sickle Medick (*Medicago Falcata*) —Black Medick or Nonsuch (*Medicago Lupulina*)— Corn Spurry (*Spergula Arvensis*)—The Tall-growing Grasses—Ray Grass (*Solium Perenne*)—Common Oatlike Grass (*Avena Elatior*)—Tall Fescue Grass (*Festuca Elatior*)—Cock's-foot Grass (*Dactylis Glomerata*)—Dog-tail Grass (*Cynosurus Cristatus*)—Common Cat's-tail or Timothy Grass (*Phleum Pratense*) —Woolly Soft Grass (*Holcus Sanatus*)—Meadow Fox tail Grass (*Alopecurus Pratensis*)—Meadow Grass (*Poa*).

SEC. VI. THE ECONOMY OF LIVE STOCK:—Horned Cattle; Breeding Cattle—Feeding of Cattle;—The Dairy: Cheese Making;—Fattening of Horned Cattle; Swine; Sheep; Horses.

☞ The subscription price to the FARMERS' LIBRARY AND MONTHLY JOURNAL OF AGRICULTURE, containing 2 vols. of 600 pages each, with numerous Engravings, is Five Dollars a year. Where five persons club together and send us $20, we send five copies. Payment is invariably required in advance. Money may be remitted through the Mail at our risk. The Bank notes of any State of specie paying Banks, are received at par. Address
GREELEY & McELRATH, Publishers, Tribune Buildings, New-York.

LECTURES TO FARMERS
ON
AGRICULTURAL CHEMISTRY.
BY ALEXANDER PETZHOLDT.

THE taste for Scientific Agriculture in the United States has created a demand for the very information which these Lectures supply. "The motive," says the author, "which has induced me to prepare such a Course of Lectures, is the complaint I have heard from many of you, that, being unacquainted with the elements of Chemistry, you have found it difficult to understand the questions which are at the present moment so warmly discussed, respecting the theory and practice of Agriculture." This work being less scientific and technical in its language than Liebig's work, is on that account better adapted for the use of general Farmers and ought to be first read. The author in his Preface says that a "perusal of this work with ordinary attention will furnish the necessary amount of chemical information for the purposes of the Farmer."

In reference to the first two volumes of the *Farmers' Library and Monthly Journal of Agriculture*, now bound up and ready for sale, the Hon. N. S. BENTON, Secretary of State of the State of New York, writes to the publishers as follows:—

SECRETARY'S OFFICE, *Department of Common Schools*,
ALBANY, July 15, 1846.

I have examined, with as much care and attention as my time would permit, the first volumes of the JOURNAL OF AGRICULTURE AND THE FARMERS' LIBRARY, published by Messrs Greeley & McElrath, New York, and do not perceive any objections to their introduction into the School District Libraries of the State; and I can have no doubt this work would prove valuable acquisitions in all, but especially to those where the subject of agriculture excites the attention of the inhabitants of the district.

N. S. BENTON, *Supt. Com. Schools.*

The Deputy Superintendent of the Common Schools of the State of New York, writes as follows:—

SECRETARY'S OFFICE, *Department of Common Schools*,
ALBANY, July 9, 1846.

Messrs. GREELEY & McELRATH:—

GENTLEMEN: I should be happy to see this work (the FARMERS' LIBRARY AND JOURNAL OF AGRICULTURE) in every School Library in the State; and I hope you will be able to afford it at a price which will place it at the command of the rural districts especially, where I am sure it can not fail of being highly appreciated and extensively read. Works of this description are, in my judgment, eminently suitable for our District Libraries; and I know of none more useful or practical than the present. Its execution is exceedingly creditable to the publishers; and the vast amount of interesting matter comprised in its pages can not fail of insuring it a wide circulation among the agricultural community—the bulwark of the State. Very respectfully,

S. S. RANDALL, *Dep. Supt. Com. Schools.*

THE FARMERS' LIBRARY

AND

MONTHLY JOURNAL OF AGRICULTURE.

THE first year of this great Agricultural Periodical closes with the June number, 1846. The pages of the Library portion are occupied with Petzholdt's Agricultural Chemistry and Von Thaër's Principles of Agriculture. The pages of the Monthly Journal portion of the work are very diversified in their subjects. The following are some of the leading articles:

No. I—(JULY).—Memoir of the late Stephen Van Rensselaer (with a fine steel portrait); Deep Plowing—An Experiment illustrating its Effects; British Agricultural Dissertations; Prize Essay on Farm Management, (with an engraved Plan for laying out a farm); Fall Plowing; On the Value and the Progress of Agricultural Science, with Extracts—from J. S. Wadsworth; The Poetry of Rural Life; Claims of Agriculture upon the Business Community; Guano—Recent Experiments in Maryland and Virginia; South-Down Sheep (with lithographic portraits); Letter from Hon Andrew Stevenson of Virginia; Southern Agriculture—Remarks of the Editor; The Silk Plant of Tripoli (with a lithographic illustration)—Letter from D. S. McCauley to Francis Markoe; Culture of Silk in South Carolina; A New Vegetable (Kohl Rabi) and New Grasses (Tussac Grass)—Recommended to be imported; Agricultural Machines patented; Effects of Electricity on Vegetation; The Disease in Potatoes—Various Theories; Notices of New Books; Great Sale of Cattle at Albany; Items, &c.

No. II—(AUGUST).—Lady Suffolk (with a portrait); A Dissertation on Horse-Breeding, and on the Trotting Horses of the U. S.; Obituary Notice of Gen. T. M Forman, of Md.; Turnip Culture in England; Under-Draining; Irrigation; Water-Meadows; Entomology; Canada Thistle (illustrated); Comparative Value of Different Kinds of Sheep for the New-York Farmer; On the Preservation of Health; The Cause of Education; Agricultural Associations and Science; Draining-Tile, Lime as a Fertilizer; XVIIIth Annual Fair of the American Institute; New-York State Agricultural Society Cattle Show at Utica; Good Signs for the South, &c. &c.

No. III—(SEPTEMBER).—Brief Sketch of the Qualities of the Short-Horned Bull (with a portrait)—On the Good and Bad Points of Cattle; St. John's Day Rye and Lucerne; N. Y. State Agricultural Fair; Sugar—its Culture and Manufacture; Comparison of Guano with other Manures; Mismanagement of Stable-Dung Manure, Entomology; Cheshire Cheese—A Prize Essay by Henry White; Silk Plant—Guano; Native or Wild Maize; Thoughts on Trees and Flowers; The Clergy—their power to improve the Public Taste for Agriculture and Horticulture—Letter from Rev. J. O. Choules; The Poetry of Rural Life, Trials of Sulphuric Acid and Bones for Turnips; Use of Sulphuric Acid with Bones as Compost; Cotton Plant (illustrated), &c. &c.

No IV—(OCTOBER).—Memoir of Liebig (with a portrait); The Sort of Information wanted at the South; To Prevent Smut in Wheat; Memoir of the Cotton Plant, by W. B. Seabrook; The Central or Red-Land District of Virginia—Letter from Hon. W. L Goggin, Various Opinions on Soiling; Principles to observe in the erection of Farm Houses; Management of Farms—Mr Hammond's Farm; Atmosphere of stables, Reflections on the Progress of Agricultural Improvement, and the Political and Moral Influence of Rural Life—Letter from Gen. Dearborn; Progress of Agricultural Improvement—Letter from Judge Rost; Improvement in the mode of attaching Horses to Wagons, Paring and Burning; The Center of Gravity (illustrated), A Review on the Past, Present, and Future State of the Wool Market; List of Premiums awarded by the New-York State Agricultural Fair, &c &c

No V—(NOVEMBER) Memoir of Hon. Richard Peters of Pa. (with a portrait); Tunisian Sheep (with portraits); History and Uses of the Cotton Plant; Letter from Dr. J. Johnson of S. C. on the Silk Plant; Thoughts on Transplanting Trees; Agricultural Address before the Queens Co. Ag. So. by J. S. Skinner; Guano as a Manure; Liebig's Explanation of the Principles and use of Artificial Manures; Wine Making, by Rev. S. Weller, with Notes by S. Clark; How to keep Farm Registers; Entomology; Management of Bees; Sulphuric Acid and Bones; The Fair of the American Institute; Sheep and Chestnuts, &c. &c.

No. VI—(DECEMBER).—Poultry (with illustrations); Successful Experiments in Soiling; Agricultural Products of the United States and Great Britain; The Potato Murrain; Consumption of Sugar in Europe and North America; Wages and Condition of Women and Children employed in the Agricultural Labor in England; History and use of the Cotton Plant (concluded); Wool-growing at the South; On Breeding Horses; Education in Virginia; Potato Starch; The Inclined Plane (with illustrations); Pea Culture in the South; Societies for the Promotion of Agriculture, Horticulture, &c.; Agricultural Premiums; Sheep Husbandry; Peters's Agricultural Account Book; Exposition of the Condition and Resources of Delaware, &c.

No. VII—(JANUARY).—Farm Buildings (with illustrations); Treatise on Milch Cows, whereby the Quantity and Quality of Milk which any Cow will give may be accurately determined (with numerous illustrations)—by M Fr. Guénon; Maryland Farmers' Club on the Right Tack; The Mode in which Lime Operates on Soil; Poultry and Useful Recipes; Thoughts on the Distribution of Labor; Jerusalem Artichoke; Cellars vs. Spring-Houses for Dairies; Flax and Hemp Husbandry; One-Horse Carts (with illustrations); The Hydraulic Ram (with illustrations); Comparative Views of the Progress of Population in different Regions of the United States; The Importance of Draining Land, &c.

No. VIII—(FEBRUARY).—Treatise on Milch Cows (with illustrations)—continued; The Potato Disease; Characteristics of different Breeds of Horses—by Hon. Zadock Pratt; On Fattening Cattle; The Language of Birds—Character and Habits of the Whip-poor-will; The Importance of acquiring a Knowledge of the Natural Science; "Lime Enricheth the Father but Impoverisheth the Son"; Capital needed for Agricultural Improvement; The Use of Salt to Man and Animals; On the Curing of Provisions for the British Markets; Sketch of Belgian Husbandry; The Flower Garden, &c. &c.

No. IX—(MARCH).—Smithsonian Fund; The Proper Position of Country Dwelling-Houses and Barns; Raising Potatoes from Seed; Scheme of Reducing the Quantity of Cotton; Southern Hemp, or Bear-Grass; Insects Injurious to Vegetation; Importing Societies; Treatise on Milch Cows—continued; Quaker or Friends' Farming; Flooding Meadows; The Shepherd's Dog, &c. &c.

No. X—(APRIL).—Guano—its Nature and Use—by Prof Hardy; Prospects in Virginia for New Settlers; The Broad-Fruit Tree (with illustrations); Sugar, and its Effects on Man and Animals; The Science of Botany and Horticulture; Ammonia and Water in Guano; General Treatment of Greenhouse Plants; Effects of Drouth on Indian Corn; Philadelphia Butter; Treatise on Milch Cows—concluded; Labor and Machinery; The Diseases of the Horse; Insects most Injurious to Vegetables and Animals, &v.

☞ Each year's Numbers contain two large octavo volumes of 600 pages each. All the Numbers of the First year can still be purchased. The First Number of the Second year commences with July, 1846. **GREELEY & McELRATH**, Publishers, Tribune Buildings, New-York.

D'ISRAELI'S
CURIOSITIES OF LITERATURE.

Every body knows that this is a very curious book, because such is its general reputation. But not known to every one why it is so curious, because comparatively few have had an opportunity amining it for themselves. We give below the headings of the different matters discussed or eml in this interesting volume, so that authors, literary and professional gentlemen, and others, may ju themselves, to some extent, at least, whether or not they can longer conveniently dispense with the tanity of personally consulting the work. Did any one ever see such a medley of oddities, or grouping of the queer things growing out of literary productions and their authors as are co what follows?

STEPHENS'S BOOK OF THE FARM.

600 ENGRAVINGS!

The following general titles of chapters and parts of the Work of Mr. Stephens, will give only a very imperfect notion of the variety and extent of the entire contents.

CONTENTS OF STEPHENS'S BOOK OF THE FARM.

Extracts from the Critical Notices published in England during the publication of the work in London.

From the London Times.

"The first part or number of this work has just been published by Messrs. Blackwood. It is written by Mr Henry Stephens, a gentleman already known to the public in his editorial character in the Quarterly Journal of Agriculture. The great merit of the work, as far as it has yet gone, is the intelligible manner in which it is written, and the strong good sense with which it is distinguished The proposed arrangement, set forth in the plan of the work, is clear and satisfactory; and the whole number is valuable as being the result of practical experience and competent theoretic knowledge. It is a book which will be received with gratitude by those who are really anxious to profit by instruction, and whose anxiety for improvement is not impeded by prejudice." . . . "The plan of the work, it may again be observed, is very good—the reasoning is logical—the assertions are the results of accurate examination and repeated experience. In addition to the information conveyed in the letter-press, the book is ornamented by accurate and handsome plates of agricultural animals, implements of farming, plans of farming, &c. &c."

From the Newcastle Courant.

"Mr. Stephens's work is divided into three portions. In the first, the pupil is shown the difficulties he has to encounter in acquiring a competent knowledge of farming as a profession, and the most easy and effectual methods of overcoming these. The second portion details the various kinds of farming practiced in the country, and points out that which the Author reckons the best for adoption under given circumstances.— The third and concluding portion accompanies the young farmer into the world, where it acquaints him how to look about for a proper farm for himself."

From Felix Farley's Bristol Journal.

"When we say that the Author is Mr. Henry Stephens, we are safe in expressing our conviction that the results of his penetration, judgment, and experience, so placed before the public, will confer an advantage on the agricultural interest of no common order. We therefore predict a large measure of success to the intended work."

From The Argus.

"We regard it as a national work; and, from the masterly manner in which Mr. Stephens handles his subjects, we feel assured it must become a standard one. His thorough practical knowledge, backed by his scientific acquirements, makes the Author's fitness for the task conspicuous; and the unpresuming manner in which his talent is displayed enhances its value still more in our eyes."

From the Midland Counties Herald.

"The entirely practical nature of this work, and the evident care with which it is produced, will, we think, render it one of the most useful public tions for the farmer which has yet appeared."

From The Times.

"The great merit of the work, as far as it has yet gone, is the intelligible manner in which it is written, and the strong good sense with which it is distinguished. It is a book which will be received with gratitude by those who are really anxious to profit by instruction, and whose anxiety for improvement is not impeded by prejudice."

From the Birmingham Advertiser.

"The farmers of England would do well to possess themselves of this work, for the variety of useful information, and the many practical suggestions it contains."

From The Britannia.

"The two parts now before us are models of clear, sensible composition, and form such an introduction to the practice of farming as has never been published before. The author brings to his task a large store of knowledge, sound sense and a lucid style." "We are quite sure that never was any work more called for, by the intelligence of the age than this 'Book of the Farm,' and believe that it could not have been entrusted to more competent hands, or produced in better style. We strongly recommend it to all classes of agriculturists as a publication of decided utility, and likely to be most serviceable to them in the successful prosecution of their labors."

From the Sporting Review.

"The work before us is one of the most practical results of so patriotic a spirit. It is a most welcome addition to our rural literature. As it proceeds, we hope to transfer some of its good things to our pages.

From the New Farmers' Journal.

"On all these important points, no one is better qualified to fill the office of a mentor than Mr. Stephens, of which the well-arranged plan, and judicious execution, of the book before us, afford irrefragable testimony."

The Concluding Paragraph.

Mr. Stephens, the Author of the above named work, was engaged for several years in writing it. Its publication was commenced in London in January, 1842, and concluded in August, 1844. The Author closes the work in the following words:

"I have now brought to a termination the task I had imposed upon myself in writing this work. If you will but follow the prescriptions I have given in it, for conducting the larger operations of the field, and for treating the various animals of the farm; and—not to mention the proper plowing and manuring of the soil—as the practice of every farmer demonstrates the necessity of affording due attention to those most important because fundamental operations, if you finish off your fields in a manner indicating care and neatness—plowing round their margins, and turning over the corners; if you keep your fences clean and in a state of repair—your fields free of weeds; if you give your stock abundance of fresh food at regular intervals in winter, and supply them with plenty of clean water on fresh pastures in summer; if you have the farm roads always in a serviceable state, and everything about the steading neat and orderly; if you exhibit skill and taste in all these matters, and put what is called *a fine skin* on your farm, you will not fail to earn for yourself the appellation of a good and exemplary farmer: and when you have everything about you 'thus well disposed,' you will find, with Hesiod of old, that profitably, as well as creditably, for you 'shall glide away thy rustic year.'"

TO THE
INHABITANTS OF THE UNITED STATES OF AMERICA!

NEW YORK IN MINIATURE.

NOTICE IS HEREBY GIVEN TO THE INHABITANTS OF THE UNITED STATES, THAT
THE RECENTLY CONSTRUCTED

MODEL
OF THE

CITY OF NEW YORK,

IN CARVED WOOD,
BY E. PORTER BELDEN,

IS ABOUT TO TAKE THE TOUR OF THE PRINCIPAL CITIES OF THE
UNION, AFTER WHICH, IT WILL VISIT EVERY PORTION OF
THE CIVILIZED WORLD.

This Model is a perfect *fac simile* of New York, representing every street, lane, building, shed, park, fence and tree; the elevations and depressions; the shipping, steamboats, wharves, railroad cars, pavements, awnings, lamp posts and every other object in the city to the number of millions. The district represented includes the whole of N. York, the harbor, the East and North Rivers, and the greater part of

BROOKLYN.

The whole rests upon a platform 20 by 24 feet in size, representing the ground, upon which are carved the elevations and depressions of the city. On this the streets and parks are laid out, and every building in the city—even every shed and out building in the interior of blocks, however small—is represented in perfect miniature, in its own exact position, with its relative size, proportions and color.

The utmost accuracy has been preserved and the minutest objects are represented—even the lines between the brick, stone or other material of which each building is composed.

The following tremendous numbers may astonish the reader, but will be found to be no less correct. There are represented upon this Model:

Over 200,000 Buildings, including Houses, Stores and Out Buildings,
2,500,000 Windows and Doors, Over 35,000 Fences and Walls,
150,000 Chimnies, 30,000 Trees,
30,000 Awnings and Lamp Posts,
5,000 Pieces of Shipping, from the Sail Boat to the Frigate.

But perhaps there is nothing that will show the immensity of the work more than the number of bricks, billions being almost too small a denomination to express the number. These statements are frequently not believed or not appreciated before an inspection of the Model, in consequence of the apparent impossibility of a representation so minute and so extensive; but every visitor acknowledges that no terms can be used to describe adequately the magnitude of the work.

But its extent is not the only merit of this Model. Its accuracy to the minutest details is astonishing. Many individual buildings are composed of hundreds of pieces, while some of the more elaborate public edifices consist of over a thousand pieces. It was in progress for more than a year, and upwards of 100 persons were employed in its construction, including the best artists, American and European.

It will be borne in mind, that this Model is vastly different from a map or a painting. It is inconceivably superior to any representation upon paper or canvass; each building being a perfect miniature building, and the whole *differing from the actual city only in point of size*.

ABOVE THE MODEL IS A

MAGNIFICENT CANOPY,
OF CARVED WORK, IN GOTHIC ARCHITECTURE,

Mounted with ornamental pinnacles, and forming compartments, in which are OIL PAINTINGS, by the first artists, of the principal

BUSINESS ESTABLISHMENTS, MANUFACTORIES, HOTELS, ETC., IN THE CITY!

This Canopy is immense, resting upon magnificent columns, and overhanging the whole area of the Model. Composed of the most delicately carved work, and highly decorated with gold and colors, it is one of the most splendid specimens of ornamental work ever executed.

PERHAPS no stronger argument can be adduced in proof of the accuracy and beauty of this Model than the universal enthusiasm with which it has been received by the New York press.

A few short extracts from the hundreds of encomiums pronounced upon it are hereby subjoined.

From N. Y. Express, Feb. 15th, 1846.
It is one of the most remarkable pieces of mechanism we have ever heard of. It is an actual miniature in carved wood of this entire city.

From N. Y. Mirror, March 3d, 1846.
We hope its persevering proprietor will receive patronage of our citizens that shall in some degree remunerate him for this expensive and laborious effort of his industry and talent.

From N. Y. Sun, March 11th, 1846.
It will in short be a perfect miniature of New York—the metropolis of America—the fourth city in the world, and from its name alone will attract more attention in this, and the old country, than any thing of the kind ever exhibited. We heartily wish Mr. Belden that success which he so justly merits.

From N. Y. Sun, March 18th, 1846.
Not only are the public buildings, churches &c. exact specimens of architecture on a small scale, but every inhabitant of New York will be enabled to recognize his own dwelling. In fact the whole expanse of streets, lanes and houses, will lie stretched out before the visiter as it would appear to a person viewing it from a balloon—with this advantage—that he will be spared the nervous feeling incidental to an aeronautic expedition, and be enabled to view it from any point he pleases.

From N. Y. Sun, March 23d, 1846.
In a word it presents as exact a view of New York, as the city itself would if viewed through the inverted end of a telescope. In conclusion we can but feel certain, that this great undertaking of Mr. Belden will be duly appreciated not only by the citizens of this metropolis and the sister cities of our republic, but by the inhabitants of those foreign countries, to whose shores Mr. Belden may see fit to transport the great city of the New World ; and that it will be to him the source of an ample fortune.

From N. Y. Tribune, April 4th, 1846.
This we conceive to be one of the greatest undertakings ever attempted. The Model is constructed upon an immense platform representing the ground with all its natural elevations and depressions, and the eye of the spectator takes in at one view every object with its relative size, proportions and color, from the Battery to Bellevue Hospital. Indeed it would seem as if by some immense mechanical power, the whole city had been compressed into smaller limits, accurately preserving its outlines and minutest traits!

From N. Y. True Sun, April 16, 1846.
This Model will undoubtedly be the most attractive and interesting exhibition ever submitted to the public, and will be viewed by a countless host in all parts of the Union.

From N. Y. Tribune, April 17th, 1846
The immense labor and great ingenuity displayed in the construction of the Model of New York, is the theme of admiration of all those persons, who have been permitted to view this great work while in progress. When completed we question if it will not be recognized throughout the United States by the *soubriquet* of *New York Junior*, from the strong family likeness it bears to its elder sister.

From N. Y. Tribune, April 22d, 1846.
This Model, with its magnificent canopy, will be the greatest work of the kind ever undertaken either in this country or Europe, and, is its exhibition in all the important cities of both Hemispheres, will be visited by thousands.

From N. Y. Evening Post, April 23d, 1846.
It is the most surprising and elaborate piece of mechanism ever achieved. Our fellow citizens cannot fail to recognize their own dwellings and other familiar objects, and the inhabitants of distant cities, by having this beautiful miniature brought to their firesides, will derive from it all the advantages of an actual visit to this great metropolis, without incurring the expenses and inconveniences attendant upon a sojourn in a large city.

From N. Y. Com. Advertiser, April 23d, 1846.
The great number of objects worthy of remark in this Model are too numerous for a single notice. We shall recur to it again, but cannot close without expressing our conviction that in undertaking this, the greatest work of the kind ever attempted, Mr. Belden has earned for himself the gratitude of every New Yorker, as well as that pecuniary reward to which enterprise and talent are entitled.

From N. Y. Com. Adv. April 29, 1846.
The advantages to our business men, not only in every locality of the United States but in all the principal cities of Europe, must be manifold at a time when increasing facilities of communication are rapidly abolishing distance.

From N. Y. Tribune, May 16th, 1846.
It is to E. Porter Belden, Esq., the talented proprietor of the Model of New York, to whom the commercial and trading interests of the community are indebted for this valuable invention—a gentleman who, in achieving one of the most extensive and elaborate works of art ever attempted, has immortalized his name.

From N. Y. True Sun, May 16th, 1846.
None but those who have seen it can form an idea of the vast attraction which this exhibition will possess for the citizens of distant states.

From N. Y. Eve. Mirror, May 13, 1846.

No exhibition that has ever been in the southern and western cities, could possess such attractions for the inhabitants, as a faithful delineation of New York, the Metropolis of the Union, the emporium of commerce and fashion, and in fact the city of which all have heard and longed to visit.

From N. Y. Herald, May 26th, 1846.

It is a gigantic undertaking, and is deserving of patronage. When completed it will be the most extensive thing of the kind in the world.

From N. Y. Tribune, July 2d, 1846.

The proprietor deserves the thanks and good wishes of the citizens of New York for the truthful manner in which he has portrayed our native city, and for the very correct idea of our vast commerce which it will convey to the dwellers in the far West, as well as to the inhabitants of foreign countries.

From N. Y. True Sun, July 2d, 1846.

Truly, this undertaking will bear comparison with the labors of Hercules.

From N. Y. Eve. Mirror, July 2d, 1846.

It is certainly one of the most gigantic projects ever conceived, and has been executed with such attention to detail, that it will be viewed with astonishment both in the United States and Europe.

From N. Y. True Sun, July 4th, 1846.

The accuracy with which every minute object is finished, is truly astounding, and we are convinced that the public at large are little aware of the immense labor bestowed upon this work to render it such a perfect *fac simile* of the city.

From N. Y. Eve. Mirror, July 9th, 1846.

The Parisians have a saying that "He who has not seen Paris has seen nothing"; if we change the name of the city the remark will apply to this exhibition, for ere long to acknowledge that one has not seen the Model of New York will be to argue oneself unknown, or what is equally disagreeable—unfashionable.

From N. Y. Albion, July 11th, 1846.

Of its fidelity and exquisite finish we can speak with unequivocal praise—not the minutest points have been overlooked; every building and object of interest in this vast metropolis has been modelled with an accuracy and finish of execution really surprising.

From N. Y. Tribune, July 13th, 1846.

The whole canopy presents a most gorgeous appearance, and combines with the Model to produce a work of art which bears testimony to the genius of Mr. Belden, its talented projector and proprietor—a work which will astonish the world. In almost no other country would such an amount of capital and talent be lavished in such an undertaking, and we cannot regard it as any other than a national one.

From N. Y. Eve. Post, July 17th, 1846.

Our friends should not let slip the present opportunity of seeing this, the only perfect model of an entire city ever constructed, and which is the result of that American enterprize and talent which has already made us rivals in the useful arts and sciences of the greatest countries in the world.

From N. Y. Herald, July [illegible], 1846.

We, with pleasure, extend our [illegible] to the originator and executor of this wonderful work. Only by the labor of months, has condensed the work of centuries, as exhibited in the accurate representation of NEW YORK in miniature. Mr. Belden has achieved a triumph which reflects equal credit upon his inventive genius and the perfect skill he has displayed in correctly portraying the beauties of this commercial city. As a work of patience, of genius and of perfection, it should be visited by every dweller and stranger in the city. The citizens of our great metropolis owe a debt of gratitude to Mr. Belden which we hope will be cheerfully and liberally paid.

From N. Y. Com. Adv., July 22d, 1846.

By no other means is it possible to embrace at a single *coup d'oeil* the whole city and surrounding waters, or to form so correct an idea of the vast extent of the metropolis, the natural beauty of its situation, and the immense commercial advantages it enjoys.

From N. Y. Sun, July 24th, 1846.

No class of our citizens, from the [illegible] to the artizan, can fail to be benefited by a visit to this stupendous work of art. The talented proprietor has certainly produced a work which, without any compliment, deserves to be patronized by all who feel a desire to see their native city set forth to the best advantage in the eyes of foreign nations.

From N. Y. *Courier and Enquirer*, July [illegible], 1846.

A visit to this beautiful and ingenious specimen of workmanship will surprise and delight every one. It is really one of the most novel and extraordinary specimens of patient and faithful labor we have ever seen, and some idea may be formed of its extent when we state that it embraces this entire city from the Battery to the 32d st. with a fidelity perfectly startling. A greater portion of Brooklyn, the Navy Yard, &c. is also represented with the same scrupulous accuracy, and altogether the exhibition is one which deserves, as we are glad to know it receives, most liberal encouragement.

From N. Y. Tribune, July [illegible], 1846.

This great exhibition continues to be well attended, and visitors express freely the pleasure they derive from it. As a work of art it is unprecedented.

From N. Y. True Sun, July 28th, 1846.

The numbers flocking to Mr. Belden's [illegible] interesting, correct and beautiful Model of our city, argues well for our public taste. In addition to the importance it has to us from its local connection, it is really the most surprising piece of mechanism in the world.

From N. Y. Eve. Mirror, July 29, 1846.

Our friends should lose no time in visiting this wonderful work of art.

From N. Y. Eve. Post, July 30th, 1846.

This interesting artistic and mechanical work is attracting crowds of visiters to the Minerva Rooms, and we think deservedly.

From N. Y. Tribune, Aug. 1st, 1846.

Strangers could not adopt a better method of making themselves acquainted with the localities of New York.

From N. Y. Mirror, Aug. 1st, 1846.

No man or paper, plan, can give so just, or anything like so spirited a conception of the city, as this Model, in itself a happy concep-tion, and executed with wonderful nicety. We are happy to hear of the great success of the exhibition; there is no doubt it must continue especially in the more distant parts of the country.

From N. Y. Tribune, Aug. 6th, 1846.

If the citizens of the other parts of the Union patronize this exhibition in a similar manner to the New Yorkers, we doubt not that it will prove the source of an immense fortune to the talented proprietor.

From N. Y. Spectator, Aug. 8th, 1846.

Visiters continue to flock to, and be delight-ed with the great Model of the Empire City, and it is amusing to observe the display of tastes so different in different persons. An exhibition where tastes so varied, yet so eleva-ted, can all be fully indulged, is not often met with.

From N. Y. Eve. Mirror, Aug. 13, 1846.

Yesterday the pupils of the Deaf and Dumb Institution visited in a body the Model of New York, by invitation of the proprietor. They expressed through their preceptors the great pleasure which they had derived from the ex-hibition, and it was delightful to witness their intelligent glances as they recognized such buildings as were familiar to them.

From N. Y. True Sun, Aug. 15, 1846.

The most popular exhibition at the present time is Mr. Belden's great Model of our city, and it is now the universal theme of conver-sation. We are happy to find that the public are so generally patronising this great work of art. It must be exceedingly gratifying to Mr. Belden to see, that after having succeeded in his arduous task, it is viewed with astonishment and delight and appreciated by thousands.

From N. Y. Tribune, Aug. 18th, 1846.

This surprising work of skill is still being exhibited at the Minerva Rooms, to eager and delighted visiters, and we believe it to be one of those works of art and skill which the public do well to encourage.

From N. Y. True Sun, Aug. 19, 1846.

We have spent much time in examining it for ourselves and feel much pleased with the result.

From N. Y. Eve. Mirror, Aug. 22, 1846.

Not an omission, however trifling, can be dis-covered. It is this fact which enhances the value of the Model, and will ensure its popu-larity wherever it goes.

From N. Y. Tribune, Aug. 22d, 1846.

High as our expectations had risen, we con-fess they fell far short of the magnificent spec-tacle which Mr. Belden had prepared for us.

From N. Y. True Sun, Aug. 22, 1846.

The numbers of fashionable visiters who, even at this dead season of the year, continue to throng the Minerva Rooms, is a gratifying proof of this great work of art being duly ap-preciated.

From N. Y. Com. Adv'r, Aug. 24, 1846.

It is the most creditable thing which has been shown for a long time, and deserves that sup-port which it is now receiving.

From N. Y. Eve. Post, Aug. 24th, 1846.

It must be seen to be appreciated, and every citizen who admires amusement and instruction combined, should visit this interesting specimen of mechanical skill and artistic excellence.

From N. Y. Tribune, Aug. 27th, 1846.

The wonderful similarity of this carved Mod-el of New York to the original city, becomes more apparent the oftener it is inspected, and fully warrants us in pronouncing it to belong to the highest order of art.

From the Knickerbocker Magazine, Aug. 1846.

Think of this entire metropolis, and a part of Brooklyn, represented by the individual street, lane, alley, house, open lot, tree—every thing in short which the city is and which it contains; the whole perfect in its proportion, and every part entirely correct in its scale. It is truly a wonderful exhibition, and reflects great credit upon its enterprising proprietor, E. Porter Belden, Esq.

From the American Review, August, 1846.

The felicitous minuteness displayed in this creation—for it is a creation—is wonderful. So minute is the work, that the very awnings, posts are given, and all the rigging on the well-known vessels and steamers in the bay and rivers. Nothing now in this city is better worth seeing, and if it is to be exhibited over the Union, it will give people in distant places a perfect idea of the American Metropolis. To see it to ad-vantage, it must be studied minutely.

From the Christian Parlor Magazine, Sept. 1846.

The other city sight, which is spoken of with astonishment by all who have seen it, is Bel-den's miniature of New York city, in which every house, public and private, every tree, post &c. is accurately copied or carved in wood. Visiters at one glance can thus obtain a perfect view of the whole city, and a part of Brooklyn. It is a monument of patient labor and curious art.

From the Knickerbocker Magazine, Sept. 1846.

Looking the other day at Mr. Belden's Mod-el of New York, (that most faithful picture in little of our great metropolis,) and admiring the admirable proportion which has been so accurately preserved in every feature of the vast miniature city, we were irresistibly led to think of Gulliver in Lilliput. Indeed, it requir-ed nothing but a thousand or two human bustling through the little streets to have made the illusion complete.

From the Protestant Churchman, Sept. 5, 1846.

The artist, Mr. E. Porter Belden, has given a perfect fac-simile of the city, representing with wonderful accuracy, every public and pri-vate edifice, with the relative proportions of the streets, lanes, elevations and depressions, and the contiguous waters. The colors of the different objects are faithfully given. We were particularly interested in the beautiful model of Grace and Trinity Churches, the for-mer of which consists of upwards of a thousand pieces, and the latter of seven hundred

Lightning Source UK Ltd.
Milton Keynes UK
UKHW011448160119
335572UK00010B/622/P